An African Volk

An African Volk

The Apartheid Regime and Its Search for Survival

JAMIE MILLER

OXFORD
UNIVERSITY PRESS

OXFORD
UNIVERSITY PRESS

Oxford University Press is a department of the University of Oxford. It furthers
the University's objective of excellence in research, scholarship, and education
by publishing worldwide. Oxford is a registered trade mark of Oxford University
Press in the UK and certain other countries.

Published in the United States of America by Oxford University Press
198 Madison Avenue, New York, NY 10016, United States of America.

Library of Congress Cataloging-in-Publication Data
Names: Miller, Jamie, 1985– author.
Title: An African Volk : the apartheid regime and its search for survival / Jamie Miller.
Description: New York City : Oxford University Press, 2016. | Includes bibliographical references and index. |
Description based on print version record and CIP data provided by publisher; resource not viewed.
Identifiers: LCCN 2016019434 (print) | LCCN 2016017655 (ebook) | ISBN 9780190274849 (Updf) |
ISBN 9780190274856 (Epub) | ISBN 9780190274832 (hardcover : alk. paper)
Subjects: LCSH: Afrikaners—South Africa—Politics and government—History—20th century. | White
nationalism—South Africa—History. | Apartheid—South Africa—History—20th century. | South Africa—
Race relations—Political aspects. | South Africa—Politics and government—20th century.
Classification: LCC DT1768.A57 (print) | LCC DT1768.A57 M55 2016 (ebook) | DDC
968.0043936—dc23
LC record available at https://lccn.loc.gov/2016019434

3 5 7 9 8 6 4 2
Printed by Sheridan Books, Inc., United States of America

Purpose

- To preserve a free, independent RSA [Republic of South Africa] grounded in Christian faith, peace, and law, for the present and the future.

Goals

- To normalize South Africa's relationships with Africa and the outside world.
- To implement healthy and productive relations between all population groups in South Africa.
- To uphold the identity of the various population groups in South Africa and in the case of the black peoples, build them up [*uitbou*] to independent states.
- To maintain law and order and a stable government and prevent communist interference in South Africa.

—Internal summary of the priorities of the Vorster Government[1]

CONTENTS

Acknowledgments   ix

Abbreviations   xiii

Glossary of Afrikaans Terms   xv

Terminology   xvii

Introduction   1

PART I   FROM CONTROL TO OPPORTUNITY

1. "We Are Not Europeans": Ideology and Identity in Pretoria's Golden Age   29

2. Into Africa: The Outward Policy   62

3. "We Must Stay Prepared": Reimagining the White Redoubt   88

4. In Search of Détente: Negotiating a Transfer of Power in Rhodesia   119

PART II   FROM CHALLENGE TO CRISIS

5. Mission Creep: South Africa's Intervention in the Angolan Civil War   165

6. The Post Mortem: Lessons from Angola   199

7. Dr. Kissinger, I Presume? The 1976 Initiatives   225

PART III   FROM COLLAPSE TO RECONSTRUCTION

8. A New Roadmap: The Development of Total Strategy   263

9. "If you say change, I'll say I can't": A New Vision   283

Conclusion   320

Note on Sources   339
Archival Abbreviations   347
Notes   349
Bibliography   415
Index   433

ACKNOWLEDGMENTS

It was not until my second stint in the South African archives, almost midway through this project, that I began to really see the story that is told here. Behind closed doors, the leaders of the apartheid regime, some of the most widely reviled figures in postwar history, were engaging in vibrant reassessments of apartheid's compatibility with the postcolonial world. Moreover, their divergent conceptualizations of race, nation, and state—as well as the interrelationships between these—led them to disagree vehemently over both the diagnosis of the regime's legitimacy problem and the suitable remedy. The resulting political conflicts were corroding the effectiveness of the regime from within. None of this fit with the assumptions and perspectives that I had initially brought to the project. In order to tease out and explain this new story, I realized that was it was not going to be enough to simply foreground Pretoria's agency, though this would be essential. I had to go further, put myself in the shoes of South African policymakers, and understand the values, norms, historical experiences, and political imperatives that shaped their views of the world and informed the various programs they developed for the regime's survival.

Many people helped me do this. On the financial front, thanks are due to the Faculty of History, the Smuts Fund, the Bartle Frere Fund, and the doctoral funds of both Sidney Sussex and Jesus Colleges, all at the University of Cambridge, as well as the Fox Fellowship at Yale University, the Royal Historical Society, the Institut Français d'Afrique du Sud-Recherche, Indiana University's African Studies Program Summer Library Fellowship, the Association for the Study of the Middle East and Africa, the Mario Einaudi Center for International Studies at Cornell University, and the American Philosophical Society. Together, these provided funds to support research in Southern Africa, as well as additional archival work in the United States, France, and Great Britain. I was also fortunate enough to gain valuable feedback at conferences from Durban to Philadelphia.

In 2012, I was the recipient of a Fox Fellowship, which gave me the opportunity to write up my doctoral dissertation in New Haven, Connecticut, and attend seminars at International Security Studies. Many thanks must go to Julia Muravnik and Julia Adams at Yale University, and Jillaine Seymour and Angela Parr-Burman at Sidney Sussex College, Cambridge, for making my transition into American academia a smooth one. Equally important to the fruition of this project was the granting of a Postdoctoral Fellowship at the Mario Einaudi Center at Cornell University. I am thankful to both Fredrik Logevall and Heike Michelsen for giving me this once-in-a-lifetime opportunity. This book would look radically different if not for the time and intellectual space that the year in Ithaca afforded me to deepen the analysis and invest in new ideas. Finally, as I brought the manuscript to publication, the Department of History at the University of Pittsburgh offered me the time and space to do it right. Many people contributed to creating a social and intellectual environment in which I felt very much at home, particularly Vincent Leung, Katja Wezel, David Leusink, Mari Webel, Molly Warsh, Pernille Røge, Lara Putnam, Marcus Rediker, and John Stoner. Special thanks must go to Patrick Manning, who not only brought me to Pitt, but also bequeathed his African history library to me upon his retirement. To those who know Pat, such generosity is no more than to be expected, but I am honored to be the recipient of it just the same.

Not every researcher gets such opportunities and I am grateful to everyone, from the funders to the administrators, who make it all possible. I must also thank the students in my classes on "State-Building and the Post-Colonial Moment" at Cornell and Pittsburgh, who helped me position my understanding of state formation in South Africa in the context of common challenges facing societies across the global south. This was the conceptual key that unlocked so much of the big picture.

A number of people offered their time and expertise during this journey, providing excellent sounding boards for ideas and my first ports of call when I encountered problems. In no particular order, Dan Magaziner, Kate de Luna, Judith Byfield, Asa McKercher, Patrick Manning, Nick Wilson, Arne Westad, Hannah Higgin, Nic van de Walle, Sue Onslow, Chris Saunders, Zach Fredman, Bernard Porter, Jack Spence, Jorge Rivera Marin, Fred Logevall, Simon Stevens, Tim Scarnecchia, Andy deRoche, Danelle van Zyl-Hermann, Fodei Batty, Matt Evangelista, Lindie Koorts, Ryan Irwin, Zhong Zhong Chen, Marc Palen, and Artemy Kalinovsky all offered ready support and answered queries. Jim Brennan, Brian Rutledge, Nat Powell, Hermann Giliomee, Peter Vale, Frank Gerits, Eleanor Bron, and John Stoner did all of these things, while also kindly sharing materials that helped to broaden the analysis.

Early in the publication process at Oxford University Press, two anonymous reviewers provided many helpful suggestions. I am indebted to their commitment to prodding me to think about my subject in new ways. Then, in the final stages of production, Saul Dubow, Chris Saunders, and Hermann Giliomee each took the time to read the manuscript and draw my attention to areas that needed more clarity or explanation. For holding me to their high standards, I cannot thank them enough. Indeed, ever since we first met in Stellenbosch in 2011, Hermann has made himself available for any and all queries over a number of years. It has been a privilege simply trying to keep up with his extraordinary knowledge of the underlying historical dynamics at play in this book. I could not have wished for a better sparring partner and my arguments are much the stronger for having withstood his queries and challenges.

Various people helped me translate tricky Afrikaans idioms, especially Zoon Cronje, Duncan Pieterse, and Rudolph van Wyk. Anna-Mart and Johann van Wyk very kindly offered me a home away from home in Pretoria in 2011 and were unstinting in their generosity. I owe them a huge debt of gratitude. The King family and the Misuri-Charkham family offered hospitality in London, Zoon and Estia Cronje in Centurion, and the Wargnys in Paris.

I am deeply grateful to the many interviewees who gave their time to speak to me. For those forever associated with the apartheid regime, it must be difficult in the new South Africa to believe that anyone might be able to utilize their recollections and construct something of value. Many interviewees gave me documents or books from their own collections, while almost all stayed in close contact long after our original encounters, enabling me to verify certain facts and conduct additional inquiries as they arose during the writing process.

A special place is reserved here for those who work selflessly in the archives. Without their dedication, historians can achieve very little. I am particularly indebted to Esta Jones, Ernéne Verster, Huibre Lombard, and Freddy Sentso (Archive for Contemporary Affairs); Steve d'Agrela, Louise Jooste, and Erika Strydom, as well as my personal declassifiers Steinman and Chambers (South African National Defense Force Archives); Neels Muller (Department of Foreign Affairs); Gerrit Wagener (South African National Archives); Tammy O'Connor (South African History Archive); Doret du Toit (Mangaung Library Services); Leonard Benjamin, Melanie Geustyn, and Zahida Sirkhotte (National Library of South Africa, Cape Town); everyone at the Merensky Library at the University of Pretoria; Jeff Peires and Liz de Wet (Cory Library, Rhodes University); Joseph Schwarz, David Langbart, Timothy Syzek and Nicholas Connico (US National Archives); Bill McNitt (Ford Library); Bert Nason (Carter Library); Marion Frank-Wilson and Todd Ramlo (Wells Library, Indiana University); and Mary Curry (National Security Archive). At Cambridge, Rhona Watson ensured that the library at Jesus College ended up with an unusually wide-ranging collection of books on South African history in the 1970s while David Lowe acquired new titles for the University Library as they appeared. At Yale, Dorothy Woodson and Melanie Maksin helped track down unusual sources, Sharon Powers was indefatigable at the Africana Library at Cornell, and Christopher Lemery welcomed my many requests at the University of Pittsburgh.

This is a decidedly unorthodox project. It straddles categories of history, rather than fitting neatly into any one box. From the outset of the publication process, Susan Ferber at Oxford University Press saw this as an asset to be developed rather than a problem to be resolved. She identified with my vision for the project and then worked tirelessly to enhance it. Both as an editor and as a friend, Susan has steered this project from dissertation to book with professionalism and empathy. A class act.

Thanks are also due to those who helped obtain the necessary copyright permissions for the images, particularly at Independent Media, the Times Media Group, the Caxton Company, and Media24. Emily Kobylecky created the superb maps and Pablo Lindsay compiled the index. Material from earlier journal articles has been reprinted or adapted with permission from Cambridge University Press, MIT Press, and Taylor & Francis.

I am deeply indebted to my family back in Sydney. They have never questioned why I would want to spend years of my life halfway across the world, trying to come to grips with a defunct regime in a country for which Australians traditionally have little more than tough love. Travel and education were the two priorities in our household growing up. Without that policy, I am sure that I would never have seen that an endeavor such as this was even an option. Together with my friends around the world, my family has been a paragon of support.

Two people came on board in the middle of this project, but had a profound influence upon it. Mid-way through, I was fortunate that Andrew Preston offered to become my supervisor, rescuing what had become a rather grim situation. Ever since, he has given assiduous support, always delivered with good humor. At one conference that I attended, a graduate student related an aphorism used at her university to refer to supervisors: "Brilliant, sociable, available; pick two." As anyone who knows him can attest, Andrew is all three. More than a wonderful scholar, Andrew is a wonderful person.

Later still, Sarah Kinkel entered the frame. Sarah has read every word published here—some of them multiple times, I fear—and her comments have improved the text immeasurably. Just as importantly, she has put up with an author possessed of a vicious perfectionist streak, which I imagine is a thoroughly undesirable experience. Through it all, she has offered love and affection, which have kept me going even when I found myself in the depths of frustration.

All errors and translations are my own.

ABBREVIATIONS

AHI	Afrikaanse Handelsinstituut (Afrikaner Chamber of Commerce)
ALCORA	Aliança Contra as Rebeliões em Africa (Alliance against the Rebellions in Africa)
ANC	African National Council (Rhodesia)
AP	Afrikaner Party
BCM	Black Consciousness Movement
BOSS	Bureau for State Security (Buro vir Staatsveiligheid)
DFA	Department of Foreign Affairs
DPC	Defense Planning Committee
DTA	Democratic Turnhalle Alliance
FNLA	Frente Nacional de Libertação de Angola (National Front for the Liberation of Angola)
Frelimo	Frente de Libertação de Moçambique (Mozambique Liberation Front)
GDP	Gross Domestic Product
HNP	Herstigte Nasionale Party
ISP	Ian Smith Papers
MFA	Movimento das Forças Armadas (Armed Forces Movement)
MP	Member of Parliament
MPLA	Movimento Popular de Libertação de Angola (People's Movement for the Liberation of Angola)
NAM	Non-Aligned Movement
NHK	Nederdeuitsch Hervormde Kerk (Dutch Reformed Church)
NP	National Party
NSC	National Security Council
OAU	Organization for African Unity
OB	Ossewabrandwag (Oxwagon Sentinel)
OCAM	African and Malagasy Common Organization

OPEC	Organization of the Petroleum Exporting Countries
PAC	Pan Africanist Congress
RF	Rhodesian Front
RSA	Republic of South Africa
SA	South Africa
SA ANC	African National Congress (South Africa)
SABC	South African Broadcasting Corporation
SACP	South African Communist Party
SADF	South African Defense Force
SALT	Strategic Arms Limitation Talks
SAP	South African Police
SBK	Sentrale Buro vir Konflikhantering (Central Bureau for Conflict Management)
SSC	State Security Council
SWA	South-West Africa
SWAPO	South-West African People's Organization
UDI	Unilateral Declaration of Independence
UK	United Kingdom
UN	United Nations
UNISA	University of South Africa
UNITA	União Nacional para a Independência Total de Angola (National Union for the Total Independence of Angola)
UNTAG	United Nations Transition Assistance Group
UP	United Party
US	United States
USSR	Union of Soviet Socialist Republics
ZANU	Zimbabwe African National Union
ZAPU	Zimbabwe African People's Union

GLOSSARY OF AFRIKAANS TERMS

baasskap: Unabashed white racial dominance. By the Vorster era, used to refer to the type of antiquated hierarchical thinking against which the regime defined its future plans for South African society.

boeremusiek: Traditional Afrikaner folk music.

Broeder: Member of the Afrikaner Broederbond.

geldmag: Big business. Traditionally seen in Afrikaner nationalist discourses as corrupting *volk* values of national solidarity, piety, and integrity.

gelykstelling: Racial mixing.

goeie buurskap: Geopolitical doctrine of "good neighborliness."

Hoofleier: National Party leader.

kragdadigheid: Literally, vigor; more colloquially, uncompromising toughness. A core value in Nationalist politics.

oorstroming: Being overwhelmed, or literally flooded, by Africans.

rooi gevaar: The red threat. This discourse both copied and merged readily with the more deep-seated discourse of the *swart gevaar*.

samesmelter: Those Nationalists who in 1934 favored "fusion" with Jan Smuts's South African Party within a new pan-white political structure, the United Party. In postwar Afrikaner politics, the term was overwhelmingly used in a derogatory sense: D. F. Malan's refusal to ally with English-speakers in favour of "national purity" formed a central part of the political mythology of Afrikanerdom's resurrection fourteen years later.

strewe: The Afrikaner national endeavor, often invoked in existential, almost mystical terms.

swart gevaar: The black threat.

veelvolkige: Literally, multinational. A foundational term in the Nationalist political lexicon used to refer to the politics of separate South African "nations."

verligte: Afrikaners prepared to countenance reforms in order to keep the separate development program compatible with the changing realities of South African society and an evolving world.

verkrampte: Afrikaners who saw any mitigation of total racial separation as opening the door to the eradication of Afrikaner self-determination, culture, privilege, and control.

volk: Afrikaner people or nation.

volksbeweging: Afrikaner national movement.

volkseie: Concept in Afrikaner thought that each national community had its own inherent and inalienable values and character.

volksfront: The people's front.

volksverbondenheid: Concept in Afrikaner thought mandating that an individual could only achieve fulfillment through membership in a national community.

volkskapitalisme: The original model of Afrikaner capitalism, with its goal of ethnic advancement. Ordinary Afrikaners were encouraged to invest their savings in Afrikaner institutions in the common interest. Starting in the 1960s, this model began to break down, as Afrikaner elites began to prioritize their own profits over the goals of the *volk* as a whole.

voortrekker: The Afrikaner pioneers who embarked on the Great Trek(s) of the 1830s and 1840s. In *volk* mythology, these intrepid purists rejected the racial policies imposed by the British in the Cape Colony in favor of staying true to their own values, even if that meant going it alone in the harsh hinterland.

TERMINOLOGY

During the period covered by this book, all South Africans were classified by race. The scope of their futures and their societal rights were functions of these imposed categorizations. Changes in classification could be devastating for entire families, resulting in ostracization by former friends and communities. Unsurprisingly, many find the terminology used in this process—such as "non-white," "Bantu," and so on—offensive, and certainly archaic. Nevertheless, in the discourses that the regime constructed, this was the language through which the white polity discussed and debated its challenges. This book must therefore use these terms.

By the postwar period, Afrikaners were generally the descendants of settlers from Dutch-, French-, and German-speaking areas of Europe, usually Calvinists, and spoke Afrikaans as their mother tongue. However, there were exceptions to each of these criteria. In this book, therefore, "Afrikaners" are considered those who self-identified as such and were allowed by the state's racial categories to enjoy the full privileges of doing so (that is, they were also classified as "white"). This racially exclusive definition of "Afrikaner" did not cover millions of other Afrikaans-speakers, especially Cape Coloreds. Both South African society and the Nationalist regime would have evolved very differently had the government chosen to define the dominant political community more broadly.

The term *volk* is deployed to denote the collective Afrikaner national movement, whether in the political, cultural, or discursive realms. It should be stressed that the identity of "Afrikaner" was just as politically functional as the other state-approved categorizations of this period. The organs of Nationalist rule relentlessly cultivated and promoted identifications as members of the *volk* to legitimize their own existence and power. In doing so, they obscured the complex and often contradictory processes at the heart of the original emergence of Afrikaner national consciousness.[2] It is important to recall that not all

"Afrikaners" were "Nationalists." Some even openly opposed the regime and its policies. However, this minority was far greater in, say, 1985 than it was in 1965.

Where unclear, the terms "English-speaker" or "anglophone" also refer to whites—those allowed to play a full role in the politics of the South African state—though this definition excludes just as many as the "Afrikaner" category. An additional concern is the term "South African." In this book, the adjective is sometimes used to denote actions of the whites-only state—"South African policy" and so on—though the government of course did not represent many who considered themselves South Africans.

Scholars and contemporary observers have often interchangeably employed the terms "outward policy," "dialogue," and (less often) "détente" to refer to South Africa's efforts to establish links with independent African states between 1967 and 1975 with a view to expanding the regime's legitimacy. In this book, "outward policy" refers to the regime's efforts to break out of isolation through bilateral constructs, while "détente" refers specifically to the multilateral, re-gional program pioneered between spring 1974 and spring 1975. (The broader détente vision remained an important factor in Vorster's foreign policy right up until the end of 1976 and the collapse of the Kissinger Initiatives.) The two dip-lomatic enterprises briefly overlapped and coexisted, but they were quite dis-tinct. This book also coins the phrase "Vorster Doctrine," which aims to resolve some of the confusion between these two sets of terms by defining the area of commonality, namely the underlying premise: Vorster's deep belief that black and white Africa did not have mutually exclusive goals and that through trade and cooperation, mutual understanding and a modus vivendi could be estab-lished. "African outreach" is used in a more all-encompassing sense, covering the desire of the existing power structure to reach out into Africa in any and all forms—diplomatically, commercially, and so on.

The names of capital cities have been used to represent the actions of a state in the diplomatic arena, such as "Pretoria realized," "Washington refused," and so on. Such labels can obscure the various interests and disagreements behind specific decisions, which in the South African context is a major focus of this book. Nevertheless, this convention is widespread in international history and is therefore replicated here, all while acknowledging such terminology for what it is: a not entirely satisfactory shorthand. The more modern "Beijing" has been used instead of "Peking," though the latter spelling was preferred at the time.

Two sets of binaries feature prominently in this book. The first, juxtaposing *verligte* with *verkrampte*, is a well-established tool used to make sense of the sharp political divergences that emerged within Afrikanerdom in the 1960s. These terms have tended to be used as personalized epithets, and this book often fol-lows suit ("leading *verligte* Willem de Klerk" and so on). However, as seen in more detail in Chapter 1, these terms should really be understood as denoting discourses, rather than individuals. This is a fine but important distinction. A person could logically espouse a position on one issue that derived from one discourse while simultaneously holding another from the other on a separate issue. It was the public sphere of the day that relentlessly classified politics into one or the other camp, with actors inside and outside parliament using the labels as political weapons. This bifurcation of political identity within Afrikanerdom distorted a much more complex conceptual terrain, as the wild swings in support for John Vorster's African outreach initiatives epitomised.

Less problematic is the use of "dove" and "hawk." In general, those responsible for the regime's statecraft and security remained dependably in one or the other camp: either they believed that the state could achieve a modus operandi with the outside world, or, due to their understanding of global dynamics, they did not. Those positions in turn consistently shaped different policy positions. Unlike the *verligte* and *verkrampte* tags, the "dove" and "hawk" labels were used only occasionally at the time. Instead, I have borrowed them from other contexts and superimposed them onto this realm to provide some intelligibility to the divisions within the regime over national security strategies. Of course, "doves" on foreign policy could be decidedly hardline on other fronts, like internal security or ideology.

Much of the research of this book was conducted in Afrikaans. Even formal documents regularly featured cultural references, low-register idioms, or colloquial language, which eluded easy translation. In such cases, I offer what I feel is the best contextual rather than literal approximation in English, with the original in italics afterwards. For instance, *geldmag* is "big business" here, rather than the more literal but awkward "money power" (or the more modern "special interests"). Afrikaans speakers will note that certain words used here—like *volk*, with its connotations of both "people" and "national community," or *strewe*, utilized by Afrikaner nationalists to mean a common, existential endeavor—are heavily laden with emotional meaning and historical connotations, rendering any translation insufficient.

An African Volk

Introduction

On August 25, 1975, the stooped, heavy-set figure of John Vorster, Prime Minister of apartheid South Africa (1966–1978), stepped out of his official car and into the warm African sunlight. Although it was the dry season, Victoria Falls roared to his left. He approached the vast chasm forged by the Zambezi River and walked onto the steel bridge constructed some 420 feet above the torrent below. In the center of the bridge sat a five-carriage train, provided by his government, which that afternoon would become the venue for talks aimed at ending renegade white rule in the ex-British colony of Rhodesia. Looking to replace building racial tensions with his own form of "détente," Vorster had come to the very border between white-ruled and black-ruled Africa. Throngs of stunned observers, journalists, and ordinary Africans looked on as the widely reviled South African leader crossed the bridge and entered decolonized Africa. Nearby, a young Zambian held up a sign that read: "Vorster becomes great today." The South African leader was promptly whisked away to the Mosi-o-Tunya Intercontinental Hotel in Livingstone, where Zambian President Kenneth Kaunda awaited him. The two sat down to lunch, with the deeply religious Vorster leading his host in a prayer for peace in Southern Africa.[1] It was a most unlikely scene. Just a few years earlier, Kaunda had asserted that apartheid constituted the "morally indefensible" counterpoint to his own governing credo of humanism. "The philosophy of Apartheid denies to the Black people the right to be; it forces them to conform to an image which the so-called Master Race has created of them to prove Black inferiority and White superiority," he had declared.[2] How times had changed. Now, Kaunda told the world that John Vorster, of all people, was "the voice of reason for which Africa and the rest of the world had been waiting."[3]

This remarkable meeting constituted the high-point of the apartheid regime's campaign to break out of isolation and secure long-term acceptance by the outside world. Situated at the nexus of African, decolonization, and Cold War history, this book explores that campaign: its motivations, its opponents, and its consequences. It is primarily concerned with the ideas that Afrikaner

1

Figure 0.1 John Vorster greets Kenneth Kaunda at Victoria Falls in August 1975. South
African Foreign Minister Hilgard Muller, officials from both countries, and the press
look on. Source: National Archives of South Africa.

elites utilized to adapt to the coming of the postcolonial world—ideas that were
powerful, contradictory, complex, original, and farcical, often all at once—and
the different strategies for survival that these ideas informed. The main geographical focus is not South Africa's relations with traditional Western powers, or with fellow white settler polities, as one might expect, but the forum in
which these efforts improbably unfolded: Africa. The chronology meanwhile
centers on the tenure of John Vorster, when the issue of apartheid's compatibility with the outside world came to a head and was addressed in the most
substantive and sustained way by the regime, with a particular concentration
on the 1974–76 period.

These years marked, in hindsight, the crossroads for the apartheid order. As
late as 1974, very few South Africans or outsiders realistically believed that a confrontation with the apartheid regime could force imminent and real change in its
social structures. The first eight years of Vorster's tenure had constituted something of a golden age for the white polity.[4] Economic growth was rampant.[5] The
regime had survived the Sharpeville insurrections of 1960. African opposition
was divided and blunted. The Afrikaner National Party (NP) had successfully
reached out to its old foe, English-speaking whites, in its quest for political and
social control. Indeed, the Nationalist vision for a future grounded in apartheid,
or "separate development"—the delineation of separate political structures, economic opportunities, and social identities for South Africa's inhabitants based

Figure 0.2 A young Zambian welcomes John Vorster to Victoria Falls. Misreading Vorster's intentions, Africans on both sides of the color line hoped that the visit was the start of a new, positive dynamic in Southern African history. Source: Ernest Stanton Publishers.

on individuals' racial and ethnic designation by a white government—seemed as unshakeable as ever. Chief Kaiser Matanzima had just accepted Pretoria's offer of political independence for the Transkei, a key step toward legitimizing the entire project. Hopes were high that other African leaders would follow suit, ultimately creating a network of formally independent statelets, known as homelands or bantustans, that the regime could oversee and control.

The Afrikaner community was therefore exhibiting a brash confidence in its future prospects.[6] In 1972, leading public intellectual Otto Krause observed that "the tough fact" was that "White South Africa's power, in real terms, is basically unchallenged—despite all the talk and all the propaganda."[7] The regime, future President F. W. de Klerk concurred, "was at the crest of its confidence and power."[8] Foreign analysts agreed. In 1970, American scholar William E. Griffith conducted a lengthy research trip in Southern Africa, cosponsored by *Reader's Digest* and the Massachusetts Institute of Technology. He concluded:

> [D]uring the next decade basic change in South Africa can only come, if it comes at all, from *within* the white Afrikaner community. . . . [The] white elite has become less provincial, less fearful, more confident, more supportive of its government, which is stable, resolute, and completely self-confident. Its black African opponents, the exiled black "freedom fighters" and the black African states themselves, have shown themselves impotent in the face of steadily more effective South African police and security operations. . . . [T]here is no realistic prospect in the near future of anything but white rule in South Africa. . . . [The Afrikaners] have both the power and the will to maintain their rule, and neither the English-speaking whites nor the Coloreds, Indians, or Africans do. The exiled African "freedom fighters" from South Africa are weak and divided and can accomplish little or nothing.[9]

The next year, sociologist Heribert Adam published *Modernizing Racial Domination: South Africa's Political Dynamics*. The book was the most comprehensive analysis yet published of apartheid as a system. "Resigned adjustment to the inevitable seems at present the dominating tendency among the politically aware non-whites inside the country," Adam wrote.[10]

This sense of stasis and white control evaporated rapidly. On either side of South-West Africa (SWA)—which the regime administered under an old League of Nations mandate—and Ian Smith's renegade white regime in Rhodesia lay Portugal's colonies in Angola and Mozambique. These constituted the bookends of Pretoria's white-ruled *cordon sanitaire*, protecting South Africa from the seemingly inexorable advance of African nationalism carried on British Prime Minister Harold Macmillan's "wind of change." On April 25, 1974, however, Portugal's right-wing dictatorship finally collapsed in a bloodless coup, which became known as the Carnation Revolution. For over a decade, Lisbon had been fighting to keep control of its five-century-old African empire. But by the mid-1970s, Portugal's colonial wars consumed almost half the government's budget.[11] A group of left-wing military officers, calling themselves the Armed Forces Movement (MFA), took power and agreed to dissolve Lisbon's colonial authority. These events transformed South Africa's geopolitical situation. Within just a handful of years, the ideological character and political outlook of the region shifted dramatically as the norms of white minority governance that had

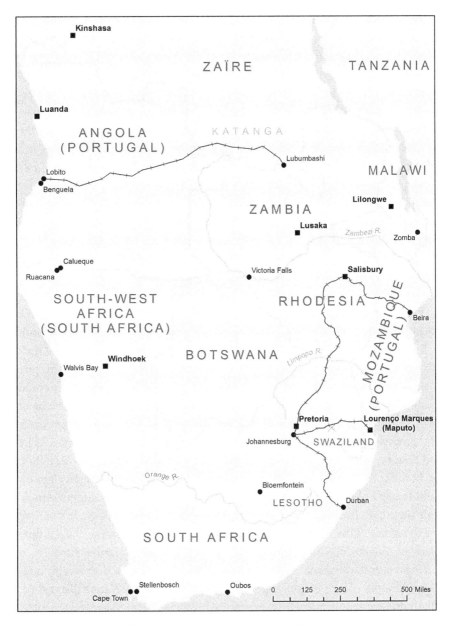

Figure 0.3 Southern Africa, 1974. Source: Map by Emily Kobylecky.

shaped the regional order receded before the ascendant forces of majority rule and African nationalism. The resulting power vacuum quickly became the next theater for the growing Cold War struggle in the developing world, as low-level conflicts between white regimes and African actors across South Africa's hinterland escalated in intensity and evolved in character.

All of this is well established in the scholarship. Yet the Carnation Revolution has often been seen as little more than the moment when the stalled teleology of decolonization restarted, leading to the fall of the regime twenty years later.[12] This is to read history backward. There was nothing predetermined about how Southern Africa evolved after April 1974, no more than there was in the fractious and keenly contested processes of decolonization elsewhere in Africa years before.[13] Equally, choosing 1974 as a starting date for this narrative ignores the intellectual and ideological shifts occurring in both the organs of NP power and Afrikaner society in the preceding years, which extensively shaped the regime's subsequent conduct. If the mid-1970s heralded the beginning of the end for Pretoria, then the regime's own actions—not to mention the worldviews, internal divisions, and political battles driving them—substantially influenced why and how events unfolded as they did. Political change in Portugal plainly heralded a turning point. However, where history turned toward, what would replace the *cordon sanitaire*, these were very much open questions—and ones whose answers Vorster was determined to influence.

Very little is known about precisely how the leaders of white South Africa sought to keep their regime viable and what obstacles they encountered both at home and abroad. How did Vorster and his colleagues understand the hostility of the outside world to their racial order? Why did they believe that despite their limited diplomatic resources and poor international standing they could manipulate global trends to the regime's advantage and change perceptions of what apartheid entailed? How did the regime successfully reach out to Africa at the same time as it brutally oppressed black South Africans at home? Why did Pretoria's efforts on this front fall short? How did the embers of this failure spark the confrontation and spiraling violence that ravaged the region right up until the end of the apartheid regime—and, in some parts of Southern Africa, well after that? The answers to these questions lie at the heart of understanding the dynamics of the Southern African theater of the Cold War, the chaotic final phase of African decolonization, and the decline and fall of apartheid itself.

These events also serve as a prism through which to reassess the evolving conceptualizations of race, nation, and state in the ideology of the Nationalist regime. On a purely geopolitical level, the regime looked to exploit cleavages on the international scene that cut across anti-apartheid sentiments and thereby gain limited forms of support and legitimacy for its internal order. However, its engagement with Africa both reflected and shaped a much deeper process of soul-searching over the identity of the *volk*, its future prospects, and what it stood for. In this way, diplomatic outreach was tethered to a broader underlying contest in Pretoria over both the feasibility of separate development in an increasingly integrated global community and the integrity of the Afrikaner nationalist mission in a new conceptual era. Foreign policy can therefore be used as a lens through which to understand the ideologies behind apartheid. And vice versa.[14]

As this contest unfolded on the levels of policy, personalities, and political philosophy, it crystallized in a caustic division between the two political titans of the era. Both Prime Minister John Vorster and his defense minister and successor in the top office, P. W. Botha, sought to forge a vision of regional stability on South Africa's own terms. However, they had divergent understandings of what this process might entail and mean. Vorster was essentially an alchemist, believing that skillful diplomacy could transform African states' hostility to apartheid into genuine acceptance. By contrast, Botha advocated unstintingly that coexistence between white and black could only be secured by using force to destroy South Africa's enemies' ability to challenge the regime. As both promoted and pursued their own solutions to Pretoria's existential crisis, they had to do so in the same context of a domestic political ethos that was isolationist, defiant, and utterly resistant to change in response to foreign pressure.[15] The fate of each model for the regime's survival therefore depended not so much on the intellectual merits of each approach, but on the ability of their respective advocates to convince their NP colleagues, rank-and-file party members, and the white electorate that their answer to the polity's problems would not cost Afrikaners their identity or way or life.

In Search of Legitimacy

So how did Vorster endeavor to secure his regime in the uncertain but certainly dangerous new environment that the Carnation Revolution heralded? His efforts to provide national security were tied to an existing search for identity and legitimacy in the unstable postcolonial world. From the mid-1950s onward, the old colonial order in Africa began to steadily disintegrate. The array of fledgling states that emerged in its place identified South Africa's apartheid system, with its entrenched racialism, as the symbolic antithesis to their emergent vision of what it meant to be a state in the postcolonial era.[16] Pretoria had previously believed that apartheid could be validated through neo-imperial norms and discourses not far removed from the "Three Cs" of the Scramble for Africa—Christianity, free commerce, and civilization—while the regime saw its legitimacy as intrinsically tied to its relationships with Western states. As these norms and discourses disintegrated, the apartheid state increasingly stressed its geopolitical role as a bulwark against communist expansion in Southern Africa in an effort to keep some form of this Western-centric support network alive. Some foreign governments, particularly the Nixon administration, responded favorably. However, the broader trend was of Western nations putting distance between themselves and the apartheid system.

Simultaneously, the regime was coming under pressure from within. The political mythology of Afrikaner nationalism relied heavily on narratives of displacement, persecution, and inferiority vis-à-vis English-speaking whites. Yet by the 1960s, Afrikaners' incomes were rising rapidly, while their culture, language, schools, churches, and values thrived due to extensive state support. The new generation of the NP's base was far more urban, educated, and prosperous than its forebears. These socioeconomic changes drove marked shifts in how Afrikaners understood themselves and their future. Traditional insularity was traded in for a fragile, outward-looking curiosity. Elites in the Afrikaans-language public sphere began to grapple with questions of *volk* history and identity, racial content and hierarchy, Africa and Africans, and development and modernity. On the political level, an alliance comprising newly confident Afrikaner entrepreneurs concerned about apartheid's impact on economic growth and intellectuals worried about the moral weight of the regime's oppression began to press the government to invest the resources needed to make the separate development vision a reality for all of South Africa's peoples.

Like his predecessor, Prime Minister Hendrik Verwoerd (1958–66), Vorster fervently believed in the virtue of the apartheid project for all South Africans and the compatibility of the homelands vision with a broad program of *goeie buurskap* (good neighborliness) on the continent. He, like his colleagues, simply could not understand why Xhosa, Zulu, and Sotho would not be as assertive about protecting their own customs and cultures as Afrikaners were, given the Nationalists' deep philosophical grounding in group rather than individual rights. Both men therefore viewed separate development as a means of allowing each group to pursue its own interests with a minimum of dangerous friction. However, on a much deeper level than Verwoerd, Vorster understood that the old framework of norms, values, and institutions that sustained the South African regime both domestically and abroad was losing currency. He therefore sought to cultivate a new framework to legitimize Pretoria's place in the world. Citing the Afrikaners' extensive anticolonial history on the continent, culminating in the Boer Wars, Vorster emphasized the identity of the regime as an inherently African rather than European entity. "[W]e are in every respect a part of Africa," he declared after only six months in office.[17] The erstwhile language of unbridled white dominance was largely discarded. Instead, the watchword became coexistence between white and black on an equal footing, both inside the Republic's borders between the regime and the homelands, and on the continent as a whole. If the foundation stones of the postcolonial world were anticolonialism, self-determination, and a rejection of racial hierarchies, Vorster resolved to appropriate the very same principles that South Africa's enemies used to attack the regime, adapt them to the Verwoerdian gospel of separate development, and use them to justify white independence and viability in Africa. The "South Africa in Africa" framework soon acquired a life of its own, providing stand-alone paradigms through which Pretoria began to construct its identity to the hostile outside world, offering sets of concepts and values with which to construct political legitimacy for the apartheid order, and lighting paths by which long-term national security and prosperity might be achieved.

Well before the Carnation Revolution, therefore, Vorster was committed to embedding South Africa's existing apartheid order, with some minimal changes, in a different network of values and norms. Sifting through established Cold War thinking and emergent postcolonial norms, he worked to identify geopolitical and intellectual frameworks that might help legitimize the Nationalist template for the future. This became a project that consumed and defined his prime ministership. Diplomats strove to construct a new regional stability. Politicians tentatively advocated new ideologies to reluctant voters. The military experimented with new strategies for national security. These were not separate processes, but part of a larger pursuit of survival in the face of threats on all three fronts simultaneously. The new agenda went far beyond a mere "rebranding" of apartheid. It comprised a quest for a vector of history that Pretoria, with its separate development program of parallel self-determination, could latch onto and ride to a secure and prosperous future.

For all the external confidence synonymous with the 1966–74 period, this was a troubling, even chaotic process for the Afrikaner regime and its leaders, as they labored to find and then reinforce structures that might allow them to preserve their independence and privileges. Vorster's campaign to Africanize the identity of the *volk* and bring separate development into alignment with the values of the postcolonial era was not even the only process of ideological reconstruction that was occurring at the time: it was concurrent with a sustained (and better known) effort on the part of the government to build a broader pan-white nationalism and thereby attract English-speaking voters.[18] Neither the rigidity of Verwoerd's apartheid master plan, nor the racist values of white society, nor the boorish culture of the National Party, nor the emotive weight of the Afrikaner nationalist history lent themselves to the political flexibility and intellectual dynamism needed to rearticulate the very legitimacy of the polity—especially one that seemed, by many measures, to be thriving.[19] It did not help that the international order was fundamentally unstable; the "years of upheaval" in one account, the "shock of the global" in another, "the diffusion of power" in a third.[20] Washington was stuck in Vietnam, its credibility on the international stage tarnished. Third World radicalism had become a force to contend with, with disparate movements forming south-south connections and coalescing around globalized discourses.[21] And the 1973 oil embargo had transformed understandings of the capabilities of smaller, ex-colonial state actors, who not only lent their weight to the international community's regular and vitupera- tive denunciations of apartheid in global forums, but often led the charge. None of this favored the steady, controlled, top-down political evolution that Vorster envisaged. It is worth remembering that the South African Cabinet approved an expensive five-year national defense plan in January 1974, several months *before* the Carnation Revolution.[22]

As South African policymakers struggled to reconcile the different paradigms through which they understood their place in the world, they found that the neo-imperial, Cold War, and "South Africa in Africa" frameworks overlapped in one area: the hostility of communism to their way of life. Wherever opposition to apartheid was to be found, whether at the United Nations General Assembly in New York, within the Organization for African Unity (OAU) in Addis Ababa, or among nationalist movements challenging the status quo in Southern Africa, the communist banner was synonymous with the most militant hostility to- ward the Pretoria regime.[23] One 1966–67 survey showed that only 9 percent of (white) respondents saw domestic African nationalism as "the greatest threat to South Africa," while fully 73 percent chose global communism.[24] Understanding how Pretoria variously tried to render its political system viable in the postco- lonial world means acknowledging the reality of such threat perceptions, rather than simply dismissing them as misguided. Anticommunism comprised a plank of consensus throughout the white political sphere, and communism (however vaguely defined) provided the focal point for debates in Pretoria over national security threats (as well as the target for policy solutions). More broadly, the sub- suming of the African nationalist challenge within—or its displacement by— the communist threat provided an ideological lodestar for the regime. However, elites actually understood the relationship between the African nationalist and communist challenges differently, both because of the diversity of worldviews prevalent in Pretoria at the time and because of the limited firsthand knowledge that the regime had of either philosophy.

In this context, two different approaches emerged as to how the NP could navigate the squalls of a changing world and establish long-term security. The first was favored by Vorster and advocated by his foreign policy team, con- sisting of Secretary for Foreign Affairs Brand Fourie, Head of the Bureau for State Security (BOSS) Hendrik van den Bergh, and Foreign Minister Hilgard Muller. These foreign policy "doves" believed that if South Africa offered to help African states achieve their goals, then their self-interest would mandate embracing mutually advantageous cooperation rather than assuming a posture of futile confrontation. This premise, coined here as the Vorster Doctrine, was the golden thread running through all incarnations of Vorster's foreign policy until the end of 1976. Through trade and diplomacy, the doves hoped to drive a wedge between those "radical" states that demanded the destruction of the Pretoria regime and those "moderate" ones that, while still opposing apartheid, did not. With African militancy quelled, Vorster believed, South Africa would have the time and space to bring the homelands vision to fruition and illustrate the validity of separate development as a mechanism of self-determination for all South Africans. Ultimately, the underlying antipathy itself would fall away.

P. W. Botha interpreted the changing contours of the global order rather differently. Supported by an increasingly proactive and cohesive bureaucratic power base in the military, Botha believed that the anti-apartheid hostility of African nationalism was merely a tool of a communist "total onslaught" aimed at the riches and strategic position of South Africa. Where Vorster concentrated on influencing the character and discourse of African nationalism, Pretoria's hawks instead relentlessly targeted the communist cancer that they saw eating away at its core. "In the situation which currently exists, an African threat and a Soviet and/or Chinese threat cannot be meaningfully discussed separately," observed one major defense force report.[25] The hawks therefore advocated that the best means of achieving national security was through rearmament, an assertive military posture, and a "total strategy" that efficiently channeled the government's resources across the board toward the countering of the multidimensional communist threat. Botha repeatedly counseled his unreceptive prime minister that instead of attempting to marginalize radical movements through uncertain processes of negotiation and diplomacy, South Africa should instead act preemptively and use extraterritorial military action to force them to submit to Pretoria's regional hegemony.[26]

Prior to 1974, these two idiosyncratic philosophies developed side by side. Although already pulling South Africa's statecraft in contradictory directions, the tension between them remained largely inchoate and did not manifest itself in debilitating policy wrangles. However, the Carnation Revolution both foreshortened the time scale envisaged by the government as being necessary to implement separate development and underlined the revolutionary consequences of failing to entrench national security. For doves and hawks alike, events in Portugal and their consequences in Africa therefore narrowed the margin for error while raising the stakes of failure. A bitter tussle for preeminence between the two factions ensued, sometimes conducted indirectly, at other times bursting into open dispute. Difficult and major policy conundrums quickly arose. Should South Africa undermine the emergent left-wing regime in Mozambique, or offer aid and assistance? Should it allow the civil war in Angola to take its course, or try to ensure the victory of a well-disposed faction? Should it help produce multiracial governments in both Rhodesia and SWA in order to influence the ideological character of the successor regimes, or bolster the white communities in both places? These issues were particularly corrosive precisely because they pointed to a basic question that went to the heart of the regime's identity and prospects: was Pretoria in fact strong enough to coexist productively with African nationalism and, if not, how was Afrikanerdom to survive? Foreign policy, so cursorily discussed in the vast literatures on apartheid, was never just foreign policy. It was the arena of a fierce battle over the direction of the regime and the future trajectory of the Afrikaner national project.

The story of how the apartheid regime sought viability and survival in the post-1974 era was therefore one of competing policy programs. This book explores the tension between these programs across three levels of analysis. The first of these is international diplomacy: what South Africa as a state actor did on the international scene in its quest for national security. From Vorster's détente agenda with Kaunda, to the intervention in Angola, to the Kissinger Initiatives, the regime lurched from one geopolitical set piece to another. The analysis explains how Vorster sought to confound Pretoria's enemies at every turn and cultivate new expectations as to the future of South Africa's role in African politics, and why his endeavors failed. This narrative thread is both juxtaposed and intertwined with the emergence of total strategy, the solution to South Africa's problems championed by Botha.

The second level of analysis is regional strategy. South Africa's diplomatic programs in the formative 1974–76 period were not predominantly responsive to international pressure, as they are commonly portrayed.[27] Instead, they reflected considered strategies based on identified (though not necessarily correct) premises and targeted (but not always appropriate) opportunities. The approaches to national survival that underpinned South Africa's negotiating positions reflected an evolution of distinct national security strategies, from outward policy, to détente, to total strategy. Each was based on different conceptions of the engines of geopolitical change in the postcolonial world and how apartheid related to them. Strategy therefore comprised the link between the philosophical and ideological debates occurring among South African leaders in the corridors of power in Pretoria and the diplomatic programs that unfolded on the global stage. To foreground and develop the role of strategy, this book connects the various literatures on Pretoria's politics,[28] foreign policy,[29] and military,[30] which have previously remained decidedly distinct.

The factors that led to the adoption and jettisoning of each strategy were often intertwined with domestic politics, the third level of analysis. This book sets South Africa's turn away from diplomacy and toward a more confrontational approach against the backdrop of both genuine conceptual differences over how to preserve apartheid in the new era and political, personal, and bureaucratic rivalries. Which vision ultimately triumphed depended not only on the suitability of each vision to the circumstances, but also on the power bases of each leader, the strength and cohesion of their supporters, and their skill in political maneuvering. It also depended upon their ability to frame their favored policies in terms of the overarching debate over the future of Verwoerdian apartheid, the central political issue in the white South African power structure at the time. This last factor was critical. The dove-hawk division *cut across* the deepening fissure in Pretoria between those prepared to countenance reforms in order to keep the separate development program compatible with the changing realities of South African society and an evolving world (more pragmatic *verligtes*) and those who saw any mitigation of total racial separation under firm Afrikaner leadership as opening the door to the eradication of white self-determination, culture, privilege, and prosperity (dogmatic *verkramptes*). This fissure provided leaders with opportunities to secure support on the domestic front for their respective national security platforms, as well as political obstacles to overcome.

Leadership styles, intraparty dynamics, and individual decisions therefore mattered substantially to the outcome of this ideological struggle, which in turn shaped the priorities and political culture of the regime as it entered its era of decline. Vorster combined his ruthless and inflexible ruling style at home with a geopolitical vision that went well beyond the stilted and confining discourses prevalent among his colleagues. However, his aversion to swift, decisive action was poorly suited to the speed with which challenges emerged during the 1970s. Only moments of real crisis drove the cautious prime minister to the far-reaching action necessary to bring his visions to fruition on the diplomatic stage. He lacked the killer instinct required for this task, feeling much more comfortable with debate and persuasion. "Vorster was warm, a nice person, a very humorous man," recalls Nationalist Member of Parliament (MP) Koos van der Merwe, who later defected to the nascent right-wing Conservative Party. "There was something different about him. We [backbenchers] felt close to him."[31] But where Vorster pioneered his agenda through building support and cultivating allies, Botha saw power as coming only from being respected and feared. Charm and persuasion were not his strong suits. Van Zyl Slabbert, Leader of the Opposition during the 1980s, described Botha in his memoirs as straight out "belligerent, abusive, and alienating."[32] Botha gained followers through accumulating debts and doling out favors as leader of the Cape NP, not by dint of his inspiring leadership or winning personality. He was also an anticommunist fanatic. He could scarcely have possessed a more rigid understanding of why the outside world was so hostile toward the Afrikaner nation, or a more reflexively bellicose way of dealing with such hostility. His various nicknames, from *Pangaman* (the axe man) to *Groot Krokodil* (the great crocodile), reflect his style of politics. Yet these shortcomings obscured that Botha was also a masterful bureaucratic operator, using his years of experience at the heart of the party to push his ideological proposals through the relevant policy channels.

Conceptualizing Apartheid

Much of the scholarship on the crisis and decline of the apartheid regime has argued for the primacy of either structural factors (like apartheid's systemic flaws, countervailing demographic trends, or incompatibilities with the outside world)[33] or the conduct of external actors (whether other states, foreign anti-apartheid movements, or South African opponents of the regime).[34] Consequently, the contrast between the volume, depth, and accuracy of scholarship on how outsiders saw the Pretoria regime, and on how the architects of apartheid understood the world around them is by any measure a stark one.[35] In the most recent overview of the apartheid era, historian Saul Dubow writes: "We now know a great deal more about resistance and the liberation movements than we did in the 1980s. . . . Conversely, concerns with central state power and ideology during the apartheid era have lagged behind. . . . What was once a corrective to master narratives has become the norm."[36] Since 1994, South Africanist scholarship has moved beyond the magnetic draw of apartheid politics to develop innovative understandings of post-war history, particularly in social and cultural history, as well as through intellectual, environmental, and literary approaches. There have been few efforts to revisit the regime through the lens of the post-linguistic turn "new" political history.[37] Consequently, our knowledge of how the regime functioned, how its leaders understood the challenges they faced, how they rationalized the hostile world around them, are little more advanced today than they were when the regime collapsed more than twenty years ago.[38] Yet these questions are just as important now as then, having left a deep imprint upon so much of South African society and, as this book details, much of the broader region. This phenomenon matters far beyond the rarified realms of the academy too. Memories and notions of "apartheid" remain central to how citizens interpret and debate contemporary South African society. Yet when viewed through extraneous prisms rather than on their own terms, in their own time and place, the architects of apartheid can appear oddly two-dimensional to modern audiences. This ultimately serves to flatten the complexity of Nationalist rule into reductionist narratives. More to the point, the less historians uncover the rationales, fictions, and contradictions of apartheid rule, the more space is left open for contemporary actors to define the past for their own ends.

As for scholars of South Africa's foreign policy, they have long identified that policy as being intimately related to the regime's domestic ideologies. In this view, Pretoria's statecraft was a function of its quest for white hegemony. Counterintuitive advances to African leaders were therefore little more than cynical realpolitik, entailing a "fundamental contradiction" with domestic racial hierarchies.[39] The archives tell a more nuanced and complex story. They reveal that while the outside world saw Pretoria as the linchpin of the "white redoubt," Vorster was eager to find ways to differentiate and distance South African whites from those in Rhodesia and the Portuguese colonies as a symbol of a new "Africanized" identity for Afrikanerdom—in spite of considerable resistance from substantial sections of both the Nationalist establishment and the white electorate. Moreover, he consistently, even obsessively, acquiesced to pleas for assistance from African leaders in the hope of proving the regime's African credentials. And yet the very same regime violently oppressed South Africa's non-white peoples, dictated the limits of their own futures, and kept them in a position of subjugation and exploitation. The key to unraveling these apparent paradoxes lies in scholar P. Eric Louw's maxim: "[I]n order to understand apartheid, one has to get inside the heads of Afrikaner nationalists and take seriously what they believed about themselves."[40] That means setting their actions in a broad context of what they thought and why—intellectual history—and the material context that shaped the evolution of those ideas—social and economic history. From this vantage point, South Africa's foreign policy was quite in keeping with emerging ideological trends in Nationalist discourse (though it violated other, older strands of thinking). Cooperation with independent African states reflected the "real" separate development ideology of the Vorster era, with its emphasis on using the homelands to both contain and promote African political aspirations. Similarly, engagement with black, anticommunist states followed the Nationalist rejection of ideologies that offered Africans alternative identities to that of the nation-state, whether pan-Africanism, black consciousness, or communism.

Yet foreign policy not only reflected domestic ideology, but also shaped it. The 1960s were characterized by marked changes in the lifestyles and outlooks of the NP's Afrikaner base. The challenge for the Vorster government was to take a *volk* identity forged predominantly in rural, blue-collar, and petty bourgeois socioeconomic contexts and update it to the mores of an increasingly urbanized, aspirational, and educated constituency. Alliances across the color line conditioned Afrikanerdom to a fresh political economy in which old racial boundaries would need to be discarded in the name of a new ethos: racial coexistence through multinationalism. High-profile meetings with leaders of other African nations fostered the awakening of an understanding of *volk* identity through the prism of a universal concept of nationalism, thereby weakening traditional isolationist tendencies and accommodating emerging middle-class perceptions of the *volk* as part of the emerging postwar global community, not its righteous counterpoint. The state's sponsoring of modernization projects in independent Africa and its embrace of the very idea of modern Africa bolstered a separate development ideology that foregrounded "development" as well as "separation." In short, the various iterations of South Africa's statecraft in this period

were closely connected to proactive campaigns to reinforce particular ideological bases for the polity and establish long-term conceptual foundations for the
apartheid state-building project.

Vorster thus saw his central mission as comprising the preservation of status
and security in the twin contexts of shifting global norms and geopolitical
parameters abroad and of a modernizing South African society at home. The
unspoken corollary of this mission was that the state's racial order was a function of specific political projects designed to harness economic, ideological, and
social resources for the benefit of a particular social group in changing circumstances. Every element of this equation—the fortunes and content of various
projects, the resources prioritized by different sectors of society, the definition
of the groups to which privileges would accrue—were vigorously contested
within Afrikaner circles, as critics mobilized different notions and discourses in
the Nationalist canon to argue for divergent forms of *volk* identity. Behind the
façade of rigid support within the party for "apartheid," ideological contest and
internal discord was actually the norm.

In sum, the unlikely geopolitical story crowned by the meeting between John
Vorster and Kenneth Kaunda is incomprehensible without foregrounding the
debates over state-building priorities within the apartheid regime, which focused on the future of the *volk* and its separate development model in a hostile
world. Existing accounts agree that the core of the regime's foreign policy lay
in resisting decolonization and African nationalism in the name of white supremacy. This book instead shows how the regime sought not so much to repudiate as to hijack the norms and values of the postcolonial era, appropriating and
adapting them to relegitimize existing racial hierarchies in new forms. In search
of long-term viability, the leaders of white South Africa endeavored to reforge
the ideological basis for their social order and corrode identifications of the regime as a brutal remnant of European colonialism in a most unexpected way: by
redefining the white polity as an African and postcolonial entity.[41] Energetic outreach to Africa became the central engine of this ideological renewal and accompanying shift in state identity.

The approach taken by this book offers a range of new and productive angles
on the regime. First, it reinterprets how the apartheid regime responded to the
emergence of the postcolonial world. The regime did not so much look to simply
reject the ideas and values shaping the emerging global order as it did to appropriate and distort them for its own purposes. Instead of presenting the habitual
picture of staunch resistance to decolonization and the very idea of independent
Africa, this book shows how Pretoria enthusiastically sought to use diplomatic
successes with the new postcolonial states to forge an alternative model of
African identity governed by discourses of mutual economic development, anticommunism, and inviolable state-sovereignty. This shift was designed to serve

twin political ends: first, to enable the *volk* to reach across the color line and lay an equal claim to the power and protection of African nationalism; and second, to create an ideological framework that would apply equally to the homelands, thereby driving an unlikely legitimization of separate development as a system compatible with postcolonial norms. South Africa was thus not just the focus of an ongoing, continent-wide conversation about what it meant to be an independent African state, it was also a major participant in that conversation.

The central battleground for these efforts was African nationalism itself. Against substantial domestic opposition, the regime no longer sought to stop the flow of African nationalism, just a few years earlier considered an existential threat, so much as it strove to divert it into desirable channels and harness its power. Of course, Pretoria did so in the characteristic style of Nationalist political culture: by arrogating to itself the sole authority to decide which channels were or were not appropriate. The gambit never quite paid off. But the fact that Pretoria was even in a position to make such claims provides a lens through which to view the crisis of African politics in the late 1960s and early 1970s. Much of the optimism attached to the immediate postcolonial period had dissipated. African leaders were mired in political instability, stuttering economic development, and the redundancy of party ideologies bereft of their colonial counterpoint.[42] Militancy against white rule had also run aground. As South African diplomats repeatedly found on their visits into independent Africa, opposition to apartheid may have been universal, but commitment to forcing its removal varied widely.

South Africa seized this opportunity to contest the content of African nationalism, challenging its foundations in black uplift, liberation from colonial rule, and pan-African solidarity.[43] This quest meant adopting the mantle of anticolonialism itself. "When it comes to colonialism and fighting colonialism, we were the very first people to do just that," Vorster told Zambian diplomats. The idea that "we're colonialists" is the "utmost nonsense."[44] It entailed jettisoning racial prerequisites; in Pretoria's view, African nationalism could apply to all of the peoples of Africa, regardless of color. And it meant introducing new content, through a heavy foregrounding of development, anticommunism, and state sovereignty. Finally, Pretoria embedded the new construct in a broader discourse with global resonance—that of the Cold War—to try to compete with existing paradigms of African identity grounded in race, anti-apartheid militancy, *négritude*, and more. The result was a novel ideological construct that served the ends of state power on the continent and rejected the transnational discourses that remained important in multilateral forums like the OAU. As historian Frederick Cooper has written of the main processes of African decolonization in the late 1950s and early 1960s: "African politics did not develop in an autonomous world, but via interaction and conflict, and the struggle itself reshaped the kind of political projects that were or were not imaginable."[45] In much the same way, the crisis of postindependence Africa at the end of its first decade improbably informed the kinds of political projects that Vorster envisaged to deal with his regime's legitimacy problem. African and South African politics did not evolve in separate spheres, but in the context of overlapping conversations about sovereignty, history, and identity.

Second, this book conceptualizes anticommunism as a diffuse ideology of social control in the global south. The Cold War system was critical in providing the apartheid regime with a new legitimacy and sense of purpose. As discourses of overt racial domination became *passé*, anticommunism offered an ideological anchor for a regime in trouble, providing a language and a common paradigm through which the preservation of apartheid could be attached to wider global causes and external discourses—and unlikely allies. It facilitated the identification of a broad panoply of anti-apartheid discourses, movements, and individuals as little more than functions of communist power and ideas. And it affected Nationalist conceptions of identity in a changing world and shaped their programs for national progress and state security. All of these processes had emerged under Vorster's predecessors. But it was during his tenure that South Africa's quest for survival came to be largely shaped by the distinctive ways in which policymakers variously interpreted the nexus between the Cold War and their own apartheid doctrines. The waving of the anticommunist banner was no mere ruse to gain foreign support in the West, whether from states, nongovernmental organizations, or public spheres. Instead, the Cold War had far-reaching and diverse impacts upon the most fundamental ways in which the architects of apartheid understood the merits of their system. This applied to how Vorster saw Africa—with his focus on driving a wedge between anticommunist regimes and militant radical ones—as well as to Botha's rival worldview, with its perception of African nationalism as an unwitting tool of global communism. Whether it was the dovish program predicated on the validity of the Vorster Doctrine, or the hawkish concepts of total onslaught and total strategy, the philosophies that underpinned South Africa's search for viability were ones derived from patterns of thought familiar to statesmen and women west of the iron curtain and expressed in the Cold War terms familiar to them, but adapted and developed in a discrete local context.

The recent trend in Cold War history has been to globalize, bringing the motives and actions of actors in the global south into the picture.[46] This book suggests that the next frontier is to look precisely at the intersection of the global Cold War and local political agendas. That is, not so much at *geopolitics*, but at *domestic* politics, specifically at how Cold War ideologies shaped contests over different political visions *within* global south states. Anticommunism as an ideology was not only diffused outward from superpowers to other actors, it was defined and redefined by those on the frontlines in the global south for their own purposes. Indeed, superpowers had very little control over the concepts and principles that they created. The iteration of this phenomenon that unfolded in South Africa mattered for actors and struggles far beyond Africa. As the apartheid regime yoked anticommunism to white supremacy, it forced anticommunist Western elites to (often reluctantly) address issues of racial justice as part of their own postwar identities.[47] Pretoria's reshapings of what the Cold War was about may have emanated from discrete processes of social construction and control in Africa, but they reverberated across the globe.

The underlying question is how ownership of the anticommunist cause could be so diffuse in the first place. The rise of Cold War discourses among the Nationalist power structure was part of a much broader global process. The Second World War broke down social orders, undermined old ideologies, and exposed those serving both on the frontlines and on the home front to new ideas and forms of social organization. In many societies, the conflict broadened the political spectrum and expanded the realm of the possible. In this context, anticommunism as a global ideology was sustained by an intersection of elite interests in diverse societies around the world. By casting domestic struggles in the Manichean mold of the Cold War, those grasping the reins of power were able to control localized social ferments and impose their own particular agendas. Drawing on his research into postwar East Asia and the United States, historian Masuda Hajimu writes: "[T]he actual divides of the Cold War existed not necessarily between Eastern and Western camps but within each society, with each [divide], in turn, requiring the perpetuation of the imagined reality of the Cold War to restore and maintain order and harmony at home."[48] The conflict was, in essence, about localized social warfare and domestic politics. In South Africa, Nationalists engaged relentlessly in this process. The rigid bifurcation of the Cold War paradigm, coupled with the Nationalist community's legendary group-think and intolerance of dissenters, flattened perceptions of the *volk*'s predicament into crude dichotomies. The African opposition was continually presented as Moscow's stooge (which it was not), while Southern Africa was portrayed as one of the prime targets of communism's worldwide march (it was not; it was just low-hanging fruit given the surging power of nonracialism in global political discourses). In the name of anticommunism, non-whites in South Africa were violently denied real political agency. But they were not the only targets of such politics. At a time when the interests and social values of Afrikaners were diverging, the mobilization of anticommunist tropes served to coalesce different social classes in order to keep the NP's claim to national representation credible. In this sense, anticommunism served as an agent of social control within the *volk*, not only within South African society more broadly. Pretoria's foreign policy both reflected and reinforced these domestic ideological needs. In anticommunist independent Africa, the attachment of local politics to a Cold War framework served similar interests. Elites utilized a globalized dichotomous discourse to tar political rivals and unwelcome ideas as "communist inspired," impose their own agendas, and keep power vested in existing state structures. African outreach not only built relationships based on this commonality, it bolstered the legitimacy of the underlying ideological framework too.

In global terms, the brand of reactive, virulent anticommunism that Masuda explores slowly reduced in resonance over time. Even in American society, the anticommunist atmosphere of the "second" Cold War of the 1980s was never quite as acute or as broad-based as during the McCarthyist 1950s.[49] Instead, the bifurcated worldviews of the immediate postwar era gradually receded before more diverse concerns—such as superpower détente, human rights, geopolitical multipolarity, north-south disputes, economic liberalization, energy sustainability, and emergent globalization.[50] Over the same time period, however, anticommunism became markedly more prominent in the reigning discourses of Nationalist power, not less. This was due not only to the growing intensity of the domestic challenges that the regime faced, but also to the hollowing out of the regime's existing ideological structure. By the 1970s, many of the concepts underpinning the regime's legitimacy were steadily declining in credibility, whether internationally, among the white electorate, or both. Languages of overt racial superiority were a currency of rapidly declining global value as early as the 1950s. More coded calls to maintain "European civilization" were largely shunned by Nationalist elites by the mid-1960s (they remained very prominent in the Rhodesian power structure, by contrast). This ideological flux led to the rearticulation of existing notions of belonging and identities in decidedly unorthodox ways, with unexpected consequences. It also led to an increasing reliance on Cold War thinking, in the forms of total onslaught and total strategy. As faith in the feasibility of the existing model for the future—Afrikaner power within a broader white power structure, at the heart of a network of independent, equally African nation-states—ebbed and then evaporated in 1976–77, anticommunism came to assume an extraordinarily dominant role in articulating what the regime stood for and why fundamental social change should be resisted.

Finally, this book argues for positioning the evolution of the apartheid state within the history of state formation in the global south. The Vorster regime committed to adapting and reenergizing the *volk*'s mission in new political and conceptual circumstances. It recast Afrikanerdom as resolutely African, while identifying in the principle of horizontal multinationalism both a panacea for the regime's troubled relations with the outside world and a means of emancipating Afrikaner nationalism from the baggage of oppressing others. The trigger for this process consisted of unique external circumstances: international opposition to apartheid incentivized some form of ideological reconstruction. But the way in which the regime dealt with this challenge actually reflected a common set of circumstances for groups of elites right across the global south: the importance of claims to "nativism" as a bedrock for legitimacy in the age of decolonization, not so much vis-à-vis colonial powers, but in contests with other internal groups. One of the most important and sudden developments of the postwar era was the creation of a singular standard for those looking to participate in the global political community and its institutions: the nation-state.[51] For diverse groups across the global south, this development created a powerful impetus to mobilize nativist claims to historical nationalism as a mechanism to legitimize claims to the apparatus of state.[52] Recent literature on decolonization has shunned the old framework of a transfer of power, identifying that the lines between colonizer and colonizee were anything but clear, unambiguous, or stable. In fact, the labels traditionally used to demarcate the latter camp, like "local," "anticolonial," and "national community," were both the weapons and site of multifaceted contests *within* each decolonizing territory over precisely which groups could lay claim to the nativist mantle and therefore ought to have the right to govern. The stoking of racial differences was often central to the fighting of these political and intellectual contests.[53] In Zanzibar and Tanganyika, for instance, sets of local elites manipulated racial identities and ethnic boundaries to legitimate particular anti-colonial and nativist narratives, establish a claim to power, and thereby shape specific postcolonial political agendas.[54]

A not dissimilar process was happening in South Africa. The gatekeepers of the white power structure reframed the meaning of the racial differences in their social order so as to legitimate new political forms that they felt would be compatible with the postcolonial world. This agenda enjoyed far from universal support among Afrikaners, but rather was pioneered by elites amid steady class diversification, evolving social mores, and changing economic conditions. To borrow Michael O'Brien's conceptualization of the American South, Afrikaner identity was simultaneously national, imperial, and postcolonial.[55] It was national in its sense of an exclusive community bound by a common heritage and culture; it was imperial both in its capacity as a settler society whose economic success depended upon the exploitation of others and in its sense of a unique civilizing mission; and it was postcolonial in its self-identification as the heir to a rejection of metropolitan authority, with a commensurate eagerness to define its place in the world on its own merits. Vorster resuscitated concepts related to this last category and moved them into the foreground of political discourse in order to create new alloys of identity; his new articulation of the *volk*'s relationship with independent Africa would never have resonated without tapping into dormant political grammar in the lexicon of Afrikaner political thought. However, the other categories in the Nationalist canon did not suddenly disappear, leaving

Vorster's agenda decidedly vulnerable to competing articulations of *volk* values from those sectors of Afrikanerdom whose status and security was closely tied to the existing racial identities. The apartheid state is often understood essentially as a colonial holdout, its system largely impervious to the discourses of legitimacy and political organization sweeping across the postcolonial world.[56] This is misleading. In fact, the regime was very much aware of the new reality and struggling desperately to adapt, trying amid caustic internal opposition to reframe its ideological foundations from one conceptual era—that of white empire—to another—that of the postcolonial nation-state.

This integration of the apartheid state into the history of state formation across the postcolonial world points to an important realization for historians of Africa. The professional discipline of African history emerged tethered to the postcolonial political project. If the goal of the new political leaderships on the continent was to regain rights and agency for Africans, then Africanist scholars' parallel mission was to regain their history—which underpinned claims to those rights in important ways. The apartheid regime served as a foil to the new movement, not only in its intellectual and political dimensions, but in its moral one too. For the first generation of African historians, however, this phenomenon obscured much of the deeply troubling nature of the formation of postcolonial societies and institutions, processes often beset by violence, exclusion, misrule, and oppression.[57] The process of recapturing rights for Africans based on their "Africanness" thus hid complex power struggles between local groups and ideas—many focused on precisely what it meant to be "African"—that went far beyond the colonizer-colonizee dichotomy. In 2003, historian Timothy Burke observed:

> [T]he problem of postcolonial Africa is treated by the majority of scholars, especially anthropologists and historians, as an extension of or continuation of the problem of the colonial, [and] the moral and political challenge of postcolonial society is subordinated to or situated within a modernity whose character is largely causally attributed to colonial intervention. . . . The moral outrage, which suffused most Africanist historical and anthropological writing about the apartheid state, is largely absent when it comes to postcolonial African misrule.[58]

But what if independent Africa and apartheid South Africa are viewed through the same historical lens, focusing on common processes of state formation in the shared environment of a global south in which legitimacy was increasingly a function of effective claims to anticolonialism and the nativist mantle? In this perspective, decolonization looks more like a contest to delineate and coalesce a dominant ethno-nationalist identity, all while vesting resources in the successful group. South Africa was no exception here, but very much part of the mainstream. By looking less at the obvious differences in domestic power structures and more at the way in which shared global contexts shaped local political contests, this approach can begin to bridge the history of early independent Africa with that of its supposed counterpoint in apartheid South Africa.

Ultimately, this book details an often dysfunctional and always divided regime in crisis, wrestling with questions about its compatibility with an evolving outside world—questions South Africa's leaders knew would result in the destruction of their way of life if they did not find effective answers. Chapter 1 outlines the political and intellectual terrain of the 1960s. It shows how and why different sectors of Afrikanerdom interpreted the corollaries of Verwoerd's separate development model in divergent ways. The next two chapters juxtapose the doves' and hawks' programs for national survival, each of which emerged in the context of these disputes over the future direction of the Afrikaner national project. Chapter 2 explores South Africa's outward policy, both as foreign policy and political agenda. It details how and why Vorster sought to bolster new ideological foundations for Afrikaner nationalism by revolutionizing the regime's relationship with postcolonial Africa. Chapter 3 illuminates the security establishment's development of the total onslaught and total strategy doctrines. It explains how the regime understood geopolitical threats in the pre–Carnation Revolution period, as well as the national security policies, foreign relationships, and bureaucratic dynamics that these worldviews informed.

Chapters 4 through 9 explore the tension between the two programs from 1974, when Portugal announced its withdrawal from Angola and Mozambique, to 1978, when South Africa attacked Cassinga, heralding the triumph of a policy of confrontation with the outside world over cooperation. Chapter 4 dissects how policymakers in Pretoria responded to the departure of Portuguese rule from their regional environment. It shows how Vorster sought to make a settlement in Rhodesia a litmus test for his vision of the *volk*'s identity and future, but failed to overcome domestic opposition to the idea of abandoning fellow whites. Chapter 5 details South Africa's military involvement in the Angolan Civil War. It explains how intervention came to be seen as satisfying both of the major policy impulses in Pretoria—working with Africa and confronting communism— and was not, as traditionally believed, designed to fortify the regime's relationship with Washington along traditional center-periphery lines of Cold War security. Chapter 6 explains how the government's processing of the Angolan débâcle became a turning point in the ongoing debate over South Africa's place in the world. It illustrates how the government's post-facto rationalizations for intervention provided important support for Botha's vision of a total onslaught and his proposals for the regime's future statecraft. Chapter 7 focuses on the Kissinger Initiatives of 1976. It shows how far from Vorster being coerced into cooperation through American pressure over apartheid, he instead saw an opportunity to pursue his personal agenda in the shadows created by Washington's massive diplomatic profile. The failure of the Initiatives against the backdrop of internal unrest buried political will for Vorster's vision within the Nationalist establishment; Chapter 8 explains the consequences. It first zooms out to explain broader structural changes in white South African society and how these affected the way in which Vorster's failure was understood, and then details how Botha and the hawks were able in this context to assertively promote their doctrines within the government. Chapter 9 then brings the two threads of the policy battle together, showing how the demise of Vorster and his visions created a vacuum for the implementation of the hawks' doctrines as government policy. Finally, the Conclusion explains the importance of these events in creating the ideological dynamics and political context of apartheid's era of decline.

Two concepts dominate the approach in this book. The first is state formation. Historians are somewhat divided on the merits of the state as a subject of historical analysis. When some three decades ago Theda Skocpol called for scholars to "bring the state back in" to the center of scholarly perspectives, historians generally sided with the humanities over the social sciences.[59] This reluctance has persisted, even as political science has moved inexorably towards data and models ("quant"), all but vacating the historical study of the state. The new generation of scholars of decolonization do not share this reluctance. As historian Jeffrey Byrne points out, "the net result of decolonization was a dramatically more state-centric world order than had been true of even the very late colonial post-World War II years."[60] To talk about the decolonizing world and *not* to talk about the global south state is to miss much of the picture. Indeed, the familiar story of post-war history—of transnational forces eroding the importance of states—is one that loses relevance when history is viewed from the global south. The phenomenon Byrne identifies heavily shaped South Africa's campaign for legitimacy. The Nationalist regime argued that it was the state, as a structure, that could entrench long-term coexistence between the *volk* and its African neighbors, both on the continent and within South Africa. However, to lay claim to the protections that the international community accorded to member states, the white polity had to be accepted within the postcolonial world as such a state. This required a transition of the party's mission from that of advancing the cause of a national movement, to entrenching and prioritizing the state. It was this transition that caused Afrikanerdom such angst, entailing shifts in understandings of racial identity, notions of membership in the political group, and narratives of *volk* history, shifts which pitted different class groups within the *volk* against each other.

The second central concept here is ideology. This book explores the apartheid regime's geopolitical struggle for survival, the forces that shaped its pursuit of this goal, and the fallout of its failure. It treats actors as rational decision makers operating within bureaucratic contexts.[61] Actors did not, however, perceive options or interests in a vacuum, but through the prism of ideological discourses shaped by historical, intellectual, and political developments. It is these discourses—the political imaginary of apartheid, rather than the on-the-ground reality to which Nationalists averted their eyes—which shaped how the architects of apartheid understood and looked to alter the world around them.[62] The analysis here follows Aletta Norval's approach in accessing the regime's ideological discourses directly, through both the public statements and private accounts of apartheid's pioneers.[63] Precisely because the separate development program was heavily infused with a moral purpose, the associated discourses contained little dissimulation of their authors' thoughts (though the discourses operated within a conceptual framework that was divorced from reality). Departures from the earlier language of unabashed white dominance were neither platitudes for foreign consumption nor mere rhetoric. Instead, they reflected real changes in how the ruling class understood the shifting nature of their political mission in changing circumstances. In studying these discourses, the approach here is simultaneously sociological, in that it explores ideas not in isolation, but in relationship to evolving political, social, and economic interests; it is historical, aware that core nationalist values were shaped by contemporary context, despite competing claims to their being frozen in time and constant; and it is contingent, noting that the particular forms of discourses isolated in any place and time were but one of many potential fusions of the various possible constituent elements, with the materialization of a given formation also subject to specific, even improbable historical events.[64] As the meeting of Kaunda and Vorster at Victoria Falls suggests, this book explores just such events.

PART I

FROM CONTROL
TO OPPORTUNITY

1

"We Are Not Europeans"

Ideology and Identity in Pretoria's Golden Age

On September 13, 1966, the NP caucus met to elect a successor to the assassinated Hendrik Verwoerd as leader of the party (*Hoofleier*) and Prime Minister of South Africa. An eloquent ideologue and the pioneer of government policy in almost every sphere, Verwoerd had cast an immense shadow over South African politics. There was no obvious replacement. In previous leadership elections, as on many other issues, the federally structured party had been split along provincial lines.[1] By the 1960s, the Transvaal and Orange Free State caucuses were committed to wholescale racial segregation and were repositories of the crudest *baasskap* racist thinking. They regarded the Cape NP as dangerously unreliable guardians of the Nationalist mantle. The southern caucus had previously supported enfranchisement for Cape Coloreds. It had also advocated the creation of a republic that stayed within the Commonwealth, rather than one that repudiated everything British in favour of a full Afrikanerization of the white polity.[2] In the aftermath of the Sharpeville massacre, moreover, key Cape ministers had questioned the very basis of the government's policy of racial separation, recommended the abolition of pass books, and urged Verwoerd to allow and encourage blacks to have a stake in the existing socioeconomic order.[3] One candidate from each faction quickly emerged: Ben Schoeman, Verwoerd's deputy as leader of the Transvaal NP; and Eben Dönges, leader in the Cape. The party was predictably divided on their respective merits, and leading ministers began to look for a compromise candidate.

John Vorster was only thirteenth in order of party seniority. However, the then minister of justice (as well as of police and prisons) epitomized the firm hand the party sought at a time of uncertainty. In spearheading the regime's post-Sharpeville crackdown, he had introduced legislation that punished "sabotage" (broadly defined) with a minimum penalty of five years' imprisonment and a maximum of death; dramatically extended the powers of the regime to censor individuals and entire organizations under "banning orders"; rendered it a criminal offence simply to belong to such an organization; and empowered the regime to detain suspects for ninety days without charge. Under the last measure, the regime had detained 1095 people. By the time the measure was suspended in early 1965, only 575 of these had even been arraigned: the law was as much designed to intimidate dissidents and dragoon them into informing on their colleagues as it was to prosecute actual transgressors.[4]

Overall, Vorster had pioneered immense damage to due process, the rule of law, freedom of association, and freedom of speech. The English-speaking community was appalled. The new agenda was "clearly the product of a dictator mentality," the *Rand Daily Mail* had declared.[5] But the effect in Nationalist circles was to inspire a deep confidence that the hardline, no-nonsense Vorster could navigate them through troubled waters. Also in Vorster's favor was that he transcended the geographical divisions in the party. Although representing a constituency in the Transvaal, he had been born, raised, and educated in the Cape. He was therefore acceptable to a broad spectrum of his colleagues: those advancing his candidacy included both the Cape faction (Vorster soon arranged for Dönges to be elected state president) and the NP's hard right-wing faction (which both nominated and seconded his candidacy). In the end, he was the unanimous choice of the party room.[6]

The polity Vorster inherited appeared to be thriving. Throughout the 1960s, the economy grew at an average rate of 6 percent per annum.[7] Incomes were rising quickly across the board, especially for whites.[8] By 1970, South Africans owned 74 percent more cars than as recently as 1960, while foreign investment had increased from US$3 billion to US$7.9 billion.[9] On the security front, the African call for concrete measures against the regime, so vibrant in the early years of decolonization in 1960–61, was running out of steam.[10] Both in South Africa and abroad, the prospect of apartheid being rolled back through diplomatic, economic, or military pressure seemed remote, or at least inchoate.[11] In keeping with the reduced sense of external threat, South Africa's defense spending declined steadily from 21 percent of the national budget in 1964–65 to 12 percent in 1972–73.[12]

However, the apparent stability that defined this era concealed important changes in how various elements of the white South African power structure perceived the regime's long-term viability, envisaged threats to the state, and understood the relationship between domestic ruling ideologies and the paradigms of decolonization, African nationalism, and the Cold War.

A Crisis of Control and Identity

Understanding how and why Vorster took the polity in unexpected directions, as well as why doing so proved controversial, requires comprehending his political context: the relationship between the apartheid system and Afrikaner nationalism in the emergence of Nationalist power; how this process informed different understandings of the mission of the *volk* in subsequent decades; and how and why Vorster understood his role as *Hoofleier* differently from his predecessor.[13] For present purposes, the apartheid system was the mechanism created to protect and advance Afrikaner nationalism, as this political force developed out of the economic and social uncertainty engendered by South Africa's rapid industrialization and urbanization.[14] Nationalist leaders saw themselves as guardians of the *volk*. To advance its interests, they coopted some outsiders and coerced the rest. Three caveats to this picture should be stated now, though they will be developed later. Afrikaner leaders in both the political and cultural realms disagreed over what those interests were and how to protect them. As the party broadened its appeal beyond Afrikaners, its interests evolved. Finally, the socioeconomic diversification of Afrikanerdom corroded both the reality and the notion that the *volk* had common, indivisible interests.

For decades, Afrikaans schools, universities, politicians, cultural organizations, and churches had incubated a resentment-filled Afrikaner identity defined against both the imperialist British and the African native.[15] Defeat and humiliation in the Boer Wars, Britain's conquest of the Afrikaner republics, and subordination in the anglophone economy were at the forefront of cultural and political discourse, all set against fears of the latent threat of black numbers, heathendom, and barbarism. From the 1930s, however, Afrikaner intellectuals, often returning from postgraduate study in the Netherlands or Germany, began to construct a positive conceptual platform for building an Afrikaner nation. Theologians developed a biblical basis for maintaining the integrity of each of God's nations. Secular political theorists borrowed heavily from the German nationalist discourses of the mid-nineteenth century to emphasize Afrikanerdom's rights as a nation with a unique culture, language, and history. The first generation of writers and historians to use modern Afrikaans provided just such a canon, though some equally warned against the group-think of nationalist enterprises and stressed the importance of independent thinking.[16]

The cumulative output of these endeavors was the political ideology of Christian Nationalism. Central to the new ideology was the concept of *volksverbondenheid*, the idea that an individual could only achieve fulfillment through membership in a national community, or *volk*. This principle applied both broadly and specifically: broadly, in that it stipulated a right to existence for each and every national community, based on its own values and character (*volkseie*); and specifically, as legitimizing the creation of an Afrikaner republic in South Africa based on Calvinist values and the reproduction of existing social structures in contradistinction to emerging "foreign" or "liberal" norms.[17] Christian Nationalism thus posed a direct challenge—with divine sanction no less—to

those who argued that political alliance with English-speakers was the path forward (*samesmelters*).

Afrikaner nationalism was thus not merely a vehicle for powerful underlying
economic forces, little more than the "form in which specific class forces came
to be organized," as some structuralists have maintained.[18] Others appear to take
Afrikaner nationalism out of the picture entirely.[19] Instead, it comprised a powerful though constructed identification that owed much to the cultivation of an
idea of the nation and the beginning of small-scale political mobilization by nationalist pioneers.[20] National consciousness developed first among the literati
and elites. The masses were the last to subscribe—and, as it turned out, the last
to let go.[21]

By the Second World War, South Africa's society and economy had been
shaped by centuries of ad hoc racial discrimination and segregation.[22] The
conflict profoundly changed labor regimes through much of Africa. Colonial
economies were heavily relied upon to support the military campaigns of their
metropoles. Economic flux led to expectations of labor rights on the part of
African workers—and ultimately political rights too.[23] The white political sphere
in South Africa was deeply concerned about the unfolding of similar processes
and their effects on traditional racial hierarchies. The war drew white workers
away for military service while simultaneously providing a massive stimulus
to the South African economy.[24] Gross national income more than doubled
between 1939 and the start of the Nationalist era in 1948.[25] Many working-
class Afrikaners migrated from farm to city; 1948 was the first year when more
Afrikaners lived in urban rather than rural areas.[26] Often very poorly educated
and insular in their cultural outlook, they generally struggled to adapt.[27] They
also found social friction with and job competition from blacks. Between
1936 and 1946, the African population of greater Johannesburg grew by nearly
60 percent.[28] As increased European demand drove a shift from small-scale
workshop-centric production to large-scale factory manufacturing, Africans
were increasingly included in the "semi-skilled" and even "skilled" labor ranks.[29]
Black labor assertiveness rose accordingly. The number of African man days
lost to strikes was nearly six times higher in the 1940s (through 1948) than it
had been in the 1930s.[30] Nor were agricultural work patterns spared the upheaval. Greater social opportunities and higher-paying jobs beckoned in the
cities, which acted as a substantial draw on the African labor pool that sustained
low-cost white farming.[31] A 1946 cartoon in *Die Transvaler* depicted a long line
of Africans heading toward the Johannesburg skyline. The ominous caption
read: "The greatest trek, 1936–?"[32]

As the use of the trek trope suggests, socioeconomic flux in South African
society fueled the growth and politicization of Afrikaner identifications.[33]
Two factors were central to this process. One was a marked erosion of "South

DIE GROOTSTE TREK: 1936–?

Figure 1.1 "The greatest trek, 1936–?" The booming war economy prompted a surge in African urbanization. As the use of the trek trope suggests, the fears provoked by this development materialized in the growth and politicization of identifications as Afrikaners. Source: *Die Transvaler*, 1946. Caxton Company.

Africanist" white identity subscribed to by English-speakers and Afrikaners alike. Events like the 1938 centenary reenactment of the Great Trek and South African involvement in the Second World War deeply divided white society. Historian Hermann Giliomee gives the example of a wartime judge asking a witness what defined "an Afrikaner." The quick reply was: "Someone who is against the war."[34] The United Party (UP) government's own ruling consensus also fell apart, as the alliance between the different economic interest groups that it represented became untenable. Where mining and agriculture wanted the state to vigorously resist African urbanization through tighter "influx control" regulations so as to sustain their cheap labor pool, manufacturing, commerce, and industry instead wanted the government to adapt to the new reality, with some even supporting the legalization of black labor unions.[35]

Such emerging conflicts of interest between major economic sectors were not unproblematic for the Nationalists when they took over the reins of government, though their more socioeconomically uniform base made the choice of hardline labor policies decidedly the more attractive one. Overall, however, the Nationalists simply shifted the political terrain by exploiting the prevailing socioeconomic precarity in the language of "nationalist" concerns. Economic insecurity was relentlessly connected to the threat of *oorstroming* [flooding] by Africans and racial degeneracy. Growing friction with other groups in urban environments was blamed on the failure of "the government" to effectively preserve Afrikaans language and culture.

Fear was thus the central catalyst for the political mass mobilization of Afrikaner nationalism and that fear found consistent fuel in changing socio-economic patterns. This sentiment extended from the grassroots to the political classes. In a letter to D. F. Malan, leader of the NP and soon to be the first apartheid prime minister, his colleague Albert Hertzog lamented that without an effective counter to "liberalist principles . . . the next generation of kaffirs will have great political authority." He concluded: "We see threats right around us—and if just a few of them are realizable, then the Afrikaner ideal will never again be realizable."[36] Political unity, however, lagged behind. As late as the end of the Second World War, no fewer than four different political organizations laid claim to the Afrikaner nationalist mantle: D. F. Malan's Herenigde Nasionale Party (Reunited National Party, the immediate forerunner of the NP); the fascist Nuwe Orde (New Order); the Ossewabrandwag (Oxwagon Sentinel, or OB), to which John Vorster belonged; and the Afrikaner Party (AP). By 1948, these battles had largely been resolved in favor of Malan's organization. The challenge for the NP was to provide a concrete, singular political program for this politically diverse nationalist movement.[37]

"Apartheid" filled this role, bringing voters behind the NP standard. Yet the details of what apartheid would constitute as a policy were notably vague. Almost the entire white political spectrum was in the market for ideas about how to entrench white supremacy; both the Nationalist opposition and the UP government commissioned major studies (the Sauer and Fagan Reports, respectively) on the issue in the immediate postwar years. The United Party could neither pin the NP down to define in which specific spheres the principle of racial separation would or would not be applied, nor could it effectively articulate how its own racial policy differed from apartheid without being labelled as pro-integration.[38] This was no accident: the purpose of the Sauer Report (1948) was not to outline a rigid policy template, but instead to create consensus behind the banner of "apartheid" between "different ideological strands within Nationalist thinking—secular as well as religious, racist, and ethno-culturalist."[39] That it did—for now. Yet the new program had an additional political strength: it was powerfully inclusive, as well as more obviously exclusive. It offered a superior mode of citizenship to all Afrikaners—which, given the racial content in Christian National ideology and the existing South African political structures, extended to English-speakers too—and attached that citizenship to a specific cultural identity and, indeed, a particular political party, the volksfront. Through its articulation and demarcation of a volk nation-state, apartheid thus ascribed a specific national identity to white Afrikaans speakers, whether they wanted it or not. Economic resources, social advantages, even existential fulfilment were all offered on the basis of that identity. No other power structures could offer superior yields based on divergent identities. This was the essence of the National Party's political strength.[40]

Though their ideological agenda emerged out of local historical processes, the Nationalists were swift to map it onto discourses with currency in the broader international community. On the racial front, they exploited British and French efforts to reenergize colonial rule in the postwar years to bolster their own white paternalist agenda. As early as 1949, the year after becoming the first Nationalist prime minister, D. F. Malan introduced the Africa Charter as a basis for cooperation with colonial powers. It committed South Africa to "retain[ing] Africa as a reserve . . . for the further development of West European Christian civilization" and preserving as much of the prewar status quo on the continent as feasible.[41] Equally, the Nationalists cited the disorder of decolonization as providing ample justification for tight government control over the existing social order in South Africa. Events like the pell-mell Belgian withdrawal from the Congo in 1960 provided ready fodder for government assertions about the dangers of enabling African political agency.[42]

The early Nationalists likewise attached their governing program to the incipient Cold War. Anticommunism had a long history within the white power structure in South Africa. Already during the Rand Rebellion of 1922, the government of Jan Smuts feverishly condemned the (largely white) miners' strike as a "Red Revolt" and "Bolshevist conspiracy." The 1925 decision of the South African Communist Party (SACP) to shift its focus from the white proletariat to its black counterpart only fueled white anxieties.[43] Communist opposition to the existing social structures accelerated during the 1930s and 1940s, as some labor organizations championed a unified working class that transcended the color bar. During the Second World War, the SACP laid out the challenge to white hegemony directly, advocating a fully inclusive polity. Under the heading "Four-fifths of the People," one banned pamphlet declared: "The non-white people of South Africa are gruesomely and shamefully oppressed. . . . Let the broad masses of the working and oppressed people of South Africa unite." The message to Afrikaners specifically was strident: "*A people which oppresses other people cannot itself be free.*"[44] Rather than reflecting upon this contention, Nationalists summarily rejected it. They attached fears of the *swart gevaar* [black threat] readily to those of a *rooi gevaar* [red threat], relentlessly animating the danger posed by communism to the existing social order. In 1948, D. F. Malan observed:

> Communism can be more destructive in South Africa than elsewhere not merely because of its ideology, but because of the fact that it makes a special appeal to the country's non-European population, and if the communists achieve in South Africa what they want to achieve as far

as the non-European population of the country is concerned, the death knell will have been sounded for white civilization in South Africa.[45]

Communism was thus presented as the barbaric nemesis to the party's mission to preserve European "civilization."

Nationalist discourses demonized communism as offering mortal challenges to Afrikanerdom in other domains too. The articulation of class interests and struggle was presented as being fundamentally incompatible with the party's emphasis on the indivisible unity of the *volk*. In 1933, for instance, Malan commented that "there were no classes or estates" among the *voortrekkers*, the Afrikaner pioneers of the Great Trek.[46] Labor quickly became the frontline of strenuous intellectual and political efforts to promote ethnic solidarity in contradistinction to class consciousness. Verwoerd wrote in one letter: "The threat to the Afrikaner is . . . that in urbanizing he would undergo a process of proletarianization in which he would lose all interest in Afrikaner culture and would become merely an international worker."[47] In 1939, the Reddingsdaadbond (Rescue Authority) was established with a singular mission: "to make the Afrikaans labourer part and parcel of national life and to prevent the Afrikaans worker developing as a class distinct from other classes in Afrikaans national life."[48]

Communism's atheism was also singled out as being anathema to the ultrareligious Afrikaners. "Communism is anti-religion, and because people are not made that way, it cannot succeed," encapsulated P. W. Botha.[49] The Calvinist churches became powerful sponsors of anticommunist writing, speeches, and conferences, providing an aggressive and united front in the Afrikaans social sphere. Another strand of the religious objection to communism drew on anti-Semitic tropes. For instance, on the eve of the Second World War, A. J. G. Oosthuizen, a minister in the Calvinist Nederduitsch Hervormde Kerk (NHK), labeled the general secretary of the influential Garment Workers Union, Solly Sachs, a "communist Jew" promoting "Russian godlessness."[50] Communism's advocacy of racial equality and internationalism was positioned as a challenge not only to political commitments to the nation and racial separation, but to sacred and immutable Christian principles too.

The Afrikaner fear of communism was thus not merely political, but existential, centering on threats to the racial, national, class, and religious components of *volk* identity simultaneously. These perceptions in turn supported the regime's identification of communism as inherently *foreign*, by definition an external menace rather than a legitimate political ideology. Though far removed from the early Cold War conflicts, South Africa eagerly volunteered its air force for the Berlin airlift in 1949 and the Korean War the next year. Moscow came in for fierce denunciation in intellectual, church, and political circles. In 1956, the South African government unilaterally closed the Soviet consulate in Pretoria.

The Suppression of Communism Act (1950), already draconian, was tightened in 1951 and 1954, as well as repeatedly during the 1960s at Vorster's own behest.[51] The public sphere was inundated with articles, books, and pamphlets, each purporting to reveal the hidden hand of Soviet-aligned agitators behind every problem the white power structure encountered.[52] Anticommunism thus became an effective tool for denigrating challenges to the existing order and demonizing potential opponents, thereby underwriting the preservation of existing forms of order and control. The Cold War did not exist as the sole applicable framework for understanding politics in a highly contested and diverse sphere. Yet the white power structure consistently perceived the world through that lens due to the prevailing political imperative in South Africa's particular socioeconomic context: mustering the requisite fear to resist the fundamental social change desired by most of the populace.[53]

Apartheid is therefore best understood as a response to twin crises of control and identity in the context of rapid industrialization and urbanization.[54] At a time when existing social boundaries were threatened, the Nationalist platform animated the fears of economically insecure voters and offered them a mirage of certainty. The NP could not have come to power without performing strongly in electorates where economic competition was most acute. In 1948, the party and its allies reached out from their rural heartland to pick up no fewer than thirteen urban constituencies on the Witwatersrand alone, including five in working- and lower-middle-class parts of Pretoria.[55] Yet the less tangible issue of identity was also critical. Apartheid constituted an extraordinarily effective mechanism for not only animating a range of fears, but also mobilizing Afrikaners to vote *as Afrikaners*—that is, for the National Party on the basis of a nationalist identity, and not for the South Africanist United Party. In areas of Afrikaner concentration, the NP and its allies were utterly dominant in the 1948 election, winning 84 percent of such seats in the Cape Province (outside of Cape Town, Port Elizabeth, and East London), 100 percent of such seats in the Transvaal (outside of Johannesburg and Pretoria), and 92 percent of such seats in the Orange Free State.[56] By contrast, at the 1958 elections, after fully a decade of benefiting from apartheid, perhaps only 1 percent of English-speakers voted for the NP.[57] Apartheid provided the most effective political framework on offer for securing an "us"—Christian National Afrikaners as an outpost of European civilization—against a malleable and shifting "them"—the barbarism of Africans, the moral corruption of the modern world, the racial integration of liberalism, the social flattening of communism.

The specific circumstances of this crudescence of Nationalist power had important consequences for Vorster's and P. W. Botha's subsequent efforts to secure the polity. Precisely because the social and intellectual spheres had been the forums where Afrikaner nationalism coalesced first while the politicians

were still fighting over issues of political organization, the party's claim to absolute leadership of the wider movement remained shaky. Other entities, particularly the Broederbond, a shadowy ethno-nationalist organization for Afrikaner
elites, were more inclined to see the power structure of the movement as diffuse,
with each arm having authority only in its own sphere.[58] Furthermore, there
was an unresolved tension between separation and domination inherent in the
apartheid program. Finally, there was a strong divide between ideologues who
saw strict apartheid as inseparable from preserving the integrity of the Afrikaner
national project and others who preferred to distinguish between the two goals.

High Apartheid

The nebulousness of apartheid as a policy was reflected in the decidedly uneven
enforcement of racial separation in the first decade of Nationalist power. The government passed overtly ideological laws designed to appeal to the crisis of identity, like the Prohibition of Mixed Marriages Act (1949) and an amendment to
the Immorality Act (1950), which respectively criminalized interracial marriage
and sex. However, the government's imposition of economic and social segregation was generally characterized by a raft of often messy legislative compromises
among the state, local authorities, labor groups, capital, and even African political
organizations.[59] Part of the reason was political weakness. The Nationalists held a
bare electoral majority, had not yet penetrated the civil service, and had yet to resolve the voting status of Coloreds and Africans, both of whom could be expected
to be hostile to their agenda.[60] Even in parliament, where it had control, the party
only maintained power due to an anachronistic weighting of rural seats; in 1948,
the smallest electoral constituency had a whopping 45.4 percent fewer voters than
the largest.[61] However, there was also no consensus within the NP over what the
future of South African society should look like and how racial separation should
be implemented. Precisely because apartheid was designed as an ideological rally-
ing point for different agendas, discourses, and interest groups, even after key pillars of racial segregation had been erected, the system was rationalized in strikingly
divergent ways within Afrikaner circles and white society more broadly.[62]

 In this context of contestation and compromise, Hendrik Verwoerd's central
achievement lay in forging a political consensus behind a far-reaching program
of social engineering. "Dr. Verwoerd's spiritual make-up was overwhelmingly
intellectual: ordered thoughts, clear doctrines, fixed future plans," observed Piet
Cillié, editor of Die Burger and no Verwoerd fan. "What was justified and correct
in principle, had to be capable of implementation. Obstacles in human nature
must give way to regulation and systemization. The ideal must be imposed on
society."[63] For the abrasive and dogmatic Hoofleier, the unique destiny of the

volk mandated the exclusion of any and all foreign elements. In 1958, soon after becoming prime minister, he set out the concept of a divinely legitimized Afrikaner state in a speech commemorating the Boer victory over the Zulus at Blood River in 1838. The Afrikaner had been "planted here at the southern point" of Africa, he proclaimed, "so that from this resistance group . . . all that has been built up since the days of Christ may be maintained for the good of all mankind." Just as the original *voortrekkers* had been decried by hostile missionaries for insisting that "the supremacy of the white man" was "necessary" for civilized development, it once more fell to whites in Africa to "be an anchor and a stay for Western civilization and for the Christian religion" in the era of decolonization. Pretoria's emphasis on racial segregation and hierarchy in an age of increasing integration and equality was presented not just as a hallowed national destiny, but as a service to all mankind: "[T]here sometimes have to be small groups that offer resistance; a resistance that can be extended until it embraces the whole pattern of nations."[64] The ideological basis for the state was thus thoroughly exclusive. Regime ideology largely consisted of the virulent canon espoused by mid-century nationalist intellectuals, expressed through religious tropes as well as neo-imperial norms and discourses that drew directly on conceptions of racial supremacy.[65]

As newly independent African states, their Asian counterparts, the United Nations General Assembly, the OAU, the World Council of Churches, and even some European powers all emerged within just a few years as critics of South Africa's racialist rule, Verwoerd remained unmoved. The rest of the world's folly, he argued, was no reason to depart from God's course.[66] In 1960 alone, Verwoerd was confronted with a series of major crises, including the Sharpeville massacre, Harold Macmillan's "winds of change" speech, South Africa's pending exclusion from the Commonwealth, and an assassination attempt. Far from wilting under pressure, the prime minister saw an opportunity to press his agenda. He exploited the global criticism and deep sense of insecurity at home to pursue a radical agenda: the establishment of a stand-alone Republic, which he presented as the modern reincarnation of historic Afrikaner nationalism; and the systematic imposition of rigid racial separation at the expense of more moderate alternatives.[67] In doing so, the former Stellenbosch academic and editor of *Die Transvaler* proved himself quite the political opportunist. By the start of the Vorster era, it was accepted throughout the NP that strict apartheid was the most effective, practicable, sustainable, and moral means of ensuring self-determination for the Afrikaner.

Verwoerd's second political success was his subsequent fusion of the pursuit of Christian National republicanism to an ideological and political framework that was articulated as providing benefits for South Africans more broadly. He reached out to English-speaking voters on the basis that what was good for Afrikaner interests was good for other whites' prosperity and status too. This unexpected move yielded profound gains, broadening the political and conceptual base for his strict apartheid vision. At the 1961 election, the NP won only 16.5 percent of votes in predominantly English-speaking Natal; by the 1966 election, Verwoerd's last, that figure had grown to 40.1 percent.[68] Simultaneously, Verwoerd utilized the principle of "own-ness" [eie] to introduce a practical solution to the emergence of African nationalism and increasing international pressure for decolonization: the creation of homelands, or bantustans, for each African "national community."[69] Blacks would be excluded from the white state and granted the opportunity to progress separately toward "survival and full development, politically and economically."[70] The cynicism of this policy was barely concealed. "A psychotic preoccupation with the rights, the liberties and the privileges of non-white peoples is sweeping the world," Verwoerd observed in a speech entitled "The Price of Appeasement in Africa."[71]

Although this vision was widely derided by outsiders as merely proscribing to black South Africans the strict limits of their political futures, the traction of the separate development concept in the white political sphere was very substantial. The long-term future of Africans was not a subject on which the NP had previously invested serious and sustained energy. Now, the *Hoofleier* seemed to have solved the entire issue and at the very first try. In Afrikaner circles, Verwoerd was lionized and his grand plan exalted. Upon his death, *Volkshandel*, the monthly periodical of the emerging Afrikaanse Handelsinstituut (AHI, Afrikaner Chamber of Commerce), lamented the passing of a "great statesman and dynamic leader":

> Hendrik Verwoerd will stand in history on the same pedestal as Paul Kruger [the leader of the Afrikaner republics in the Boer Wars]. He is the political as well as economic father of our white Republic. . . . His sincere efforts to help non-white races develop independently in their own areas has laid the foundation for a future template of a multi-racial state with independent ethnic groups.[72]

Even the liberal *Rand Daily Mail*, a fierce critic of the regime, stated that Verwoerd had taken "the simple, crude concept of racial domination known as *baasskap* and refined it into a sophisticated and rationalized philosophy of separate development."[73]

The State-Builder

Upon Verwoerd's assassination, Vorster's central policy priority comprised the fulfilment of his predecessor's separate development vision: the creation of ethnic homelands or bantustans for Africans while not disturbing the central role that cheap black labor played in overall white prosperity and control. No other Nationalist prime minister had ever had a clearer sense of his political constituency and what they wanted for the future. However, this consensus was a function of a rigid ideology—by definition any racial integration could not be total separation—that served as both a guiding light and a straightjacket for future leaders.

In truth, Verwoerd had bequeathed little more than a blueprint. He had summarily rejected the Tomlinson Commission's recommendation (1955) that sustainable white independence required substantial investment in the viability of the homelands.[74] It was up to his successor to find the funds, ideologies, and materials to build the modern South African state. The scale of the challenge soon became apparent. By the end of the 1960s, new research revealed that Verwoerd had severely underestimated the growth of the black population. "The projections imply a doubling of [black] numbers between 1970 and 1994," economist J. L. Sadie found in a landmark study. "The need for a sustained and vigorous family planning program, which will reduce [black] fertility more rapidly than is implied in our projections, is obvious."[75] In 1970, Vorster chose a different path, latching onto the idea of accelerating the preparation of the homelands for independence and stripping blacks of their South African citizenship.[76] Unlike Verwoerd, he acknowledged the need for the economic development of the bantustans. In 1971, the South African Treasury contributed 200 million rand to the South African Bantu Trust Fund, compared to less than 10 million rand in 1960.[77]

This was nowhere near enough funding to achieve real viability for the homelands. But it was a major policy shift, and one that brought into sharper view the importance of solving apartheid's underlying legitimacy problem. Vorster realized that the old framework of norms, values, and institutions that had sustained the South African regime both domestically and abroad was losing currency, such that pursuing the separate development goal within the existing conceptual framework would lead only to unsustainable isolation. "The practice [of separate development] requires pragmatism. . . . We must take notice of the circumstances of the times and deal with them accordingly," he told the NP caucus.[78] The new prime minister therefore resolved to forge a framework of legitimacy that applied to all South African "nations" on the same basis, one that could support the existing physical structures sketched out by Verwoerd. He later reflected: "I set myself two goals, first, to create better relations between people, Afrikaans and English-speaking, White, Colored, Indian and Black; second, to do my utmost to normalize relations between South Africa and other countries."[79] These goals were, in fact, deeply interrelated.

Vorster sought new scaffoldings of legitimacy for the state in a most unexpected way: by corroding identifications of his regime as a brutal remnant of

European colonialism and redefining the white polity as part of independent Africa. After only six months in office, he launched this campaign with a speech in the Afrikaner heartland in Bloemfontein. In the nineteenth century and culminating in the Boer Wars, he stressed, Afrikaners had formed "the first African state to have revolted against [British] imperialism. It [was] the first state in whose midst there were cries for emancipation and independence." From this anticolonialist history emerged a claim to the nativist territorial nationalism of the postindependence era: "[W]e are in every respect a part of Africa."[80] On the face of it, this was simply an extension of a preexisting strand in the Nationalist canon. The *volk* represented "the only white nation which was born here," echoed Hertzog, increasingly among Vorster's most implacable right-wing foes.[81] However, Vorster then used this reformulation of the historical foundations of Afrikaner nationalism as a platform from which to conceptually reshape apartheid around norms of interdependence and coexistence rather than dominance and hierarchy. "[I]f Nationalism was right for my people then it is right for anyone, irrespective of his color or identity," he continued.[82] The ideological watchword became coexistence of white and black on an equal footing, both inside the Republic's borders between the regime and the homelands and on the continent as a whole. Building on this subtle shift in how Pretoria articulated the conceptual foundations for apartheid, Vorster looked to appropriate the very same principles South Africa's enemies used to attack the regime—anticolonialism, the elimination of racial hierarchies, and self-determination—adapt them to the Verwoerdian program of separate development, and use the new constructs to justify Afrikaner independence and control at the core of a broader white power structure.

From the outset, Vorster's ideological campaign had clear limits. The new ideas remained centralized in his office, rendering them vulnerable to competing interpretations of the polity's identity from others. The new program was beset by logical contradictions, not the least being how Afrikaners could outline a nativist territorial claim while affording the same rights of citizenship in the polity to English-speakers, who made no parallel claim of their own. And, of course, local black leaders were never allowed to shape the new ideological framework, but instead had to subscribe to it as a precondition of being allowed to engage formally with the regime.

Vorster offered no mere shift in emphasis or style from his predecessor. Despite his creation of the homeland vision, Verwoerd's conceptualization of Afrikanerdom retained a fundamentally inimical relationship with African nationalism. Just before his death, Verwoerd met with Leabua Jonathan, soon to be leader of independent Lesotho, but pointedly refrained from dining with him.[83] Moreover, the ideological basis of the regime remained unchanged by decolonization. "[T]his Republic is part of the White man's domain in the world. . . . He, and the spirit with which he is endowed . . . will always be needed where order and peace and progress are desired," Verwoerd said in 1966.[84] This was a fundamentally European and colonialist vision of the cultural and political identity of the state. In contrast, Vorster believed that the emergence in the postcolonial era of the nation-state as the sole repository of legitimate sovereignty opened a path to justify Afrikaner independence on the very same basis as that claimed by new African states. African nationalism, previously viewed as an existential threat, could actually be used to strengthen the regime's claim to legitimacy. In this thinking, the articulation of separate development as creating a multi*national* polity in contrast to a vertically stratified multi*racial* one only reinforced "the inalienable right of each national group"—Afrikaner and African alike—"to its own particular territory."[85]

The argument that the morality of separation derived from its facilitation of parallel nationalisms was not new. It had been stressed in what appears to be the first written mention of the term "apartheid" in its modern usage, by Dutch

Figure 1.2 "You see, we're not really part of Africa at all!" John Vorster's heavy emphasis on a nativist Afrikaner identity and a concomitant rejection of a European whiteness differed from the ideas of his predecessor, Hendrik Verwoerd. Source: *Cape Times*, 13 March 1961. Independent Media.

Reformed Church pastor J. C. du Plessis in 1929. Rejecting an existing policy that offered blacks no "independent national future," du Plessis had advocated that the Gospel be brought to bear in a way that fitted the African "character, nature and nationality."[86] Du Plessis's call intersected with developments in interwar segregationist thinking, which sidestepped scientifically untenable categories of racial hierarchy in favor of emphasizing respect for the uniqueness of each culture. While providing a foundation for the idea of separate progress, this new trend in social science nevertheless "fe[d] upon a wide range of racist assumptions."[87] This concept of "positive" apartheid reappeared periodically when Nationalists sought to deflect accusations that their policy's sole effect was white oppression by gesturing at a broader value for black South Africans. In 1944, for instance, D. F. Malan had argued for a policy that would "give the various races the opportunity of uplifting themselves on the basis of what is their own."[88] Vorster revived and foregrounded this subordinated element of apartheid discourse:

> [W]hat is the basis of separate development? It is, in the first instance, the right of the Whites to preserve their white identity. . . . But what he wants for himself he does not begrudge those of other colors in South Africa. . . . [I]f [the black man] comes to you and says, I want political rights, then I say to him you may have your political rights, but not in my territory. . . . I say to him he can develop into a free independent nation in his own territory. . . . Our whole policy is aimed at leading [South Africa's blacks] to independence, to self-determination.[89]

Crucially, the audience for such messages was more domestic than foreign; this speech was delivered in the tiny rural town of Naboomspruit. Continuing, Vorster told his fellow Afrikaners outright: "[W]e have too long described ourselves as Europeans to the outside world. We are not Europeans, we are of Africa as any other person is of Africa."[90]

The National Project

In pursuit of this program to reshape the ideological basis of the *volk* and its state, Vorster was in a powerful domestic position. By 1966, the NP was largely unchallenged among Afrikaner voters, while Verwoerd had bequeathed Vorster a huge majority of 126 out of 166 seats in parliament. The rules for Nationalist MPs were strict but simple. Debate could be vigorous within caucus, but policy disputes were to be resolved in-house. Once the leadership had taken a decision, ranks were to be closed. Willem Kleynhans, a scholar at the University of South Africa, once memorably commented that the NP's discipline was "the strictest of any party this side of the Iron Curtain."[91] The NP also enjoyed overwhelming support from other sources of Afrikaner identity and cohesion, including the main Calvinist churches and the Broederbond.[92] This striking symbiosis between the political and cultural arms of the nationalist project gave Afrikaner rule a hegemonic, impenetrable guise. It also created an additional deterrent for would-be dissidents: social exclusion. One journalist who refused to toe the line found himself subject to "total ostracism in every sphere and spectrum of Afrikaner society," including not being allowed to baptize his daughter.[93] Writer André Brink later recalled:

> [B]ecause Afrikaners had such a *beleaguered* sense of identity, of identity under threat, the possibilities for normal discussion and argument were almost non-existent. . . . [O]ne felt that in such conditions the individual's very existence was at stake in every utterance, every attempt at compromise, every attempt at reasoning. And over the years Afrikanerdom had devised diabolically efficient ways of dealing with "aberration." . . . To be branded a "traitor of the *volk*" was devastating. Since identity itself was tied up with, determined by, the *volk*, expulsion from that safe laager was a form of death.[94]

The apparent strength of the South African government obscured three sources of instability, each of which became increasingly apparent as South Africa's system struggled with the challenges of the post-1974 period.[95] The first comprised the limitations of Vorster's own style of governance. Just as Verwoerd had come to power on the back of his ministerial power base in the Department of Native Affairs, and P. W. Botha later did likewise with Defense, Vorster relied heavily on his contacts and support in the internal security bureaucracies. However, the unusual circumstances of his accession deprived the new prime minister of a political home or patronage network in any of the provincial congresses of the federally structured NP, an important weakness. A year after his accession to the premiership, Vorster told an interviewer: "I never saw it as my task to push forward policy, either in Parliament or outside. A person can never become a good leader unless he is also a good follower. No leader chooses himself. He is pushed forward by his own people to fill that position."[96] This statement was not false self-deprecation; it was a telling reflection of Vorster's political limitations. In contrast to the hands-on, *dirigiste* approach of Verwoerd, he endeavored to retain support within the party by allowing his ministers substantial leeway to run their portfolios as they saw fit and governing by Cabinet consensus. Meanwhile, Vorster subtly encouraged his colleagues in new directions with provocative, paradigm-breaking statements, loaded with unsaid corollaries. His reluctance to dictate also reflected his low-key, cerebral, and unpretentious

personality. In virtually all meetings except caucus, the prime minister allowed
his interlocutors to present their case first. P. W. Botha's authorized biography
tellingly related: "Often you did not know what [Vorster] was thinking, and you
just had to come to your own conclusions."[97] Heinrich du Toit, Head of Military
Intelligence, agreed: "[T]wo ministers would walk out of a Cabinet meeting
interpreting what had to be done in completely opposite ways."[98]

The detriments of this leadership style were particularly marked in the foreign policy and national security realms. At the start of Vorster's tenure, most
NP leaders had no interest in or feel for foreign affairs. Partly due to the country's
isolation and partly due to an Afrikaner ethos that was distinctly introspective,
few had traveled abroad at all. One observer was not far from the mark when he
wrote that Afrikaners "knew little about the outside world and only wished to be
left alone to run their own affairs and those of other South Africans as they saw
fit."[99] However, Vorster refrained from designating clear government procedures
for how foreign policy was generated, discussed, and approved. The Department
of Foreign Affairs (DFA) saw itself as the executor rather than the originator
of policy ideas. Coupled with Vorster's reluctance to provide clear direction
to bureaucracies over the scope of their responsibilities, this meant that the
DFA, the South African Defense Force (SADF, the military), the Department
of Information (Information, propaganda), and the Bureau for State Security
(BOSS, intelligence and domestic security) repeatedly encroached on the others' self-defined policy preserves within the broad remit of South Africa's interactions with the outside world. By the early 1970s, the relationship between the
bureaucracies that comprised South Africa's foreign policy and national security
apparatus varied from difficult to poisonous.[100] Former Ambassador to the UN
Jeremy Shearar recalls that the military saw the diplomats as "the lavender boys,"
while to the DFA, "everything the military did complicated our job."[101]

A second source of instability was that by the 1970s Verwoerd's model of
complete segregation was becoming visibly unrealistic and counterproductive.
South Africa's macroeconomic success belied that apartheid's limitations of
the educational and economic opportunities of black South Africans were increasingly unsuited to the needs of the Republic's evolving, industrializing, and
diversifying economy. Into the 1960s, when agriculture and mining still formed
the core of the South African economy, apartheid remained reasonably compatible with the overarching economic need for large amounts of unskilled labor.
However, by 1970, manufacturing contributed 24.2 percent of GDP, mining
10.3 percent, and agriculture only 8.3 percent.[102] The new economy required
a skilled workforce, which, in the absence of sufficient whites, mandated the
education and training of blacks.[103] The government had no solution to this
fundamental conflict between economic and ideological imperatives, respond-
ing with ad hoc exceptions to the programs of pass laws and job reservation,

which respectively controlled blacks' geographic and socioeconomic mobility. These quickly became so numerous as to undercut the entire system's integrity. Between 1966 and 1975, the state launched no fewer than 5.8 million prosecutions for breaches of various influx control laws.[104]

This process had major economic and ideological consequences for the government. Economically, South Africa's growth was both reduced and inconsistent by the mid-1970s. In 1974, gross domestic product (GDP) growth was 7 percent, in 1975, 2 percent, in 1976, an anemic 1.5 percent, and in 1977, negligible.[105] Unhelpful global conditions did not help, but it was outdated economic foundations that were the major culprit and rendered recovery elusive. Ideologically, the observable incompatibility between an apartheid doctrine that mandated the centrifugal expulsion of blacks to rural homelands and the reality of a centripetal economy drawing them inexorably into urban centers undermined both the authority of the government and the credibility of its ideological program.[106] Overall, Afrikanerdom and the National Party were willfully blind to these developments and their implications. Signs of major strain were inescapable. In 1973, for instance, black labor unrest culminated in a series of massive wildcat strikes centered in Durban.[107] Yet the Vorster-era NP lacked the flexibility or openness to respond creatively. The concept of "group rights" was inviolable, the ironclad Verwoerdian corollary of the party's mission of *volk* advancement. Every proposed policy, in every area, was predicated upon the ideal of separate futures. At the same time, however, important figures and constituencies within the Nationalist movement were beginning to realize that reform *within* this framework was essential—few more so than P. W. Botha, with his ties to key Cape elites and businesses.[108]

Finally, Afrikanerdom itself was slowly but irrevocably diversifying.[109] The ideology of Christian Nationalism stipulated a homogeneous, classless *volk* in which individuals held equal membership in the group by dint of a common heritage, language, religion, and customs.[110] This self-image was rooted in a historical reality of Afrikaner economic marginalization vis-à-vis English-speaking whites. In 1939, Afrikaners comprised only 3 percent of white engineers, 4 percent of white accountants, 11 percent of white lawyers, and 15 percent of white doctors.[111] However, by the Vorster era, socioeconomic progress was corroding both the reality and the self-image. State protection of private Afrikaner interests and promotion of Afrikaners into public sector employment had substantially narrowed the income gap with English-speaking whites. Where Afrikaner per capita income was around 47 percent of that of English-speakers at the end of the Second World War, already by 1960 that figure had risen to 64 percent.[112] Then, from 1961 onward, the economic boom lifted all boats (including non-white ones). Afrikaner per capita income increased one-and-a-half times faster between 1960 and 1976 than it did from 1946 to 1960.[113] The types of work Afrikaners were engaged in were changing too. In 1946, 30.3 percent of Afrikaners were employed in agriculture, 40.6 percent in blue-collar jobs, and 29 percent in white-collar positions.[114] By 1970, those figures were 9.7, 32.4, and a massive 57.9 percent, respectively.[115] As they climbed the socioeconomic ladder, Afrikaner breadwinners faced less direct competition for jobs from blacks. Their livelihoods depended increasingly on specialized training and qualifications, and less on their membership of the Afrikaner group.[116] This process not only weakened the collective interest with each passing year, it also damaged earlier forms of racial thought underpinned by economic rivalry. It was no coincidence that it was during the boom years that Afrikaners began to understand Africans and the concept of "Africanness" differently.

New jobs meant new patterns of life too. In *volk* myth, the quintessential Afrikaner was a resourceful farmer, eking out a living from the harsh environment. By contrast, cities were traditionally seen as centers of capitalism instead of self-reliance, fluid social mores instead of Calvinist piety, and cosmopolitanism instead of cultural integrity.[117] Yet already by 1960, 76.8 percent of Afrikaners self-identified as urban.[118] Historic towns like Pretoria and Bloemfontein were growing into metropolises that were thoroughly Afrikanerized in character. The new generation was also decidedly more educated than its forebears. By 1965, almost two-and-a-half times as many Afrikaner schoolchildren who completed Standard 6 (the eighth year) went on to complete their high school education compared to just a decade before.[119] This education transformation not only entailed a revolution in the life opportunities available to individuals, it posed a challenge to the younger generation's ability to interpret their social and individual identities through the paradigm of the historic *volk*. The Afrikaner of nationalist myth was generally vocational, even anti-intellectual; even through the 1880s there was just one high school across both Boer Republics, and no universities.[120] Such self-images were increasingly incompatible with the educational milieu and intellectual outlook of young Afrikaners, many of whom flocked to spend their formative years at booming tertiary institutions. When John Vorster gave his commencement address at Stellenbosch in 1971, he honed in on one theme, identified in his speech notes by the underlined English term: "Generation Gap."[121]

The new generation began to articulate their identities as Afrikaners in ways that transcended the rigid normative boundaries of their forebears. By the Vorster era, young Afrikaners were just as likely as their English-speaking counterparts to use their shortwave radios to tune into the rock music played on airwaves out of Mozambique, and far more likely to do so than listen to the traditional *boeremusiek* played by the South African Broadcasting Corporation (SABC).[122] Miniskirts and golf may have carried associations of promiscuity and capitalism, respectively, but the new generation embraced them regardless. Rather than defining itself against the anglophone-dominated economy, the new Afrikaner middle class instead looked for advancement within it. A spate of newspapers emerged during this period to cater to this new market. Titles like *Rapport, Dagbreek en Sondagnuus, Die Beeld* and *Beeld* all targeted an urban and educated readership. With their editorial offices headed up by prominent *verligtes*, the new sheets articulated a more confident and outward-looking Afrikaner world view. Venerable broadsheets like *Die Transvaler* (1937) initially struggled to adapt, before realising that they too had to get with the times if they were to retain their traditional political and cultural relevance.

In the realm of high culture, a cohort of writers known as the *Sestigers* openly challenged apartheid society. Barely concealed social critiques had long been prominent among English-speaking elites. The plot of the 1971 best-selling thriller *The Steam Pig* hinged on the murder of a woman whose family was ruined when the state changed their classification from White to Colored. But now, criticism of the established order came from Afrikaner writers. Drawing their inspiration from the intellectual and political world of 1960s protest, the emerging canon embraced cosmopolitanism, racial tolerance, urban life, secularism, and sexual permissiveness. André Brink's *Kennis van die Aand* (1973) portrayed a love affair between a colored man and a white woman—always more controversial than the other way around—as well as depicting torture by the regime. It achieved the distinction of being the first Afrikaans work to be banned by the state. Just as important as the *Sestigers*'s confronting depiction of South African society was their depiction of Afrikaners themselves. Instead of the heroic, resolute Afrikaner protagonists of old, main characters were now conflicted, introspective, and often living on the peripheries of a troubled and tragedy-filled society.[123] Or they were not white Afrikaners at all. Replacing nationalist dogma with curiosity and soul-searching, the *Sestigers* asked what it meant to *be* an Afrikaner in the new socioeconomic environment. This was a question increasingly on the minds of the new Afrikanerdom—and its leaders. Aggravating the government's angst was that the new movement both portrayed and personified the enemy as coming from within. The fathers of both poet Ingrid Jonker and novelist Etienne Leroux were Nationalist MPs.[124]

Afrikaner businessmen came into their own too. Under the old model of *volkskapitalisme*, Afrikaner entrepreneurs had explicitly harnessed commerce to the advancement of overarching *volk* interests.[125] Ordinary Afrikaners were enlisted to become shareholders in or invest their savings with Afrikaans institutions for the common good. In the mid-1960s, however, this mind-set receded in favor of private profit. When the Cape-based Afrikaner insurance giant Sanlam struck a major deal with the archetypal villain of English-speaking capital, Harry Oppenheimer, the result was public outcry. *Die Vaderland* angrily declared that *volkskapitalisme* was "dead and buried . . . in a twenty-four carat coffin."[126] Such landmark deals signaled a shift in how ordinary Afrikaners understood the very pursuit of individual wealth, which was detached from its historical mooring to capitalist exploitation and instead was increasingly to be found yoked to the rugged adventurism of the *voortrekkers*. Businessmen suddenly began to be seen less as selfish moneygrubbers, seeking fulfilment in private prosperity, and more as intrepid pioneers, furthering common and personal interests simultaneously. Conspicuous consumption and the pursuit of status goods swamped an ethos that had recently derided such practices.[127]

Figure 1.3 After years of ascetic public mores, the economic boom of the 1960s drew Afrikaners into the world of consumerism. Here, Lexington uses one of the new fads, golf, to make a sexualized appeal to the upwardly mobile, urban male Afrikaner: "After action, satisfaction." Source: *Volkshandel*, March 1967. Promedia Publikasies.

These striking changes in how Afrikaners understood themselves and the world around them provoked a backlash. There was no shortage of concern that South Africa's untrammeled economic growth would lead to liberalism, hedonism, and moral relativity, not to mention a decline in *volk* solidarity and integrity. "[A] large portion of the Afrikaner people, and in particular its more well-to-do class, are becoming worshippers of Mammon," lamented *Die Transvaler*.[128] This message resonated with those alienated by the socioeconomic changes transforming Afrikaner lifestyles. The party's base of farmers and blue-collar workers bemoaned the erosion of cultural shibboleths by the material interests of the growing, upwardly mobile middle-class. Equally, traditionalist elites espousing the immutability of Afrikaner identity felt threatened by newly prominent writers, professors, and technocrats offering an alternative intellectual leadership for the *volk*. Together, this alliance would furnish major obstacles to Vorster's efforts to reshape Afrikaner identity.

The *Verlig-Verkrampstryd*

The Verwoerdian model presented apartheid as a unitary, inseverable program. The principle of racial separation was sacrosanct. If apartheid was, in Verwoerd's phrasing, "a rock of granite," then conservatives rationalized that any crack weakened the whole.[129] Vorster saw things differently, distinguishing between "petty" apartheid, which discriminated among South Africans based on race alone, and separate development, which drew distinctions based on (attributed) ethnic or national identities.[130] Shortly after becoming prime minister, he reportedly told a group of Nationalist MPs:

> No, chaps, you have all got it wrong. The cardinal principle of the NP is the retention, maintenance and immortalization of Afrikaner identity within a white sovereign state. Apartheid and separate development is merely a method of bringing this about and making it permanent. If there are other better methods of achieving this end, then we must find those methods and get on with it.[131]

Such statements were at the time little short of heresy—and from the *Hoofleier* no less.

Why did Vorster conceptualize the party's mission in such ways? Part of the answer, as seen, lay in circumstances: the need to shore up the state's legitimacy; the changing fortunes of apartheid economics; and the shifts in perspectives and interests within Afrikanerdom. In these circumstances, alternate *Hoofleiers* might also have seen petty apartheid as increasingly dispensable or begun to understand the *volk* in new ways. But Vorster's own politics and background mattered too. Unlike his predecessor, Vorster had never been part of the Afrikaner intellectual circles of the 1940s and had little time for ideological rigidities. Nor had he been a long-time party man, suppressing his own views in order to climb the ladder, like P. W. Botha.[132] Instead, for decades he had defined his zealous faith in Afrikaner nationalism on his own terms, on two occasions even at the risk of destroying his political career before it really started. In 1941, he had resigned his membership in the NP when Malan insisted that he choose between it and the smaller, more radical OB (most others, including P. W. Botha, made the opposite choice). Then, in 1951, the NP refused to endorse Vorster as a candidate in the Brakpan constituency. Verwoerd himself wrote a powerful editorial in *Die Transvaler* urging voters not to support the former OB man. Vorster continued as an independent candidate anyway. (He lost on recount by just four votes.)[133] On both occasions, he risked being cast into the Nationalist wilderness. However, Vorster was fanatically devoted to the *volk* rather than any specific policy or organization. His commitment to Verwoerdian apartheid as the roadmap for the future was an intellectual one, not an article of faith. And while the new *Hoofleier* still rationalized that separate development would preserve *volk* agency and independence, he also felt that in the postcolonial age petty apartheid was starting to outlive its usefulness and become a liability.

Vorster was also particularly susceptible to the opening up within Afrikanerdom of new ways of thinking about Africans. As minister of justice, he had served on the frontlines of the regime's counterrevolutionary campaign of the early 1960s. His experiences had heavily influenced his understanding that the threat to the *volk* derived from communists—whether white agitators, black radicals, or activist students of any color—but not from Africans as such. This thinking became foundational to his worldview, a principle he never violated or departed from. The minutes of one meeting with homeland leaders in the mid-1970s recorded the following rationale on the issue of the safe return of political exiles:

> The Prime Minister said if people left [South Africa] (a) who did not commit a crime (b) who were not Communists but whose only crime was to have left the country without a passport, then he would consider their request to return sympathetically, should the homeland leaders vouch for them. . . . Referring to a certain specific case, the Prime Minister said that the person was a communist and had boasted about it in court. He, the prisoner, had not changed his mind. All people in South Africa, Blacks and Whites, needed protection against the aspirations of Communists such as this individual who did not speak on behalf of the Black people but on behalf of the Communist Party.[134]

The regime's unyielding focus on communism as an external, corrupting force provided space in Nationalist circles to move away from the blunt tropes of *oorstroming* prevalent in right-wing circles. Free of communist influence, the thinking went, there was no reason to think Africans would not buy into the separate development vision, giving it real legitimacy abroad. The state's interest therefore no longer lay in ignoring, obliterating, or making no accommodation for African aspirations, but in channeling them into the strict confines of the multinational vision. This belief had major consequences for Vorster's political agenda moving forward.

Vorster was careful to emphasize that his new thinking remained consistent with and indeed built upon the policies of his predecessors. He habitually mentioned previous *Hoofleiers* when broaching any new idea or policy direction in an effort to market his reform agenda as merely the extension of principles already in the Nationalist canon. Nevertheless, his new concepts, pregnant with implications of alterations to South Africa's rigid racial order, proved destabilizing to an Afrikaner community accustomed to Verwoerd's uncompromising assertions of white unilateralism, hierarchy, and supremacy. Early in Vorster's tenure, even very minor reforms designed to represent a more parallel rather than hierarchical conception of the relationship among South Africa's ethnic communities provoked a vicious conservative backlash. The most incendiary of these were the government's torturous efforts to dismantle the color bar on the sports field. Proposals in Vorster's first term (1966–1970) included allowing non-white athletes to represent the Republic in sporting competitions (although without competing alongside or against white South Africans) and allowing Maoris to tour as part of New Zealand rugby teams (although not allowing Basil D'Oliveira, by birth a Cape Colored, to tour with the English cricket team). Both measures departed from Verwoerd's hardline stance on an issue that set one white fear against another: the trepidation that social mixing might lead to full racial integration on the political level against the anxiety that white South Africa's steady exclusion from the rapidly growing arena of international sport might lead to political and economic isolation.

What began as an undermining of Vorster within the Broederbond by a hardline subgroup known as the *Afrikaner-Orde* exploded into a public conflict over the future of the *volk* and its relationship with other peoples. The result was the internecine *verlig-verkrampstryd* (1968–70), fought between those prepared to countenance some minor reforms in order to keep the separate development program compatible with the changing realities of South African society and the outside world (more pragmatic *verligte* Afrikaners) and those who saw any mitigation of total racial separation as opening the door to the eradication of Afrikaner self-determination, culture, and control (dogmatic *verkramptes*). "Vorster had big shoes to fill," reflects Stoffel van der Merwe, then a diplomat and later a Nationalist MP. "Times were changing and many people saw the situation as if Verwoerd [had] stopped changing the scene in 1966. They wanted things to continue as in 1966."[135]

The *verlig-verkrampstryd* severely damaged party unity, ultimately prompting the departure of four Nationalist MPs to Hertzog's new Herstigte Nasionale Party (HNP). It also consumed Vorster's first term as prime minister and waylaid his reform agenda.[136] Numerous Afrikaners saw his reframing of the Verwoerdian gospel as little short of apostasy. A letter to the editor of the HNP's periodical *Die Afrikaner* noted: "I was always a Nationalist until Dr. Verwoerd came to his end. Then the appeasement started and today I ask myself the question: what is more important, to build your proud nation or to submit to integration? Where is Mr. Vorster taking the nation?"[137] Dr. Andries Treurnicht, then editor of the Pretoria daily *Hoofstad*, remained in the NP, but became known in the press as "Dr. No" for his opposition to any and all reforms. The well-spoken former pastor provided the intellectual heft to a political cause more often articulated in cruder terms: "If petty apartheid lapses completely, then grand apartheid is senseless, superfluous, and unnecessary, because if white and non-white are acceptable to one another at all levels of everyday life and they mix everywhere without reservation, then it is senseless to force them to live in separate states or residential areas."[138] And yet, with one eye on developing international norms and ever-increasing isolation, Vorster sought to create just such a distinction between sacrosanct national separation and dispensable racial discrimination and position that distinction at the core of the government's plan for the future. Even from an early stage, Pretoria's tentative outreach toward independent Africa was central to the articulation of this conceptual shift. At the height of the intraparty furor in October 1968, Vorster spelled out to the Broederbond the corollaries of his new approach with uncharacteristic bravado:

> There are people now who are worried about where the children of black diplomats . . . will swim. Here too there should be no misunderstanding. There is no such thing as a first class or a second class diplomat. Black diplomats will come to South Africa. I want you to know it, and if you have any objection in principle then you must put it to me because then I cannot be your leader. This is the road I am going to take.[139]

At its core, the *verlig-verkrampstryd* was fought over different conceptions of the *volk* and therefore what interests the Nationalist state should be seeking to preserve and entrench. For *verkramptes*, the success, security, and stability of the

1960s was due to Verwoerd's willingness to forge a political reality that reflected and perpetuated the unchanging essence of Afrikaner national existence. The *volk* was unique as a guardian of God's values. The separate development system served to isolate and preserve its *genie*. Therefore, South Africa's political evolution was finished. Any departure from the Verwoerdian model was seen as a betrayal of the nation, not a political adjustment to reflect evolving state interests. "Precisely because the National Party is the *volk's* party, it has the inalienable interests, inviolable convictions, and Christian calling of the *volk* as a guiding star indicating the way forward," *Hoofstad* stated, encapsulating this thinking. "Its leaders are [only] leaders because they follow these."[140] In this view, Afrikaner unilateralism lit the path toward righteousness. The polity's isolation only underscored the unique purity of the *volk's* mission.

This political conflict mapped onto a more intangible battle between different claims that Afrikaners could make upon the state. It pitted a group that saw the *volkstaat's* role as entirely congruent with providing privileges to and defending the interests of those who were members of the *volk* on the basis of that membership, against another that viewed the state as having plural functions depending on circumstances, which might mandate delivering benefits to other groups. It was precisely in this broadening gap between nation and state, in a polity explicitly marketed by elites as a pure "nation-state," that the *verlig-verkrampstryd* unfolded.

In the political realm, therefore, *verkramptes* became vigorous defenders of the status quo in the name of preserving *volk* purity. The government is fond of saying that "the times have changed," which is "another way of apologizing for deviating from tested policy and principles," *Die Afrikaner* typically editorialized.[141] This not only meant resisting Vorster's proposed softening of racial divisions, but also railing against a much broader class of agents driving the economic and social evolution of Afrikanerdom in the 1960s. "Five years of 'verligte,' 'outward,' liberal policy," prominent HNP defector Jaap Marais wrote in 1971, had meant that "it is a group of businessmen, newspapermen and academics who today have the political initiative in their hands."[142] Through this virulent anti-elitism, *verkrampte* discourses targeted the rural and working-class Afrikaners who felt most threatened by the dismantling of racial boundaries. Verwoerd had once famously claimed that it was better to be "poor and white than rich and mixed."[143] *Verkramptes* agreed wholeheartedly. "Today [the NP] has become the party of the rich man and big monied interests," *Die Afrikaner* proclaimed. "The time where the common and poor man could rely on the Government for the protection of his interests is finally over."[144] *Verkramptes* were also hypervigilant against any foreign ideas or influences. It was telling that one of the other flashpoints of the *verlig-verkrampstryd* centered on government attempts to encourage white immigration. More whites improved the demographic equation for the regime. *Verkramptes*, however, stressed that new arrivals could not be expected to readily integrate with the Afrikaner community, learn Afrikaans, or convert to Calvinism.[145] Hertzog told the far-right publication *Veg* that the National Party's immigration plan was undermining the *volk* through the acceptance of "all sorts of heterogeneous elements which cannot subscribe to the endeavor [*strewe*], the call, and the worldview of the Afrikaner."[146] The mythologized national community of the *verkrampte* ideal was not only resolutely white, it was defined on class and cultural grounds too.

Verkramptes thus unapologetically saw the separate development framework as a tool to entrench Afrikaner power by unilaterally excluding undesirable cultures, trends, and peoples from the *volk's* domain. However, others felt that the logical corollary of Verwoerd's creation of the bantustans was the creation of viable and meaningful futures for Africans. The Afrikaner nation "cannot, will not, and does not want to rule South Africa as if only Afrikaners lived in the country," proclaimed Schalk Pienaar, editor of the newly founded Johannesburg newspaper *Die Beeld*.[147] Afrikaners had been the "pioneers of anticolonialism" in the Boer Wars, *Die Burger* editor Piet Cillié added, and yet had succumbed to some of the same practices of colonialism. "We cannot and should not become the last bastion of a wrong order when the Afrikaners as a people had been forged in resisting a similar order."[148] The rapidly changing socioeconomic environment of the 1960s may have threatened the status and identity of some Afrikaners and driven them toward chauvinistic nationalism, just as in the 1940s. But for others, "high apartheid" brought a new confidence in the ability of the *volk* to co-exist with the outside world. Newly eligible voters at the 1970 elections, for instance, had never known anything but Nationalist power. They had no personal experience of the widespread feelings of political exclusion, cultural inferiority, and economic precarity that had shaped and scarred older generations. Their worldview was accordingly quite different. "[D]oes a group wish to bottle itself up, or does it wish to survive with healthy interrelationships between all the multifarious groups that live in the land?" asked leading public intellectual Otto Krause, channeling this new zeitgeist.[149] There were also pragmatic imperatives driving these reconceptualizations of the *volk* and its future. The 1960s heralded an end to the world of empires and the age of white supremacy. In its place, the global south welcomed self-determination and the era of the nation-state. "[T]hat the country should have a multiple power structure now seems inevitable, simply because White South Africa, which now holds the power, knows (or is coming to know) that it will go under if power is not shared out separately in this way," reasoned Krause.[150]

For *verligtes*, the solution to these moral and practical conundrums was the same: real separate development. "[S]eparate freedoms" for South Africa's different communities was "the means, the way, the goal of NP policy," Pienaar reflected.[151] The removal of antiquated petty apartheid was vaunted as the corollary of the creation of separate political spheres. "Considerable prejudice still has to be overcome and much capital and energy will have to be expended by Whites and Non-Whites to wipe out forms of intentional and unintentional discrimination which have become part and parcel of our history," admitted Willem de Klerk, then a professor at Potchefstroom University and considered the preeminent *verligte* of the day. However, he continued, "[t]here is a growing insistence on equal treatment, equal facilities and equal opportunities for all in South Africa."[152] Pienaar went further; petty apartheid was "offensive" and "insane."[153] Vorster's tentative breaking down of old canards of white supremacy even emboldened *verligtes* to position their agenda in the center of Afrikaner politics. "Verligte Afrikaners are essentially separate development people; verkramptes essentially believe in *baasskap* apartheid," Krause provocatively declared.[154]

The issue of homeland development provides a microcosm of the emerging gap between the two camps, as discrete policy disputes mapped onto these volatile identity issues. In addition to strictly limiting state contributions, Verwoerd's prohibition on private white investment in the homelands ruled out their becoming even vaguely viable entities. Although the Tomlinson Commission had suggested that 50,000 jobs needed to be created in the homelands every year, between 1960 and 1972 only 85,544 jobs had been created in both the homelands *and* the border areas within the Republic.[155] "Even now the White community of the Republic of South Africa has not constructed a definite framework for Bantu homeland development," observed Jan Lombard, a member of the Bantu Affairs Commission, in 1972.[156] Reasoning that the white polity's fate and that of the homelands were intertwined, *verligtes* campaigned for a new policy. "Bantu homelands are the essential cornerstone of our [ethnic] relations policy over the longer term," underlined Pienaar.[157] Pretoria needed to embark on "determined development" of the homelands "in all fields," Willem de Klerk chimed in, including "the consolidation and expansion of their territories."[158] The Broederbond's Committee on Relations with the Bantus concurred. "[W]here there in the past was domination by Afrikaners over non-Whites . . . [t]he [new] approach to the non-White communities must derive from the Christian faith in people, from the doctrine that you must accept responsibility for your neighbor, but may not rule over him, and may not use him as a slave for your own ends."[159] On the committee's recommendation, the Broederbond's Executive Council petitioned the Cabinet to consolidate the "impractical, disjointed" homelands and give blacks a share in the development corporations.[160]

The *verligte* intellectuals were joined by less idealistic allies. Like their counterparts abroad, Afrikaner businessmen fiercely advocated a low-tax, antiregulation, and free-market business environment right up to the point where public projects would be directed into their hands. Homeland development offered massive new opportunities in nearly every commercial sector, from education to infrastructure. After years of preferential treatment in government contracts, Afrikaner capital backed itself to be Pretoria's chosen agent in this new endeavor. Just months after Verwoerd's death, *Volkshandel* observed that the current policy of restricting development to the border areas would "offer a livelihood to ultimately only a small part of the possibly 30 million Bantu by the end of the century." Real separate development, however, mandated the "development of the Bantu homelands with the help of white initiative and capital."[161] Along with increasing the skilled black workforce, homeland development became a top-tier concern for the Afrikaner business lobby over the ensuing years. In 1970, *Volkshandel* revealed that the AHI was "plead[ing] [with the government] for a blueprint and a masterplan for development of the white areas, border areas, and homelands as the foundation and guarantee for our future."[162] By the following year, "economic decentralization" was described as "the key to continued White existence."[163] Such ideas, delivered in increasingly strident tones, were very much in line with Vorster's own interpretation of the separate development roadmap: the ideal of political independence coupled with the reality of economic integration.

Verkramptes saw such policies as beyond the pale. *Die Afrikaner* attacked "the provision of services in the homelands and to Bantu in urban areas" as a "most injudicious spending of [white] taxpayers' money."[164] An in-depth, front cover exposé entitled "R40 000 000 in one year for Bantu education out of white pockets" related, in outraged tones: "There are 800 more schools for Bantus than for Whites; more than 500 000 Bantu children in school; the Department of Bantu Education is twice as large as all the white education departments put together. Consequently, Bantus stream into the white cities in greater numbers and drive Whites from their jobs. Many of them become communists. Are we on the road to a second Blood River?"[165] The newspaper repeatedly connected homeland development to the broader narrative of the government selling out to big business. While Verwoerd's "cardinal principle was that the Bantu must be educated to provide for his own economic needs," Vorster's stipulation that blacks had to be educated to provide for "the needs of White capital" was just "recklessness."[166] Another editorial said the government was "prisoner to economic forces which don't care about the color line and ... [was instead] only interested in the cheap labor which an available black mass can deliver."[167] The heated tenor of this debate derived not so much from fiscal concerns as from the policy's ramifications for the relationship

between the *volk* and outsiders. Was Afrikanerdom's mission compatible with
political independence and economic advancement for Africans, or not? This
was precisely the issue that Vorster's foreign policy would tackle head on.
"[A]*volk* wishing to preserve itself must isolate itself by means of the boundaries of race, culture, religion, customs, and language," Jaap Marais insisted.
"[O]ur isolation is our strength."[168] The prime minister's counter resonated with
an increasingly educated, confident, and outward-looking Afrikanerdom: "We
want to go into the world we live in."[169]

Vorster ultimately emerged triumphant from the *verlig-verkrampstryd*. Only 4
out of 126 Nationalist MPs left the party in 1969, though at one stage it appeared
that perhaps as many as 40 would do so.[170] Vorster crushed the HNP at the 1970
national elections and then used his new political mandate to force Broederbond
leaders to purge renegades from the organization in the name of preserving *volk*
unity. In 1972–73, 8859 out of 9027 Broeders signed a pledge that they would
have nothing to do with the new party.[171] The mainstream newspapers threw
their weight behind Vorster too. *Verkrampte* rebels had "not only diminished the
leaders but also undermined the strength of the Party in managing the nation's
problems [*landsvraagstukke*]," editorialized even Treurnicht's *Hoofstad*, with the

PILGRIM'S PROGRESS

Figure 1.4 Vorster's efforts to reshape apartheid were weighed down by consistent
verkrampte opposition. Source: *Cape Times*, early 1976. Independent Media.

recalcitrant preacher assessing which way the political winds were blowing. "The NP is the political people's front [*volksfront*] of Afrikanerdom and if Afrikaners in the Party split [*verdeel raak*], not just their own interests but also those of the Party and the whole country are undermined."[172]

Throughout the 1970s, the HNP struggled to gain political traction. The leaders of the renegades were unable to move beyond negation and outrage. They labored to present their cause as a realistic path for the future, rather than just a reproduction of the past. And they refused to disavow the conspiratorial and even batty ideas advanced by fellow travelers in the public sphere; the HNP needed all the support it could get.[173] All of these were needed to challenge Vorster's massive institutional advantages as *Hoofleier*: stewardship of the NP offered a nationwide political network, stature throughout the Afrikaner social sphere, and a machinery to patronize supporters and blacklist defectors.

Nevertheless, the emotive pull of *verkrampte* discourses on Afrikaners substantially transcended the limited political strength of the undisciplined HNP. Opposition foreign affairs spokesman Japie Basson said aloud what Nationalists desperately did not want to admit: "Mr. Vorster's difficulty is this: Verkramptheid is not an organized movement in the party, which can be rooted out by expulsions and technical victories at congresses. It is a widespread state of mind, an attitude and a distorted way of thinking which he and other Nationalist Party leaders helped to create."[174] Quite so. Indeed, much of the resonance of *verkrampte* thinking derived from history. Memories and narratives of an earlier Nationalist split in 1934 cast a long shadow over the politics of the late 1960s. As the Great Depression exposed and exacerbated Afrikaner poverty, then *Hoofleier* Barry Hertzog (Albert's father) had argued that the best way of alleviating the situation lay in a pan-white merger. D. F. Malan countered that Afrikaners needed a political party of their own and that "fusion" with English-speaking whites was a betrayal of *volk* integrity. His breakaway faction became the modern NP, and Malan eventually established a ruling coalition on Afrikanerdom's own terms, much as he had predicted. *Verkramptes* were therefore well placed to position their cause as in line with the party's hallowed traditions and lay claim to the mantle of ideological purity. By contrast, *verligtes* struggled to offer even vaguely plausible historic anchors for their brands of *volk* identity. Starting in the 1950s, Krause suggested, "Afrikaner thinkers" had grown "more and more restless with the prospect of *baasskap* apartheid" as "[i]t was obvious to many that a horizontal division with Whites on top and Non-Whites below was morally wrong and untenable in the long run."[175] Equally unconvincingly, Willem de Klerk contended, "Color and chauvinism should never form the basis of South African racial policy and where these motives become evident, they should be resolutely opposed, as has been done up to the present."[176] Such transparent projections of modern day *verligte* thinking backward in time struggled to compete with the much more easily articulated *verkrampte* claim to Afrikaner traditions.

The very existence of the schism forever damaged whatever unrealistic assumptions existed of a homogenous nationalist entity, with all Afrikaner interests represented in the political sphere by the same party with one set of policies.[177] In 1969, no less a figure than Broederbond chairman and chair of the SABC Piet Meyer told the Broederbond's Bondsraad [annual congress] outright that the idea that good relations between South Africa's different groups could develop through "the removal of so-called "petty apartheid" was "very unrealistic" and the mark of "a spineless Afrikanerdom."[178] Into the 1970s, the persistent claims of *verkrampte* elites to be the true representatives of Afrikaner values and history directly challenged the party's identity as the political incarnation of the *volk*.[179] One letter to the editor of *Die Afrikaner* asserted that the HNP was "ultimately more Nationalist than [the NP], because they still uphold what we value. . . . [The NP] just has the name—the skin; but the lion has left it."[180] Although politically latent, the ideological threat was potent indeed. Treurnicht's *Hoofstad* asked Afrikanerdom pointedly: "The question is: who is deviating from the principles of the National Party and who is rejecting the Christian National basis of our entire social, educational, political and national life? Without false piety: Who stands for God's Word?"[181] In subsequent years, such critiques, usually voiced outside the party room but resonating deeply within it, formed an emotive intellectual and political counterpoint for any debate over the future direction of the polity, as well as a substantial obstacle to any effort at domestic reform or deviation from Verwoerdian doctrine.

This domestic opposition and its existentialist challenge to Vorster's claim to ethnopolitical leadership was a critical factor in the acceleration of Pretoria's African outreach. After the *verlig-verkrampstryd*, the prime minister had little incentive to seek long-term viability for the polity through far-reaching reforms at home, thereby risking entanglement once more in destructive internal battles over Afrikaner nationalist purity. He had been shaken by the whole experience.[182] Even after receiving his first personal mandate in the 1970 election, winning no fewer than 118 of 166 parliamentary seats, his second term (1970–74) was notable for the unadventurous scope of the government's legislative agenda. Instead, Vorster turned resolutely to foreign affairs, where he was slowly gaining traction with African leaders, where he as prime minister had the most freedom of maneuver, and where he was least constrained by the entrenched racial and nationalist norms of his party.

2

Into Africa

The Outward Policy

Hendrik Verwoerd had seen little need to reach out to independent Africa. "It is not that we are not willing to enter into friendly relations with any well-disposed African state," he explained in 1962. "But they must first abandon their hostility towards South Africa."[1] Where Verwoerd saw an impasse, John Vorster saw an opportunity. While DFA and Information were entrusted with improving South Africa's image in Western countries and stopping the disintegration of its traditional relationships, Vorster simultaneously launched an audacious campaign targeting the crux of the anti-apartheid movement: African states themselves. The prime minister placed the execution of his highly sensitive outward policy in the hands of a small team of trusted advisors, comprising Foreign Minister Hilgard Muller, Secretary for Foreign Affairs Brand Fourie, and BOSS chief Hendrik van den Bergh.[2] The feared head of South Africa's domestic security was an unusual choice as one of Pretoria's new ambassadors-at-large to Africa. A former policeman, van den Bergh had no relevant qualifications or expertise. However, he had been interned with Vorster during the Second World War as a member of the OB and enjoyed his trust. Such an emphasis on personal relationships and ad hoc decision-making networks was typical of the Vorster era, especially in the foreign policy realm. Reporting directly to Vorster, the three men worked discreetly to open doors to Africa. They reasoned that if South Africa offered to help African states achieve their goals, they would embrace mutually advantageous cooperation out of self-interest.[3]

On a purely diplomatic level, Pretoria looked to exploit cleavages on the African scene that cut across anti-apartheid sentiments and thereby gain limited forms of international acceptance.[4] The regime explicitly sought to prevent any repeat of the coalescing of Western states behind a united Afro-Asian anti-apartheid campaign, as had occurred after the Sharpeville massacre.[5] Pretoria accounted for no less than two-thirds of the total GDP in the greater Southern African region, with an economy ten times as prolific as the next largest contributor.[6] It exploited this disparity to invest in political benefits in Africa.[7] For example, the regime agreed to furnish 70 percent of the capital needed for the construction of a hotel in northern Madagascar at the decidedly below-market rate of 6 percent annual interest. It also provided a government-to-government loan earmarked for the construction of tourist infrastructure, amounting to US$3.2 million at a paltry 4 percent.[8] However, understanding what African outreach was designed to do on a deeper level means resisting the temptation to interpret Pretoria's engagement with independent Africa through external understandings of its relationship with Africans at home (that is, vertical, exploitative racism), and instead foregrounding the *regime's* understanding of that relationship. The sudden projection of South Africa into Africa was not just about the short-term goal of preventing a resuscitation of international isolation through cultivating new relationships. It was at least as much designed to create a forum in which Pretoria could advance a new state identity underpinning longer-term security and legitimacy: the acceptance of the Afrikaner community as part of independent Africa through an "Africanization" of separate development as a social order.

Like their imperial predecessors or white neo-imperial counterparts elsewhere on the continent, Nationalist leaders had to keep Africans in a position of subjugation and exploitation while simultaneously being seen to govern for the benefit of the social order as a whole.[9] Vorster's strategy for meeting this challenge in a changing world was to reshape the ideological basis for the regime's existing racial hierarchies by embedding South Africa's existing sociopolitical system, with some minimal alterations, in a different network of values and norms. As James Brennan and Jonathan Glassman have variously demonstrated, the racial divisions stratifying postcolonial social orders were not innate, but constructed and contested structures, shaped alternately by specific processes of pre- and postindependence governance, tensions between communities for resources and status, and self-identification through metaphor and discourse.[10] Amid substantial opposition, Vorster sought to navigate a similar process and manipulate it to the Afrikaners' advantage. Apartheid would be rearticulated both to Africa and to the white electorate as representing a network of interdependent nations—each with an equal claim to African nationalism—rather than a system entrenching vertical racial dominance. Pretoria's relationship with independent Africa became the central engine for reforging the ideological foundation of the regime and its plan for the future. If Africa's opposition to South Africa was largely a function of the perception that apartheid was among the last and most oppressive vestiges of colonialism, then Vorster's African outreach was an attempt to shatter this perception by redefining apartheid into the normative context of the postindependence era. Statecraft was conscripted in the service of state-building; diplomacy in the service of ideological renewal. This was not an effort merely to divide and lure African leaders, but a campaign to contest and shape the definition of a legitimate African state.

From High Apartheid to High Modernism

The key to understanding why some African leaders engaged with Vorster's outreach lies in the parlous condition of the postcolonial African state. By the late 1960s, a decade of misrule, dictatorship, poverty, and political instability had provoked widespread disillusionment as to what was possible in the aftermath of colonialism. Many leaders were seeking new templates of governance. Additionally, African state identities—how citizens, leaders, and elites understood their polity's character and purpose—were in flux. The campaign against white rule, long a clarion call for African states, had calcified into futility and demoralization. It bears remembering that before being overruled by his ANC Executive, Zimbabwean nationalist leader Abel Muzorewa had agreed in autumn 1974 to a version of Ian Smith's qualified franchise that would have left blacks with only 24 percent of the seats in Parliament and limited access to the educational or economic opportunities needed to increase that proportion over time.[11] Lusaka was also prepared to accept a qualified franchise in Rhodesia, even after the Carnation Revolution.[12] Pretoria, operating from a position of economic prosperity and political stability, exploited this confluence of trends. To find common ground and reach across the color line, Vorster articulated a new vision for Africa's future grounded in material progress and continental cooperation: interdependence between independent states, regardless of color. This vision appealed to certain African leaders on three fronts.

The first was development. After years of colonial rule, calls for African initiative to deliver the bounties of modernization to "the people" were prominent across the continent. Many leaders echoed Kwame Nkrumah's famous boast to make Ghana a paradise within ten years. On the whole, African states performed just as well in terms of GDP per capita in the 1960s as countries of similar incomes across the global south.[13] Yet by the turn of the decade, much of the economic promise of the early years of decolonization had evaporated. Independent African polities had inherited colonial-era economies that had been consciously designed to extract particular resources. In some ways, this was a boon. Postcolonial governments took over existing monopsonistic marketing boards, which became the dominant mechanism for raising revenue. These boards not only typically secured the mandatory purchase of a state's given cash crop (or, less often, core mineral), they also compensated peasants at considerably less than the crop's market value. Just as the difference had previously found its way into colonial coffers, now the same funds were used by postcolonial leaders for ideological, developmental, internal security, or patronage purposes. However, these structures did not provide enough income to meet local expectations of a self-sufficient, African-led, industrial future. The singular focus of the marketing boards militated heavily against the establishment of any real economic or political pluralism, which might have broadened the base of the polity, while building major tensions among exploited and neglected rural populations.[14] Consequently, these economies were far too narrowly structured to weather unfavorable economic conditions. When the 1970s brought drought, oil shocks, falling commodity prices, and surging interest rates on vast state loans, sub-Saharan African leaders found themselves under even more pressure to deliver modernization and fewer resources with which to do so.[15]

South Africa offered to address this problem squarely. "Africa and Providence have been good to us," Vorster told voters at home, and "it is our Christian duty to return in some measure what Africa has given us."[16] To this end, Pretoria sponsored development initiatives in a variety of African countries. These ranged from furnishing Chad with geological equipment for the exploration of mineral resources to providing major technical and financial contributions to an unlikely pilot project on livestock rearing in Gabon.[17] In contrast to the large hydroelectric schemes built in Portuguese Africa, at Cabora Bassa in Mozambique and Ruacana-Calueque on the Angola-SWA border, most of the projects Pretoria pioneered with independent African states fell far short of their economic goals. However, South Africa's ends were largely ideological. Not only did the Pretoria-funded projects provide a tangible link between the regime and independent African governments, they also gave some substance to the model of African identity that the regime was proposing. "The problem of the Third World is not political rights, but the very basic necessities for existence like bread and butter and employment," Cape MP L. A. Pienaar summarized.[18] This represented the essence of Vorster's vision for Africa's future: the displacement of inconvenient political agendas by a new agenda of material progress, both in the homelands and on the continent. In a conversation with Kaunda's foreign policy point man, Mark Chona, Vorster stressed that development and modernization, not liberal conceptions of political pluralism and participation, were the key to political viability. Referring to recent unrest in Uganda, he observed quizzically: "Don't people appreciate that in the years ahead it is more important to feed your people than anything else? The world is moving into the stage where those countries who can feed their people . . . will pull through and . . . the others will go under. . . . [G]ood administration and the standard of living of the people must be paramount." Chona's reply reflected just the juxtaposition that Pretoria sought to promote between material progress and stability on the one hand and the opportunism of communist neo-imperialism on the other. "Exactly. But that is where the tragedy of Uganda lies, and the Soviets, whom, you know, feed on the existence of conflict, are ready."[19] The new focus on aid and assistance to Africa therefore not only served discrete diplomatic ends, it bolstered a much broader conceptual agenda.

At home, political support for this new agenda derived from its potential to reconcile emerging tensions in the Afrikaner national project. The new focus on African modernization—from homeland development, to funding dams in Angola and Mozambique, to technical assistance programs across the continent—reproduced deep-seated notions of racial and cultural superiority.[20] However, like so much of the *verligte* agenda, the new policy reframed these notions in altruistic terms. "[T]he opportunity for the White African to effectively apply his intimate knowledge and experience in helping the Black man" was ultimately "the only method by which the West's role in Africa can metamorphose from colonial outsider (who simultaneously created work and growth) to that of guardian and benefactor who shares and builds," *Volkshandel* editorialized.[21] As colonialist supremacy gave way to the new creed of developmentalist partnership, racialized paternalism was rechanneled and renewed. Equally, African development served to address underlying concerns within Afrikanerdom over the *volk's* sudden embrace of materialism and industrial modernity by repositioning these as necessary for the state's security, identity, and destiny. "Growth and development in Southern Africa is the only effective method to keep Africa for the Africans," *Volkshandel* purred.[22] Corporate interests and *verligte* thinkers swooned over the potential of Afrikaner entrepreneur Anton Rupert's notion of "mutual prosperity" to offer precisely the sort of communal economic basis for Africa's future that might complement Vorster's advocacy of a shared conceptual foundation of self-determination, anticolonialism, and nativist nationalism.[23] Pretoria's sudden embrace of development thus reflected something of a high modernist mentality, as the regime searched for its own political and ideological fulfilment in the "development" of others.[24] The details of the South African–sponsored initiatives are highly illuminating in this regard. Pretoria enlisted engineers and technocrats to develop entirely schematic projects for its African partners. Templates were superimposed onto target societies with little or no consideration given to local contexts or peoples. And limited attention appears to have been paid as to whether South Africa's contributions were yielding results on the ground. Simply contributing the assistance was what ultimately mattered.

The second front of the charm offensive was geopolitics. As former colonial powers steadily shed their imperial commitments in Africa, Washington and Moscow, and to a lesser extent Beijing, filled the void. Each sought to bolster its state creed through its diffusion in the global south.[25] For African states dealing with the challenges of postcolonial rule, this process had important ideological as well as the more obvious material attractions. As leaders searched for ideological tools to help them govern their increasingly fractious and unstable societies, they became more receptive to those with external legitimacy and currency on the new global stage, whether radical-communist or conservative-"free world." The extent to which domestic policy in fact reflected nominally "capitalist" or "socialist" principles varied. Plenty of leaders continued to market their legitimacy through appeals to other discourses, particularly home-grown "authentic" nativisms.[26] Yet the division of Africa into Cold War camps was more than a pattern of allegiance of convenience. Many leaders and parties had in fact been deeply influenced in their formative years by Western or Leninist ideas.[27] Consequently, those regimes that professed fealty to a particular Cold War camp did, in fact, tend to conceptualize their state-building goals and develop matching strategies within the corresponding discourse.[28] This trend accelerated in the late 1960s, as the Vietnam War shifted the focus of ideological competition from Europe to the former colonies. In the new ideological environment, few African states could remain ideologically "neutral," and leaders increasingly articulated their ruling ideologies in Cold War terms.[29]

A microcosm of this narrowing of the available ideological space can be seen in francophone Africa, where South Africa made its most unexpected headway. By the late 1960s, the dominant model in francophone Africa of close ties with Paris, or *françafrique*, was rapidly disintegrating.[30] Institutions like the African and Malagasy Common Organization (OCAM), created in 1965 to promote a vision of moderate francophone African unity under French leadership, collapsed into irrelevance; only three heads of state attended its 1973 summit in Mauritius.[31] Leaders found that close cooperation with the old metropole did not guarantee stability; between 1963 and 1966, there were thirteen coups d'états in francophone Africa alone.[32] This well-documented crisis of governance provoked a crisis of state identity. A succession of francophone ex-colonies sought changes in or cancellations of their existing defense agreements with France. The power structures of the societies, their social orders, or the fact that France usually remained the security guarantor of last resort remained unchanged. Instead, the new agreements were overwhelmingly symbolic, designed to "affirm [the African states'] political identity in contradistinction to the old colonial power."[33] In place of the *françafrique* state identities, leaders increasingly looked to wed their ideologies to Cold War models. The result was bifurcation. Some began channeling more radical brands of anticolonialism not far removed from Ahmed Sekou Touré's Guinean platform; Congo-Brazzaville, the Malagasy Republic, and Mauritania all publicly broke with Paris.[34] Equally, moderate leaders like Ivorian President Félix Houphouët-Boigny and Senegalese leader Léopold Senghor suddenly found themselves looking for ways to invigorate their conservative, top-down agenda for the future. Just as the norms and consensus of the postcolonial moment a decade earlier had worked against Pretoria, by the end of the 1960s, divisions over the direction of the African project played into South Africa's hands.

In seeking a discourse through which to advance its new model of postindependence African politics and a network through which to connect South Africa with potential fellow-minded states, the language and structures of the Cold War provided Pretoria with ready tools. Given the "Russian penetration and violence that Africa is facing" and "the Red-Chinese belt in Africa," Vorster suggested in 1971, "the leaders in Africa who are concerned about the peace and the security and the prosperity of Africa should find and understand each other."[35] Three years later, he extended this vision, predicting that South Africa's engagement with its black neighbors would form the basis of "a power bloc . . . against communism."[36] Such positions mapped onto widespread concerns in independent Africa, as well as reflecting regime ideology in Pretoria. Signal moments like Chinese premier Zhou Enlai's famous 1965 declaration in Tanzania that Africa, Asia, and Latin America were all "ripe for revolution" terrified those anticommunist (or "moderate") regimes whose state ideologies prioritized evolutionary change and stability over broad-based social transformation. In this context, Vorster and his team appreciated that anticommunist African states were distinctly more receptive to their overtures than radical ones whose ideologies dictated a more militant brand of anticolonialism. Constructing relationships with the former could help deepen the cleavage between the two blocs.[37] By overlaying Cold War affinities onto continental divisions over the importance and urgency of removing white rule from Southern Africa, Pretoria aimed not merely to take advantage of African regimes' Cold War loyalties, but to strengthen those identifications and commensurately weaken the importance of anti-apartheid militancy as an ideological pillar of consensus in postcolonial African state identity.

The final front of Pretoria's charm offensive was the promotion of state sovereignty. For the first generation of postcolonial African leaders, the pull of the nation-state ideological model was irresistible, trumping alternatives such as federations or pan-Africanist ideals, both popular as late as the 1950s.[38] Nation-states were mandatory for membership in the new international community and global organizations. Courtesy of colonialism, they usually came with a preexisting apparatus of governance, including established borders. Nation-states were even "seen as the very essence of modernity by nationalists."[39] Though colonialism as a concept was to be condemned, the vehicle and form of European power had left a lasting impression upon new African leaders. However, precisely because so few of the successor entities in Africa emerged organically, they were states first and national communities later—if ever. While the UN Charter opens with "We, the Peoples of the United Nations," the OAU Charter (1963) tellingly begins "We, the Heads of African and Malagasy States and Governments."[40]

The embrace of the state did not abate. By the end of the 1960s, the African state had largely spurned broad-based pluralism in favor of centralized authoritarian rule grounded in clientelism and periodic, sector-based popular mobilization.[41] This trend owed much to geopolitical context. Even where leaders held tenuous control over their nominal territory and exercised limited "empirical" sovereignty, they nevertheless were treated as legitimate by virtue of controlling the "juridical" institutions of the former colonial structure.[42] Postcolonial African rulers thus found themselves in charge of "gatekeeper" states: legitimacy and other political resources derived from foreign recognition of their ownership of the gate rather than the consent of the governed at home.[43] Executive power therefore ruled supreme. Once in control, gatekeepers had little to gain from broadening the narrow avenues to power that they themselves had successfully trodden. Conversely, they had strong incentives to tightly define the literal and conceptual boundaries of political contest in the foreign-recognized political structure, the nation-state, and shun any transnational claims on citizens' identities (and, potentially, loyalties).[44]

In this context, Pretoria's boldest gambit lay in seeking to detach the antiapartheid discourse from its traditional transnational bases in postwar antiracialism and opposition to colonial exploitation, and instead reducing it to nothing more than the advocating of interference in another state's sovereign affairs.[45] The cardinal principle of Nationalist South Africa's foreign policy and its primary defense against anti-apartheid activism had long been an insistence on mutual noninterference in domestic affairs as the bedrock of geopolitics. Vorster now sought to build upon the foundation of noninterference a renewed emphasis on the nation-state as the apotheosis of national fulfillment in postcolonial Africa and therefore the sole repository of legitimate sovereignty—a contention with obvious resonance for the homelands program. By engaging with African states on the international stage rather than ignoring them, South Africa hoped to strengthen the notion that nation-states were the only acceptable political entity in the postcolonial era, thereby bolstering the contention that they were the only possible future for Sotho, Zulu, and Xhosa too.

This pitch to contest the contours of African geopolitics was well-timed. By the late 1960s, militancy against white rule had run aground: in 1968–69, only four African states bothered to pay their OAU Liberation Committee dues.[46] In 1969, fourteen Eastern and Southern African leaders, including those with unimpeachable anti-apartheid credentials like Julius Nyerere of Tanzania and Kaunda of Zambia, signed onto the Lusaka Manifesto, qualifying the previously unrelenting support of armed struggle to overthrow apartheid: "If peaceful progress to emancipation were possible, or if changed circumstances were to make it possible in the future, we would urge our brothers in the [South African] resistance movements to use peaceful methods of struggle even at the cost of some compromise on the timing of change."[47] Within months, both the OAU and the UN General Assembly, two forums at which South Africa was routinely excoriated, had endorsed the manifesto.

As for the resistance movements, they were isolated and wrong-footed by Pretoria's new agenda, which posed a direct threat to their claim to have the whole continent's support. The outward policy received heavy coverage in publications like the South African ANC's journal *Sechaba*, where editorials conveyed dismay and anger. One editorial observed that the cause of isolating the regime internationally, successfully pioneered through a "coordinated initiative of African, Asian and Socialist states at the United Nations," was now being undermined by "individual states" who had "succumbed to timidity," displaying "an extraordinary poverty of spirit" in an act of "sheer folly."[48] A July 1971 cover story put the issue more pointedly still: "Dialogue is betrayal."[49]

South Africa's vision of a future defined by material progress, state-centric status quo rule, and cooperation between African nation-states had its appeal. Indeed, the concerns that South Africa put on the table must have been decidedly important to African leaders for them to sideline their deep antipathy for apartheid and hand the regime a series of public relations victories. At the June 1971 Addis Ababa summit of the OAU, a body largely defined by the twin causes of pan-African unity and opposition to white rule, no fewer than six anticommunist states—Gabon, Côte d'Ivoire, Lesotho, Malawi, the Malagasy Republic, and Mauritius—risked being seen as sell-outs on both fronts by voting against a resolution that rejected engagement with Pretoria, in effect repudiating the existing approach of confrontation and isolation. A further five out the thirty-nine states present abstained.[50] Such a spectrum of moderate African leaders risked opprobrium not because Pretoria bribed or coerced them, but because South Africa had accurately identified and creatively foregrounded areas of common interest that cut across an anti-apartheid dynamic that had for the moment become tired and inert.

The Showcase

Vorster's broadening of the conversation with independent Africa did not eliminate the fundamental abhorrence many African leaders felt toward a system deeply redolent of the racism and exploitation they associated with their own experiences of colonialism. But it was enough to launch a dialogue across the color line, create new diplomatic dynamics, and open previously closed doors. By the height of the outward policy in 1971, South Africa had regular diplomatic discussions with just under half of all the countries in independent Africa.[51] Even these limited successes were rapturously received by Vorster and his foreign policy team. Domestically, any productive contact with black African leaders strengthened Vorster's hand in making a difficult case to the electorate: that the regime could coexist productively with its erstwhile nemesis, African nationalism. Geopolitically, South Africa did not need to win over its most vehement critics in Bamako or Lagos to show progress. It only needed to prevent consensus by diluting and reshaping the singular focus on apartheid in African perceptions of the regime, bolstering ideological alternatives, and dividing independent Africa. This Pretoria had done. "We have cut the black countries to our north completely in half—they are at one another's throats," Vorster exaggerated to Rhodesian Prime Minister Ian Smith.[52]

Malawi had even become a showcase for Vorster's new model of African relations. Following behind-the-scenes contacts, in 1967, leader Hastings Banda formally requested South African support for his development agenda.[53] He planned to construct a new capital at Lilongwe, closer to his political and ethnic base among the Chewa than the old colonial center at Zomba, while also building a railway line to the port of Nacala in Mozambique, alleviating his landlocked country's difficulties in getting its goods to port. Vorster was happy to acquiesce with a soft loan: the projects became a symbol both of Banda's ability to modernize his country and of Pretoria's capacity to help African leaders achieve their development goals. The agreement also laid the foundation for a burgeoning relationship. In May 1970, Vorster embarked upon a state trip to Malawi, his first to independent Africa. The visit surpassed Pretoria's expectations. Banda told his guest deliberately, "You and I, your country and mine are pioneers and explorers in a new way of international relations and interracial relations."[54]

In August 1971, Banda completed a five-day return visit, the first to South Africa by the head of an independent African country. Pretoria spared no expense to illustrate that black African leaders would be treated like any other head of state. Banda was welcomed with a twenty-one-gun salute at Waterkloof Airport in eastern Pretoria and fêted at state banquets. He met with many of the regime's leading figures as well as (government approved) local African leaders, was taken on a tour of Simonstown naval base, and addressed a group of Malawian migrant laborers. The public responded too. A multiracial crowd of between one and three thousand converged upon the President's Hotel in Johannesburg upon his arrival.[55] Banda did not leave his hosts disappointed, extolling the futility of the OAU's policy of overthrowing the South African regime and acknowledging the right of whites to live and thrive on the continent.[56] He told the press that the OAU's militancy was a thing of the past and that "the Africans of South Africa" had told him that "Dr. Kenneth Kaunda of Zambia and Dr. Julius Nyerere of Tanzania do not speak for them."[57] He went further. "South Africa doesn't need a certificate of respectability," he added. "It already has one."[58]

Figure 2.1 In May 1970, Vorster travelled to Malawi, completing his first visit to independent Africa. Source: Archive for Contemporary Affairs.

Banda came under fierce criticism from independent Africa. Uganda's state paper, *The People*, advocated the expulsion of Malawi from the OAU, labelling the country the "rotten egg" of Africa, "as bad if not worse than the racist countries."[59] From the north, Algeria's *El Moudjahid* called Banda "the apostle of treachery."[60] While some in radical Africa were outraged, others were simply in denial. Bamako's mouthpiece, *L'Essor*, conveyed to its readers its own picture of Banda's visit to South Africa. The newspaper made no mention of the effusive welcome at Waterkloof Airport or of the crowds thronging Banda's hotel in Johannesburg. Instead, it portrayed Banda's arrival at Waterkloof as a humiliating snub, reflecting "the inability of the racist regime to mask its hideous face." As for Banda, Bamako presented him alternately as an economically captive supplicant—"the poor President" trying to thrive in "a sinister and fearful atmosphere of an aggressive militarism"—and a quisling, striving "to camouflage his treason of the African cause."[61]

Yet Banda's ongoing relationship with Pretoria was driven neither by economic obligation nor by any quid pro quo. It derived from a dove-tailing of short-term interests set against similar state-building models and overlapping (though hardly congruent) worldviews. Banda's authoritarian centralism—encapsulated in the governing mantra "Kamuzu knows best"—was not entirely dissimilar from the Nationalists' arrogation of control over the scope of permissible African agency within the Republic.[62] His chief focus was development and growth; the state-owned *Malawi News* was full of articles about new roads, building projects, agricultural advances, and foreign investments. The synergy with Pretoria extended to geopolitics, where Banda's virulent anticommunism trumped his distaste for neo-imperialism and its associated racial essentialism. In a major 1964 speech entitled "A Threat to World Peace," he made this clear: "Make no mistake about it at all . . . to Communists the state is not only all powerful but has the absolute right to do anything with your goods and even your breath itself. That is Communism for you."[63] In the mid-1960s, Beijing twice offered much-needed economic aid.[64] Banda refused, but he had no such qualms when it came to accepting South African assistance. In the wake of his rapprochement with Pretoria, he brushed off criticism by insisting that communist power, not white rule, was the "other" against which he defined his rule. In a private letter he told Kaunda that he "bitterly resented" the Zambian president's criticism of cooperation with Pretoria: "More than once, you have sent your Ministers to Russia, China and other countries for discussion or negotiations on trade and other matters. Neither I nor any of my Ministers or anyone else in this country, has ever said a single word against you personally . . . [b]ecause, we feel it is none of our business whatsoever."[65] Banda's statement encapsulated at one stroke the fusion of anticommunism and state-based geopolitics grounded in noninterference that Pretoria was promoting on the continent.

Engagement with South Africa and a concomitant rejection of the OAU policy of blanket confrontation became a wedge issue between moderate and radical African states. In West Africa, Houphouët-Boigny found in South Africa's promotion of neo-European nation-state entities and associated territorialized identities the materials he needed to reenergize a waning moderate francophone cause. "We will not achieve the solution to the problem of apartheid in South Africa by resorting to force of arms," he declared in November 1970. "We must open talks with this country."[66] At a press conference in April 1971, Houphouët-Boigny went further, counseling dialogue with the Republic "on an equal footing" and even referring to apartheid as "a matter within the domestic jurisdiction of South Africa."[67] If anything, the virulence of radical Africa's responses to the outward policy's successes, epitomized by the reaction of *L'Essor* to Banda's meetings with Vorster, only played into Pretoria's hands by sharpening the correlation between Cold War blocs and engagement-confrontation alignments.

As Vorster advanced his agenda more aggressively in the post–Carnation Revolution era, moderate leaders even competed to assert their leadership of the new dynamic.[68] Not only was Banda's visit to South Africa featured in a series of front-page articles in Côte d'Ivoire's major daily, *Fraternité-Matin*, but the paper repeatedly stressed Houphouët-Boigny's own role in laying the foundations for the materializing "dialogue" through his earlier speeches advocating engagement

Figure 2.2 In February 1975, Vorster visited President William Tolbert in distant Liberia. Here, his dovish advisors revel in their coup. From left, Secretary for Foreign Affairs Brand Fourie, Ambassador to the the UN Pik Botha, Foreign Minister Hilgard Muller, and Tolbert. Source: National Archives of South Africa.

with Pretoria.[69] Likewise, when Vorster met with Liberian President William Tolbert in early 1975, the *Malawi News* was careful to remind readers that both Tolbert and Vorster were actually following Banda's lead: "He [Banda] is the pioneer of the ideology . . . [of] contact and dialogue. . . . At the time he began to preach and practice this ideology he was alone and some leaders in Africa were against him. . . . Today it has grown popular."[70] For his part, Banda crowed as Malawi was chosen to host the inaugural meeting of the new African, Caribbean, and Pacific organization in 1975; so much for the "rotten egg" of Africa.[71] Far from distancing themselves from the rapprochement with South Africa, anti-communist African leaders were jostling for the credit.

The Home Front

Reaching out into Africa was a venture into the unknown for white South Africa. When Vorster first met with Banda in 1970, he hedged by visiting Ian Smith on the same trip. But by the return visit a year later, a good deal had changed. Newspapers avidly followed every aspect of Banda's tour, publishing multiple articles each day. "Dr. Banda's visit puts the stamp of success on the outward policy of our Prime Minister, Mr. Vorster," adjudged *Hoofstad*.[72] By the time news broke of Vorster's meetings with Houphouët-Boigny and Senghor in Côte d'Ivoire in 1974, *Die Beeld* carried a multipage color spread, full of photos of the visit.[73]

However, Vorster sought not only to build new relationships with African states in an effort to alleviate the regime's international isolation, but also to parlay Africa's engagement with the regime into a more enduring ideological foundation for the state's legitimacy. He duly mobilized the new and tentative co-existence with African nationalism on the continent behind the Verwoerdian argument that separate development was the only means of enabling each of South Africa's ethnic groups to exercise their right to self-determination. On one front, Pretoria's new willingness to engage with independent African states was advertised as proving its good faith regarding coexistence within South Africa. In the wake of the highly successful June 1971 OAU summit, Vorster used the diplomatic gains abroad to energize his domestic agenda, embarking on a week-long "listening tour" of the homelands. Simultaneously, the white polity's ability to interact productively with the new homeland entities was presented as a symbol of its readiness to coexist with African nationalism across the continent. In a 1969 speech at the Akademie vir Wetenskap en Kuns (Academy for Science and Art), Vorster spelled this out: "[W]hat I consider most important of all, what will eventually turn the scale in our policy of co-operation with Africa, is that, slowly but surely, it is becoming clear to the African states that we are absolutely honest towards our own black peoples within our borders."[74] In this way, the regime's new policy toward Africa was refracted through reconsiderations of the state-building template at home. Within little more than a decade, the dominant Nationalist ideology had shifted from denying that there was a need to stipulate a political future for Africans at all, to committing to the homelands vision but seeing its fulfilment as entirely a matter for Africans, to openly acknowledging that the viability of the homelands as African nation-states was integral to the future of the white polity. This was substantial change, and at a breakneck pace. The regime's openness toward independent Africa followed these shifts.

Better ties with Africa and Vorster's state-building agenda at home thus became mutually reinforcing programs. This was not a charade intended for foreign consumption, but a top-down campaign to promote a new ideological foundation for a particular set of social, political, and economic structures—and one that readily captivated its advocates. Muller scrawled excitedly on one letter from Fourie:

> Most [foreign observers] fail to see that the position in SA is changing—
> not as a result of pressure from without, not in the form of concessions
> for favors (eg. Respectability)—not as a quid pro quo—not as a result

of fear or eagerness to win friends—but as a result of the implementation of the policies of the Govt, re the various non white peoples.
Policies consistently declared & maintained and implemented with
increasing speed . . . to achieve self-determination.[75]

To Vorster's team there was no contradiction between hosting Banda and imposing apartheid. Rather, the two phenomena were decidedly compatible under
the principle of respecting each national community's own inviolable right to
fulfilment and independence. This emphasis on multinationalism equally provided the rationale for Vorster's intensified efforts to break South Africa out of
sporting isolation. The 1973 boxing bout between Pierre Fourie and African
American light-heavyweight Bob Foster in Johannesburg would have been unthinkable just a few years earlier. The same year, African American tennis star
Arthur Ashe received a visa to play in South Africa after being rejected on three
prior occasions. The regime even included non-whites in its South African Open
International Games for the first time, with the centerpiece being a soccer match
between white and black South African teams. *Verligtes* could only applaud. In
pushing through sports reforms, Vorster had shown "a cool head in emotional
circumstances," Schalk Pienaar wrote in his regular column in *Rapport*, in the
face of both "foreign and domestic hostility."[76]

The "international" format of these sporting encounters was highly revealing
of the whole enterprise. Save for the most radical *verligtes*, there was no conceptual route for Afrikanerdom to embrace "Africanness" that did not first pass
through multinationalism. Acceptable "Africanness" had to be already bounded
by states and thus not a political challenge to the regime. Foreign black athletes, soul and funk bands, businessmen, and government officials were all now
welcomed. Many stayed at the Pretoria International Hotel (formerly the Paul
Kruger Hotel—*verkramptes* had forced a renaming).[77] But black South Africans
were not allowed to enjoy the fruits of such changes until the homelands had
been established—that is, until they were not black South Africans any more.
The same barriers existed for Afrikanerdom's understanding of black South
African culture too. Journalist Rian Malan, a relative of D. F. Malan, recalled his
experiences as part of the awakening of Afrikaner youth to the outside world
in the 1960s: "I . . . knew the words to 'We Shall Overcome' and 'Marchin' to
the Freedom Band' by heart. In contrast, I doubt that any of us could so much
have as hummed the melody of 'Nkosi Sikalel' iAfrika.' . . . It was hip to be into
black culture. . . . [However, i]n white Johannesburg, black culture was inclined
to mean James Brown and James Baldwin, not the culture of that old black man
in the mountains or the black people in our back yards."[78]

For Vorster, the acceptance of an Africanized identity for the white polity and
steadily abandoning the ways of the past were fundamentally intertwined. To

fully embrace the new, a line had to be struck through the old. As African leaders began engaging with Pretoria on a regular basis, he exploited the atmosphere of flux created on the domestic political scene to signal a move away from hierarchical racism. "Under no circumstances should you slight a person who speaks a different language, whose skin is a different color, who has a different standard of civilization," Vorster declared in 1970. "You must never adopt the attitude that you are better than another person."[79] The next year, he went further: "If your policy is founded on your being better than someone else because you have a white skin, it is wrong, foolish and vain. What are you but a creature of God, as he is, to raise yourself and think you are better than he?"[80] These were truly radical statements in the context of the racial policies of his party and the mores of his electorate. More was to come. During Banda's state visit in 1971, Vorster allowed himself to be photographed sitting between two black women. This was nothing short of scandalous to *verkramptes*: the photo appeared in every copy of *Die Afrikaner* for months afterwards.

Much of Vorster's constituency remained wedded to the racially supremacist identities, policies, and ideologies cultivated by Verwoerd and felt alienated by the outward policy. *Die Afrikaner* savaged Vorster's foreign policy as an "obsession with seeking friendship where friendship is not to be found."[81] A 1973 editorial related: "How can the South African Government . . . pump in millions and millions of Rands in the form of cheap loans if there exists irrefutable

Figure 2.3 When Hastings Banda visited Pretoria in 1971, Vorster dined between two black women and allowed himself to be photographed doing so. This image was seen by the right-wing as exemplifying the elite's moral decay. It was still being reproduced in the HNP's journal *Die Afrikaner* two years later. Source: *Die Afrikaner*, 25 May 1973. Herstigte Nasionale Party.

proof that these African countries give active support and help to black death squads?"[82] A letter to the editor posited that African leaders were only engaging with Pretoria with a view to changing the apartheid policy. The receptiveness of certain African leaders to dialogue was "nothing other than interference in South Africa's domestic affairs."[83] Vorster saw things differently. It was true that Leabua Jonathan, Hastings Banda, and others did not approve of apartheid. But African outreach did not "weaken" or "threaten" the separate development plan, he insisted behind closed doors to the Transvaal NP. "To the contrary," the establishment of diplomatic ties entailed "an acknowledgement of sovereignty, and an acknowledgment of sovereignty brings with it an acknowledgement of the way in which you govern your country."[84]

Yet for all the ostensibly strategic objections, the ardour of the *verkrampte* backlash emanated from the intended implications of Vorster's new approach for the relationship between nation and race at home and for the content of Afrikaner nationalism. Vorster's outward policy "waters down and undermines the principle of separation between the races," lambasted Hertzog.[85] "The slogan [*wekroep*] is that we must be one with Africa because we are of Africa. With this it is implied that our links with Europe and European civilization must be broken," *Die Afrikaner* editorialized. "We hope for the white man's sake that there is still time to reflect on this perilous situation and turn back to the path which assures security and safe existence for the White man."[86] *Verkramptes* quickly yoked their criticism of the outward policy to their broader agenda of defending unbridled white supremacy against the caustic pressures of an increasingly integrated economy and society. Under the heading "Poor man throttled by rich man's party," *Die Afrikaner*'s 1971 New Year's editorial juxtaposed the government's largesse in black Africa with its neglect of the Afrikaner base. "In the name of the 'outward' policy R8,000,000 has been 'lent' to Malawi and R2,300,000 to Madagascar at 4 per cent interest, while the poor man in South Africa must pay 9 per cent to own his own house. . . . [The government] doesn't give a damn what becomes of the common man."[87] Readers parroted back versions of this critique. "The Government hands out plenty of money willy nilly [*om los en vas*] to black states, but for the farmers there is very little [*bloedmin*]," one suggested.[88]

For leading *verligtes*, however, Vorster's program provided the overdue intellectual complement to the separate development vision. Otto Krause lauded the shift to a multinational vision of "a South Africa of many equal nations, each based on its traditional territory," including an "Afrikaner nation, as a new nation living among other nations in Africa."[89] Willem de Klerk concurred. "[T]he Afrikaner nation is of Western origin, but is *of Africa*, and its people are not part of a colonial settlement," he wrote. "We are inseparably connected to the other nations of Africa and with them we have to seek our destiny."[90] Again, Afrikaner capital bolstered such calls in the name of commercial self-interest, while steering clear

Figure 2.4 "For that freshly roasted taste of genuine, real coffee—use Malawi beans." John Vorster depicted in a right-wing publication not as a noble ethnic leader, but as nothing more than a radio sponsor. The visual cues—the DJ's flashy cravat and long sideburns, the rock band in the background—conveyed to readers a criticism of Vorster's foreign policy embedded in a much broader opposition to the modernizing forces sweeping through Afrikaner society—and the cosmopolitan ideas and new social identities that they were bringing. Source: *Die Afrikaner*, 29 January 1971. Herstigte Nasionale Party.

of the more politically sensitive corollaries and identity issues. Outward policy offered untold new markets. As early as 1967, the AHI had offered full-throated support for "cooperation with African countries in the economic realm."[91] Leading businessmen had frequently been seconded by the government to help design development projects in independent Africa. Now, as African outreach materialized into a core government policy, Afrikaner capital roundly endorsed Vorster's efforts. "[C]ommunication and dialogue between black and white in Africa," *Volkshandel* averred, was "of the utmost importance."[92]

Once again, the fight for South Africa's future was waged on the battle-ground of the past. The government increasingly portrayed African outreach as a long-standing Nationalist norm. "Even the Voortrekkers established relations with Bantu chiefs for diplomatic affairs," the 1974 election manifesto informed voters.[93] "It may surprise you to know," Vorster told the Transvaal NP, "that in 1863 the Free State House of Assembly held a banquet for Moshoeshoe in a hotel in Bloemfontein, and received him as Head of State of the Basotho. So [African outreach] is nothing new in our people's history."[94] Such limited truths inspired a much more expansive reinvention of Nationalist tradition across the party. "The White Nationalist has never at any time seen himself as a colonialist in Africa. He has never at any time been afraid of the upsurging nationalism among the Blacks and he does not disregard the right of the Blacks to self-determination," declared Cape MP J. J. Engelbrecht.[95] "Running like a golden thread through the statements of the leaders of the National Party over the past decades is one main desire, namely the desire for co-operation with the countries of Africa," echoed G. P. D. Terblanche, representing a far more conservative constituency in the Free State.[96] This was in line with the hard *verligte* position articulated by Willem de Klerk: "The traditions of the Afrikaner do not include the racial rejection of the Non-Whites. Although there were numerous clashes between Whites and Non-Whites in the history of South Africa, the basic tendency was one of openheartedness and readiness to further the development of the Non-Whites."[97] The shift in the historicization of Afrikaner nationalism's relationship with black Africa since Verwoerd's Blood River speech was unmistakable. L. A. Pienaar even used Vorster's new ideology to hammer the opposition United Party for maintaining an antiquated policy of "one united colonially inspired South Africa." The United Party "had only one idea: of the White man governing the Black man in South Africa." This stood in stark contrast, he insisted, to Nationalist policy: "[W]e have changed to a South Africa which is being shared.... The ceiling has been lifted. The decolonization process has been tackled successfully.... When the winds of change blew through Africa it was the National Party which conceived the idea of the liberation and decolonization of the Bantu peoples of South Africa."[98]

Although the realities of oppression and exclusion on the ground did not change, this notion of horizontal coexistence between the white polity and black Africa became the core of a new identity for the regime, providing the NP with much needed ethnonationalist direction in the wake of the *verlig-verkrampstryd*. On the whole, Nationalists were responsive to the new African identities proposed for Afrikaner nationalism and the white polity. Fewer were willing to validate what Vorster saw as the inescapable complement to this shift: the removal of day-to-day racial discrimination and a commensurate foregrounding of multinationalism as the foundation for social, economic, and political life. Again, Vorster's movement on this issue both fueled and reflected *verligte* calls for change in the public sphere. In a landmark 1973 editorial in *Die Transvaler*, the historic organ of the Transvaal NP, Willem de Klerk wrote: "Separation which is unnecessary and unfair can destroy its own goal—it can inflame rather than prevent racial friction. Repugnant measures, double standards, humiliating discrimination and inconsequential [regulations] will need to be reviewed. These clash with Christian fairness, realistic human interactions, and good relations between peoples."[99] Later that year, the emboldened de Klerk even grasped the third rail of Afrikaner politics: mixed sport. Until each people became independent for itself, he wrote, "as an interim measure . . . every sportsman of whatever color, as an inhabitant of South Africa, ought to be included [in national teams] based on merit alone."[100] New Transvaal MP and recent Springbok rugby captain, Dawie de Villiers, went even further. "There is no reason why mixed [*veelvolkige*] cricket and rugby teams from the Republic cannot compete internationally."[101]

However, though Vorster's vision of separate development was gaining plenty of currency within the center of the party, there were strict limits to the appetite of an inherently conservative Nationalist community for the social corollaries of his geopolitical vision. In 1971, the hardline Minister of Information Connie Mulder headed to London to give a major speech on South Africa's new foreign policy. A full decade younger than Vorster or P. W. Botha, Mulder was a rising star in the party. He became head of the Transvaal caucus, the largest in the NP, the following year, and was frequently referred to in the press as the regime's "crown prince." His speech reflected just how rapidly Vorster had transformed the regime's sense of the white polity's identity and role in the world. First, Mulder established the historical basis of Pretoria's anticolonialism. "South Africa claims to be one of the first African countries to obtain full independence, after its long history of colonial government." Then, he offered South African aid as part of a positive vision of Africa's future grounded in modernization and development. "[T]he continent of Africa is finding its own feet. . . . South Africa not only sincerely wishes [the new African states] well, but also claims to be part and parcel of the awakening Africa, doing its share in its own way to assist African countries wherever possible." He then embedded this vision in a binary, positioning communist subversion as the alternative to economic cooperation:

[T]he different ways in which different countries run their own domestic affairs, can be regarded as relatively insignificant compared with other challenges facing Africa. Then we shall all realize that we are wasting time and energy criticizing one another, and that we should rather provide for the real needs of Africa, which are better education, more health facilities, bigger economic development, improvement in the field of agriculture, further industrial expansion, better housing and improved living conditions for all. Then we shall also realize that the real danger is communist infiltration—whether it be Russian or Red Chinese—and that we should forget our small squabbles and differences and create better understanding amongst all African countries.

Mulder then articulated how the same principles underpinned the regime's domestic policy: "We believe that these nine nations [the homelands] must become sovereign independent states in their own right, exactly as free as Ghana, Nigeria, or the United Kingdom, with full membership of the United Nations if they so desire. We also believe that they are entitled to maintain their own languages, cultures and identities in their own way according to their own wishes in their own geographical territories." Mulder then completed the circle, using the new concepts to reinforce the white polity's security and legitimacy. "At the same time we also believe that the South African nation is similarly entitled to self-determination and the maintenance of its own identity in exactly the same way."[102]

As a whole, the speech was indistinguishable in language, tone, and structure from Vorster's own thinking. The Verwoerdian model of white solidarity as the cornerstone of Pretoria's foreign policy had been supplanted by a vision of cooperation across the color line. Yet Mulder could have greatly helped Vorster both at home and abroad with even a few bromides hinting at a dismantling of petty apartheid. Even in front of a receptive foreign audience, Mulder demurred. There simply was not enough support in mainstream Afrikanerdom to cushion such statements from a rising conservative.

A Vulnerable Agenda

For all Vorster's efforts at carefully marshaling changing conceptions of Afrikaner nationalism and utilizing his foreign policy to feed favorable political trends, three interrelated phenomena weighed his agenda down. First, in a process that would be replicated over the coming years, Pretoria's national security strategy undercut its foreign policy. Vorster's inability prior to the Carnation Revolution to bolster his embrace of African identities with more than token reductions in his support for Salisbury and Lisbon, as well as South Africa's continued dominion over SWA, substantially undermined the government's efforts to dispel widespread perceptions of the regime as a form of neo-imperialism. In 1968, Kaunda underlined just how counterproductive these relationships were in a personal letter to Vorster: "In actual fact, nobody, at least in this part of the world, had considered the question of lumping together South Africa with the rest of [the] minority regimes. It is only South Africa's apparent decision to throw her lot in with the rebel regime in Rhodesia which has brought her into the full focus of criticism by the rest of the international community." That aside, the Zambian president continued, he "certainly would be interested" to learn more about Pretoria's envisaged program of leading its African communities toward self-determination.[103] The Lusaka Manifesto reiterated this distinction, standing firm on militancy toward Portugal and Rhodesia while qualifying the previously unrelenting support of armed struggle to overthrow apartheid.[104] However, Vorster did not fully appreciate the urgency of widening this opening or of harmonizing his foreign policy and P. W. Botha's national security strategy until after the Carnation Revolution.

Second, the lack of a far-reaching repeal of petty apartheid legislation meant South Africa's efforts to recast identity politics on the continent never succeeded in overcoming entrenched perceptions of apartheid as a symbol of Africa's colonial past. There was extensive talk in *verligte* circles about granting meaningful rights to Africans living in urban areas, repealing large swathes of the most offensive petty apartheid measures, and deracializing public spaces en masse. "In South Africa we have a government and a people that is moving away from racism, that is moving away from discrimination, that wants to rectify it and get it out of its system," announced rising MP Louis Nel.[105] In 1973 alone, for instance, the Bantu Labour Relations Regulation Amendment Bill made strikes by Africans legal under certain conditions; there was a limited opening of the color bar in the employment market, enabling blacks to move into more skilled and higher paid roles; the government established mechanisms to direct foreign aid to the homelands; and the military allowed Cape Coloreds to become commissioned officers.[106] Even such ad hoc measures were enough to alienate the right-wing, from whose perspective the pace of change was dramatic. Simultaneously, however, the lack of a broad-based rather than piecemeal reform agenda to give effect to the vaunted flattening of South Africa's racial hierarchies was a major obstacle to recalibrating African understandings of what separate development entailed. Even in his landmark April 1971 speech in Abidjan, Houphouët-Boigny did not hold back in his criticism of "the revolting system of apartheid."[107]

Finally, Vorster's efforts to represent his polity's relationship with the homelands as similar to the new relationships with independent African states met with limited success in Africa. Even those African leaders receptive to discussions with Pretoria remained unconvinced that grand apartheid itself was a sufficient formula for the exercise of all South Africans' postcolonial rights, as that concept was accepted internationally at the time. "In some respects I am a man for dialogue [with Pretoria]," Senegalese President Léopold Senghor told a press conference in April 1973. However, "[i]n the first place dialogue would have to take place, not between us and Mr. Vorster, but between the Vorster government and the black majority in South Africa."[108] His government told South African officials much the same thing in private on numerous occasions.[109]

Even Banda, the leader with whom Pretoria found the warmest reception, reflected the tension between these two impulses. Upon Banda's accession to the prime ministership, Ghanaian leader Kwame Nkrumah had looked to cultivate him to the pan-African standard: "[W]e in Africa cannot afford to compromise our stand with the colonialists or neo-colonialists in any shape or form." Africa, he argued, had "to stand together in a united front."[110] However, Banda had little time for the politics of racial identity or using hostility toward apartheid as an ideological anchor for his regime. His diplomats saw the OAU as "vocal" and "emotional," and its anti-apartheid militancy as yielding only "popular but unrealistic pronouncements or policies."[111] Instead, Banda anticipated that multiracialism would inevitably constitute the future across the region; Africans would have to see "today's imperialists" as "tomorrow's fellow Africans, tomorrow's fellow countrymen, tomorrow's fellow citizens."[112] However, having worked as a young man in the mines near Johannesburg, where racial oppression and economic exploitation went hand in hand, he was under no illusions about the power structures of apartheid. Banda's unpublished autobiography, which he wrote while imprisoned by the British at Gwelo in 1959–60, relates: "The idea behind the policy of apartheid, is not justice and equity to the Africans, but rigid control over them, in order, the better and more effectively, to keep them in perpetual subjection and serfdom. . . . It is a design to re-enslave all the Africans in South Africa."[113] Even as he accepted a soft loan from Pretoria to build a new capital city and fulfill his modernization agenda, Banda told South African officials, "I am as strongly opposed to apartheid, colonialism and discrimination as is any other African leader."[114]

For "moderate" African leaders, the outward policy targeted three dynamics: their need for economic development, their fear of communist challenges to their rule, and—given Pretoria's apparent stability—their powerlessness to dismantle apartheid. Some African states were willing to engage with the new ideologies and state identities that Pretoria was promoting. It suited several to reemphasize the inviolability of the postcolonial state or to attach their legitimacy to Cold War discourses, especially if these shifts reinforced structures and norms that could bolster their security as gatekeepers. They were simultaneously often prepared to eschew militancy on the pragmatic grounds that the existing OAU norms of blanket hostility, informal economic boycott, and support for liberation movements were proving ineffective. However, Vorster's success in changing the focus and nature of the conversation over apartheid hardly eradicated the preexisting discourses by which African leaders felt a fundamental abhorrence of an apartheid system that recalled their own experiences of colonialism. This rendered the relationships established by outward policy both hollow and unstable.

A Global Discourse

South Africa's failure to fundamentally redefine African perceptions of apartheid left the outward policy vulnerable to changes in the international environment.

In the early 1970s, radicals across the global south reinvigorated the anticolonial cause by connecting their disparate political struggles within a broader global militancy.[115] Inspired by successes in Cuba, Algeria, Vietnam, and elsewhere, African radicals harnessed the new discourses of revolutionary liberation to their existing anticolonial narratives. Militant states increasingly set the agenda at the OAU, jostling for prominence on the continental political scene through ever more inflammatory exhortations to insurrection against Lisbon, Salisbury, and Pretoria alike. In 1972, the OAU generated a renewed campaign, the Year of Liberation, targeting the elimination of the remnants of white rule in Africa, including a 50 percent increase in funding and resources for the Liberation Committee.[116] By mid-1972, the momentum of the outward policy had stalled.[117] In May, the Johannesburg *Financial Mail* asked "Is Dialogue Dying?"[118] By October, the *Star* across town provided an answer: "The outward policy may not be quite dead, but these days it is looking very moribund."[119] By early 1973, one BOSS analysis of the African scene observed starkly: "In the face of the stronger military disposition and the formal rejection by the OAU of dialogue with South Africa as a path to reaching a modus vivendi, the enthusiasm of supporters of dialogue has faded and with it our hope for the expansion of our outward policy."[120]

This change in the tone of African politics accelerated during 1973 as the South African–sponsored paradigm for African relations grounded in anticommunism, economic cooperation, and status quo political stability was displaced by an alternative that Pretoria could not have foreseen: the idea that white rule in Southern Africa constituted a neo-imperial historical phenomenon of the same type as the Afro-Asian bloc's new *bête noire*, Zionism. In 1967, French scholar Maxime Rodinson had famously argued that the Israeli state was essentially colonialist in character, much like the apartheid state and the French occupation of Algeria.[121] In reshaping the lenses through which the Arab-Israeli conflict was understood, his arguments also recast opposition to Pretoria across the global south. By 1973, sub-Saharan Africa was enlisting Arab states in a militantly anti-apartheid stance, broadening the anti-Israel front far beyond the Middle East in exchange. The synergy between these two antitheses to postcolonial ideals was a prominent theme at the tenth anniversary summit of the OAU in May— that is, even before the Yom Kippur War in October—and became a focal point for the reconstitution of the Afro-Asian anti-apartheid unity of the early 1960s. For North African states in particular, the new discourse conveniently reconciled both their Arab and African identities. Instead of sub-Saharan leaders like Kaunda and Nyerere, it was Algerian President Houari Boumedienne who led the anti-apartheid charge at the 1973 OAU summit: "Africa cannot adopt one attitude towards colonialism in southern Africa and a completely different one towards Zionist colonization in Northern Africa [in the Sinai]."[122] The result was a drastic recalibration of African attitudes toward Israel. As late as the start of 1972 thirty-one African countries maintained relations with Israel. By the end of 1973 that number had been slashed to just five.[123] All of these—Côte d'Ivoire, Botswana, Lesotho, Swaziland, and Malawi—were among the strongest supporters of engagement with South Africa.[124]

This refocusing of the African political scene on opposition to apartheid through the prism of anti-Zionism proved the turning point for the outward policy. In October 1973, the UN General Assembly rejected South Africa's credentials for the first time and declared apartheid a "crime against humanity." The representatives of every African state except Malawi walked out of the General Assembly as Muller began to plead South Africa's case.[125] The following month, the Organization of the Petroleum Exporting Countries (OPEC) extended the oil embargo enacted during the Yom Kippur War to South Africa, Rhodesia, and Portugal. And at the March 1974 meeting of the UN's Special Committee of Twenty-Four on decolonization, the South African mission in New York observed that "frequent reference was made to the 'collaboration between Portugal, the United States, Israel and South Africa against the liberation movements.'"[126] South Africa's efforts to dissociate apartheid from perceptions of neo-imperialism had suffered a telling setback. The public gains of the outward policy and the extension of a moderate African norm in favor of noninterference in South Africa's affairs stalled.

The circumstances of the collapse of the outward policy in 1972–73 were vital in shaping both the regime's conceptions of its place in the world and its future policies. The unravelling of a moderate, anti-interference African bloc could have been interpreted as proof of the need to reevaluate South Africa's foreign policy or reassess the appeal of Pretoria's alternative models for African politics. Instead, policymakers perceived in the recent international reversals only a case for renewed efforts to stop Pretoria's relationship with independent Africa being from hijacked by communist-backed radicals. "If it were not for the interference on the part of Russian militarism and Chinese insurgence [sic], we would reach an agreement with Africa," said Defense Minister P. W. Botha.[127] It was true that the 1972 Mogadishu Declaration had reestablished the pan-African consensus on the need for apartheid's overthrow by force of arms or sanctions. But Vorster's team accentuated the positives. Behind the scenes, they still met regularly with their African counterparts. Though top-level public summits remained elusive, documents show that between mid-1973 and mid-1974, Muller even met clandestinely with the heads of state of Gabon, Mauritius, and Côte d'Ivoire.[128] By the Carnation Revolution, South Africa traded not just with Rhodesia and the Portuguese colonies, but with almost all anticommunist African states. The value of South African goods heading north of Southern Africa was still minute as a proportion of the Republic's total exports, but it was still nearly 50 percent greater in 1973 than as recently as 1970.[129] And although the OAU advocated blanket isolation of South Africa and a full trade embargo, Pretoria understood that many member states paid only lip service to such calls. Consequently, far from apartheid constituting a barrier to the regime's acceptance on the continent, the government rationalized that it was *especially* in Africa, as Muller put it, that South Africa's "bona fides [would] not be generally accepted until we have taken our policy to its full consequences, in other words, until the homelands have become independent states."[130]

This reasoning met with little internal resistance. The regime's unwillingness to fully commit to dismantling petty apartheid only reinforced the political appeal of continuing to push the ideological envelope through foreign policy. Petty apartheid affected nearly every minister's portfolio. Vorster was hardly willing to strong-arm all of his colleagues simultaneously; that was the antithesis of his consensus-seeking approach to governance. Equally, among the bureaucracy, the issue of precisely who spoke with Africa had become a prestigious and coveted policy terrain and the subject of substantial interdepartmental conflict. As the DFA's conventional efforts increasingly ran aground in 1972–73, Information and BOSS became more heavily involved in cultivating bilateral relationships behind the scenes, particularly in laying the groundwork for Vorster's historic meetings with Houphouët-Boigny and Senghor in Côte d'Ivoire in 1974.[131] By that year, all three bureaucracies were involved in pursuing their own programs for establishing relationships in Africa. This competition in and of itself likely contributed to the ongoing centrality of African outreach in South Africa's foreign policy.

Therefore, despite the outward policy's demise and Africa's renewed commitment to apartheid's removal, when the Portuguese regime collapsed there was considerable momentum across the board in Pretoria for the idea that engagement with Africa rather than confrontation was the way forward. After five hundred years, the Carnation Revolution may have suddenly changed South Africa's strategic environment. But Pretoria's response drew extensively upon the experiences of the previous years, specifically the emergence of the idea that the regime could solve its legitimacy problem through an Africanization of its identity.

3

"We Must Stay Prepared"

Reimagining the White Redoubt

Even during its "golden age," white South Africa remained distinctly conscious of its isolation and vulnerability. The readiness of the regime to enforce censorship laws, lash out at foreign critics, and crack down upon nongovernmental organizations critical of its racial policies revealed the deep-seated anxieties of the ruling elite, at least as much as the ease with which it did so pointed to the government's strength. In this context of bullishness interwined with insecurity, white South African society initially responded to the steady departure of European authority from Africa and the profusion of new states in its place with nothing short of fear and dismay. Lurid stories of Africa unleashed mesmerized the public sphere. Between 1952 and 1955, the Mau Mau uprising and associated conflict over Kenya's future featured in no fewer than 804 reports in *Die Burger* alone. Forty-two percent of these appeared on the front page.[1] Equally resonant for South African whites was the chaotic Belgian withdrawal from the Congo in July 1960. Newspapers produced an endless stream of accounts relating the killing and raping of whites.[2] In the early 1960s, the dominant impulse driving the regime's national security policy was a desire to simply keep such chaos as far away as possible. Simultaneously, the government invoked decolonization as posing a mortal threat to whites across Africa, a move that paid major electoral dividends. For all the overblown rhetoric and civil liberties abuses, hardline rule gained a new appeal for all whites when juxtaposed with the alternative of a black takeover. "We fight as a *volk* for our survival, and there is now nothing so important as that we have the consciousness of strong internal unity," as Verwoerd put it on the campaign trail in 1966. "That is why it is so important that Afrikaans- and English-speaking people stand side by side in the struggle for our survival."[3] Anglophone voters were suddenly targeted relentlessly on the basis of a shared white interest: standing firm in the face of decolonization to the north.

As the existential fear of the early 1960s gave way to the bullish optimism of the mid-1960s, Afrikanerdom began to reflect more soberly on what the new global environment meant. In particular, Nationalist elites increasingly interpreted decolonization through the prism of the *volkseie* concept. This concept held that the key to harmonious and moral social construction lay in each national community existing according to its own culture and characteristics. If *volkseie* mandated the maintenance of the Christian National character of Afrikanerdom and freezing out foreign influences, it equally legitimized the creation of spheres in which African peoples could enjoy similar autonomy.[4] This logic not only underpinned Verwoerd's creation of the separate development vision in 1959, it also shaped Pretoria's responses to African nationalism abroad. *Volkseie* mandated that "legitimate" African nationalism could only exist in Africans' innate socioeconomic context and stage of development; that is, tribal structures and traditional chiefdoms. Commenting on the Mau Mau violence, Verwoerd observed: "The tribal authority is the natural ally of the [civilized, white] government against such rebellious movements. It was the chiefs with their authorities who sided with the forces of law and order and who assisted European authority."[5] This thinking had the additional benefit of splintering Africans into smaller, more controllable groups, implicitly rejecting pan-Africanist claims to common cause and shared identity.

From this perspective, Nationalists saw the creation of independent African nation-states beginning in the late 1950s as little more than foreign-educated elites, or *évolués*, hijacking the idea of self-determination for their own ends. E. G. Louw, then Minister for Native Affairs, put it thus:

> [S]trong influences have been at work in the effort to destroy everything connected with the national character of the Natives. That steady background of his tribal consciousness . . . is gradually disappearing, and the Native [consequently] . . . has a feeling of instability which is nourished by people who are only too eager that he should be torn away from all his anchors, so that he can become easy prey to their propaganda.[6]

The new African elites pressing European empires for self-determination were perceived as divorced from the essential tribal nature of their respective national groups. It followed, by definition, that they could not be true nationalists. Their ideas, from pan-Africanism to communism, were seen as foreign imports, little more than vehicles for the manipulation of "real" African aspirations. In this analysis, the Mau Mau uprising and the violence in the Congo simply reflected the dangers of removing Africans from their cultural context and corrupting their essential nature.[7]

DIE DONKER STROOM STYG.

Sy kan nog gered word, maar die water styg nou vinnig. Oormôre kan
dit te laat wees. Red haar betyds deur môre HNP te stem.

Figure 3.1 Traditionally, white South Africa saw Africa as foreign and full of latent
threats. In this election-eve appeal, entitled "The Dark Current Rises," Afrikaner
nationalism is presented in true nineteenth-century European style, personified as a
pure, Marianne-like figure, surrounded by a sea of forboding blackness. The threats of
Liberalism, Communism, and Racial Mixing loom. The text reads, "She can still be saved,
but the water is rising quickly. The day after tomorrow could be too late. Save her by
voting for the National Party tomorrow." Source: *Die Transvaler*, 1948. Caxton Company.

Not until the Vorster era was this thinking first joined and then slowly
eclipsed in Nationalist discourses by an acceptance of the concept of the modern African, a trend that accelerated into the P. W. Botha period. At home, the
Vorster government looked to develop the homelands through the construction
of schools, hospitals, and industries, albeit slowly and in the context of domestic

Figure 3.2 Decolonization as seen by English-speaking whites. The winds of change blow the fire of black nationalism down from the Congo, to Rhodesia, and beyond. Hendrik Verwoerd is depicted complacently relaxing on his stoop. Source: *Daily News,* 25 February 1961. Independent Media.

political opposition. And in the field of foreign affairs, Vorster realized that if African nationalism could be contained within the boundaries of the nation-state, such that any links to pan-Africanism were neutralized, then co-operation with the previously derided *évolués* could prove very useful indeed. In this way, decolonization prompted a shift from the traditional colonialistic racism, replete with tropes of primitive, darkest Africa, to the more subtle, home-grown, but equally dangerous discourses of the Vorster era, grounded in the principle of parallel nationalism and a claim to unique knowledge of Africa and its peoples. The ideology behind the separate development vision was updated and recast to allow for a no-longer-deniable reality: African nationalism.

South Africa's national security profile was thus not so much closely tied to domestic racial *policies*, as has long been axiomatic in the literature,[8] as it was reflective of underlying *discourses*. And as understandings of African nationalism, communism, and the trajectory of the *volk* changed, so too did its approach to national security. These changes initially connoted reconceptualizations of the same enemies. But the new strategic thinking of the 1960s opened up new and unintended paths for statecraft, thereby laying the groundwork for the dramatic shifts of the post–Carnation Revolution era.

Controlling the Conversation

At the start of the Vorster era, the apartheid regime saw its central security interest, both at home and abroad, as lying in vigilantly controlling the political conversation over the regime's legitimacy. The first frontline involved marginalizing
those who sought to bolster damaging perceptions of South Africa's social order.
Pretoria remembered well the international alienation of the early 1960s, when
the emergence of apartheid as a counterpoint to the nascent Third World project had powerfully (though not always decisively) disincentivized South Africa's
traditional Western friends from providing even limited validation of its social
order.[9] Vorster inherited Verwoerd's solution to this problem: mitigating criticism
of apartheid in elite Western circles. Under the demure and phlegmatic Minister
for Foreign Affairs, Hilgard Muller, the DFA sought to blunt attacks on apartheid
and to advocate the merits and feasibility of Pretoria's model of separate development. The DFA's mission statement was clear: "[W]e must succeed in convincing
the world that we can resolve our internal issues and are busy doing so."[10] Pretoria
also underscored South Africa's role as a reliable Cold War ally, stressing its strategic location at the Cape of Good Hope, its reserves of rare and important miner-
als, and its unflinching anticommunism.[11] "The South Africans believe that even
informal military cooperation with [the] West would provide them with protection against any future external threat to ⌊the⌋ maintenance of white supremacy
in South Africa," American Ambassador John Hurd cabled home in 1974. "South
Africans . . . look forward to the day when we will need port facilities on [the]
African mainland. And what single African country, they ask rhetorically, can offer
a stable political situation, has a government with firm anticommunist convictions, and would be fully willing to give us what we need[?]"[12]

    In the detached and unhurried tenor of these activities, its focus on Western
powers, and in the core arguments advanced, this dimension of Vorster's foreign
policy represented a marked continuum with Verwoerd's. Additionally, amid
concerns that the DFA was not being assertive enough in its advocacy of South
Africa's case, in 1972 Vorster authorized the Department of Information to
wage a more vigorous and underhanded campaign designed to shape the debate
on apartheid within Western countries themselves. Under the direction of its
minister, Connie Mulder, and the department's young, suave secretary, Eschel
Rhoodie, Information worked assiduously behind the scenes to court, fund, and
sometimes simply manufacture foreign mouthpieces for South Africa's views. Its
clandestine efforts included attempting to buy the Washington *Star* newspaper,
cultivating influential American and other Western politicians through expensive lobbyists, and organizing visits by South African ministers operating in
ostensibly private capacities to Western capitals , thereby circumventing foreign
governments' efforts to avoid public meetings with South African officials.[13]

That much more was going on behind the scenes at Information than simply producing glossy brochures on South Africa's wildlife and economy should have been evident from the mismatch between the department's ostensible functions and the party rank of its minister: Mulder had recently been chosen as the new head of the Transvaal NP, replacing the outgoing Ben Schoeman.[14]

The primary target of these campaigns was the United States, whose disposition toward South Africa was seen in Pretoria (and elsewhere) as the key factor in the capacity of international opposition to apartheid to translate into meaningful action against the regime. That disposition changed repeatedly throughout the 1960s.[15] By the end of the Kennedy Administration (1961–63), Washington's position was that by encouraging self-determination and supporting African nationalism, the United States could promote its position in postcolonial Africa and preempt any expansion in communist influence there. While this inclination continued under Lyndon Johnson (1963–69), the Vietnam War drove a wedge between Washington and the Third World. In this context, a less idealistic argument won favor: the white regimes could be counted upon to virulently oppose radicalism in the region; undermining them might create a fluid situation ripe for communist penetration. By the end of the Johnson Administration, American policy had reverted to "moderate pressure and a posture of official aloofness," in the phrasing of one internal account.[16] This meant criticizing racialist rule and championing self-determination in Southern Africa, but without providing the concrete initiatives, political capital, or diplomatic resources needed to actually encourage a transfer of power.[17]

From the outset, the Nixon Administration's policy—enshrined in the adoption of Option Two in the infamous National Security Study Memorandum 39 of 1969—amplified this trend, positioning the United States squarely behind Pretoria.[18] The American interest in the region, the new administration decided, lay above all in stability:

> The Whites are here to stay and the only way that constructive change can come about is through them. There is no hope for the blacks to gain the political rights they seek through violence, which will only lead to chaos and increased opportunities for the communists. We can, by selective relaxation of our stance toward the white regimes, encourage some modification of their current racial and colonial policies. . . . There is virtually no evidence that change might be forthcoming [on apartheid] as a result of any approach on our part.[19]

In theory, the Nixon Administration's policy committed the United States to encouraging incremental reform by working through the white power structure. In practice, this amounted to a relaxation of even the token pressures applied

by previous administrations. Washington repeatedly rallied its Western allies
to help blunt UN resolutions introduced by nonaligned or communist countries criticizing Pretoria, winning itself few friends in the process. Equally sym-
bolically, the Nixon White House did nothing to stop the passage of the Byrd
Amendment allowing imports of Rhodesian chrome, thus placing the United
States in the company of Portugal and South Africa as the only nations to openly
flaunt the mandatory UN embargo on trade with the renegade Smith regime in
Salisbury. South African ministers were even received in Washington by leading
officials. Mulder was photographed at the White House with Vice-Presidents
Spiro Agnew and Gerald Ford[20]; he also met openly with numerous congress-
men, senators, and governors, including Ronald Reagan and John Connally, all
of whom evinced various levels of understanding of South Africa's racial situation.[21] Secretary of State Henry Kissinger promised Muller: "Sometimes the
African countries press us on matters affecting South Africa. Then we may have
to say something to please them but we shall avoid harassing you and we shall
always do so with understanding and goodwill. . . . I will curb any missionary
zeal on the part of my officers in the State Department to harass you."[22]

South Africa was greatly comforted by the Nixon Administration's position.[23]
"As long as President Nixon stays in power, we can expect that our relations with
the United States will remain reasonably stable," a major DFA report on bilateral
relations stated. "Its rejection of ideology and interference in the domestic affairs
of other states, its pragmatism, and its support for dialogue and the peaceful
resolution of international disputes, are all to the advantage of South Africa."[24]
Another report observed: "Stability in Southern Africa is in the US national interest and it is for this reason that the US continues to oppose the use of violence
in our area and refuses to give recognition or assistance to the terrorists. . . . We
shall . . . continue to enjoy a period of grace for as long as Dr. Kissinger remains
at the helm of US foreign policy—even if President Nixon does not serve his
full term as President."[25] In a March 1971 letter to Vorster, Nixon did not refer
even obliquely to American disapproval of South Africa's racial policies, but instead explicitly underlined the "immediate and broad applicability of the 'Nixon
Doctrine' in Africa."[26] The message the South Africans received was precisely
that intended: while Washington would keep Pretoria at arm's length, the regime
would continue to be given a relatively free hand to maintain control across the
region in whatever manner it saw fit. Pretoria duly did so, using force to combat
and contain African groups who sought to define their own futures in ways that
impinged upon the polity's freedom of maneuver. For Nixon and Kissinger,
there was little more to the relationship than that. Washington still saw South
Africa's racial policies as repugnant and its long-term program for their resolution, separate development, as unfeasible. In 1972, when South Africa was more
stable and prosperous than at any time until the demise of the apartheid regime

two decades later, a major CIA National Intelligence Estimate noted in no uncertain terms: "The program of separate development of white and non-white communities is not working and almost certainly will not work."[27] While the Nixon Administration made such views clear in public, where they were usually understood in Pretoria as posturing, the State Department did likewise in private, earning the enmity of South African officials.[28]

As an insurance policy, the Vorster government also began to develop nuclear weapons. Since 1965, the regime had been utilizing American uranium in the Safari-1 research reactor at Pelindaba. Although Pretoria refused to sign the new Non-Proliferation Agreement in 1968, a series of agreements with the Johnson and Nixon Administrations increased the quality and quantity of the imported uranium fuel. In exchange, the regime renewed its commitment not to develop a weapon. Simultaneously, however, the South Africans developed a home-grown enrichment technique capable of producing weapons grade uranium-238 from uranium-235. In 1970, they announced the construction of a new plant at nearby Valindaba to run the process; around the same time, American uranium began to go unaccounted for. In March 1971, well before the Carnation Revolution, Vorster decided to explore the construction of a weapon that might act as a deterrent to would-be aggressors. In May 1974, the first rudimentary device was successfully tested. Later that year, Vorster authorized the production of an ostensibly peaceful nuclear explosive. By 1978, under renewed global pressure and faced with an array of geopolitical threats, the regime formally decided to develop an offensive nuclear capability. The program quickly accelerated once P. W. Botha succeeded Vorster in September of that year.[29]

The second front of South Africa's efforts to control the political conversation over the regime's legitimacy saw Pretoria confront those who sought to claim the mantle of African nationalism for themselves; that is, outside the Nationalist framework of tribalism and *volkseie*. This impulse manifested itself daily, in the actions of a vast internal security apparatus largely designed to suppress independent African political agency. It also extended to rigorous control over undesirable ideas. Perhaps the most notorious example of this occurred in 1971, when the government simply censored Leo Kuper's chapter in volume II of the *Oxford History of South Africa*, which focused on the history of African nationalism in a nationwide perspective.[30] For the regime, African nationalism could only attach to each of the country's African "peoples" and be fulfilled within the homeland structures.

The Simba Rebellion in the Congo (Kinshasa) in 1964 saw the regime take the fight against African nationalism into new realms.[31] As communist-backed rebels overran the eastern half of the new country and challenged the tenuous control of the pro-Western government of Moïse Tshombe, Portuguese officials became concerned about instability across the long border with Angola and sought out South African help.[32] In a meeting in Lisbon with Vorster's special emissary to Southern Rhodesia, Harald Taswell, Portuguese dictator António Salazar described a wave of black nationalists threatening "European" rule, a specter that mirrored Pretoria's views of the dangers of decolonization for Southern Africa:

> We have certain problems in "Southern Africa." ... What will happen is that African states, after receiving their independence, will follow the experiences of Indo-China and Algeria, in other words, they will organize sabotage, terrorism, etc. The collapse of Southern Africa will spell the end of the work of civilization. ... It is in the interests of Portugal and South Africa to therefore ensure that stability in Southern Africa is maintained.[33]

In Salazar's Southern African domino theory, the battle was best fought in the Eastern Congo. "If there is to be a war in Southern Africa," he told Taswell, articulating the principle that would become the bedrock of South Africa's national defense policy through the 1970s and 1980s, "South Africa would prefer to see the war at a distance of 2000 km from its own borders rather than on its own territory."[34] Portugal transported to Tshombe the arms, material, and transport aircraft it had in Angola, and despatched several thousand armed "Katangan gendarmes" and five thousand automatic weapons acquired through NATO. South Africa bore the financial burden.[35] The Simba Rebellion provided the exemplar for a new strategy of forward defense. Pretoria resolved to work with Lisbon and, after Smith's Rhodesian Front government issued its Unilateral Declaration of Independence (UDI) in 1965, with Salisbury, to keep African nationalism as far away from South Africa's borders as possible.

Through the end of the 1960s, South Africa provided a limited but important contribution to Portugal's efforts to maintain control in its overseas territories. In 1967, Defense Minister Botha visited Lisbon and made it clear that South Africa would respond favorably to requests for military equipment.[36] The following year, the South African Air Force began supporting Portuguese operations in south-eastern Angola out of bases in SWA, though at great expense and with little success. The SADF's review concluded that the occasional "terrorist" killed or cache of weapons captured "does not justify the vast financial cost involved in the air effort."[37] In mid-1969, South Africa agreed to a 25 million rand loan to Portugal, as well as the donation of 8.5 million rand in old military equipment.[38] The 1970 agreement laid bare the basis of the bilateral relationship:

> The purpose of the loan is to help Portugal eliminate insurgency in Angola and Mozambique, to regain control of and to re-establish good

govt administration over the populations there. It is important for the security of Southern Africa generally and for the RSA particularly that these two Portuguese provinces be peaceful, politically stable, economically sound and developing and friendly towards the RSA. By helping them to realize these aims we will be making it less likely that they will become sanctuaries for the further spread of insurgency in Southern Africa or bases for the launching of more conventional enemy military action here.[39]

This military aid developed against a background of increased cooperation in other spheres too. In 1969, South Africa agreed to fund approximately 45 percent of the cost of constructing the Cabora Bassa dam in Mozambique, an investment of some 190 million rand. The agreement secured hydroelectric energy for South Africa at far less than market price, thereby bringing the two governments together economically as well as geopolitically.[40] However, recalls Kaas van der Waals, the South African military liaison in Luanda from 1969 until 1973, South Africa "didn't provide troops and that is what the Portuguese needed."[41]

The other pillar of the forward defense effort was Rhodesia, though given Salisbury's dominance over the insurgents there prior to December 1972, the focus of South Africa's attention and resources was on the relationship with Portugal.[42] After UDI, South Africa played an important role in ensuring the survival of the internationally unrecognized regime, particularly in refusing to comply with the UN trade embargo against Salisbury.[43] Moreover, from 1967, South Africa deployed helicopters and South African Police (SAP) units along Rhodesia's northern border to prevent the infiltration of insurgents from Zambia.[44] To outside observers, that South Africa should become the "regional patron of the Rhodesian regime" was a logical manifestation of a white racist axis extending from Pretoria to Salisbury.[45]

However, assumptions that Pretoria's assistance was predictable and dependable, given the pan-white foundations of the relationship, obscured a more complicated picture. At the societal level, cultural links, business relationships, and family ties all transcended political borders. Ian Smith himself had attended Rhodes University in Grahamstown; his brother-in-law was South African Finance Minister Owen Horwood. Rhodesian rugby and cricket teams played in South African provincial competitions, while leading Rhodesian sportsmen regularly represented the Republic at international level. Even the Broederbond had a handful of chapters in Rhodesia among the Afrikaner population there. "[T]he vast majority of [white] South Africans" therefore wanted to see UDI "succeed," stated *Die Volksblad* at the time.[46] Decolonization to the north further fueled white solidarity. "It is in the interest of the Republic that the whites remain in power in Rhodesia, otherwise Pan Africanism will [progress] from the Zambezi [Rhodesia's northern border] [to] the Limpopo [South Africa's northern border]," observed *Veg* in 1968. Any "handover" would be a "departure" from the Nationalist mission of "maintaining the white man's authority," the right-wing periodical warned.[47]

However, by the Vorster era South Africa and Rhodesia as polities differed substantially from each other in political culture, historical experience, and identity.[48] The levers of state power in South Africa were overwhelmingly in the hands of Afrikaners, long inculcated with a distrust of the British colonial heritage valued by the Rhodesian whites—in spite of their repudiation of London's current decolonization policy. Equally, Rhodesians had a long history of opposition to Afrikaner culture and power. In 1922, the fifteen thousand overwhelmingly British settlers had rejected incorporation in the Union of South Africa, fearing domination by Afrikaners. Even into the 1970s, elements of Smith's Rhodesian Front disapproved of the inclusion of Afrikaners in national politics.[49]

Moreover, Pretoria and Salisbury each looked upon the others' systems for dealing with their multiracial societies—separate development for the South Africans, and (from 1969) the qualified franchise for the Rhodesians—as primitive, unenlightened, and misguided.[50] As Broederbond Chairman Gerrit Viljoen later wrote in a circular to Bond chapters, the Smith regime had haughtily rejected South Africa's policy of separate freedoms and instead chosen a sociopolitical system that reflected an "unchanged British colonial mentality which cared little for honesty towards underlings [*onderhoriges*]."[51]

Against this backdrop, it was the emerging *verligte* conception of Afrikaner identity, shepherded and cultivated by Vorster and his allies, which provided the most important conceptual grounds for Pretoria's decision to ultimately distance itself from Salisbury. As seen, the new ideas of Afrikaner identity grounded the polity's legitimacy in discourses of national identity—histories of culture, belonging, connection to the land—rather than the older discourses of racial rights. In this thinking, that national identity was indeed white, and resolutely so, but the legitimacy of its nation-state did not derive from a notion of racial superiority; it derived from Afrikaner history. As this paradigm gained in popularity among public intellectuals, business elites, mainstream Afrikanerdom, National Party MPs, and others, it became accepted that the Smith regime could not lay any such parallel claims to nationhood, but instead relied precisely on the outdated concepts that the new discourses left in the past. In her history of the Smith regime, Luise White draws a distinction between two types of white settler regimes. The first looked to rebrand their legitimacy in the wake of empire and articulate their own legitimacy as nation-states.[52] The second was typified by the Rhodesians. They "utilized a hodgepodge of institutions and practices . . . to maintain what they refused to call white rule but instead relabeled as responsible government. They did not claim to be "the people" worthy of sovereignty but instead proclaimed membership in an empire, or the West, or an anti-communism that had no national boundaries."[53] The new Afrikanerdom certainly looked for external geopolitical and conceptual anchors, both in "the West" and "anticommunism." Overall, however, the centrality of discourses of nationhood to Afrikaner political discourse place the white South African polity firmly in the first category. Indeed, Afrikaner elites condescended to a Rhodesian power structure that lacked a deep, unified national history. All they saw was an entity that comprised huge numbers of postwar immigrants and, overall, wanted to reproduce in Africa a lost, imagined Britain—an identity that was "literally reactionary," to use White's term.[54]

In short, whatever singular affinity of race existed between the two peoples was resolutely undercut on the South African side by a range of other perspectives and concerns, some of which went right to the core of the regime's newly dominant worldviews. In fact, viewed from Pretoria, the relationship with Salisbury rested not so much on the commonalities identified by foreign observers, but on two basic principles. First, South African state support for Rhodesia (and Portugal) was based on an alignment of national security interests. As historian Sue Onslow succinctly identifies:

> [the] growing perception of mutual interests [in the years preceding UDI] stemmed directly from the Congo crisis, and accelerated European decolonization in Central and Southern Africa. Both governments were transfixed by the perceived dangers of African nationalism and associated political extremism, stimulated by superpower (Russian and Chinese) meddling in the region. This threatened the explosive cocktail of political instability and racial strife. Both Pretoria and Salisbury thus regarded white African "civilization" to be under threat.[55]

However, South Africa's continued support for Rhodesia depended on the continued centrality of this paradigm to Pretoria's designation of its foreign policy interests, which was something that could—and indeed would—change. Second, although South Africa's forward defense commitments, such as the SAP contingent on the Zambezi, were highly valued in Salisbury, they represented just one part of Pretoria's evolving and expanding foreign policy profile and had to be balanced against other considerations. Vorster realized that support of Salisbury came at a diplomatic cost, as it impinged heavily on South Africa's efforts to avoid alienating Western countries at the UN, a major priority in the campaign to prevent further post-decolonization isolation. As early as 1968, Vorster surreptitiously approached Zambia's Kaunda with a view to orchestrating a long-term solution in Rhodesia. It was Kaunda's reluctance to work with the apartheid regime, not Pretoria's desire to uphold a white racist axis in the region, which meant that the opening ultimately came to nothing.[56]

South Africa's support for Rhodesia was therefore consistently less strident or automatic than was often perceived. In 1964–65, Pretoria had not been an enthusiastic supporter of UDI or the Smith regime, but was loath to support a regime of UN sanctions that might well be used against Pretoria in the future.[57] Likewise, when Rhodesia subsequently asked for more South African assistance, Pretoria demurred. In early 1969, after several efforts at pushing the conversation toward closer defense ties, Smith flatly told Vorster that "he felt very strongly . . . that South Africa, Portugal, and Rhodesia should meet to discuss common threats and problems in the field of defense." Pretoria's reply amounted to a pointed rebuff: "South Africa considers it unwise that there should be any closer formal links than already exist between Portugal in Africa, Rhodesia and the Republic of South Africa for the time being."[58] When the Rhodesian insurgency escalated in mid-1973 and Salisbury again sought more extensive military support, including aircraft, SADF training units, and Pretoria's help in recruiting South African volunteers, Vorster again refused to see the Republic's national interest as congruent with pan-white racial solidarity.[59] He told Salisbury: "[T]he [anti-South African] sanctions proposals now before the Security Council underline the need for us to weigh up the pros and cons of every step that would, rightly or wrongly, be regarded as provocative by those Western countries which are still trying to avoid an escalation [of regional conflict]." He duly refused to provide the military hardware or SADF personnel, and only provisionally allowed Rhodesia to recruit in South Africa. It was imperative, he said, to "avoid possible charges of complicity against the South African Government."[60] A blind-eye approach would have to suffice.

In sum, Vorster's decision not to increase aid to Rhodesia's military effort, much like his later decisions to downscale existing commitments, was based on a cold-blooded assessment of South Africa's security interests rather than any ideological affinity or sense of loyalty to a government or society of the same kind. This shift away from a pan-racial framework of understanding geopolitics toward a nation-state centric approach reflected evolving thinking in Nationalist circles on the identity of the *volk*, the future of postindependence Africa, and the nature of the separate development system. The change in how the regime conceptualized whiteness was soon to become a major problem for Ian Smith's beleaguered, landlocked regime. But even in 1973, as the Rhodesians began to lose control of the security situation, the Nationalist regime struggled to straddle the new and old ways of thinking. Rejecting another request for more military help, Vorster told the patently unconvinced Rhodesians: "The more we draw the fire on ourselves, the more we reduce our practical ability to assist you in the future. To put it bluntly, if we were to allow ourselves to be hanged, it would be equally disastrous to you."[61] The conclusion was true enough. But the underlying reasoning did not make a great deal of sense: in order to help in the future, Vorster was saying, South Africa could not help now, when the Rhodesians needed it.

Pretoria's Praetorians

If Vorster and his foreign policy lieutenants saw openings for constructive outreach in Africa's changing geopolitical landscape at the turn of the 1970s, others in Pretoria saw little cause for optimism. From the military's perspective, communist countries were supporting insurgencies and revolutionary movements across the developing world, from Indochina to Southern Africa. As Britain withdrew its forces east of Suez, the Soviet Union was increasing its naval presence in the Indian Ocean. And radical African states, even when in desperate need of Pretoria's aid, continued to be the most ardent critics of South Africa and the least receptive to the outward policy.[62] None of these developments went unnoticed outside the SADF. "[W]e see the communist threat unfurling before our eyes in this part of the world," Vorster noted in one typical speech.[63] However, these developments sparked a subtle but important transformation in how first the military and, later, the regime as a whole understood the postcolonial world.

The SADF began to see the Republic as being under assault from communist-backed insurgents as part of a Moscow-orchestrated "total onslaught" against the Western world, within which Southern Africa, with its mineral resources and strategic position, constituted a coveted prize.[64] The international revolution of Marxist doctrine, Soviet and Chinese foreign policy, radical African states, and liberation groups like the African National Congress (ANC) or South-West African People's Organization (SWAPO) were viewed as parts of a constant and singular threat aimed squarely at the polity's viability and the self-determination of the Afrikaner. Western state and nonstate actors supporting the Third World's campaign against apartheid were seen as simply playing into the communists' hands. All geopolitics, from African nationalism to calls for decolonization in the region, were to be understood through the prism of the Cold War. This idiosyncratic, homegrown philosophy would have an enormous influence on South Africa's threat perceptions and national security policies right up until the end of the apartheid era.[65]

The notion of "total onslaught" built upon, extended, and systemized pre-existing anticommunist paradigms of threat perception. Yet it differed from existing perspectives in three important ways. First, it excluded other threat perceptions. The total onslaught was "total" and therefore responsible for all of the anti-Pretoria hostility. Second, it saw South Africa not as one of many targets for communist expansion, but as one of Moscow's highest priorities. Finally, it did not distinguish between the intentions of various communist actors, especially Beijing and Moscow, nor between radical African calls for the destruction of apartheid and the willingness of more moderate states to countenance dialogue with the regime while remaining opposed to South Africa's racial order. Any and all opposition to Pretoria was seen as communist-inspired and a function of the total onslaught.

While the SADF rapidly became ideologized, neither the monolithic and aggressive communist penetration of sub-Saharan Africa on which total on-slaught was predicated nor the sense of extreme urgency with which it was artic-ulated was quite borne out by the steady stream of foreign intelligence reports compiled by van den Bergh's BOSS agents. Instead, these reports usually stressed the complexities and limits of communist relationships in Africa. While still seeing Moscow and Beijing as enemies of the state, BOSS tended to downplay the extent of actual communist penetration in Southern Africa and to (accu-rately) emphasize a demise in interest in the region by 1973–74. "China's policy in Africa constitutes an inseparable part of her universal policy ie. Her effort to consolidate her position as a leading power within the 'Third World' and the undermining by any means of Western and Soviet influences," one report com-mented. However, the report concluded, Chinese influence was in fact limited to a small number of African countries and these remained more wary of Beijing than welcoming.[66] Another BOSS assessment anticipated that Moscow could be expected to "take what opportunities occur to further their aims, which are in ge-neral to build up their influence; to demonstrate their position as a super-power; to enlist African countries as clients or at least 'non-aligned' sympathizers; and to counter Western and Chinese influence." However, in practice, the assessment found, "Soviet policy towards Africa south of the Sahara has been and can be expected to continue to be cautious and opportunist; during the last three years Soviet penetration of Africa has been slow and uneven. The Russians do not give Africa a high priority."[67] This last sentence was heresy in military circles, not least because it undermined the SADF's raison d'être. Other BOSS reports insisted that major divisions and differences existed between Beijing's and Moscow's approaches to Africa. "The USSR is for China the single biggest threat to Africa and to world peace," observed one.[68] "What is clear is that China's battle with the Soviet Union, its most ardent enemy, has become not only an important factor in its policy towards Africa in general, but also in its position on involvement in the 'liberation' of Southern Africa [in particular]," noted another. "China will remain unsympathetic to [the SACP and the ANC], which are predominantly Soviet tools."[69]

These observations and the challenges they posed to the idea of a monolithic, orchestrated threat were ignored by the military. Instead, African nationalism came to be seen as nothing but a function of communism. "The threat to [South Africa, Portugal, and Rhodesia] comes from two main sources: Communism and African Nationalism. The latter is the instrument selected by the former to achieve its deepest aims," opened one set of SADF strategic guidelines in 1972.[70] The rest of the analysis built on that premise. A major threat assessment report from 1973 concurred: "[T]he USSR and China . . . [are] the primary manipulators behind the scenes of the OAU against the white controlled states of Southern Africa."[71] By the early 1970s, total onslaught had substantially subsumed the black-white paradigm as a system of threat perception in the military.

Total onslaught found a ready adherent and zealous advocate in P. W. Botha. As far back as 1937, he had warned his very first Cape NP congress of "the steadily increasing communist danger in South Africa."[72] There was plenty of political mileage to be gained in pursuing his anticommunist inclinations too. By 1966, Botha must have been reconsidering his career trajectory. He and Vorster were born within a month of each other. They had moved in the same political circles as young men, even sharing rides between party meetings in Cape Town and Stellenbosch.[73] They had been appointed deputy ministers on the same day in 1958 and full ministers again on the same day in 1961. However, though Botha's service to the party was much more extensive, he kept getting overlooked for the top roles in favor of his rival. By the mid-1960s, Botha had served the Cape NP for twenty-two years in nine different roles; Vorster had held precisely no comparable offices.[74] Nevertheless, party elders approached Vorster, though he represented a Transvaal constituency, to succeed Dönges as Cape leader (Vorster declined).[75] Botha had paid his dues on the federal level too, and with similar results. He had been an MP for five years longer and had not left the party for the OB during the Second World War. And yet upon Verwoerd's death, it was Vorster who was elevated to the premiership while Botha was never more than a fringe candidate.

Botha's experience at the heart of the party was not wasted effort. Vorster, a lawyer by training, retained an unrealistic faith in the power of argument to win the day in the political arena through logic alone. Botha, by contrast, had instead developed a deep understanding of how bureaucracies and policy processes could serve as the keys to wielding power. After being elected leader of the Cape NP in 1966, for instance, he used his unparalleled knowledge of the hierarchies and architecture of the organization to exert rigid control over a caucus previously known for its free-thinking ways. This modus operandi died hard. After Botha became prime minister in 1978, he immediately issued a flurry of directives aimed at streamlining the way in which the Cabinet functioned, while simultaneously narrowing the number of committees considering proposed legislation. Both measures centralized power in his own hands overnight.[76]

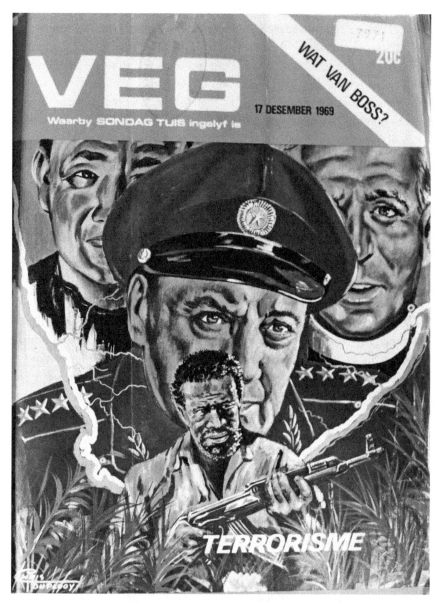

Figure 3.3 Total onslaught built upon, extended, and systemized preexisting anticommunist paradigms of threat perception. This 1969 cover from the Herstigte Nasionale Party's short-lived journal, *Veg*, identifies the puppet-masters utilizing African militants for their own ends. From left to right, an Asian communist leader, a Soviet general, and a third figure bearing a strong resemblance to Anglican bishop Trevor Huddleston: the religious arm of the anti-apartheid movement was widely perceived in pro-apartheid circles as a stooge of foreign communist powers. For all their differences on issues of Afrikaner identity and social policy, the far-right was just as militantly anti-communist as the Nationalist mainstream. Source: *Veg,* 17 December 1969. Transmond.

Figure 3.4 Born one month apart, John Vorster and P. W. Botha climbed the political ladder at much the same pace. Here, in 1961, Hendrik Verwoerd introduces his two new Cabinet ministers to the State President, C. R. Swart. From this point onward, however, Vorster's career would soar, while Botha would be forced to wait his turn. Source: Archive for Contemporary Affairs.

Botha approached his other new role, as minister of defense, with the same zeal. He cannot have failed to realize that managing intricate but necessary port-folios like Colored Affairs (1961–66)—always delicate, and all the more so for a Cape politician—might be less politically advantageous than others. He doubt-less hoped for a new portfolio from the incoming prime minister and was duly rewarded. Yet the SADF was anything but an established engine for advance-ment in Nationalist politics. The South African military had no track record as a power base for ambitious politicians. However, the lack of a secretary overseeing the Department of Defense gave the minister and the chiefs of staff a great deal of leeway, particularly if they were of one mind. Equally, increasing international isolation created a rationale for the military to assume a newfound prominence, if its leadership were willing to assume that responsibility. Botha ensured both conditions were met. However, he also looked at his new role as providing an opportunity to emulate Vorster's own route to a national political profile. In the early 1960s, Vorster had personified the anticommunist defiance that infused

Nationalist political culture through his brutal campaign against internal dissidents. Now Botha sought to do much the same, only using his ministerial remit of foreign threats as the springboard.

In a landmark speech to the House of Assembly in July 1970, Botha began articulating the vision of a global, multifaceted communist assault that would drive much of the regime's subsequent strategic thinking. "This is not a struggle about apartheid," Botha told Parliament. "It is an onslaught by Communism under the guise of religion or freedom or whatever else, directed against stability, security, and progress. . . . Today, virtually every sphere of life is part of that overall strategy and that total onslaught on the free world and the people of the West."[77] Where Vorster saw South Africa's strength and prosperity as an ideal platform from which to reach out to Africa, for Botha the communist threat mandated the assertive and proactive preservation of national security. Vigilance and rearmament were required in place of what he perceived to be complacency and naïveté. In a rousing speech at Boksburg in late 1973, for instance, he fleshed out his emerging worldview:

> There are forces trying to bring about revolutionary conditions in South Africa. A revolution in this country can perhaps—if it succeeds—hurt and wound white South Africa—but it will eventually lead to the enslavement of the colored as well as Indians under a Communist controlled dictatorship—which will bring no freedom to the black masses. We are witnessing today how through Chinese efforts a strong grip is being applied by Communist forces on Tanzania and Zambia. They are not being liberated, but gradually enslaved under the false pretenses and slogans of the liberation of Southern Africa. . . . We must stay prepared. . . . We must have the capacity to fight back purposefully and decisively.[78]

He revisited many of the same themes in another speech in March 1974:

> Let there be no doubt in our minds—behind these agencies of subversion and terrorism there exist strong forces of militarist imperialism in Moscow, Beijing and their satellites . . . [who] make the Free World believe that they want peace, that we are in a period of "détente." But in the meantime, they continue to build up their own military strength. . . . Terrorism in Southern Africa will have no success unless it is supported from outside by those forces from Moscow and Beijing who, although they have their own quarrels, are determined to overthrow the stability in Southern Africa and destroy this bastion against Communism. This

whole threat against Southern Africa is part of a global strategy against America, Europe and the Free World.[79]

Within the NP more broadly, it was not until the mid-1970s that Botha's fulminations on the total onslaught were echoed by those other than his loyal and ambitious Cape acolytes.[80] Few other MPs, BOSS analysts, or figures outside military circles were converts to the new ideology or used the phrase "total onslaught" themselves. However, the central notion of a systematic communist assault on the regime resonated deeply with a polity searching for a broader framework for comprehending the diverse forms of sustained opposition to the regime even as it went from strength to strength. In 1972, a major CIA National Intelligence Estimate observed:

> Many whites, including South Africa's leaders, believe that the current social and political ferment throughout the continent is Communist-inspired and managed; that it would be no problem without communist instigation. They point to materiel and training provided by Communist countries to insurgency groups operating against white minority governments in southern Africa. They see foreign-based black liberation groups operating against the Portuguese, Rhodesians, and South Africans as the spearhead of a Communist thrust into southern Africa.[81]

Total onslaught gained traction not only because it provided cohesion to existing anticommunist sentiment or a straightforward paradigm for understanding the hostile world outside the Republic, but also because it fit with and reinforced the NP's approach to domestic governance. Total onslaught allowed the Nationalist establishment to fully externalize the African nationalist challenge to the regime by depicting that challenge as a function of Cold War dynamics. Just as the ironclad insistence on the Afrikaners' right to self-determination provided a powerful ideological imperative for the development of apartheid in the first place, total onslaught supplied a paradigm that positioned the grievances of black South Africans as part of an externally orchestrated assault on the government and simultaneously denied them any legitimacy. If black Africa was not the source of the anti-Pretoria hostility, then total onslaught provided a potent framework for the assertion that communism was. Drawing on his experiences managing South Africa's counterinsurgency cooperation with the Portuguese, Lieutenant-General Alan Fraser soon encapsulated the foundation of South Africa's new official threat perception: "Revolutionary warfare must be recognized for what it really is—aggression from *outside*."[82] This interpretation of opposition to the regime enabled the government to focus on external foes and avoid confronting the issue of the white regime's continued viability in South Africa in the light of the black population's actual political aspirations. For South Africa's leaders of this generation, University of South Africa (UNISA) scholar and SADF-affiliated strategy consultant Deon Fourie recalls: "[T]here was no alternative in their minds but apartheid.... [They] lacked the political and historical and sociological sophistication to think of alternatives."[83] As demographic and economic realities began to corrode the basis for the Verwoerdian vision of complete separation in the mid-1970s, total onslaught provided a system of threat perception to bolster the regime's preconceptions and deny the need for real change.

Counterrevolution and Reform

Concomitant with the crystallizing perceptions of a state of total onslaught was the emergence of its envisaged antidote, total strategy. The term "total strategy" originated in French general André Beaufre's *An Introduction to Strategy*, which appeared in English in 1965.[84] Informed by France's colonial counterinsurgencies in Vietnam and Algeria as well as Paris' complicated relationship with its nominal Cold War patron in Washington—both geopolitical phenomena to which Pretoria could relate—Beaufre's thesis was that in the nuclear age, challenges to state power were less likely to be of a conventional military character. Instead, they would manifest themselves as a multifaceted "indirect" threat that could only be countered through the coordinated deployment of all the elements of a state's power. By taking the initiative on multiple fronts at once—economic, political, psychological, and military—the state could use its broader range of resources to sap the insurgents' will and capacity to continue. This model of international statecraft and conflict management riveted Fraser and others in the SADF searching for a greater strategic cohesion to South Africa's approach to national defense.[85] By the mid-1970s, many of the concepts introduced by Beaufre, such as the exterior and interior maneuver, and direct and indirect strategy, were repeated as dogma at the SADF's headquarters at Voortrekkerhoogte, even if their meaning and policy implications had changed substantially.

Following a series of lectures on strategic thinking by Deon Fourie in 1968 and a week-long SADF seminar in 1969, Fraser began to rigorously apply Beaufre's doctrines to the Southern African context.[86] He conceptualized the threat to the nation not as a diffuse insurgency requiring ad hoc military containment in different places at different times, but as a coordinated revolutionary onslaught requiring a systematic strategic response. "Revolutionary warfare ...

differs fundamentally from the wars of the past in that victory does not come from the clash of two armies on a field of battle," Fraser wrote in *Revolutionary Warfare: Basic Principles of Counter-Insurgency,* soon a core text for aspiring officers. "Military operations, as combat actions carried out against opposing forces are, in fact, of limited importance and are never the total conflict. Instead, revolutionary wars are conducted as a carefully coordinated system of actions, political, economic, administrative, psychological, police and military."[87]

Beaufre inspired some of the early total strategists to think about South Africa's strategic conundrum and the underlying geopolitical impasse between the government and the international community over apartheid in original ways. In *Revolutionary Warfare,* Fraser developed a set of strategic guidelines for South Africa's struggle against the insurgent threat. Among these was an appreciation that South Africa's geopolitical conundrum needed to be resolved politically rather than militarily. "In some revolutionary wars the military campaigns have been won by government troops or nearly so, but the wars have finally been lost politically," Fraser noted. "The inescapable conclusion is that the overall responsibility [to resolve conflicts] rests with the civilian power at every possible level." Fraser then observed that in order to survive and thrive, South Africa had to address the political aspirations of the insurgents. "A government must retain the political initiative over the insurgents by having a cause even more attractive than that inspiring them," he wrote. "Communist agitators identify themselves with, and act on, popular grievances. . . . As long as . . . the legitimate grievances that gave rise to the insurgency have not been eliminated, the danger of revolutionary wars will persist." Finally, Fraser peered into the future with perspicacity. "Time is on the side of the insurgents," he mused. "The only effective and permanent counter to insurgency is good government, which alone will gain and maintain the steadfast support of the people."[88] Such ideas had political implications that greatly exceeded the narrow limits of acceptable Nationalist discourse.

Fraser was not alone in using Beaufre's ideas to think about South Africa's position in new ways. In mid-1973, Jan Robbertze, the head of the SADF's new Directorate of Strategic Studies, wrote a speech for the Chief of the SADF, Admiral Hugo Biermann, entitled "Total Strategic Policy."[89] In one section, it articulated the challenge South Africa faced in striking terms:

The problems posed are:

- How much compromise is required to satisfy our critics? How much is possible without sacrificing our way of life?
- What evolutionary reforms can be introduced to prevent revolution & yet still to remain within our means? How can we ensure that these do not lead us to pre-empt our options or get into positions from which we cannot retreat? . . .

- How can we ensure that we are leading the move towards change rather than becoming the casualties of change, and yet not surrender to change for its own sake? . . .
- A sobering thought is that, whereas our enemies could attack time and again, and lose, we shall have only one opportunity to lose.[90]

With an emphasis on compromise and conciliation that was at odds with the Nationalist program for the future, this was probably the most comprehensive and thoughtful consideration of the need for political change being advanced at such a high level of the regime at this time. Others were also prompted to think outside the box. In a November 1973 lecture to the defense ministers and senior officers of both Rhodesia and South Africa, including P. W. Botha and Biermann, Ken Flower, the Head of Rhodesia's Central Intelligence Organization, went right to the core of the ideologies underpinning Pretoria's understanding of the world. "Communism as such does not constitute as great a threat to our respective governments, to the white man in southern Africa, as say, African nationalism."[91]

These flashes of unorthodoxy were quickly forgotten or sidelined. The SADF as an institution was unable to escape the anticommunist straightjacket and address the challenge posed by African political aspirations outside of a Cold War framework. Instead of providing the theoretical tools for innovative solutions to the regime's problems, total strategy remained irreversibly tethered to total onslaught. Magnus Malan, then a mid-level officer rising quickly through the ranks, encapsulated this association in his memoirs: "In order to launch an effective counter against a total onslaught, the target country has to initiate, at the highest level, measures that are managed in accordance with that country's total national strategy."[92] Total strategy thus became a function of a particular worldview, incapable of being interpreted in other contexts. Though they saw themselves as much more pragmatic, innovative, and forward-thinking than their political masters, the hawks had merely traded in one ideology, white supremacy, for another, total onslaught. Deon Fourie reflects: "Everyone jumped on this bandwagon of communist agitation, and nobody was ever able to stand back and say, 'Let's look at this and see it in a more general way, and understand that we are looking not just for ways of dealing with what we think is the enemy, but in dealing with any kind of conflict generally.'"[93]

The long shadow of anticommunism subsumed the potential of total strategy thinking to provide the regime with innovative solutions. Subsequent South African policy largely failed to reflect Fraser's principles. Instead of taking the political initiative and addressing black political desires in a concerted manner in the pre-Soweto era, Pretoria failed to make any real concessions until it was forced to do so, thereby abnegating control over the pace and scope of long-term change. In *Revolutionary Warfare*, Fraser had emphasized the need to establish a clear line between the adversary and the state: "It is essential to identify the enemy exactly—and then to isolate him from the population."[94] Instead of squarely addressing the challenge posed by postcolonial norms of nonracialist governance and fighting the battle of ideas, Pretoria spent immense intellectual, financial, and human resources fruitlessly combatting "communism," all while isolating itself from its own non-white population.[95]

New Paradigms of Security

The consequences of the emergence of total onslaught as a system of threat perception and the development of total strategy as an approach to national security were soon perceived on the battlefield. From 1967 until 1970, South Africa contributed to Portugal's counterinsurgency efforts, but did not share cash-strapped Lisbon's sense of urgency. In 1969, for instance, the Portuguese requested a 130 million rand loan to support their military operations in Angola and were profoundly disappointed when South Africa offered only 25 million rand and insisted on repayment with interest.[96] However, starting with a major December 1968 analysis, Fraser began to express serious concerns about the logic of South Africa continuing to fund Portugal's efforts in a piecemeal, limited manner. He argued that, despite all the money and equipment that Pretoria supplied, as long as South Africa had only a small stake in the operation, the Portuguese would continue to focus their efforts on the more heavily populated north of Angola, where they had twenty-two battalions, rather than in the southern areas that concerned South Africa, where they had just one.[97] Fraser's identification of a need for a more comprehensive South African contribution was as much informed by total onslaught's insistence on a broad-based external assault and total strategy's impulses toward a more coordinated approach to national defense as it was based on on-the-ground reports of an inefficient Portuguese counterinsurgency. This was strikingly evident in his developing characterization of the insurgencies:

> A factor which the RSA and our friendly neighbors will ignore at our peril is the increasing co-operation between the stronger liberation movements, which together with evidence of co-ordination of action between these insurgent organizations under the auspices of the Russian inspired Liberation Committee of the OAU, spells a heightening of danger for the RSA and her friends in southern Africa.[98]

This realization that the insurgent challenge that Portugal faced in the Angolan bush was part of a larger and more coordinated threat to South Africa's sovereignty had significant consequences for how the SADF perceived its relationships with Lisbon and Salisbury. "There can be no doubt in any of our minds that we have a common enemy: we, i.e. Portugal, the RSA and Rhodesia," Fraser wrote in 1970. "Unless we are to lay ourselves open to the possibility of defeat in detail [ie. individually], we must fight this enemy jointly—if not simultaneously."[99] The SADF even explicitly transposed the domino theory from Southeast Asia to Southern Africa: if the white-ruled states to the north fell to communist-inspired black insurgents, then South Africa would be next.[100]

From 1970 onward, therefore, high-ranking South African, Portuguese, and (from 1971) Rhodesian military officials began to meet regularly as part of a new ALCORA (Alliance Against the Rebellions in Africa) structure to streamline military planning, share intelligence, and coordinate counterinsurgency operations. Outside of the ALCORA structures, South Africa also began to seek more control over and involvement in the Portuguese counterinsurgencies. Under the 1970 bilateral agreement, Pretoria provided Lisbon with 100.7 million rand earmarked for the purchase of war supplies and 35 million rand for the socioeconomic development of Angola and Mozambique, sums equivalent to around half South Africa's existing annual defense budget.[101] In return, the agreement established the inclusion of South African representatives on the Portuguese counterinsurgency councils, stipulated that Lisbon would "make available to the [SADF] direct from Angola and Moçambique operational military intelligence information," and mandated that the Portuguese achieve specific South African security goals, namely ensuring "the integrity of the borders of the RSA and SWA by the elimination of insurgents in the adjoining districts of Mozambique and Angola."[102] The agreement spelled out the South African interest in the stability of the Portuguese colonies:

> It is important for the security of Southern Africa generally and for the RSA particularly that these two Portuguese provinces be peaceful, politically stable, economically sound and developing, and friendly towards the RSA. By helping them to realize these aims we will be making it less likely that they will become sanctuaries for the further spread of insurgency in Southern Africa or bases for the launching of more conventional enemy military action here.[103]

One high-ranking SADF officer noted in retrospect: "The decision to support Portugal in her war against the terrorists in Mozambique and Angola, was a political one. . . . [N]o conditions whatsoever were laid down as to the return of any of the equipment or stores by Portugal for whatever reasons. It was accepted that equipment so supplied became the property of the recipient."[104]

As the SADF began to embrace total strategy in 1972–73, the ALCORA coordination deepened. In June 1972, ahead of Botha's meeting with his Portuguese counterpart, Dr. Joaquim Moreira da Silva Cunha, Fraser wrote to Biermann advocating still more South African involvement in the Portuguese counterinsurgencies: "This is our war as much if not more than Metropolitan Portugal's."[105] Instead of South Africa's regular financial contributions, which represented "just another drop in their bucket and which will result in no guarantee of victory nor even a stemming of the tide of insurgency," Fraser advised that Pretoria should "make a massive financial contribution . . . to allow us a say in the conduct of their operations. . . . The Portuguese will never accept any say in the conduct of their operation by us as long as the SADF speaks as an armchair critic."[106] South Africa had to "assum[e] the joint responsibility with [the Portuguese] for the overall conduct of their counter insurgency campaigns in Angola and Mozambique" and deepen the ALCORA relationship.[107] Biermann and Botha agreed. In mid-1973, South Africa succeeded in persuading Portugal and Rhodesia to establish a Permanent ALCORA Planning Organization based in Pretoria and tasked with coordinating the logistics of joint military operations in Southern Africa.[108] In November, Botha again visited Portugal to conclude Operation Cadiz, under which South Africa offered a five-year undertaking to bankroll Portugal's counterinsurgencies to the tune of 150 million rand.[109] This long-term commitment represented a marked departure from the much smaller annual agreements that had existed previously and was offered in addition to the 20 million rand in basic assistance that South Africa by now provided on a yearly basis.[110] Botha was concerned that Portugal was using South Africa as an open checkbook; "It just keeps getting greater," he scrawled on one Portuguese request.[111] However, Biermann reassured him that "the RSA is under a *moral* obligation . . . to help to the maximum of its capacity."[112]

In the months preceding the Carnation Revolution, Operation Cadiz was on the verge of materializing. In March 1974 the Portuguese Ministry of Defense wrote to Botha to inform him of over 100 million rand worth of military purchases that Lisbon was in the process of making with Pretoria's money.[113] The Cadiz funds were going toward not only high-end equipment, but also everything from mechanical saws to paraffin refrigerators.[114] In the space of just a few years, Portugal's war had to a degree indeed become South Africa's war too. A further memorandum sought to schedule a May meeting between Portugal's top officers and their South African counterparts, including the head of Krygskor, the South African government's armaments production arm, to discuss how Pretoria might help Lisbon obtain the most suitable equipment.[115] The meeting never took place.

Figure 3.5 Defense Minister P. W. Botha inspects Portuguese troops on a visit to Mozambique in 1972. Even as Portugal's control of the security situation was declining steadily, at Botha's behest South Africa was sharply increasing its financial and military assistance to Lisbon behind the scenes. Source: National Party.

Thus, by April 1974, Pretoria was giving Lisbon an immense amount of military equipment and money to fight as its proxy against what it saw as communist-inspired African nationalism. In all but name the relationship had quickly come to resemble a full—if covert—military alliance. [116] If the increase in assistance given to Portugal between 1969 and 1973 was substantial in absolute terms, it was downright dramatic as a proportion of the total resources allocated to national defense. Over the same period, the share of South Africa's budget devoted to defense was slashed by almost 30 percent, in line with the outward policy's fragmentation of Africa's anti-apartheid consensus.[117] However, the renewed appreciation within the SADF of the value of the *cordon sanitaire* to South Africa's national security derived from a framework of threat perception that was distinct from that of the early 1960s. The battle lines remained the same, but the enemy was conceptualized very differently; the focus now lay on "reds", not on blacks. Some SADF files, for example, even referred to Malawi as a perimeter ally; so much for the "white" redoubt.[118]

Outside military circles, however, the anticommunist paradigm resonated easily among subscribers to the old discourses. *Die Afrikaner* observed, in language indistinguishable from that of the hawks:

> South Africa must realize that its northern border is now the Zambezi; that Rhodesia is engaged in an action which exhausts its resources more than those of the enemy; that the continuation of civilization, not only in Rhodesia, but also in the whole of Southern Africa and beyond, requires greater participation from South Africa; and that the war will not end until it is waged deep in the enemy's territory and its bases and communication links are destroyed.[119]

Veg concurred. The "handover of the country [Rhodesia] to a black authority would simply concentrate the full international pressure in all its intensity on the Republic."[120] *Verkramptes* were thus fully on board with the forward defense policy, even if their focus on racial affinities as the glue holding the white redoubt together was decidedly in eclipse among the strategists at Voortrekkerhoogte.

By 1974, the government had also broadly validated the hawks' total onslaught paradigm. That January, Biermann addressed the Cabinet on the threats to South Africa. Citing Russian and Chinese influence in the OAU member states, Africa's potential to develop a conventional military capacity through Chinese influence in Zambia and Tanzania, and the dangers of increased Russian involvement in the Indian Ocean with the reopening of the Suez Canal, he concluded: "The RSA is indeed already involved in an undeclared war."[121] The Cabinet promptly approved his proposed forward defense strategy as the core of Defense's new Five Year Plan.[122]

However, while the government accepted total onslaught and forward defense's primacy in the security sphere, Vorster and his foreign policy team did not believe that these superseded or displaced South Africa's other foreign policy concerns. Where Botha and the SADF saw indications of Moscow's and Beijing's increased interest in Africa as mandating an ever more militarist South African approach to Africa, Vorster saw only further impetus to redouble his African outreach efforts. Before the Waterberg byelection in 1971, Vorster launched into an animated exposé of the dangers of communist penetration in Africa very much reminiscent of his defense minister. Chinese interest in the Tanzam railway to the north indicated Beijing's intentions to "come down systematically to push South Africa against the sea," he warned the voters. "Have you already considered," he asked his audience, "that it is one thing to fight Black terrorists on the Zambezi, but another thing to fight Red Chinese on the Limpopo?" The hawks' policy recommendations were that such a threat mandated the deployment of South African military force on the Zambezi, but Vorster's worldview led him to a very different imperative. "I have to bring about an understanding between South Africa and other African states," he concluded. "I seek the peace and friendship of all non-communist states in Africa and I do not apologize for this."[123]

By the eve of the Carnation Revolution, this essential divergence between the hawks and the doves was particularly evident on the issue that would soon dominate Pretoria's foreign policy: South Africa's relationship with Rhodesia. Despite Botha's, Biermann's, and Fraser's zeal for a "joint defense strategy" with Portugal and Rhodesia rather than just ad hoc, small-scale cooperation, Vorster and his dovish advisers evinced a notable lack of urgency or enthusiasm for such. Flower recalls that in late 1973: "The military leaders had been holding tripartite discussions and had agreed in principle that there should be a common strategy of "Joint Defense of the Zambezi River Line," but there seemed little prospect of translating theory into practice."[124] In a March 1974 report to Smith, he expanded on this:

> Although all the South Africans seen on my visit displayed a commendable interest and some keenness in trying to counter the increasing threat to South Africa by tripartite effort between themselves, the Portuguese and ourselves, I regret to say they are still disorientated in many ways. . . . [O]ne is left with the impression that they [the South Africans] still have a long way to go before really committing themselves to the concept of "joint defense of Southern Africa."[125]

Salisbury was not so much disappointed with Pretoria's refusal to provide substantive military assistance in 1973 as it was exasperated at the mixed messages it was receiving. "What we want are the hard facts. Assuming there is not to be a Settlement with Britain, how far and in what form is the Republic of South Africa able to help us to maintain our air deterrent and COIN [counterinsurgency] aircraft? We must know where we stand," Rhodesian Defense Minister Jack Howman complained to Ian Smith.[126] The SADF was enthusiastic about the Rhodesian request.[127] Its major threat assessment analyses from the time positioned the "white controlled states of Southern Africa" as a given whole and concluded that "[t]he RSA must take this into account and ensure at all costs that the status quo in the white neighbor states and in Malawi is maintained."[128] Far from seeing this as a matter of the highest priority, Vorster overruled the hawks and decided that no major military aid to Rhodesia would be forthcoming at all.[129]

Instead, the Vorster government committed to helping Rhodesia and Portugal hold the line, but no more. If anything, cooperation with the latter was more attractive; Portugal was a member of NATO, while Rhodesia had no defenders on the world stage. Fundamentally, this was why Pretoria had fewer qualms about aiding Lisbon than Salisbury. But Vorster's decision also reflected two overarching principles. First, while the idea of a broad-based communist onslaught on the Republic had gained substantial currency within the government, Vorster and his foreign policy team did not see the dynamics of international politics in quite the one-dimensional way that Botha and the SADF did. And second, fighting insurgents was seen as a short-term holding operation, not a proactive, long-term solution to the *volk's* security and legitimacy problems.

By 1974, therefore, two distinct paradigms had developed for interpreting the world outside South Africa's borders, identifying external dangers to the state, and assessing how the regime could best resist these. Both saw the intersection between radical black nationalism and global communism as the primary threat. Both conceptualized the national interest in ways that transcended the old principles of pan-white solidarity. And both reflected Afrikanerdom's growing desire to make the *volk's* mission compatible with the reality of independent Africa, rather than merely denying or ignoring it. Indeed, both paradigms comprised the same intellectual ingredients, precisely because they came from the same small pantry of Nationalist political thought. However, the ingredients were combined in divergent ways—and that made all the difference. For Vorster and his foreign policy advisers, the phenomena of decolonization and an emergent global south setting a new normative agenda were the ascendant forces of geopolitics. They therefore advocated the use of diplomacy to drive a wedge between those radical African and communist states calling for the overthrow of the regime and those more moderate African states whose support was needed for the anti-apartheid clarion call to receive acceptance as a norm among the international community as a whole. Further, the doves believed that through careful diplomacy and judicious use of its substantial resources, South Africa could provide solutions to Africa's problems and be accepted by other African states as one of them. This was a fundamentally optimistic and proactive policy program that drew strength from the regime's vitality and prosperity. Botha and the SADF, however, perceived the Cold War as the primary paradigm of international affairs and fixated on a multidimensional total onslaught against Southern Africa in general and Pretoria in particular. They advised cooperating with Lisbon and Salisbury to keep the liberation movements on the frontline of this onslaught disjointed, ineffective, and as far away from South Africa's borders as possible; military power had to be employed to *force* independent Africa to live with South Africa. This was essentially a defensive vision, articulated in the language of fear and vigilance and fueled by the insecurities undercutting the *volkstaat's* newfound success and stability.

The result was a national security policy that contradicted and undermined South Africa's foreign policy. Even as Pretoria enthusiastically advocated its compatibility with decolonized Africa, its military co-operated with Portugal and Rhodesia in an effort to maintain white rule in Southern Africa by force of arms. Vorster must have seen the two programs as compatible, or at least not incompatible. Forward defense could be used to keep radicals at bay while South Africa targeted its charm offensive toward moderate black Africa. But both as policies and philosophies, the respective approaches to national security advocated by the hawks and the doves did not form a coherent whole. Colin Eglin, leader of the Progressive Party, pointed out the incongruity at the heart of Pretoria's foreign policy: "When I was listening to the hon. the Minister of Foreign Affairs, I found it very difficult to believe that I was listening to a member of the same party, let alone the same Cabinet, as the Minister of Defense who had spoken only about half an hour before him. . . . One cannot have it both ways."[130] In Africa's eyes, either South Africa welcomed decolonization and could deliver it to its black peoples through separate development, or it colluded with reactionary forces in Lisbon and Salisbury. It could not credibly do both.

Like a flame to fuel, the Carnation Revolution and the pending decolonization of Portugal's African colonies would lay bare the conceptual differences, policy divergences, and interbureaucratic animosities that this divide had riven in Pretoria. While for Vorster events in Angola and Mozambique only underlined the urgency of realizing his vision of peaceful coexistence with independent Africa and a concomitant escape from international isolation, for the hawks the ascendancy of nominally Marxist movements in both places had the effect of a fulfilled prophecy, confirming their deepest fears of the advent of global communism to South Africa's borders.

In Search of Détente

Negotiating a Transfer of Power in Rhodesia

On April 24, 1974, John Vorster went to bed a happy man. South Africa's white electorate had gone to the polls earlier in the day. The outcome was never in doubt. When the counting was over, the National Party had been reelected with 123 of 171 parliamentary seats. That same night, a continent away, Portugal's right-wing dictatorship finally collapsed in a bloodless coup. The Carnation Revolution came as a surprise to Pretoria.[1] Despatches from Ambassador R. J. Montgomery in Portugal had given Pretoria very little indication that the Lisbon regime was on the verge of falling.[2] DFA reports had downplayed the impact of General Antonio Spínola's critique of Portugal's colonial policies, which had appeared months earlier and sparked the coup.[3] Moreover, the prognoses emerging from Portugal's Southern African colonies were decidedly varied. Veteran Consul-General Mike Malone's cables from Angola unequivocally (and accurately) related that the situation on the ground was actually improving rapidly in favor of the Portuguese. In November 1973, Malone surmised: "It is no doubt an exaggeration to say—as did a senior Portuguese Security officer in the course of a conversation with me a few days ago—that 'the war in Angola has been won.' That it is well on the way to being won is, however, beyond dispute."[4] By February 1974, little had changed: "The tide of war in Angola, as has now been the case for some time, continues to flow strongly in favor of the Portuguese," Malone cabled home.[5] Kaas van der Waals, the SADF's point man on Angola, reflects: "The situation was excellent. For all purposes, the war had been won—but you don't win that [kind of] war militarily."[6]

The news from Mozambique was somewhat worse. In spring 1973, a lengthy DFA report cited a "deterioration" of the situation, with the Mozambique Liberation Front (Frelimo) expanding southward "relatively fast."[7] Following a visit to Mozambique at much the same time, Montgomery agreed:

> Where armed terrorism is in Angola an incidental nuisance and even then is limited to certain regions, one is soon made aware that it

constitutes the crux of the problems in Mozambique. . . . Despite the
losses which FRELIMO has suffered, they are nevertheless continuing
to send reinforcements to the areas in which they operate. . . . It cannot
be reported optimistically on the country's future.[8]

SADF reports concurred: Frelimo's penetration of the central and southern provinces, and even urban peripheries, was substantial.[9] Despite the more ominous
reports emanating from Mozambique, however, noone in Pretoria in April 1974
believed that South Africa's geopolitical foundation was about to disintegrate.
Just four months before the coup, *Time* magazine encapsulated the conventional
if misguided wisdom: "The situation is in stalemate . . . [but] the Portuguese
are still firmly in control in all three [African] territories."[10] The Portuguese had
simply been there too long and the messages were too mixed to drive a major
change in Pretoria's policy.

 Although caught off guard, South African policymakers soon realized that
the Carnation Revolution was both an important and a broadly negative development. "There was an immediate sense that . . . there was a change and it was
a change not for the better," remembers Jeremy Shearar, Chargé d'Affaires in
London.[11] By the end of April 1974, the MFA had already announced its intention to dissolve the Portuguese empire. The halcyon days of the *cordon sanitaire*
and the buffer states were over. Defense spending had already been increased
in 1973 in response to the resurgence of African radicalism on the global stage;
the Portuguese coup ensured that trend continued.[12] Furthermore, policymakers realized that a major psychological fillip had been accorded to Pretoria's enemies. "It is clear that our adversaries smell blood," reported the South African
mission to the UN.[13] South African opponents of the regime were also galvanized. Black Consciousness Movement (BCM) national organizer Nkwenkwe
Nkomo recalls that political change to the east soon inspired a new line of activism: "Mozambique has done it, why can we not be next?"[14]

 Although it was evident that Portugal would soon divest itself of its colonies, it remained unclear to Pretoria what form decolonization would take,
over what time period, and what the attitudes of the new regimes toward South
Africa would be. Decolonization had involved transfers of power both to radical
regimes eager to project their revolutionary credentials onto the African scene
and to moderate states more focused on social and economic development at
home. It had occurred both peacefully and chaotically. Which categories would
Angola and Mozambique fall into? "[N]obody seems to have the faintest idea of
what is going to happen next," Shearar observed.[15] The potential influence of the
ascendant Portuguese left-wing on the decolonization processes was a concern
from the outset.[16] However, as long as Spínola sat at the head of the junta and
remained dominant over the socialist and communist elements in the MFA, a

form of "managed" decolonization featuring important elements of social, economic, and political continuity rather than a swift, Congo-style transfer of power appeared a distinct possibility.[17] Marius Oelschig, Malone's vice-consul and the SADF representative in Luanda, recalls: "When moves were made to give the Angolans 'statehood,' with independence in the form of some loose Portuguese Federation consisting of the Metropole and the Overseas States, I believed that there could be progress."[18]

Accordingly, the tone in Pretoria was one of watchful concern rather than panic. Neil van Heerden, then a junior officer at the South African embassy in Washington, remembers: "There was a firm belief on all sides—both pro- and anti-government in South Africa—that these were things that we could contain, we could manage. It would take a lot more out of the fiscus [budget] than we had been prepared to put in before, but . . . we [we]re still masters of our own destiny."[19] Vorster accordingly instructed his Cabinet in mid-May: "The position is unclear and South Africa is taking a wait and see stance."[20] To the prime minister, this new wave of decolonization posed little threat to South Africa:

> We must view the developments in Moçambique in the light of our own policy, which is based on self-determination. Several neighboring countries are under Black governments and we ourselves are in the process of creating some more by leading our own Black homelands to independence.
>
> The emergence of a Black government in Moçambique therefore does not upset us in the least.
>
> OR
>
> is but another proof that our policy based on self-determination [in contrast to Portugal's policy of assimilation] is a sound one.[21]

From late May, therefore, Pretoria repeatedly and publicly emphasized its desire to work with whatever regimes came to power in both Angola and Mozambique. South Africa was "not concerned about the color of the governments in these territories," Vorster declared to the world, but "only about there being stable governments which would maintain law and order."[22] Noninterference, however, ran both ways:

> [W]e shall not allow mercenaries or any other groups to attack Moçambique from our soil. Neither shall we support any group with such intentions. On the contrary, we would like to help Moçambique to create conditions of stability and progress. At the same time we accept

and expect that the new government of Moçambique will from its side
also ensure that no such unfriendly acts would be directed against us,
from their soil.[23]

Even the normally unreceptive English-language press lauded the maturity of
Vorster's "impeccably correct" stance.[24]

Over the winter of 1974, that maturity was tested on a number of fronts.
The Vorster government had hoped that neighboring Mozambique's heavy
economic reliance on South Africa would encourage any new regime to seek
constructive bilateral relations.[25] The Cabora Bassa hydroelectric dam, tour-
ism, Lourenço Marques' harbor facilities, and remittances from Mozambican
mine workers were all major earners dependent on South Africa's continuing
goodwill. However, Portugal's moves to effect a straight hand-over to Frelimo,
without a local referendum or elections, raised the specter of increased communist influence, including possible military bases, on South Africa's doorstep. In
late July, Muller met with American Ambassador John Hurd to stress the dangers to both countries of communist naval facilities on the Mozambican coast.[26]
In accordance with Washington's habitual response to South Africa's efforts to
point out shared geopolitical interests, Hurd sought to dampen Muller's ardor.[27]
In private, though, the Americans were just as concerned. "Muller's approach
raises important policy considerations which we will have to face sooner or
later," the American consulate in Lourenço Marques observed. "There is no
doubt in our mind that post-independence Frelimo-run Mozambique will be
heavily influenced by [the] Soviets and Chinese."[28] Even at this early stage,
the game-changing potential of events in Mozambique for the regional situation was all too evident. BCM leaders soon announced that they had been in
"secret talks" aimed at bringing Frelimo leaders to address rallies in Durban
and Johannesburg, as well as at the University of the North in the Northern
Transvaal. When Pretoria took the unusual step of preemptively banning the
meetings, the emboldened BCM activists went ahead anyway. By the end of
1974, over sixty remained in detention. Their defiance reflected the increased
sense of possibilities among black South Africans engendered by geopolitical
changes in the region.[29]

Angola's greater distance from South Africa coupled with Portugal's greater
control over the security situation there meant policymakers were initially less
alarmed about events in Luanda than those in Lourenço Marques.[30] However,
as early as May, Malone began to foresee Angola's decline into chaos. Regardless
of who ultimately came to power in Lisbon, he wrote home, it was unclear how
they would organize a peaceful handover of power to "no less than *three* mutually
antagonistic terrorist movements, each one of which regard themselves as the
rightful future rulers of Angola. . . . [T]alk of a 'negotiated solution' in Angola

appears to me to be basically unrealistic."[31] As the country descended into periodic violence over the winter, the political situation became even murkier. In early August, Malone cabled home: "[I]t is not an exaggeration to say that Angola is at present a country which, in the opinion of many, is heading slowly but steadily in the direction of civil war."[32]

Over the ensuing months, officials became increasingly concerned about the predominance in the Portuguese government of leftists who, in their plans for decolonization, prioritized speed and social justice over stability and continuity.[33] With evident alarm, the South African military attaché in Lisbon reported in late July that Vasco Gonçalves, the new prime minister, was "an out and out communist."[34] Oelschig likewise observed that Admiral Rosa Coutinho, the newly appointed president of the Governing Junta of Angola, was "a known communist and this fact can only add fuel to the argument that Lisbon intends selling Angola down the river."[35] By spring, South Africa's consul in Lourenço Marques, I. A. "Dolf" Kotzé, lamented that the "shift to the left" in Portugal was producing the feared results: "What we always expected, namely that South African policies are turned on as unacceptable, has come to pass."[36]

Despite the uniformly pessimistic messages reaching Pretoria from its DFA, BOSS, and SADF personnel in Angola, Mozambique, and Portugal, Vorster maintained his "hands off" policy.[37] However, Pretoria's continued assurances of noninterference were reflexively greeted with skepticism from independent Africa, Lisbon, Paris, Washington, and others.[38] Foreign governments were not alone in assuming that Pretoria might try to preserve some form of neo–*cordon sanitaire* in Southern Africa. The archives reveal that Pretoria was approached by white settler or multiracial but right-wing groups seeking support, funds, and arms for UDI-style coups in both Angola (by at least five separate groups between April and September 1974) and Mozambique (at least three groups). South African support was even sought by similar organizations in Portuguese Guinea and Equatorial Guinea.[39] Closer to home, Ian Smith had already tried to persuade Vorster to support Mozambican separatists in establishing a rump state friendly to both Salisbury and Pretoria south of the Zambezi.[40]

All of these parties overlooked that Vorster was less interested in maintaining a neo-imperial status quo than in creating a new architecture for what he saw as postcolonial coexistence on the continent. Consequently, although Pretoria had ample opportunity (and means) to interfere in the Portuguese colonies in 1974, both openly and covertly, the government rejected all invitations. In September, when white settlers launched a major coup attempt in Mozambique in response to Lisbon's announcement of a handover to Frelimo, South Africa deliberately kept its distance. Instead, Vorster set up an interview with *Newsweek*, in which he struck a statesmanlike chord in reiterating South Africa's position on Portuguese decolonization:

INTERVIEWER: How do you view the disorder and economic chaos in Mozambique and the recent unrest in Angola?

VORSTER: I don't like it. Unrest in any part of the world gives cause for concern—especially in a neighboring country. Whoever takes over in Mozambique has a tough task ahead of him. It will require exceptional leadership. They have my sympathy and I wish them well.[41]

Although the MFA's ideological leanings continued to cause concern, Pretoria agreed to Lisbon's request to publicly dispel any notions of South African support for the white settlers, thereby helping Portugal control the uprising and smooth the way for Frelimo's accession to power.[42]

"The greatest potential threat which the RSA has ever had"

Vorster's wait-and-see response to the Carnation Revolution was built on three assumptions that had crystallized over the course of the outward policy: first, that a meaningful distinction existed between African states' declared opposition to apartheid and their willingness to act to overturn it; second, that this distinction was congruent with the fissure between moderate and radical regimes on the continent, not with the division between white and black ones; and finally, that through judicious diplomacy this distinction could be maintained and exploited, buying South Africa time to grant its black peoples self-determination through the homelands, convince the world of the legitimacy of these polities, and eventually overturn Africa's opposition to Pretoria. "The policy of separate development can be sold in Africa," the prime minister assured his caucus behind closed doors.[43]

Total onslaught, however, dictated that no such distinction existed. Instead, it promoted the idea that due to their Leninist doctrines, communist powers were inherently expansionist and would exploit any opportunity to use African opposition to apartheid as a vehicle to penetrate further into Southern Africa. In this view, black governments open to left-wing influence in Angola and (especially) Mozambique would provide just such opportunities and bring the communist threat closer in both time and space to South Africa's borders. In his January 1974 security briefing to the Cabinet, just prior to the Carnation Revolution, Biermann had mulled over the then-hypothetical fall of Mozambique in just such terms: "In the event of the withdrawal by Portugal from [Mozambique] and/or the takeover of [Mozambique] by anti-RSA elements, the threat will naturally, as far as the time scale is concerned, be considerably increased."[44] Consequently, even as Vorster was at pains to emphasize to skeptical foreign ambassadors that South Africa would not intervene either overtly or covertly in Mozambique, in early May the SADF developed an invasion plan of the country to support white interests, replete with strategic points for gathering troops, key targets to disable in Lourenço Marques, and lists of the forces and equipment needed for success. The rationale given for such an operation reflected the seamless way in which the total onslaught paradigm had fused with the older neo-imperial and racist geopolitical perspectives: "[T]he building up and strengthening of white solidarity in the white-controlled states" was critical "[f]or combatting the communist bear."[45]

As it became clear that Lisbon was turning away from the conservative approach to decolonization advocated by Spínola, the hawks' concerns sharpened. A major Military Intelligence threat assessment from August 1974 predicted:

> These [post-Carnation Revolution] governments will, although forced to a degree to rational action to achieve political consolidation and economic growth, become a factor which will strengthen th[e] terrorist onslaught against the RSA. . . . [B]oth SWAPO and the SA ANC will enjoy much greater freedom of movement through Angola and Mozambique while they will receive more direct and indirect moral and material support. . . . The timescale according to which events will likely develop will be defined chiefly by the USSR and China: the two powers who have the greatest incentive to create and manipulate tension in Southern Africa.[46]

The SADF became riveted by the idea that a Frelimo-ruled Mozambique would provide a conduit for antiregime insurgents—tools for communist powers, in this view—to strike against South Africa's industrial heartland in the Transvaal. "The changed situation in Mozambique offers our enemies the opportunity to take action directly against South Africa," the threat assessment declared.[47]

P. W. Botha duly wrote to Vorster on October 2, the day before he was due to attend a national security meeting with the prime minister, Biermann, and other leading generals at Groote Schuur, the prime minister's Cape Town residence.[48] Botha's views diverged sharply from official policy. "[T]he change of government in Mozambique is certainly the greatest potential threat which the RSA has ever had," the defense minister declared. "The RSA would be foolish to allow itself to be deceived through sweet talk [*mooi praatjies*] of economic ties, Cabora Bassa power, non-interference and the like."[49] Instead of seeing the decolonization of the Portuguese colonies as an opportunity to prove the regime's much-vaunted ability to coexist peacefully with black African governments, Botha saw events through the prism of a communist-backed OAU assault against white rule in Southern Africa. Reflecting the SADF's August threat assessment, he told Vorster that the new governments in Luanda and Lourenço Marques would be inherently hostile to South Africa for ideological reasons and would therefore "in all likelihood be terrorist oriented." He argued that the dominant framework for South Africa's security policy should be that of a Southern African domino theory: "[T]he potential frontlines can *not* be seen in isolation—each is an outpost on the OAU's path to its central goal—the RSA." The minister therefore counseled full support for the Smith regime as part of a strategy of forward defense—not because of an ideological or racial affinity on South Africa's part, but because the *OAU* saw Salisbury and Pretoria through the same lens. The OAU's "ideology has already for a long time declared war on the white ruled states—because they are white, and because the power is in white hands," he wrote. "[T]he longer Rhodesia can remain standing the more advantageous it will be for RSA."[50]

Botha's letter illustrates that even as early as October 1974 a sharp cleavage existed between himself and Vorster both on how South Africa related to forces of geopolitical change in the postcolonial era and on the nation's strategy for self-preservation. It also shows that in private he was becoming increasingly strident in his dissent. Botha closed the letter with a series of rhetorical questions urging Vorster toward a more proactive and assertive approach to South Africa's defense. If Mozambique embraced subversion and terrorism, "must the SADF merely defend or may the SADF strike at bases over the border in Mozambique?" If Lourenço Marques began preparing a conventional force for use against South Africa, "are we going to wait until we are attacked or shall we take the initiative?" To the north, "are we going to do everything in our capacity to keep Rhodesia standing, including the sending of SA troops in sufficient quantities to hamper [*kortwiek*] the terrorist attacks?" And—most significantly in light of subsequent events—"[i]f there is a coup in Angola and the RSA is asked for help, what will our stance be in this regard and to what degree will we assist?" He pleaded with Vorster to address these issues urgently: "Without answers to these questions, there can be no planning of any consequence, and the SADF will be groping in the dark. The time has arrived that military strategy be joined to political strategy and that the SADF be unequivocally informed where its responsibilities lie."[51]

Vorster had little time for any of this: he saw opportunities where his excitable defense minister saw threats. When he met with Botha and the generals the next evening, he dismissively told them: "In the long term there may be problems but in the short term we see no immediate problems," let alone indications that Angola and Mozambique would be used by guerillas as "launchpads" [*afspringbasisse*].[52]

Détente and Confrontation

Botha could not have known it, but instead of thinking about increasing South Africa's support for Rhodesia, Vorster was actually busy reconsidering the rationales for the existing relationship. By mid-1974, negotiations on Rhodesia's long-term political future had returned to a familiar stalemate. As ever, the central sticking point was the mechanism of franchise. Salisbury's 1969 constitution stipulated two electoral rolls: an A roll, with high educational and financial qualifications, which elected fifty MPs; and a B roll, with lower qualifications designed to encourage black participation, which elected a number of MPs proportionate to the electorate at a given time (in 1974, just twenty). Even as more Africans qualified for the vote, the constitution did not allow the B roll to elect a majority in Parliament, but instead only permitted "parity."[53] Salisbury insisted that any negotiations over a future political dispensation had to take place within this framework. To expand the franchise, the regime would consider adjustments to the number of African MPs elected by the B roll, but not a lowering of the electoral qualifications. In this way, Rhodesia's electoral system epitomized one of the major contradictions of colonialism: whites had established their own European forms of modernity as the benchmark for full political participation, while simultaneously restricting the ability of Africans to attain that standard.[54] While Muzorewa's ANC had nevertheless shown a willingness to negotiate with Smith on this basis, the guerrillas, including Joshua Nkomo's Zimbabwe African People's Union (ZAPU), operating out of Zambia, and Ndabaningi Sithole and Robert Mugabe's Zimbabwe African National Union (ZANU), with strong support from Tanzania and Frelimo, remained committed to a nonracial polity based on one-man-one-vote.

Vorster realized that the context for this impasse was changing. On a purely military level, it was evident that the Smith regime would find it harder to control the insurgencies, particularly if a full second front opened in Mozambique. Politically, the pending transfer of Angola and Mozambique to African rule had both increased the sense of inevitability of black rule in Rhodesia and radicalized the demands of the African opposition.[55] In June, the ANC's Executive rejected the constitutional settlement that Muzorewa had tentatively reached with Salisbury in May. Muzorewa told an angry Smith that events in Mozambique had "made the position more difficult."[56] The Zambians likewise explained to Brand Fourie that "in previous years the black Rhodesians should have accepted equal representation as a foundation [for a settlement] but in light of the events in Portugal and Mozambique this was no longer acceptable and black majority rule ha[d] become the only [feasible] solution."[57] Nor was Salisbury the only target of the revitalized international effort to resuscitate the stillborn process of African decolonization. For the first time, the Afro-Asian bloc in the General

Assembly had successfully managed to put the issue of South Africa's expulsion from the UN on the Security Council's agenda.

Prior to the Carnation Revolution, Vorster had resisted offering Rhodesia major military assistance for fear of an international backlash. In the new geopolitical climate, Vorster and his foreign policy team realized that to maintain the remnants of the white redoubt (as Botha in effect advised) would only expose South Africa further. The Smith regime had become more of a liability than an ally. Vorster decided to seize the initiative. If South Africa were to coexist peacefully with independent Africa in the new environment, the cautious and piecemeal approach of the outward policy would not be enough. A dramatic gesture to seize the initiative and wrong-foot South Africa's enemies was required. Instead of trying to turn back the tide of decolonization, he resolved to ride the wave of reenergized African nationalism and work with Africa to broker a settlement in Rhodesia.

Complementing this move, Vorster sought to accelerate the transition to majority rule in SWA. As late as May 1969, the Nationalist government had passed the SWA Affairs Bill, which portended even closer association between the Republic and the governed territory. That vision was now left resolutely in the past. In August 1973, Vorster had announced at the NP Congress in Windhoek his intention to usher SWA toward moderate majority rule.[58] Now, in mid-1974, a top-secret committee known as Bronze—featuring Fourie, van den Bergh, Biermann, local white representatives, and others—started convening to explore ways in which SWA could become independent through separate and ethnically defined political entities, much as in South Africa.[59] "It was not only a question of self-rule for South West Africa, it was a question of self-rule for the individual tribes," recalls Riaan Eksteen, then head of the DFA's SWA section and the secretary of Bronze. "If you [want to] use the word homelands, it was also for that."[60] Largely due to the less developed political and military capabilities of the dominant liberation movement in SWA—ZANU and ZAPU together had at least five thousand trained insurgents by 1975 as opposed to only a few hundred for SWAPO[61]—the overwhelming focus of détente would be Rhodesia.

From the outset, détente as a geopolitical program confounded observers. In one sense, the decision to facilitate political transitions toward moderate black majority rule in Rhodesia and SWA was transparently a recognition of the evident shift in the balance of power between white minority rule and African nationalism. Détente was thus largely about damage control, designed to buy the regime time to accelerate the development of the homelands and thereby acquire long-term legitimacy. In one cable, Pretoria's new Ambassador to the UN, Pik Botha, articulated this defensive vision: "Rhodesia is ultimately not our land and South-West Africa was never part of our sovereign territory. . . . Our problems will not end if we effect the resolution [*ontknoping*] of these two sticking points but we will get breathing space to resolve our internal problems."[62] Almost forty years later, he characterized South Africa's détente aims in much the same way: "We saw clearly that if we could reduce the severe African assault and attack on us, then of course—in the UN and elsewhere—the insistence on greater sanctions which would have harmed the economy would also calm down and give us perhaps time to consult here with [the homeland] leaders."[63] Salisbury likewise saw détente as a defensive maneuver. The South Africans, Smith told his Cabinet, "wanted to buy time in order to adequately equip themselves against the possibility of a major confrontation with the rest of Africa at some future date."[64]

Yet détente was also designed to use Portuguese decolonization as an opportunity to prove the regime's vaunted commitment to addressing the priorities and solving the problems of independent Africa. In exchange, Vorster sought initially implicit and ultimately explicit recognition of the white polity as an African entity, with all the connotations of permanency and noninterference that entailed, rather than a remnant of colonialism. In this sense, the core aim of détente was very much a proactive one. When he first broached détente in October 1974, Vorster told the Rhodesians that "[h]e had always felt that Africa would have to come to an accommodation with RSA . . . and he is more sure than ever that this is going to come about."[65] In the annual no-confidence debate in January 1975, Vorster argued that détente had indeed begun to fulfill this vision:

> [T]here has been a clear acceptance that we are of Africa. It follows from that that we on our part take Africa into account. But the other side of the coin is that Africa takes us into account. . . . [W]e are not a minority group here in South Africa. . . . We are a people of Africa in our own right and in our own country, and no one can deprive us of that right and that country. We do not interfere, nor do we permit anyone to interfere in our affairs.[66]

In April 1975, he told the NP caucus much the same thing. Through détente, he summarized, "we have indeed achieved a great deal: (a) We have shown our good faith regarding Africa and have gained a lot of good publicity overseas (b) It is to our benefit [*Dit kom ons ten goede*] that we offer cooperation to Africa (c) To our own people, especially young people, we can say that we have done everything in our capacity to avoid confrontation (d) We have convinced Africa that our efforts are not out of weakness."[67] Vorster thus sought to mobilize this new diplomacy in support of his promotion of a new identity for the white polity. Transvaal MP Dawie de Villiers, fast becoming an influential *verligte* voice, encapsulated the new thinking:

> The events in Angola and Mozambique and the withdrawal of the Portuguese have brought home to us afresh to what extent we are a part of Africa. . . . [It is] important for us in South Africa to realize that we too are Africans—people of Africa, and not Europeans. . . . I believe we shall have to bring about a greater orientation towards Africa across a broad front. We shall have to give more content to our African identity. . . . In order to be able to do this, we shall have to give up many of our prejudices concerning Africa and the people of Africa.[68]

Détente was therefore not just about damange control, but also counterattack.

Observers failed to grasp détente in this incarnation and tended to see it as little more than an extension of outward policy.[69] In part, this was because détente both coincided with and fueled a final burst of outward policy successes. In addition to the frequent African visits of his foreign policy team, Vorster himself clandestinely met with Houphouët-Boigny and Senghor in Côte d'Ivoire in September 1974.[70] He also visited Liberia in February 1975 and even traveled to South America in August to build relationships with right-wing authoritarian regimes in Uruguay and Paraguay.[71] African guests continued to arrive too, including Laurent Dona-Fologo, the Ivorian Minister of Information—a black man with a white wife.

Certainly, détente inherited its broad aims from the outward policy. Both diplomatic programs were designed to prove to African leaders the value of coexistence with Pretoria over confrontation; to foreground common interests in place of the previous ideological hostility; and to dilute the singular focus on apartheid in Africa–Pretoria relationships in a broader range of concerns and interactions. Both programs also reflected the Vorster Doctrine: the core belief that if Pretoria offered to solve Africa's problems, then acceptance both of the offer and eventually of the regime would be forthcoming. Both endeavored to bolster South Africa's case for a moderate and interdependent Africa as an alternative to the African radicalism that demanded the destruction of the Afrikaner regime; the appropriation of the "détente" label itself was a clear nod to South Africa's desires to embed African interstate relations in a Cold War context and to foreground common geopolitical interests over ideological differences.[72] But the two diplomatic programs were otherwise distinct. Where outward policy was invariably clandestine, unhurried in tenor, bilateral in focus, and aimed at Africa *in toto*, détente was largely public, infused with a sense of urgency, multilateral, and restricted to Southern Africa. More fundamentally, their central mechanisms to achieve the common end were different. While outward policy sought to garner international legitimacy by building bridges to African countries on a state-by-state basis, Vorster aimed through détente to facilitate peaceful transitions toward moderate black majority rule in Rhodesia and SWA and to thereby put distance between itself and the other members of the white redoubt.

Ex Africa semper aliquid novi

Kenneth Kaunda was a particularly unlikely partner in peace for John Vorster. As the chairman of both the OAU and the Non-Aligned Movement in the early 1970s, the Zambian president had been at the forefront of the international anti-apartheid campaign. He had also been a key sponsor of both the SA ANC and ZAPU. To the apartheid regime, Brand Fourie later recalled, Zambia was "one of the terrorists' most important host countries."[73] An accord reached between Muller and his Portuguese counterpart Rui Patricio in June 1971 stated specifically that "both South Africa and Portugal agreed that President Kaunda of Zambia was a danger to the peace and tranquility of Southern Africa" and urged cooperation with Rhodesia to counter his influence.[74] In addition to the ideological and political hostility, there was also a great deal of personal animosity between Kaunda and Vorster. The latter's efforts to engage Lusaka through the outward policy had descended into an exchange of acrimonious letters, which Vorster then publicized in order to embarrass Kaunda. As for Lusaka's subsequent official reproduction of the letters, it concluded: "There has never been any question of President Kaunda meeting Vorster"—in bold type and in capitals.[75]

As the Rhodesian conflict escalated, however, Kaunda foresaw increasing damage to Zambia's fragile economy.[76] As historian Miles Larmer observes, he abandoned an "idealistic vision of political liberation" in favor of "a ruthless pragmatism based on [his] interpretations of Zambia's national interests."[77] This change in foreign policy served domestic political interests for Kaunda too. The pursuit of regional stabilization reflected internal pressures to focus on domestic rejuvenation amid increasing economic stagnation, rather than continuing to bear the heavy costs of being a frontline host for liberation movements.[78] Even in a one-party state, these pressures were important factors in Lusaka's rapprochement with the apartheid regime.

From Pretoria's perspective, it was obvious that Zambia would be the linchpin for any initiative aimed at regional rehabilitation. By the start of the 1970s, Zambia's per capita GDP of US$431 was not only one of the largest in Africa—three times greater than that of Kenya and twice that of Egypt—but substantially greater than that of middle-income nations across the global south like Brazil or South Korea. As anthropologist James Ferguson observes, it is easy to forget today that at the time "Zambia was not reckoned an African 'basket case,' but a 'middle-income country,' with excellent prospects for 'full industrialization' and even ultimate admission to the ranks of the 'developed' world."[79] None of this could realistically be said about Botswana, Tanzania, the future Mozambique, or Malawi. Pretoria's road to acceptance in Africa therefore inevitably ran through Lusaka.

Already in 1973, South Africa had been looking to reestablish contact with Zambia.[80] The Carnation Revolution gave these efforts urgency. From winter 1974, BOSS representatives began meeting clandestinely with Zambian officials with a view to jointly sponsoring a revival of the settlement talks in Rhodesia. At first, the contacts were tentative. However, the departure of Spínola from the Portuguese government at the end of September pointed to increased regional tensions and radicalization as Lisbon moved to the left. On October 4, Kaunda's right-hand man, Mark Chona, visited Vorster in Pretoria. As he welcomed his guest, Vorster paraphrased Pliny the Elder, "*Ex Africa semper aliquid novi*" [From Africa, always something new].[81] Both sides agreed to explore the opening.

On October 15, Vorster secretly sat down with Chona in Cape Town. The busy prime minister prioritized the meeting; his organizer reads: "Chona [Keep the whole afternoon open]."[82] Chona told the leader of the apartheid regime that he spoke not just for Kaunda, but had come from meetings with Julius Nyerere of Tanzania, Seretse Khama of Botswana, and Samora Machel and Joaquim Chissano of Frelimo. "All to a man" had reiterated the Lusaka Manifesto's acknowledgment of Pretoria's noncolonial status "in the strongest possible terms." They saw South Africa as an "independent and sovereign state" and agreed that the Afrikaners were "not merely people in Africa, but people of Africa":

VORSTER: We are just as much part of Africa as you are.
CHONA: Exactly.

As Chona stressed in various formulations on no fewer than five occasions during the conversation, Africa would not "take the fight" to the Republic and there was "no question of interfering in the internal affairs of South Africa." Instead, the presidents wanted South Africa's cooperation on the Rhodesian issue. The situation there was "a stumbling block in trying to get Africa to understand the South African problem," which was "totally different."[83] Decades later, Chona portrayed all of this as dissembling. "What else could I say?" he suggested, smiling.[84] But it seems he was not just telling the South Africans what they wanted to hear. Kaunda told the British the same thing: "Zambia and other members of the OAU considered South Africa to be in a different position from Rhodesia. They abhorred apartheid but did not consider South Africa to be a colonial power except in Namibia."[85] There was no reason to mislead the British, the Zambians' partner in opposing and pressuring the Smith regime. The African presidents had seemingly accepted that avoiding a brutal racial war across the region required

Pretoria's cooperation regardless of the signal it sent to black South Africans. For his part, Vorster was more than receptive. He and Chona spent the afternoon constructing a detailed framework to remove the "stumbling block" to Pretoria's acceptance as a full part of Africa.

Even as the détente plan was being hatched, everything was very much on a need-to-know basis. In late August, Progressive Reform Party MPs visited Zambia. Upon their return, P. W. Botha assumed the familiar role of the National Party's hatchet man, telling the press that leader Colin Eglin was "a guest of the Government where the rapists and murderers of South African women are being trained."[86] Vorster had kept everyone in the dark about his changing thinking. His team was keenly aware that the enterprise they were undertaking could backfire dramatically. After meeting with Zambia's ambassador to the UN in early November, Pik Botha, quickly becoming an integral member of Vorster's foreign policy brain trust, cabled home that he felt somewhat like *voortrekker* leader Piet Retief walking into an African trap. But, like Vorster, he felt that, on balance, South Africa had little choice: "[T]he alternative is unavoidable large scale conflict with [black] Africa and the possibility of great power intervention which . . . would place us ultimately in a position where we have no more bargaining power and destructive and humiliating terms would be forced upon us. Currently we can still dictate our own terms."[87] Vorster duly summoned Rhodesia's Accredited Diplomatic Representative, Harold Hawkins, for a one-on-one meeting. "[I]t could be the correct psychological moment to take an initiative regarding a settlement in Rhodesia," he told Hawkins. There was no arm-twisting. Instead, Vorster sought to persuade the Rhodesians that seeking a settlement was in their own best interests. After extolling the "really exciting possibilities" offered by a new era of peaceful coexistence in Africa, Vorster suggested: "If [the Rhodesians] played [their] cards right, the present impasse could be solved from [their] current position of strength while Black Africa was at the crossroads."[88]

In the second half of October, Smith twice visited Pretoria, where Vorster tried to convince him to commit to holding a constitutional conference.[89] The African nationalist leaders in Rhodesia's prisons would have to be released in order to attend, Vorster pointed out, but any such move would be predicated upon the establishment of a much-needed ceasefire.[90] Smith was deeply skeptical of the merits of even temporarily releasing ZANU's Sithole and ZAPU's Nkomo and dubious that any unity could be achieved among the notoriously fractious nationalist factions. However, he was equally wary of being branded as the obstreperous party.[91] Moreover, mere participation in Vorster's détente promised a concrete benefit—a ceasefire that would enable him to regroup and strengthen the government's military position—while in exchange requiring only an open-ended commitment to meet with the nationalists. He therefore signed on, agreeing to release Nkomo and Sithole from detention so they could travel to Lusaka and meet with the four "Frontline" Presidents—the leaders in Zambia, Mozambique, Botswana, and Tanzania.[92]

On October 23, Vorster invited the entire diplomatic corps to the Senate in Cape Town in expectation of a major address on South Africa's place in Africa. "Southern Africa has come to the crossroads," he declared. "[The] choice lies between peace on the one hand or an escalation of strife on the other. The consequences of an escalation are easily foreseeable. The toll of major confrontation will be high. I would go so far as to say that it will be too high for Southern Africa to pay."[93] Vorster committed South Africa to avoiding these consequences. Through the outward policy program, he again volunteered South African capital, technology, and skills to address independent Africa's central desire for development:

> South Africa is prepared, to the extent to which this is asked of it, and to which it is its duty, to play its part in and contribute its share towards bringing and giving order, development and technical and monetary aid as far as this is within its means, to countries in Africa and particularly to those countries which are closer neighbors. Africa has been good to us, and we are prepared, as far as our means allow us, to return to Africa a measure of what we have so generously received over the years.[94]

In addition to the economic program, Vorster offered a new political contribution to coexistence: détente. He emphasized the importance of self-determination in SWA and indicated his government's renewed desire for a lasting settlement in Rhodesia. "I know it is being said in some quarters . . . that South Africa is holding the Rhodesian Government back" from concluding a settlement, he announced. "I want to say that that is not so. . . . I believe that now is the time for all who have influence to bring it to bear upon all parties concerned to find a durable, just and honorable solution."[95]

The second act of this diplomatic gambit unfolded the next day, as his new Ambassador to the UN, Pik Botha, addressed the Security Council. For the first time, South Africa's UN delegation included three non-whites: a black, an Indian, and a Cape Colored. In the first part of the speech, Botha stuck to the well-worn script of the Vorster era. The characteristic defiance, the warning to potential meddlers, the claims of a rich Afrikaner anticolonialist heritage, the insistence on separation not domination as the core of apartheid, and the professions of a willingness to cooperate with independent Africa were nothing new. Then, in a passage reproduced in newspapers worldwide, Botha appeared to signal the scaling back of apartheid: "I want to state here today very clearly and categorically: my Government does not condone discrimination purely on the grounds of race or color. . . . We shall do everything in our power to move away from discrimination based on race or color."[96] Both at home and abroad, this was often seen as a stark departure from existing South African policy. The United States, the UK, and France all felt they had sufficient cover to veto an African resolution to expel South Africa from the United Nations—the first triple veto in UN history. Yet Pik Botha's careful wording was entirely in keeping with the Vorster vision for South Africa's domestic political evolution. Pretoria was signaling its intention to progressively repeal certain petty apartheid regulations that discriminated among the citizenry by race alone and attracted plenty of unwanted international criticism. But it had no intention of moving away from separate political development, with the population divided not by "race or color" but by ethnicity or, in Pretoria's terminology, "nation."

Nevertheless, Vorster had fulfilled his part of the deal with Kaunda. He had provided the Zambian president with the support he needed to avoid criticisms that he was selling out the pan-African cause by working with the apartheid regime: an apparent commitment that the reform of apartheid was indeed part and parcel of working with Pretoria. Now Kaunda played his role in the carefully choreographed drama. "This is the voice of reason for which Africa and the world have waited for many years," he declared at the University of Zambia, the epicenter of the strident student movements that bitterly opposed his new policy. If South Africa was committed to opening the path for peaceful change, then "Africa, in accordance with the principles laid down in the [Lusaka] Manifesto on Southern Africa, stands ready to help create conditions for peaceful change. . . . [W]e also pledge our commitment to help find a peaceful solution in Rhodesia provided it is based on criteria which meet the demands of the people."[97]

Mozambique also responded to Vorster's new approach. In mid-November, Fourie and BOSS agent Hans Brummer visited interim Prime Minister Chissano in Lourenço Marques. Chissano confirmed that while Lourenço Marques saw apartheid as "unacceptable," it was the responsibility of South Africans rather than Mozambicans to do something about it.[98] Postindependence Mozambique, he echoed in public, would not allow anti-apartheid insurgents to operate out of its territory. "We are not going to interfere in the internal matters of South Africa. . . . [W]e think that it belongs to the South African people to solve that situation, the same way the Mozambican people solved the situation in Mozambique."[99] The elated South Africans hastened to build a constructive if unlikely bilateral relationship on this platform. As a contingency plan in case Frelimo closed Mozambican ports to South African trade, the regime had begun looking intently at expanding port facilities in Durban. Now, Pretoria chose instead to invest in *Mozambique's* railways so as to both ensure the viability of Lourenço Marques' harbor and provide for ongoing economic interdependence.[100] South Africa also began a large-scale program to help with

Mozambique's food shortages, including the delivery of massive quantities of fertilizer.[101] As with Malawi, Vorster was determined to build a relationship that could serve as an exemplar to independent Africa of the benefits to be reaped by embracing cooperation with Pretoria.

Overcoming Domestic Opposition

In encouraging the Smith regime toward a settlement in Rhodesia, the Vorster government possessed two forms of leverage. First, it controlled the amount and types of the military assistance it gave Rhodesia. In winter 1974, this consisted of a limited amount of equipment and a SAP contingent of no more than two thousand men.[102] Pretoria's contribution was more psychological than militarily decisive.[103] Second, South African railways were major arteries for carrying Rhodesia's exports to port. If escalating warfare prompted Mozambique to close its border, these would only increase in importance.

At the same time, Vorster had major domestic restrictions on his freedom of maneuver. In addition to the hawks' opposition, the white public was resistant to the notion that Pretoria might "sell out" the Rhodesians to placate militant African states. It likewise failed to see how abandoning one of South Africa's few allies constituted wise foreign policy. In June 1975, Vorster and Smith attended a rugby match between South Africa and France in Pretoria. When Vorster's presence was announced by loudspeaker, he received warm applause; when Smith was introduced, the crowd went into raptures.[104] Vorster had to avoid getting too far out in front of these popular attitudes and allowing détente to become a focal point for the "fifth column" of far-right wingers who remained in the NP even after the traumatic HNP breakaway of 1969.[105] From the NP's own backbenches, Treurnicht underlined the cultural, historical, and religious links between whites on either side of the Limpopo. He lamented the "voices in South Africa urging that South Africa should dissociate itself from Rhodesia. In saying that, they do not only mean that South Africa should only dissociate itself as regards religion and culture, but politically too, and that Rhodesia should stew in its own juice. . . . [W]e do not want to be written off as people who want to leave Rhodesia in the lurch."[106] Right-wing concern over SWA—where unlike in Rhodesia, the whites were overwhelmingly Afrikaners, often considered themselves "South Africans," and were sometimes members of the NP too—was just as acute. As early as 1971, when the earliest moves toward a shift in South Africa's control over SWA were launched, *Die Afrikaner* had editorialized:

> That this proposal is coming from an Afrikaner Government known for fighting for the interests of the White Man in Southern Africa borders

on the unbelievable. . . . The dangerous implications of this decision go much further still. If the South African Government gives the Non-Whites of SWA the right to decide the future of whites on the grounds of their great numbers in that territory, then on what principled grounds can a similar right be refused to the Non-Whites of South Africa?[107]

As Vorster subsequently went further, sponsoring an embryonic SWA government, the periodical lambasted the new policy as "meaning a handover to a black government, Uhuru, [and] the destruction of all rights and security for the White man."[108] It was not only on the far-right that this public opposition to détente reverberated. In October 1974, Ben Schoeman, Vorster's recently retired former deputy prime minister and leader of the arch-conservative Transvaal NP, launched a blistering attack on détente in a controversial speech in Kimberley:

> I think that we as White people must be under no illusions. The Black military states with their Communist allies, have only one aim and object in view and that is the surrender of the White man in South Africa. Nothing less than Black majority rule will ever satisfy them. Those misguided people who believe that appeasement will satisfy them are living in a fool's paradise. . . . I do not trust President Kaunda and have no faith in him. He is not and never will be a friend of South Africa.[109]

These arguments were deeply redolent of the critique advanced by P. W. Botha. Vorster must have wondered how many others in his ranks quietly agreed with the two NP titans.

The reality was that white South Africans were fundamentally conflicted over détente. They were excited by the prospect of an end to the status quo. "There is a curious mood in the Republic today which is almost euphoric," observed London's *Financial Times*. "For the first time for well over a decade White South Africans, pilloried and isolated in the international community, now believe they are well on the way to acceptability. They find it a heady experience."[110] *Verligtes* needed no encouragement. If Vorster's foreign policy pitted a future of multinational coexistence against the neo-imperialist racial dominance of the past, then they were only too eager to throw their weight behind the prime minister's efforts to construct an inclusive ideological architecture of separate development on the ruins of *baasskap*. "The Rhodesians cannot expect that Afrikaners . . . must throw their own principles of multi-nationality [*veelvolkigheid*] and separate nationalisms overboard just because the Rhodesians don't believe in them. We also have to look after our own affairs," wrote Otto Krause in *Die Transvaler*.[111] However, others were reluctant to stomach the steps Vorster was outlining as being necessary to achieve these ends—a move away from the old frameworks of white solidarity—and remained unconvinced that Pretoria's détente program was realistic, given the militant tone emanating from Africa. Schoeman encapsulated the feeling of most when he reflected in his memoirs that he would "welcome rapprochement between South Africa and the Black states of Africa, but impossible demands must not be made."[112]

Vorster worked hard to defuse this critique and condition public opinion to support his diplomacy. Through confidential briefings of newspaper editors and feature writers—some of which he conducted personally in the Cabinet room—he ensured that both the Afrikaans and English-speaking dailies showed striking support for his often counterintuitive initiatives.[113] The press was duly careful to avoid any implication that South Africa was interfering in Rhodesia's affairs and explicitly assured readers that a settlement there would not create momentum toward a transfer of power in South Africa because the racial orders in the two were different. On January 18, 1975, the day after just such a briefing, *Die Transvaler* stressed:

> In South Africa many people argue emotionally about Rhodesia because whites are involved. They consider South Africa's position as analogous to Rhodesia's. Our policy however guarantees separate development and the authority [*seggenskap*] of each group over its own affairs. This eliminates the whole question of majority rule in South Africa. In Rhodesia's policy, the [eventual] outcome of a majority [black] government is built in . . . For now, the details of the settlement agreement are Rhodesia's responsibility. In no way have we in our commentary supported the demands of the ANC for immediate black majority rule for Rhodesia.[114]

This delicate recalibration of the argument over détente and the subtle neutralization of the population's pan-white sympathies was just what Vorster sought. To the same end, he ensured that Muller told the Perskor newspapers not to publish a word of Schoeman's Kimberley speech. The task of speaking to the Cape-based Nasionale Pers papers was delegated to P. W. Botha, a member of its board, but he somehow neglected to convey the message.[115] Overall, opponents of détente could not match Vorster's offer of access or proximity to power and found their perspectives marginalized, even where they might have expected a sympathetic hearing. When a group of conservatives led by Vorster's brother, the well-known reverend, Koot, held a congress to express solidarity with the white Rhodesians, *Hoofstad* pointedly critiqued their cause as tantamount to offering Salisbury a "blank check" that we "can no longer honor [*instaan*]." The two states did not have identical interests, the newspaper stressed.[116] Schoeman later raged in his memoirs against a rare "unholy alliance between the liberal English press and certain of our Afrikaans newspapers ... on Rhodesia they spoke with one voice."[117] If the Afrikaans press had anything to apologize for on Rhodesia, Krause countered, it was that they had not spoken up sooner and more forcefully.[118]

Vorster also used the Broederbond to market détente within elite Afrikaner circles. On August 24, 1974, while Parliament was in session in Cape Town, Vorster secretly flew to Pretoria to address the organization. Even as BOSS began discussions with the Zambians about a settlement, the prime minister maintained that South Africa and Rhodesia were in the same geopolitical boat and that Pretoria would never leave the Rhodesians in the lurch. One right-wing Broeder said after the meeting: "I myself could not have hoped for a more conservative line."[119] Once détente was launched, however, Vorster changed tack. In November 1974 and February 1975, he appeared before the Broederbond's Executive Council [*Uitvoerende Raad*] to stress that events compelled the government to act decisively. "Urgent action is necessary," he told the Broederbond

Figure 4.1 John Vorster had no respect for press freedom. Throughout his career, he threatened independently minded editors with ever more draconian censorship, while allowing BOSS to habitually harass and intimidate journalists. It was therefore no small irony that he was able to enlist almost all the white press to support his détente initiatives in 1974–75, including even the deeply mistrusted English-language cohort. Source: *Daily News*, 1973. Independent Media.

in November; "We must consider what is necessary to maintain control over our political destiny and ensure our White identity," he echoed in February.[120] Although such views were doubtless distributed to each of the Broederbond chapters, Vorster did not have it all his own way. In May 1975, the Executive Council tabled an extended study of détente. The study was careful to display support for the merits of Vorster's overall vision: "Détente must serve as a pre-requisite for the development of a situation of real peace, where sovereign states exist alongside each other and where simultaneously there reigns cooperation on all levels of common interest, without ceding one's own identity and without the interference of one in the internal affairs of the other." However, the study continued, while the OAU had at times embraced negotiation (the Lusaka Declaration) and other times confrontation (the Mogadishu Declaration), its commitment to the removal of white rule as a whole remained unchanged. "One thing remains however consistently clear, and this is that African countries will never change course on their ultimate aims in Southern Africa," the study stated. Africa and Pretoria had "irreconcilable aims." The unmistakable implication, namely that Vorster's dream of peaceful coexistence could not be realized, was left unsaid—to say so would have been a direct rejection of NP policy and the *Hoofleier* himself—but it was clear enough. Instead, détente was presented solely as a mechanism for postponing confrontation with black Africa and buying the government time to prepare for the inevitable conflict.[121] This was very much the soft hawkish interpretation of détente: the study did not overtly repudiate negotiations over Rhodesia as a waste of time or advocate shifting the SADF's remit to the Zambezi and the Angolan border, but it did see such negotiations as incapable of yielding an African modus vivendi. For all Vorster's efforts, opposi-tion to détente evidently persisted in elite forums. When Vorster addressed the NP caucus in late February 1975, with détente appearing to falter, his words pointed to the divisions within his own party: "We have to stand together. We can never always stand together, but standing together [now] is essential. Our calling is to live in Africa."[122]

Vorster's difficulties in gaining support for his détente endeavors were a func-tion of foreign policy style, as well as content. Throughout his prime ministership, South Africa's foreign policy was formulated by a very limited coterie. This was partly due to Vorster's proclivity for informal decision-making structures. But it was also partly due to the jealous guarding of policy terrain by Fourie and van den Bergh, both of whom were eager to maintain their central roles in Vorster's exciting African outreach endeavors.[123] This arrangement had its advantages. The "small circle" approach lent South Africa's foreign policy dynamism and flexibil-ity; major decisions could be taken and implemented with remarkable speed. But it also meant a lack of civil service support, including the marginalization of experts in the DFA. C. A. "Bastie" Bastiaanse was the head of the Southern

Africa desk at the DFA at this time, yet he remembers being excluded from every aspect of the détente program.[124] In interview after interview conducted for this book, diplomats recalled that the DFA did not function as an engine of foreign policy strategies or as a support system for their implementation, but as a bureaucracy whose chief task was to report back foreign views of apartheid. "Foreign policy was badly formulated. There was very, very little [by way of] formal foreign policy statements [at the DFA]," remembers van Heerden. Foreign policy "was always something that was produced . . . in the mind of the Prime Minister."[125] J. S. F. Botha, then ambassador to the United States, put it even more bluntly: "There really was no foreign policy [at the DFA]."[126] Vorster was thus depriving himself of the institutional support he needed to bolster and market his foreign policy at home. If even South Africa's diplomats could not be relied on as strident advocates for détente, how could Vorster convince doubters at home and abroad of its merits? Van Heerden reflects: "We had unfortunately a weak tradition, if one at all, of developing a dynamic foreign policy that was practical and that was pursued in a way that we would go out and gain public support [for it]."[127] Without a strong support base at home for his innovative détente initiatives and facing opposition from two potent and separate critiques, Vorster simply could not bring himself to force the obdurate Smith to reach a settlement. Flower recalled: "[I]t was not until 1976 that Vorster, for his part, realized that he would have to twist Smith's arm to the last painful gasp if he was to make any progress in Africa."[128]

The Lusaka Agreement

On November 8, 1974, Nkomo and Sithole were secretly released from prison, boarded a South African plane, and arrived in Lusaka to establish a unified nationalist negotiating position under the auspices of the Frontline Presidents.[129] From November 1974 until the Victoria Falls conference in late August 1975, countless meetings were held between various South African, Frontline, Zimbabwean nationalist, and Rhodesian representatives. The central mechanism remained the same throughout. The nationalists would halt operations and agree to a ceasefire. In exchange, Salisbury would release all political detainees and lift the ban on both ZANU and ZAPU.[130] Both sides would then meet "without preconditions" at a conference to negotiate a new constitution. Vorster would act as guarantor for the Rhodesian commitments and Kaunda for the nationalist ones. Détente consumed Vorster's attention: it was central to his state-building agenda for the polity. In November 1974 alone, he had no fewer than seventeen scheduled meetings with Fourie and eight with van den Bergh, even though both were frequently out of the country.[131]

Figure 4.2 John Vorster and Ian Smith. Often perceived as close allies, the professional and political relationship between the two was in fact fraught. They held divergent notions of how race informed their respective constituencies' identities and futures. Source: National Archives of South Africa.

Initial progress was swift. On November 15, Kaunda wrote privately to Vorster that, as promised, the Frontline Presidents had successfully:

> urged [the nationalists] to desist from armed struggle if negotiations are possible and to accept a formula which falls short of One Man One Vote as long as its results go beyond parity. So having gone this far, I earnestly urge you to use your influence on Mr. Smith to cross at this opportune moment the Rubicon of Rhodesian political development. . . . In accordance with our November program, he should now move to release all political detainees and political prisoners, remove restrictions on the movement of leaders, lift the ban on ZAPU and ZANU and all the other measures which are outlined in the program.[132]

Yet even before Smith could fulfill his part of the deal, talks broke down. Kaunda and Vorster had agreed upon a given framework for negotiations. In

Pretoria, Chona had even said that the Presidents were willing to work within Salisbury's existing qualified franchise framework.[133] However, the parties directly involved had their own ideas for Rhodesia's future political dispensation, some of which lay outside that framework. The more militant nationalists supported Nyerere's contention that any settlement must ensure that "[o]n independence the majority of the voters of Rhodesia must be Black."[134] As for the Rhodesians, they were a long way from realizing the need to transfer power to a black majority at all, regardless of the formula. "[P]rogression to parity in Parliament," Smith told his main lieutenant, Secretary to the Cabinet Jack Gaylard, in private, "would be measured in centuries and not decades."[135] How the existing rate at which Rhodesia's blacks qualified for the franchise could be accelerated toward majority rule without a "lowering" of the franchise qualifications was a fundamental, even irreconcilable, disjuncture that appeared at the very earliest stages of the détente process. Yet when Smith raised this point in a private letter to Vorster, the South African prime minister avoided addressing the issue.[136] Vorster saw Pretoria's job as restricted to bringing the parties together and keeping them talking. He refused to get involved in the details of any settlement so as to render credible his position that South Africa was not selling out Rhodesia's whites, uphold the principle of noninterference in other states' affairs, and keep his domestic critics at bay. He despatched Fourie first to Lusaka and then to Salisbury, where the veteran diplomat reassured a deeply suspicious Smith that Kaunda did not share Nyerere's insistence on majority rule at independence.[137]

Finally, on December 11, Smith announced to a stunned world his support for the Vorster-Kaunda deal, which became known as the Lusaka Agreement. The *Malawi News* observed that at the start of the year, such events "seemed as remote a possibility as man walking on Jupiter."[138] The newly liberated Nkomo and Sithole returned home to Rhodesia for the first time in years. But the central issue remained conspicuously unresolved. Smith's statement on December 11 stipulated that Salisbury "was not prepared to deviate from our standards of civilization"—meaning no lowering of franchise standards—while the ANC's reply the next day explicitly designated the purpose of the conference as being to deliver "independence on the basis of majority rule."[139]

None of this affected the mood in South Africa. Just two months earlier, independent Africa had driven South Africa to the brink of expulsion from the UN. Now leaks from government sources fueled heated speculation in both the domestic and international press of a dramatic reversal.[140] Had Vorster really persuaded Smith to secretly release Sithole and Nkomo—designated outlaws whose names were not even allowed to be seen in print in Rhodesia—to participate in settlement discussions in Lusaka? Had he flown to Côte d'Ivoire in the dead of night in September to meet with Houphouët-Boigny and Senghor?

Was the current progress in Rhodesia the precursor to a Southern African summit, at which Vorster and South Africa's sworn enemies would establish a new regional order? Was the Republic about to apply for membership in the OAU?[141] "Give South Africa six months," Vorster told South Africa's critics during a visit to his constituency in November 1974, and "[you] will be surprised at where the country will stand."[142]

Figure 4.3 In September 1974, Vorster secretly flew to Côte d'Ivoire to meet Ivorian President Félix Houphouët-Boigny and Senegalese leader Léopold Senghor. When his hosts permitted him to break the news in May the next year, it caused a sensation in the South African press. The front-page headlines here read, "Vorster in guard of honor in Black Africa" and "Premier reveals secret trip", as the photo shows an anything but low-key welcome in Yamoussoukro. From left to right, an unknown Ivorian officer, Head of the Security Police Mike Geldenhuys, Secretary for Foreign Affairs Brand Fourie, Houphouët-Boigny, BOSS chief Hendrik van den Bergh, and Vorster. A raft of color photos and heavy coverage of the visit featured on the inside pages. Source: *Beeld*, 15 May 1975. Media24/Gallo Images.

What did Vorster mean by this? The speculation pointed to a fundamental reconfiguration of the relationship between the apartheid regime and black Africa. And as 1975 began, Vorster reaped the rewards. "For Mr. Vorster, the present progress has been a personal triumph," observed *Die Vaderland*. "He is a statesman of international stature and if peace comes to southern Africa, his name will be immortalized as the man who took the initiative."[143] Vorster "deserve[d] the honor and admiration he was receiving on all sides for his détente success in Africa," concurred *Die Transvaler*.[144] The prime minister's star would never shine brighter. Nationalist MPs competed to laud their leader; so much for the intra-party recriminations and schisms of recent years. Engelbrecht told the House:

> South Africa stands with a strong and dynamic leader, a leader unassail-
> ably strong within his own party, a leader who enjoys the support of all
> population groups in this country. . . . The Prime Minister, following
> the course he does, with the peace ventures he has already undertaken,
> will lead Southern Africa out of the valley of suspicion, mistrust and
> bloodshed to the highlands of peace and mutual confidence. . . . These
> events over the past weeks and months in Africa have proved unequivo-
> cally that the solution of the problem of Southern Africa and peace and
> progress in South Africa can only be built on the policy of separate de-
> velopment because only that policy guarantees the sovereignty which
> is sacred to every people.[145]

Even staunch *verkrampte* Tom Langley, MP for Waterkloof, declared: "I be-lieve that 1974 will go down in the history of South Africa as the Year of John Vorster. . . . In all these matters, he enjoys the support, love and esteem of my colleagues, of myself and, I believe, of millions of people in South Africa."[146]

Vorster promptly utilized his newfound stature to advance his domestic vision. Behind closed doors, he told his caucus that now was the moment to act on petty apartheid:"There are still points of friction and we must eliminate them. At the moment, we have the attention of the world and we must keep it at all costs."[147] Stoffel van der Merwe, then at the DFA, reflects: "It seemed to me, our road back to the world runs through Africa. But our road back to Africa runs through the Free State."[148] First, Vorster announced the repeal of the notorious Masters and Servants Act, which criminalized infractions of contracts of employment and thus served to ruthlessly control black labor. Days later, the regime accepted the credentials of Malawi's new ambassador, the first black top envoy to be sta-tioned in apartheid South Africa (Malawi's previous ambassador had been white). Vorster then held a major roundtable with the homeland leaders—and ensured that the Department of Information published the minutes. For the first time, white voters could see the prime minister not only telling the homeland leaders that they could "discuss matters with him as equals," but also engaging in pointed disagreements with his interlocutors about separate development. At one point, Cedric Phatudi, Chief Minister of Lebowa, criticized the regime's resettlement policy in no uncertain terms, noting that people "suffered when they were 'dumped,' penniless, in areas without any facilities."[149] The *verkrampte* response from Langley and his ilk to these events was noticeably muted, such was the prime minister's popularity.

Here was Vorster's dream politics in action: foreign policy success facilitating tightly controlled, top-down domestic reform. Predictably, *verligtes* applauded. "In modern South Africa, [petty apartheid] must be simply eliminated, and it is being eliminated, with remarkable acceptance by the public," observed Schalk Pienaar.[150] But it was the mainstream Afrikaans press that provided Vorster with the crucial political cover by echoing the argument that the new moves were merely the natural consequence of the separate development philosophy. The removal of petty apartheid was "already foreseen by the late Dr. Verwoerd. It is nothing new," stated *Die Transvaler*.[151] This was an extraordinary recasting of history.

Vorster's new politics received substantial support from outside the National Party too. Upon returning from his own trip to independent Africa, Eglin told the House that Pretoria concentrated all too often on the militant statements of the OAU and ignored the heterogeneity of African states. These, he insisted, provided openings for government-to-government dialogue, which in turn could provide a platform for a shift of identity at home, with white voters seeing themselves less as neo-imperialists and more as "white Africans." Naturally, he continued, this would require concrete moves away from racial discrimination, but "not a radical restructuring" of society.[152] The next month, Dick Enthoven, on the left wing of the United Party, told the House:

> If the Government were showing the imagination which this task of launching our Africa policy demands, they would be more sensitive to the stumbling blocks which make it difficult for Black leaders to talk to us. . . . They would realize that this Government is seen by these people as the last bastion of racialism and colonialism in Africa and they would take steps to prove that they are not racists and colonialists. They would do this by phasing out the negative aspects of their policy which we call petty apartheid.[153]

Across the floor, Vorster must have been almost unable to contain himself. Neither Eglin nor Enthoven could have known that he was already deep in discussions with Lusaka behind the scenes. Indeed, there were plenty of actors outside the Nationalist caucus who, like Vorster, were keen to use African outreach as a springboard to greater viability. No friend of the government, the *Cape Times* was simply effusive: "Vorster must be awarded the highest marks by political friend and foe."[154] Such perspectives coexisted with more sanguine analyses. Stanley Uys, the *Sunday Times*'s veteran political editor, applauded Vorster's efforts to use statecraft to help him remove racial discrimination. "[E]verybody should be enjoined to support the new diplomacy to the hilt," he wrote. However, Uys predicted with foresight, the prime minister would need to both consistently enact domestic reforms and secure a settlement in Rhodesia to sustain the momentum.[155]

Such was Vorster's apparent progress on the Rhodesia issue that in early January, British Foreign Minister James Callaghan hastily endeavored to involve the UK in the negotiations. At a meeting in Port Elizabeth, Vorster was in rare form. There was "agreement among all the parties" for a qualified franchise, he told his guest. The specific terms would presumably be based on educational qualifications, but the franchise would "of course be irrespective of color" and "everybody realized that the majority of voters would be black at the time when the new franchise comes into effect." (In fact, these statements reflected what Vorster wanted, not what the Rhodesians had accepted.) The important thing, however, was that the parties themselves determined the details. For his part, Vorster promised that "[h]e would go on seeking peace until it was clear he had failed." If an agreement was reached, he equally "would be responsible for seeing it carried out." Callaghan's visit was the first to South Africa by a top-level British leader since Macmillan gave his famous "winds of change" speech in 1960. His host simply could not resist getting his own back on behalf of a spurned *volk*. "[I]f the British were to come in at this moment," Vorster told Callaghan, choosing his words carefully, "they would wreck the whole thing."[156]

Obstacles

No sooner had the Lusaka Agreement been announced than two new obstacles arose. The first concerned the security commitments. Did the "gentleman's agreement" ceasefire require the guerrillas to leave Rhodesia, disarm, report to the authorities, or simply halt active operations? And how many political detainees did Smith have to release and when? The second obstacle comprised the details of the planned constitutional conference. Salisbury insisted both that a conference on Rhodesia's future had to take place in-country and that no chairperson was necessary. The former meant that certain nationalists would have to obtain legal immunity just to attend proceedings and would be subject to arrest at the government's whim (as had happened in May 1974, when Salisbury had deemed Edson Sithole to be hindering its efforts to reach agreement with Muzorewa).

The latter helped to fortify the advantage of incumbency held by his government: without a neutral chairperson, Smith would assume the role much as he
had in previous negotiations. The ANC sought instead to hold a conference outside Rhodesia with a neutral, possibly British chairperson. Such arrangements
would internationalize the process and ensure the parties had equal standing.
Both developments would act in the ANC's favor.[157]

In late January, after six weeks of fruitless and acrimonious discussions
with the nationalists and the Zambians, the Rhodesian delegation of Smith,
Gaylard, and Flower met with Fourie and van den Bergh.[158] An insistent Smith
beseeched the South Africans to press Rhodesia's case on the arrangements for
a conference and "enlist the support of Zambia" to make the nationalists observe the ceasefire. He also pleaded with Pretoria to curb the "consistently hostile" anti-Salisbury sentiment in the South African newspapers, as it conveyed
the impression that Pretoria did not stand shoulder to shoulder with Salisbury.
"[T]he Afrikaans press and particularly 'Die Transvaler' were regarded as
mouthpieces of the South African Government," Smith complained, and their
line only strengthened the African nationalists' belief that he "must hand over
Rhodesia to them."[159] On both points, the South Africans promised their cooperation. However, in response to Pretoria's low-key, almost apologetic repre-
sentations that Rhodesia fulfill its side of the Lusaka Agreement too, Salisbury
was resistant. Van den Bergh suggested that Rhodesia contribute to the ceasefire by keeping their forces in their positions rather than ordering them to patrol; Fourie requested that Salisbury not publicize future killings of guerrillas to
avoid increasing tensions. Smith unequivocally refused both requests.[160] When
both parties met with the Zambians a week later, an emboldened Smith abruptly
rejected van den Bergh's desperate efforts to broker a new ceasefire.[161] Détente
again seemed on the brink of collapse.

As in December 1974, only the prospect of a complete breakdown compelled
Vorster to apply the requisite pressure on Smith. In early February 1975, Muller
and Fourie flew to Lusaka to meet with Kaunda, Khama, Nyerere, and the nationalist leaders.[162] The Zambians said that they shared the South Africans' concern that continuing incidents involving out-of-control ZANU insurgents were
endangering détente.[163] The Frontline Presidents confirmed that they were willing to make ZANU observe the ceasefire, but they needed something in return, if
only to assuage the radical faction at the OAU. The next day, Muller and Minister
for Police Jimmy Kruger told a stunned Hawkins that although a ceasefire was
not in place, the South Africans had decided to confine the SAP contingent on
Rhodesia's northern border to their camps.[164]

The Rhodesians were shocked. Even years later, lingering feelings of betrayal
and anger infuse Smith's account in his memoirs.[165] Just days earlier, van den
Bergh had reiterated to Smith Pretoria's long-held and oft-stated policy that

the SAP units would not be withdrawn from Rhodesia until the violence had ended.[166] But the South Africans were fed up with the lack of tangible progress. In an effort to convince the Rhodesians to negotiate with the nationalists in good faith, they had changed their policy.[167] The manner in which they did so, however, only exacerbated Rhodesian angst. Throughout the phased withdrawal of the SAP through mid-1975, South African ministers avoided mentioning Vorster's decision to distance Pretoria from Salisbury.[168] Instead, they insisted that the SAP contingent had always been in place to protect against anti–*South African* insurgents—a plainly unconvincing distinction that denied the common cause of the white redoubt security paradigm.[169] Some in Salisbury got the message. After Muller and Kruger had informed him of the initial SAP confinement, Hawkins relayed the new reality to Stanley O'Donnell, the Rhodesian minister for external affairs:

> The [South African] visit to Lusaka is also an indication of the view I have been expressing to you that whether a solution is found in Rhodesia or not, South Africa intends to press on with détente and to increase contact with African states who matter, whilst gaining the maximum kudos she can from her efforts to help reach a solution in Rhodesia. . . . [The South Africans] see it as essential that the fighting should end and that we should get on with the talking.[170]

Gaylard likewise observed: "[T]he South Africans are hell bent on détente. . . . In particular they will disregard the evidence of their own military authorities— if these are ever permitted to penetrate to Prime Minister level."[171] Flower had already observed as early as November that "Vorster [had] made it clear to Mr. Ian Smith that he must get a settlement, and get it quickly, or South Africa would cut off our water. . . . South Africa, in search of 'détente' with Black Africa, is prepared to ditch us."[172]

Smith, however, was intractable. When he arrived in Cape Town a week later he was surprised to find himself meeting with no fewer than four South African ministers. To convey a united front, Vorster had brought Muller, Kruger, and a recalcitrant P. W. Botha along to Groote Schuur.[173] The South Africans were open about how they understood the relationship between a Rhodesian settlement, détente, and Pretoria's international rehabilitation. They reiterated Vorster's grand plan: "[S]ubject to a settlement in Rhodesia and the resolution of the South West African problem, the African states would then concur with South Africa and its policies." Vorster added that given South Africa's recent diplomatic coups, invitations to meetings with Kaunda and even the OAU itself were just a matter of time. Muller also reminded Smith of the consequences if a settlement was not forthcoming: "[U]nless Rhodesia gave way there would be a war and the Europeans would eventually be pushed out of the country." Smith was incredulous. "[T]he ultimate objective of the OAU," he reminded his hosts, "was to liquidate South Africa in the same way as Mozambique and Angola, the next objectives being Rhodesia and South West Africa and then South Africa." This being so, Rhodesia and South Africa simply had to stick together. He stressed that he had repeatedly "disabused the South Africans of any idea that Rhodesia would capitulate to the African. . . . It was quite incomprehensible why the South Africans should not appreciate that in reaching a settlement with the ANC, the Prime Minister [Smith] was not prepared to do anything which would weaken the position of the Europeans in Rhodesia." Smith reminded the South Africans that "they only had to look at the present [Rhodesian] Constitution to see that majority rule was very far from [the] Government's intentions."

Rather than forcing compliance, Vorster still sought to persuade Smith of the virtues of the détente vision and to convince him that a settlement was in Rhodesia's best interests. However, Smith unequivocally rejected every aspect of that vision and saw no need to transfer power to the African majority at all. Vorster's belief that Pretoria could manipulate geopolitical forces to its advantage and use anticommunism to cut across the postcolonial consensus on nonracialist governance was incompatible with the Rhodesian prime minister's more conventional understanding of the role of race in postcolonial African geopolitics. Both the briefing Smith gave to his Cabinet after this meeting and his memoirs suggest that he was not simply being obstinate, or desperately pushing back against Pretoria's wishes, or playing dumb. He simply found it impossible within his own worldview to understand how what the South Africans were articulating could possibly be in white Rhodesia's best interests, not to mention those of Pretoria. In this meeting, he even broached the possibility of the SADF replacing the SAP or Rhodesia embracing an apartheid program itself. The South Africans responded that both propositions would destroy détente overnight. The latter, a horrified Muller averred, would be an "absolute disaster": such a move would immediately destroy the distinction between the Rhodesian and South African political systems that the South Africans were trying to draw.[174]

Ironically, Pretoria was experiencing more success in convincing independent Africa that they had common interests than it was with Smith. In this context, Vorster needed to make it unequivocally clear that South Africa would, in effect, sell out the Rhodesians to save its own skin. This he signally failed to do. When Smith again pressed the South Africans on the continuing calls in the Afrikaans press for early majority rule, Vorster avoided pointing out that such views did in fact represent those of his government. Similarly, when Smith asked the South African prime minister about the existence of a "Vorster Plan" circulating in Lusaka, outlining a framework for a potential settlement, Vorster falsely denied the existence of any such plan.[175] Indeed, far from applying pressure on

Smith to conclude a settlement, Vorster managed to instead convey his refusal to force Rhodesia's hand. Smith concluded his report to his Cabinet of the Groote Schuur meeting thus:

> [O]ne thing had come across loud and clear and that was that [the South Africans] wanted a settlement and wanted Rhodesia to give way. . . . At the same time they had made it plain that they would not interfere in this matter and would like to be able to say that Rhodesia had taken the decision itself and it had been nothing to do with South Africa. It was also apparent that the South Africans had no intention of dropping Rhodesia or selling her out. They were merely looking for an easy way out of the situation.[176]

Vorster had thus managed to both seriously alienate Smith and convince him of South Africa's unwillingness to twist his arm. The Rhodesian prime minister therefore neither trusted nor feared him.

Emboldened by Pretoria's position, Smith arrested Sithole in a transparent effort to scuttle the settlement negotiations. The South Africans were furious.[177] Within days Kruger announced the withdrawal from Rhodesia of a first SAP contingent.[178] On March 17, Smith travelled to Cape Town to explain Salisbury's actions to Vorster and his advisers. The discussions started at 10:30 a.m., lasted into the evening, and continued the next morning.[179] Smith argued that as the Frontline Presidents had refused "to abide by the undertakings to bring an end to terrorism which were given when the concept of détente was proposed . . . Rhodesia reserved the right to retaliate in even greater strength than before and, if necessary, would expect the support of the South African army."[180] The South Africans countered that the detention of Sithole merely gave the nationalists "an excuse for not coming to the negotiating table."[181] Moreover, Kaunda had just told Pretoria that if the Frontline Presidents could not show at the forthcoming OAU summit in Dar es Salaam that détente was producing tangible progress, then they "would be unable to prevail over the extreme militant OAU members and the call for an escalation and intensification of the terrorist campaign could prove irresistible."[182] Pretoria therefore asked Smith to temporarily release Sithole to attend the summit. This "would strengthen the hands of the Presidents in convincing the rest of Africa that progress could be made," Muller told Smith. "If this were not to be done, their position would be hopeless."

Smith was deeply reluctant. He told Muller and Fourie in early April that this was "the most difficult thing" that the South Africans had ever asked him to do. Releasing Sithole would amount to an astonishing reversal and erode his government's credibility. It was, in short, "impossible." He again stressed that when he had originally committed to détente "he had had an assurance from the

South African Prime Minister that if [détente] failed, the South Africans would be back stronger than ever with troops instead of police." He asked "whether when the chips were down, the South Africans and Rhodesians would stand together." However, the request from Lusaka for something to show for their efforts at the OAU meeting was the impetus Pretoria needed to stand firm. Regarding the issue of SADF support, Fourie clarified that whatever undertakings had been given by Vorster—presumably at the outset of détente in late October—were not issued "in that form of words." Muller added that South Africa had promised only that they would "reevaluate the situation" if détente were to collapse.[183] The bottom line, they told Smith, was that "in the absence of a settlement South Africa would not continue to support Rhodesia indefinitely."[184] Much to Pretoria's annoyance, Smith continued over the ensuing months to refer to a perceived South African commitment to send in its military to defend Rhodesia.[185] There is no credible evidence that Vorster ever gave such an assurance (though others in his government may have done). Instead, Smith's move appears to have been a reprisal of a strategy he had often used with the British: redefining others' statements as categorical assurances and then tenaciously using these to allege betrayal on the other party's part regardless of context or subsequent events.[186]

In the short term, South Africa's straight talk worked. Smith temporarily released Sithole and left little doubt about who was behind the decision. "In all honesty, I must tell you that it is not a decision to which the Rhodesian Government readily agreed. However, we were assured that to do so would significantly assist the cause of détente," he said publicly.[187] White Rhodesia was appalled. It suddenly became clear that to Pretoria détente was no mere "exercise," as the Rhodesians insisted on calling it, but an altar on which white control in Rhodesia might well be sacrificed.[188] Smith had finally gotten the message that Pretoria was serious too. "The South Africans were sensitive to the point of obsession over the need for a successful conclusion to the détente exercise," he told his Cabinet. "The South Africans appeared to hold this view with complete conviction, irrespective of the realities or otherwise on which it was based, and it would be foolish to disregard this fact."[189] Smith even began to look in earnest at a framework for a transfer to majority rule—however flawed and contrived—probably for the very first time. He explained to his Cabinet ministers that if Rhodesia were to supply South Africa with its census figures, showing that under the 1971 Home-Smith settlement proposals majority rule "could" be obtained within fifteen years, then this would enable Pretoria to effectively broker a favorable settlement with Lusaka on its behalf.[190] The idea soon lapsed, but it was South Africa's firmer approach—spurred again by a desire to show Africa the benefits of cooperation with the apartheid regime—that had borne fruit.

Discourses of Appeasement

After P. W. Botha's meeting with Vorster in early October 1974, he and the military fell into line with the détente campaign, but they did not change their views on its merits. In party forums, such as the annual congress of the Cape NP in September 1975, Botha declared that he "identified wholeheartedly with the détente policy."[191] In his written statement to the Truth and Reconciliation Commission in the mid-1990s, Botha would declare much the same: "I identified wholeheartedly with Vorster's détente policy."[192] However, Botha and the SADF continued to believe that the OAU's drive "to force the existing order in white-ruled Southern Africa to change" would be relentless due to the inherently expansionist doctrines of its communist backers.[193] Accordingly, they did not subscribe to the Vorster vision that through détente Pretoria could earn Africa's respect, neutralize its determination to overthrow white rule in the South Africa, and provide a foundation for long-term coexistence. In handwritten notes-from February 1975, Botha revealed his true feelings: "Nie détente nie—maar appeasement—paaiery! [Not détente—but appeasement—appeasement!]"[194] From within the military, Jan Robbertze expressed much the same view, though in less colorful terms. "[D]étente or dialogue is the key to peaceful co-existence and therefore to the stability and economic well-being of the inhabitants of this region," observed the head of the SADF's Directorate of Strategic Studies. "[S]uch an idea, however, is anathema to the communist powers and to many revolutionary black leaders in Africa."[195]

In this assessment, the hawks were guided by their belief that the communist powers had used the period of superpower détente to build up their military capabilities and improve their global strategic positions. "Russia and China understand something entirely different by the concept 'détente' from what the Western World and the free world usually understands by it," Botha told Parliament. "What the free world understands by it is co-existence and non-interference in each other's internal affairs, while what Russia and China understand by it amounts to world domination by means of world revolution and even violence."[196] Botha's personal papers reveal an utter derision of the West's willingness to believe that Beijing and Moscow—"in spite of their façade of competition," as he scrawled in notes for one speech—could ever be persuaded to abandon ideologically driven imperialism.[197] Even in public, Botha's support for détente was heavily undercut by his focus on the communist threat:

> The broader pattern today is typified by the belligerence of certain African States, a strengthening of the Soviets' presence in the Indian Ocean, an expansion of the footholds the Soviets and Red China have

Figure 4.4 P. W. Botha did not believe that Vorster's détente schemes were realizable. He and his generals told the Rhodesians as much, undermining Vorster's initiatives. Here, Botha meets with Smith and his defense minister, Jack Howman. Source: Cape National Party.

gained on this continent, and the collapse of democracy's resistance in much of Asia. This is the background against which South Africa must view its own defense measures. . . . This means that we must not only *have* an adequate capability but also have it *conspicuously* so that it may serve both to deter and to repel those who may have designs on our country, its stability and its sovereignty. We would be foolish not to give our full support to these [détente] efforts, but equally foolish to allow ourselves to be lulled into a false sense of security, to neglect out military capability, and to be ultimately reduced to speaking from a position of weakness.[198]

Furthermore, to the hawks, events in the region appeared to bear out this thinking. A highly critical SADF study observed that in Rhodesia the ceasefire had only tied Salisbury's hands while the insurgents flouted the agreements and regrouped. Détente had therefore done nothing to deter the OAU from pursuing its goal of removing white rule from the continent.[199] As for Mozambique, the hawks saw events there as a barometer for South Africa's post–Carnation Revolution relations with independent Africa, much as Vorster did. However, they took a very different reading. As early as November 1974, the SADF's annual threat assessment observed that despite Frelimo's need for political and economic consolidation, even under the interim government, "it is clear that Communist powers are being given opportunities to exert and extend their influence."[200] By June 1975, on the eve of Mozambican independence, these concerns had sharpened. Citing "unmistakable" current cooperation between the USSR, the SA ANC, and Frelimo, Military Intelligence predicted that regardless of Chissano's assurances of noninterference, "[i]t can be expected that there will be extremist elements in the future Frelimo government who will want to lend all possible support to SA ANC activities against the RSA."[201] Independence in Mozambique, another Military Intelligence report concluded, would merely assist South Africa's enemies in waging the political and military struggle against South Africa with "greater zeal and purpose."[202] Ultimately, the hawks felt that South Africa's approach to decolonization in Mozambique provided an exemplar of what *not* to do when dealing with independent Africa. By preaching cooperation and pursuing coexistence, South Africa had created a détente dynamic under which it relinquished the initiative and abjugated its ability to use its relative strength vis-à-vis Lourenço Marques to create a favorable strategic position. Meanwhile, its enemies merely "seized upon the détente approach as a means of exploiting [the post–Carnation Revolution] gains."[203] Botha was determined to prevent the government repeating the same mistakes in Angola.

Breakthrough

For all Vorster's efforts to secure Sithole's release, the results of the OAU summit in April 1975 were mixed. The ensuing Dar es Salaam Declaration stated that "any talk of détente with the apartheid regime is such nonsense that it should be treated with the contempt it deserves."[204] The OAU "reject[ed] dialogue and détente," Vorster duly briefed his Cabinet.[205] However, he remained undeterred. Behind the scenes, Kaunda reiterated to Fourie that the Frontline Presidents' ongoing commitment to noninterference in South Africa's affairs was distinct from their public criticism of apartheid.[206] Moreover, Sithole's release coupled with the assassination of Herbert Chitepo, ZANU's chairman and an implacable opponent of détente, enabled Kaunda to push the ANC back toward negotiations.[207] As winter approached and the two sides edged fitfully toward meaningful discussions, Vorster used South Africa's leverage to bring Smith to the table. Even as Hawkins "practically begged" him not to, the South African prime minister continued to withdraw SAP contingents.[208] Vorster's foreign policy lieutenants, meanwhile, kept conveying the message that "South Africa could not become involved in an open ended commitment to Rhodesia."[209] There was also a "carrot" to accompany the "stick." In late May, as Smith met with the ANC, Vorster approved loans to keep the Salisbury regime afloat.[210]

The problem with this strategy was that while carrot and stick could—and eventually did—encourage Salisbury to go through the motions of negotiations with the nationalists, it had a negligible impact upon Smith's perceptions of a comprehensive settlement as inevitable, let alone desirable. Even as Salisbury–ANC talks resumed in June, Smith continued to tell his regional patron openly that he still had no intention of handing power to a black majority "with the inevitable instability which would result."[211] South Africa's strategy was therefore in many respects counterproductive. Every time Vorster agreed to handle more Rhodesian trade, or offer the regime a much-needed loan, or represent Salisbury's interests to the Frontline Presidents, the Rhodesians were reassured that when push came to shove Pretoria would ultimately stand by it—just as South Africa's military was consistently telling them.[212] In the wake of the approved loans, for instance, Smith reported to his Cabinet that Vorster was "now seeing things more clearly" and was back in alignment with Salisbury's interests.[213] He added that negotiations were not going to happen; it was time to embark upon an internal strategy based on the evisceration of ZANU through the redetention of all "ex-detainees, other than the nationalist leaders" and "encouraging Mr. Nkomo to form a moderate breakaway group with whom the Government would be able to negotiate."[214] Vorster's carefully tailored new strategy was merely producing mixed messages.

By July, the June "talks about talks" had broken off. In a strident missive to Vorster, Smith wrote: "[T]he time has come to show that the white man in Southern Africa is going to take a stand. The blacks respect strength and they despise weakness and this is a lesson of Africa which we ignore at our peril."[215] The only way "to salvage the present détente exercise" was to reactivate the SAP and reinforce them through military personnel "in keeping with the assurance you gave me when we first embarked on this exercise, that if there was a resurgence of terrorism your forces would re-enter the battle."[216] Smith's letter backfired badly. Given the power relationship between Rhodesia and South Africa, Smith's confrontational tone and his open rebuke of Vorster's decision to scale back the SAP commitment were both unwise.[217] The timing was also poor. Smith could not have known it, but just the day before Chona had hosted Fourie in Lusaka and told him that Kaunda thought the time had come "to make a move."[218] Finally, the continued references to the alleged assurance of South African military support—dispelled by Muller and Fourie at the April 3 meeting—must have been little short of galling to the South Africans.[219] In a pointed but correct reply, Vorster unequivocally dispelled any expectation of South African military support.[220] He stressed that to deploy the SADF would "lead to a furor" in the UK, France, and the United States—the three countries united in vetoing the introduction of further UN Security Council sanctions against South Africa. Such action would be perceived "as the final throwing down of the gauntlet and a decision to seek solutions through military means," the South African prime minister wrote. "Escalation would be inevitable."[221] To underscore the point, he promptly removed the last SAP contingent.[222] Vorster finished his letter on a sour note. "In spite of a deep difference in domestic policy, South Africa has supported Rhodesia in the face of a hostile world for ten years and in the process spared no effort to do so," he pointed out. He was therefore "surprised to note an undertone that it is in fact Rhodesia which has carried the burden of South Africa" and not vice versa.[223]

Vorster had had enough. He invited Smith, Chona, and their entourages to a secret meeting in Pretoria on August 8 and 9. Vorster made it clear he would "wash his hands of Rhodesia" if Smith refused to attend a conference, Brand Fourie recalled.[224] "[T]here was no alternative but to co-operate in this new initiative, otherwise Rhodesia would be branded in the eyes of the world," Smith subsequently told his Cabinet.[225] The resulting Pretoria Agreement stipulated that the Rhodesians and the nationalists would meet no later than August 25 to "express publicly their genuine desire to negotiate an acceptable settlement."[226]

One of the long-running disputes between the parties had been ingeniously resolved: the parties would meet in South African Railways carriages on the bridge between Zambia and Rhodesia at Victoria Falls. But other issues remained outstanding. The agreement stipulated that following the Victoria Falls conference, the details of a settlement would be worked out in committees "within Rhodesia." This clause quickly became a sticking point: more than a few of the nationalists would have to risk being redetained just to attend. In any case, they had not themselves signed onto the agreement and did not feel bound by its stipulations. As for Smith, he still had little intention of actually reaching a settlement. He continued to see the détente negotiations as just a means of ensuring the upper hand against the insurgents. Noting that as a result of the détente ceasefire over the past few months Zambia had finally "severely restricted and almost entirely prevented" guerrillas from operating out of its territory, Smith told his Cabinet: "If terrorism could be effectively halted [in Mozambique too] there would be less urgency to reach a settlement and it could be expedient to go on talking to the ANC for years."[227]

Nevertheless, the South Africans were elated with the elusive breakthrough.[228] The agreement was their initiative—"almost entirely drafted by Vorster," Gaylard noted.[229] Both the South African carriages and the joint opening of the conference by Kaunda and Vorster would render Pretoria's contribution to the landmark summit and its indispensability to solving Africa's problems unmistakable in the eyes of the world. As the parties met before the world's media, against the backdrop of the falls, on the symbolic boundary

between black-ruled and white-ruled Africa, Vorster had reason to feel optimistic that his détente efforts had—at the very least—finally reaped a publicity
bonanza for the apartheid regime. Expectations in the public sphere were high
too. The "historic meeting . . . could be inscribed in history as the beginning
of peaceful coexistence in Southern Africa," editorialized *Hoofstad*.[230] As a not
insignificant ancillary benefit, by offering Lusaka progress on the Rhodesian
issue, Pretoria had disincentivized Zambian support for South African liberation movements. Shortly afterward, the Zambian authorities asked the SA
ANC for the real names and addresses of its operatives present in the country;
Oliver Tambo and his colleagues had little reason to think these would not be
forwarded to the Nationalist regime. As historian Hugh Macmillan points out,
for the liberation fighters stationed in Zambia, the Victoria Falls conference
was the "lowest ebb" of their struggle, as they had to endure watching their
hosts breaking bread with the enemy.[231] SA ANC journals like *Sechaba* simply
ignored the conference entirely, preferring to focus on the more comforting
stories of national independence emanating from Mozambique. "Frelimo =
ANC" ran one typical headline.[232]

...Suid-Afrika se stories klink baie mooi, maar wie sal ooit vir óns werk gee as vrede skielik uitbreek?"

Figure 4.5 Liberation fighters around the campfire respond to Vorster's détente
campaign: "South Africa's stories sound great, but who is ever going to employ us if peace
suddenly breaks out?" Source: Die Burger, 25 October 1974. Media24/Gallo Images.

Figure 4.6 The five-carriage South African Railways train that hosted the Victoria Falls conference, perched above the Zambezi River. Source: National Party.

Once the conference began, however, South Africa's optimism quickly faded. Muzorewa opened by producing for Smith's signature a "Declaration of Intention to Negotiate a Settlement." It read: "We publicly state that the only genuine settlement to the majority of the people of our country is the one that shall be based on the transfer of power from the minority to the majority people of the country—that is to say majority rule now."[233] The ANC also insisted that the committee work in Rhodesia could only be effectively carried out if the delegates of their choice could attend. Salisbury would have to guarantee blanket immunity for even the most militant among them. Both objections provided all the grounds that Smith needed to claim that the ANC had refused to abide by the Pretoria Agreement.[234] Fourie paced the length of the train long into the night and again the next morning to try to produce some accord, but Smith wasted little time in returning to parliament the next day to announce that the talks had broken down.[235] He soon resolved to seek an internal settlement with non-ANC African leaders and redetained Sithole to underline his intentions.[236] Relations with South Africa soon descended into public recriminations.[237] For all intents and purposes, détente was over before it ever really got going.

The Missed Opportunity

Détente may have appeared suddenly on the international diplomatic scene in late 1974, but it drew heavily upon intellectual undercurrents that had developed over the previous years. The most important of these was the principle that stability and security were not to be secured through collaboration with white regimes, but rather through cooperation with anticommunist ones regardless of their color. South Africa had even promised not to interfere in left-wing Mozambique so long as the new government did nothing to undermine South African sovereignty. This policy was fully in keeping with Vorster's guiding notion that African nations could live and trade together so long as they did not interfere in each other's internal affairs. When seen in this broader context, Pretoria's surprising response to the Portuguese coup actually reflected a measure of continuity in South African foreign policy, even in substantially changed geopolitical circumstances.

If a rapprochement with black Africa was one part of Vorster's statecraft program, then a distancing of Pretoria from other forms of white rule on the continent was the other. In stark contrast to the pan-white patron-client model generally perceived by both contemporary observers and later historians, Pretoria's relationship with Salisbury throughout détente varied from cool to icy, while it responded enthusiastically to the entreaties of independent Africa. Vorster saw securing a political transition in Rhodesia as central to his plan to bring Pretoria into alignment with the postcolonial world on its own terms. In this way, he believed that South Africa could not only reduce regional tensions in the short term, but also prove Pretoria's ability to solve Africa's problems, outflank the radicals at the OAU, and provide a clear basis for acceptance in Africa.

His foreign policy had ideological as well as geopolitical ends too: displaying the regime's willingness to engage fruitfully with nation-states of all colors both reflected and was intended to bolster the entire underlying philosophy of separate development. This was the logic behind his belief that he could compartmentalize the fate of white minority rule in SWA and Rhodesia while avoiding creating momentum toward an abdication of white power in South Africa itself.

However, domestic opposition acted as an albatross around Vorster's neck, restricting his confidence in taking the drastic action needed to push Smith toward a settlement. Kaunda understood this all too well. "Vorster needs pressure to move forward or else he will do too little too late," he told the Americans.[238] On closer examination, this opposition to détente consisted of two separate critiques: the *verkrampte* paradigm, which drew upon the racism underpinning South African society and dictated sticking by the Rhodesians based primarily on racial affinity; and the hawkish view, which mandated that as the OAU was an instrument of expansionist communist powers, coexistence was an illusory and foolish aim. Vorster's efforts to use the press and the Broederbond to overcome this opposition were insufficient to quell his own doubts about the political dangers of being Salisbury's executioner. This alone can explain his insistence on restricting South Africa's role to merely bringing the parties together and his concomitant reluctance to push the obdurate Smith toward capitulation. Vorster only applied pressure in response to African entreaties or when it looked like a total breakdown in the negotiations was imminent. Even after ten months of South African cajoling, by the time Smith arrived at Victoria Falls he had agreed to do no more than attend a constitutional conference, as he had already agreed to do back in December 1974. Ironically, détente collapsed not because Vorster had failed to diminish the all-consuming role of race in African leaders' perceptions of relations with South Africa, but because he refused to do more to vigorously address the obsession with racial hierarchy within his own society.

Ultimately, the 1974–75 window constituted a major missed opportunity for South Africa. The Southern African theater of the Cold War was essentially still a "phoney war": the relentless international pressure on the white regimes and the reinvigorated African military campaign against them were not yet realities. It took events in Angola, where the security situation had been quietly deteriorating, to bring that scenario to life.

PART II

FROM CHALLENGE TO CRISIS

5

Mission Creep

South Africa's Intervention in the Angolan Civil War

From the Carnation Revolution until the autumn of 1975, Pretoria's foreign policy was heavily focused on Rhodesia and, to a lesser extent, Mozambique. Throughout this period, however, the political situation in Angola was deteriorating rapidly. By early 1975, Lisbon was keen to relinquish its responsibility for Angola as swiftly as possible.[1] "My friend, if I could get out of this damn place tomorrow, you wouldn't see my **** for dust," High Commissioner General Antonio Silver Cardoso told South African Consul-General Mike Malone.[2] Angola looked destined for a civil war fought between three rival nationalist movements.[3] The Marxist People's Movement for the Liberation of Angola (MPLA), led by Agostinho Neto, had its stronghold in Luanda and the regions east of the capital. It had a history of support from various Eastern bloc countries, especially Yugoslavia. A decline in such aid had accompanied the waning fortunes of the movement's guerrilla campaign in 1972–73, but by early 1975 the USSR had decided to align itself squarely behind the MPLA's claim to power.[4] The National Front for the Liberation of Angola (FNLA), led by the corrupt and unimpressive Holden Roberto, was based in northern Angola.[5] Roberto preferred to run his operations from Zaïre, only very rarely entering Angola itself. "[I]t is widely believed that [the FNLA] is a sort of 'private army' of Mobutu's and that its leader, Holden Roberto, is a mere puppet in the hands of the Zaïrois Government," observed Marius Oelschig, the SADF's military attaché in Luanda. "It is general knowledge that this movement receives almost unlimited support from Government sources."[6] The movement barely attempted to hide its ties. One FNLA report, "L'Intervention des Soviétiques en Angola," published in 1975 in an effort to draw international attention to Moscow's support for the MPLA, carries the official stamp of its ministerial origin: "Départment de Relations Extérieures, Kinshasa."[7] Finally, the National Union for the Total Independence of Angola (UNITA) was based in the south. Though less politically organized than the others and lacking any real military capacity or cohesion, UNITA was led by the charismatic and capable Jonas Savimbi. He was "an excellent person, a brilliant strategist, very disciplinarian with his forces [sic]. . . . We got on very well with Savimbi," SADF Director of Operations Constand Viljoen recalls.[8] "He was a very nice person. He spoke a number of languages. He was a poet," agrees Koos van der Merwe, then working in Military Intelligence at Grootfontein.[9] As for the whites who dominated the Angolan economy, as the prospect of all-out conflict loomed larger and with South Africa refusing to support a UDI, the trickle of emigrants that had started in winter 1974 became a steady flow.[10]

The Alvor Agreement, concluded in January 1975, confirmed that political power would be shared between the three movements until Lisbon formally granted independence on November 11. "The Treaty of Versailles, it is generally agreed, was a standing invitation for the outbreak of future strife," observed Malone. "In that respect it had nothing on the attached document!"[11] The interim coalition government quickly became untenable. "The picture in Angola at the moment is very gloomy. . . . There is no beer, there is no bread, there is no hope," Oelschig cabled home.[12] The factions' paramilitary wings spent their time skirmishing with each other, while their diplomatic representatives went abroad seeking recognition of their claim to the throne, as well as arms and funds. These distant events would ultimately lure South Africa into precisely the sort of military conflict with racial overtones that it had sought to avoid through the careful statecraft of détente, establishing the widespread expectation of regional confrontation where Pretoria had tried so hard to nurture the fragile prospects of stability and coexistence.

Threat Perception

South Africa's response to the ominous situation developing in Angola was tentative and cautious. As early as winter 1974, Malone and his BOSS colleague, Dirk Visser, suggested that Pretoria send a high-level BOSS emissary to Luanda to talk with "some of the more prominent emergent politicians."[13] From the outset, however, the South Africans' instinct was to deal only with the FNLA and UNITA. Malone—who had no sympathy for any of Angola's "Kaffirs with machineguns,"[14] regardless of their politics—suggested that there was "at least a possibility, I think, that we might be able to reach some sort of accommodation with either one or both of these Western oriented Movements."[15] By contrast, negotiation with the MPLA—whom Malone described for Pretoria as "in effect nothing more than Communist puppets"—was quickly excluded.[16] Oelschig recalls that he suggested making contact with Neto's movement, but this prospect "was not well received in Pretoria. I was summoned to report personally and was given a 'dressing down' by the Director of Counter-Intelligence. I had the feeling that some sort of 'black mark' had been entered onto my personal record, as back-handed references to my 'communist sympathies' arose from time to time thereafter."[17] From then on, Oelschig remembers, "[c]ontact with the MPLA, with its strong Soviet connections, was out of the question."[18]

Among white South Africans, the excitement and cautious optimism engendered by détente continued to be counterbalanced by the deep-seated, visceral fear of the dangers of communist expansion. The public remained acutely sensitive to any perceived expansion of communist influence in any part of Africa or the Indian Ocean. Even a minor Soviet military build-up in distant Somalia in June sent South Africa's editors into hyperbolic overdrive. "USA, China and Russia Involved: Arms Race in Africa," declared *Hoofstad*.[19] Furthermore, viewed from Pretoria, the situation in Angola differed in two important respects from that in Mozambique. First, unlike in Lourenço Marques, South Africa had little economic leverage to ensure neighborly behavior from whichever group ended up governing in Luanda. And second, where Frelimo had been the only plausible successor to the Portuguese in Mozambique, none of the movements was similarly preeminent in Angola. In the three-way power struggle developing to the north, Pretoria perceived a unique opportunity to shape the nature of the postcolonial government to its advantage. The temptation was too great to resist.

South Africa therefore launched a series of exploratory overtures to the FNLA and UNITA to see if an Angola ruled by either would provide the regional stability and security that the government desired. During the second half of 1974, the SADF held a series of meetings with UNITA representatives and subsequently supplied the movement with small quantities of arms and ammunition, as well as food and clothing.[20] From February 1975, Military Intelligence and BOSS officials began meeting separately with the upper echelons of both the FNLA and UNITA in Africa and in Europe.[21] Both movements were desperate for help and said what South Africa wanted to hear: that an Angola under their control would form part of an anticommunist bloc in Southern Africa built on the three pillars of economic interdependence, good neighborliness (*goeie buurskap*), and noninterference in each other's affairs.[22] Crucially, both committed to denying SWAPO facilities in southern Angola. "Dr. Savimbi promised that SWAPO attacks on South-West Africa would not be permitted," wrote F. J. du Toit Spies in the official SADF history of the intervention in Angola.[23] The FNLA, not to be outdone, said it would allow the SADF to conduct "hot pursuit" operations against SWAPO operatives up to 50 miles inside Angola.[24] Over the coming months Pretoria supplied limited military aid and funding to both organizations, but there was no sense of urgency to its actions.

What transformed the situation in Angola from concerning to threatening was the increasing realization over spring 1975 that the MPLA was becoming

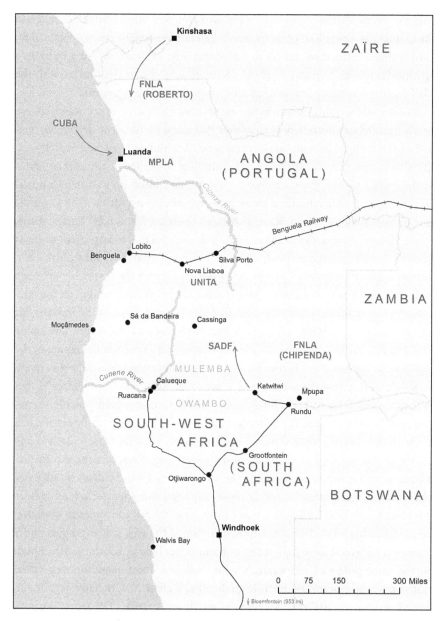

Figure 5.1 Angolan civil war, 1975–76. Source: Map by Emily Kobylecky.

the most dominant of the three factions. A BOSS assessment from January 1975 described a situation of three viable contenders with—if anything—the FNLA predominant.[25] One Malone despatch from March—after a split in the MPLA led to Daniel Chipenda taking around two thousand relatively well-trained troops over to the FNLA—was even more confident: "There is more and more evidence that the communist-dominated MPLA Party is losing ground in Angola . . . and, although they are still definitely a force to be reckoned with, it is my personal opinion that a FNLA/UNITA combination is likely eventually to come out on top."[26] But from late May onward, the MPLA began to slowly gain the upper hand in Luanda, besting the well-armed but ill-disciplined FNLA forces around the capital.[27] Simultaneously, having been despatched to the south to open a second FNLA front, Chipenda approached Pretoria to request assistance.[28] Finally, a series of skirmishes involving the SADF broke out on the SWA border, reminding Pretoria that events in Angola could not be ignored.[29] Together, these developments attracted Vorster's attention. Having told caucus that he expected "a violent civil war in Angola,"[30] he asked for a comprehensive review of the situation from both the SADF and BOSS.[31]

The SADF submission presented by Botha to Vorster on June 26 was categorical. "Although the MPLA enjoys the least political support among the Angolan people," due to "sustained support" from the USSR and the communist bloc, they "can for all intents and purposes be considered the presumptive ultimate rulers of Angola," it observed. "Only drastic and currently unforeseeable developments could alter such an outcome."[32] With time of the essence, four courses of action were outlined. South Africa could:

- Provide help to FNLA (Chipenda). This would cost relatively little. However, there was no guarantee that he alone could bring stability to southern Angola or prevent an MPLA takeover.
- Help UNITA and both wings of the FNLA to form a united anticommunist front. To support them would yield benefits in the long term, including the formation of a friendly neighboring state and a secure Angola-SWA border.
- Furnish socioeconomic assistance to southern Angola. This would further South Africa's détente aims and help future Angola-South Africa relations. However, the exclusion of SWAPO from the border area by a future government in Luanda would not be guaranteed. Moreover, in light of the fierce fighting between the three movements, it was doubtful whether any of them would be interested in such assistance.
- Contribute no assistance to any party. This would give South Africa no control over events.[33]

All indications are that BOSS agreed with the SADF that the second option—supporting an FNLA-UNITA coalition so as to prevent an MPLA takeover of Angola—was the preferred course of action.[34] Vorster concurred.

The significance of the SADF submission lay not only in its role in Vorster's decision, but also in its establishment of the total onslaught paradigm through which Pretoria would perceive subsequent developments in Angola. The

submission characterized the MPLA as an organization that was unrepresenta-
tive of the Angolan people—it noted that one opinion poll registered just 10 percent support among the populace—and therefore should be seen as a vehicle for
foreign communist interests. These characterizations reflected a distorted filter-
ing of information through the central paradigms of Nationalist political philosophy: both the FNLA and UNITA were seen as representing ethnic groups
seeking to govern their traditional areas in line with the notion of *volkseie*, while
the MPLA was pigeon-holed as a foreign puppet. This provided a potent and
durable rationalization for South Africa's hawks to argue that Pretoria's involvement in Angola was a response to preexisting foreign intervention. Explaining
South Africa's presence in Angola to Parliament in January 1976, for instance,
P. W. Botha would point out: "Everyone who knows Angola knows that UNITA
and FNLA represent the majority of the Angolan people. If peaceful methods
had been employed and the people had been allowed to elect their governments
without interference, South Africa would not have been interested in this matter
other than in the role of the observer."[35] Brand Fourie, no supporter of intervention in Angola, likewise recalled: "It was our standpoint that the inhabitants of
Angola, without interference or prescription from outside, had the right to decide
for themselves who would rule them. . . . Our military involvement in Angola
was the consequence and not the cause of Russian/Cuban intervention."[36]

This last statement was not accurate. In July 1975, foreign communist support
for the MPLA was decidedly limited.[37] While Havana, Pretoria, and, for that
matter, Washington all became concerned at the course of events at roughly the
same time—in mid-July—Cuban assistance was slow to actually materialize. It
was not until late July that modest financial support of only $100,000 appeared,
not until early September that Cuban advisers arrived to train and bolster the
MPLA's forces, and not until the third week of October that the training centers
were fully operational.[38] Acute Soviet interest in support of the Cuban effort was
similarly delayed. It was only on November 2—two weeks *after* South Africa had
sent regular forces into Angola—that the SADF received positive confirmation
that the Cubans were indeed supporting the MPLA on the ground.[39] None of
this stopped a relentless stream of post facto justification by the South Africans.
In another account authorized by the SADF, historian Sophia du Preez notes
that by the end of July, the MPLA "had 1000 fully armed troops deployed in
Southern Angola and further trained soldiers were en route from Cuba. With
extensive Russian-Cuban support, Neto was ready to clear [*weg vee*] all opposition before him."[40] None of this future support was apparent to the South
Africans when they made their decisions.

The clarity with which the SADF submission's conclusions depicted a pending Cold War confrontation between a foreign-backed MPLA lacking any real
domestic support and the anticommunist forces of Roberto, Savimbi, and

Chipenda masked the complexities of the on-the-ground situation. Far from two ideological blocs naturally developing in Angola, the FNLA and UNITA were at least as much rivals with each other as they were with the MPLA. "The relationship between the FNLA and UNITA in Southern Angola cannot be considered a good one," the SADF submission itself observed in the fine detail, away from the strident conclusions. "The differences between Chipenda and Savimbi are too great to allow an alliance between the two to work."[41] Military clashes between the two "allies" were commonplace even into late 1975.[42] Furthermore, while it was readily assumed that as a Marxist liberation movement the MPLA would actively support SWAPO, the future compliance of the FNLA and UNITA themselves with South Africa's security aims was far from guaranteed. "Although Savimbi earlier made it clear that he would not interfere in the internal affairs of RSA or support South Africa's enemies, SWAPO terrorists were [previously] trained in Southern Angola by UNITA instructors and housed in UNITA bases," the submission stated. "UNITA leaders are currently doing nothing to restrict the UNITA-SWAPO understanding in Southern Angola."[43] Even in mid-November 1975, Military Intelligence admitted that "certain UNITA elements can be expected to warn SWAPO of any SADF action against them."[44] Finally, very little effort was expended in assessing whether the FNLA or UNITA could actually help South Africa achieve its goals. Those working on the ground were unimpressed with both groups from the start. The SADF submission described Roberto as "exceptionally proud, jealous, dictatorial, and racist" and portrayed UNITA as way out of its depth.[45] Both became key allies. Policymakers simply superimposed the Cold War template onto the developing conflict and overlooked these shortcomings.

Equally crucial was the ideologically driven manner in which the submission linked the situation in Angola to the security of SWA and South Africa. The border clashes that occurred from April 1975 onward provided the vital tangible security threat that anchored the hawks' characterization of the Angolan situation as an opportunity for the expansion of the total onslaught through an MPLA-SWAPO alliance.[46] However, the clashes were not in fact with SWAPO or MPLA cadres, but with UNITA.[47] More fundamentally, the designation of the integrity of the northern SWA border as a vital national security interest was not a preexisting one but in fact flowed from the characterization of the situation in Angola as a conduit for total onslaught. The national security overview that P. W. Botha forwarded to Vorster ahead of the hawks' critical meeting with the prime minister in early October 1974 exhibited an exceptionally alarmist vision of regional threats in the post–Carnation Revolution era.[48] Yet in contrast to the crucial South African security interests it identified in Rhodesia, Mozambique, and even Botswana, the overview had specifically downplayed the importance of a revitalized insurgency in northern SWA to South Africa's national defense: "[T]he loss, or rather the rule of the northern [SWA] homelands by insurgents, would not constitute an immediate threat for the RSA, although it would be a morale setback for the RSA which our enemies domestic and foreign would [use to] spur our enemies to intensified efforts."[49]

Plainly, in mid-1975, Angola was at the chaotic intersection of a variety of historical forces, with many possible outcomes. In this context, the SADF's superimposition of a Cold War dichotomy onto a considerably more complex postcolonial power struggle was not just misguided, but also counterproductive and self-fulfilling. In winter 1975, influenced by the doctrines of total onslaught, the South Africans perceived a massive alignment of communist support behind the MPLA that only developed later. It was the SADF's involvement in the conflict that both galvanized and provided the diplomatic justification for a dramatic escalation in Soviet and Cuban support for the MPLA (and, in the immediate aftermath, for other liberation movements too). It was thus South Africa's intervention in Angola that brought about the materialization of the feared total onslaught and the drawing of the battle lines of the Cold War in Southern Africa, at least as much as the other way around.

A Supporting Role

Pursuant to Vorster's decision to explore tangible support for the FNLA and UNITA, Viljoen and BOSS Head of Foreign Operations Gert Rothman flew to Kinshasa on July 4, 1975, to consult Savimbi and Roberto as to their military needs. Viljoen recalls:

> Savimbi was there. Holden Roberto was there. They explained to me the situation. They said "Can you give us any support that will be able to assist us in holding our positions?" . . . I then made certain recommendations to the government that the two forces of Roberto and Savimbi cannot hold themselves against the MPLA forces supported by Cuba and the USSR, and they had to find another way of fighting, which was the more conventional way.[50]

Viljoen compiled a list of weapons, supplies, and equipment—mortars, machine guns, rockets, grenades, plastic explosives, vehicles, and radios—to send to UNITA and the FNLA. The total cost amounted to some 20 million rand.[51] Even as he did so, the situation in Angola deteriorated sharply. By mid-July, alarmist South African despatches informed Pretoria that the MPLA was all but in control of the capital.[52] The FNLA and UNITA left the interim government. Fears of a full-blown Cold War conflict in Southern Africa began to materialize. *Die*

Burger editorialized: "What is looming then is a spreading proxy war between China and Russia in Africa, in which the two Red powers, not ready for the long predicted day of reckoning on the Asiatic borders, are skirmishing, as Hitler and Stalin did in Spain, for imperialist advantages."[53]

In this tense atmosphere, van den Bergh, Fourie, and SADF Chief of Staff Ray Armstrong flew out on July 14 to see Vorster on his winter holiday at Klippen.[54] The prime minister approved Viljoen's list and empowered van den Bergh to source the necessary arms from abroad to hide Pretoria's role.[55] (The first shipment of weapons and supplies arrived from Europe in Matadi, Zaïre, in August. UNITA's chronic disorganization meant that the FNLA received everything.[56]) To the extent that South Africa had a clear goal in Angola, it was a limited one. Viljoen recalls: "The MPLA were getting the best [of it] in Angola because of support from the USSR and support from the Cubans. So the whole idea of participating in action against them was to maintain UNITA and the FNLA in a position where they would be able to participate in a government of national unity which was due to start on 11 November 1975."[57] The decision to spend 20 million rand on weapons and supplies must be seen against the backdrop of South Africa's earlier policy of outsourcing the effecting of its national security goals to avoid drawing attention to itself and its apartheid policies. For almost a decade, South Africa had supplied substantial equipment and training, as well as some personnel, to help both Lisbon and Salisbury fight their counterinsurgencies against liberation movements (which in the former instance ironically included both UNITA and the FNLA, as well as the MPLA). Likewise, in 1964 in the Congo, it had bankrolled Portuguese efforts to bolster Moïse Tshombe's anticommunist forces with arms and mercenaries and thereby crush the Simba Rebellion. In this way, Pretoria's decision in 1975 to support the FNLA and UNITA at arm's length fitted with preexisting templates for influencing regional events.

That template was, of course, far from unique to South Africa. As Pretoria funneled arms to FNLA and UNITA, so too did Paris and Washington. French archives reveal few specific details. But Spies's work gives a sense of the contribution: "At the beginning of November . . . approximately nine C-141 cargo planes delivered arms to Kinshasa from France. This created the impression in South Africa that France would continue to pursue the desired goal. Much of this ammunition and weapons was transported by South African aircraft to various bases in Angola."[58] American assistance started earlier. On July 18, the Ford Administration committed to its own covert program in support of the loose FNLA-UNITA coalition. It did so in spite of heavy opposition from the State Department, which counseled staying out of a deteriorating situation in a country in which America had very limited interests.[59] Ford told Kissinger, "I have decided on Angola. I think we should go . . . if we do nothing, we will lose southern Africa. I think we have an understandable position. I think we can defend it to the public. I won't let someone in Foggy Bottom deter me."[60] By the first week of August—the same time that the first South African arms arrived—the CIA program, codenamed IAFEATURE, had "grown into a full-fledged covert action program," in the words of one operative.[61]

At this point, BOSS and the SADF, the two bodies responsible for South Africa's national security, began to disagree on the merits of involvement in Angola. "Already at this stage the SADF was of the opinion that weapons deliveries would not suffice, but had to be complemented by logistical support . . . and the provision of a few officers . . . to help plan an appropriate political and military offensive," wrote Spies.[62] But while the SADF was already looking ahead to deeper involvement, BOSS was uncomfortable with even the present level of commitment. Johan Mostert, then a junior BOSS officer, remembers: "It so happened that I was working in General van den Bergh's office when the [weapons] request from the Military came through. Van den Bergh, to the best of my knowledge, had no hand in drawing it up. I had to process it. . . . It was in conversations with him during that time that I got the impression that he was not very keen on the war effort."[63] Piet de Wit was Chief of Evaluation at BOSS, in charge of collating the incoming information and processing it for the daily intelligence reports. "We were definitely advising to stay out [of Angola]," he recalls.[64] At one stage, van den Bergh set up a meeting for him and colleague Mike Louw to present Botha with a report Rothman had received from the CIA casting doubt on the likelihood of achieving a positive outcome in Angola. "P. W. just looked at us. We gave him the report. . . . And he just said 'Thank you very much. There's the door.' He was not impressed at all."[65]

Van den Bergh harbored what turned out to be well-founded doubts about where South Africa's open-ended and ill-defined commitment to the FNLA and UNITA would lead and the impact it would have on the détente program with which he was heavily involved.[66] By August 1975, negotiations over the future of Rhodesia, Pretoria's overwhelming foreign policy priority, were at a critical stage. The meeting at Victoria Falls loomed. The uncertain consequences of South Africa's covert involvement in Angola could derail everything.

Bureaucratic rivalry provided an additional underlying dimension to the BOSS-SADF divergence. The crux of the dispute between the two organizations tasked with preserving South Africa's security concerned the delineation of intelligence collection and analysis responsibilities and, ultimately, the roles of each body in informing policy choices. This had long been a gray area in the South African government's structure; the Potgieter Commission (1969–71) convened to resolve just this issue had achieved little. By the mid-1970s, BOSS believed it sat at the pinnacle of South Africa's intelligence structure, with Military Intelligence reporting to it. The SADF, however, saw itself as the only body responsible for countering extant national security threats. In its view, it was Military Intelligence's responsibility to detail specifically military threats and BOSS's duty to report on broader threats in the "social, political, economic, ideological and psychological" spheres, with the SADF sitting on top of the two, developing strategic responses to threats of all kinds.[67] The SADF ultimately saw it as its responsibility to "make a synthesis" of the factual intelligence evaluations compiled by both BOSS and Military Intelligence and use its understanding of "a broad spectrum of other factors" and the "capacities and potential" of would-be adversaries to project into the future and recommend appropriate counter-measures.[68]

The turf war led to bitter recriminations on both sides.[69] Rhodesian Central Intelligence Organization head Ken Flower recalled: "It was depressing for us on our visits to South Africa to have to listen to BOSS reviling the Military, the Military berating BOSS and, toward the end, BOSS railing against the Police—in short, almost everyone denigrating almost everyone else."[70] Fueling the rivalry was the personal animosity between Botha and van den Bergh. "It was amazing that two Afrikaner leaders should fight like that," remembers an animated de Wit.[71] Angola finally broke their already fraught relationship. Botha was ambitious, aggressive, and prickly at the best of times. But from the first perceived materialization of the total onslaught in Angola in mid-1975, he became ever more assertive in his advocacy of the SADF's remit and his disdain for what he saw as the doves' pursuit of coexistence with black Africa through "appeasement." The impact on the policymaking process of this multilayered animosity between the two organizations was stark. "Van den Bergh was at that time one channel of communication to the Prime Minister," Spies wrote. "The second . . . was through Military Intelligence to the Minister for Defense and thereby to the Prime Minister." The two channels only converged at the top.[72] Vorster's organizer bears out this depiction. His meetings at this time on regional issues—whether concerning Angola, Rhodesia, or other security topics—often featured the foreign policy double team of Fourie and van den Bergh (Muller often being abroad), or P. W. Botha, but only rarely all three.[73] Inevitably, how Vorster chose to approach the problem developing in Angola became heavily influenced by the rivalry between the SADF and BOSS and their differing conceptions of the nation's security priorities.

South Africa's Gulf of Tonkin

Ironically, it was security issues at one of South Africa's showcase industrial developments that triggered the final collapse of Pretoria's vision of modernization and material progress as the cornerstones of Africa's future. On the

Cunene River that formed the western part of the border between Angola and SWA, South Africa and Portugal were building a hydroelectric project, mirroring a much larger collaboration at Cabora Bassa in Mozambique. A weir dam was being constructed at Calueque, in Angola, while an associated hydro plant was located fourteen miles downstream at Ruacana, in SWA (henceforth the "border sites"). Both were largely financed by Pretoria. The idea was for the two countries to literally use the borders that divided their domains to hold their territories together in the long-term, through powering African development. However, a deterioration of the security situation at the border sites transformed South Africa's interest in the situation in southern Angola, with quite divergent results from those the two governments intended.

Throughout July 1975, the MPLA and UNITA had been involved in skirmishes across anarchic southern Angola, where the Portuguese presence was only nominal.[74] Into early August, workers at the border sites reported repeated harassment by UNITA bandits. (At this stage, South Africa's relationship with UNITA was covert and inchoate. The bandits would not have known about the emerging alliance.) This was brought to the attention of the SADF's upper echelons at a meeting in Pretoria late on the afternoon of Friday, August 8, where a contingency plan was developed for the sites' protection. That evening, the workers were again stopped and threatened by local UNITA fighters; the next morning, a small border patrol unit unilaterally moved in. The plan was immediately put into action. According to du Preez's authorized SADF history, "people in Pretoria" ordered both reinforcements from Otjiwarongo and the deployment of an entire battalion out of distant Walvis Bay to secure the region surrounding the sites. By Monday, the South African army was established across the border in southern Angola. The seizure of the border sites soon became a useful front for further South African involvement. The DFA, Cabinet, and (eventually) the press were told that the SADF was merely holding the border sites, which provided a plausible explanation for increased operational activity as South Africa sent troops and war materiel deep into Angolan territory under the cover of reinforcing the existing position.[75] This much of the deception, at least in its broad outline, has long been known.

However, a closer inspection of the evidence suggests that the seizure of the border sites should be understood quite differently. Botha and the SADF were intensely concerned about the possibility that southern Angola might provide a rear base for SWAPO forces striking into SWA. From late July, these concerns sharpened. Having effectively secured control of Luanda and its environs, the MPLA began an offensive into the south. Reports reached the SADF of a Soviet ship unloading equipment for the MPLA as well as continued favoritism shown toward the movement from the left-wing government in Lisbon.[76] On July 25, Military Intelligence told the SADF high command: "The MPLA realizes that it has the necessary support from the USSR and the Portuguese authorities and it will follow the communist template as it is laid out, namely revolution and the eventual takeover of Angola."[77] Elements within the SADF duly began to agitate for a decisive response to halt the MPLA's surge.[78]

In this context, the border sites affair became something of a Gulf of Tonkin incident, manipulated by Botha and the SADF so as to force the pace of involvement in Angola and justify further engagement. In this respect, the minutes of a tense interdepartmental meeting held at the Union Buildings in Pretoria on Monday, August 11, are especially illuminating. The meeting had been convened specifically to address the continued viability of the Ruacana-Calueque project in the broadest sense, not just the SADF's security concerns. The twelve-person meeting featured just one military representative, Biermann, but three officials from the Department of Bantu Administration and Development, and two from the Department of Water Affairs, including the head of its SWA division. In the event, however, Biermann simply informed the meeting that the border sites had been seized over the weekend by the SADF "on the authority of the Minister who had consulted with the Prime Minister."[79] (Dirk de Villiers and Johanna de Villiers's authorized biography of Botha, written with his close involvement, does not mention any prime ministerial sanction and instead depicts a decisive and commanding minister for defense.[80]) Neither Fourie nor van den Bergh had been consulted; both immediately vented their opposition. The urbane, mild-mannered Fourie, chairing the meeting, angrily pointed out that it was "an act of aggression to send troops across the border" and stressed that when he was in Zaïre just a week before, Mobutu had specifically warned him that any South African involvement in southern Angola would have "serious repercussions." He demanded to know "on whose authority the SAW [the army] had acted" and could scarcely believe Biermann's assertion that the seizure was indeed executed with the proper authorization.[81] Van den Bergh agreed with his partner in détente, characteristically stressing that regional "confrontation must be avoided at all costs."[82] Handwritten messages between Muller and P. W. Botha illustrate that the doves' anger was only assuaged by an agreement that South Africa would control the border sites temporarily until the Portuguese could reestablish their authority and take over from the SADF.[83] As Botha well knew, the Portuguese were quite unwilling to do so.

One of two things had occurred. When Botha heard that the patrol unit had taken over the border sites, he telephoned Vorster, seeking approval for reinforcements for the exposed troops and workers until the Portuguese could provide protection themselves. The prime minister, who had his hands full convincing Smith to sign on to the Pretoria Agreement, assented to a request he could not reasonably refuse. Alternatively, Vorster was not consulted and was told of the fait accompli later. Either way, the hawks and not Vorster were

behind the seizure of the border sites and, in what would become a familiar pattern in the months and years to come, Botha circumvented communal decision
making to obtain his desired end. In doing so, he was motivated by his view of
South Africa's complacency in the face of the total onslaught and by a lack of
support from his colleagues for the hardline security measures he felt that the
threat required. Shortly afterward, for example, Botha proposed to Cabinet that
Pretoria "declare SWAPO a banned organization"; his colleagues, not sharing his
alarm, demurred.[84] This lack of urgency was mirrored within the DFA: Hans van
Dalsen, Head of the Africa Division, suggested that Muller talk directly to Botha
about the SADF's "trigger happy" ways.[85] For his part, Viljoen suspected that the
seizure of the border sites not only became a convenient cover for South African
involvement after the fact, but that Botha had in fact utilized a minor incident to
justify a much-desired presence in southern Angola: "Let me put that straight.
[The seizure of the border sites] was used in order to explain the presence of
South Africa in Angola. . . . I must be honest, I always got the impression it was
a handy way of explaining an operation that didn't have the intention of protecting Calueque and Ruacana. It was a handy explanation to use to the rest of the
world."[86]

The Breytenbach-Viljoen Recommendations

Throughout August, the SADF's confidence in the ability of the anticommunist
coalition to hold its own faded. The MPLA continued making inroads into the
south, as well as east toward the Zaïrian border.[87] On August 14, Botha ordered
the SADF in SWA to begin covertly supplying weapons to the southern arm of
the FNLA, led by Chipenda; his authorized biography confirms that he only
later informed Vorster of this action.[88] Two weeks later, under operational order
8/75, a large quantity of arms was delivered.[89] However, the SADF believed that
training was also required. On August 29, a number of SADF officers, headed
by Lieutenant Colonel Jan Breytenbach, held talks with Chipenda at the SADF
base at Rundu in SWA. They developed an operational plan to help him retake
the south and sent it back to Viljoen in Pretoria.[90]

The Breytenbach-Viljoen recommendations stated that the FNLA had a
"great need" for more than just the existing small-scale material support and
training programs that South Africa was currently providing.[91] "Personally,"
wrote Breytenbach in the original operational plan, "I believe that the success
of the operation depends on good leadership at every level, that is to say, white
South African command and logistical support."[92] A four-stage support program
was proposed. First, South Africa would provide a variety of weapons to compete with the MPLA's Soviet equipment and would show the local forces how

to use them. Then, it would train the guerrillas in semiconventional warfare, enabling them to hold major centers. Next, the SADF would run a two- to three-week crash course to create nine separate offensive units tasked with driving the MPLA (and SWAPO) forces from southern Angola. In the final stage, South Africa would help train a regular force that could provide security in the south and allow "normal government functions" to be carried out.[93]

At the annual congress of the Cape NP at the start of September, Botha sought to persuade Vorster that South Africa should adopt these recommendations and take a more assertive role in training and arming the anticommunist movements. In his speech as leader of the Cape caucus, Botha portrayed events in Angola even at this early stage as posing a major national security threat in the context of the Cold War:

> Weapons pour into the country in the form of Russian help to the MPLA. Tanks, armored troop carriers, rockets, mortars and smaller arms have already been delivered. The situation remains exceptionally fluid and chaotic, and provides cover for SWAPO terrorists out of South-West Africa. Russian help and support, both material and [illegible] in moral encouragement, constitutes a direct threat.[94]

He gave the recommendations to Vorster, with a short handwritten note: "I think we have to do it. We will implement [*toepas*] with great secrecy."[95] The next day, as they flew back from East London to Pretoria together, Vorster assented.[96] Training for around four hundred men from FNLA (Chipenda) soon began under Breytenbach at Mpupa in southern Angola. When the disorganized UNITA leadership finally reestablished contact with Pretoria shortly afterward, the SADF launched a parallel program for around eight hundred of Savimbi's men.[97]

This single decision was pivotal to South Africa's subsequent escalating commitments in Angola. Before Vorster's approval of the Breytenbach-Viljoen recommendations, South Africa's commitment amounted to little more than the 20 million rand arms package, supplied under plausible deniability. At this point, Pretoria could have walked away. Beijing had been training the FNLA in the north—yet another indication of how the situation in Angola defied the hawks' crude Cold War classifications—but had already wisely extricated itself from the burgeoning conflict.[98] BOSS was advocating a similar course of action. At the conclusion of the Breytenbach-Viljoen recommendations, Viljoen candidly observed: "I have reason to believe that General van den Bergh will not be entirely on board largely due to the impact that any leak will have on the détente campaign. It may therefore be necessary to keep our Minister [Botha] fully informed throughout so that at the Prime Ministerial level the matter is

put by both sides."[99] This evidence, coupled with Mostert's and de Wit's recollections, contradicts the myth that BOSS was at least as keen for intervention
in Angola as the SADF was—a myth that features prominently, for instance, in
Botha's authorized biography.[100]

Van den Bergh's concerns were, however, ignored. Vorster's approval of the
four-stage plan, dubbed Operation Savannah, became the point of no return.
By committing the SADF to bolstering the FNLA and UNITA, the prime minister had inadvertently provided the framework for the military to subsequently
recommend that it had insufficient means to achieve the sanctioned end, which
remained constant. It was this mechanism by which all subsequent escalations—
including the insertion of SADF forces in mid-October—would be effected and
then rationalized.[101]

How exactly did Botha gain control of the policy process and convince Vorster
to intervene in Angola over the objections of the influential van den Bergh and
Fourie? A range of factors were important. First, the issue of involvement in
Angola was presented as a function of preserving the security of SWA. Whereas
BOSS and the SADF tussled for preeminence on other issues under the national
security rubric, the SADF had a free hand in SWA, which gave Botha's recommendations a particular salience. Second, the decisions to commit resources in
Angola were made incrementally. This facilitated a much greater level of involvement than Vorster could have originally envisaged. Third, Botha's consistent
focus on the concept of national security threats within a Cold War paradigm—
which suddenly seemed to be materializing in a total onslaught alliance between
the Marxist MPLA, SWAPO, Yugoslav arms, Soviet funds, and (later) Cuban
advisers—helped him outmaneuver his dovish rivals. South Africa's involvement gave socialist countries plenty of motivation to intervene for ideological
gain and, ultimately, a diplomatic free pass for doing so. But powerbrokers in
Pretoria drew different lessons at the time: Botha looked like the man who had
been right all along—the voice from the wilderness, as another of his biographies is titled.[102] By contrast, even as events in Angola escalated, Muller continued to focus on his traditional job of marketing South Africa—essentially
ensuring that apartheid did not receive too much bad press in Western countries
and promoting Pretoria's reliability as an anticommunist bulwark. In September,
he told the Waldorf Club in London: "We regarded the events in Moçambique
as a challenge. It was seen as an opportunity to prove that we, as is the position in
the case of our relations with our other neighboring states, are prepared to, and
can, live together with our neighbors."[103] He could not have known how quickly
and dramatically South Africa's foreign policy was departing from that much-
vaunted model even as he spoke. Meanwhile, van den Bergh and Fourie were
preoccupied with détente and gave little attention to Angola. Instead, Viljoen
and Rothman were usually employed as the contact points with Roberto and

Savimbi.[104] Even in the unpublished extended manuscript of Fourie's memoirs, Pretoria's policy toward Angola right up until mid-December 1975 features extraordinarily sparsely. The powerful Secretary for Foreign Affairs had no role in the decision-making process over intervention in Angola and only came into the picture to negotiate the subsequent withdrawal. The doves may have disdained Botha's hawkish approach and crude thinking, but they had no alternative conceptual framework with which to tackle the deteriorating situation in Angola. And by absenting themselves from the policymaking process over Angola, the doves effectively left a vacuum that Botha readily filled.

The final factor explaining Botha's success in securing the escalation of South Africa's involvement was his ability to use the mechanisms of Vorster's policymaking system to his advantage. Vorster afforded his ministers substantial leeway to run their own portfolios, a *primus inter pares* model that had dangerous consequences. "The more powerful ministers were effectively in a position to determine overall government policy by presenting the Prime Minister with a fait accompli, and the Cabinet was reduced to an almost peripheral role in the overall elaboration of policy," scholar Dan O'Meara explains.[105] The hours before Cabinet meetings would often be full of one-on-one meetings with Vorster: ministers sought to reserve even five minutes of the prime minister's time, presumably in an effort to get direct approval for important items and immunize their proposals from unpredictable Cabinet oversight.[106] Botha had all the attributes needed to thrive in this system. An MP since 1948, a minister since 1961, head of the powerful Cape caucus, and leader in the House of Assembly, he was very senior in a rigidly hierarchical party. He had plenty of favors to dole out and debts to call in. He was uncompromising and difficult to argue with. And he had an interpretation of the consequences of not granting the SADF the resources and power to do its job that provided plenty of rationale to push the envelope. As Annette Seegers put it in her history of South Africa's military: "Should they seek justification for what they did, [Botha and the SADF] needed to look no further than Total Onslaught. Its apocalyptic vision of a South Africa caught in a deadly bipolar world struggle contributed to the belief that South Africa was indeed at war [and that o]nly extreme and unconventional measures could prevent political and military demise."[107]

Consequently, throughout 1975–76, as his alarmist views concerning the total onslaught crystallized against the backdrop of events in Angola, P. W. Botha began to flex his muscles. The number of motions he proposed in Cabinet rose exponentially; as per Vorster's system, the vast majority were naturally approved. He also began to act more autonomously. When he needed explicit prime ministerial approval, he went straight to Vorster, bypassing the Cabinet and the ministers concerned. On other occasions, Botha acted in pursuit of broad ends sanctioned by Vorster but without consulting him as to the specific decision.

There appears to be no reliable or verifiable indication in any of the archives or sources, including the SADF-sponsored histories by du Preez and Spies, that the Cabinet or the prime minister were consulted prior to the first (minor) weapons delivery to UNITA in October 1974, the granting of more substantial assistance to the same in February 1975, the decision to start assisting FNLA (Chipenda) in late August, or the support for Holden Roberto's last-minute attack on Luanda on November 10. Spies claims at one point that on September 24 the Cabinet "approved" Botha's "plan of action" for training UNITA, but there was no Cabinet meeting that day.[108] There was a meeting on the 23rd, but the minutes not only show that Botha failed to brief the Cabinet on South Africa's strategy in Angola in any way, they suggest he was not present at the meeting at all.[109] Similarly, then Head of the Army Magnus Malan's memoirs relate that Botha kept the Cabinet informed before the taking of the border sites.[110] This is not accurate either. Malan, the SADF, its historian Spies, and probably the Cabinet itself all thought that there was more prime ministerial authorization and oversight for Botha's actions than there really was.

Boots on the Ground

By the end of September, South Africa was supplying arms and advisers to the FNLA in the north of Angola and operating full-scale training and logistical support programs for the FNLA (Chipenda) and UNITA in the south. Due to the diplomatic volatility of South Africa's apartheid system, secrecy was deemed integral. Within the government, perhaps only Vorster, Botha, and van den Bergh understood with any clarity the overall picture of South Africa's involvement in Angola. The DFA and the Cabinet were shut out entirely. The government also knew it could rely on the sweeping censorship powers it held over the publication of news on security matters to keep the press and the public uninformed too.[111] Even within the SADF itself, the flow of information was very heavily regulated. The Breytenbach-Viljoen recommendations spelled out that the officers involved in the programs, both in Pretoria and operating out of SWA, were to be specified in advance by name.[112] The Angolan organizations were ordered to do the same for their contacts with the South Africans. "The FNLA soldiers are to be told that they are being trained by mercenaries," the recommendations stipulated. All equipment, weapons, and ammunition were delivered using nonconventional channels and unmarked vehicles. SADF uniforms and insignia were avoided. Everything, on the ground as in the corridors of power in Pretoria, was strictly on a need-to-know basis.

Van der Waals, formerly the SADF's contact with the Portuguese military in Angola, was tasked with running the UNITA training program. He recalls that his "impossible orders" were to train two brigades of UNITA fighters in conventional warfare, launch an operation to stop "at all costs" the MPLA's advances on the UNITA capital of Nova Lisboa—and to do it all before November 11, just seven weeks later, when he would be withdrawn. "I had one day to prepare everything. That evening I had to brief the army general staff. . . . And the next day I had to fly in [to Angola]. . . . A week later all the personnel that I had chosen would go in." The South African goal remained constant: "We wanted to put UNITA—and the same with the FNLA, where I was not involved—in such a strong position that the world and the Organization of African Unity would have to recognize both the FNLA and UNITA as well as the MPLA as equal partners. . . . That was the broad concept."[113] However, Botha and top generals were already planning something more than a training and support role. An internal SADF summary of the chronology of the war notes that on September 24:

The following operational plan was approved in principle by the Minister:

Phase One: Land and cities must be brought under UNITA/FNLA control.

Phase Two: Occupation and pacification [*skoonmaak*, lit. cleansing] of the south-western corner of Angola, including cities like Sa de Bandeira and Mocamedes.

Phase Three: Attack on harbor cities Benguela-Lobito and opening of the Benguela railway before 11 November.

Phase Four: Conquest of Luanda.[114]

The plan was never carried out.

As the reinforced anticommunist coalition attempted to reverse the MPLA's recent gains, it encountered a number of obstacles. The local fighters could not use advanced equipment, while the emphasis on secrecy and the corresponding insistence on a limited intervention severely restrained the coalition's ability to quickly dominate the inferior MPLA before the intervention of Cuban forces in October.[115] The central challenge for the SADF was how to rapidly transform hit-and-run forces of limited discipline into armies capable of taking and holding territory. "The problem which Savimbi and Roberto experienced was their troops were guerrillas and they had the habit of fighting and running away in order to be able to fight another battle," explains Viljoen, who oversaw both training programs.[116] It is difficult to understate the scale of the task van der Waals faced in molding UNITA into a cogent fighting force. Many of the men lacked boots and basic military clothing; few had handled firearms before, let alone mortars or mines.[117] Initial advances consequently met with little success. On October 5, a

week after the arrival of van der Waals's training team, the UNITA column fled
from a skirmish near Nova Lisboa, as had been their instinct throughout their
decade-long insurgency against the Portuguese. The outspoken van der Waals
told his superiors that, given the scale of the conflict and the deficiencies of its
allies, South Africa's aims would never be achieved through a covert, small-scale,
equipment-lite intervention.[118] From his experiences with the FNLA at Mpupa,
Breytenbach concurred.[119]

Their recommendations came at a crucial time. By early October, the MPLA
had control of the capital, most of the harbors, and large parts of the south and
east. A massive Cuban military training program aimed at stiffening its forces
was almost fully operational.[120] It was evident to all that despite South Africa's
material assistance, the training programs, and the deployment of SADF command, logistical, and operational support, the MPLA would be in a position to
seize power on November 11. "The MPLA enjoys at this stage an advantage over
the other two movements and will in all probability emerge from the struggle
as the victor," Military Intelligence reported. "The MPLA . . . will probably rule
Angola."[121] On October 8, the SADF's upper echelons agreed with the consensus
emanating from the front: the FNLA-UNITA-South Africa alliance could not
achieve the desired political end by staying on the defensive, but had to go on the
offensive and employ a conventional warfare capacity.[122]

On October 6, Vorster saw his foreign policy team of Muller, van den Bergh,
and Fourie, and met again with the latter two on the morning of October 7 before
a Cabinet meeting.[123] Vorster then told the Cabinet, surely based on these discussions, that both Zaïre and Zambia had told South Africa that the MPLA was going
to win in Angola.[124] Kinshasa's interest in events was plain, but Lusaka's was also
important. As early as April, Kaunda had visited the White House and presciently
told Ford that the situation in Angola was about to become a major problem.
Just as regional stability had been reason enough to incentivize a rapprochement
with Pretoria over Rhodesia, for the same reasons Kaunda could ill afford to see
chaos emerge across Zambia's western border. Again claiming to speak for a coalition of regional actors spanning the Cold War divide—specifically Mozambique,
Zaïre, Portugal, and Tanzania—Kaunda strongly urged American support to render Savimbi a viable compromise candidate between the then dominant warring
factions, the FNLA and MPLA.[125] There is no reason to think he told the South
Africans anything different. Ultimately, the concerns of Pretoria's African partners must have assuaged Vorster's doubts that the intervention in Angola might
undermine détente and instead held out the tantalizing prospect that the two foreign policy ventures might prove complementary.

This amber light was all Botha needed to press his case. Viljoen singularly
agreed with van der Waals's and Breytenbach's diagnoses of the situation, and
had begun agitating for the introduction of armored cars and other advanced

equipment.[126] Accordingly, upon the general's return from consulting with Roberto and Savimbi on October 9, Botha invited him to deliver the SADF's recommendations to a meeting five days later of the State Security Council (SSC).[127] The SSC had been created in 1972 along the model of the United States' National Security Council (NSC) in an effort to coordinate South Africa's disparate national security bureaucracies. By law, BOSS, Defense, Justice, Police, and the DFA were all represented, while the prime minister, as the chair, could request the attendance of other parties.[128] Until the Angolan Civil War, the SSC had rarely been convened and was of limited importance. However, Botha realized that if he could strengthen its role, he could ensure that national security policy was developed in the coordinated manner in which total strategy dictated it must, while also creating an institutional vehicle that he might be able use to extend his influence over policy generally. As early as 1974, for instance, he had sought to strengthen the SSC by staffing it with a permanent secretariat[129]; in time he would use this secretariat to control the SSC's agenda and dominate policymaking.[130] And by making the SSC the forum at which intervention in Angola was decided upon, Botha ensured that the body would stand at the heart of South Africa's subsequent national security decision making.

Yet even as Viljoen addressed the SSC, the operational orders had already been issued. On October 9, Eland armored car squadrons were despatched from their base in Bloemfontein to the SWA-Angola border, ready to be airlifted deep into Angola, surely not coincidentally, on the 14th. A further column, code-named Zulu, was also assembled, seemingly again without any prime ministerial approval.[131] Botha was taking matters into his own hands. On September 4, Vorster had committed the SADF to the goal of preventing an MPLA takeover in Angola. Now, the prime minister had conveyed the urgency with which events in Angola were being perceived by his détente partners in moderate independent Africa. The corollary, surely, was that whatever reservations he had about intervention and détente being conflicting priorities were dissipating accordingly. P. W. Botha therefore arrived at the SSC with broad prime ministerial approval for action and would treat it—not for the last time—as a rubber-stamp body. Yet this analysis actually understates the degree of autonomy that P. W. Botha was arrogating to himself. The Zulu column was despatched from Rundu toward the Angolan border at 2 p.m. on the 14th.[132] But the SSC did not even convene until 2.30 p.m.[133] A fait accompli indeed.

On October 14, therefore, South African regular forces crossed the border on a short-term mission to reinforce the advisers and logistical staff already with UNITA and the FNLA and increase the two movements' chances of participating in Angola's postindependence government on November 11. This action represented an escalation of means to achieve a long-standing end, rather than a qualitative shift in strategy. Even so, the injection of regular forces constituted a watershed moment. South Africa could have folded its hand and withdrawn its advisers unobtrusively, leaving Havana and Moscow open to censure by African moderates for their long-distance intervention. Instead, Pretoria took the decision to double down, departing from the cardinal principle of South Africa's foreign policy and the key mechanism for excluding its own apartheid policies from its relationships with independent Africa and deflecting international pressure: the principle of noninterference in states' internal affairs.

Staying the Course

Initially, the two South African armies—Zulu in support of FNLA (Chipenda) and Foxbat in support of UNITA—made swift progress.[134] The isolated MPLA units in southern Angola, even with Cuban support, were pushed back by South Africa's professional forces. By the end of October, the FNLA and UNITA together held around 80 percent of Angolan territory.[135] However, following a counterattack by the MPLA in late October, the coalition's rapid advance northward stalled. "With the power of the supporters of the MPLA, [the anticommunist front] couldn't hold the fort. And quick as a flash, towards the 11th, the MPLA started occupying all the traditional UNITA and traditional northern cities," remembers Viljocn.[136]

The approved plan had always been for a short-term mission with a firm deadline of independence day. However, it soon became clear that the MPLA would declare itself the legitimate ruler of Angola and that the socialist bloc would recognize it as such. True to form, the SADF recommended that far from withdrawing as planned, in the face of a revitalized MPLA opposition, further South African assistance was needed to maintain the FNLA-UNITA position.[137] Military Intelligence reports from the time reveal the enduring power of the total onslaught paradigm in its assessment of the Angolan conflict: "For the continent as a whole, a continuation of what is happening in Angola sets a most alarming precedent. . . . What is to prevent a modernday [sic] 'scramble for Africa' with the USSR setting the pace and all the horrors of war and social and economic retrogression that would accompany it?"[138] Furthermore, an assault by the FNLA on Luanda on November 10 proved a disaster, all but wiping out Roberto's military capability in the north.[139] "The morale of FNLA is dangerously low and they are deserting their posts," a Military Intelligence report from the front noted.[140] Freed from heavy fighting on the northern front, the MPLA, strengthened by a sizeable and growing Cuban force, was now able to hold the SADF in the south.

Vorster remained deeply ambivalent about maintaining South Africa's military involvement. It was one thing to covertly influence an open power struggle,

quite another to overthrow an internationally recognized government, especially with faltering allies. However, on November 10, Savimbi secretly flew
to Pretoria to implore Vorster to maintain and indeed augment South Africa's
role.[141] "Our presence is according to Dr. Savimbi a precondition of his own
troops' participation," the prime minister subsequently told his Cabinet.[142] As
if the scene of an anticommunist African leader begging in person for South
Africa's help did not appeal enough to Vorster and his particular vision of the
continent's future, the UNITA leader added that Zambia and other moderate
African states were behind him—and, by implication, behind Pretoria too.[143]
In the context of the coalition's deteriorating fortunes, Savimbi's plea was crucial. Suddenly the intervention in Angola was no longer perceived as a threat to
South Africa's broader détente agenda. Instead, an ongoing South African presence in Angola could satisfy both the hawkish desire for a proactive repulsion of
communist expansion in the region and Vorster's own fixation on cooperation
with independent African leaders. While he had previously remained detached
from the intricacies of the intervention, on Friday, November 14, Vorster met for
almost two hours with Botha, Biermann, Muller, and Viljoen to help strategize
how South Africa would help UNITA and the FNLA form a credible alternative to the MPLA administration.[144] The theory remained that if South Africa
could keep the FNLA and UNITA in a strong position while simultaneously
avoiding detection, the international perception would be that Angola was split
among three roughly equal claimants, and the inevitable conclusion would be
that power must be shared between them. Viljoen was despatched to Kinshasa
to tell Savimbi and the increasingly irrelevant Roberto that South Africa was
going to stay the course.[145] Simultaneously, General André van Deventer moved
a new unit, 101 Taskforce, into Angola. His instructions were to push the MPLA
north of the Cuanza River and help the FNLA and UNITA establish themselves in the south.[146] The rare consensus among the hawks and the doves was
not, however, universal: van den Bergh was still not on board. He was excluded
from the strategy meeting and instead met separately with Vorster straight afterward.[147] The same day, CIA Africa Division chief Jim Potts told Washington's 40
Committee, the body in charge of covert operations: "[The South Africans] have
been worried. [*Not declassified*] has been pushing for them to pull out and use
mercenaries."[148] Doubtless, the unnamed person was Potts's opposite number
and sometime interlocutor.[149]

Allies and Covert Ops

If South Africa was going to serve as the first line of defense against communist penetration in sub-Saharan Africa, the emboldened Vorster wanted support

from the Western powers who would reap the Cold War benefits. Pretoria, Washington, and Paris had all been bolstering the FNLA and UNITA in various ways. Months earlier, South Africa had approached the Americans about a fully coordinated joint effort in Angola prior to Vorster signing off on the 20 million rand assistance package. The newly declassified version of the minutes of a NSC meeting on June 27 records Director of Central Intelligence William Colby as saying: "South Africa would like us to join with them in an effort, but we can avoid the problems that would create and deal with the black [African states]. Some [of these] would be encouraged for the US to take a role, and that would activate them."[150] Washington followed Colby's advice and rejected Pretoria's entreaties. In November, NSC staff member Hal Horan told the 40 Committee: "The South Africans have an interest in this themselves; they asked for help but when we didn't give it they stayed because of their own interests."[151] For Washington, Angola was a very low priority until the arrival of Cuban forces drove the conflict's sudden escalation in Cold War significance. The budget for IAFEATURE was not even increased from the original $24.7 million until November 27.[152] By that point, South Africa was already deeply involved in the conflict and looking for a way out.

Two enduring and widespread misunderstandings therefore need to be corrected.[153] First, the Americans did not have to solicit South African involvement. Pretoria was keen to be involved for its own reasons and Washington was happy to allow the South Africans to surreptitiously represent the anticommunist cause. In January 1976, Kissinger told his inner circle: "We didn't encourage them to go into Angola, but we certainly—they did the only fighting that was going on there for a while."[154] Second, South Africa's intervention was not initially rationalized as a means to strengthen the bilateral relationship with Washington. That line of thinking only materialized much later, as events threatened the viability of Pretoria's original calculus. With the war entering a new phase in mid-November, Vorster felt it was time to bring the relationship out of the shadows. In June, Pretoria had proposed that Vorster visit the United States; Washington thought that this was "a ludicrous idea" and decided that the best response was to not respond at all.[155] The newly confident prime minister likely entertained a dream scenario whereby South Africa's intervention in Angola not only promoted Pretoria's geopolitical aims as conceptualized by hawk and dove alike, but also provided a basis to prove South Africa's value to the "free world" in a concrete way. To this end, late on the afternoon of November 14, he and Muller met successively with the French and American ambassadors for the first time since the Angolan imbroglio had arisen.[156]

In his meeting with the American Ambassador, William Bowdler, Vorster was composed and confident about Pretoria's position in Angola. He painted a broadly positive picture of events, suggesting that "without Soviet intervention

[the] FNLA and UNITA could more than hold their own," and asked that the ambassador convey this to Ford.[157] Tellingly, he emphasized that the heightening of tensions in Angola threatened the negotiations between Smith and Nkomo in Rhodesia, the stability of anticommunist black states in the region, and the ongoing constitutional negotiations in SWA.[158] The prime minister's focus was still firmly on the big picture: détente and the acceptance of the *volkstaat* as an African state. Vorster refrained from making any specific requests for assistance and "confined himself to expressing concern at the inflow of Soviet arms and Cuban soldiers."[159] The subtext, however, was clear. Bowdler cabled home that when Vorster indicated that "only the US 'as our leader' could dissuade the Soviets from further involvement, he was implicitly asking that we do something to prevent the MPLA from receiving reinforcements that would enable them to move on the offensive."[160]

Over the weekend following these meetings, Vorster's optimism drained rapidly. Following a scoop by Reuters journalist Fred Bridgland, from November 15 mainstream Western newspapers slowly began to report the presence of South African troops in Angola.[161] Unconfirmed reports of "white mercenaries" and the like had been around since late October. However, confirmation that the forces of the apartheid state were attempting to influence a power struggle in black Africa revolutionized the diplomatic dimension of the conflict. "The desperate gamble of Holden and Savimbi to snatch victory from defeat by making a devil's bargain with Pretoria has now rebounded against them," editorialized *West Africa*. "By taking aid from South Africa, UNITA and her ally have broken the unwritten rules of Pan-Africanism."[162] Publicly, Pretoria's African allies moved to distance themselves from the apartheid regime. Savimbi not only denied that he had received South African aid, he also claimed that SADF forces were killing and seizing UNITA fighters and that Pretoria's goal was to weaken all three movements by sponsoring an internecine conflict.[163] Kinshasa, not to be outdone, categorically denied any cooperation with "the kingdom of the white racists."[164] With enemies like South Africa's, it was forced to keep friends like these.

The response at home to the fitful revelations of the SADF's role in Angola was equally dramatic. Vorster's détente policy had attracted broad support in the press, even among the usually hostile English-language newspapers. Pretoria's deception over Angola ended the honeymoon abruptly. "The whole situation has become very unfunny," the *Pretoria News* stated. "South Africans now know that there has been international speculation [on the presence of South African troops in Angola] which the government clamped down on."[165] The Johannesburg *Star* opined that the government had "a policy of censorship and equivocation which does no good at home and is palpably harming us abroad."[166] On November 15, the *Rand Daily Mail* simply published a blank column where

Figure 5.2 Although South Africa's intervention in the Angolan Civil War was slowly reported in the foreign press from mid-November 1975 onwards, Pretoria continued to use sweeping censorship powers to obscure the truth at home. When casualties began to emerge, the English-language press resorted to novel methods of doing their job. Over the censored area, the insert reads: "For reasons totally unrelated to military considerations or the security of the State, an announcement of the death in action last Thursday of South African servicemen has been delayed by the Defence authorities. This information, of vital concern to the country, will be released officially only today." Source: *Rand Daily Mail*, 15 November 1975. Times Media Group.

Bridgland's revelations would have featured. Underneath was written: "A report on Angola which would have occupied this space has not been published because permission, which is required in terms of the law for such publication, has not been granted." Botha was apoplectic.

When he returned to the office on Monday, November 17, Vorster resolved to contain the fallout from Bridgland's revelations. First, he decided to maintain the fiction. Over the coming days, both Botha and Muller publicly and vociferously insisted that South African forces were doing no more than protecting the border sites.[167] When querulous South African diplomats wrote home seeking permission to continue upholding this line, as they had since mid-August, they were instructed to do so.[168] Even as late as mid-January, after the SADF's involvement had become universally accepted, South African ambassadors were still officially in the dark. A plausible denial required a credible front, and the DFA was it. Second, Vorster resolved to take key parties, who might find out the truth from other sources, into his confidence. On November 18, Botha and Vorster brought the Cabinet into the picture. Botha described the military situation, outlining for the first time the degree of South African involvement. Vorster then gave an overview of the international dimension, mentioning that he had been in contact with Savimbi, the French, and the Americans about Angola. His ministers, so long accustomed to a large measure of delegated responsibility and authority, must have been astounded to find that the country they ran had been directly engaged in a major armed conflict for over a month.[169] Later the same afternoon, Botha and Vorster jointly briefed the editors of the major Transvaal Afrikaans news outlets on the situation, while using the government's sweeping censorship powers to prevent them from publishing what they learned.[170] The English-speaking press suddenly found themselves excluded from the inner circle. The South African embassy in Washington was also finally informed around this time.[171]

Vorster's public relations strategy yielded little success. In the weeks to come, Pretoria's denials did little to dent the emerging global consensus that the SADF was deep inside Angola, though they did help to obfuscate the precise nature of its presence. "In spite of the clear denial by South Africa that RSA forces are taking part in the fighting against the MPLA, it has been accepted by all the media that RSA forces are indeed involved," observed Military Intelligence just two weeks after Bridgland's story.[172] Vorster thought he was regaining control of the information flow and even skillfully coopting the press, in an effort to prevent the media from "prejudicing our position."[173] In fact, all he had done was buy some time while rendering the government's credibility hostage to the vicissitudes of the battlefield, not to mention alienating powerful editors by making them complicit in the deception. When on December 16 the MPLA paraded four captured SADF soldiers in front of the world's media, whatever fragile credibility Vorster's government had built up among the broader international community over the previous eighteen months evaporated.[174] At home, South Africans, black and white, were left bewildered as to how this had occurred. "Lack of the real facts can only fan the wildest rumors," suggested the major black daily, the *World*.[175] The public was left to guess the worst—especially when Botha announced that national service would be extended from three weeks to twelve, without acknowledging why.[176] Still, official statements over the ensuing weeks continued to contain only as much information as was required to explain the latest reversals on the battlefield. "The British newspaper reader still knows far more about the South African involvement in Angola than do the South African families whose men have been fighting there," the London *Guardian* pointed out as late as the end of January 1976.[177] Even those at the front itself had little knowledge of the overall operation. "I knew [that Zulu had entered Angola] because I had intercepted it on the radio," van der Waals, at the head of its partner column, Foxbat, recalled. "I was never [actually] informed."[178] Spies admitted, even in an authorized history: "For the South African public, the whole process—from the initial secrecy, to gradual hints [*geleidelike deurskemering*], to the final divulging of the real state of affairs, was at the very least a traumatic experience."[179]

Internationalization of the Conflict

The growing media furor also made Vorster acutely aware of South Africa's diplomatic exposure in Angola and the need to secure concrete support from South Africa's would-be Western allies. In his meeting with Bowdler on Friday, November 14, Vorster had refrained from making specific requests for aid. Just four days later, however, South Africa made a formal request to both the State Department and the Quai d'Orsay through the SADF Chief of Staff, General Ray Armstrong, that Washington and Paris increase their assistance to the FNLA-UNITA coalition.[180] From Vorster's perspective, the negative press was far from ideal, but the vision that he had committed to a week earlier of South Africa leading a broad, multiracial, anticommunist front in Angola, was still achievable. Influential radical states like Nigeria and Tanzania had been quick to recognize the MPLA in the wake of Bridgland's revelations. But moderate Africa had taken a wait-and-see approach. Success on the battlefield and on the international stage might bolster the existing efforts to cut across anti-apartheid sentiments by entrenching Cold War loyalties as a central issue in African geopolitics.

However, Vorster did not realize that the prospect of being exposed as allies of apartheid had transformed the already finely balanced cost-benefit analyses in both Paris and Washington. French President Valéry Giscard d'Estaing had been distinctly unenthusiastic about the whole enterprise from the start.[181]

He soon pulled back France's contribution. As for the Americans, at the November 14 meeting with Vorster, Bowdler had been noncommittal but supportive in response to his overview of the situation; a South African presence in Angola served Washington's ends so long as it remained covert. Yet even before Bridgland's article appeared the next morning, the Ford Administration was acutely aware of the dangers of even the appearance of cooperation with Pretoria. "The problem is, if we get more South Africans [in] we get more political trouble," Colby told the 40 Committee.[182] Revelations of the SADF presence only sharpened these concerns:

NATIONAL SECURITY ADVISOR BRENT SCOWCROFT: Option B, encouraging South Africa. What does that include specifically?

COLBY: They'd like to get their troops out, and hire mercenaries. They say that they don't have the money to do this and have turned to us. I think that this is political dynamite. The press would be after us. They and [the] Africans would say that the MPLA is supported by the big, brave Russians, while the others are backed by the bad South Africans and Americans. That would be unpleasant.

UNDER SECRETARY OF STATE FOR POLITICAL AFFAIRS JOSEPH SISCO: More than that. Your description is too mild. What is in the interests of the South Africans? They have more interest in being there than we do and they don't need our help. I do not favor giving any support to the South Africans.[183]

Articles in major newspapers alleging direct collusion, like one entitled "South Africa Seeks US Angola Aid," which appeared in the *Washington Post* on November 26, only aggravated the situation—while also ensuring that the post–Vietnam Congress would be hostile to requests for more covert funding. Realizing that its capacity to support the FNLA and UNITA militarily was finite, the Ford Administration turned to a diplomatic solution. "The trend is against us in Angola," Kissinger told Ford as early as November 19. "I think we should appeal for a cease-fire to the OAU [Organization for African Unity] and the Soviet Union."[184] By this stage, as he wrote in his memoirs, "the South African intervention represented both a political embarrassment and a bargaining chip."[185] While the beleaguered South Africans desired an increased American commitment to offset their military overexposure, ironically Washington sought the converse: foreign assistance to compensate for the limitations on its own scope for action. When Beijing, Paris, and London proved equally reticent to throw in their lot with the pilloried South Africans, Washington resolved to induce Pretoria to keep its forces in place and prevent an MPLA rout.[186]

As an emergency OAU meeting was announced for December 9, then postponed until early January, the issue of Angola's future became a diplomatic

free-for-all. In general, African states' positions on Angola's future were determined by their Cold War loyalties; radicals favored the MPLA, while moderate
countries favored a unity government. Any idea that a FNLA-UNITA coalition
would be crowned had been dead in the water since Bridgland's revelation of
South Africa's supporting role. The United States and France, as well as Zambia
and Zaïre, lobbied African states hard. Giscard d'Estaing urged the heads of
thirteen francophone African countries to support a unity government and the
withdrawal of all foreign forces.[187] Bill Schaufele, Assistant Secretary of State for
African Affairs, visited five key moderate African countries, as well as London,
Paris, and Bonn.[188] By January 3, Ford had written to no fewer than thirty-two
mostly African heads of state on the issue of Angola's future.[189]

This was the context for Kissinger's carefully crafted response to General
Armstrong's request for more American military assistance. The message
rejected the request for additional American weapons for the coalition, insisting that "the FNLA and UNITA have received enough and adequate arms for
their defense." At the same time, it expressed that Washington "shar[ed] the
concern of the RSA over the danger of the provocative role of the Russians and
the Cubans in Angola" and would "regard the imposition by force of a Soviet/
Cuban/ MPLA regime in Angola with great concern." It was a masterclass in diplomatic obfuscation. Kissinger's message invited the recipient—especially one
diplomatically exposed and desperate for Washington's acceptance, like Pretoria
was—to perceive an expression of solidarity between the two countries, while
carefully avoiding anything that could be identified as either a positive American
response to Armstrong's request or an appeal for an additional South African
commitment.[190]

The South Africans were duly confused. How could Washington be simultaneously alarmed at communist bloc success in sub-Saharan Africa, which from
its perspective was a major issue for the "free world," but not be prepared to
contribute the resources to push back the incoming forces?[191] Vorster urgently
summoned Bowdler for in-person clarification on November 29, a Saturday.[192]
As the American ambassador reiterated Kissinger's message, the prime minister perceived the desired reassurance that the United States shared its goal of
preventing communist expansion in the region. He left the meeting satisfied,
telling the Cabinet on December 3 that the Americans were "*heeltemal positief*"
[entirely positive] about Angola.[193] At an SSC meeting two days later, van den
Bergh remained skeptical, reporting that his attempts to elicit concrete help from
the French and Americans had been unsuccessful. Without them making good
on their promises, he surmised, the war could not be won. Botha did not share
his nemesis's pessimism. The proactive defense minister outlined a three-phase
plan to help extricate the SADF while not abandoning South Africa's aims: a
propaganda campaign aimed at highlighting communist interference in Angola;

further training of the FNLA and UNITA to "Angola-ize" the conflict; and additional entreaties to France and America to contribute more than just weapons, including substantial economic development assistance in southern Angola.[194] Still hopeful of a positive outcome, Vorster ignored van den Bergh's misgivings and approved Botha's plan.[195]

Washington continued to string the South Africans along into December, even as the military situation deteriorated. The SADF had lost the military initiative. Defeat at the Battle of Ebo in late November, the arrival en masse of Cuban forces, and the onset of the rainy season meant that military advance had ceased to be a realistic possibility.[196] One report for P. W. Botha's eyes only concluded ominously: "FNLA-UNITA relationship could explode at any time. [They h]ave already fired on each other in Lobito and Serpa Pinto. Similar incidents have already taken place in other large towns."[197] On December 12 and 13, P. W. Botha and Viljoen visited the front in Angola to assess the military situation for themselves. Van Deventer, the local commander, was profoundly pessimistic. A military solution could not be obtained so long as Luanda remained in enemy hands, he said. More soldiers were needed to break the stalemate, but even if such were forthcoming, the logistics were not in place to support them over the distances involved. As for South Africa's allies, van Deventer had "no confidence in UNITA or the FNLA," whose troops were "prone to disappear." With no sense of self-awareness, Botha mused: "We are possibly more deeply involved in this operation than anyone had originally foreseen." Botha congratulated van Deventer on the fine work of his troops and told him that he would "urgently" seek out Roberto, Savimbi, and Mobutu and inform them "that RSA feels that its part is now done and that we want to withdraw from the area as soon as possible."[198]

Simultaneously, Deputy Assistant Secretary of State for African Affairs Ed Mulcahy told South African embassy diplomats in Washington that "American aid was being supplied at off-the-record requests of at least five [African] heads of state." He added that around US$25 million had thus far been spent by the United States in support of the FNLA and UNITA and "that [the] United States would continue along these lines as long as it felt necessary."[199] Like Kissinger's reply to Armstrong's request for arms, Mulcahy's message was carefully crafted to hit the emotional buttons of the isolated South African government without making unequivocal commitments. It suggested that Washington would stay the course when it was in fact looking resolutely for the exit. The Americans were not the only ones using and misleading the South Africans. The Zaïrian Minister for Foreign Affairs, Mandungu Bula Nyati, told Kissinger in Paris: "For the time being we don't want them [the South Africans] to get out. We will be Machiavellian. Let the South Africans use their forces and we will then use this to get the Africans to get the Russians out."[200]

Figure 5.3 In mid-December 1975, P. W. Botha visited the Angolan front at Silva Porto and received a uniformly negative prognosis from the SADF command. "We are possibly more deeply involved in this operation than anyone had originally foreseen," he concluded. From left to right, General André van Deventer; Head of the Army Magnus Malan; Botha; Jonas Savimbi; Commissioner-General for the Indigenous Peoples of South West Africa Jannie de Wet; and Minister for Economic Affairs Chris Heunis.
Source: National Archives of South Africa.

Yet Vorster had little countervailing information at this point to suggest that things were not as they seemed. Since having been brought into the picture, his Ambassador to the US, Pik Botha, had been canvassing opinion in Washington to see whether aid would be forthcoming. Ever since, Botha has often told the same story of what occurred. He says he phoned Vorster in mid-December and told him that in light of events in Vietnam, America was unlikely to provide the help South Africa needed. Vorster apparently replied: " 'But Pik I have it from the highest level that the Americans will keep on supporting whatever we do there.' The Prime Minister then scolded his Ambassador and told him to go 'do some homework.' "[201] According to Botha, he conducted more inquiries and phoned back to reiterate his original diagnosis that "the Senate would inevitably cut off funds."[202] The documents tell a different story. On December 17, Botha's cable home was guarded but optimistic. "Reliable sources inform me that there is a more than fifty per cent chance that the Senate will approve help to the FNLA and UNITA out of the defense budget."[203] Two days later the US Senate passed the Tunney Amendment by the margin of 54 votes to 22—hardly a close vote— preventing the Ford Administration from contributing further funds to the anti- communist coalition.[204]

The demoralized South African leadership was shocked. Echoing their rec- ommendations from a month earlier, Viljoen and Malan emphasized that South

African troops were exposed and static. They counseled swift withdrawal.[205] However, since the passing of the Tunney Amendment, moderate Zambia and radical Nigeria had asked the South Africans both to keep the SADF in place until the OAU vote was taken and to promise, behind the scenes, to withdraw thereafter.[206] Vorster was not convinced. However, new National Security Adviser Brent Scowcroft summoned Ambassador Botha and requested that the South Africans "stand fast for now in their own national interest."[207] He also arranged for Mobutu to invite Muller and Fourie to Kinshasa to assure them that the moderate African coalition wanted South Africa to stay at least until the OAU meeting too.[208] Vorster agreed to hold the line. He had nothing more to lose.

A Diplomatic Resolution

On January 12, the OAU finally met in Addis Ababa to decide Angola's future. The member states were evenly divided: twenty-two favored recognizing the MPLA and twenty-two supported a unity government. The chairman— Uganda's Idi Amin—cast his deciding vote with the socialist camp. It was all over. Two days later, the SADF withdrew to the border sites. For all the FNLA's and UNITA's myriad shortcomings, the furor over Pretoria's involvement, and the restrictions on the Ford Administration's freedom of movement, Vorster had nearly secured the most unlikely of victories.

The vote is revealing of the shifting patterns of identity politics in postcolonial Africa. South Africa's intervention in Angola greatly reenergized African radicalism. The narrative of an expansionist, deceitful apartheid regime attempting to forcefully impose itself on a process of African decolonization took root easily. In Brazzaville, for example, Congolese radio condemned a "South African crusade to reconquer independent African countries."[209] Recent events gave such statements major credibility. Yet South Africa was not the only party whose intervention in Angola had raised African ire; Nigeria's entreaties during the Angolan endgame are indicative in this regard.[210] Long after the revelation of South Africa's real role in the conflict, major regional players, especially Zambia and Zaïre, were still fearful of communist expansion in Africa and eager to keep the SADF in Angola to prevent an MPLA walkover. Vorster's central argument—that African politics could play out in Cold War terms rather than remaining hostage to the legacy of the continent's colonial past and anchored to the overthrow of apartheid as a symbol of that past—had gained some traction on the continent. In an open vote that in many ways had become a proxy over South Africa's role in Africa, fully half of the states in Africa were not afraid to be seen alongside their colleagues at the OAU voting for the cause widely associated with the apartheid regime.

Vorster's program of unhurried bilateral diplomacy, his emphasis on development and economic aid, and his prioritization of a conservative pragmatism over ideological activism had proven attractive to numerous of the "second generation" of postcolonial African leaders. Vorster's strategic mistake—in addition to countless tactical ones—was forcing African leaders into an open vote on whether their identification with Cold War blocs and their fear of communist-backed conceptual and geopolitical challenges to their state-based vision for Africa's future cumulatively superseded their hostility toward apartheid. As the experiences of the previous years should have conveyed to Vorster, although the first two concerns had become more important as African leaders struggled with the economic downturns and political chaos of the 1970s, apartheid was still a foundation stone of postcolonial African identity, especially at the OAU. And as Angola receded from the focus of the Cold War lens over the subsequent months, the familiar paradigm of traditional pan-Africanism returned to heal the deep rift across the continent. Within six weeks, forty-one of the forty-six OAU members had recognized the MPLA government. The OAU ultimately censured only South Africa's intervention and made no mention of its communist counterpart.[211] Moderate African leaders were burned by the vote too and fled to the safety of old ideological staples, leaving Pretoria isolated once more. Even Kenneth Kaunda refused to carry on the fight and fell into line in support of an MPLA regime.[212] As a final insult, the UN Security Council voted 9-0 (with six Western states, including the United States, the UK, and France, abstaining) to condemn South Africa as the aggressor and call for reparations to the new Angolan state. The architects of apartheid could not believe it.

6

The Post Mortem

Lessons from Angola

The Angolan adventure was an unmitigated disaster for the apartheid regime. Despite all the efforts and expense—some 90 million rand[1]—Pretoria had ended up with the precise outcome it had sought to avoid: SWA would have a Marxist government on its northern border. But the consequences of South Africa trying to prevent this eventuality and failing were worse still. Its intervention had animated the latent anti-Pretoria hostility of a number of distinct actors—including Moscow, Havana, the MPLA, SWAPO, and radical African states—who coalesced into a resurgent alliance. Additionally, by being caught in the act of trying to influence the outcome of an African civil war, Pretoria had undermined the image it had been painstakingly constructing of a white South Africa that could coexist peacefully, prosperously, and constructively with black Africa. Finally, the Angolan experience had entrenched communist powers as reliable vanguards of postcolonial nationalism and provided a clear template for combating the racialized social orders in Southern Africa through militant action rather than dialogue. Together, these developments shaped a potent alignment of communist bloc power and African radicalism on the ground in Southern Africa—rather than just in Addis Ababa or New York—and one explicitly aimed at the overthrow of the South African government.

Pretoria ended up in this predicament for a range of reasons. These included a failure to contribute overwhelming force before October 1975, when the Cuban mission reinforced the limited MPLA forces; the extensive political and military shortcomings of the FNLA and UNITA; loose decision-making procedures within the Vorster government; the lack of a clear overarching strategy that alloyed political, diplomatic, and military factors; geopolitical calculations made on the basis of ideology with scant weight given to the facts on the ground; and an inability to rally international support to the cause. Yet none of these were the main focus of what the government took away from Angola.

Lessons Learned

The first lesson learned from the Angolan Civil War was that the convergence of communist support for the MPLA constituted a classic example of Moscow's relentless drive for world domination. In hawkish terminology, recent events heralded the long-predicted arrival in Southern Africa of the total onslaught.[2] Operation Savannah was therefore understood solely as a response to the feared communist drive for hegemony. This line of thinking ignored Pretoria's own role in shaping the dynamics of the conflict and, therefore, the geopolitical aftermath. The level of the Soviet Union's and Cuba's interest and engagement in Southern Africa was indeed much higher in early 1976 than it had been just a year earlier. However, it was South Africa's intervention in Angola that had enabled both countries to justify their involvement in antiracist and anticolonialist terms and allowed them to escape any serious international censure for their own long-distance campaigns. There was never any grand communist design on far-flung Angola. Rather, Soviet and Cuban involvement was opportunistic and incremental. "Soviet involvement in Angola in 1975 … lacked any clear strategic plan or goal," historian Vladimir Zubok writes in his landmark study of Moscow's foreign policy. Instead, as the conflict escalated, "[t]he Kremlin masters felt obliged 'to save Angola' and support the Cubans, as Soviet prestige was now at stake."[3] That prestige derived from the situation's intensification from a low-level power struggle in a part of the world of very limited interest to superpowers, to a conflict that became seen as a Cold War test of wills. South Africa's role in that intensification was very substantial. As for Havana, its initial response to the MPLA's requests for support was sluggish.[4] However, as other parties (like the South Africans) committed more resources and the stakes rose, the Angolan Civil War presented an opportunity for the regime in Cuba to register an ideological victory and bolster its revolutionary credentials. Pretoria thus played into Moscow's and Havana's hands. When Cuban emissary Major Raúl Díaz Argüelles returned from Angola in early August, he told Raúl Castro:

> [Neto] wants to make the situation in Angola a vital issue between the systems of Imperialism and Socialism in order to obtain aid from the whole Socialist Camp. We consider that he is right on this issue since at this point in Angola the sides are clearly defined, the FNLA and UNITA represent the international Imperialist forces and the Portuguese reaction, and the MPLA represents the progressive and nationalist forces.[5]

South Africa's intervention was critical in solidifying this definition internationally, while also tainting its side with the baggage of institutionalized racism.

Other optics for the conflict were available. It is hard to avoid the conclusion that Pretoria would have been better off either staying out entirely and allowing events in Angola to play out, or at least refraining from sending in regular troops and allowing Havana and Moscow to be widely condemned in Africa for their unprecedented intercontinental forays.[6]

The second lesson learned from Angola was that the failure of Operation Savannah to enable the FNLA and UNITA to take part in the postcolonial government was overwhelmingly (if not solely) due to the refusal of the US Congress to fulfill America's commitments to the anticommunist alliance. Following a frank February 1976 meeting with the South African prime minister, Bowdler cabled home: "Vorster believes US has done itself irreparable harm in Africa by its failure to block [the] Soviets in Angola, and regards us as indecisive and unreliable. The Angolan experience has made him lose confidence in the US."[7] Vorster soon commented to the Rhodesians that "anyone who relied on the USA has his deepest sympathy,"[8] and told *Newsweek* that "US Secretary of State Henry Kissinger had urged the SADF incursion into Angola and then failed to provide the necessary back-up."[9]

This thesis—that American abandonment was the cause of South Africa's failure in Angola—gained extraordinary traction across the polity. In 1978, P. W. Botha told Parliament:

> I know of only one occasion in recent years when we crossed a border and that was in the case of Angola when we did so with the approval and knowledge of the Americans. But they left us in the lurch. . . . The story must be told of how we, with their knowledge, went in there and operated in Angola with their knowledge, how they encouraged us to act and, when we had nearly reached the climax, we were ruthlessly left in the lurch.[10]

"The turning point of the war . . . was the new law passed by the American Congress forbidding military support to any Angolan Party," echoed then Director of Operations for the Army Jannie Geldenhuys in his memoirs.[11] Various versions of this thesis were repeated by highly placed South African diplomats, generals, and politicians alike in interviews for this book. Certainly, Washington supported the involvement of the armies of the apartheid regime in a power struggle in independent Africa, encouraged feelings of solidarity in Pretoria, and then left South Africa bearing the military and diplomatic cost of the joint effort. Further, although the American and South African covert programs were designed, motivated, and implemented separately, there was some constructive cooperation between them, even if the details remain unclear or unverified.[12]

Yet Washington—and Congress more specifically—was just the scapegoat for a thoroughly ill-advised and poorly planned venture. Three factors together explain why South Africa intervened in Angola: the regime's understanding of events in Angola and their relationship to the security of SWA as perceived through the prism of total onslaught; P. W. Botha's relentless advocacy for a pro-active response and his skillful navigation of the decision-making process; and the incremental nature of the intervention, by which each escalation was based on recurrent realizations that the existing means the state was deploying were insufficient to achieve the constant end of preventing an MPLA takeover. South Africa needed very little encouragement to deepen its involvement. As early as June 1975, the SADF was already portraying an MPLA victory in decidedly alarmist terms and advocating decisive countermeasures: "The anti-communist groups will need to quickly build up the support programs of both the FNLA and UNITA in the limited time available in order to prevent a full communist takeover in Angola. . . . The available time is at this stage critical."[13] Washington was content to have South African troops secretly bolster the FNLA and UNITA forces, and South Africa, long spurned by the United States, was equally satis-fied to know that the two states were fighting on the same side. In the months following the intervention, Bowdler saw all too well what the South African gov-ernment was doing in recasting history. "[Botha] has carefully restated official position on SAG involvement in Angola this time without himself charging that US had given assurances or instructions, although that is the inevitable conclu-sion most are reaching from present as well as past exchanges on the issue," he cabled home in May 1976.[14]

The reality is that the Americans knew full well what the South Africans were doing in Angola, all while trying to tilt the balance of power in Angola through a low-priority, ham-fisted CIA operation of their own. As for the South Africans, they were under the impression that the Americans would ultimately come to their aid in more concrete forms, given their shared interest in the conflict. But this expectation flatly ignored the political costs of open alliance with the apartheid regime, the realities of congressional oversight in the US system, the dominant mood in American politics regarding covert operations in the post–Vietnam War/Church Committee era, and the very low priority accorded to Southern Africa in American worldviews. Information on all of these factors was readily available in reports from South Africa's diplomats, as well as local English-language and international newspapers. However, the regime's leaders ignored the reams of countervailing evidence and simply hammered reality into the forms they preferred.

The old patron-client model of center-periphery Cold War relations was evi-dent in Pretoria's thinking. But the relationship with Washington was of mar-ginal importance in policymaking conversations until November 1975, and was much less important than how Pretoria adapted Cold War concepts to its unique regional and racial context. Policymakers did not see events in Angola through the prism of South Africa's relationship with the United States, but rather through the optics of their own homegrown philosophies. That Pretoria was caught unawares by Congress's cessation of funding and the American failure to provide more tangible support to the anticommunist coalition is at least as much an indictment of Vorster's failure to develop a cogent strategy based on the input and expertise of BOSS, the SADF, and the DFA—not to mention the embassy in Washington—as it is of Kissinger's shameless realpolitik. Contingent factors, such as Vorster's unique policymaking structures and the inability of UNITA and the FNLA to hold their own without substantial South African support, also contributed to the final outcome.

The harsh truth was that it was apartheid that lay at the root of the key restraints on South Africa's scope for strategic action in Angola. Hostility to apartheid was central to the disastrous emphasis on secrecy and deception, to the resulting tentative commitment of diplomatic resources and military manpower through spring 1975, and to the inability to attract decisive political and military support from foreign allies. Everything Pretoria did—its Bantu education program, the development of the homelands, its regulation of the labor market, the ethnic federalism it proposed for SWA, the emphasis on group rather than individual rights—stemmed from a deep faith in the necessity and desirability of the separate political development of ethnic groups as the only means to guarantee *volk* self-determination and fulfillment at the core of a broader white power structure. Consequently, apartheid never came under any serious scrutiny in the post-Angola post mortem. Instead, South Africa's leaders developed their own narrative of what had happened in Angola and simply externalized their failures.

This was especially problematic as the intervention in Angola had substantially alienated Africans at home. Behind the regime's façade of stability, young urbanized Africans were becoming increasingly radicalized through new politics like the BCM.[15] Just as the early 1970s saw new generations of Afrikaners reinterpreting their identities and aspirations in the context of a shifting material context and global norms, their counterparts in the black underclass were doing likewise.[16] In the decade prior to the Angolan crisis, black newspapers had been unable to mount a consistent or effective challenge to the regime's authority. They asserted African rights and exposed appalling living standards, but ventures into direct confrontation were infrequent.[17] Instead, the predominant mentality was often one of resignation, with many African elites seeking reform within the structures and discourses created by the regime. Homeland leaders continued, for instance, to receive plenty of positive coverage in the mainstream black press.[18] Vorster's African outreach resonated deeply with this mentality. The Victoria Falls conference received blanket coverage in the *World*, a tabloid owned by the white, English-language Argus Group and hegemonic in the black market. "Dr. Banda's visit has given us dignity," its stablemate, the *Weekend World*, declared during the Malawian leader's 1971 tour.[19] The regime's new deal, inchoate and limited as it was, fueled not insubstantial support for its pioneer. As late as January 1976, a Market Research Africa poll published in the *World* showed that fully 53 percent of black respondents thought Vorster was doing a "good" or "excellent" job. The accompanying letters to the editor lauded the détente program, the removal of certain job reservations, and the development of the homelands. "Mr. Vorster is the 'problem solver' between our various nations," one letter to the editor observed. "Next year, there will be a Black Prime Minister in his own independent Black state here in South Africa, all given by Mr. Vorster. He is good," chimed in another.[20] "It appears that never before in the history of our country has a leader enjoyed such widespread backing," concluded Joe Latakgomo's editorial the next day.[21]

Angola changed all of that.[22] Once it was confirmed that Pretoria had intervened in Angola and then been driven into a hasty retreat, black South Africans' perceptions of the future changed notably. "Our restless youth is espousing the cause of the MPLA. People are saying 'The devil we don't know cannot be worse than the devil we do know,'" said Hudson Ntsanwisi, Chief Minister of the Gazankulu homeland.[23] The tone emanating from the *World* and its readers likewise shifted. In November 1975, for instance, the paper had featured an extensive profile of development in the Transkei, advertisements for people wanting to join the future homeland government, and positive coverage of the selection of Bophuthatswana's future capital. As the truth emerged from Angola in early 1976, the disposition of the paper shifted markedly. "We accept that, to a certain extent, there is consultation with homeland leaders, but it is the nine million Blacks in the urban areas who really need to be consulted," ran one editorial.[24] "While the Government is telling the world that it is moving towards eliminating race discrimination, there is little evidence to justify this claim," challenged another.[25] More pointedly still, the *World* ran a survey asking blacks whether they would take up arms in defense of the Republic. Eighty percent said no. One canny respondent pointed out that he was now "a Bantu Homeland citizen, so I'd be indulging myself in foreign politics—South Africa's." Several others bitterly pointed out that their fathers had fought in the Second World War, only to be denied a share of postwar prosperity; why would they make that mistake again?[26] Homeland leaders were emboldened too. Just months earlier, Zulu leader Chief Mangosuthu Buthelezi had publicly advocated the idea of a referendum among Zulus over whether to accept homeland independence.[27] Now, he gave a landmark speech in Soweto in which he explicitly called for majority rule across the country. In doing so, he insisted that he spoke not only for Zulus, but for all black South Africans—a rejection of the framework of "nation-based" African leadership that Pretoria tolerated.[28]

Responsibility and Accountability

Pretoria's perception of the materialization of the total onslaught in Angola, coupled with the perceived Western failure to stand against it, bred a debilitating feeling of isolation. "The Angolan experience has greatly heightened South Africa's sense of vulnerability," Bowdler explained after his February meeting with Vorster. "[The] South Africans had banked on the strategic importance of Southern Africa and the Cape Route to the 'West' (read us) as overriding [our] scruples about apartheid. . . . [T]his article of faith has now been shattered."[29] Defending Operation Savannah in Parliament, Vorster declared: "We have learned a lesson in Angola. . . . [W]hen it comes to the worst, South Africa stands alone."[30] Such words were a far cry from the surging confidence with which the prime minister had been promoting regional détente just six months earlier. However, it was widely recognized that events in Angola had provided a major fillip to South Africa's enemies. Intelligence reports predicted a renewed subversion campaign by a reenergized SWAPO operating out of southern Angola, a sharp escalation of the nationalist insurgency in Rhodesia, and increased support for liberation movements operating out of Mozambique.[31] Behind all of these, the DFA and the SADF now agreed, there was the distinct possibility of Soviet or Cuban support, either through direct military force or "surrogate intervention."[32]

Despite this foreboding picture, there was little post-Angola demoralization within the SADF. A debriefing conference held at Voortrekkerhoogte on March 15–19 entrenched the narrative that the defense force had performed admirably. South African troops had "handled themselves well" such that "we won every battle," an internal review noted.[33] What limitations the SADF had experienced on the battlefield were squarely attributed to outdated arms. Magnus Malan recalled that the conflict had revealed "an enormous lack of comparable firepower. It was a shock to compare the Defense Force's obsolete weaponry with that of the enemy."[34] Strategically, the SADF internalized that it had been thwarted by poor planning in Pretoria and American abandonment in the face of communist aggression; it saw Angola as a political and diplomatic, rather than military, defeat.[35] Yet Pretoria's hawks, led by Botha, had a played a major role not only in the operational execution of Operation Savannah, but also in the interpretation of intelligence and even the individual decisions that brought South Africa into the conflict in the first place. The distinction between political and military decision making had been anything but clear-cut.

As for Botha, he was able to avoid bearing responsibility for the Angolan disaster entirely. Right from the first stage of the intervention, he had advocated military escalation to combat the perceived total onslaught. He then continued to do so long after escalation had become unfeasible and damage limitation had instead emerged as the order of the day. With the MPLA "appearing to be making progress," Botha briefed the Cabinet on December 2, "it was necessary that the West help with troops."[36] This was never on the cards, not least two weeks after Bridgland's revelations. Botha was just engaging in wishful thinking. Similarly, when van Deventer issued his roundly pessimistic prognosis during Botha's visit to the front on December 12 and 13, the defense minister was still torn between the harsh reality and his instinctive preference for seizing the initiative. He told General van Deventer that if the MPLA destroyed any further bridges, South Africa would have to consider an attack on Luanda. Botha then elucidated—in quite some detail—the logistics of such an operation, including possible American support for "action instigated from Luanda harbor." Van Deventer's reaction is not recorded.[37]

How did Botha keep his job? Despite ongoing censorship, there was some criticism of the intervention in the public sphere and even calls for Botha's resignation.[38] Johan van der Vyver, a law professor at the University of Potchefstroom, forthrightly declared that "South Africa's escapade in Angola will probably prove to be the blunder of the century."[39] With tongue planted firmly in cheek, Schalk Pienaar described Operation Savannah as "a slight mistake" ('n ligte mistykie).[40] However, Vorster was too heavily implicated himself to cut his difficult but powerful defense minister loose. No sooner had the decision to withdraw the SADF from Angola been taken than the NP began to close ranks. This was no easy task. MPs had no idea what script to stick to, because they knew next to nothing about the entire venture. When P. W. Botha finally opened up to caucus in late January 1976, the minutes show that he fielded a slew of the most basic questions from his colleagues:

> Why did we interfere in a foreign country?
> Why did we withdraw?
> Can our forces seize the border?
> If the USA won't give us weapons, then what? . . .
> Are we manufacturing enough weapons [ourselves]?
> To what extent are we involved? . . .
> To what degree are we there on the request of Africa?
> Can we win? . . .[41]

Botha responded with verve: "Everyone in Africa knows how far we are involved. From here on out, there will be an anticommunist front in Africa and

SA and Africa will openly act in concert. We will not get much help from others. The French actions are disappointing. . . . [T]he USA is on board at the highest level but Ford and Kissinger are in a battle with Congress." Meanwhile, Vorster spelled out the way forward in his customary style. In light of recent events, "the greatest [party] unity is necessary."[42] For all their philosophical disagreements and long political rivalry, the two men had effectively formed a common front in an effort to save their careers.

When Parliament resumed a few days later, the government's defense of Operation Savannah was vigorous and disciplined. Its case relied heavily on unverifiable assertions, specious reasoning, and outright falsehoods. At one stage Botha's number two, Deputy Minister of Defense Kobie Coetsee, told the House that "as far back as May 1975 . . . the Cubans ha[d] been streaming into Angola."[43] This was pure fiction. Nevertheless, the government successfully entrenched the narrative that South Africa had acted honorably and in concert with African and Western allies to combat extracontinental communist aggression, a line that contained enough of the truth to gain traction. Those who questioned this narrative were viciously attacked and often had their patriotism challenged. Botha took the lead, using those journalists who had sought answers from the government over how and why South Africa had invaded Angola as a focal point. During the no-confidence debate in January, he criticized "some of South Africa's own reporters" for violating the government's "trust" and "certain newspapers of both languages" for doing the government "a disservice."[44] Prior to the defense vote in May, he went further, savaging by name the *Rand Daily Mail* and the *Cape Times* as "newspapers which brim over with disloyalty to South Africa."[45] The combative defense minister singled out *Cape Times* deputy editor Gerald Shaw as a "fifth columnist" who wrote "subversive" articles.[46] He also labeled the author of a Progressive Reform Party pamphlet criticizing the intervention as a "cockroach" spreading "blatant lies" in a "base and vile attempt to disparage the Defense Force and to create mistrust."[47] The opposition United Party was thoroughly cowed. In Parliament, Vorster told the UP's spokesman on foreign affairs, Japie Basson, "Why don't you stick your head up your arse?"[48]

The creation of this "with us or against us" paradigm, launched under the protection of parliamentary privilege, was as effective as it was unedifying. In May, a Johannesburg *Star* poll of one thousand white South Africans found that fully 64 percent of respondents thought that the government had been right to send troops into Angola. Only 18 percent disagreed.[49] After the Broederbond Executive Council conducted hearings into the intervention—fulfilling the role one might expect elsewhere to be performed by a parliamentary or legislative committee—its final report strongly reinforced the government's narrative of events. South Africa had been "*asked* by the pro-Western forces to help stop the Russian-Cuban supported MPLA. This request for aid was supported by certain African governments and other governments. We were therefore there *on request*."[50] The Broederbond report also laid blame precisely where the government desired: "It is already well known how President Ford and Dr. Kissinger's efforts to lend help . . . were thwarted by the US Congress. . . . The West is however currently too wishy washy [*pap en slap*] to expect any help from."[51] Such was the newly alarmist atmosphere within which Pretoria understood national security that Botha managed to push through legislation that retrospectively legalized his deployment of South African national servicemen during the conflict outside South Africa and SWA, no minor infraction.[52] There was never any serious investigation by the Broederbond or any other body into precisely how the intervention had occurred, the specific chain of events, the diplomatic dimension, or Botha's central role as a relentless advocate of intervention.[53] Not only did the minister for defense escape any repercussions for his headlong pursuit of the disastrous intervention in Angola, he emerged stronger than ever.

Rearmament

As South Africa's leaders searched for new ways of securing the regime's future in the new environment of reenergized communist involvement in the region, the pervasive sense of fear produced a renewed focus on national security priorities and the hawks' policy recommendations. With the Cabinet's adoption of Defense's Five Year Plan in early 1974, there was already broad approval for directing more state resources toward defense.[54] However, in accordance with Vorster's chaotic style of government, there was no concrete plan in place for exactly how much money would be budgeted for this purpose. Events in Angola enabled Botha to force the issue and finally secure the large increases in defense spending that he had sought for years.[55]

In October 1975, Botha had vigorously championed the need for extra funds, informing Treasury of his intention to deliver a major submission to the Cabinet in the new year, focusing on "the threat to and preparedness of the SA military."[56] Angola brought his point home for him. At the Cabinet meeting on December 3, with his colleagues having only recently been informed that the SADF was deep inside Angola, Botha opportunely raised the issue of South Africa's defense needs. The Cabinet promptly approved his submissions: 1 billion rand of the main budget would be allocated to Defense for 1976–77; the SADF would "define its own priorities"; the Armaments Board would be empowered to make use of scarce foreign export credits; and the military would "be accorded the highest priority in the supplementary budget."[57] The Cabinet also agreed that the entire issue of military preparedness would be revisited after the summer parliamentary break. On February 25, Botha duly underscored to his colleagues

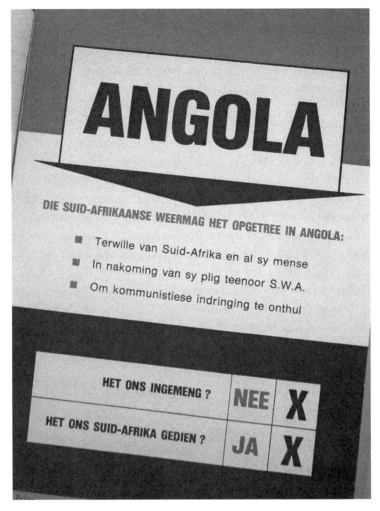

Figure 6.1 In the aftermath of the SADF's intervention in the Angolan civil war, John Vorster and P. W. Botha led a disciplined government effort to manipulate the truth and thereby manage public perceptions of the event. This pamphlet formed part of that effort: "The South African Army acted in Angola: In the interests of South Africa and all its people; In compliance with its duty to SWA; To reveal communist intrusion. Did we interfere? No. Did we serve South Africa? Yes." Source: National Party.

the gravity of South Africa's security vulnerabilities. The Cabinet promptly voted to increase Defense's allocation from the main budget from 988 million rand for 1975–76[58] to 1250 million rand.[59] At the next meeting on March 3, this was augmented to 1350 million rand, an increase of almost 37 percent on the previous year's figure.[60] At every stage, Botha's Cabinet submissions drowned his colleagues in a potent combination of broad-brush alarmism and an unmatchable control of the figures, rendering his proposals hard to second-guess. The public mood was also strongly in favor of such fiscal reprioritization. In March 1976, a poll of 2300 whites conducted by the newspaper *Rapport* found that in the post-Angola climate 76 percent of respondents were in favor of building up the military.[61] In June, Botha again highlighted the inadequacies of the defense allocation and lamented the national security cutbacks that would be required to stay within budget. The Cabinet yielded once more and agreed that any extra funds found in the budget would be redirected to Defense.[62]

These extra funds fueled an extensive rearmament campaign. In 1976 alone, the SADF embarked on a major upgrading of its tanks and armored cars,[63] purchased everything from 13,000 AK-47s to air-to-air missiles,[64] and began liaising with Armscor to improve its artillery, which had proven to have a vastly inferior range to the Soviet equipment encountered in Angola.[65] Whereas previously the SADF had focused heavily on counterinsurgency threats, arms, methods, and operations, in light of the new Cuban presence to the north, over the ensuing years much of the new expenditure went toward building a conventional warfare capacity through the purchase or (increasingly) domestic development of artillery, tanks, and fighter aircraft.

Figure 6.2 Beginning in the mid-1970s, P. W. Botha successfully argued that defense needs had to be given the highest priority in the annual budget. The result was a massive rearmament campaign and a relentless redirection of resources towards the military. Here, Botha takes a flight in a French-designed Mirage IIID fighter jet.
Source: National Party.

Botha and the military also secured increased leeway to execute their more assertive national security strategies. As a key February 1976 SADF policy paper approved by Botha made clear, in the post-Angola era the military began to focus heavily on the SWA border area, through two separate but related lenses. One perceived threat came from a rejuvenated SWAPO. "The greatest negative effect which a general withdrawal [from Angola] will have is that it offers SWAPO the opportunity to regroup along the SWA border," the policy paper stated.[66] Accordingly, the SADF resolved to maintain a strong and active deterrent presence in SWA that could also operate into southern Angola: "[T]he RSA's counter-insurgency forces will take strong action against SWAPO centers in the border area. Such clandestine action can always be linked to 'hot pursuit' should it become known."[67] The other perceived threat along the SWA border was conventional: a Soviet- or Cuban-supported MPLA drive into southern Angola, and perhaps beyond. The SADF's proposed countermeasure was essentially to repeat the same strategies at the core of Operation Savannah. As early as February 1976, Biermann recommended to Botha that "[a] continued UNITA guerrilla-campaign, with covert RSA support, is a necessary element in the limiting of the capacity of the MPLA to consolidate captured territory and simultaneously form a conventional force against SWA."[68] Chris Thirion was part of the SADF unit that subsequently sought out Savimbi's defeated forces in the bushland of southeastern Angola. He recalls that they told the UNITA leader: "We have a message from South Africa, from Pretoria. We will support you. We will help you. We will arm you. We will train you. But you must then help us."[69] Both South Africa and the United States duly supported UNITA forces as a buffer between Luanda and SWA and as an irritant to the fledgling MPLA government.[70] By October, South Africa had agreed to run four- to six-week training courses for groups of 30-40 UNITA guerrillas at a time. Those trained were then equipped with infrared equipment for night-time warfare and deployed in the Cunene region of southern Angola.[71]

In this way, the post-Angola sense of vulnerability produced an important shift not only in South Africa's willingness to use force to shape its regional environment, but also in the ways in which it would do so. Prior to the Carnation Revolution, South Africa had given military support to anticommunist states in the region, such as Portugal and Rhodesia, as part of a strategy of forward defense. When this strategy became impracticable, it had tried to use diplomacy to create a new regional order in Southern Africa. Then, through Operation Savannah, Pretoria had supported nonstate actors with a claim to sovereignty. Now, in the post-Angola era, it became established practice for South Africa not only to preemptively attack guerrilla cadres outside its borders, but also to support rival anticommunist insurgents in an effort to weaken established and recognized but hostile states.[72] In a few short years, South Africa had thus moved from being a status quo power heavily invested in the integrity of existing state structures in the region to one that fostered instability and actively undermined those structures. This was a massive shift in the regime's statecraft, and one that made substantive cooperation with nearby African states on the basis of mutual non-interference and *goeie buurskap* all but impossible.

A corollary of the government affording the SADF more leeway to enact its preferred security strategies was a decline in civilian control over how it did so. In April, the doves were dismayed (if somewhat unsurprised) to learn that the SADF had been violating the parameters of South Africa's assistance to Rhodesia's defense. The airplanes and pilots that Pretoria had seconded to the Rhodesians to hold the line may not have been directly involved in attacks on Mozambican soil, which Vorster would hardly have allowed, but they were being utilized to scout and map potential targets inside Mozambique.[73] Then, in July, an SADF raid on a SWAPO camp in Zambia proved deeply embarrassing for South Africa's diplomats in the context of ongoing negotiations over Rhodesia. The raid, in which twenty-four were killed and forty-five wounded, summed up the disdain the hawks had for Vorster's priorities. Lusaka fumed: Pretoria had been its partner in both peace and war over the previous twelve months.[74] In a subsequent cable home, Bowdler was highly critical of the lack of civilian oversight of military operations. "There is a good possibility that civilian instructions to the military have not been as tightly drawn as they should be and that the military, lacking experience in the international milieu, have been insensitive to the political implications of their actions," Bowdler opined. Amid a "certain looseness" in government decision making, he concluded, "[w]e believe much leeway was left in the hands of a highly emotional and sometimes erratic Minister of Defense."[75] Similarly, when the SADF resurrected its support for UNITA, the US Defense Intelligence Agency observed: "The South Africans probably hope a revitalized UNITA in southern Angola can prevent the Cuban and MPLA forces from providing effective support to the SWAPO guerrilla movement. It is still [however] uncertain as to whether this training program is sanctioned by Pretoria or another independent operation by the military, as has been suggested by previous reporting."[76]

Thus, the Angolan Civil War proved a watershed in the ongoing conceptual, political, and policy battle in Pretoria between the security-conscious hawks and the détente-favoring doves. Within the apartheid regime, the entire conversation on national security changed decisively. Justifying the Angolan intervention before Parliament in January, Vorster for the first time appropriated the hawks' term "total strategy."[77] Whether as formal policy or unofficial practice, early 1976 marked the beginning of rearmament and large defense budgets in Pretoria coupled with preemptive strikes and covert destabilization outside South Africa's borders. The postwar alarmism also set in motion a steady deterioration of civilian control over security matters, particularly in the border areas.

All of these developments would have a crucial influence on the white polity and the unfolding of conflict in Southern Africa over the ensuing years.

The Resurrection of Détente

The more surprising legacy of the post-Angola sense of isolation and vulnerability was that it simultaneously produced a renewed impetus toward détente, whose resurrection in 1976 ran counter to all expectations.[78] South Africa's intervention in Angola had severely alienated the fellow lusophone regime in Lourenço Marques, the exemplar for independent Africa of the merits of détente. At the UNGA in late October, Mozambique's representative lambasted apartheid as "the heavily disguised maneuvers of the fascists and racists to maintain the peoples of those territories in perpetual slavery" and "a brutal torture system" with "new types of concentration camps," tantamount to "colonialism and nazism" and "a constant menace to the independence and the freedom that our people has just regained after 10 years of untold sacrifice."[79] Such calumnies were no worse than what a number of radical African regimes said on a regular basis, but what followed next was more perturbing to Pretoria: "We should thus like to express our militant solidarity with the people of South Africa, led by their national liberation movement, in their courageous struggle against apartheid."[80] If the central tactic of Vorster's diplomacy was to drive a wedge between independent Africa's opposition to apartheid and its willingness to act to redress it, and post-Carnation Revolution Mozambique was a showcase for the validity of this tactic, then détente appeared to be failing.

The prospects for a Rhodesian settlement looked bleak too. Following the Victoria Falls summit, negotiations had stalled. Subsequent internal talks between Salisbury and Nkomo, with no direct South African involvement, had produced little progress. In Salisbury's view, to focus on providing for majority rule was short-sighted; what mattered was stable political development and, in its narrow and disingenuous construction, ensuring "the best possible government irrespective of color."[81] Smith continued to insist that a qualified rather than universal franchise was the only way of ensuring responsible government and avoiding "a revolutionary rather than evolutionary process."[82]

At the negotiating table, the main parties were far apart. Salisbury's position built directly upon the 1969 and 1971 Rhodesian constitutions, neither of which had been voted on by the black population. It envisaged a parliamentary system in which:

• Sixty seats were voted by and reserved for Europeans. To qualify, one needed either income of 1980 Rhodesian dollars or 3960 dollars' worth of property;

or four years of secondary education, as well as either income of 1320 dollars
or 2640 dollars' worth of property.

- Thirty seats were reserved for Africans. Some would be elected by tribal electoral colleges. Others would be elected by Africans who qualified on a separate African roll by having 660 dollars in income or 1320 dollars' worth of
  property, or two years of secondary education, as well as either 440 dollars in
  income or 880 dollars' worth of property.
- Finally, there would be up to thirty more African seats, which would be
  elected by Africans who achieved the European standards of the first electoral
  roll. The number of seats would increase over time as the number of qualified
  voters did, but to a maximum of thirty. In this way, only parity between whites
  and blacks could be achieved.[83]

After the Victoria Falls conference, Nkomo tried to work within these broad
structures. He proposed a system of three nonracial electoral rolls:

- An "A" roll of 36 seats with high qualifications, which in practice would over-
  whelmingly comprise white voters.
- A "B" roll of 72 seats with much lower qualifications.
- A "C" roll of 36 seats, based on universal suffrage, without qualifications.
  Nkomo stipulated that all Rhodesians must have a say in how the country
  was governed, even if this fell short of "one man one vote."[84]

Nkomo also maintained that the goal of any settlement had to be a form of majority rule. Smith was unreceptive, insisting that there could be no "lowering of
standards." Exasperated by Smith's continued refusal to commit to extending the
franchise to all, Nkomo told him in a heated February 1976 meeting that he was
missing "the whole point—the ANC did not accept that a citizen of Rhodesia
required extra qualifications to be a citizen."[85] By March 1976, the talks had collapsed entirely.[86] Smith told the press: "I don't believe in majority rule—black
majority rule—not in a thousand years."[87]

For Smith's adversaries, the experience only served to underscore the futility of seeking to redress the racist political systems of Southern Africa through
negotiation, right as the Angolan Civil War was illustrating the effectiveness of
the use of force and the diplomatic toxicity of cooperation with the apartheid
regime. In early 1976, the Rhodesian nationalists and Frontline Presidents were
therefore unusually united and forthright in their advocacy of military overthrow as the only remaining solution. "We were committed to the search for a
negotiated solution in Rhodesia and we have travelled the road all the way down
to Cape Town to honor the commitment," a Zambian official declared. "That
search has finished and we shall now leave no stone unturned in aiding an armed

struggle against Rhodesia."[88] Without the cooperation of Lusaka and with the relevant African states leery of working with Pretoria, it was difficult to see how détente had a future.

Vorster, however, saw much in the events surrounding Angola to validate his détente agenda and justify new efforts in that direction. Angola "was a great success for SA. We have come further in Africa than what we expected," he told caucus, extolling an improvement in Pretoria's diplomatic position on the continent.[89] "In Africa, we have built many bridges. Many of them are still standing. Our channels to Africa remain open. Africa has respect for us."[90] Other elements of the government outside Vorster's circle were just as encouraged by the behind-the-scenes support shown by moderate African states for South Africa's military involvement. At the Cabinet meeting on January 14, held just after the OAU meeting on Angola in Addis Ababa, the prevailing sentiment was not one of disappointment. Instead, the consensus was that the meeting had "gone reasonably well."[91] In Pretoria's view, South Africa had demonstrated that when it came to communist expansion in Africa, it could be relied upon to stand by its rhetoric. And judging by the OAU meeting, fully half of Africa, including key regional states like Zaïre and Zambia, appeared to have appreciated that. "Most of these [moderate] states approve—in private—of the South African presence in Angola as an opposition to Russian dominance," a Military Intelligence report observed.[92] The Broederbond Executive Council report on the Angolan intervention, based on extensive consultation with the government, reflected these views:

> A long term goal [of the intervention] was to offer proof to moderate African leaders through a positive (if limited) response to a request for help from blacks of our preparedness to offer our own lives in the interest of blacks and to confirm our reliability as an African ally. In this we apparently succeeded beyond expectations (see the vote at the Addis Ababa conference of the OAU) and it can be hoped (in spite of the unfavorable disposition of the MPLA) that the goodwill and confidence that the RSA has awakened in Africa will *in time bear more fruit*. By contrast, if we had turned a blind eye to the requests for help, we would today stand discredited among moderate African leaders.[93]

Pretoria also believed it had demonstrated through its military and political cooperation with the FNLA and UNITA one of the key principles underpinning détente: that the interests of the apartheid regime and black Africa need not by definition be mutually exclusive, and South Africa, for its part, was willing to go to considerable lengths to help achieve common goals.[94] Addressing the

Broederbond Executive Council in February, Muller explained: "From conversations with African leaders, it has become apparent that they see cooperation with SA as necessary. We have opened the road to cooperation between Black and White in Africa. We are trying to find solutions and in the process Africa has found that we can be trusted."[95]

The prospect of increased communist intervention in Southern Africa also acted as a powerful incentive for renewed détente efforts. By March 1976, Cuba had over ten thousand troops in Angola, as well as MiG aircraft and over 300 tanks.[96] The foreboding situation in Angola was accompanied by a sudden increase in militancy from Frelimo in Mozambique. The government in the newly renamed capital, Maputo, broke off bilateral contacts with Pretoria at the foreign ministry level, sending a clear signal that the uneasy post–Carnation Revolution modus vivendi was at an end.[97] Mozambique closed its border with Rhodesia, preventing trade coming through to the key port of Beira, and declared war on Salisbury.[98] An ominous BOSS report stated that hundreds of insurgents were flooding into rural Rhodesia, with more expected.[99] Most concerning of all, reports began to arrive of a sharp increase in Soviet military aid to Maputo, including T-34 and T-54 tanks—arms that could only feasibly be used in conventional warfare rather than the existing low-level guerrilla conflict.[100] In this context, Vorster was deeply concerned that communist powers might exploit the ongoing political impasse in Rhodesia to provoke a full-blown Cold War conflict in Southern Africa that the West was evidently unwilling to fight.[101] The SADF agreed. A military study of the effect of events in Angola on Rhodesia's security observed: "This Soviet and Cuban intervention has introduced a new dimension in the previously assessed threat. Whereas formerly the emphasis had been on supporting 'liberation movements,' the precedent of direct intervention by a foreign military power has now been established."[102]

For Vorster, this alarming prospect underlined the urgency of working with moderate African states in the region to promote an alternative to the insurgency, radicalism, and militancy represented by the Havana-Moscow-MPLA axis. He launched a major though unsuccessful effort to mend the relationship with Maputo,[103] while the DFA started holding discussions on a broad range of issues with the new government in Luanda.[104] As Vorster strove to repair South Africa's regional relationships, he also sought to preempt foreign involvement on the SWA issue by accelerating progress toward independence there. By early 1976, events in Angola, the prospect of a reinvigorated SWAPO, and the passing of UN Security Council Resolution 385 condemning South Africa's occupation of SWA had together highlighted the need to produce a viable, anticommunist state that would allow South Africa to divest itself of a commitment that was proving more trouble than it was worth. Since September 1975, representatives of each of SWA's designated ethnic groups had been meeting in Windhoek under South African auspices.[105] The incipient organization, known as the Turnhalle Conference, soon acquired an unlikely significance for Pretoria. "It is very necessary that the constitutional conference in SWA make swift progress," Muller told the Broederbond in February.[106] Pik Botha likewise told Kissinger in April that independence could be expected within three years, as South Africa "had no interest in keeping that territory."[107] *Verligtes* agreed. "Rhodesia and South-West soon need to find a fair dispensation for all races and nations as a foundation for national unity and stand together against the threat to freedom and democracy," *Volkshandel* opined in a major editorial on foreign policy.[108] Such views could scarcely have been farther away from those on the right-wing of Afrikaner politics.

Vorster's room for maneuver in orchestrating a settlement in SWA was circumscribed on two fronts. He had to avoid the domestic backlash that would accompany perceptions of selling out fellow whites, who overwhelmingly self-identified as Afrikaners to boot. And he had to ensure that South Africa kept a certain distance from proceedings, so that in opening the door to multiracial government, Pretoria was not seen to acquiesce to institutions and norms that it did not—and would not—allow at home.[109]

Despite the risks, Vorster soon realized that Turnhalle might be just the vehicle he needed to achieve the desired end. "Once the thing started, I think they [the South Africans] had the idea that the whole thing [Turnhalle] might work and they tried to influence it in many ways—infiltrators, and agents, and things like that," Turnhalle chairman Dirk Mudge recalls. "They tried to hijack the thing."[110] In particular, Pretoria hoped that Turnhalle would attract international legitimacy as a multiracial conduit for self-determination, which became the primary theme in official South African policy statements on SWA. Vorster told the international media: "Our attitude all along has been that Southwest Africa . . . does not belong to South Africa. . . . It belongs to the people of Southwest Africa and those peoples have the inherent right to decide their own future. They are busy at the moment doing just that."[111] At the same time, the independent state envisaged by Pretoria was transparently one in which South African interests—especially its security concerns—would be firmly safeguarded. "On the military level and the economic level, the territory will remain linked to South Africa," Muller assured the Broederbond, with understatement.[112]

South Africa's occupation of SWA and the illegal minority regime in Rhodesia were both issues of roughly equal salience on the international scene. However, Vorster had made it clear that any external assault on SWA would be treated in Pretoria as an attack on South Africa itself and resisted as such.[113] By contrast, Rhodesia's lack of international legitimacy, ongoing civil war, and weaker armed forces meant it was seen as the soft underbelly of the remaining white redoubt.

Furthermore, the Salisbury regime's control over the security situation was in sharp decline. One major SADF assessment from April 1976 concluded:

> The Rhodesian security forces are still currently in a position to control the terrorism situation. If however it is taken into account that around 4000 Security Forces members (SAP excluded) are involved in combatting around 800 terrorists, it is to be doubted whether Rhodesia can succeed in controlling a strengthened onslaught by approximately +-1000 terrorists without taking manpower out of civilian life which would be to the serious disadvantage of the domestic economy.[114]

The assessment also stressed that as the insurgency escalated, Rhodesian "hot pursuit" operations against insurgents based in other sovereign states, particularly Mozambique, might provide just the sort of pretext needed for direct Soviet and Cuban intervention.[115]

Therefore, as Vorster looked to resuscitate his détente vision, he sought to reinvolve South Africa in the negotiations over Rhodesia's future. As early as January, he had contacted Hawkins, seeking observer status in the abortive internal talks with Nkomo.[116] At the same time, Kaunda came under attack from backbenchers within his own party. They implored him to ease the country's economic plight by opening the southern border to trade with Rhodesia and South Africa.[117] Kaunda duly contacted Vorster in late February to request that South Africa reprise its power-broking role on the Rhodesian issue, and the South African prime minister responded favorably.[118] Events in Angola had heightened the expectations of African nationalists and radicalized the discourse on decolonization. However, despite his rhetoric, Kaunda's commitment to militancy was never as strong as Nyerere's or Machel's.[119] For Lusaka as for Pretoria, the prospect of an expansion of communist-backed military force in the region provided a powerful catalyst for renewed diplomatic efforts; the road from Angola to Rhodesia literally passed through Zambia.[120]

As in 1974, it was the combination of pending regional deterioration and entreaties from independent Africa that brought out the statesman in the naturally cautious Vorster. Unlike in 1974, however, the tensions and expectations were such that it was going to take more than just Zambia's and South Africa's good offices to force the disparate parties into a settlement.

A New Cold War Problem

From late February 1976, the Ford Administration also began looking at how it could prevent the Cubans and Soviets from shifting their military presence from Angola toward influencing the struggle in Rhodesia.[121] The problem was perceived quickly and clearly. If Havana and Moscow threw their weight behind the black nationalists, the United States would be left with two exceptionally unpalatable options. The first was to allow them a free hand and be perceived as powerless in the Cold War. "We must make the Soviets pay a heavy price. If the Cubans move, I recommend we act vigorously. We can't permit another move without suffering a great loss," Kissinger told the National Security Council.[122] The alternative was to confront the communist coalition and be cast as a de facto ally of white minority rule. "It must be enormously tempting to the Soviets to press for a polarization of forces in Southern Africa," Winston Lord, Director of the State Department's Policy Planning Staff, wrote. "The United States, even under the 'best' of circumstances, would hardly commit resources to support white minority regimes; in the present political atmosphere this approaches the unthinkable."[123] An interagency review of Washington's Southern Africa policy stressed that time was of the essence: "Although the Soviet-Cuban role in Angola arouses deep concerns among many African countries, it is doubtful that there would be significant African opposition to an active Soviet-Cuban role on behalf of guerrilla movements in Rhodesia or Namibia. Practically all Africans—even the most conservative—have a commitment to the struggle against the white minority regimes controlling both territories."[124] Britain saw the situation in much the same way. "I do think the Angolan episode will have encouraged the Russians and Cubans to look for other opportunities to exploit, one way or another, to their own advantage and to the discomfiture of the West," Callaghan wrote to Kissinger. "We therefore have to pre-empt them. . . . I am more than ever sure that the right course is to continue to work for an early and peaceful transfer of power to African majority rule in Rhodesia."[125] With British support, the Ford Administration resolved to orchestrate a negotiated settlement in Rhodesia.[126]

Vorster was skeptical about working with Washington again after Angola.[127] "The USA's bark, since Vietnam, is much worse than its bite," he reflected.[128] However, the Ford Administration realized that if South Africa for whatever reason did not approve of the evolution of events, it could sustain Rhodesia both militarily and economically.[129] It acknowledged that getting Pretoria on board was therefore a precondition for a successful settlement. To this end, the Administration's own blaming of Congress for Washington's failure to support Pretoria in Angola helped reestablish a basis for bilateral cooperation. "Congress is insane on this issue [US assistance in Angola]," Scowcroft bluntly told Les de Villiers, South Africa's Deputy Secretary for Information.[130] This mechanism enabled Kissinger to recultivate a sense of common geopolitical interests and shared disappointments, and then use these to repair the relationship between the Ford Administration and the Vorster government. In his meetings with Pik

Botha, he played the part masterfully: "Those bastards [the Soviets]. When I think of Angola, that was a set up. We could have so bled them."[131] He did likewise in person with Vorster later in the year:

KISSINGER: My South African colleagues had a very painful experience last year because I overestimated what we could do in Angola.
VORSTER: Hear, hear.[132]

Kissinger's first move was to summon Pik Botha to the White House to inform him of his plan for Rhodesia and to explain how the plan related to a broader recalibration of American policy on Southern Africa. In order to avoid a Cold War conflict, he said, Washington was going to launch a major diplomatic offensive aimed at forcing the capitulation of the Smith regime. The South African role that Kissinger envisaged was implied but clear: "I must be very tough on Rhodesia. . . . I get the impression your government would understand that."[133]

Over the subsequent weeks, Kissinger secured Pretoria's support in four ways. First, as the quid pro quo for Pretoria's refusal to sustain the Smith regime, Kissinger openly stated that while he would come out in favor of majority rule throughout Southern Africa, both in his speeches and in practice he would distinguish between the various polities. "I differentiate between South Africa and Rhodesia, with Namibia in between," he told the South Africans straight out.[134] It was this device that enabled Kissinger to castigate South Africa in the language necessary to win African approval of the American proposals—"Apartheid must end,"[135] he pronounced in his landmark Lusaka speech on April 27, though the *Washington Post* accurately noted that otherwise his speech "skipped lightly over South Africa"[136]—while simultaneously securing South African assistance on Rhodesia. Second, on precisely the issue on which South Africa was unwilling to compromise—apartheid—the questions of what reforms were needed and when they needed to be in place were deliberately left undefined. "I see virtually no possibility of [Vorster] agreeing to any fundamental changes in racial policies within South Africa," Bowdler had told Kissinger in no uncertain terms.[137] Kissinger therefore avoided the issue entirely. Consequently, instead of seeing Washington's new Southern African policy as encouraging the dismantling of South Africa's social order, the Vorster government perceived that by stressing the need for change in the other white-ruled territories, the new American policy reinforced the notion that multinationalism rather than racial hierarchy had to be the ordering principle of Southern Africa's politics. In this way, Washington's new approach was seen not only as being compatible with the government's separate development agenda, but even as facilitating it.[138] Third, Vorster was enticed by the prospect of further high-profile meetings with Kissinger, providing recognition of the regime's importance—and permanency—on the world stage.[139] No NP prime minister had ever met an American secretary of state. Now, a series of meetings loomed, with the first set scheduled for West Germany in June. Pretoria's delight at finally being courted by Washington was palpable. "We ha[ve] been ignored by the United States for years, but for the first time now South Africa ha[s] an opportunity to talk to them," Muller crowed to the similarly frozen-out Smith.[140] Finally, Kissinger offered Pretoria American assistance in forestalling communist intervention in Southern Africa. That assistance was only diplomatic for the moment, but the secretary of state explicitly left the door open to military involvement too:

PIK BOTHA: One thing: A Cuban invasion of Rhodesia would cause insurmountable problems for us.
KISSINGER: If that should happen, I assure you we will act.[141]

Notably, there appears to have been no real consideration by anyone within the various arms of the South African government as to whether the Ford Administration could be any more militarily effective in the region than six months earlier. Hope trumped logic. Obtaining an American commitment to defend shared "free world" interests in Southern Africa spoke directly to Afrikanerdom's increasing fears of isolation. In the aftermath of Angola, Vorster had told his caucus: "The Russians are not abandoning their plan for world domination.... The only power that can stop them is the US."[142] Kissinger's new involvement was therefore a ray of hope in an otherwise gloomy geopolitical picture.

More subtly, the insertion of American power into Southern Africa at this stage provided Vorster personally with invaluable domestic political cover. In the post–Carnation Revolution era it had taken all of his political skill and capital to convince the inherently conservative NP establishment that distancing South Africa from Rhodesia rather than galvanizing the remaining white redoubt was a necessary precondition for regional stability. Resistance to Vorster's emphasis on bridge-building and to his faith in coexistence with independent Africa on an equal footing remained strong, particularly within the military and on the party's right wing. That resistance had only strengthened since Angola. Early in the new year, Vorster's office circulated a proposal that spelled out in detail his regional vision of long-term, multiracial cooperation. The prime minister's vision entailed anticommunist Southern African states—both white and black, including the homelands—being steadily brought together through mutual economic benefit to form a NATO-style defense union, involving a common headquarters, a mutual defense pact, and troops from each country.[143] The SADF considered such an idea, though attractive, completely unfeasible in the radicalized post-Angola environment: "The difficulties involved in setting up such an arrangement would, in view of the fundamental differences between participating states, be immense. . . . Tremendous resistance from the outside world and especially the OAU could be anticipated and black member states would be subjected to great pressures."[144] Similarly, when Vorster had tried to coopt the opposition within his party by bringing it into the détente process in autumn 1976, he had little success. In March, he chose to despatch the conservative Connie Mulder to Salisbury in an effort to persuade Smith to move toward majority rule. In the event, as Smith's memoirs make clear, the two ended up getting along famously and nothing was achieved.[145]

In this context, Washington's new role meant Vorster was able to assuage the doubters' concerns by presenting South Africa's involvement in the Rhodesia negotiations as a function of the United States' renewed interest in regional stability. This new factor was pivotal in enabling the prime minister to push Smith much farther than a year earlier. As in 1974–75, Vorster committed South Africa in 1976 to applying targeted pressure to Rhodesia, while simultaneously going to great lengths to deny that he was doing so. In one such articulation of the standard line, he told the press: "We have advised, we have pointed out alternatives, we have made suggestions, but never have we prescribed or twisted Mr. Smith's arm. This attitude stands. The decision that will be taken in Rhodesia must be taken by Rhodesians."[146] The received wisdom ever since has been that such cynical protestations of noninterference were "just for public consumption," in one scholar's phrase.[147] Yet Vorster's public line was indistinguishable from what he repeatedly told the Cabinet and caucus: "South Africa's position remains unchanged, that it is not prepared to exercise pressure on Rhodesia. South Africa has not pressed or influenced Rhodesia to hold negotiations."[148]

In fact, Vorster's insistence on South Africa's noninterference in the long-running Rhodesian negotiations was just as much designed to provide himself with cover against political opposition as it was to insulate his innovative diplomacy from the vicissitudes of South African public opinion. Within the party, Treurnicht and his followers were opposed to any alteration to the Verwoerdian model of white regional dominance, *baasskap* in a new guise. They were always going to be implacable, to be overcome rather than persuaded. The leaders of the two largest caucuses in the NP's federal structure—the Cape and the Transvaal—were a different matter. It was common knowledge that P. W. Botha's solution for the predicament in which South Africa found itself was preemptive forward defense, at the Zambezi if necessary. For his part, Mulder's prescription amounted to more aggressive marketing of the virtues of separate development through his Department of Information, coupled with negligible changes at home, whether in petty apartheid or (as Vorster advocated) in ideology and identity. Vorster therefore developed a new strategy to neutralize and blunt their opposition. He opted to exclude both from the 1976 negotiations, instead working closely through his foreign policy brains trust of Fourie, Muller, and van den Bergh; use his meetings with Kissinger to boost his own personal prestige and thereby neutralize opposition within the party; and simply pretend that the real pressure for a settlement was coming from the Americans rather than from him, with South Africa's cooperation presented to his colleagues as a prerequisite for the longed-for rapprochement with Washington. In this way, not only did the Ford Administration ask of South Africa what Vorster was fully prepared to deliver—pressure on Salisbury and independence for SWA—it even helped him domestically to do so.

Détente II

In all other respects, however, Vorster's task in seeking a Rhodesian settlement was more difficult in 1976 than it had been in 1974–75. As before, Pretoria had to encourage the intransigent Smith regime to accept a transfer of power from the white minority to some form of pluralism that would inevitably entail rule by the black majority. Nothing else would be acceptable abroad and get Rhodesia off the international agenda. As previous experience showed, this would be hard enough. However, Angola had raised African expectations and radicalized the entire discourse on decolonization. In 1974–75, Vorster had viewed a settlement as an opportunity. By 1976, it was a necessity. He was caught between the urgency of producing a settlement before regional tensions escalated and the imperative of avoiding Smith's replacement by radicals who might provide safe havens for revolutionary cadres bent on the Republic's overthrow, or even invite military support on their behalf from extracontinental communist powers. For South Africa, the margin for error had narrowed substantially. Vorster had to be careful not to encourage a hasty transfer on terms that overly disadvantaged whites and moderate blacks and instead facilitated the emergence of a radical government on its borders. He had to press Salisbury hard enough to avoid ending up with a settlement that was so belated that in the interim moderates would be discredited and militants strengthened.[149] And he had to avoid undermining Salisbury to the point where radical insurgents took over by military rather than constitutional means, thereby lending a further boost to the cause of militant decolonization. In sum, South Africa's interest in 1976 lay in sustaining Salisbury's viability just enough to conclude a reasonable settlement, but not so much that it could hold out indefinitely. This was always going to be a delicate balance to achieve.

The likelihood of an escalation in Rhodesia and the possibility of communist intervention had also narrowed Vorster's room to maneuver on the domestic front. As in 1974–75, Vorster was all too aware of the need to avoid the impression among his white electorate that South Africa was selling out the Rhodesians. As he told Bowdler, if "white women and children were being slaughtered," he "would be under intense pressure to intervene in Rhodesia."[150] In order to ensure that Salisbury ceased procrastinating, South Africa had to forswear the prospect of intervening militarily on behalf of the white Rhodesians. However, as Vorster candidly told his Cabinet in early March, this was a contingency he could not actually rule out: "We have informed Rhodesia that in the event of war, they must work on the assumption that they are alone. The more difficult decision for the Government is however whether South Africa CAN stay out if Rhodesia gets involved in war."[151]

The final obstacle, as ever, was Smith himself. By 1976, Vorster was exceptionally frustrated by Smith's refusal to yield to the inevitability of a transfer of power. "The Rhodesians know what cards are on the table," he told Brand Fourie in March. "They must get on and play the hand accordingly."[152] In a long briefing on regional policy the same month, Vorster began to take the caucus into his confidence to build support for a more concerted approach on Rhodesia. "We have held Mr. Smith's hand. He is, however, not an easy person to deal with. . . . He has achieved nothing and lost a great deal," he told the party room with candor. "We have told Smith that if he seeks out the warpath, he will have to walk it alone."[153] Yet the Rhodesian prime minister continued to see détente as little short of appeasement of the common Marxist foe and a recipe for disaster for both regimes.[154] He told the South Africans that they had an "emotional obsession with détente" and howled that "détente had been elevated to the status of a sacred cow and no criticism of it was tolerated."[155] Smith was astounded that Pretoria continued to provide only lukewarm support to Salisbury even after détente had so visibly failed at Victoria Falls.[156] Moreover, the Rhodesians were fully aware of the sympathies of South Africa's white populace and also knew from their frequent liaisons with the SADF that South Africa's security establishment was far from on board with Vorster's foreign policies.[157] For all these reasons, Smith still refused to believe that when the decisive moment arrived, Vorster would actually pull the trigger.[158] The Rhodesian leader reflected in his memoirs: "It was unrealistic to me to believe that Vorster would go so far as to attempt to jettison us, to use us as the sacrificial lamb for some end which could only be speculative and might end, like all his previous efforts, in disaster. However, I was wrong."[159]

7

Dr. Kissinger, I Presume?

The 1976 Initiatives

At the end of April, American Secretary of State Henry Kissinger delivered the Lusaka Address, seemingly heralding a reversal of Washington's long neglect of both Africa and the issue of majority rule.[1] No sooner had he done so than Pretoria announced an end to additional military aid to Rhodesia—a clear signal to Salisbury (and the Frontline states of Tanzania, Mozambique, Botswana, Angola, and Zambia) that the American initiative had prima facie South African support.[2] Over the subsequent weeks, Smith repeatedly sought a meeting with Vorster. But the South African prime minister kept his distance, presumably hoping time and isolation would help his counterpart realize that a transfer of power at last had to be effected.[3]

Finally, ten days before he was due to meet with Kissinger in West Germany, Vorster invited Smith to Libertas, the official prime ministerial residence in Pretoria. He again tried to convince the Rhodesian leader that a settlement was in his own best interests. Vorster "pointed out the alternatives" once more, repeatedly suggesting that Smith preempt an escalation of the insurgency and avoid the prospect of Soviet or Cuban intervention by offering the black population a better deal at the negotiating table. He also issued a stern warning about the dangers of conducting cross-border operations into Mozambique, which increased the risk of escalation and attracted negative publicity internationally. Smith was as inflexible as ever. He maintained that the insurgency was well under control; the only acceptable solution was an orderly transfer to responsible majority rule (that is, a qualified franchise); no real progress in the negotiations could be obtained until the insurgency had first come to a halt; his government was actually attracting steadily increasing levels of black support; and "the alternative to what he was trying to do was a certain communist take-over."[4] The regime, he improbably assured his South African counterpart, "could go on indefinitely, as it was not on the verge of collapse."[5]

An exasperated Vorster asked Smith to give him something tangible to take to Kissinger. Under Smith's plans, what would "responsible government" look like? What specific voting arrangements would be acceptable? And most importantly, what sort of time period was Salisbury willing to accept for a transfer of power? The questions came thick and fast, but Smith steadfastly avoided providing any concrete answers that might limit his scope for negotiation in the future. For Pretoria, Lusaka, and Washington alike, the threat of expanded communist intervention in Rhodesia may have served as a powerful incentive for a settlement, but for Salisbury, events in Angola had merely made the consequences of hastily agreeing to an unfavorable settlement all too real. "Premature handover to black government would make Angolan-type chaos certain with ZANU enjoying full Marxist backing and RSA as hamstrung as they are in Angola," Jack Gaylard told Harold Hawkins. "Continuing white government is the only insurance against that situation."[6] The Rhodesians also saw American involvement as a valuable new factor in the equation, one that would increase the resonance of their anticommunist message and strengthen their hand at the negotiating table.[7] The tense and unproductive meeting between Vorster and Smith only served to expose the chasm between the two regimes' priorities in any Rhodesian settlement. Brand Fourie recalled that so little had been agreed upon during the meeting that the ensuing press release noted only that "[t]he two prime ministers had discussed the situation in Southern Africa."[8] The experience was a timely reminder for Vorster of the scale of the challenge he had before him.

Meeting Kissinger

Reminded of just how difficult it was going to be to convince Smith to abnegate power, Vorster traveled to meet Kissinger in West Germany over June 23 and 24. In addition to two private meetings with the secretary of state, at which no minutes were apparently taken, two plenary sessions were held.[9] The first of these focused on Rhodesia; the second, held the next morning and considerably shorter, on SWA. The encounters, held in the Bavarian villages of Bodenmais and Grafenau in an effort to avoid anti-apartheid protesters, were surreal. They produced a large amount of substantive progress; featured lengthy iterations of the unique Nationalist view of Southern African politics and history, punctuated by the prime minister's idiosyncratic humor and homespun wisdom; and took place in an unmistakably convivial atmosphere, replete with banter and jokes from both sides. "The rapport established between Vorster and Kissinger was quite remarkable," recalled Donald Sole, present as South Africa's Ambassador to West Germany.[10] At no stage did Kissinger criticize apartheid or suggest that

Figure 7.1 In June 1976, American secretary of state Henry Kissinger invited John Vorster to Bavaria, West Germany, to discuss the future of Rhodesia and South-West Africa. With Kissinger uninterested in talking about South Africa's domestic situation, the two men got on famously. Source: National Party.

separate development was not sustainable. Instead, he simply sought—and obtained—Pretoria's support for his Southern Africa plan.

As for Vorster, he had five aims in West Germany and achieved all of them. First, he wanted to emphasize the strength and resilience of the Salisbury regime to Kissinger, who saw a sharply deteriorating situation in Rhodesia. "They [the Rhodesians] can liquidate the terrorists, and they're doing quite well," Vorster purred.[11] Based on his dismissive attitude toward Smith's similar arguments just ten days earlier in Pretoria, such statements went far beyond what Vorster believed to be true. He was exaggerating in order to persuade the Americans that Salisbury was not on the verge of collapse and therefore would not accept any deal that was too unfavorable to white Rhodesians. Second, Vorster sought to emphasize Pretoria's indispensability to any settlement: "You have to realize it was South Africa that brought them [Salisbury and the nationalists] together and South Africa that created the climate. Kaunda asked us to get Nkomo and Sithole out of detention. We did it. We arranged the meeting at the bridge and we provided the amenities at the bridge. I brought Smith and Kaunda together for the first time since 1962. Everything they've [the parties] asked us to do, we've done."[12] Far from being coerced, Vorster was eager to get involved. Third, he wanted to see exactly what framework Kissinger planned to utilize to produce a settlement. He must have been elated to find that the Americans did not want him to take the lead in effecting Smith's downfall. "Majority rule was in their opinion unavoidable and it was for Mr. Smith to decide whether he wanted to bring it about himself," Fourie, present at the meetings, recalled.[13] Fourth, Vorster wanted more meetings with Kissinger in order to gain international respectability.[14] Securing the limelight was crucial not only to halting the ongoing deterioration of South Africa's international reputation, but also to bolstering his own credentials within his party. Finally, and most importantly, Vorster wanted concrete progress toward a Rhodesian settlement amenable to South Africa. This last was achieved with remarkable speed and ruthlessness, as Kissinger and Vorster quickly came to an understanding to help the supposedly pro-Western Nkomo take over. This understanding included a package of financial aid and property rights designed to encourage the white community to stay, thereby contributing to the economic viability and stability of the new state. The package was a key ingredient for the South Africans, who were keenly aware that any premature suggestion that they were preparing to ditch Smith without adequate guarantees for the whites would prove explosive within the electorate. "Our people are very emotional about Rhodesia," Muller pointed out. "Once this issue gets into the emotional field and I play it wrongly, I'm out," Vorster bluntly concurred.[15]

Vorster ultimately agreed to use his influence with Smith so long as a suitable package could be designed. However, the South Africans repeatedly emphasized that while the details of such guarantees were still being figured out, secrecy was vital. "It's absolutely essential this be kept quiet," Pik Botha stressed.[16] "If anything leaks beforehand to suggest that Vorster is preparing to sell out Smith, the South Africans say the whole deal is off," Kissinger reported back to Ford after the meetings in West Germany.[17] This suited Washington just fine. For their own domestic reasons, the Americans were hardly keen to have the arrangement with the South Africans publicized either.[18] Moreover, it was important to Kissinger's overall strategy that South Africa's acquiescence be seen to be outstanding, thereby comprising a bargaining chip that he could use to urge cooperation from independent Africa later.[19]

As Vorster returned from West Germany, Salisbury strove frantically to find out what had transpired in the meetings with Kissinger. At the first of two post-summit meetings with Hawkins, Fourie concealed that Vorster and Kissinger had essentially come to an agreement to support Nkomo. The talks, he said, had been merely "exploratory." The veteran Secretary for Foreign Affairs then crafted something of a "good cop, bad cop" scenario, in which it was the United States, rather than South Africa, that was insisting on Salisbury taking substantive steps toward majority rule. He (accurately) related that Vorster had put Rhodesia's position to the Americans, namely, that Salisbury had enjoyed substantial successes against the insurgency and it should never be forgotten that "the aftermath of a terrorist victory, or of a poor settlement, would be economic chaos and a break down of law and order." However, Fourie continued, "the points made by Vorster did not have any great impact."[20] Instead, Kissinger—whose position Fourie described as "amazingly tough and utterly cynical"[21]—had insisted that the only means of averting an escalated conflict was substantive and immediate movement by Salisbury toward majority rule.

The ploy worked. With no equivocation, Hawkins relayed to Salisbury: "The Americans had emphasized they were not prepared in any circumstances to come in on our side. They believed the only way to avoid chaos and to thwart Marxist ambitions was for us to come to a quick solution to our constitutional problems ourselves. . . . They had said again and again the only way to avoid chaos was for us to reach a solution."[22] Pretoria had tried for two years to persuade Salisbury to take what it saw as a realistic approach to negotiating Rhodesia's future. Now, it was shamelessly coopting Washington's substantial diplomatic heft to push Salisbury in the desired direction. In a second meeting with Hawkins a week later, Fourie spelled out the way forward. Observing that "the [Kissinger] initiative represented the very last chance for Rhodesia," he encouraged Salisbury to open negotiations with Nkomo. "This would be [the] only hope for [a] settlement of our own making," a resigned Hawkins cabled home.[23]

This became a central tactic for Vorster over the ensuing months. Despite having been burned by America during the Angolan Civil War, he enthusiastically supported Washington's efforts to engineer a transfer of power in Rhodesia and construct a framework for independence in SWA. Observers thought he did so to avoid American interference in the apartheid program. Scholars have likewise perceived American leverage at work, even speculating that Kissinger had manipulated the gold market to bring Vorster on board.[24] However, far from being coerced, Vorster was just as eager for settlements in Rhodesia and SWA as the Americans. He therefore not only fell into Washington's slipstream and let Kissinger make the running for him, but also exploited America's involvement to neutralize the opposition that had plagued his plans in 1974–75.

The meetings in West Germany also yielded substantial progress on SWA. Unlike on Rhodesia, Pretoria was eager to take a visible role in designing a stable settlement in SWA, and was already doing so. "The big difference from Rhodesia is that [Vorster] is in the driver's seat," Bowdler noted in one cable. "[T]he [Turnhalle] conference is so structured that by proxy nothing will be decided that is not generally acceptable to him."[25] However, Turnhalle was substantially

Figure 7.2 Observers believed that John Vorster cooperated with the Kissinger Initiatives to deflect American pressure over apartheid. Instead, Vorster utilized Kissinger's high profile and diplomatic heft to help him bypass domestic opposition to pursuing his preexisting goals of multiracial settlements in Rhodesia and South-West Africa.

Source: Johannesburg *Star*. Independent Media.

hampered by its lack of international acceptance. It featured representatives from no fewer than eleven designated ethnic groups; the paramountcy of group rights and the importance of separate ethnic identities were concepts as diffi-cult to transcend in SWA as they were in South Africa. However, whites formed the dominant faction and drove the agenda. As for the non-white groups, "most of the representatives were indoctrinated homeland leaders and well dis-posed toward the South African government," Mudge reflected.[26] Pretoria also liaised frequently with Mudge's white delegation so as to protect South African interests.

Accordingly, the international community saw Turnhalle as essentially Pretoria's puppet. It demanded the inclusion in any independence process of SWAPO, whom the OAU and the UN had designated the sole legitimate rep-resentatives of the SWA people. However, the South Africans were implaca-bly opposed to the participation of what they saw as a Marxist terrorist group with no domestic legitimacy. The NP cultivated a SWAPO creation myth that focused heavily on the role of white communists in the movement's foundation; just months before, Vorster had referred to SWAPO as being "born in communist sin."[27] Equally, the Nationalists saw SWAPO's claim to represent everyone in SWA-Namibia as ample proof that it represented no one nation or people; it therefore could scarcely be a legitimate political actor in a world of nation-states. Vorster held a personal repugnance of the organization that transcended the usual South African hostility to communism. In an interview with the SABC, the prime minister's loathing of SWAPO and its leader, Sam Nujoma, was unmistakable:

> [Nujoma] is not an elected leader of SWA, he is not even a genuine leader of SWA and SWAPO is but one of twenty or more political parties which do not enjoy majority support in SWA, but rather who enjoy minority support in SWA. One must clap one's hands together that a body like the UN can take it upon themselves to say that a specific organization and a specific person is the organization and the man to whom SWA must be entrusted.[28]

Thus while SWAPO's inclusion remained taboo for Pretoria, its exclusion all but guaranteed that a resulting settlement would lack international acceptance. What one side saw as a deal-breaker, the other saw as a sine qua non, hardly a recipe for a successful settlement.

Washington's involvement offered a way out of this impasse. The United States sought much the same moderate and stable government in Windhoek that South Africa desired.[29] It also needed Pretoria's cooperation on Rhodesia. Washington therefore resolved both to allow South Africa a free hand on SWA and to work behind the scenes to secure international support for the process, thereby offering Pretoria an alternative route to legitimacy.[30] Kissinger told Vorster in West Germany: "I couldn't care less whether [the new state is] unitary or federal. Whatever is internationally accepted, we'll accept. . . . We have no fixed ideas about how the constitution is drafted, as long as it leads to independence."[31] Kissinger was more concerned with the appearance of a democratic or at least pluralist process rather than the reality. However, he made it clear to Vorster that concessions would need to be made on South Africa's part to achieve international acceptance. Specifically, Turnhalle would need to convene outside of SWA or South Africa in order to appear independent of Pretoria, while SWAPO would need to be included in some form.[32] Pretoria balked at both proposals. However, Vorster realized that while the Ford Administration would allow South Africa substantial control over the independence process, all indications were that if Jimmy Carter were elected, he would seek direct UN involvement and a much more prominent role for SWAPO.[33] Vorster was therefore receptive to both of Kissinger's suggestions.

"Not a nightmare which will disappear"

These behind-the-scenes discussions over the future of white rule in Southern Africa played out against a dramatic backdrop: on June 16, systematic repression gave way to wholescale rebellion in the Soweto township. Over the subsequent weeks and months, unrest spread rapidly to other urban areas, where it was met with a violent crackdown.[34] The sudden, spiraling chaos caught the government off-guard. Just the month before, Manie Mulder, chairman of the West Rand Administration Board (and Connie's brother), had reassured the media that "the broad masses of Soweto are perfectly content, perfectly happy. Black-white relationships at present are as healthy as can be. There is no danger whatsoever of a blow-up in Soweto."[35] The regime had also somewhat recovered from the fallout from the intervention in Angola and was looking ahead with cautious optimism. Just the day before, Vorster had briefed his caucus on what he saw as a critical turning point in the fortunes of the *volk*. The Transkei was about to become independent. This would allow the regime to finally display the feasibility and virtue of the much-maligned separate development model. Simultaneously, Washington needed the regime's help, seemingly highlighting Pretoria's centrality to Africa's future. The timing could scarcely have been more fortuitous, extolled the impassioned prime minister to his caucus. "This is where we want to be, [at the center of] the world's attention. We have never had such good publicity," he said. "We did not arrange it so. Someone higher than us made it so." The regime was on the verge of great success, Vorster concluded. "There is hope for the future."[36]

Within just twenty-four hours, this remarkable optimism had dissolved as events buried the Nationalist pretension that the grand apartheid vision was moral, just, and wanted by blacks. "One thing should be abundantly clear. South Africa can never be the same again," declared a newly ebullient *World*. "By its divisionary nature the present policy of separate development creates mistrust and does very little to eliminate tension among the various race groups." What was needed, the newspaper suggested, was a jettisoning of the homeland framework in favor of convening "an immediate national conversation" representing all of South Africa's peoples.[37] Moreover, the uncompromising international response to South Africa's subsequent ruthless crackdown, culminating in unanimous UN Security Council condemnation, underscored Pretoria's status as a pariah in the global community. The regime was under a level of global pressure not experienced since the Sharpeville massacres sixteen years earlier.

How these events affected the regime's long-term viability was the subject of a post–winter break Cabinet meeting on August 3, one of the most crucial in Vorster's twelve-year tenure as prime minister. The unusually detailed minutes provide a unique window onto the intellectual debate within the corridors of power in Pretoria over how the apartheid regime might secure its future.

The atmosphere in the Cabinet room was very tense. South Africa's leaders were plainly worried that they were on the brink of losing control entirely, none more so than the prime minister. The meeting quickly agreed on a predictable crackdown at home. "Domestic order must be maintained," Vorster summed up. There could be "no more Sowetos." But what about the bigger picture, long-term viability for the *volk*? The Cabinet saw the challenge before South Africa as an integrated one, with internal unrest intimately interconnected with the negotiations with the Americans, regional security, and the separate development state-building agenda. Vorster insisted that his grand plan remained viable and that movement on Rhodesia and SWA remained prudent policy. The nation was indeed subject to "icy winds," he told his colleagues, but "[w]e must not become panic stricken, or take crisis decisions."[38] His basic argument that settlements could lead to long-term regional stability stood on two pillars: first, that South Africa's cooperation would be seen by the international community, and Africa in particular, as proof of the regime's ability to be a constructive force on the world stage; and second, that the new majority black governments in Salisbury and Windhoek, having seen first-hand the benefits of working with the apartheid state, would not promptly turn around and help undermine the regime themselves. By reinforcing the breadth and depth of anti-apartheid sentiment in the world, recent events had gravely undermined the credibility of both notions.

The prime minister proceeded to handle the situation deftly, turning the crisis to his advantage. Prior to the meeting, he had circulated a key cable that he had just received from Pik Botha in New York. Botha's "Long Telegram" constituted a seven-page wake-up call explaining South Africa's position in the post-Soweto international environment.[39] This cable constitutes perhaps the most comprehensive and considered assessment of how South Africa's renewed isolation in the post-1976 environment was understood at the highest levels of the apartheid regime. As a rule, Vorster's ministers had very little experience of international affairs or feel for global events. In contrast, Pik Botha had been a diplomat for most of the previous sixteen years. He was worldly and well read. Though the rising star of the party was widely mistrusted in *verkrampte* circles for his free-thinking ways and pragmatic instincts (and valued by Vorster for the same reasons), his knowledge of international affairs relative to other party members' was unquestioned.

Pik Botha recalls that the aim of the Long Telegram was to "suggest which national and international activities or actions will give us the best chance to survive. . . . What we can do to avoid the actions against us while we still have the power to take the decisions to avert our own destruction."[40] The tone was suitably bleak and direct. He reported that following the UN Security Council's post-Soweto resolution, South Africa was in dire straits. Pretoria had to face up to the full extent of global opposition to its system: "Even among those who believe that our internal order can be maintained, there is nevertheless a fear that repetitions of Soweto will soon lead to international sanctions. . . . A final warning has now been issued to us."[41] Moreover, Botha emphasized, whatever lingering hope there was in Pretoria that the United States would come to South Africa's rescue in the case of a Cold War conflict had to be jettisoned. A more realistic appraisal of American attitudes and politics should be adopted:

> The current American government is seemingly the only Western government which still displays a willingness, however vague, to consider as a possibility a political solution in the Republic which is not necessarily based on one man one vote. A new USA government under Carter will not support such a favorable policy which is not based on [the] political integration [of ethnic or racial groups]. We are now reaching the stage, therefore, where we are not only not going to have any support for our policy, but when it is actively combatted by the whole world.[42]

Botha's message was unmistakably ominous: "It is my considered opinion, based on personal knowledge and evaluation over a period of 16 years that the above explanation is a realistic analysis of what stands right in front of us [*onmiddellik voor die deur*]. It is not a nightmare which will disappear. It is the harsh reality of waking up."[43] All of this, Botha concluded purposefully, underscored the urgency of prompt progress in the ongoing regional negotiations. South Africa could "buy a little time to control our domestic situation only if we can cold-bloodedly and urgently get rid of the Rhodesian and SWA problems."[44]

This was precisely the argument advanced by Vorster early on in the Cabinet meeting, setting the tone for the subsequent discussion. Through facilitating settlements in Rhodesia and SWA, he declared, "We can buy time to see through the implementation of the [separate development] policy." Emphases and approaches differed, but his Cabinet colleagues concurred overall. Even the hardline Mulder, though skeptical as to whether South Africa's post-Soweto international position was quite as grim as Pik Botha had suggested, recognized that South Africa "had to dispose of [the] Rhodesian and SWA issues. . . . [I]n Rhodesia a moderate government of white and black had to be formed. This applies to SWA too." P. W. Botha also eventually supported the prevailing consensus, though without enthusiasm. "We must find a solution for the Rhodesian question," the defense minister parroted. "We must buy time."[45]

Figure 7.3 In 1976, Pretoria's doves fought one last rearguard action aimed at securing international legitimacy for the white polity. Although he had only recently joined the team, the young, dynamic Pik Botha soon took on a leading role. From left to right, a visibly ailing John Vorster, Pik Botha, Brand Fourie, and Hilgard Muller. Hendrik van den Bergh is absent, presumably busy suppressing the uprisings sweeping through South Africa's townships. Source: South Africa Department of Information.

On the surface, Vorster had skillfully coopted Pik Botha's expert and independent analysis to gain support for his diplomatic agenda and preempt opposition amongst his colleagues. Yet upon closer inspection, there was in fact little resolution of the underlying differences within the Cabinet over the direction and focus of South Africa's geopolitics. The hawks, for instance, read Botha's cable very differently. In the middle section of the Long Telegram, the ambassador had asserted that the UN resolution served to confirm both that most African states accepted that the Soviet Union and its satellites would provide the manpower and equipment to combat majority rule in Southern Africa and that there were "clear and even eager" indications coming from Moscow that it was prepared to fulfill these expectations.[46] Noting that P. W. Botha and Magnus Malan had told him that South Africa could not withstand a conventional assault along the entirety of its borders, the ambassador reasoned: "There is no doubt that the Russians are aware of this, that they are planning such an assault under the pretext of the African clarion call [*Afrika wekroep*] and that they have considered that the West, including the USA, will not come to help South Africa. This is the reality which we now must stare in the face and [which] within the next few months will be put into action."[47] Such predictions of impending Soviet penetration into Southern Africa were predictably seized upon by the hawks.[48] Military Intelligence's analysis of Botha's cable focused entirely on his characterization of an opportunist Soviet Union exploiting local liberation movements, neighboring black states, political and economic crises, and international incidents to further its influence in the region and ultimately provide a pretext for direct intervention.[49]

Thus, although Pik Botha and Vorster saw Soweto and the resulting international obloquy as reinforcing the need for immediate progress on SWA and Rhodesia, South Africa's hawks saw in events a confirmation of the need for a strengthening of conventional security measures. Never one to miss an opportunity, P. W. Botha promptly informed Cabinet that in the new climate "South Africa had additional defense problems along its borders which must be defended."[50] Although numerous budget increases had been approved over the previous months, Botha nevertheless asserted that "[t]he Defense budget is R200 million too little" and "if the R200m is not forthcoming" then the military's "preparedness on land and in the air" would be compromised.[51] For years, he had tried to draw attention to South Africa's strategic vulnerability and seek approval for increased funding and responsibilities for the military. Often, he had been ignored. How times had changed. At the August 3 meeting, four more ministers openly echoed his call for stronger defenses. These included three senior figures: Louwrens Muller, Deputy Leader of the Cape NP and a very close ally of the minister for defense; Jimmy Kruger, Minister for Police, a hardline *verkrampte* supporter of Mulder and a member of the Transvaal NP; and S. P. "Fanie" Botha, a *verligte* Transvaler who would run against Mulder from the left in the contest for the NP leadership in September 1978. Evidently, policy was more of a coagulant in this unlikely coalition than politics. Through his advocacy of total onslaught, Botha had effectively monopolized the conceptual framework for the long-time Nationalist proclivity for externalizing opposition to the regime as a communist project. Now, in a moment of crisis, Botha's assertive, radical prescriptions were finding a warm reception from right across the Nationalist spectrum.

Enthusiasm for Vorster's détente endeavors within the Cabinet therefore coexisted uneasily with the desire for stronger conventional defense measures. For the time being, both could be pursued. This was the compromise course that Vorster followed in the wake of Angola to maintain Cabinet support for his détente diplomacy; hence the large increases in the defense budget during the first half of 1976.[52] But the two policies in fact represented fundamentally divergent approaches to the security challenges that South Africa faced. One approach was constructive, cooperative, and multilateral, the other assertive, defiant, and unilateral. One was derived from the idea that South Africa could change the world's views of apartheid and ultimately erode international hostility; the other saw little point in trying. And as long as the prospect of successful, completed settlements in Rhodesia and SWA seemed nebulous, the Cabinet was decidedly ambivalent over the feasibility of the diplomatic route and reticent to apply the requisite serious pressure on Smith and the SWA whites.

That ambivalence was not restricted to the Cabinet. In winter 1977, Broederbond Chairman Gerrit Viljoen, a close ally of P. W. Botha, wrote a circular to the Bond chapters. Drawing on briefings from "government figures," the *verligte* Viljoen explained and endorsed Vorster's renewed effort at reshaping South Africa's regional context: "We must not subordinate *our* interests to those of Rhodesia, however tight the ties between us might otherwise be." However, the arguments mustered behind this position were of two distinctly different types. Vorster's unique brand of idealism was not overlooked. Rhodesia comprised "a painful dilemma," Viljoen wrote, but those African leaders who were prepared to acknowledge that Afrikaners "had a right to exist as an African *volk*" nevertheless saw the white governments in SWA and Rhodesia as "colonial remnants." This argument, however, featured less prominently than the rationales of hard-headed realism, articulated in emotive tropes. A move on Rhodesia was necessary "to try to keep the wolf from the door" and prepare for a "hot confrontation" when it eventually materialized, Viljoen stressed.[53] The language in which the policy of regional settlements was sold to Afrikanerdom had shifted from the inexorable optimism of summer 1974–75.

Vorster nevertheless pressed on. With renewed though hardly fulsome Cabinet approval for his strategy for the regime's survival, he decided to withdraw South Africa's air crews from Rhodesia, which were integral to Salisbury's counterinsurgency efforts.[54] The Rhodesians were piqued rather than persuaded. The South Africans had told them nothing of the details of the Kissinger Plan. All they knew was that Kissinger had declared his support for the British timetable of independence within two years, which seemed incompatible with Salisbury's own insistence on an "evolutionary" transition. It was becoming clear to Salisbury that what Kissinger was proposing was to be a diktat; Hawkins could only plead with Fourie that it was "obscene to discuss our proposed fate without our participation."[55]

The Rhodesians responded by taking matters into their own hands in an effort to torpedo the emerging diplomatic momentum. On August 9, Rhodesian forces destroyed a major insurgent camp at Nyadzonya in Mozambique. Perhaps over eight hundred guerrillas, including twenty-eight Frelimo fighters, were killed.[56] Pretoria was enraged.[57] In just the past few months, Vorster, Fourie, and van den Bergh had each stressed to the Rhodesians the need to refrain from controversial cross-border actions.[58] Although the operation had clearly been meticulously coordinated, the Rhodesians claimed it had been a "hot pursuit" raid rather than a cross-border attack and, as such, was not covered by their prior assurances of restraint.[59] Moreover, Hawkins reminded Fourie, the Nyadzonya operation "closely paralleled the recent attack by RSA forces against the SWAPO base camp in Zambia, and other hot pursuit operations carried out by them."[60] He spelled out the corollary: "If we were to concede the principle that we could not hit back at our attackers in hot pursuit we would be crippled. . . . Furthermore, a precedent would be set that would certainly be applied against South Africa in due course."[61]

Rhodesia's intransigence only strengthened Vorster's resolve. Just as Vorster never understood Smith, the Rhodesian leader never grasped that it was clear setbacks that brought the defiant gambler out of the naturally cautious South African prime minister. Vorster immediately instructed Pik Botha to work with Kissinger on the wording of a public statement indicating South African support for the Kissinger Initiatives.[62] Just four days after the Nyadzonya attack, on August 13, Muller read from the supplied script at the annual Natal NP congress in Durban. "[A]lthough it is not for the South African government to determine how the problem should be tackled and solved, I want to declare once again that the South African Government welcomes this initiative and that we are prepared to comply with the request to demonstrate our commitment to Africa by giving our full support for a peaceful outcome."[63] Muller's speech had the desired effect. The South African diplomatic mission cabled from Salisbury: "We believe that the overall impression left here by Dr. Muller's speech is that South Africa regarded a settlement as urgent and that Rhodesia could not rely on South Africa much longer to sustain it in the absence of progress toward a settlement."[64] Salisbury was finally getting the message that Pretoria was serious about prompt progress toward majority rule.

Vorster's Comeback

By September, Kissinger had laid the groundwork and was ready to bring the various stakeholders together. His strategy was to first draw the various parties—the UK, the Frontline states, Rhodesia, and South Africa—into a loose agreement, and then use their support to bring Salisbury and the nationalists to the negotiating table, where they could hammer out the details. Kissinger told Pik Botha: "My experience in negotiation is, once the parties have made the decision to settle, they have [a] vested interest in settling the details. If they haven't agreed to settle, every detail is insuperable."[65] Swift progress was vital. With presidential elections in November, the Ford Administration might not be in office in a few months' time. Whatever momentum had been built up could not be allowed to dissipate. And with South Africa finally on board, progress in the negotiations over Rhodesia, so often elusive and illusory, suddenly seemed within reach. At the same time, the parties realized that in the post-Soweto environment Pretoria's support was tenuous. In a conversation with British Foreign Secretary Tony Crosland, Kissinger mused:

> Is his [Vorster's] domestic situation strong enough? Especially because some in his country can plausibly say his getting into this negotiation has weakened his situation in South Africa. In June [that is, before Soweto] my argument to him was that this would buy him time for his own problems. I can't tell him this now.[66]

As a British adviser pointed out to the secretary of state, South Africa had just received television. Images of the "kidnapping and killing of white women" in a lawless Rhodesian transition would rapidly corrode public support for South Africa's role and make Vorster's cooperation untenable.[67]

With such issues in mind, Vorster and Kissinger met again in Zurich in early September.[68] Kissinger outlined the details of the package for the Rhodesian whites. Existing land ownership rights would be protected. If citizens wished to sell their homes or farms they would be able to sell them to a public authority underwritten by an international Zimbabwe Adjustment Fund for a percentage of their preindependence market value. That percentage would rise every year for five (later adjusted to ten) years, a clear incentive to remain in the new Zimbabwe. Vorster approved; the package was just what he needed to sell the deal to his domestic electorate.

The meeting was not, however, without its surprises. Vorster was under the impression that South Africa would move last in Kissinger's choreographed initiative; that is, the African presidents were to have signed onto the Kissinger Plan before he persuaded Smith to accept it. The secretary of state instead stipulated that Vorster secure "99 per cent" of Smith's agreement first. For all his frustration with Smith and the urgency of avoiding a major Cold War conflict on his borders, Vorster still had serious reservations about taking on the role of Salisbury's executioner as opposed to facilitating an international process.[69] He told Kissinger: "[W]e cannot be seen to be deposing Ian Smith. The Rhodesians can depose him but not us.... [I]t's immoral for me to do it."[70] Morality aside, Vorster knew that given *verkrampte* sentiment it might well prove political suicide. Kissinger assuaged Vorster's concerns by appealing to the bigger picture— and by issuing a crucial, implicit, but hollow assurance:

> What we're doing is preventing Communist foreign penetration into Rhodesia.... If the war continues, even a Rhodesian victory has the paradoxical consequences that it brings nearer foreign intervention, which we won't be able to resist, given our domestic situation.... [But] If we have brought majority rule, with British cooperation, and there is still foreign intervention, then it's not in the name of white against black.[71]

The implication was clear: if communist intervention occurred against a predominantly black, post-Smith Zimbabwean government, Washington would find it easier domestically to intervene. Vorster fell into line, later telling his Cabinet: "If all this leads to conflict, he [Kissinger] can give no guarantees because it is the US Congress that must decide. However, [the Ford Administration] will be especially amenable [toward intervention]."[72] Kissinger cabled back to Ford: "It is clear that Vorster has not swerved from his earlier promises to us; this is an extremely courageous decision for him, particularly in light of the domestic problems erupting in his country. It looks now as if real progress on Rhodesia is possible unless the black side collapses on us."[73]

Vorster was similarly amenable on SWA. He agreed to both of Kissinger's requirements: holding the constitutional conference in Geneva, rather than Windhoek; and allowing SWAPO participation. As seen, the latter ran counter to Vorster's every instinct. But he was eager to conclude a settlement on SWA that sidelined the UN, which he saw (with some justification) as biased in favor of a transfer to SWAPO rule. Even as Vorster met Kissinger in Zurich, Sean McBride, the UN Special Representative on SWA, publicly stated that South Africa should first withdraw from SWA and then initiate talks with SWAPO and only SWAPO.[74] Vorster therefore agreed to Kissinger's demands, while attaching three conditions of his own: first, SWAPO could take part only if they were "prepared to state publicly they will support peaceful solutions in South-West Africa and will stop terrorism immediately"; second, Vorster himself would not negotiate with SWAPO, but the Turnhalle representatives could do so if they chose; and third, SWAPO would be present in Geneva as just one of several bodies representative of the peoples of SWA. He told Kissinger in no uncertain terms: "If SWAPO and Sam Nujoma think they can come to negotiations, whether in Geneva or in Timbuctoo, as the only recognized representative then the Conference will be in a shambles on the first day."[75] Kissinger raised no objections.

On his return to South Africa, Vorster promptly convened his Cabinet. It had been just a month since the tense August 3 meeting. Yet as he divulged the results of his discussions with Kissinger in Switzerland, the mood could hardly have been more different. The prime minister reported progress on every front. On Rhodesia, South Africa would not be required to be the hangman: "South Africa's position was that interference in Rhodesia's internal affairs, such as to remove Ian Smith as Prime Minister, could not be permitted. This was accepted." On SWA, "South Africa has won," Vorster declared. There would an all-parties conference, with both the UN and South Africa as observers, designed to achieve independence for SWA by the end of 1978. On South Africa's position at the UN, at a new low after Soweto, Vorster announced that Kissinger had committed to blocking any move at the UN to declare apartheid a threat to world peace: "[The] US will veto any decision under Chapter 7 [of the UN Charter] so long as the Ford Administration remains in power." Finally, Kissinger had agreed to visit South Africa itself—and would meet with homeland as well as Indian and Colored leaders. The validation that this last might provide for South Africa's besieged separate development policies could not have gone unnoticed. The minutes concluded: "The result that has been achieved is almost unbelievable. . . . [T]he cause of peace has been substantially promoted."[76]

Vorster must have been ecstatic. His colleagues had responded to his briefing with rapturous praise for what they saw as his skillful diplomacy and mature statesmanship; "our Prime Minister's integrity and capability are accepted [internationally]," the minutes purred. He was about to complete ten years as prime minister, more than any of his apartheid-era predecessors. The first homeland in the Transkei was due for independence in October. And to crown it all, South Africa seemed on the path back to acceptance by the West. In public, however, the Ford Administration continued to keep Pretoria at arm's length. Kissinger told Bowdler that acquiescing to Vorster's request to mention to the press a "drawing together" of the two countries would be "a most unwise move."[77] But in private, what Kissinger told Vorster was music to his ears: "In my judgment our meetings over the past months have laid more solid foundations for relations between the United States and South Africa."[78] After the devastating disappointment of Angola and the arresting shock of Soweto, Vorster's stock had once more returned to near the heady heights of summer 1974–75. "I do not want to put it any higher than this [*hoër stel as dit nie*]," the ebullient leader told the Free State NP congress a few days later, "but it can possibly flow from this that the matter of Southern Africa is settled."[79]

Safari Diplomacy

Having secured South Africa's commitment to persuade Smith to accept his settlement proposals, Kissinger embarked upon his "safari diplomacy" in sub-Saharan Africa. Nyerere and Kaunda were both more than receptive to the unfolding scheme.[80] Meanwhile, Smith headed to Pretoria. For the first time, the South Africans revealed to him the details of the Kissinger Plan. The Five Points, often referred to as Annex C, were:

1. Salisbury would accept majority rule within two years.
2. Salisbury would meet immediately with nationalist leaders at a conference to organize an interim government.
3. The interim government would consist of two bodies. The Council of State would consist half of blacks, half of whites, with a white chairman with no casting vote. Functions would include passing legislation and supervising the drafting of the new constitution. The Council of Ministers would be the executive branch of the interim government and have a black majority and a black first minister. Decisions would be taken by a two-thirds majority.
4. The UK and Salisbury would both enact the necessary legislation to give effect to the interim government.
5. Upon establishment of the interim government, sanctions would be lifted and all guerrilla violence would cease.[81]

The Five Points were not unattractive to Salisbury. The Zimbabwe Adjustment Fund in particular, which essentially constituted a Sixth Point, was a major and concrete reassurance that Rhodesia's white community would have a future in the new Zimbabwe. Pretoria made it clear what they expected Smith to do and reiterated that no last-minute assistance to the regime would be forthcoming. The South Africans repeated Fourie's earlier tactic of pretending that the real pressure was coming from Washington, rather than Pretoria. "It is not Ian Smith who is being pressurized so much as it is a case of John Vorster having his arm twisted," van den Bergh told Flower disingenuously.[82] The Rhodesian leadership "accepted in principle," but insisted on discussing the details with Kissinger before they took it to Cabinet.[83]

Kissinger duly arrived in South Africa on September 17. His presence was a landmark experience for both the South African electorate and its government, still reeling from the waves of civil disorder sweeping through South Africa's townships. Now, the American secretary of state—"Super K," the 1973 Nobel Peace Prize laureate, one of the most famous and powerful people in the world—had arrived in sleepy Pretoria to ask for white South Africa's help. *Die Burger* covered the arrival of "Superman Kissinger" in no fewer than six articles across the first two pages.[84] Yet the same day that Kissinger touched down at Waterkloof Airport, police in Soweto killed six demonstrating children and injured thirty-five more.[85] "[T]here is a definite anti-American feeling among many Blacks," editorialized the *World*. Black youth, in particular, viewed Kissinger's enterprise with "deep suspicion" and "fear[ed] another American 'sell out' of their aspirations."[86] It was a stark reminder of the vast and growing distance between Vorster's vision and African hopes.

With his state-based view of geopolitics, Kissinger considered Pretoria's domestic policies essentially extraneous to his need to engage with its leaders on the diplomatic level. However, the negotiations were not occurring in a vacuum, but were intimately connected to the imperative to restore domestic control. One Broederbond circular from the time makes this all too clear:

> During a recent meeting with a friend in a responsible position [read: a high-level NP official or government minister] it became clear that, depending on the development of foreign relations, considerably increased action can be expected in the interest of the restoration of law and order in black townships, especially in Soweto. In this connection the [Broederbond] Executive wants to stress that our black population is substantially different from the white Westerner, especially in terms of respect for power, violence, and strong action. It has become urgently necessary to give conclusive proof to the vast majority of non-rioting blacks of the Government's *will* and *power* to maintain law and order in everybody's interest.[87]

As in West Germany and Switzerland, Kissinger and Vorster quickly found common ground in Pretoria. Vorster fulsomely agreed to deliver Smith: "On Annex C . . . I think I can persuade him to come in. And if he does come in, I am prepared to guarantee personally that he will go through with it—as a person and as a party. I am prepared to stand in as guarantor for his commitments, in toto."[88] This was much further than he had gone in 1974–75. But if Kissinger's central role in the overall settlement architecture was liberating the prime minister from his domestic political restraints, Vorster was performing a similar function for the Americans: the secretary of state was loath to sit down with Smith, thereby according Salisbury a measure of recognition and perhaps offering the Rhodesians room to maneuver, unless he was assured that a positive outcome would ensue.[89]

With Vorster covering him, however, Kissinger sat down alone with Smith at the American ambassador's residence on Sunday, September 19. The secretary of

Figure 7.4 In September 1976, with the South African state and the black majority
locked in daily armed conflict in the townships, Henry Kissinger flew to Pretoria
to ensure that John Vorster would force Ian Smith to agree to a multiracial political
settlement in Rhodesia. From left to right, emerging from Libertas, Vorster, his wife
Tini, Henry Kissinger, and Hilgard Muller. Vorster's heir apparent, Connie Mulder,
and the towering figure of General Hendrik van den Bergh, head of BOSS, loom
behind them. Source: National Archives of South Africa.

state again hit the right emotional notes, expressing his sorrow at what needed to
happen.[90] The two then drove across town to Libertas, where they carefully went
over the details of the Five Points. Vorster said very little, but his presence spoke
volumes to Smith. The Rhodesians emphasized that they wanted the Defense
and Law and Order ministries in the interim government to be controlled by
whites so as to ensure a "stable transition." Kissinger would not guarantee this,
but he repeatedly assured the Rhodesians that he would strongly support their
wishes on this point:

KISSINGER: I'll tell them [the African presidents] orally [that] you insist on the
    Law and Order and Defense Ministries, and I will support it . . .

The conversation soon circled back to this central point, with much the same
result:

MINISTER FOR FINANCE DAVID SMITH: It is essential that the two security ministries
    be white. There is no alternative.
KISSINGER: So I can tell them [the African presidents] that you accept a two-thirds
    majority of blacks, with a veto for the whites, in the Cabinet [the Council

of Ministers], provided the two security ministers remain white for the two years of transition?

IAN SMITH: Yes.

KISSINGER: That is not unreasonable.[91]

The copy of the Five Points sent to the Rhodesians by Kissinger on September 22 duly stipulated in writing that the two ministries would indeed be controlled by whites.[92] It also reiterated the agreed-upon structure for the Council of State: equal representation between blacks and whites, with a white chairman with no casting vote. Yet even as Kissinger visited Pretoria, the British were reminding the secretary of state that they were far from committed to the Five Points and had serious reservations over the make-up of the Council of State in particular.[93]

Kissinger proceeded regardless. He made it clear to Smith that he had only two choices. "Our option was to accept or reject. If we rejected, the next offer would only be worse," Smith recalled.[94] Kissinger promised Smith that if the interim government came under communist attack, "we would at least give you diplomatic support and look favorably on others who give military support."[95] However, if a Democrat were to win the US presidential election, he pointed out, things would be different. For his part, Vorster warned Smith in a private side-meeting that South Africa was no longer going to support Rhodesia either economically or militarily.[96] To bolster the point, South Africa closed its border with Rhodesia while Smith was in Pretoria, leaving less than twenty days of oil in the country's stockpiles.[97] Smith would later lament the "South African eagerness to throw us to the wolves in their desperate panic to try to buy time and gain credit for solving the Rhodesian problem."[98] But Vorster continued to obscure the nature of his involvement. In November, in his first interview on American television, he told *Face the Nation*:

> All that I did was to give Mr. Smith the position as I saw it. We discussed the various alternatives, but the decision—and I want to make that quite clear—the decision that Rhodesia arrived at was its own decision, and Rhodesia wasn't pressurized [*sic*] in any way by South Africa at that time or at any time before that. . . . I've always adopted the attitude . . . that I was not prepared to twist Mr. Smith's arm, but that any decision arrived at would be his own.[99]

None of this was true.

Smith agreed to recommend the Kissinger Plan to his Cabinet. The parties concurred that pending its approval, the Rhodesian prime minister would make a public announcement on the Friday, less than a week later. Kissinger's entire strategy hinged on this moment. If Smith publicly committed to a transfer of power, the secretary of state believed that the skeptical but long-suffering African Presidents and nationalists, as well as the increasingly apprehensive British,[100] would embrace the entire process. Accordingly, as deliberations continued in Salisbury in the lead-up to the Friday announcement, Kissinger sent Smith numerous messages designed to sweeten the deal for the Rhodesian whites. In these, he indicated to the Rhodesians that both a qualified franchise and a white blocking mechanism in parliament, the two means that Salisbury had proposed to maintain additional white control in the new state, were not precluded by the Kissinger Plan and would remain on the table at any subsequent conference.[101] Kissinger was also at pains to stress that there would be no bait and switch. He assured Smith in a cable: "It is our considered judgment that the best course for the Rhodesians at this moment is to accept the Five Points as they are, coupled with our assurance that we will not repeat not allow new demands to be raised from the other side beyond what is agreed in Annex C [sic]."[102] He told the South Africans the same thing: "Whatever the British do, we will not deviate from or ask for any more concessions than we've agreed to."[103]

On September 21, Smith duly advised his Cabinet to accept the Kissinger Plan. Although the deal amounted to "an ultimatum," he nevertheless told his colleagues that "[t]hese proposals represented the best offer Rhodesia could expect from the free world. Furthermore, South Africa had emphasized the need for a settlement now otherwise Rhodesia would be faced with a deteriorating situation with the prospect of being forced to accept a less favorable settlement at a later stage."[104] As Central Intelligence Organization head Ken Flower later recounted: "The South African political, economic and military arm-twisting, which had been growing steadily more painful, had finally proved too much for Smith, his government and his country to bear."[105] Smith recalled the experience more dramatically: "On that fateful day in Pretoria, Vorster placed the proverbial pistol to our head."[106] After further discussion the next day, the Rhodesian Cabinet backed Smith's position.[107]

The Side Deal: SWA

Kissinger's visit to Pretoria also yielded major breakthroughs on SWA. Vorster and Kissinger swiftly agreed upon a Seven Point structure for a transition to independence by the end of 1978:

1. A constitutional conference in Geneva.
2. The UN would have observer status only.

3. South Africa would send a representative to maintain contact with the participants and negotiate on issues that bore directly on South Africa's relationship with an independent Namibia.
4. The conference would decide the modalities of the SWA election and the nature of its supervision.
5. The agenda would be entirely open to whatever issues the participants might wish to raise.
6. Pretoria committed itself to accepting the outcome of the conference.
7. Independence would be obtained by December 31, 1978.[108]

Vorster agreed that SWAPO could attend the constitutional conference, provided it first gave an undertaking to renounce violence and ceased all insurgent activity.[109] Having spoken to Mudge, he told Kissinger that "if SWAPO should make a declaration that they seek a peaceful solution and call off their dogs and stop the terrorism, he [Mudge] feels there is no question the [Turnhalle] conference will talk to SWAPO."[110] South Africa's acceptance of Kissinger's SWA framework was therefore explicitly conditional on this matter, yet it was not included in the Seven Points themselves. This mirrored how the financial guarantees for white Rhodesians, equally important to Pretoria's acquiescence there, were not included in the Five Points. Kissinger's tactic of prioritizing bringing the parties to the table, coupled with his eagerness for a swift settlement, meant that major areas of disagreement were being papered over or obscured.

The Seven Points gave South Africa a number of tangible benefits. First, the withdrawal or reduction of the SADF presence in SWA was not a precondition of any stage of the envisaged political process. This would allow South Africa, whether through the SADF or UNITA, to continue to eradicate SWAPO cadres in the border area even as constitutional discussions took place. Second, the Seven Points provided the first international acknowledgment of the legitimacy of the Turnhalle delegates as representatives of the SWA people and of their centrality to the drafting of a constitution. This development correspondingly diluted SWAPO's importance and implicitly negated its claim to be the sole representative of the SWA population. Third, the Seven Points enabled SWAPO to be brought into the process, but on South Africa's terms. SWAPO would have to lay down its weapons simply to gain a seat at the table, and as one of many parties present, it would not gain any of the recognition that would have accompanied bilateral negotiations with Pretoria. Finally, the deal was accompanied by an American promise to veto any UN resolution calling for sanctions over South Africa's ongoing presence in SWA—a major lightning rod for international pressure—while Kissinger also agreed to bring the French and British on board at the Security Council.[111]

Overall, the Seven Points thus constituted a very good deal for South Africa. However, the likelihood of the framework producing a durable settlement depended on two assumptions, both of which proved rash: that Turnhalle would conform to Pretoria's wishes, and that SWAPO could be forced to settle for a lesser role at the constitutional conference. In August 1976, Turnhalle had agreed to create an interim government with a view to independence by the end of 1978. At its annual congress, the SWA NP had then given approval for a three-tiered structure that shared power between national, regional-ethnic, and local authorities.[112] But over the ensuing months, major differences arose between Mudge and his more reactionary and doctrinaire fellow white Turnhalle delegates, led by A. H. du Plessis and Eben van Zyl. The central issue was how racial differences would be represented in the new polity and what the precise role of the second-tier structures would be. Mudge wanted a multiracial, pluralistic, and unitary state, in which the second-tier ethnic structures had limited authority over each group's "own affairs," defined narrowly. By contrast, du Plessis and van Zyl prioritized the preservation of white privileges, identity, and control. Accordingly, they supported strong second-tier structures that attached SWA's various ethnic groups to geographically-based units in keeping with the ideology of separate development. As in South Africa, these would splinter the black majority into a series of ethnic minorities. If independence had to come, then they wanted a central government that amounted to little more than a federation of these second-tier entities.[113]

The differences amongst the white delegates were not only based on divergent intentions for the role of race in the new polity, but were also informed by different conceptions of political identity. Mudge envisaged Namibia as an independent, mutiracial country with links to both South Africa and other states. He was something of a Namibian nationalist at a time when such an identity was inchoate and undeveloped. Blacks are asking us to "decide whether we are South-Westers or South Africans," Mudge vented in private. "We must throw in our lot with the future of this country, regardless of the consequences." After all, he continued, "we get so little out of this association with South Africa. . . . The party here needs to walk its own path."[114] By contrast, the old guard saw strong links to Pretoria as essential to the white community's future. They struggled to countenance any real divergence from the policy of the South African NP, let alone reconcile themselves to the need for discussions with SWAPO about Namibian independence.[115]

Publicly, Pretoria insisted that the Turnhalle delegates were largely in agreement and on the verge of implementing an interim government.[116] The reality was very different. At one Cabinet meeting in October, a despairing Vorster told his colleagues that regardless of the public line emphasizing Pretoria's noninterference in the process, Turnhalle "had to be pressured to draft a constitution."[117]

Indeed, the divide at the heart of the SWA NP was only growing wider. In October, part of a transcript of a conversation between Mudge and a Mr. X, later revealed as P. W. Botha's biographer Daan Prinsloo, ended up on du Plessis's desk. "[T]he whites of South-West must identify themselves with South-West, number one. Second, they must identify with the black man's desire for independence and do so with enthusiasm," the transcript recorded Mudge as saying. They had to "avoid ending up in the same position as the white man elsewhere in Africa" by being seen as opposing black freedom. Instead, vehicles like Turnhalle offered a great opportunity to build a "multi-racial politics" that could serve as a "counterweight" to SWAPO and provide for an inclusive future.[118] Mudge's frank remarks severely damaged the already fraught relationship between the two factions. While insisting in a subsequent letter to du Plessis that the conversation had been both "private" and "informal," Mudge did not distance himself from his comments.[119] Instead, in a speech at Kamanjab a few days later, he declared his opposition to two pillars of SWA's apartheid structures, the laws on mixed marriages and interracial sex.[120] These were seen as essential elements of the existing social order by the right wing of Nationalist politics on both sides of the Orange River.

These incidents rendered compromise among the SWA whites improbable. The American embassy in Pretoria observed: "Frustration at Turnhalle mounts as [the] anticipated new white position has yet to materialize. . . . Turnhalle talks [have] teetered on brink of collapse for weeks."[121] On November 24, an exasperated Vorster convened a crisis meeting.[122] As well as the white Turnhalle delegates, he also invited Magnus Malan, the new Chief of the Defense Force, to attend the meeting and help illuminate for the feuding leaders the concrete consequences of not reaching an accord. Malan obliged. He detailed at length that SWAPO would soon have three thousand trained insurgents, while the likelihood of a Cuban-supported conventional attack would increase as the MPLA consolidated its rule in Angola. To ensure that the SWA delegates were under no illusions, he added that in the coming years the SADF would likely face problems on multiple fronts and would inevitably prioritize a threat on the eastern flank near the industrial heartland of the Transvaal over one in distant northern SWA. His conclusion was crystal clear: the likelihood of South-West Africans escaping the full force of the total onslaught "depend[ed] on the political progress made by the [Turnhalle] Conference."[123]

For all Malan's warnings, the distance between the two white factions remained vast. Du Plessis stressed that "the blacks in the [Turnhalle] Conference were becoming ever more aggressive and uncontrollable," while SWAPO's influence was increasing in the relatively populous north.[124] In a private letter to Vorster written a week earlier, he had pointed out that a recent visit to refugee camps in northern SWA had been exploited by the non-white Turnhalle groups to convey that the camps "ought to be a lesson . . . of what could happen to the Whites if we did not satisfy their demands. This was indeed said in so many words."[125] Du Plessis insisted that the stability and viability of the future state in SWA ultimately depended on a constitution that was acceptable to whites.[126] Mudge agreed that Turnhalle was increasingly divided, but rationalized that this was only to be expected: each of the ethnic groups had their own priorities and constituencies. To him, the only viable solution was a division of power between them in the constitution. However, he stressed, "if the outcome of the Conference amounts to anything that looks like a homeland, the Conference will be rejected by the various population groups."[127]

Despite South Africa's best efforts, Turnhalle had developed a life of its own. Not only were different population groups expressing their own views on the construction of the new multiethnic state, but the one faction Pretoria thought it could rely upon to stick together and dictate proceedings was deeply divided. Such differences could not be swiftly resolved through some seven point agreement between Washington and Pretoria, because they reflected a much deeper normative fluidity sweeping across the entire region. The rules of what constituted a legitimate political and social order were falling apart. Angola and Soweto had contributed to this sentiment among African groups, certainly. But in questioning old shibboleths of unbridled white dominance Vorster had also done his part to break down ironclad certainties among the descendants of white settlers across the region. Mudge's vision of a multiracial, nation-state based politics coupled with a prompt scaling back of petty apartheid clearly owed much to Vorster's own hesitant signposting of this model for Southern Africa's future.

Just as SWA's whites were not fulfilling the role envisaged for them by Kissinger and Vorster, the feasibility of the Seven Points was also being undermined by SWAPO. In early November, Ford lost the American presidential election. The incoming Carter Administration was both less willing to compromise on the prospect of a genuinely broad-based successor state in SWA and more open to an active American role on the issue.[128] Both were good news for SWAPO. Meanwhile, as Turnhalle struggled to reach an agreement, SWAPO leaders spent the last months of 1976 consolidating their support from the USSR and Cuba and entered the new year galvanized in their desire for total control in SWA. On the battlefield, SWAPO units proved increasingly effective against UNITA and soon regained the initiative.[129] From a position of military strength, SWAPO had no incentive to lay down its arms and accept a lesser role alongside Turnhalle in Geneva. Mudge remembers: "SWAPO's attitude was 'Why should we talk to Dirk Mudge? He's got no army, he doesn't control the country. Who is he? We talk to South Africa. And we only talk to South Africa about handing over Namibia to us.' That was their point of view."[130] By January 1977, Bowdler observed, "[t]alk of bringing SWAPO into the Turnhalle discussions, or a meeting between SWAPO, South Africa, and South Westers, has vanished."[131] By early 1977, the process on SWA that Kissinger and Vorster had sponsored had collapsed entirely, while the new Carter Administration swiftly distanced itself from the Seven Points and everything connected with them.[132]

The Five Points Unravel

The negotiations on Rhodesia fared little better. On September 24, Smith had announced his reluctant acceptance of the Kissinger Plan on both radio and television:

> I would be dishonest if I did not state quite clearly that the proposals which were put to us in Pretoria do not represent what in our view would be the best solution for Rhodesia's problems. . . The American and British Governments, together with the major Western powers, have made up their minds as to the kind of solution they wish to see in Rhodesia and they are determined to bring it about. The alternative to acceptance of the proposals was explained to us in the clearest of terms, which left no room for misunderstanding.[133]

Two days later, the five Frontline presidents met in Lusaka. They publicly rejected the Kissinger proposals, objecting particularly to white control of the two security ministries.[134] For Pretoria, this was the first sign that anything was amiss. Only Kissinger had been in contact with the Africans and had any idea what they were thinking. Vorster had energetically fulfilled his obligations and thought everything was running smoothly. Smith had even acquiesced to the plan, and in public too. Now everything was in jeopardy.

On the surface, the impasse existed over just two issues: who would control the security ministries in the interim government, and the racial balance of the Council of State. This divergence was, however, representative of a more fundamental problem, namely, that Kissinger had represented the status of Annex C differently to different parties. The Rhodesians perceived it as an immutable contract representing the full extent of their concessions and believed they would not have to concede any more ground.[135] The African presidents saw it as a basis for negotiation.[136] And the British understood it as merely a working draft.[137] On the basis of the documentary record (and in contrast to Kissinger's memoirs), all parties were justified in their views.[138] Accordingly, although Nyerere and Kaunda had been initially receptive to Annex C, neither felt committed to it as an ironclad framework for a final settlement.

This was not the only flaw in Kissinger's settlement framework. The decision reached by London and Washington to allow Smith to make the initial announcement, though in wording meticulously vetted by them, was a tactical error. For the African presidents to sell the deal as a victory for decolonization and African nationalism, the initiative for a final settlement had to at least appear to come either from them or the international brokers, but certainly not from the hated Smith.[139] Similarly, in order for the enterprise to have credibility in Africa, London and Washington needed to be in lock-step, when they rather resembled a three-legged race.[140] Their differences could not have passed unnoticed by their interlocutors in the Frontline states. In one remarkable exchange in mid-September, for instance, Callaghan told Kissinger, with more than a little snark, that "we cannot from 5000 miles away, and without any Cabinet (or Treasury) commitment, publicly endorse every particular proposal that you may make."[141] Kissinger replied pointedly: "There is no way you can avoid involvement. If the conference fails, you will have Rhodesia on your hands again and the options now open to you will be closed."[142] The working relationship between the two never recovered. Finally, Kissinger had not consulted all of the Frontline presidents, much less the nationalist leaders themselves.[143] He had shunned the more radical Machel and Neto, so they had no direct stake in the Kissinger Plan's success. Both had plenty to gain from championing the militant pan-African cause and banging the anti-American drum; doubtless their presence at the multilateral Lusaka meeting contributed heavily to the ultimate rejection by the presidents of the Five Points.

Vorster suddenly found himself politically exposed by the prospect of the Kissinger Plan's failure. Smith, he acknowledged to Cabinet, had done everything that was required of him. However, with the Africa having "repudiated the agreement," there was now "a great deal of confusion." Vorster endeavored to limit his political liability by again emphasizing to his colleagues that "South Africa [had] exercised no pressure on Rhodesia, [but only] handed over the written proposals to Smith." Demoralized and uncertain, he sought further cover, telling his Cabinet: "As for Rhodesia, we have to give them the weapons to maintain their position, regardless of the cost."[144] Smith was stunned to find Vorster suddenly offering to train Rhodesia's Mirage pilots free of charge and authorizing a long-delayed 20 million rand loan.[145] Meanwhile, Kissinger met with Pik Botha in Washington and assured him that a Rhodesia conference convened by the British would go ahead as planned: "[T]he way to a negotiated settlement is open. . . . There has been no significant rejection of the five points, nor, in fact, has there been a conclusive rejection of the two ministries being held by the Europeans."[146] This was a decidedly optimistic interpretation of the Frontline presidents' expressed views, but it was enough to persuade Vorster. Much like in December 1975, he had little choice but to stay the course. From

Pretoria, William Schaufele, Assistant Secretary of State for African Affairs, assured Kissinger that the South Africans were still on board and would continue to "use their substantial influence" to keep Smith in line.[147]

When the Rhodesia conference convened in Geneva on October 28, a consistent dynamic quickly emerged. As each nationalist delegation presented its proposals, the Rhodesians stuck firm to Annex C. The minutes of one typical session recorded: "Mr. [P. K.] van der Byl [Rhodesian Minister for Foreign Affairs] stressed that the Rhodesian Delegation was present in Geneva purely to assist in the implementation of those proposals [Annex C], anything else being outside what the Rhodesian Government had accepted. Concessions had been made beforehand and no more could be considered."[148] Much like the Africans, the British saw the Five Points as decidedly pliable and their chairman, former UN Ambassador Ivor Richard, was disinclined to force the nationalists to stick closely to them. With progress proving elusive, the South Africans realized that the Geneva Conference was not going to produce a settlement.[149]

"It is time for reassessment"

With the Geneva Conference deadlocked, Richard visited Southern Africa in an endeavor to persuade Salisbury and Pretoria to agree to a new, British-designed deal. The Richard Plan differed from the Kissinger Plan in two important respects, each designed to address the major impasses between the parties: it proposed an interim government under black control, effectively constituting an immediate transition to majority rule; and it provided for Britain to assume the contested security ministries and temporarily to resume its colonial role through a Resident Commissioner.[150] The Richard Plan thus both minimized the role that whites would play in shaping the contours of the future state and featured a humiliating handover of executive power by Smith to the distrusted British. On both counts, the new proposals amounted to a substantially worse deal for Salisbury than the Kissinger Plan that had already been agreed to.

As for South Africa, the problem for Vorster was that the already fragile domestic support for a settlement was collapsing. Throughout 1976, he had been increasingly hemmed in on two fronts. First, repeated Rhodesian raids into Mozambique, the Soweto insurrections, and the post-Angola resuscitation of anti-Pretoria norms had together fueled a marked rise in militancy in black Africa. In one editorial typical of the new era, the *Times of Zambia* stated that South Africa's system meant "a ruthless subservience to domination by an alien people. . . . The salvation of the black man lies in his total refusal to cooperate with apartheid."[151] Victoria Falls must have felt a long time ago, though Vorster and Kaunda had in fact prayed together just a year earlier. This sentiment resonated well beyond Southern Africa too. Liberia's President William Tolbert, who had been very receptive to the outward policy, issued a similar verdict on South Africa to a joint session of the US Congress in September 1976: "I am convinced Africans would prefer death to continued repression."[152] If the violence of Soweto had not made it hard enough for even moderate African leaders to engage with Vorster, then the government's response, infused with all the *kragdadigheid* (literally, vigor; more colloquially, uncompromising toughness) of traditional Nationalist political culture, had made it impossible. M. C. Botha, the deeply conservative Minister for Bantu Administration, displayed all the callousness toward Africans that Vorster was trying to purge from his regime: "I do not react to statements which Bantu leaders make in public."[153] The year of 1976 was notable for the paucity of the government's direct contact with independent African leaders and Vorster's reliance on Kissinger as an intermediary instead.

Second, Vorster was subject to increased pressure from his right wing. In January, he had attempted to neutralize criticism from the right by bringing Treurnicht into his outer Cabinet to replace Punt Jansen, a renowned *verligte* pragmatist. The move did nothing to silence the ambitious and articulate archconservative. Instead, it only succeeded in giving Treurnicht a platform closer to the center of Nationalist political circles from which to express his dissent—often subtly and while staying just within the limits of party policy. In June, for instance, he publicly criticized the recent opening of the Nico Malan Theatre in Cape Town to non-whites. The prime minister responded by bringing up the issue in caucus. But when Treurnicht subsequently offered an apology, unconvincingly suggesting that he had been trapped by insistent newspapermen, Vorster could only lamely reiterate that MPs should not "disturb [party] unity."[154] As the government considered limited reforms in the wake of Soweto, the emboldened *verkrampte* leader resolutely opposed any and every measure, galvanizing the right wing of the party. Koos van der Merwe, who followed Treurnicht out of the NP in 1982, recalls the right-wing's ethos toward the broad coalition of enemies of the *volk*: "We'll show the bastards!"[155] Yet it was Treurnicht who as Deputy Minister of Bantu Administration and Development had insisted on the instruction of Africans in Afrikaans, the trigger for the Soweto unrest. Vorster could easily have made his bête noire the scapegoat and dropped him from the Cabinet. Or, when Treurnicht inevitably defended his actions, Vorster could have engineered to expel the renegade from the party and used the isolation of the right-wing to energize his own agenda.[156] He did neither.

Vorster's overall response to this signal challenge of his tenure was a microcosm of his leadership. Although he had utilized the Soweto emergency to furnish momentum for his cherished campaign for legitimacy and rehabilitation abroad, his creativity in statecraft was matched by a chronic inability to use domestic crises and the flux they created to fulfill his vision at home, rather than perceiving them solely as challenges to his ability to maintain support within the party. *Verligtes* were clamoring for reform within the overarching separate development framework: home ownership for urban blacks; an acceleration of homeland development; investment in training and education for Africans; increased black living standards as an exemplar to radical Africa. "It is time for reassessment," declared *Volkshandel*.[157] "Greater power for urban blacks over their own affairs must come," echoed *Die Burger*.[158] The annual Broederbond Bondsraad, held at the end of September 1976, epitomized the prevailing climate. In the shadow of Soweto, *verkrampte* Carel Boshoff, the new chairman of the Broederbond's Committee on Relations with the Bantus and Verwoerd's son-in-law, dominated discussion of new avenues for the future. What was needed, he said, was a return to Verwoerdian apartheid: the rigid application in policy of the theory of full separation, grounded in biblical norms, and a renewal of Afrikaner unilateralism based on the unique mission of the *volk* (as opposed, by implication, to recognizing the rights and goals common to all national communities, as emphasized by *verligtes*). However, under Gerrit Viljoen's chairmanship (1974–1980), the Broederbond had already accepted, within the bounds of multinational thinking, the essentially interdependent reality of South African society. "The likelihood of maintaining political control over our White homeland depends on the degree to which Blacks—including those who are located in White areas—can exercise meaningful political rights in their [respective] homeland, as an alternative to political partnership within our White fatherland," read one memorandum.[159] Accordingly, when Boshoff's proposals came up for discussion, unconvinced senior Broeders responded that they were unrealistic. From the chair, Viljoen summed up (and doubtless shaped) the overall feeling. "We are not immobile people of granite," he said, deliberately invoking Verwoerd's famous metaphor. The goal had to be to further adapt the separate development model to economic and social realities.[160]

Polls likewise showed that the pulsating violence in the townships was breaking down entrenched attitudes within the electorate. A survey in the Afrikaans weekly *Rapport* showed that 57 percent of whites were willing to abolish job reservation by race, the central pillar of apartheid in the economic sphere. Another poll found that as many as 44 percent of whites were willing to support a form of restricted franchise for blacks. Importantly, this poll also indicated that support for the NP itself remained constant.[161] The message to Vorster should have been crystal clear. "White opinion was badly shaken; was willing to consider reforms if that was what was required to make the troubles go away; but was clinging tight to its party allegiances," scholar R. W. Johnson assessed at the time. "[F]aced with crisis and uncertainty, [the electorate] looked to strong government and a strong leader as never before. This left the ball very much in Vorster's court."[162] There were plenty of prominent Nationalists who increasingly saw the *verkramptes* for what they were: obstructionist flat-earthers without any feasible template for the future, playing relentlessly to the basest racist instincts of the electorate. These included P. W. Botha, Fanie Botha, and Piet Koornhof, as well as rising stars of the next generation, like Pik Botha and Barend du Plessis. However, just as Vorster was unable to free himself from the millstone of right-wing dissent, equally he was unable to fully articulate a coherent reformist vision and rally support around himself on that basis. When he met with the Broederbond Executive Council in November, he could only offer that after serious self-examination and reflection, he had concluded that "separate development" was the way forward.[163] This formulation avoided all of the important questions on the minds of Afrikaners, not least the elites. If P. W. Botha was already upset with what he saw as Vorster's disorganized style of governance and reluctance to take the fight to global communism, then the prime minister's refusal to pioneer much-needed reform spelled the irreversible breakdown of their relationship.

Vorster's failure to exploit this atmosphere of change in spring 1976 was the final, fatal mistake of his premiership. He understood the crucial importance of reducing petty apartheid for his project of relegitimization. Time and again, he had taken politically damaging stances on perhaps the most emotive issue for grassroots Afrikaners: playing sport, especially rugby, with other races. In the aftermath of Soweto, he did so again, pushing through legislation to allow clubs, if they so chose, to be multiracial at all levels of competition. He also announced the wholescale abolition of "hurtful" and "discriminatory measures serving no purpose," an express commitment that would have been invaluable in bolstering his African outreach just two years before.[164] When Louis Nel energetically took up the reformist mantle in caucus, the prime minister was equally unequivocal in his support of the *verligte* agenda in principle. "What do we want to keep?" Nel inquired rhetorically. "1) Principles 2) Security 3) Sovereignty 4) Identity. Thus far we have done this through 'peoples policy' [read: separate development] and 'separation policy' [read: petty apartheid]. The problem is where separation exists 'on the grounds of color.' . . . [I]t is this that the world holds against us. They question whether our racial policy does not in effect damage our separation policy." Vorster concurred and in pointed language: "Mr. Nel is right in his views on racism."[165] Such was the atmosphere of flux in party circles that racism itself had become a designated negative.

However, the embattled Vorster did not understand that the time had come for more, much more. Soweto had broken the sense of stasis in South African politics, thereby providing a unique opportunity to head in new directions. But instead of leading, Vorster tried to keep the peace: sports reforms and a number of ad hoc concessions toward urban blacks for the *verligtes*, juxtaposed with ruthlessness toward the protesters and strong law and order rhetoric for the *verkramptes*. The overall result was dysfunction, rather than balance. At one Nationalist rally in September, he carelessly remarked that extra funds originally earmarked for improving non-white living conditions would now have to be directed to the repairing of property damaged during the disturbances.[166] For all his unexpected skill at discerning and shaping what foreign African leaders wanted, Vorster had a remarkable lack of understanding of how he could use his power and political weight to reorient African demands at home. This was just one of the many ironies and contradictions of his premiership.

Exasperated *verligtes* responded by taking matters into their own hands. In November, editors from *Die Transvaler, Beeld*, and *Rapport* launched a coordinated attack on Treurnicht's obstructionism. Minister for Water Affairs Braam Raubenheimer vigorously defended his colleague and accused Willem de Klerk, the editor of *Die Transvaler*, of disloyalty to the cause.[167] In the Nationalist lexicon, there were few bigger insults: nothing short of labeling the man who had coined the very terms "*verligte*" and "*verkrampte*" an enemy of the *volk*. Such a breach of Cabinet solidarity could not have occurred without Vorster's tacit consent, and the prime minister lent weight to such conclusions by refusing to repudiate Raubenheimer's accusations.

The divisions that had been papered over since 1969 had turned into a gaping fissure. Nationalists both within and outside the political arena disagreed on the importance of racial separation to the Afrikaner nationalist project, and what form it should take. In this context, Vorster's attempts to straddle the divide and keep the peace did nothing but take the ground out from underneath his feet. Even powerful hardliners like Mulder had previously supported Vorster's lead out of deference to his prime ministerial authority, his achievements on the international stage, and his prioritization of party unity. But Vorster's refusal to use this unique moment to bolster his vision with a platform of reforms that simultaneously took the initiative away from the protesters in the townships and Treurnicht's *verkramptes* sapped his authority within the party. Vorster, so effusively, even obsequiously, praised in September by his Cabinet, never again commanded the same respect among his colleagues.

"We have stuck our necks out as far as we can"

These events had a major impact on the pending settlements for Southern Africa. In January 1977, Richard traveled to the prime minister's holiday house at Oubosstrand to ask Vorster to persuade Smith to accept his plan. He found his host in two minds. On the one hand, the geopolitical equation was still essentially the same.[168] If a transition to majority rule in Rhodesia could not be achieved peacefully, then the guerrilla war would escalate, communist powers might increase their African commitments, and Pretoria would come under pressure to intervene. All of this militated in favor of ongoing South African pressure on Salisbury. On January 3, Vorster told Richard that if there was a "bankable assurance" that under the Richard Plan guerrilla activity would stop upon the establishment of an interim government, then he might be willing to try to persuade Smith to comply.[169] However, by January 11 he had changed his mind. He had already assisted Smith in publicly ending his regime. But there were "limits" to what he could do that "could not be exceeded," Fourie recalls. The prime minister "had to guard against a 'backlash.' "[170] Indeed, the day after Smith announced his capitulation by radio, a group of HNP supporters had even broken into Libertas to protest the sell-out of Rhodesian whites.[171] Vorster's willingness to defy both public opinion and substantial rumblings in his Cabinet over his pursuit of an internationally brokered settlement in Rhodesia had reached its full extent.

Vorster also felt deeply disenchanted by the way in which the Kissinger Plan had unraveled. He was especially dismayed that in Geneva Richard had allowed the Africans to escape the commitment to the Five Points that he had been led to believe that they had made.[172] The prime minister was "unhapp[y] with the fact that every concession on Rhodesia and Namibia had been met by escalating African demands," Pik Botha frankly told the Americans.[173] Further, Richard was offering none of the courtship or respect that Kissinger had skillfully deployed to woo Vorster and accord his government the recognition it craved. When the prime minister suggested to Richard that his new proposed transition government, featuring ten whites and twenty blacks, "looked like majority rule at once," Richard tactlessly replied that the change was necessary because "the Africans did not trust [the Rhodesians] to carry the deal through to majority rule in the agreed timeframe."[174] This, as Vorster quickly pointed out, ignored that the South African prime minister himself had explicitly been Smith's guarantor under the original plan.[175]

Ultimately, Vorster was only willing to pressure the Smith regime, defy his Cabinet and his party, and risk public opprobrium if he felt that South Africa's cooperation would bring about both a stable Zimbabwe *and* international respect and appreciation. Achieving a settlement was desirable, but what really mattered was how a transition to majority rule could be leveraged into regional détente in the medium term and international rehabilitation in the long term. Unlike Kissinger, Richard had failed to appreciate the importance of this equation to obtaining Pretoria's assistance and ultimately securing a durable settlement.

For all these reasons, Vorster ultimately told Richard that he was not prepared to reprise the same role he had played for Kissinger.[176] While stressing his ongoing desire for a settlement, he stressed that "in this matter we have gone as far as we can possibly go. If you can agree with the Rhodesians, fine, but we have stuck our necks out as far as we can."[177] He did promise that he would suggest to the Rhodesians that they not reject Richard's proposals outright.[178] But while Pik Botha told the Americans that Vorster had put the hard word on Hawkins to accept the Richard Plan,[179] the Rhodesian minutes of the meeting show he did no such thing.[180] Without South African leverage, the Richard Plan was a nonstarter. When Richard met with Smith a few days later, the Rhodesian leader rebuffed him in no uncertain terms, insisting that the new proposals "would have such a devastating effect on Rhodesian morale that it was incomprehensible how the British side could expect him to accept them."[181] The meeting broke up acrimoniously. Vorster's détente vision, long on life support, was finally dead and buried.

The collapse of the Kissinger Initiatives on Southern Africa constituted a major turning point in the evolution of Pretoria's approach to regional security, the regime's survival, and the international community. In the first half of the 1970s, Vorster had tried to make the running himself, strengthening Cold War identities in Africa and then exploiting them in an effort to increase South Africa's legitimacy. Now, he had exploited more familiar models of Cold War power relations, allowing Washington to act as the superpower while simultaneously maintaining enough agency to maneuver for every advantage he could behind the scenes. The context had, however, changed. Not only were the expectations of other parties—from Lusaka to SWAPO, and from Soweto to Havana—much higher, but Vorster's own constituency increasingly understood the connection between regional settlements and its future prospects in different ways. The discrete goal in 1976 was the same as it had been a year earlier: creating stable multiracial states in both Rhodesia and SWA. However, for all Vorster's salesmanship, the way in which the Afrikaner power structure articulated the broader goals of the enterprise was changing. Whether in the arresting Broederbond circular spelling out how progress for the Kissinger Initiatives would facilitate a more brutal and efficient crackdown in the townships, or in Cabinet's effusive commitment to a security buildup, there was a shift away from a faith in the construction of a long-term conceptual and political architecture for the region based on multinationalism to a more hard-headed pursuit of the narrower goal of buying time at home. These two lines of thinking about the regime's future coexisted through 1976, but the collapse of the Kissinger Initiatives rendered the former a mirage. With the evaporation of his grand vision went Vorster's authority. By 1977, the prime minister had run out of ideas and energy. To a degree heretofore unappreciated, South Africa's cooperative stance on the Kissinger Initiatives was a highly personalized endeavor—and Vorster took the failure of those initiatives personally. He never again took the lead on national security. Deeply disillusioned, he would soon completely reevaluate South Africa's security strategies and reluctantly follow the more unilateral approaches advocated by his hardline colleagues.

PART III

FROM COLLAPSE
TO RECONSTRUCTION

A New Roadmap

The Development of Total Strategy

The year 1976 marked a turning point not only in the struggle against the apartheid regime, but in the mission and power structure of the regime itself. Since 1948, the regime's ideology had centered on the advancement of a class-less national community with constant, common interests. However, the post-Sharpeville economic boom had created contradictions between this ideal and the demographics of Afrikanerdom, damaging the synergy between class and "national" interests that was central to the National Party's strength. In the 1950s, it had been relatively easy for the party to advance the economic interests of Afrikaners as a group. Policies like agricultural subsidies, influx control, job reservations, and state sector expansion overwhelmingly favored farmers, blue-collar workers, and low-level civil servants—the three categories that together accounted for the vast majority of Afrikaner bread winners.[1] Already during the 1960s, however, the socioeconomic picture of Afrikanerdom was changing in important ways. First, as seen, its labor profile was diversifying substantially. Second, the remarkably uniform wage structure of Afrikanerdom was slowly but steadily becoming more unequal.[2] Not only did Afrikaners increasingly have divergent material interests, but there was an increasing consciousness of this fact. In 1975, the Broederbond's Executive Council observed with concern that Afrikaner businessmen no longer highly valued nationalist goals. Instead, they "considered economic growth and materialist considerations a higher priority than the freedom and sovereignty of the Afrikaner people."[3] Elites increasingly valued employment in the private sector over jobs whose purpose was to sustain public goods.[4] Finally, and not unrelatedly, there was a decline in the authority and prestige of traditional elites. In the public sphere, Calvinist *dominees* and socially conservative educators had acted as vigilant gatekeepers, ensuring the primacy of *volk* solidarity over other forms of identity or alternate paradigms for understanding society. However, increased urbanization and education, greater access to information about the outside world, and the rise of public intellectuals with power bases in the new *verligte* press together informed a more disparate intellectual universe for Afrikanerdom—one that, as the now regular bannings of major works of Afrikaans literature underlined, was much harder for the NP to control under the broad banner of "nationalist unity."

The changing occupations of the Broederbond membership provide a neat optic on each of these processes. In 1952, almost 60 percent of Broeders were "educators" and 10 percent were Calvinist clergy. Another quarter were farmers heavily dependent on public subsidies for viability. Precisely none described themselves as a "businessman." By 1968, the situation was quite different. Where educated Afrikaners had previously flooded into the education sector—whether as headmasters, school teachers, professors, or university staff—the next generation branched out into law, medicine, and, above all, commerce.[5] Fully 14 percent of Broeders now ticked the "businessman" box, forming the third-largest category behind the rapidly dwindling ranks of educators (21 percent) and the steady numbers of farmers (22 percent).[6] That the new entrepreneurs identified as such is in itself a telling indicator of how rapidly capitalism and its associated values took root in Afrikaner culture.

By the 1970s, the diverging interests of a socioeconomic constituency that was more varied in occupation, more oriented toward private gain, and more diverse in outlook were harder for the NP to satisfy uniformly in its existing guise as the explicit vanguard of the *volk*.[7] The party responded by increasingly aligning itself on policy issues with the educated, upwardly mobile classes. The concerns of employers in particular began to receive very favorable consideration in political circles, even where their calls for more training and fewer job bars for blacks ran directly counter to the desires of working-class Afrikaners whose social status and competitive advantage depended on the maintenance of a black underclass. More broadly, the NP traded in the puritan austerity of Afrikaner tradition for the politics of aspiration.

The NP's decision to prioritize an ethos of consumption over that of ethnic solidarity made reaching out to other whites of similar means and outlook to middle-class Afrikaners the logical gambit. Ideology adapted to achieve the new goal. There was now one "nation, composed of Afrikaners and English-speaking people," Vorster claimed, as the party diluted its exclusivist nationalist appeals in favor of a broader language of white inclusion.[8]

A number of factors facilitated this shift. First, Verwoerd had already broken down some of the barriers, with an electoral campaign that aggressively targeted English-speakers before the 1966 polls. Second, the increased focus in party circles on modernization and living standards as the standard of good governance against which its homeland and Africa policies should be judged provided a conceptual bridge to the acceptance of a more consumerist party ethos. Since a universal franchise was out of the question, it was increasingly accepted within

Nationalist circles that the continuation of white status and privileges would depend on the polity's ability to provide for the rapid *material* advancement of blacks instead.[9] Third, the party's grandiose homelands agenda needed capital. The right-wing was animated by few issues as much as the spending of "white" taxpayer dollars on black benefits. One typical *Die Afrikaner* exposé entitled "Bantu in homelands get 104,000,000 rand from Whites," bemoaned: "While thousands of Whites must struggle to get housing, to get hospital services, or to start a business, deputy minister Piet Koornhof boasts: 'Our best and most modern hospitals are being built in the homelands.'"[10] To avoid this political minefield, the government increasingly looked to mobilize private capital to achieve its development goals. This reliance on the private sector became even more profound as the country progressively shifted to a war economy. As P. W. Botha told his fellow ministers: "In order to be able to enjoy the necessary freedom of action, it is essential that the RSA be strategically self-sufficient. This implies that the SADF must, to an increasing extent, be able to rely on the SA industry regarding the supply of materiel (armament, ammunition and supplies). In fact, it can be categorically stated that the SADF cannot execute its task without an effective contribution by industry."[11] Fourth, the model of Afrikaner identity that saw anglophone culture as its nemesis was breaking down rapidly. Rather than defining themselves against the anglophone-dominated economy, members of the rising Afrikaner middle class instead looked for advancement within it. Equally, this same social stratum no longer repudiated global culture, but instead looked to go beyond the closed realm of the *volk* and experience foreign music, sport, and culture. In the 1960 census, only 1.6 percent of whites were bilingual. Already by 1970, that figure was 18 percent.[12]

Finally, like any political party, the NP was innately drawn toward increasing its share of the vote. As much as its founding ideology militated against attracting English-speakers, the color of the franchise pulled in the opposite direction. The latter increasingly trumped the former, though not without plenty of ideological contradictions and working-class casualties. This was no overnight change. By 1982, polls suggested that one in four English-speaking whites supported the NP. However, this figure was just one in seven at the 1977 election, even as the government ran a virulently xenophobic campaign that aimed to bring whites resolutely together on the basis of a shared fate: either whites would hang together, or they would hang separately.[13]

The NP's electoral dominance in the 1970s therefore rested fundamentally on the contention that the interests of all whites, of all classes and language groups, could be satisfied simultaneously, a difficult political agenda to sustain.[14] In terms of ideology, the NP's outreach to English-speakers did not displace the existing party mission of pioneering *volksverbondenheid* so much as it created an unlikely amalgam, larger in electoral appeal but inherently unstable. Race was the coagulant, though the constituent parts were in other respects less than compatible. Most obviously, much of the Afrikaner lore from which NP leaders drew to energize initiatives had been created in opposition to English-speakers. Vorster's African outreach provides a case in point. The logic of his articulation of Afrikanerdom as an African *volk* turned largely on the audacious claim to Afrikaner anticolonialism, a claim that rested entirely on historical enmity toward the very community that the NP now cultivated. The government engaged in contortions to avoid addressing such paradoxes. To this end, Vorster extended the remit of the anticolonial claim beyond all plausibility, even within the idiosyncratic universe of Nationalist discourse. "[T]he Whites, the Afrikaners and the English-speaking people," he posited, were "not colonialists."[15]

In the short term, this compact proved hugely successful at the polls. However, by the mid-1970s, there was a fundamental and growing tension within the NP between its traditional incarnation as the vanguard of the *volksbeweging* [national movement] and its new role as a pan-white, economic growth-promoting entity. At *stryddae* [party rallies], Nationalist politicians tried to mobilize support as they always had, by evoking the symbols and tropes of Afrikaner history, usually in chauvinist tones.[16] But such calls no longer had the same traction.[17] Party figures likewise tried to reassure the base that English-speakers were essentially only being coopted into the *volkstaat*, such that their inclusion would ultimately strengthen Afrikaner interests, even as Vorster's own articulation of a pan-white national identity pointed to a more complicated reality. This led to ill-judged, half-hearted, and contradictory policy choices in an effort to sustain the illusion. The issue of educating Africans in Afrikaans, the flashpoint for the Soweto uprising, was just such a concession to culture-centric *verkramptes*—even though calls for a policy of Afrikanerization of English-speaking whites had long since been quietly dropped from the Nationalist agenda.[18]

Vorster papered over this central tension in party identity by claiming that the party's traditional philosophy of group rights could simply be extended from Afrikaners to all whites. His vision held that the white South African state would sit at the center of a network of independent nation-states, with all entities recognized as peers in the international community. In this way, it built directly upon Verwoerd's blueprint and was sold explicitly as such (though not without difficulty). In a situation where national and class interests were increasingly incompatible, Vorster's program was a last-ditch effort to entrench a communal national interest at the core of the polity's future and sustain the increasingly tenuous notion that nationalism was still the essential principle of the party. Nationalism was, after all, the core concept infusing his vision for the future at every level.

Yet Vorster's plan deliberately left vague where the conceptual boundaries of the national entity lay. Instead, he advertised the core benefits that would be

Figure 8.1 This image of the South African Defense Force withdrawing from the Angolan Civil War in March 1976 illuminates the contradictions between the National Party and its evolving base. On one level, the image conveys the National Party's commitment to nationalism and *volkseie* as the ordering principle of social organization, one of the hallmarks of the Vorster era. While P. W. Botha receives the troops back into SWA, he is flanked by Peter Kalangula of the Owambo legislative council on his right, and Pastor Cornelius Ndjoba, chief minister of the Owambo, on his left. Even in defeat, the central optic of the war was to prove the regime's ability to co-operate productively with black Africa in the pursuit of common interests. The foreground tells a different story. The young soldiers, many of them conscripts, have named their tank: "Proud Mary," keeps on rolling. If this is a reference to Creedance Clearwater Revival's 1969 original, that underlines the new generation's openness to global culture. Afrikaans was the lingua franca of the armed forces by this time, but the youth were circumventing the state's cultural controls and norms to worship rock music all the same. If it is a reference to the more recent Ike and Tina Turner version (1971), African-American music, then this points to something more: the growing though fragile understanding among young people that blackness might not have to be simply feared and spurned—if African political desires could be channeled into, and contained within, the homeland framework. Source: National Archives of South Africa.

shared by all of the different constituencies in the Nationalists' newly broad church. Unlike on most economic or social policy issues, the interests of working-class or rural Afrikaners in the resolution of the country's legitimacy issue or the entrenchment of long-term national security were actually closely in alignment with those of wealthy English-speaking whites in the suburbs of

Cape Town. In some ways, even though *verkramptes* recoiled at Vorster's engagement with African leaders, if he could establish long-term viability for the polity then his plan offered to rigidly and permanently define privileged citizenship in purely racial terms. This was even more of a core concern for traditionalists than it was for the middle classes.[19] However, precisely because Vorster had anchored his foreign policy in the principle of multinationalism, its failure only served to highlight the increasing instability of the underlying political and conceptual bedrock.

This eclipse of the NP as a fundamentally *national* party, pursuing a future of multinational separate development, was both sudden and unequivocal. One story illuminates the vastness of the ideological vacuum that emerged.

By 1976, Joseph Rhodes was a rising star in the US Democratic Party. Having already served two terms in Pennsylvania's House of Representatives and briefly enjoyed the political limelight for his work with the Nixon Administration's Commission into Campus Unrest, he began to turn his attention toward Southern Africa. He had repeatedly broached the idea of a fact-finding visit to Ford officials, only to be brushed off. He made the same offer to the incoming Carter Administration, who sent him to South Africa for a month to gauge the political climate and establish contacts with local black leaders. Rhodes was just twenty-nine and African American.

Little was expected of the trip. "Relax and enjoy yourself," incoming Ambassador to the UN, Andrew Young, advised the overeager politician. "You learn more that way."[20] However, at an event at the American ambassador's official residence, the aggressively *verligte* Nationalist MP Louis Nel sought Rhodes out. Nel told Rhodes that on November 23 there had been a secret meeting of the party's central committee. Vorster had told the assembled that the only way "to save Afrikanerdom" was to make major changes during the next parliamentary session, including the wholescale removal of racial discrimination. Influx control, the Group Areas Acts, race classification, and the Immorality Act would all be "scrapped." However, Nel stipulated, there was a precondition: "[N]one of this would happen unless there could be an informal understanding between the US and South Africa on what was "significant" change for this year, next year was another matter." Rhodes could not believe his ears and insisted that he had to hear it for himself from someone higher up. On December 20, he duly met with both Nel and Connie Mulder. The Transvaal leader repeated much the same message. In Rhodes's account:

> [Mulder] state[d] that his government anticipated a new, more aggressive American policy toward South Africa, and indeed only such a policy would give his government the out it needed to make real changes, changes that the enlightened members of his party knew had

to come if South Africa was to have a peaceful future but changes they could not make if they appeared to come as a result of black unrest.[21]

The Carter Administration quickly saw that getting involved in quid pro quos with the apartheid regime would be foolish, and the opening came to nothing.[22]

Yet the Nel–Mulder approach raises plenty of questions. Was Mulder used as the high-level mouthpiece because he was Nel's superior as head of the Transvaal NP, because of his extensive experience with American officials, or because Vorster had acknowledged that he was his likely successor? Why was P. W. Botha not deputized to make this approach? His politics and power base were markedly more reformist than Mulder's, which straddled both suburban Johannesburg *verligtes* and rural Transvaal *verkramptes*, and everything in between. Or were Nel and Mulder in fact working without Vorster's assent at all? There is no record in the prime minister's diary of such a meeting of the party's central committee in the whole month of November. The answers to all of these questions remain outstanding. The big picture, however, is clear. The regime had lost any and all sense of its long-term goal, of what it was trying to actually preserve beyond mere survival. Many aspects of the previously hallowed separate development template were now on the table. Verwoerdian apartheid was no longer considered a valid roadmap for the future and had been unceremoniously consigned to the past. The question now was, what would replace it?

In short, the regime needed a new ideology, one that incorporated the tropes and narratives of Afrikaner identity without alienating non-Afrikaners. It had to provide for continuity with the *volkstaat* cause of the past, while simultaneously mobilizing all whites for the sacrifices that would be needed to face the new challenges emerging at home and abroad.[23] Vorster continued to vaunt nationalism as the answer to this problem. In November 1976, he told the Broederbond Executive Council that "the recent trying months and weeks had convinced him anew that there is no way to handle race relations but the way of separate development. . . . He called on the [Broederbond] to take stock and throw everything into the battle to maintain and promote this policy."[24] However, it was increasingly common ground within the party that South Africa's future would have to depart from ideas that were seen as sacrosanct just a few years before. In their place would be the construction of a black middle class, an entirely new approach to urban blacks, and a political path for Coloreds and Indians. The NP constitutional committee, which began sitting in spring 1976 under the chairmanship of P. W. Botha, was the initial engine for driving many of these ideas into the center of Nationalist discourse and, later, policy. As these ideas emerged from the shadows into mainstream Nationalist forums, horrified conservatives pointed the finger firmly at *suidelike geldmag* [colloquially, "Cape big business"]. Doubtless, the white upper classes strongly supported the proposed measures.

But the committee was broad based and included the heads of the other major regional caucuses, Alwyn Schlebusch (Free State) and Connie Mulder. Such was the increasingly broad acknowledgement of the need to change from the future of Verwoerd's and Vorster's dreams to a new dispensation that acknowledged the realities on the ground.[25] The challenge was whether the party could find a new language and identity to manage change, instead of being consumed by it.

The last part of this book explains why and how it was the hawks and their apolocalyptic security threats that began to fill the vacuum, becoming both a partner and a vehicle for the NP's fitful and abortive transition to a new sense of self and purpose. This development was most unanticipated. No ideological concept or policy of any importance in the Nationalist canon had ever originated in the military. Yet total strategy suddenly evolved from a counterinsurgency doctrine of interest to a few generals interested in colonial wars to a governing template for the state, one whose slogans were common knowledge among the populace. Indeed, while Angola drove Vorster to embark on a last-ditch effort to reengage with the international community and resuscitate regional détente, the hawks saw the same events as heralding a critical mass in the expansion of the total onslaught. They therefore pressed the government to adopt a total national strategy. In doing so, they not only challenged how Pretoria developed and executed national security policy, but also established a conceptual and policy foundation that offered an alternative to the dominant dovish approach to South Africa's interaction with the outside world and, later, a mechanism for the reconstitution of the state's plan for the future.

A New Approach

In late May 1976, P. W. Botha, outgoing Chief of the Defense Force Biermann, and his designated replacement, Malan, twice sat down together to assess what had gone wrong during Operation Savannah and how those mistakes could be avoided in the future.[26] Reflecting on these conversations, Biermann wrote that while the full consequences of Angola "ha[d] still not yet been fully evaluated," all three men had agreed that "preliminary partial analysis indicate[d] unmistakably that there were weaknesses in our planning and execution that could have been avoided if we had implemented a coordinated strategy. . . . At times during the operation there was an uncomfortable ad hoc feeling—rather than a considered and planned strategy."[27] For his part, Malan stressed that Angola had hardly been an "isolated occurrence," but instead "[t]he list of examples" of uncoordinated policy formed an "unbroken series" emanating from "all areas" of the government and whose "effect [wa]s cumulative."[28] Meeting in June, the Defense Planning Committee (DPC), whose central role was to prepare the military for future challenges, endorsed these conclusions: "It was agreed that the major problem confronting Defense was the lack of a national strategic policy. Until this policy is laid down Defense will be planning in a void."[29]

It was not only the perception of strategic shortcomings during Operation Savannah that brought the issue of strategy, long on the hawks' minds, once more to the fore. In the post-Angola environment, Botha and his generals had become painfully aware that they lacked the means to combat the range of renewed threats to South Africa's security. In part, the issue was simply the amount of government funding. Botha worked tirelessly throughout the second half of 1976 to ensure that every surplus rand in the government's coffers was redirected to Defense.[30] But Biermann, Malan, and Botha agreed that the underlying issue was not so much how much money was being channeled to national defense, but that those funds were not being used as efficiently and systematically as they could be due to the lack of a coordinated, interdepartmental approach to national security.[31] They felt that in the new regional climate the development of a conventional warfare capacity was urgently needed. Equally, without the government designating the areas of national strategic priority, the hawks realized that they did not know how to plan such a buildup or how much money to ask the government for.[32]

For the hawks, the Soweto unrest underlined the disastrous results of allowing this situation to continue.[33] On June 14, just two days before the first insurrections, the DPC "emphasized that with the present financial provision Defense can barely cope with a situation of insurgency in South Africa. If any other actions are contemplated eg. offensive action beyond South Africa's borders[,] greater funding will be required."[34] As the unrest unfolded and spread to townships across the country, Biermann duly reflected that even with the expanded defense budget secured on the back of Botha's strenuous advocacy, the SADF did not have the resources to simultaneously neutralize both internal and external challenges. If a need arose for "any further actions, like eg. a police action in Rhodesia or eg. an attack on a hostile neighboring state, the SADF will currently not be in a position to ensure success," the departing chief wrote ominously.[35] Botha told Vorster much the same thing. In the current climate, he stressed, "the Defense Force must be prepared to fight internal subversions as well as border insurgencies, as well as to deal with [*hoof te bied*] an escalation to a conventional regional confrontation like Angola."[36] With this realization, the hawks resolved to take the initiative.

While the townships burned through the winter of 1976, Botha and Malan worked together to develop a plan aimed at convincing the government to adopt a national strategy. The two men quickly formed a close and dynamic partnership. When Botha finally relinquished his position as defense minister in 1980, it was Malan whom he trusted to take over the mantle he had held for fourteen years.

"They had a father-son relationship. And it was very clear who was the father and who was the son," recalled Military Intelligence officer Chris Thirion.[37] "Magnus Malan had a lot of respect for P. W. Botha," remembers Stoffel van der Merwe, who worked extensively alongside both men. "He stood under the discipline of P. W. Botha willingly."[38] Under the Botha-Malan axis, Defense and the SADF enjoyed a marked synergy, reinforcing each other's conclusions about the nature of South Africa's external challenges and the most appropriate responses.[39] Both men saw the national security threats of the mid-1970s as functions of the total onslaught and, as disciples of Beaufre, supported the adoption of a total strategy as the antidote to global communism. Beyond that commonality, the relationship was one of complements, not mirror images. Malan was something of the philosophical engine. As a young officer, he had been seconded to the French army in Algeria in the late 1950s, before further developing his counterinsurgency thinking at Fort Leavenworth, Kansas, where he spent 1962–63. He vigorously promoted the diffusion of the ideas and strategies that he had picked up during these experiences, including sponsoring Deon Fourie's 1969 SADF seminar on strategy. The rising star of the SADF was a "very enthusiastic" follower of Beaufre, Fourie recalls. "P. W. was quite profoundly influenced . . . by Magnus, and Magnus was very much a thinker about counter-insurgency."[40] For his part, Botha offered a mastery of bureaucratic processes honed over four decades as a career politician and NP powerbroker, as well as an extraordinary energy and persistence. Just as total strategy particularly appealed to Malan because of its epiphanic insights into counterinsurgency, Botha was drawn by its potential to impose order on the chaos of the South African government.

Botha's direct style was both an impediment and an asset to the cause. In both February 1973 and June 1974, he and Biermann had successfully lobbied for the creation of committees designed to facilitate a more multifaceted and coordinated approach to the insurgency threat.[41] Botha advised the SSC: "The effective countering of the entire hostile effort in the fields of subversion, propaganda, insurgency and terrorist aggression, will require the coordinated efforts of a wide spectrum of governmental bodies . . . in order to . . . [m]ake the most effective use of all the resources at our disposal."[42] The Cabinet duly created a new Interdepartmental Counterinsurgency Committee, headed by Biermann and reporting to the SSC.[43] But much like its predecessor—the Joint Interdepartmental Counterinsurgency Committee—the new institution proved too weak to effect the designated end, let alone promote total strategy ideas and principles more generally.[44] This failure reflected the central shortcoming of Botha's heavy-handed approach to the promotion of total strategy. His indefatigable willingness to take the initiative and the reluctance of his colleagues to confront or question him consistently resulted in the creation of the committees and institutions that he desired. It was easier to say yes and move on than to stand in his way. However, so long as he was only defense minister and therefore one of many relevant actors in Pretoria, the effectiveness of these bodies in executing the ambitious task of providing more cohesion to South Africa's national security policy depended not on the institutions' existence alone, but on the actual commitment of the participants across the government to the total strategy vision. This required Botha to persuade other departments, Cabinet ministers, and key civil servants of the benefits of his philosophical vision on its intellectual merits—and the abrasive defense minister was anything but well suited to this task. Malan later recalled: "There were times when we butted heads . . . oh, yes. At one stage when I was Minister [for Defense] I made a decision and he queried it to the extent that I said I'd resign. It was about buying submarines. We didn't speak to each other for three months. . . . He could be nasty, boy there were times when he was nasty. But you had to take it."[45] Another close ally, the Head of the National Intelligence Service, Niël Barnard, likewise resigned himself to Botha's forceful personality: "P. W. was a tough man, [but] Africa is a tough place."[46] These perceptions of Botha constituted a major obstacle to the hawks' efforts to persuade independent stakeholders, including elected representatives and top public servants, to alter their perspectives on South Africa's relationship with the world, undertake the transformative reforms they proposed, and effectively place the nation on a war footing.

When the Cabinet reconvened after the winter recess in August, Botha and Malan embarked on an all-out lobbying campaign, simultaneously advocating the development of a national strategy at the SSC, before Cabinet, and on the prime ministerial level. The centerpiece of this effort was Botha's submission to Cabinet.[47] The government was reeling from Soweto. However, as in the post mortems following the intervention in Angola, the questions Soweto raised regarding the shortcomings of apartheid—specifically the reluctance of blacks to embrace the identities, structures, and political rights that Pretoria had designated for them—were ignored. Instead, Botha told his agitated colleagues that the recent urban unrest was but another manifestation of the total onslaught. In order to achieve "the overthrow of the current government's authority and the imposition of a black majority government," South Africa's enemies were engaged in "a psychological onslaught to indoctrinate the local people to revolt and to undermine the state's actions." The goal was "the activation of the black masses to agitate for baseless political rights."[48] Much the same message was voiced by Malan in a foreboding speech delivered in Rustenburg around the same time, entitled "Shoulder to the Wheel":

> The world persists in seeing [the situation in South Africa] as a conflict between white and black. This is far from the truth, however, for what we face is really an ideological attack aimed against black *and* white, an

attempt to destroy the harmonious and peaceful way of life in a civilized country in order to replace it with a puppet regime based on communistic doctrines.[49]

In his Cabinet submission, Botha suggested that the worst might be yet to come. "The Communist onslaught from Black Africa escalates daily," he outlined. "The current security situation can escalate overnight, as happened in Angola, to a semi-conventional war. It is indeed the strategy of the Communist to escalate from insurgency to conventional."[50] All of this led to a predictable conclusion: "From the nature of the enemy's strategy it is clear that the RSA must institute comprehensive action . . . [with] the efforts of all State Departments coordinated and orchestrated at the highest level."[51]

Building upon the Cabinet submission, over the first two weeks of August, Botha and Malan successfully sought government approval for three structures that they had identified as potential forums for the development of a national strategy. In doing so, they endeavored to avoid the impression that they sought to dictate to the government what that final strategy might be. In a draft submission to the SSC, Malan purposefully declared in his introduction: "[I]t is already acknowledged that the deployment of the Military takes place under parliamentary control. The freedom of action of the Military is defined, limited, and circumscribed in the Defense Law. As Defense is an instrument of policy, it is necessary that its actions be realized by national security objectives which are identified by the Cabinet."[52] Botha and Malan also consistently cited as the basis for their submissions the recommendations of the Venter Commission into security policy chaired by J. J. Venter, Head of the Public Service.[53] Since its publication in early 1975, the Venter Report had attracted little attention within the government. However, it served the hawks' ends to frame their proposals in terms of the Commission's impartial and independent recommendations, thereby mitigating perceptions of a radical Defense-driven overhaul of the state's national security apparatus.

First up was the creation of a Sentrale Buro vir Konflikhantering (SBK, Central Bureau for Conflict Management) as a permanent secretariat to the SSC, a proposal taken from the Venter Report.[54] The hawks however envisaged the SBK as having a much more expansive role. In a submission to the SSC in early August, Malan pointed out that while current statutory authority accorded the SSC a dual role—to advise on security threats and responses and to define intelligence priorities—the body needed to take on a more specifically "strategic" function.[55] In a Cabinet memorandum, Malan expanded on how the SBK might provide this. Although the "proposed functions of the SBK were described" in the Venter Report, he recommended that "[t]hese must be broadened to include all aspects of national or total strategy. The influence of political, military, economic, psychological, and technological factors in the formation of the total strategy in a non-conflict situation must be controlled by the same body, namely the SBK."[56]

Second, Botha and Malan advocated the creation of an interdepartmental committee to pilot the development of a national strategy.[57] On August 10, the SSC duly created a five-man body, featuring Malan, Brand Fourie, van den Bergh, Piet Rautenbach, chairman of the Public Service Commission, and L. Botha, from the Prime Minister's Office.[58]

Finally, Botha and Malan sought government sanction for a one-day strategy symposium to be held at Voortrekkerhoogte.[59] Botha asked Vorster and other members of the inner Cabinet to ensure that key civil servants attended. In his characteristically direct style, Botha reminded his colleagues of the under-lying national security imperative: "It is such that, in today's world, the scope of strategy is 'total', meaning that it includes the whole field of State activities. Unfortunately many of our civilian leaders still do not see strategy in this light but consider it as a matter which belongs solely in the armed forces. This is natu-rally a completely wrong view."[60]

Overcoming Opposition

In arguing the need for a total national strategy, Botha and Malan encountered substantial resistance from those outside the defense establishment. Vorster's foreign policy team in particular did everything they could to impede the hawks' agenda. Far from seeing the need for an SADF-driven national strategy, they resented the military's constant distraction from—and often undermining of—Vorster's diplomatic agenda. Despite Defense's best efforts, the interdepart-mental committee therefore never actually met, because Brand Fourie, the des-ignated chairman, consistently declared himself unavailable.[61] Similarly, instead of engaging with the symposium, Brand Fourie and Eschel Rhoodie attended only very briefly, perhaps for just half an hour each, while van den Bergh did not turn up at all.[62] In hawkish circles, Deon Fourie recalls, this was interpreted as "very clearly a signal" to other civilian attendees of the low priority they accorded the entire event. "It was so obvious," he reflects.[63] The doves were not alone in their opposition. One post-symposium SSC memorandum drafted by Defense acknowledged that the occasion had highlighted the "diverse opinions of the government departments over the influence and influencing of a body on State Security."[64] Some invitees "felt that the creation of a permanent body on the prime ministerial level was incompatible with the principles of parliamen-tary rule under the Westminster parliamentary system."[65] Others thought that a Cabinet committee could discharge the envisaged strategic responsibilities.

Still others believed that the entire chain of command within the government needed to be reshaped.

Plainly, outside Defense and the SADF, other government departments were suspicious that the creation of the proposed structures and the adoption of a total strategy would lead to an increased role for the hawks in decision making within their own policy preserves and the abrogation of parliamentary control. "[I]t was really a problem of bureaucratic politics," Deon Fourie remembers.[66] Thirion agrees. "They [Botha and Malan] tried to do it in a more democratic way. They formed a secretariat of the State Security Council. . . . And it didn't go off well, because it was somewhat dominated by the military. The concept was seen as a military concept."[67] The hawks' advocacy of a strengthening of the SSC in particular, where the military featured prominently and many civilian departments were not represented at all, likely did nothing to allay suspicions. The make-up of the symposium must have also caused alarm. While a wide range of stakeholders in South Africa's future were invited, including representatives from DFA, Information, Justice, Treasury, BOSS, the Prime Minister's Office, academia, and the private sector, the military nevertheless accounted for fully half the invitees.[68] Similarly, of the lecturers speaking at the symposium, Venter, M. H. A. Louw from the Institute for Strategic Studies at the University of Pretoria, Wim de Villiers from General Mining and Finance Corporation, and S. S. Brandt from the Prime Minister's Economic Advice Board, represented a reasonable cross-section of civilian interests and expertise. However, this still left five of the nine lectures on the day to be delivered by SADF officers.[69] Also notable was the type of experts who were being enlisted to create and shape the state's future. There were zero invitees from the ranks of those whose prestige derived from their role in the cultural defense of the *volk*. In their place were experts chosen on the basis of their technical expertise: business leaders in place of pastors, security experts instead of university rectors, political scientists instead of theologians.

For Brand Fourie in particular, it must have been difficult to see how the development of a national strategy designed explicitly to channel the government's resources toward the maintenance of national security could not result in a greater voice for the military on regional policy and a commensurate devaluation of the role of the DFA. The content of the hawks' national security proposals and their disagreements with existing policy were no secret. Attached to the hawks' Cabinet submission proposing the creation of the interdepartmental committee and the sanctioning of the strategy symposium was an SADF-Defense document entitled "A Proposal of Possible Policy Guidelines for RSA's Total Strategy." The "Proposal" predictably advocated a markedly more proactive and assertive regional posture. At a time when Vorster was struggling to repair South Africa's fractured relationships with the former Portuguese colonies and desperately trying to orchestrate a transfer of power in Rhodesia, the "Proposal" suggested preemptive action to prevent an unfavorable military buildup in Angola and Mozambique and that "Rhodesia be supported in its conflict with a common enemy on all levels (Covert)."[70] Fourie and his foreign policy colleagues therefore resolved to ignore the hawks and their ideas. Even in the extended version of his memoirs, the military and total strategy hardly feature, though they had a crucial influence on South Africa's overall foreign policy, particularly from the late 1970s onward. This decision not to engage with the new structures was a tactical error. The real threat to the balance between military and civilian elements in the policymaking process, particularly on foreign and national security policy issues, did not lie in the development of a national strategy per se. The doves could have participated in the new structures, working together with other departments to neutralize, influence, or dilute the hawks' concrete proposals. Instead, the absence of other proposals or ideas merely indirectly validated the hawks' insistence that a national strategy could only be informed by total strategy ideology.

This ideology posed an inherent challenge to the existing division of responsibilities at the highest levels of government. Its all-encompassing nature not only provided the hawks with a justification to go beyond reshaping government structures or advocating purely military policies, it constituted an ideological imperative to embrace a more holistic approach to their remit and to engage with otherwise extraneous policy areas affecting military performance, such as industrial production, economic affairs, and manpower regulations. For the hawks, the nature of the Cold War mandated an expansive view of national defense. "According to the current modern concept defense is not just limited to military actions, but includes also actions in other fields which can be used in the indirect mode of strategy to exercise pressure on an enemy," one Department of Defense Cabinet submission stated. "An effective defense strategy must cover/include all of these terrains, and what is more, provisions must be made for coordination and the orchestration of actions in and between the various terrains. . . . The whole problem revolves around the concept of a Total Strategy (on a national level)."[71] The development of a comprehensive national strategy was not seen as a policy option, but an objective necessity. Moreover, total strategy, as advocated by Beaufre and interpreted by the hawks, was self-evidently not restricted to the reform of government structures and policymaking procedures with a view to creating a coordinated strategic approach to the regime's problems. The ideology equally entailed a specific global outlook or paradigm for interpreting threats—total onslaught—as well as a set of particular conventions as to how those threats were to be combatted according to given postwar counterinsurgency practices.[72] Both in Beaufre's ideology and in Botha's practice, these elements were inseparable, two halves of one whole. Pretoria's doves were justifiably

worried on a purely bureaucratic level that the new structures would provide a
gateway to increased military influence in policymaking. However, perhaps the
more significant challenge existed on the ideological plane: the creation of the
new structures in the context of the doves' disinterest constituted a limited but
substantive recognition of total strategy ideology that served to validate and later
institutionalize the accompanying total onslaught worldview and proactive military doctrines.

Although the doves believed that Botha and Malan's restructuring of government policymaking would marginalize civilian input, the hawks saw things differently. To them, the new institutions were designed specifically to engage the
civilian government in designing a new national strategy. "We went a long way
in trying to coerce other departments into realizing they had a very important
part to play in the revolutionary war," Malan's replacement as chief of the army,
Constand Viljoen, admits.[73] Though doubtless the hawks wanted a major input
on the military aspects of that strategy, to take a leading role in its drafting would
have run directly counter to Beaufre's own insistence on the primacy of civilian authority in this area. It was "under direct control of the Government—ie
political authority" that total strategists were "to define how total war should be
conducted," Beaufre had pontificated.[74] As political scientist Chris Alden points
out in the leading study on Botha's approach to governance: "The functional
requirements of total strategy demand that the military play a role in conjunction with other governmental departments but there is clearly no room in total
strategy for the dominance of the military side of the equation."[75] One of the
most commonly heard axioms during the total strategy era was that the solution
to neutralizing the total onslaught was only 20 percent military and 80 percent
political. "At the end of the day, there is no military answer to insurgency warfare,
revolutionary warfare, whatever you want to call it," Thirion remembers. "[T]hat
is what General Malan would have told you."[76]

In the years to come, Afrikaner capital and *verligte* elites would each find in
total strategy's inherent claim to overarching policy authority a vehicle conducive
to their reformist agendas. Changes to influx control, the altering and repealing of
job reservation legislation, the legalization of black labor unions, and more were
all rationalized as national security priorities. As Dan O'Meara put it: "In Botha's
vision, clinging to policies that did not work represented the greatest danger to
Afrikaner survival simply because it handed to the enemies of Afrikanerdom ever
greater opportunities to mobilise ever more powerful forces against the beleaguered volk."[77] Total onslaught was thus explicitly mobilized to legitimize reform.
This often happened above the heads of the existing government bureaucracies,
in the new security apparatus created in the name of total strategy.

Yet in these early stages of the advocacy of total strategy, practice within the
military reflected Beaufrean doctrine. The imperative remained to coordinate,

not to dictate; the entire endeavor was very process oriented. Even when the SADF attempted for the first time to develop a more comprehensive national strategy of its own for a given problem—in this case, Rhodesia—it arrived at precisely no specific policy recommendations, concluding merely that inter-departmental action was more vital than ever: "Due to the lack of a national strategy, the formulated military strategy [for Rhodesia] is not comprehensive enough to deal with all aspects of the total onslaught. . . . The formulation of a Total Strategy based on a joint strategic evaluation by all state departments is now an exceptionally critical need."[78] This tendency was even more pro-nounced outside military policy. While Botha and the military had begun to broach a broader approach to defense that incorporated the nonmilitary fields in which the country needed to impose its will, their memoranda and studies in these areas were notable primarily for their vagueness.[79] There were occasional references to the need to create parallel but subordinate institutions enabling Coloreds and Indians to govern their "own affairs," for example, or to the idea "that the people as a whole be engaged in the defense of the country."[80] However, the understanding that Beaufre's emphasis on undercutting the appeal of revo-lutionary action would require the sort of pervasive political reforms associated with the early Botha era (1978–83) remained very much undeveloped in 1976.

In this context, it was to the hawks' alarm and frustration that the civilian leadership refused to engage with the new structures and assume the central role in designing a national strategy that the hawks had designated for them. "The military people complained bitterly about the fact that the civil servants refused to chair the State Security Council or the subordinate councils. They [the civil servants] always pushed the military people into taking the chair. . . . The lack of enthusiasm on the part of the civil servants was actually the reason why the Defense Force took such a leading role," Deon Fourie remembers.[81] Thirion offers an alternate but compatible explanation. "The creation of the secretariat of the State Security Council was [designed] to give other departments the op-portunity to join in there and second people and have a say," he recalls. "But because, let's be honest, the military understood the concept of total war and total strategy as a department better than anyone else, the first secretaries—the heads of the Secretariat—was [always] a General [*sic*]. That probably wasn't the correct move. It didn't go off well with the rest of the administration."[82]

There was—and would continue to be—a tension between the Beaufrean edict on the primacy of civilian authority in articulating national direction and the hawks' urgent desire in light of the strengthening total onslaught to get a strategy in place regardless of which department was in the driving seat. In the short term, the hawks resolved this tension by interpreting the reservations expressed by nonmilitary officials at the symposium as little more than con-cerns "that their positions of power would be undermined."[83] They rationalized that such concerns could not be allowed to impede a process that they saw as meriting the highest priority. In October, Military Intelligence's annual threat assessment was completed, depicting an ever-increasing total onslaught. "The intensity and circumstances of violence and hostile actions has increased during 1976 and the onslaught has strengthened on various levels," the assessment found. "Communist powers still aim to isolate the white power structure in Southern Africa further and to bring about its collapse through a range of political, economic, military and other means of coercion."[84] The assessment detailed that Angola had recently signed a cooperation treaty with Moscow, Mozambique's assistance to the onslaught was predicted to increase as Frelimo solidified its authority there over the coming year, and the OAU was exhibiting "a great degree of solidarity against white governments."[85]

Accordingly, from October 1976 onward Botha and Malan began to reevaluate. If the government refused to take the initiative in developing a national strategy, they would assume a more hands-on role. This important transition was reflected in Defense's postsymposium SSC submissions, in which the hawks claimed that the symposium provided a clear mandate to start formulating a national strategy. One submission recorded: "a) Without exception the need for a national/total strategy was identified and accepted. b) Without exception the need for coordination of the activities of the various state departments in the pursuit of joint national goals was identified and endorsed."[86] Another noted that the symposium had unanimously adopted a resolution citing "a need for a permanent body which on the authority of the Prime Minister could deal with strategic matters on a coordinated basis"—without mentioning whether any alternative resolutions had even been advanced.[87] With the civil service's input and approval having already been supposedly ascertained, the hawks then advocated that henceforth the bureaucracies' self-interested opposition based on "departmental views and loyalties" needed to be excluded.[88] Botha and Malan proposed that in place of the five-man interdepartmental committee, which had still never met, a new committee needed to be convened under the aegis of the SSC.[89] In contradistinction to the previous emphasis on the primacy of civilian institutions, the SSC became the engine for the drafting of a national strategy.[90]

A New and Total Strategy

These intricate bureaucratic tussles during the second half of 1976 had a major and wholly unanticipated impact on the future of the regime, its statecraft, and the Southern African theater of the Cold War. P. W. Botha and Malan had identified in national strategy an effective conceptual and bureaucratic terrain on which to promote their alternative approach to the regime's long-term security.

Those outside the SADF and Defense were initially bemused by the seemingly sudden obsession with "strategy" and failed to quite grasp the possible long-term implications of the hawks' innovations. However, by early 1977, the foundations for an entirely new brand of statecraft, governance, foreign policy, and national security policy had been laid. Initiative, force, and assertiveness would be promoted as replacements for Vorster's existing tenets of cooperation, diplomacy, and persuasion. Moreover, total strategy further entrenched the position of total onslaught as the central overarching paradigm through which events outside South Africa would be understood within the regime. The events of the second half of 1976 therefore provided both the opportunity and the compunction for the convergence of three factors that came to have a major influence on how the apartheid regime interacted with the world outside its borders: a newly assertive defense establishment feeling impelled to action by global events; a dogged and powerful minister who tirelessly represented their interests at the political level; and a holistic, inflexible, and (ironically) limited ideology that mandated a national posture incompatible with Vorster's constructive and cooperative approach to geopolitics.

Total strategy thus developed through the realization of the national security establishment that they lacked the mandate and resources to effectively counter the broad range of security threats facing the country. It subsequently both became the ideological vehicle for reform and shaped the structures of governance that facilitated that reform.[91] Anticommunism was therefore not just a mode of threat perception or a domestic ideological staple. In the form of total onslaught, it provided the bridge from an essentially ethnic politics to authoritarian reformism, one of the signal changes in the history of the apartheid regime.

The emergence of total strategy also had important consequences for *who* would be assessing the threats to South Africa and the institutional context in which they would do so. Disingenuously or not, the hawks claimed a mandate for a national strategy from the broad array of stakeholders at the symposium. This created an entirely new policy area in which the hawks' preeminence was unchallenged; "total strategy" comprised the only ready template for the content of such a "national policy." The hawks had originally intended their new institutions to encourage civilian departments to take a leading role in developing a national strategy. However, given the refusal of unenthused mandarins to engage with the new institutions, the hawks came to believe that the weight of saving the nation would have to fall on military shoulders and changed their attitude accordingly. In other words, just as the hawks had established an bureaucratic platform from which to advocate their ideas, they were simultaneously overcoming whatever reluctance they had previously felt to wade into the policy arena.

As a bonus, BOSS had been resolutely outmaneuvered and marginalized. Botha and the military had not so much moved the goalposts of their feud from intelligence to strategy as they had created an entirely new game which, given their respective remits, only they could play. To the extent that the hawks sought to work with nonmilitary personnel to fashion their total strategy and broaden its support base, they largely ignored BOSS and the DFA in favor of reaching out to a new breed of expert. As late as the early 1970s, the regime relied heavily on a class of traditionalist elites to bolster the case for the Nationalist agenda. Theologians articulated the moral and religious case, while conservative social scientists provided the pseudoscientific justification. All were Afrikaners, all owed their status to their furtherance of the *volk*, and all were far too close to the NP to provide truly independent perspectives let alone a sustained critique of government policy. Those few who did were marginalized as suspect elements or even enemies of the *volk*.[92] In the era of total strategy, however, *verligte* elites, businessmen, and a new breed of political scientist looking primarily toward the scholarship of globalized academia were all brought into the inner circles of policymaking, including both English-speaking South Africans and even foreigners. All had long been viewed with varying degrees of mistrust by mainstream Afrikanerdom. Many would prove to have little attachment to the ideal of an Afrikaner *volkstaat*.

9

"If you say change, I'll say I can't"

A New Vision

By the start of 1977, pessimism again reigned in Pretoria. With the collapse of the Kissinger Initiatives and Africa's post-Soweto embrace of militant decolonization, it seemed that Southern Africa was destined for an armed conflict fought along racial lines and infused with Cold War imperatives. The negotiations over Rhodesia's future had come to naught. But when Smith signed on to a two-year period for a political transition, he foreshortened the time frame within which his opponents expected regime change, whether through elections or fighting. In February 1977, the OAU Liberation Committee voted to channel all of its Rhodesia funds toward the ZANU-ZAPU Patriotic Front, isolating and weakening moderate leaders like Muzorewa.[1] In SWA, meanwhile, the communist bloc was steadily increasing its military assistance to SWAPO, even as Turnhalle continued to debate the structure of a new Namibia.[2] Ominously for South African interests on both fronts, Soviet President Nikolai Podgorny and Cuban leader Fidel Castro were both due to arrive in Southern Africa in March. Their twin visits reawakened the specter of full-scale communist intervention against the minority regimes in the region. Increased confrontation and military escalation appeared inevitable. Muller, never a wartime consigliere, quietly resigned after a decade as Vorster's foreign minister.[3]

These events prompted a stark reorientation of the apartheid regime's statecraft and ideology. Precisely because Vorster had attached so much political capital to his campaign of international rehabilitation, the sudden deterioration of South Africa's international standing damaged his personal authority. Equally, the domestic fallout of this process created a conducive atmosphere for Botha's prescriptions of unilateralism and defiance, as the NP shifted decisively to the right. Total onslaught and total strategy became entrenched at the heart of the apartheid regime's understanding of its place in the world, its sense of self, and its existential predicament in the region—where they would remain right up until the end of the Cold War.

The Full Court Press

The very day after he took office as Ford's successor, Jimmy Carter issued Presidential Review Memorandum NSC-4, requesting a full multi-agency review of Washington's policy toward Rhodesia, SWA, and South Africa.[4] Principals at the highest level, including Vice President Walter Mondale, Secretary of State Cyrus Vance, National Security Adviser Zbigniew Brzezinski, and Carter himself were personally involved. If "human rights" was to be foregrounded in the new administration's foreign policy, then Southern Africa would be one place where the administration would take a visible stand.[5]

The reorientation of American policy was a milestone. As the various negotiating positions of Zimbabwean nationalists after UDI indicated, and as the settlements proposed for Rhodesia and SWA in 1976 confirmed, the international community was willing to accept much less than a fair deal for all Southern Africans. When it came to racist minority rule in the region, America was no exception. Kissinger told Vorster as much: "Whatever is internationally accepted, we'll accept."[6] The actors involved saw right through American claims to a higher motivating principle. "Kissinger doesn't give a stuff who takes over," Mudge told the NP caucus. "[F]or Kissinger it all boils down to one thing, he wants a solution ... What the consequences might be for South-West, he does not care, he just wants it off the table."[7] From the other side of the color divide, Dar es Salaam saw things much the same way. "We suspect that[,] despite their claim[s,] the Americans are up to something regarding Rhodesia and Namibia," Tanzanian intelligence noted, with clear eyes. "There is every reason to believe that their objective is to install puppet regimes to forestall any possibility of revolutions by armed struggle in Rhodesia and Namibia[.] We are therefore initiating a diplomatic offensive against these designs[.]"[8] Overall, the West wanted to do anything but lead on the issue of white rule and even the most steadfastly pro-Western African leaders knew it. "You Americans have been anti-South African only because you believe that to be otherwise will incur the wrath of black Africa," Zaïrian government adviser Barthélémy Bisengimana told American Ambassador Walter L. Cutler in January 1976. "If we ourselves were to ally with South Africa—you cannot be more papist than the Pope."[9] American administrations had done much to suggest that this perception had substance. In February 1974, outgoing American Assistant Secretary of State for African Affairs, David Newsom, told South African Ambassador J. S. F. Botha: "[T]he establishment of a *modus vivendi* with the Black African countries would, of course, presuppose a significant change in the general acceptability of South Africa's policies and this fact would of itself be of greater importance in bringing about a more positive attitude toward South Africa in the United States."[10] Carter's policy repudiated

Bisengimana's point by establishing that the United States had a direct national interest in the removal of apartheid, rather than the issue largely mattering only insofar as it affected Washington's relationships with the global south.

This was not a perspective that came instinctively to all members of Carter's foreign policy team. One National Security Agency list of American foreign policy priorities from November 1976 put Rhodesia on page 18 and Namibia on page 19. The Middle East, a new Panama Canal treaty, a new Strategic Arms Limitation Talks (SALT) agreement, even civil violence in Cyprus: all were viewed as more important geopolitical issues. Yet even for the more hard-headed Cold Warriors like Brzezinski and his allies, Southern Africa quickly came into the foreground because of the risk of regionwide confrontation. "[T]he possibilities are there to transform this from a black-white conflict into a red-white conflict," he told a major meeting on Southern African policy in February 1977. "There is very little time left. We should start squeezing [Pretoria]."[11]

The Carter Administration's hardline approach toward minority rule in Southern Africa thus not only derived from moralistic-human rights concerns, it also represented a new strategic-geopolitical calculus. Like its predecessor, the Carter policy recognized that in order to resolve the political problems in Southern Africa peacefully and avoid ending up on the wrong side of a racialized Cold War conflict, active and prompt American diplomacy was needed. But unlike Ford and Nixon, the Carter White House adjudged that apartheid was no longer a guarantor of regional stability or a bulwark against communism, but instead actually engendered instability and attracted communist influence.[12] Mondale explained the new approach in an interview with the *Rand Daily Mail*:

> The communists only prevail when there are great human issues that they can exploit and take advantage of. On their own, trying to make headway in a just society, their ideology and their political appeal is minimal and always has been. . . . [S]upport for the minority regimes and an unwillingness to recognize the rights of the majority through racial discrimination, oppression, injustice, and failure to permit political participation, all these things can lead to advancement by communist and other extremist groups. If the South African Government can get itself on the path towards true dialogue and accommodation and political participation by all segments of its own society, it will greatly strengthen itself and it will greatly strengthen the entire region against communist penetration. . . . [T]he best way to silence [the communists] is to move promptly toward social justice so that those profound grievances that otherwise would exist disappear.[13]

This was the most significant conceptual shift in how the US government as a whole viewed apartheid in the entire Nationalist era. It laid bare a major miscalculation by Vorster and his colleagues, who had consistently assumed that the more Washington viewed regional events through a Cold War prism, the more it would feel compelled to offer real protection for its ostensible, if estranged, Western ally. Not so. From the new administration's perspective, apartheid South Africa had ceased to be a reliable anticommunist partner and was now a liability to the West's capacity to contain communist expansionism in the Third World. Instead of having to choose between fighting communism and pursuing social justice, the United States suddenly viewed the two goals as in alignment.

While the Ford Administration had prioritized progress on Rhodesia and SWA over change in South Africa's social order, the Carter Administration resolved to seek progress on all three fronts simultaneously.[14] In this "full court press," Washington would use its leverage to encourage—in Carter's words—"gradual *but persistent*" change within South Africa itself.[15] The Carter Administration did realize that it needed South Africa's cooperation to forestall conflict in Southern Africa.[16] But it sought to persuade Pretoria to do America's bidding out of its own self-interest. Whereas the Ford White House had incentivized Pretoria's cooperation on Rhodesia and SWA by offering the implicit quid pro quo of time to reform on South Africa's own terms at home, Carter's approach was more akin to "stick and bigger stick" than "carrot and stick."[17]

From the outset, the administration was cognizant of the dangers of this approach. In the early stages of policy formation, Carter was concerned that demands for a profound overhaul of South Africa's social and political system "could be counter-productive and drive them [the Nationalists] into a closet." The president continued: "We should alleviate South Africa's concern that we are going to put immediate and absolute pressure on them for a revolution."[18] The National Security Council (NSC) similarly recognized that the South Africans were "stubbornly resistant to change." Too much pressure might "stimulate more obdurate resistance" and corrode Washington's influence entirely.[19] Nevertheless, it concluded, "This is a risk the NSC has decided to take."[20]

In late March 1977, Pik Botha, about to leave his post as ambassador to Washington in order to become South Africa's foreign minister, was summoned to the White House to meet with Carter, Mondale, Vance, and Brzezinski. The administration was determined that the new position on Southern Africa not be misunderstood, or be interpreted as lacking the full support of all the relevant arms of government. Carter opened the meeting by making it clear that if a deterioration of relations was to be avoided, the United States expected a swift transfer to majority rule in Rhodesia and SWA, as well as major steps toward real pluralism in South Africa. Botha was defiant. Separate development was not commensurate with whites "dominating blacks" but rather was the only means of allowing each of South Africa's racial groups to exercise its own "right to self-determination." Moreover, he clarified, petty apartheid was already on the way out. "Discrimination on the basis of color," Botha repeated, "is, in my view, indefensible." On Rhodesia and SWA, Botha pointed out, South Africa's policy remained unchanged. In both, he said, "[w]e are ready to accept a black majority government but not a minority government on the basis of armed force." South Africa badly wanted settlements, but "[e]very time we have done something, we encounter more radical demands." The two sides largely talked past each other. Carter finished the meeting with a stern warning: "The longer we delay settlement[s] the more certain it is that future radical leaders will reject changes that would be possible now. The situation will deteriorate rapidly. Your government will suffer."[21]

Pretoria saw this message as little more than a brazen attack on its internal affairs. Jeremy Shearar, then the number two at the South African embassy in Washington, was present at the meeting. "This was really a cold, hard, no-brakes-barred line from the new administration," he recalled. "When we got back, Pik said to me, 'Jeremy, this is no good. . . . I'm going to send a message back to South Africa to say we cannot work with this administration. . . . They have told us to take certain steps that we cannot take.'"[22] When he heard from his ambassador, Vorster was flummoxed. He pleaded with Carter in a remarkable private letter that channeled pure desperation. There was no introduction, not even a "Dear Mr. President." Instead, the letter opened: "Why must we confront one another, why must we quarrel with each other? Is there no way in which we can sort out our differences?"[23] Vorster sought a private meeting to ascertain exactly what the Carter Administration's position meant for his people and the regime's search for legitimacy.

Vienna

On May 19 and 20, 1977, Vorster met with Vice President Mondale in Vienna. Riaan Eksteen was present as South Africa's newly appointed Permanent Representative to the UN. From the outset, he recalls, "[t]here was no rapport between Vorster and Mondale, as there was with Kissinger."[24] Sole, Botha's replacement at the embassy in Washington, concurred. "The atmosphere was . . . completely different" from that in West Germany the year before, "when Vorster and Kissinger clicked from the outset. . . . Although they were both speaking English they were not talking the same language. . . . There was no meeting of the minds whatsoever."[25]

The first meeting focused on Rhodesia. Although he recognized that the Kissinger Plan itself was moribund, Vorster wanted to reproduce the basic architecture of the 1976 negotiations. "You will look to me on Smith and I will look to you on Nkomo and Mugabe," the South African prime minister outlined. "If you can guarantee Nkomo and Mugabe will fall into line, I will guarantee Smith does."[26] Mondale indeed wanted Vorster to deliver Smith, just as he had done in 1976.[27] But he wanted the focus of the renewed push for a settlement in Rhodesia to comprise the emerging Anglo-American proposals, also known as the Owen-Vance proposals after their primary sponsors, British Foreign Secretary David Owen and the American Secretary of State. The new plan was that London (with Washington's support) would take the lead in drawing up a draft constitution, which could then form the basis for negotiation at a conference attended by the various nationalists and the white Rhodesians—with or without Smith himself.[28] Vorster did not want to see a repeat of the free-for-all in Geneva, nor did he welcome negotiations on the basis of new proposals inevitably less favorable to white interests than the Five Points or even the Richard Plan. Moreover, the South African prime minister had his own political constraints to consider. Bowdler had stressed this to the new administration. Vorster was keen "to see a solution in Rhodesia, preferably on terms favorable to the whites, in order to avoid catastrophic developments there that would inevitably involve South Africa," the ambassador had informed Washington, but he had to avoid "accusations of a sellout" of Rhodesia's whites.[29] The Carter position took no account of such constraints. Indeed, a central weakness in the West's approaches to both SWA and Rhodesia throughout 1977 and 1978 was an inability to seriously acknowledge the realities of South Africa's (and, for that matter, Rhodesia's) domestic political terrains. In Vienna, Vorster was therefore forced onto the defensive. He ventured that no solution was possible through the Anglo-American route so long as the Zimbabwean nationalists were divided and violence continued. Instead, a referendum needed to be held so that Smith could find a black leader to negotiate with. After nearly three years of persuading Smith to abandon his positions, Vorster was suddenly trotting out well-worn lines straight from the Rhodesian prime minister's playbook.[30]

No issue laid bare the chasm between the roles envisaged by Pretoria and Washington for white Rhodesians in a future settlement—and indeed the different perceptions of the future for whites in Southern Africa more broadly—like the Zimbabwe Development Fund. The Fund represented the latest incarnation of the West's economic support for a political transition, packaged the previous year as the Zimbabwe Adjustment Fund. As in 1976, Vorster insisted that white viability was central to the stability and prosperity of the future Zimbabwean state. "A guarantee is needed for the whites from you or Owen," he told Mondale. "A guarantee is needed of law and order, that there will be no expropriation, no confiscation. Otherwise, the whites will leave. Mugabe has said that they will

take over property, that there will be trials by people's courts, a Marxist government and expropriation. If this is so, forget about a solution." Mondale's reply
gave Vorster no comfort. "We hope for a multi-racial Zimbabwe, and the possibility for all who wish to stay [to be able to do so. But] I can't guarantee the
results. . . . We can't guarantee that the people of Zimbabwe will choose a government that will reject public ownership." Moreover, the vice president added,
dropping a bombshell: "The Zimbabwe Fund . . . can't be used simply to buy out
whites. . . . [T]here has been a change. . . . We couldn't support and pass a bill in
Congress for a buy-out fund." The South Africans were astounded. Strategically,
the Fund was seen by Vorster as the critical guarantee of constancy in the new
Zimbabwe, stability being South Africa's foremost geopolitical concern on the
Rhodesian issue. And politically, the "sliding scale" package had been essential
in 1976 to enabling Vorster to apply pressure on Smith while not losing support among his own electorate and within his party. "This is a dramatic and radical change. It will make it impossible for us to continue," Pik Botha responded
sharply. "Originally, the Zimbabwe Development Fund had a dual purpose. It
was to help develop infrastructure, and it was to do everything it could to help
the whites remain," Vorster chimed in. "This is a radical departure now from
what we and Smith were told."[31]

The parties reassembled later that day to discuss SWA.[32] The Contact
Group, also known as the Five—an ad hoc grouping featuring the permanent
Western members of the UN Security Council (the United States, the UK,
and France), as well as the two leading temporary Western members (West
Germany and Canada)—had begun meeting with Vorster on the SWA issue
in April. While Vorster had made all the right noises at this first encounter
in Cape Town, including committing to not ratifying Turnhalle's template
for independence (hereafter, the Turnhalle Constitution) and instead leaving space for an international process to emerge, Washington remained
unconvinced that the South Africans would not reprise Turnhalle in another
role.[33] After all, Pik Botha had told Vance in early March that "the Turnhalle
Conference is so far along that it is too late to change."[34] Mondale therefore
resolved to spell out the Contact Group's position in no uncertain terms: there
would need to be "national elections with all Namibians participating, leading
to a constituent assembly, which would create a constitution. The [interim]
structure would have free and equal elections, without an intimidating environment."[35] The vice president conveyed to Vorster that any interim authority
would have to draw on support beyond the narrow foundations of the existing
conference: "If it is only Turnhalle, it will not be accepted. If it is broadly created, it could be." To ensure there was no confusion, Don McHenry, Deputy
Ambassador to the UN, added bluntly: "Turnhalle has not been a fully par-
ticipatory organization." Vorster refused to back down. "The leaders in South

West Africa have [already] been elected," he insisted. "Turnhalle is representative, no matter what you think." In fact, Vorster continued, Turnhalle already fulfilled the function of a constituent assembly and was in the process of drawing up a constitution. Although Turnhalle was his "enemy," he was duty bound to accept the wishes of South-Westers and allow them to proceed toward independence, if they so chose.[36]

The third meeting, held the next day, focused on apartheid.[37] If the previous two meetings had been tense, the atmosphere of the third was glacial. A year earlier, Bowdler had strongly counseled Kissinger that any endeavor to lecture the South Africans on separate development would prove futile and counterproductive.[38] Mondale was nevertheless unrelenting. "We don't believe [that] apartheid or separateness is workable or just," he told Vorster. He refused to draw any distinction between petty apartheid and grand apartheid. "Progressive transformation is necessary. Basic elements of that transformation are an elimination of discrimination—for us, this includes separateness." Vorster was incensed. The principle of the separate political development of "national" groups was sacrosanct within his party—and had been for decades. "This is a real and workable policy," he insisted. "No one can change [it]. No one will dare to. If you say change, I'll say I can't. It is ingrained and I won't."[39]

Relations soured further after Mondale's postsummit press conference, in which the vice president commented that there would need to be a system of "one man, one vote" in the Republic:

JOURNALIST: Mr. Vice President, could you possibly go into slightly more detail on your concept of full [political] participation as opposed to one man one vote? Do you see some kind of compromise?
MONDALE: No, no. It's the same thing. Every citizen should have the right to vote and every vote should be equally weighted.[40]

To Pretoria, this amounted to a foreign power not just criticizing its internal order, but calling for the destruction of Afrikaner autonomy, as well as rejecting the broader white community's right to determine its future. Even the other side of the House joined the Nationalists in their pique.[41] "It was this statement," Sole recalls, "which in truth was the real beginning of the confrontational build up between South Africa and the United States that became the dominant feature of the relationship between the two countries from 1977 to 1981. Mondale's dreadful faux pas deprived the US Government of all credibility in the eyes of the South African Government, whose attitude owards the United States progressively hardened."[42] Pik Botha's response to Mondale was widely reported: "We shall not accept [one man one vote]. Not now, not ever, never ever."[43]

The Winter of Discontent

In the months that followed the Mondale-Vorster summit, the international community followed Washington's lead and began to marginalize South Africa on a number of fronts. The Commonwealth sought through the Gleneagles Agreement to further cut sporting ties with South Africa. Western governments began to discourage investment; South Africa's net capital outflow rapidly increased.[44] Moves to exclude South Africa from the Atomic Energy Agency accelerated. Even France, long resistant to the international clamor over apartheid, announced it would not sign any new arms contracts with South Africa.

In Pretoria's eyes, Mondale's press conference had made it clear that the regime was no longer considered part of the solution to Southern Africa's problems, as Kissinger had recognized. Instead, as Pik Botha told the Rhodesians, the Americans regarded white minority rule "as a single problem" such that "South Africa was no longer considered separately from South-West Africa and Rhodesia."[45] This was a fair reading of Washington's position. The Americans viewed the various white communities as a collective obstacle to progress. Little effort was made to distinguish between their leaders, political cultures, social norms, domestic compacts, or ideologies. Race alone was perceived as the determinant factor in their behavior. "Vorster probably rejects the idea of genuine elections in Namibia. Even if he believes that the Turnhalle group would outpoll SWAPO, he would likely load the electoral rolls disproportionately with whites," predicted one NSC briefing paper. "The point is that neither Smith nor Vorster wants to yield up power [in Rhodesia and SWA, respectively] and will do so only under duress. Elections do not provide duress; they are what Smith and Vorster might turn to after duress has been applied, as a way of avoiding more intense pressure."[46] This might have been true for Smith and for the vast majority of white politicians across Southern Africa, but it was not for Vorster. He was virtually alone among the higher echelons of the NP in his eagerness to find ways to work with the international community to bring about multiracial (if inevitably unbalanced) polities in both Rhodesia and SWA. The Carter Administration's policies made such a position untenable.

By the winter of 1977, it was widely recognized across the polity that a new era had begun for Pretoria's relationship with the world. At the end of August, Sole cabled home, identifying "a new watershed in South Africa's international relations. Nothing can be the same again. . . . The whole pattern of developments has thus produced a situation where South Africa is far more exposed than ever before in her history to political, psychological, and economic pressures. . . . We should accelerate to the extent necessary the tempo of our contingency planning against the possibility of sanctions."[47] The government simply could not understand why it was being singled out, especially given its peers on the continent. In Vienna, Vorster had challenged Mondale: "I dare you to tell me which African country to accept as a model."[48] This oft-repeated plea may have been self-serving, but it pointed to a valid, if limited, truth: white South Africa was held by the West to substantially higher standards of pluralism, human rights, and democracy than the new postcolonial black states, to which it often turned a blind eye.[49] The late 1970s was the nadir of African political pluralism; perhaps just over 10 percent of states on the continent had a competitive multiparty system.[50] It was equally inconceivable to Nationalists why the West continued to engage with the Eastern bloc countries that posed a mortal Cold War threat, but chose to lecture and isolate distant South Africa. "The West is prepared to co-operate with the Soviet and Marxist States. Although they condemn these States, they are not forever asking them: 'Before I co-operate with you, tell me what your domestic policy is,'" P. W. Botha told the House. "Surely we are dealing with extreme hypocrisy here, and three-quarters of our problems stem from this. The Republic of South Africa is being subjected to double standards."[51] Such points resonated throughout white South Africa.

Figure 9.1 Jimmy Carter: "Away with the South African homelands," he says sternly; "Create a Palestinian homeland in Israel . . . ," he says enthusiastically. Below, a little bird asks, "Mommy, mommy, what's a double standard?" Also of note is the United States crest on the podium, on which the national motto has been altered to read: "Interchangeable values." Source: *Hoofstad*, 19 October 1977. Caxton Company.

The regime's latent insecurity exploded into a full-blown siege mentality fueled by deep-seated xenophobic currents within the body politic. Afrikaner nationalism had long been ethnically exclusive and often hostile toward other national or ethnic groups. These attitudes were reproduced by the historical lore of the *volk*: the Great Trek legend; Afrikaners' treatment by the British in the Boer Wars; the years of political, cultural, and economic subordination within the Union of South Africa. The potency within Afrikaner nationalist mythology of narratives of mistreatment by the "other" was a vital element driving the entire idea of the separate development of South Africa's different ethnic groups; only in isolation, so the thinking went, was cultural integrity viable.[52] And despite the substantial successes of Nationalist rule—the vast improvement in Afrikaners' socioeconomic position, the tight grip on political power, the creation of the Republic in 1961 as the institutional fulfilment of *volk* nationalism, the forging of a pan-white political alliance formed overwhelmingly on Afrikaners' terms, the reaching out into Africa through the outward policy—the fear of all things foreign remained deeply embedded in the culture of the party.

The *verkrampte* right-wing was particularly quick to defend Afrikaner integrity in such terms. "The onslaught which is today waged against the party-political structure in South Africa," Jaap Marais announced upon accepting the leadership of the HNP in late May, "is a left-wing power grab [*magsaanslag*] which has its origins in the English speaking world."[53] His predecessor, Albert Hertzog, opined: "President Carter was carefully selected and prepared for his post by American Capital [*Geldmag*]."[54] Both lines of attack were designed to connect the current crisis to preexisting themes in the far-right's political canon. The former reflected the deep distrust of anglophone culture and ideas, and implicitly rejected Vorster's embrace of English-speaking South Africans. The latter played upon Afrikanerdom's traditional mistrust of capitalism, also historically dominated by English-speaking whites.

Opposition from the right provided fertile soil for a powerful indictment of Vorster's foreign policy and strategic vision in particular. " 'Détente' is not a word that exists in the Afrikaner's vocabulary or dictionary. Our Volk's Voortrekkers never knew such a thing," Hertzog proffered.[55] On Rhodesia, he pointed out sarcastically:

> On the one hand the Blacks must be appeased and their demands satisfied and on the other the will and the spirit of the whites to endure [*staan*] in Rhodesia must be broken. Step by step, [Vorster] has done that. . . . Before Mr. Vorster started with his détente policy and his arse kissing [*flikflooiery*] of the blacks . . . there were scarcely a hundred terrorists in Rhodesia. Since his policy, the terrorists have infiltrated

on a large scale.... First it was Mozambique; then Angola, and now Rhodesia. All under one South African Prime Minister.[56]

Marais struck much the same chord:

> In recent weeks and months, we have again seen how the most drastic concessions are made to hand over Rhodesia, to part with South-West Africa, and to weaken us here in South Africa by tearing down our ramparts [*plat slaan ons skanse*], by tearing away our defenses, in an effort to acquiesce to the demands of these enemy forces. We have now seen that all the concessions on Rhodesia, on South-West Africa, and on South Africa's internal policy are not enough for the enemies of South Africa. What use is it to try to be accommodating towards your enemies when they demand nothing less than your life?[57]

Such critiques rapidly gained traction. *Die Vaderland* observed: "[I]t would appear that Dr. Andries Treurnicht [now] has the support of the majority in the caucus. It would probably be justifiable to conclude from the present climate that the majority of Nationalists are now to the right of the center."[58] The steady shift of the NP towards *verligte* positions, ideas, and discourses over the last decade stopped. With memories of the party turmoil of late 1976 fresh in his mind and his country already facing more than its share of problems, the last thing Vorster wanted was for the HNP, joined by conservatives within the NP, to use foreign hostility to Pretoria to outflank him on the right. A direct challenge to his state-building agenda grounded in charges of liberalism, coddling blacks, diplomatic appeasement, and progressive (or "Prog") politics would be difficult to defeat.[59] "They were [even] more afraid of their right-wing than they were of the communists," Mudge recalls. "To go against sentiments in the Party especially right-wing sentiments was very difficult ... absolute political suicide."[60]

In dealing with this situation, Vorster was caught between fear and temptation: fear of the long-term consequences if he tacked to the right and adopted the unilateralist standard, abandoning his cherished vision of rehabilitation grounded in international cooperation; and temptation to reap the electoral rewards if he did so. There was also the matter of how to reenergize a fracturing party. The HNP breakaway of 1969 had reverberated throughout every level of Afrikanerdom and the party. "Schism," wrote Alf Ries and Ebbe Dommisse, two of South Africa's leading journalists, "is one of the most feared concepts in the vocabulary of Afrikaner politics.... For the National Party 'causing a split' is a deadly sin."[61] The 1934 division between Barry Hertzog's *samesmelters* and Malan's "purists" was likewise etched deep into party lore. The prospect of destroying Afrikaner political unity again weighed heavily on Vorster, P. W. Botha, and their contemporaries. "People of that generation . . . did not want to see the Nationalist Party ruined again," Deon Fourie recalls.[62]

Yet the gap between the different factions of the party was wider and more evident than ever. Koos van der Merwe, who entered Parliament later that year and soon identified with the conservative wing of the NP, recalls the tenor of the times. "Politicians in the National Party and elsewhere slowly started to ask themselves, 'But will [separate development] work? Can we apply it practically?' "[63] Stoffel van der Merwe, from the opposite wing of the party, remembers things similarly. "The Afrikaners were between a rock and a hard place at that time, because it was becoming clear that separate development was not going to be the savior of the Afrikaner. If not that, then what?"[64] Right-wing leaders exploited the unease. Stoffel van der Merwe remembers Treurnicht's resuscitation of an old appeal. "The NG Church tells us that differences between nations is ordained by God. We're back to the Tower of Babel," he recalls. "It is the will of God that nations should be kept [separate]. Apartheid is the will of God." In the political realm, this could only mean one thing: "Separate development is the way to go and nothing else."[65] By appealing to a higher authority, the charismatic preacher was able to circumvent some of the restraints acting upon career politicians. When Treurnicht again breached party practice by airing his dissent in public, the prime minister once more refused to rein him in, displaying a mercy withheld from the HNP splitters. Instead, Vorster feebly told the caucus, "[W]e must preserve [our] unity."[66]

Meanwhile, *verligtes* were tired of following the government's lead and increasingly took up the mantle of reform themselves. For the first time, the AHI invited black capitalists to their annual congress in Cape Town. Blacks already formed "an integral part of . . . our White economy," announced Jan Hupkes, a leading figure in the AHI. "In the foreseeable future, the homelands will not provide enough work opportunities to accommodate the fast growing black peoples."[67] The message was clear: urban blacks had to be brought into the fold; complete racial separation was a thing of the past. As for Coloreds and Indians, "we must make them part of our world," declared Willem de Klerk.[68] The recommendations of P. W. Botha's constitutional committee, released in August 1977, sought to do just that by establishing parliaments for both groups to rule over their "own" affairs, and enabling them to have a limited say in "common" affairs. The outcry on the right was fierce. Vorster pleaded with his divided, disoriented caucus. "[I] remain convinced that the NP's principles are broad enough for everyone, and everyone can be accommodated," he insisted. "We have channels to discuss problems. . . . My door is always open to everyone and you can use it. It is not necessary to talk [about them] in public."[69] The barely camouflaged public sparring between different party factions continued unabated.

In this context, Vorster could not resist embracing chauvinist nationalism, focusing on the foreign hostility, and riding the surge of indignation sweeping across the polity. When called upon to clarify what Mondale had meant with his "one man, one vote" remark, Pik Botha, the worldly face of the government, could have assuaged domestic concerns by pointing to the Carter Administration's subsequent efforts to walk back Mondale's impolitic remarks.[70] Instead, he fanned the flames: "What is it they want us to remove in this country? They have said that they want us to remove the whole basis of the structure of our society. They want to remove our right to govern ourselves and our right to be ourselves."[71] From late July, the *Citizen* newspaper, later revealed to have been directly controlled by the government, launched a series of nine anti-American feature articles published over three weeks.

But even as the government sought to benefit from the backlash against the Carter Administration, it could not control the fire it was fueling. In September, the death in custody of BCM leader Steve Biko and the government's callous response provoked universal condemnation. Police Minister Jimmy Kruger's famous response to Biko's death—"*Dit laat my koud*" ("It leaves me cold," or, more colloquially, "I don't care")—created a public relations nightmare for the regime. Moderate African leaders who had once welcomed Vorster and engaged

Figure 9.2 Anti-Americanism became a staple of Nationalist discourses in 1977. Here, a Hoofstad cartoon depicts Vorster as David fighting against the Goliath of America, with Jimmy Carter unsheathing the sword of sanctions. In the background, the international community clamors. Source: *Hooftstad,* 24 May 1977. Caxton Company.

with his outward policy viciously turned on him. William Tolbert, the President of Liberia and Vorster's host in February 1975, lectured his erstwhile guest in a private letter: "The oppressed masses of South Africa have now demonstrated, even more than ever, an irrepressible will to be free and to enjoy human dignity and, together with all South Africans, become masters of their own destiny. . . . While your Government has made some seemingly positive gestures, real issues remain unresolved; and it seems to me that they *must be resolved*."[72] Sole baldly admitted: "The South African Government's handling of the whole [Biko] episode reduced its international credibility to near zero."[73] In a vicious cycle, more South African defiance brought more international pressure, which in turn sparked more white anger, inflamed social tensions, and fed right-wing pressure on Vorster to regain control. In October, an editorial appeared in the *World* calling for political change in terms far outside the realms of discourse acceptable to the government: "We have realized that it is no longer of any use appealing to the morality of the much vaunted Christianity of those who rule. Now instead we appeal to their instinct for survival. We say to the government and to the whites in general, either abandon your privileges now and submit yourselves to majority rule in a non-racial society or face certain destruction in the future."[74] The attack on the Nationalists' Christianity was intended to provoke, and it did. Vorster responded by arresting forty-nine black leaders, banning eighteen civil rights organizations, and closing down the *World*. The international reaction was immediate, intense, and widespread. Washington withdrew Bowdler and promptly resolved to support a mandatory UN arms embargo.[75] American congressional petitions deplored Vorster's crackdown, as did a demarche from the European Economic Community.[76]

Vorster responded by calling an early election. The Nationalists campaigned on a virulently anti-American, xenophobic, and fear-mongering platform. "The only thing acceptable to the world is radical, Marxist Black rule by the barrel of a gun," Pik Botha announced during the campaign—and in a predominantly English-speaking constituency. "This is the type of rule you will have in South Africa if the National Party is destroyed."[77] The Afrikaans press stoked the flames. "South Africa can no longer trust America," editorialized *Hoofstad*. "America has very clearly finally chosen sides against the Whites in Southern Africa."[78]

The NP won a record 134 out of 165 seats. Vorster was "our hero," remembers Koos van der Merwe.[79] Much as in the crisis years of the early 1960s, playing to acute foreign threats served to coalesce white voters behind the Nationalist banner at the expense of other political players. Both the HNP and the official opposition, the New Republic Party (the successor to the United Party), were thrashed, winning zero and ten seats (as compared to zero and forty-one seats in 1974), respectively. Yet rarely had a landslide victory obscured such political weakness. A better measure of the strength of the government was that 1977 was

„AS Pa nie nou ophou dut en Nasionaal gaan stem nie, is my toekoms daarmee heen!"

Figure 9.3 "If Dad doesn't stop dozing and go vote National, then my future will be gone!" the young girl says. In supporting the National Party's "with us or against us" 1977 election campaign, the Afrikaans press abandoned any pretence of journalism in favor of electioneering and propaganda. Source: *Volksblad*, 30 November 1977. Media24/Gallo Images.

the first year of Nationalist rule in which white emigration exceeded immigration.[80] Nor had Vorster won by triumphing in the battle of ideas; instead he had simply appropriated those of his right-wing. Scholar Christopher Hill estimated that in the new House of Assembly, 77 Nationalist MPs were broadly *verkramp* and only 56 broadly *verlig*.[81]

The events of the long winter of discontent of 1977 undermined Vorster's authority and leadership on a fundamental level. Without a personal political base in any of the provincial caucuses, Vorster had traded heavily on his statesmanship, specifically his ability to offer South Africa a measure of rehabilitation within the international community on its own terms. It was he who had visited Liberia, Malawi, and the Ivory Coast; he who had brought Smith and the Rhodesian nationalists together at Victoria Falls; he who had hosted none other than Henry Kissinger in Pretoria. All of these foreign policy successes had excited the electorate with the promise of an end to isolation without the abandonment of their identity, privilege, and way of life. And he had achieved them not by giving in to South Africa's critics and giving up the party's segregationist politics, but while accelerating separate development, most notably through the independence of the Transkei the year before. Pretoria's humiliation in Vienna and its alienation over the subsequent months was therefore not just destabilizing and arresting to the polity, it also struck at the core of Vorster's premiership. His efforts to put a good face on the Vienna disaster were deeply unconvincing. The chance to get South Africa's point across to the Americans had been "a fantastic experience" and "a wonderful opportunity," he told his caucus. "It went well and we will reap the fruits going forward." A senior British journalist had apparently even remarked that the prime minister reminded him of "the Churchill of old." His trusted acolyte, Pik Botha, was scarcely more plausible. When Vorster told the press in Vienna that South Africa would stand alone, the foreign minister informed the party room, "there was 5 minutes of standing ovation."[82]

The reality was different. Koos van der Merwe recalls seeing Vorster at Libertas on his return from Vienna. "He was shaken, visibly shaken."[83] As Vorster's campaign for the *volk*'s future descended into futility, his effectiveness as a leader evaporated too. He was a "lame duck," Stoffel van der Merwe remembered. "The people around him start[ed] looking to someone else. Who's next? How can I place myself?"[84] Koos van der Merwe agrees. "It was as if [Vorster] stopped," he remembers. "He stopped believing."[85] On August 2, Vorster told his Cabinet that he was considering stepping down. His colleagues persuaded him to stay on, but uncertainty remained over the national leadership.[86] By the second half of the year, it was obvious to all that the government was unable to generate new ideas for the array of issues confronting the country.[87] This provided an opening, for the first time in thirty years, for major political ideas to come from organizations outside the Nationalist family.

Pushing Total Strategy

The collapse in South Africa's international standing in 1977 created a vacuum in the regime's geopolitical policy. Pretoria no longer believed that Western brokers acknowledged the very validity of its interests in constructing and brokering their proposals on Rhodesia or SWA. More fundamentally, the international community had signaled that Vorster's grand vision of a future forged by multinationalism was not achievable. The mood within South Africa had shifted in favor of unilateralism and defiance; the public and the caucus had no more appetite for cooperating with a hostile international community than the leadership did. The minister of defense was no longer alone in advocating a full reevaluation of how Pretoria understood its place in the world, assessed threats, and approached national security at the most basic level. In July, Pik Botha mused to the Rhodesians: "We must discuss a viable strategy together—a total one for

Southern Africa."[88] The language was not accidental. Total strategy was the only developed vehicle for navigation toward a new future, though the course it might take and the precise nature of the destination were decidedly unclear.

In his study of authoritarian politics in postcolonial Southeast Asia, political scientist Dan Slater offers a useful tool for understanding why powerful sectors of the white power structure came on board with a total strategy vision that imposed higher taxes, suppressed the growing cultural, social, and intellectual richness of white society in the name of national security and political ideology, and increased the reach of the state into society and the economy. Slater argues that when challenges to the existing social order are acute and existential, elites can be expected to form "protection pacts—broad elite coalitions unified by shared support for heightened state power and tighter authoritarian controls as institutional bulwarks against continued or renewed mass unrest." Specific conditions have to be met. The popular challenge needs to focus elite anxieties through specific trigger events. The underlying source of the unrest needs to be seen as endemic to the social order, rather than episodic. There needs to be little confidence among elites that desirable change can be effected through a transition to a more open society, but instead requires a more closed one. Finally, the unrest needs to be rooted in class conflict, such that elites readily identify as such and know where the line between ally and foe lies. If these hold true, Slater concludes, elites will support an authoritarian regime, even as it draws upon more of their resources and limits their autonomy in various spheres.[89] Much of this picture can be seen in South Africa in the wake of 1976. Afrikaners remained less well-off than their partners in the white power structure. On average, per capita Afrikaner incomes were only 71 percent of those of English-speaking whites.[90] However, the interests of educated whites in security and an aspirational economy were increasingly similar regardless of whether they spoke English or Afrikaans, while a relatively thin but highly influential slice of Afrikanerdom had entered the white upper class. Moreover, all of these groups saw much the same picture: a nexus of external pressure and internal unrest; a model of ethnic politics that was unable to address the current crisis; and a system that would continue to provoke regular, escalating challenges to the existing social order without fundamental reform. Total strategy addressed each of these issues. It married foreign and domestic policy in a singular statecraft; it paid scant attention to traditional Afrikaner loyalties in favor of developing a diverse socio-political organism with a shared interest in resisting revolutionary change; and it vaunted the importance of imaginative and transformative change to the status quo. From this perspective, total strategy was not unattractive to stakeholders in the middle and upper echelons of the existing white social pyramid.

With the landmark 1977 Defense White Paper, Malan and P. W. Botha had elevated three of the core tenets of total strategy from SADF philosophy to government policy, while simultaneously launching the language and terminology of "Total Strategy" into the public domain.[91] First, there was an acknowledgment that South Africa was currently involved in an ongoing but low-intensity conflict: "[W]e are today involved in a war, whether we wish to accept it or not."[92] Second, there was the characterization of that conflict as a struggle not against liberal internationalist norms or African nationalism, but against a multifaceted Moscow-driven total onslaught. The aims of that onslaught were defined as: "The expansion of Marxism by fomenting revolution in Southern Africa"; "The overthrow of the white regimes in Southern Africa so that the militant Africa bloc can realize its aspirations with regard to the destruction of so-called colonialism and racialism and the establishment of pan-Africanism"; and "The striving after an indirect strategy in order to unleash revolutionary warfare in Southern Africa and, by means of isolation, to force the RSA to change its domestic policy in favor of Pan-Africanism."[93] Finally, there was the insistence that only a "total" response mobilizing all of the resources of the state in an integrated fashion could provide an effective counter to this onslaught. "The process of ensuring and maintaining the sovereignty of a state's authority in a conflict situation has, through the evolution of warfare, shifted from purely military to an integrated national action," the White Paper stipulated. "The resolution of a conflict in the times in which we now live demands an interdependent and coordinated action in all fields— military, psychological, economic, political, sociological, technological, diplomatic, ideological, cultural, etc."[94] These ideas became the foundational pillars of how the regime understood its geopolitical predicament through the 1980s.

Having established total strategy as the conceptual framework within which national security threats would be officially perceived and tackled, Botha traveled to Oubosstrand on August 13–14 to lobby Vorster to follow his lead on policy, a week before caucus was due to meet in Cape Town. It was time, Botha argued, to face up to reality. South Africa faced a buildup of weapons and insurgents in Angola, Rhodesia, and Mozambique. There was increased Russian involvement in the region and an apathetic response by the West. And the Republic was for the first time subject to a conventional threat too: as well as the low-level "indirect" onslaught to which South Africa had long been subject, "the possibility that the Republic might in the medium term be threatened by conventional onslaught, supported by forces of superior military capability, is not merely a far-fetched academic hypothesis."[95] These threats could not be countered by diplomacy alone, he counseled. One internal strategic assessment from Botha's ministerial files noted tellingly: "The aim of total war is to impose the aggressor's will unconditionally on the target country. This aim is similarly 'total' and can only be assuaged by the unconditional capitulation of the target country. In the aggressor's perception 'normalizing relationships,' 'détente,' 'concessions,' 'negotiations' etc. are not solutions, but simply interim steps to the objective."[96]

In this new era, Botha advised Vorster, South Africa had to embrace a more unilateralist and assertive approach to national security. On SWA, Vorster and Botha were in one sense in agreement as to Pretoria's broad aims and policies: South Africa should only be prepared to withdraw from SWA provided that a state friendly to the Republic could be established there. But Botha saw the results of an unfavorable settlement in much more alarmist terms. The August 1977 "SADF Strategic Guidelines on SWA and Angola" put this plainly:

> It cannot be overemphasized that the SWA matter is the current focus of the struggle against the RSA. For us there is much more at stake than just the political future of SWA—our credibility, and therefore the further course of our entire resistance is directly at issue. . . . Once we are out of South-West Africa, we will never be able to get back what we perhaps already now at this critical stage cannot consolidate. The possibility of the emergence of an anti-RSA state on the banks of the Orange River cannot in the medium or long term analysis be lost sight of. The likelihood of anti RSA actions from Angola would be dramatically increased in the event of the emergence of a hostile or even neutral SWA.[97]

For the hawks, this realization mandated that South Africa simply could not afford to conclude a settlement on anything other than its terms. One SADF policy paper on the SWA negotiations stated: "The more political concessions are made, the more political demands will be issued for military concessions. The situation in SWA has already reached the stage where further concessions are unacceptable."[98] The hawks therefore advised that South Africa should not restrict itself to merely ensuring that "[a] broad-based multi-ethnic Turnhalle political party [was] mobilized to combat SWAPO politically," which was the core of Vorster's existing policy.[99] Indeed, Pretoria should seek not to outsmart and outmaneuver SWAPO, but to crush it. The hawks' recommendations included:

> Extended clandestine offensive actions must be conducted against the MPLA, Cubans, and SWAPO in Angola . . .
> Strategic force application plans must be drawn up to implement limited, well-defined retaliation measures over the SWA/Angola border. Aerial actions must be included in these . . .
> Operational plans must be made for clandestine attacks on SWAPO bases in Angola and Zambia . . .
> Security Force members must be trained to covertly pose as election officials . . .

A Department of National Security for SWA which is incorporated in an overarching defense treaty organization with the RSA must be created . . .

Former FNLA/UNITA refugees must be mobilized in a clandestine manner to operate against MPLA/SWAPO.[100]

On Rhodesia, South Africa's hawks were similarly dismissive of an approach that foregrounded diplomacy. Malan advised Botha:

Rhodesia is confronted with a total war which is waged by the black states of Africa, the communist world, and also the Western world. . . . The main goal for the communist countries as well as the African states is to annihilate white authority in Rhodesia and to install a black regime in its place, regardless of the consequences that this might entail for the whites [in terms of] orderly progress, stability, and economic wellbeing.[101]

In this context, the likelihood of a settlement being reached that would produce a moderate and stable government of the sort that South Africa would desire was remote: "A black majority government in the medium term and possibly even in the short term is inevitable. But a peaceful solution, which is an unlikely possibility, will only lead to continuing and even increasing violence . . . [because] Russia will oppose any agreement which does not lead to a Marxist takeover in Rhodesia." This left only one option. While negotiations "still hold the greatest advantage for Rhodesia as well as for RSA, even if it is just to buy extra time," nevertheless, "[t]o prevent a Marxist or hostile government coming to power in Rhodesia, with all the resulting security disadvantages which this would entail for the RSA. . . . [South Africa must] through covert military means, offer a contribution to maintain the white government, and with it law and order, in Rhodesia for as long as possible."[102] That contribution would have to be tightly defined. Malan acknowledged that South Africa could not afford to fight a conventional war in Rhodesia; any overt presence would provide an ideal pretext for communist intervention. They would need to restrain the Rhodesians from rash actions, like raids into Mozambique, for much the same reason.[103] Nevertheless, the bottom line was that Pretoria should realign its power firmly behind Salisbury. It was this policy recommendation, anathema to Vorster, that Botha proposed.

The defense minister was advocating a full reconceptualization of the relative roles accorded to diplomacy and force by the South African state. Even with relegitimization for the regime seemingly a broken dream, Vorster still sought to resolve the disputes in SWA and Rhodesia in order to forestall communist intervention, dampen regional tensions, and buy time to advance separate development within the Republic. This seemed the best of a poor set of options. The increasingly important business community agreed. The government had to find "practical solutions for South-West Africa and Rhodesia," *Volkshandel* offered.[104] For Botha, however, the settlements were seen as ends subordinate to a much larger goal of asserting South African hegemony over the region as a whole, by force if necessary.[105] Niël Barnard, the man Botha would handpick to succeed van den Bergh as head of South Africa's intelligence services, recalled the prevailing strategic view within the military:

> They broadly believed there was a communist onslaught . . . and our main challenge is to fight—through proxies—wars in Mozambique and Angola. It was almost like . . . the Schlieffen and von Moltke doctrine in the First World War, where the argument would be: to defend the homeland you must control the *raum* area. . . . For us to survive in South Africa . . . we must be able to control what goes on in Angola, in Zimbabwe, in Zambia . . . and in Mozambique as well.[106]

The implications of this perspective were far-reaching. Whereas Vorster had been impelled to international cooperation by the realization that any delays on SWA and Rhodesia would lead to a strengthening of opposition forces and thus a worse deal for South Africa down the line, it was a corollary of Botha's "security first" approach that no settlements would be pursued until South Africa had already achieved its security interests. For Vorster, settlements offered an opportunity for the regime, given the circumstances; for P. W. Botha, they were an imposed irritant. Nodding, Thirion recalls Botha's attitude to diplomacy: "Yes, we will negotiate, but we will negotiate from a very strong point. That was his thing."[107]

Conflicting Policies

By the second half of 1977, the public mood had shifted substantially, providing a much more conducive context for P. W. Botha's advocacy of total strategy outside Voortrekkerhoogte. If the times were changing, Botha seemed to be the man for them. In the November election, the minister for defense won his seat of George with extraordinary ease, securing almost 94 percent of the vote.[108] He did not, however, receive the carte blanche he sought from Vorster. In large part, this was due to the unlikely successes Pretoria's diplomats secured under the leadership of the new Foreign Minister, Pik Botha.

In the aftermath of the collapse of the Richard Plan, Pretoria pursued a two-track strategy. The regime aimed to keep the strained international negotiations over SWA and Rhodesia on foot, while creating feasible alternative governments on the ground through "internal settlements." These would involve only the parties "directly involved" in the outcome and simply excluded those unamenable to settling. Momentum and leverage secured on one track was mobilized to produce desired progress on the other. "Keeping the international proposals alive," as Pik Botha spelled out to the Rhodesians, "would also give time to develop the internal solution as a possible alternative."[109] However, the foreign minister's real strategic masterstroke lay in his realization that there was essentially a third route to stable settlements: internal solutions that satisfied enough of the requirements emerging in the parallel international negotiations to ultimately secure recognition from the Western brokers.

To this end, South Africa's relationship with Rhodesia experienced a decided rapprochement throughout 1977. The two governments, somewhat in the roles of executioner and condemned in 1976, suddenly found their interests once more in alignment, if not entirely congruent. Meetings between representatives featured none of the palpable tension of the previous year's encounters; instead the atmosphere was more often "warm and fruitful," in the words of one set of Rhodesian minutes.[110] Between 1968 and early 1976, Pretoria had furnished Salisbury with 82.1 million rand in direct military help.[111] In 1977 alone, South Africa gave Rhodesia nearly 70 million rand worth of defense equipment, including aircraft, armored cars, dual-use vehicles, shotguns, telecommunications equipment, mortars, rockets, mines, grenades, spare parts, parachutes, and medical and camping equipment.[112] More was to come. By December, it was clear that an exhausted Muzorewa would accept some form of a "blocking third" of white-reserved seats in the new parliament. These could be used to prevent constitutional change on issues central to continued white economic privilege.[113] When this commitment persuaded Smith to finally agree to form a multiracial polity, Pretoria began to funnel the assistance the bishop needed to monopolize black support and build a major political operation.[114] In May 1978, Vorster approved a massive $150 million loan to the new, multiracial transitional government; its economic viability was all South African.[115] Suddenly, after years of disappointment and frustration, a settlement in Rhodesia seemed within reach.

Meanwhile, in SWA, NP conservatives led by A. H. du Plessis and Eben van Zyl had refused to abandon petty apartheid. Mudge therefore quit the party altogether and formed the multiracial Democratic Turnhalle Alliance (DTA) with other Turnhalle delegates. Ironically, the sidelining of the NP in this way actually created a more representative and internationally acceptable vehicle for Vorster to work through. Mudge recalls his frequent meetings with the South African prime minister: "I thought John Vorster had the idea that I could make it. He did not admit it [openly]. But I just got the idea that he wanted to put me in a stronger position."[116] Pretoria agreed to supply political consultants to help the DTA run a "sophisticated machine," all while engaging in military actions against its foremost adversary, SWAPO.[117]

The face of these unexpected coups was not the declining Vorster, but the young, energetic foreign minister. It was telling that upon the Cabinet's ratification of the April 1978 Contact Group proposals on SWA, Krugersdorp's executive council awarded the "freedom of the town" honor to Pik Botha. Despite his previous foreign policy adventurism—not least on SWA—the prime minister was passed over.[118] In December 1977, the *Pretoria News* likewise selected Pik Botha as its Man of the Year, though he had been the country's top diplomat for just nine months.

Botha's appointment as foreign minister at the age of forty-five heralded a major generational change in South Africa's diplomatic corps. Prior diplomats tended to be "old school" and very much enamored of a low-key approach to defending South Africa's interests against foreign pressure. Muller represented "the old British tradition of diplomacy," C. A. "Bastie" Bastiaanse, then Ambassador to Malawi, recalls. However, he adds with understatement, South Africa's predicament "needed a little more than Muller's approach."[119] Muller agreed. In his resignation speech, he candidly told his colleagues that "in SA's best interests . . . a new style of foreign policy is [now] needed."[120] Pik Botha, with his enigmatic combination of resolute defiance and reformist zeal, all wrapped in a telegenic, cosmopolitan package, personified that new style. The entire tone of South African diplomacy changed abruptly. "Pik had an approach to Foreign Affairs where he thought we should be more assertive because of the nature of the problems we were in at that time," Bastiaanse reflects.[121] Van Heerden concurs: "Until Pik came, we never had ministers who were dynamic, who drove this as a policy that they believed in."[122] Into the 1980s, the foreign minister surrounded himself with a very different breed of like-minded diplomats: young, dynamic, silver-tongued, and tenacious in fighting off foreign criticism. But already in 1977, he stood out for his ability to manage the different elements of South Africa's complex negotiating position on SWA, using these to prevaricate and stall the progress of the talks as required back in Pretoria.

Central to Pik Botha's success was that he realized the importance of controlling bureaucratic processes to obtaining his goals. As the SWA issue in particular developed into a series of complex and drawn-out negotiations, he increasingly made these his personal responsibility, supplying the Cabinet members with regular memoranda on the course of the talks—his renowned "*Geagte Kollega*" [Dear Colleagues] letters. As seen, Vorster had exploited his party room's lack of foreign policy nous to provide himself with freedom of maneuver on the world stage. Pik Botha came to the opposite conclusion: he could better achieve his diplomatic objectives if his colleagues felt well informed and invested in each step of the process. In this sense, Pik Botha in fact shared much with P. W. Botha. Both understood that the laxness of Vorster's governing style made controlling the paperwork, files, and ultimately the decision-making processes more important to securing desirable policy outcomes, not less. And as Pik Botha entrenched his centrality to the information flow surrounding the government's development of negotiating positions, he ensured the continued importance of the diplomatic avenue within South Africa's overall national security policy.

Apart from his diplomatic and bureaucratic skills, Pik Botha's public image also helped him to prevent the disappearance of negotiations and statecraft from Pretoria's political lexicon—despite the evaporation of any broader ideological framework in which to root the strategy. In 1977, the flamboyant foreign minister had few loyal followers in the NP caucus. He had been in the diplomatic corps, then an MP from 1970 to 1974, then ambassador to the United Nations and the United States, before being shoe-horned into a safe parliamentary seat in May 1977. Botha had experienced a meteoric and unconventional rise—and therefore had no power base in the party to speak of. He was also widely seen as among the most radical *verligtes* in the party. In his maiden parliamentary speech, he had called for the government to sign the Universal Declaration on Human Rights, a move that shocked conservatives. In May 1977, when the entire polity was shifting dramatically to the right, he had told a campaign rally: "I am prepared to die for our right to exist. But I am not prepared to die for [segregation] signs on a lift."[123] Arrie Paulus, leader of the powerful Afrikaner Mineworkers Union and a future Conservative Party MP, condemned such distinctions in the most cutting terms: "For me the definition of an Afrikaner is someone who is prepared to lay down his life for apartheid. A person who says he will fight for South Africa but not apartheid is not a real Afrikaner—he is a liberal." Petty apartheid was "an essential part of the grand design."[124] Pik Botha was undeterred; in July, he declared his support for the repeal of the Immorality and Mixed Marriages Acts.[125]

With his ability to strike the right note with the right crowd, shifting easily between traditional *kragdadigheid* and reformist thinking, Botha quickly attracted a huge grassroots following. Television had only arrived in South Africa in 1976. From his time abroad, Pik Botha knew how to use it effectively. He quickly became the eloquent mouthpiece of the government, the first identifiably modern South African politician. The contrast with the stern, dour image cultivated by Nationalist leaders in the past was unmistakable. Van Heerden recalls: "There was one magic factor that worked for Pik and that was his mass appeal. Whenever the party was in difficulty they would bring in Pik to come and save the day. . . . Pik got away with things because of the standing that he had."[126] Botha himself likewise reflects: "When it came to elections I was expected to hold meetings from Cape Town to Messina, and from Komatipoort to Upington, from Springbok to Pofadder."[127] Furthermore, as the Information Scandal began to tarnish a succession of major political figures, including Mulder and Vorster, Pik Botha, by virtue of his recent entry into the Cabinet and his frequent absences abroad, emerged unscathed.

The foreign minister also enjoyed real access at the highest level. The Vorster– P. W. Botha relationship had long been strictly professional and had by this point substantially disintegrated.[128] By contrast, as the protégé of Vorster's long-time head of foreign policy, Brand Fourie, the foreign minister enjoyed the prime minister's confidence. This was an important asset in Vorster's highly personalized foreign policy processes. When the prime minister retired in September 1978, it was Pik Botha who sat by his side at the press conference.[129]

Thus even though the diplomatic approach was no longer attached to any end goal for the regime, any future vision other than survival and buying time, P. W. Botha's vision of regional hegemony confronted a potent and unexpected counterweight at the highest level. The result, particularly on SWA policy, was chaos. Vorster gave the military substantial leeway on security issues, while simultaneously allowing Pik Botha to vigorously keep diplomatic avenues open. As during the Angolan Civil War, this division of responsibilities ignored that the two areas—security and diplomacy—were inherently interrelated. The conflict came to a head in a heated meeting on December 29, 1977, when Vorster invited Pik Botha, Brand Fourie, P. W. Botha, Malan, and Viljoen to Oubosstrand to hear their views on South Africa's SWA strategy.

The foreign minister, as was his wont, spoke first and decisively. He advised that Pretoria should keep talking to the Western Contact Group. The Five had just recognized South Africa's supposedly neutral administrator-general in SWA and acknowledged its need to keep South African forces there right up until independence, two of the regime's key priorities in influencing the outcome of any election. The two sides were not too far apart on the outstanding issues, he added; a settlement that would be internationally acceptable was "within our reach." However, he reassured his hawkish colleagues, the ultimate aim remained to draw the sides together and then maintain the initiative through the internal electoral process.[130]

For all the shared optimism over South Africa's success on the diplomatic front over the last few months, divisions between the doves and the hawks quickly reappeared. P. W. Botha vouched that the key to a successful election result lay in preventing SWAPO from gaining ground among the Owambos, the most populous of SWA's ethnic groups. The time had come, he said, to use military force to make this happen. "We must successfully wage the political battle in Owamboland and that depends on military successes. . . . [W]e must make

SWAPO hurt and the SADF must obtain the right to go in there [*effectief ingaan*] and take care of the[ir] bases."[131] Earlier in the month, Malan and his minister had agreed that the SADF needed the right to operate in Southern Angola. Simply waiting across the SWA border for SWAPO to infiltrate from Angola was to yield the initiative, a cardinal sin according to Beaufre's doctrines.[132] Jannie Geldenhuys, then General Officer Commanding in SWA, remembers: "They were on the other side of the border, you could not get to them, so they did what they liked."[133] Malan now asked for prime ministerial authority "to cross the border . . . for clandestine operations and also for open [that is, conventional] operations."[134]

Vorster was immediately receptive. The prime minister, the minutes note:

> agreed that it is necessary to hurt SWAPO militarily [but] asked that we pay a little attention to the [diplomatic] repercussions in this respect. He was convinced that if you do not hurt SWAPO over the border-wire, you increase the danger of losing the political battle in Owambo. If SWAPO is accepted as the strongest in Owamboland, then we will undoubtedly lose the [political] battle. The ideal [situation], for the Prime Minister, would be if we could hit SWAPO in such a way that it would be deniable and South Africa would not openly be linked to it.[135]

The diplomats were aghast. Pik Botha pointed out that plausible deniability would be impossible if South Africa lost an aircraft, or equipment, or prisoners of war across the border. He also reminded his colleagues that if any resulting diplomatic incident caused a collapse of the international negotiations on SWA, South Africa would face renewed sanctions, this time "with teeth." Fourie added that there would be major consequences at the UN if South Africa was again caught crossing into Angola. The two men pleaded, at the very least, for permission to only be given for "clandestine operations and not open operations." Characteristically, Vorster opted for a compromise course. Open operations in Angola would not be allowed without his specific authorization; clandestine and hot pursuit operations would. The use of aircraft would not be permitted; tanks would.[136] No one left the meeting happy with this incoherent outcome. Vorster's relentless instinct to seek balance and compromise was as counterproductive to policy as it was damaging in politics.

The Road to Cassinga

But what would the new approach mean in practice? An answer was soon forthcoming. In spring 1978, the Contact Group's detailed proposals for a settlement

in SWA materialized, the culmination of nearly eighteen months of intense negotiations. Pik Botha's relentless haggling and stubborn brinkmanship had secured
a number of major concessions to South Africa. The UN Transition Assistance
Group (UNTAG) presence would consist of around two thousand troops and
one thousand observers, not the five thousand and one thousand that SWAPO
sought. The future status of the disputed port of Walvis Bay, the economic life-
line of any future Namibian state, would be excluded from the proposals and
settled later. And UNTAG personnel would not be drawn from countries overtly
supportive of SWAPO.[137] When the proposals were formally handed to Pretoria
on April 10, an enthused Pik Botha resolved to convince a skeptical Cabinet to
approve them.

The foreign minister laid out three arguments for his colleagues. First, true
to form, he underlined that rejection would have serious consequences internationally, including the possible introduction of economic sanctions. South
Africa would appear the obstructionist party, particularly as many of the political groups in SWA, including Mudge's DTA, had already come out in favor
of the proposals.[138] Had South Africa now rejected the proposals, Eksteen
reflects, "it would have been . . . a middle finger to the world."[139] Second, Pik
Botha was able to point to significant South African victories in the negotiations. South Africa would keep control of SWA up until independence and
remain responsible for the maintenance of law and order. "Acceptance of the
proposals," Brand Fourie recalls, "therefore did not put the security of the territory in jeopardy."[140] Additionally, the foreign minister triumphantly told the
Cabinet, "it is clear that Walvis Bay is not negotiable—they [the Five] have
yielded it."[141] Control of SWA's future trade held out obvious potential for ongoing South African leverage over any independent successor state. Finally,
there was some red meat for the hawks. He emphasized that acceptance of the
proposals would not be the last word on SWA. Instead, as Sole recalls, the proposals still left "a great deal of room for maneuver with respect to [their] implementation."[142] Eksteen agrees. Acceptance of the proposals indeed connoted
a commitment to self-determination in SWA, but what "self-determination"
meant was a fluid concept. "You wanted to use the international vocabulary,
but you give different meanings to the words. [It was all in] how they're being
interpreted."[143]

In the Cabinet room, debate continued well into the afternoon.[144] Several ministers thought that agreeing to the Contact Group's April proposals amounted
to forever yielding the initiative on SWA to the UN, to the detriment of South
Africa's national security.[145] P. W. Botha in particular was virulently against the
whole idea. "I myself was strongly opposed to certain elements of the settlement
plan. My colleagues, who were at the time with me in the Cabinet, will confirm
that," he told a joint sitting of Parliament a decade later. "However, I abided by the

Cabinet decision and after I became Prime Minister I honored [*gedoen gestand*] my predecessor's international undertakings. This meant that I no longer had reservations."[146] This was disingenuous. The defense minister never reconciled himself to the regime's acceptance of what in September became UN Security Council Resolution 435. Both as prime minister and then as president, he did everything he could to delay the implementation of the agreed-upon plan in the name of security concerns.[147] "P. W. always said, this 435 thing, he inherited [it] from John Vorster. He never really liked it," Mudge recalls.[148] Van Heerden is more categorical. The defense minister "hated the idea."[149]

P. W. Botha and the military had concrete security reservations about the Cabinet's decision. In March, the DFA had asked Malan under what conditions the military would accept the proposed reduction in the residual SADF force to just 1500 men, as raised in negotiations in New York. Malan replied that as the SADF reduced its numbers over a period of no less than thirty weeks, a total ceasefire needed to be maintained. He added that during the withdrawal process, SADF troops could not be restricted to bases or camps, and after withdrawal, the remaining forces would have to be restricted to no fewer than nine bases. Finally, and crucially, Malan stipulated that when the ceasefire was declared and withdrawal began, an election date be set that was "in no way dependent" on whether the ceasefire was in fact subsequently observed. This meant that if a ceasefire did not hold, valid elections would nevertheless be held in an SWA under full South African control.[150] While the Contact Group's April proposals did provide for a ceasefire (though not on the terms outlined by Malan), none of the SADF's other caveats were satisfied by Pretoria's acceptance of the April proposals.[151] Instead, to the hawks, South Africa was now committed to allowing an electoral process that might permit a SWAPO victory and, given the extensive UN involvement agreed to, rendered that outcome a very real possibility.[152] In this view, the Cabinet had undermined South Africa's control over SWA in the short term and its ability to continue its forward defense strategy in the long term.[153] "The 25 April proposals are not acceptable from a military standpoint," Malan lamented to his minister, "and I consider it an impossible political breakthrough to get the 25 April proposals now altered . . . such that they are militarily acceptable, given that we have already accepted them."[154]

Entering May 1978, therefore, Pik Botha had earned South Africa some breathing space. Acceptance of the international proposals on SWA had thwarted the UN General Assembly's call for further sanctions and strengthened the case of those few abroad who argued that dialogue with South Africa, rather than confrontation, could bear fruit. Within days, all of this was to be undone.

While the foreign minister was in New York trying to stave off new UN sanctions, P. W. Botha and Malan were following the other policy track approved by Vorster, planning how best to cripple SWAPO in order to ensure a favorable electoral result. A Military Intelligence assessment written in mid-February underscored the need for action:

> It is absolutely imperative that SWAPO's military prospects—externally but especially within SWA—be dismantled before the elections. The political aim, namely the influencing of the population of Owambo, by means of military action against SWAPO bases in Southern Angola is our highest priority. . . . The current time is relatively favorable for South Africa to go on the offensive.[155]

Malan advised his minister that the SADF's existing strategy was proving insufficient. In the last few years, he wrote, the military had concentrated on winning the hearts and minds of the locals, while launching limited counterterrorism operations in the border area. However, given that the SADF was not permitted to deploy the military and air force against targets deep inside Angola, these latter efforts had proved inadequate. With the SADF's "hands tied behind its back" and UNITA increasingly ineffective in Cunene province, SWAPO had gone from strength to strength; the number of insurgents was expected to increase from 3700 to 5000 trained men by the end of 1978. He concluded categorically: "We can never win the war against SWAPO if they are allowed to operate in secure areas north of the border and concentrate on attacks on our forces in northern South-West Africa." South Africa had to hit SWAPO bases in southern Angola "with all forces, including the air force." Malan added that a successful strike would do much to repair the image of South African military might, tarnished abroad during Operation Savannah. Finally, he addressed potential counterarguments, concluding that the broader political context was conducive to action now. While "this sort of operation will unleash violent diplomatic reactions," the increasing preoccupations with events in the Horn of Africa limited the likelihood of a communist military response. "The situation," he concluded, directly quoting the Military Intelligence assessment, "is therefore at the moment probably relatively favorable for such action."[156] Again, it was typical of Vorster's decentralized style of government that generals, rather than experts at the DFA or BOSS, felt that they both needed to make such evaluations and had the expertise to do so. The minister for defense was nevertheless convinced, writing on the memorandum: "Go forward with planning as discussed."[157]

As per the Oubosstrand compromise, however, P. W. Botha still had to convince the Cabinet to authorize an overt cross-border operation. Time was of the essence. Military Intelligence had ascertained that while SWAPO's headquarters were currently at Cassinga, around 170 miles north of the SWA border, they were shortly due to be moved to an unknown location in the Mulemba area to the south.[158] In other respects, however, events were playing into Botha's hands.

In mid-February 1978, Nujoma had given an interview to the SABC in which he rejected the prospect of elections in SWA. "Majority rule is [now] out," the SWAPO leader declared. "We are fighting to seize power in Namibia for the benefit of the Namibian people. We are revolutionaries."[159] Then, in late March, DTA President Clemens Kapuuo, a key black leader broadly amenable to Pretoria, was assassinated.[160] As tensions rose, Vorster responded, detaining 120 figures connected with SWAPO and banning all "unregistered" political meetings.[161] This was the climate in which the defense minister pitched his case for a unilateral cross-border action against SWAPO. On April 11, Cabinet gave the go-ahead to begin preparations for Operation Reindeer, a simultaneous strike on Cassinga and another base just across the border.[162] (Planning had already been under way for almost six weeks.) On May 2, Botha's colleagues issued the green light for action.[163] Years later, Pik Botha agitatedly recalls the decision-making process after the April proposals had been agreed upon:

> Within a week . . . almost the next Cabinet meeting, he [P. W. Botha] came with the idea that they want to attack Cassinga. I opposed it *vehemently*. . . . I pointed out here we've just approved Resolution 435. Britain, France, America, Canada and [West] Germany—we might have to face a Security Council meeting, with severe, incalculable consequences for us. And now in the Cabinet, one after the other speaks. We were divided, split in two. Most of the time, we finished Cabinet meetings [by lunch]. On a few occasions, like this one, over after lunch. Again, split in two. And eventually, P. W. Botha said "Prime Minster, we're not making any headway. May I suggest," he said, "if it is successful, it is your credit. If it is a failure, you can blame me and I'll take the blame." Vorster then said to his colleague, "I am the Prime Minister and not you. . . . Whether it is a success or a failure, I take the responsibility." In that way, the previous session I got through my Resolution 435, and now P. W. got his Cassinga attack.[164]

The approval of Operation Reindeer epitomizes the development and execution of South Africa's national security policy by the end of the Vorster era. Even from Washington, Sole could reflect: "We [were] notorious in South Africa for our compartmentalization, with plans being prepared by one department independently of what is being done by another department."[165] But it was not so much the compartmentalization of policy planning that was the problem. That South Africa's military and its diplomats should have differing approaches to, and recommendations for, the complex challenges that the regime faced was only to be expected. The problem was Vorster's propensity to try to satisfy every recommendation simultaneously, even when they were contradictory. Rarely was this

quite as evident, or damaging, as on the Cassinga strike. Agreeing to the courses
of action advocated by both Bothas was a means to keep the peace in an increasingly divided Cabinet, particularly as Vorster's personal authority deteriorated.
However, it made for incoherent and ineffective policy. In the space of little over
a week, South Africa both agreed to and then undermined the international proposals on SWA, not to mention brazenly insulting the Western parties who had
brokered them.

The strike on Cassinga was a resounding military success. Following an
aerial bombardment, SADF parachute troops conducted a "mopping up" operation. Perhaps more than 600—insurgents, women, and children alike—were
killed.[166] Internationally, however, the attack utterly undermined everything
that had been earned through Pretoria's acceptance of the April proposals. The
Security Council condemned South Africa's actions; the General Assembly
reacted with predictable outrage; and the issue of Chapter VII sanctions was
promptly reopened. As for the Contact Group, whatever fragile perceptions had
developed that South Africa was a reliable partner interested in regional stability
evaporated. Vorster's legacy of bridge-building in Africa must have seemed nothing but a distant memory. The regime was now roundly viewed as an obstacle
to any peaceful settlements, to be treated with hostility, disdain, and suspicion.

"The Rest is History"

In Nationalist circles, however, the Cassinga strike was rapturously received.
"South Africa hits hard" in response to "threats and intimidation," beamed
Hoofstad as part of its heavy coverage.[167] Just as the battered public sphere clung
to the strike as the first bit of good geopolitical news since the false dawn of
Kissinger's visit to Pretoria, Cassinga likewise had a galvanizing, empowering
effect on the regime's leadership. "Cassinga . . . pulled them [the politicians] together," Viljoen recalls.[168] For all the international pressure and increasing total
onslaught, the global humiliation and existential soul-searching, the operation
suggested that the regime could still manage the situation in SWA and ultimately
control its own destiny—if it followed P. W. Botha's approach. This belief was
only intensified by the continued lack of benefits accrued from cooperating with
the international community. On May 3—before the Cassinga attack but after
South Africa's acceptance of the April proposals—the UN General Assembly
had voted 119–0 in favor of the Security Council introducing economic sanctions against Pretoria and requiring a full and immediate SADF withdrawal from
SWA, regardless of the progress of the Contact Group negotiations.[169]

Cassinga thus became a signal moment in how the regime engaged with the
outside world. The attack was the prototype of the much-talked-about total

strategy; Nationalists of virtually all stripes liked what they now saw. The P. W. Botha way provided a guiding light to a regime in trouble—and one that did not shine on domestic affairs, the real source of its problems. South Africa was savaged internationally for the attack, especially for the civilian deaths involved, but such criticism simply drove Botha into his element: "No self-respecting country can allow itself to be dictated to from outside. If ever South Africa's interest within the Republic or the integrity of our borders are jeopardized we shall strike back."[170] The operation had been very much his proposal and its success was his success. At the next Cabinet meeting, Vorster openly congratulated his defense minister.[171] Military incursions into neighboring countries quickly became accepted within the Cabinet as the new norm. In June, for instance, P. W. Botha told the Cabinet of a SWAPO buildup in the Caprivi Strip; his colleagues promptly gave him a blank check to respond.[172] The final months of Vorster's premiership saw a marked hardening of South Africa's position on SWA, its stance toward the international community, and its approach to national security. The regime moved past its recent demoralization and began eagerly looking to seize the military initiative on the regional stage. Even in his resignation speech, Vorster committed South Africa to holding internal elections in SWA as soon as possible, damaging the credibility of Resolution 435 and instead moving the regime behind Malan's strategy.[173]

Cassinga also heralded the marginalization of the DFA, the only significant remaining critic of the Botha way within the government. The balance between defiance and force on the one hand and persuasion and diplomacy on the other tilted decisively. Eksteen reflects:

> I was in New York. [I] listened to the news: Yes, South Africa had entered into Angola and bombarded a place called Cassinga. What the hell? So I called someone in Foreign Affairs and said "What are you going to do about Cassinga?" [He replied:] "Where the hell is Cassinga?." . . . So the head of Defense Force public relations, a guy that I knew from way back . . . It was 9 o'clock South African time, I said to him "Listen man, can you tell me, is this true about Cassinga?" He said "What about Cassinga?" I said "Well, that we bombarded Cassinga and heavy casualties and so on." He said, "What does that have to do with you? . . . Mind your own business." And he hung up the telephone. The rest is history."[174]

What was the DFA's reaction when they found out the SADF had hit Cassinga? Viljoen laughs. "Terrible."[175] Sidelining the DFA (and any other doubters) became the dominant pattern of national security decision making in the Botha era. "Everything the military did complicated our job. But we just had to soldier on, keep the doors open," remembers Shearar.[176] "The enemy offers you a target," Thirion muses. "Pik would come up with an answer like, say, 'Look on such and such a date in the United Nations, the Security Council has a meeting. This and this and this and that, the timing is not good internationally, and so on and so on.' And then we [in the SADF] would either laugh it off or do it anyway."[177] With a wry smile, Viljoen reflects, "We very seldom liaised with Foreign Affairs, because they were always anti-, and we had to do these things for military purposes. . . . They wanted to know, but unfortunately the secrecy of such operations is so important."[178]

These developments unfolded against a backdrop of profound political uncertainty. Already by winter 1978, Vorster's career was in terminal decline. His capacity to lead the party in a time of crisis had been greatly diminished by the long, slow death of his state-building agenda: a policy of separate development grounded in an ideology of African multinationalism. However, in the year preceding his retirement, new factors catalyzed a freefall in his political stock. Steady leaks exposing the Information Department's rampant misuse of government funds earmarked for the clandestine promotion of South Africa's image abroad exposed his government as both inept and corrupt. Additionally, Vorster's health faded rapidly. In September, he emerged from a short spell in hospital and announced, definitively this time, his intention to resign.

Connie Mulder had long been presumed Vorster's successor due to electoral math alone. Out of the 133 MPs and 39 senators who made up the 172-strong Nationalist parliamentary caucus in 1978, the Transvaal supplied no fewer than 80 members, while traditional allies in the Free State accounted for another 24 votes. If provincial loyalties were consistent, Mulder should have had enough support to win on the first ballot. However, his candidacy, tarnished by persistent questions in the English-speaking press about his department's misuse of government funds, imploded spectacularly in the days leading up to the election.[179] Even so, P. W. Botha could not have won without support from some unlikely quarters. Pik Botha, who received 22 votes on the first ballot, subsequently threw his support behind his fellow *verligte* and namesake.[180] Additionally, party veteran Alwyn Schlebusch, whose insider status meant he had learned more of the details of the Information Scandal than most, directed his Free Staters away from the toxic Mulder.[181]

Without Botha as prime minister, some of the key internal reforms of the next few years—particularly the creation of the National Security Management System, the reorganization of much of the bureaucratic apparatus of government, and the strengthening of the SSC at the expense of the Cabinet—would likely never have happened. All of these were close to Botha's heart. Equally, Mulder had long aligned himself with center-right positions in the party, cultivating an image within the party as a reliable conservative. His support base and influences would have been more doctrinaire than P. W. Botha's. However, the broader political equation facing Mulder would ultimately have been the same: a working-class base and traditionalist elites fiercely patrolling the boundaries of *volk* identity and seeking to entrench Verwoerdian norms in perpetuity, juxtaposed with the steady socioeconomic divergence of Afrikanerdom, the dissolution of old animosities between Afrikaans and English-speaking whites of certain classes, and an evaporation of *verligte* faith in the capacity of multinationalism to provide the intellectual anchor for the polity's future. None of the candidates were in a position to imagine and pioneer the kind of revolutionary change that the country actually needed. In this context, the ongoing shift toward a pan-white political ideology, the growing international hostility, and the need to mobilize capital for national defense and a war economy—these were now realities, regardless of who became *Hoofleier*.[182] And as one lengthy interview Mulder gave shortly before his political downfall made all too clear, he too was very much aware of the range of challenges the regime faced, even as he characteristically avoided showing his hand as to what, precisely, he would do to address them.[183] The structural changes both in South African society and in the regime's political environment, exacerbated by short-sighted policies and poor leadership, *required* a new sociopolitical dispensation, regardless of who was at the helm. After all, P. W. Botha did not leave the *volk* norms that he had been committed to for decades because he wanted to, but because he had to.

On foreign policy in particular, there would have been little or no difference between a P. W. Botha government and one led by Mulder. Cassinga had entrenched the validity both of total onslaught as a system of threat perception and of total strategy as an effective paradigm for national security. The overarching policies of securing regional hegemony, forward defense, and preemptive strikes would have stayed much the same. There simply was no alternative approach with political support. Mulder and his old ally van den Bergh might have wanted to reach out again to independent Africa, but the terrain of African politics was indistinguishable from 1975. Angola and Soweto had ensured that. Any notion of a resurrection of dialogue and African rehabilitation was pure fantasy. Even if Mulder had succeeded Vorster and even if he had been able to escape responsibility for the emerging scandal—both big ifs—P. W. Botha would still have been the second most powerful figure in a divided party. He was the unchallenged head of the Cape caucus, the government's leader in the House, the longest-serving MP, and the most senior minister in the government. In short, he would have had immense leeway over national security policy moving forward.

Moreover, Botha's foreign policy would have been just as attractive for other Nationalist leaders precisely because total strategy was never just a national security policy, but performed vital political and ideological functions too.

Afrikaner political unity on the polity's future and the basic forms of social organisation was collapsing. In early 1982, Treurnicht led 15 other MPs out of the NP (out of 131) to form the Conservative Party. It was the most wrenching split the party had experienced since gaining power.[184] But the anticommunism of Treurnicht and his followers was no less vigorous than that of Botha and his military advisers. "This assault is being made by communism upon democracy in South Africa," declared J. J. B. van Zyl, MP for Sunnyside and a Conservative Party defector. "We are experiencing a struggle against the human spirit. It is a struggle of atheism against Christianity, against the believers."[185] Koos van der Merwe, van Zyl's fellow defector, recalls things similarly. "It was very easy to convince somebody that we have a total onslaught.... I believed in the total onslaught."[186] There is no distance at all between such characterizations of South Africa's geopolitical conundrum and that offered by Stoffel van der Merwe, who became a close associate of P. W. Botha:

> The Russians, the Soviet Union, was very imperialistic. They wanted to subject the whole world to communism. Communism, as it was preached, fell well on the ears of poor people, disadvantaged people.... I *still* feel today that those concepts were in actual fact good concepts. "Total" onslaught because it was not only a guerrilla onslaught, but also an economic, and also international, also moral—in all spheres of life you were under pressure. So it was a total onslaught in that sense. And then to fight against a total onslaught you need a total strategy. So for me it makes sense.[187]

As the interests and values of different sectors of the electorate continued to diverge, anticommunism became ever more important to channeling the electorate's emotions toward a common enemy and ultimately sustaining the regime's increasingly tenuous claim to political control. For all their differences on social policy, bilingual Johannesburg businessmen fearful of international isolation and traditionalist Northern Transvaal farmers looking nervously at events across the border in Rhodesia shared a fear of a revolution advocating material expropriation, antiwhite violence, and social flattening. With its intellectual arsenal rapidly dwindling, the regime relied ever more on animating anticommunist anxieties to justify its rule. This was, of course, a new variant of an old Nationalist tactic. Just as Verwoerd had exploited fears of *oorstroming* in the early 1960s to bring English-speakers into the Nationalist fold while advancing Afrikaner cultural hegemony, P. W. Botha plumbed new depths of hyperbole and alarmism, as anticommunism served to legitimize unpalatable reforms that greatly benefited some sectors of society over others. Unlike Verwoerd, however, Botha had a new and potent method of providing his rhetorical appeals with real body. The regime's swift, decisive strikes against shadowy antiregime militants deep inside foreign territory, ideally suited to sensationalist media publicity, periodically provided an emotionally distraught electorate with an illusion of agency and control. The underlying fears of a communist takeover remained, however, ready for the government to exploit again. This stratagem was not enough to keep Vorster's broad Nationalist coalition together, but it was enough to offer an area of substantial consensus for the white polity as a whole. Into the 1980s Progressive politicians, English-speaking journalists, some business leaders, and more than a few Afrikaner academics and public intellectuals lamented Botha's reflexive belligerence. However, no serious or sustained political challenge to his "security-first" unilateralism materialized within either the Nationalist or Conservative Parties (though if politicians and the public knew more about the Angolan intervention, it might have done).

Cassinga thus introduced the model of confrontation between the regime and the world that would dominate the next decade: diplomatic stand-offs and unadulterated hostility on the international stage, set against a backdrop of savage violence on the ground across Southern Africa. The precepts of total onslaught, entrenched in the government's national security doctrines, themselves rejected diplomacy as a means of negating foreign opposition to the regime. Instead, confrontation was deemed the only effective countermeasure. The regime never again reconciled the potential of diplomacy to ease its predicaments at home with its instinctive preference for combative solutions to its many security problems. In 1985, long after Vorster's demise, the scenario that unfolded in autumn 1978 would play out almost identically. Just as the Commonwealth's special diplomatic mission, the Eminent Persons Group, was due to deepen its engagement with the regime, the military launched coordinated cross-border operations in Zambia, Zimbabwe, and Botswana (as well as in Angola and Swaziland shortly afterward).[188] To those who remembered Cassinga, this must have seemed all too familiar. Indeed, until F. W. de Klerk decided to take the polity in a new direction in August 1989—a decision he decided to signpost by meeting with Kenneth Kaunda at Victoria Falls—African heads of state would not meet freely and on an equal footing with Pretoria's leaders in the way that they had with Vorster; they would do so only with the threat of South African military force hanging over them. In Pretoria, there was no longer any talk of African rehabilitation or reacquiring international legitimacy; the focus had narrowed to crisis management at home and stalling the insurgency abroad. "The burning question is to what degree I can accommodate the West and buy time," Pik Botha confessed in a 1978 meeting with P. W. Botha and Chris Heunis, Minister for Economic Affairs.[189] This was still the essence of South Africa's statecraft fully a decade later.

Conclusion

The apartheid regime strove not so much to ignore the values and norms of the postcolonial world, but to hijack, manipulate, and redefine them, in an effort to legitimize their social order. The causes of this phenomenon were both external and internal. The unfolding of decolonization and the danger of further international isolation provided an important impetus for the regime to look for new geopolitical and conceptual foundations. Equally, changing ethoses among a newly prosperous, urbanized, and outward-looking Afrikanerdom prompted new conceptualizations of the *volk* and its relationship with the outside world. The centerpiece of the regime's campaign for rehabilitation comprised deploying diplomatic engagement with independent Africa to drive a rearticulation of the ideological basis of the separate development system. This improbable initiative was launched on two fronts: persuading black Africa that apartheid meant something new by rearticulating existing racial hierarchies in the languages of the nation-state and development; and convincing white South Africa that the discrete racist measures of petty apartheid could be jettisoned from the program of separate development in such a way that reform would actually enhance the viability of the white polity rather than dooming it. By foregrounding a future of parallel nationalisms both at home and abroad, Vorster hoped to definitively detach the *volk* from the conceptual universe of colonialism and embed it in a new foundation that would ensure the long-term future of the Afrikaner at the core of a broader white power structure. This agenda may have been inchoate and was ultimately unfulfilled, but it was not superficial. Both the confidence aroused in *verligte* circles and the animosity of right-wing critics reflect that key constituencies realized that much was at stake in Vorster's new expressions of identity. It was also not without consequences. While Vorster focused intently on placating critics of his new paths for the *volk* in the political and public spheres, P. W. Botha waged a successful campaign to advance his own prescriptions for the polity's statecraft behind closed doors and beyond public scrutiny. The spectacular collapse of Vorster's efforts to construct a new ideological foundation for the *volkstaat* helped facilitate the rise of Botha's program, which not only prescribed confrontation with the same actors that Vorster had sought to woo by labelling them tools of a global communist conspiracy, but was predicated upon that confrontation, creating a relentless, self-perpetuating cycle. Botha's program soon became the vehicle for the reincarnation of Nationalist power around a new set of ideas: the cooption of other racial groups within the central political structure; the energetic cultivation of a black middle class; and the solidifying of a new NP alliance increasingly based on race and security fears, rather than on shared language, culture, and religion.

The story detailed here emerges from a focus on the nexus of foreign policy, state-building, and political ideology. But even this tranche of the South African experience clarifies much established wisdom. The Vorster government was not committed to the white redoubt, either geopolitically or conceptually. Instead, it eagerly, even desperately, looked to distance itself from its erstwhile partners in Rhodesia and SWA and to undermine notions of pan-white identity across the region to facilitate that end. The regime's plan for the future of the *volk* and the white power structure may have spurned global discourses on the connection between race and political legitimacy, but it was heavily influenced by other norms in the emerging postcolonial canon. National self-determination, postcolonial development, and anticommunism were precisely the designated vehicles for finding common ground with would-be allies in Africa. Anticommunism was not a cause disingenuously invoked by Pretoria to protect white privilege, but an ideology that shaped how Nationalists understood their identity and mission on the most fundamental levels. The state's foreign policy was not the subject of consensus within the NP, let alone across the white polity more broadly. Instead, bitter conflicts over the regime's statecraft both reflected deep philosophical differences over the *volk*'s place in the world and served as the terrain for struggles between different leaders and power bases. Finally, the separate development idea may have started out as a cynical manifestation of white unilateralism. But it spawned a genuine faith in the principle of parallel nationalisms that ultimately undercut the original intention of preserving the *volk*'s capacity to dictate its own future and hampered the regime's ability to competently execute statecraft of any kind.

Legacies

"[A]s opposed to the here-today-gone-tomorrow idea of the colonialists," Vorster once remarked, "We are Africans. We are of Africa and to my last day in politics I will strive to have us accepted by the people of Africa."[1] Long before that day, however, Vorster's cherished vision of productive coexistence between the white polity and independent Africa was in tatters. The debate between moderate states willing to engage with Pretoria and radicals advocating militant action aimed at the regime's destruction had shifted decisively in favor of the latter. Nationalist political will to seek diplomatic and normative coexistence disintegrated shortly thereafter. Terms like "dialogue" and "détente" evaporated from the Nationalist lexicon, never to return, displaced by "total onslaught" and "total strategy." When John Vorster died in 1983, he did so in the political wilderness, where scholars have largely left him.

His foreign policy lieutenants experienced divergent fates. Muller enjoyed a quiet retirement out of the public eye. His successor, Pik Botha, became one of the longest-serving foreign ministers of any modern state. Throughout the 1980s, he mounted what at times seemed like a one-man rearguard action against further isolation and sanctions, all while having to repeatedly justify the very merit of diplomacy to a deeply skeptical P. W. Botha and his Iagos in the military establishment.[2] Brand Fourie also acclimatized himself to the new order, continuing in his role as head of the Department of Foreign Affairs before a late-career sojourn as ambassador to the United States. With all the bitterness of a former crown prince ousted out of his inheritance, Connie Mulder briefly dabbled in far-right politics, though to little effect. His sons Corné and Pieter did the same, teaming up with Constand Viljoen to form the Afrikaner nationalist Freedom Front in the early 1990s. Showing much of his father's political fluidity, Pieter served for five years in Jacob Zuma's Cabinet (2009–2014) while remaining the leader of a party championing the creation of a state exclusively for Afrikaners. For Mulder's ally, Hendrik van den Bergh, there was no future. On the very day P. W. Botha took office, the former BOSS chief offered his resignation to his long-time adversary. The new team for ensuring the regime's survival was soon installed, with P. W. Botha at the head, Magnus Malan in charge of the military, and Niël Barnard looking after domestic security. This troika would remain in place for the rest of the decade, though their formal titles changed along the way.

As for Vorster, after resigning the premiership in September 1978, he was promptly elevated to the ceremonial State Presidency, despite his visibly ailing health. However, continued revelations of the misuse of funds to market South Africa's image abroad rendered his holding of even this office untenable. The initial government reports into Information's "irregularities" had unconvincingly (and inaccurately[3]) whitewashed the prime minister's involvement, ascribing political responsibility solely to Mulder. However, soon after P. W. Botha assumed office, the very same author of the ostensibly definitive investigation, Judge Rudolph Erasmus, released a "supplementary" report that laid much of the blame at Vorster's feet.[4] No one who knew the Cape leader's skill at behind-the-scenes political skullduggery was surprised. When reporters occasionally sought out the embittered former prime minister, Vorster sharply criticized the policies and approach of his successor. In 1982, when Andries Treurnicht left the NP to found the Conservative Party, the former *Hoofleier* even issued a statement supporting the rebel cause. His change of heart was not inspired by a new affinity for the reactionary policies of his old bête noire, but was simply the cost of entry to a coalition of rancor: lining up alongside Vorster were more than a few of the other casualties of P. W. Botha's brutal rise to power, from his former Cape ally Louwrens Muller to his old rival Connie Mulder.[5]

The enduring political legacy of Vorster's statecraft lay less in his foreign policy than in its associated conceptions of the *volk*'s identity and its relationships with other peoples. Vorster was the first Nationalist prime minister to commit the regime to the idea that Afrikanerdom did not have to cling to the concept of unilateral vertical dominance, consciously isolating itself from other communities. Instead, he pioneered the notion that Afrikaners could band together with other peoples—specifically those of other races—to successfully form a common, long-term conceptual and geopolitical foundation for coexistence. That foundation was, of course, tightly defined: nationalism and autonomy for each, in politically separate nation-states. However, the first logical corollary of separate development, as Vorster and *verligtes* successfully contended by the early 1970s, was that the polity's interest lay in functioning, stable, and independent African states, both at home and abroad. It became accepted that homelands needed to offer opportunities and viability, rather than the neglect and destitution pursued by Verwoerd. Both visions were cynical in motivation and devastating in their human effect, but they were fundamentally different in nature. The concept of feasible coexistence also underpinned Vorster's call for the removal of petty apartheid on the grounds that it imperiled the future of integrated, multinational development. This argument resonated rapidly and deeply. In 1970, only 4 percent of Afrikaners supported sports competition between whites and blacks; by 1978, 76 percent supported racial mixing within the same team.[6] For mainstream Afrikanerdom, if not for *verkramptes*, there was no going back to Verwoerdian norms. On both the homelands and daily discrimination, grand and petty apartheid, the positions that Vorster nurtured were pillars of the Nationalist agenda by the middle of his tenure. Both were fringe ideas within the party when he entered office just a few years before.

Simultaneously, however, Vorster clung to the idea that separate development constituted the dominant framework for South Africa's future. In this view, only smoothing the rough edges of the existing approach was required. At the post-Soweto Cabinet meeting, he told his colleagues: "If we make the adjustments to our [apartheid] policy that the circumstances require from a position of strength, we will get support." Solving the problem was all about "examining policy implementation," not reassessing the merits of the policy itself.[7] Yet it was precisely those forums that he set up to pursue such "adjustments"—the Theron

Commission on the situation of Coloreds, the Wiehahn Commission on black labor rights, the Riekert Commission on influx control, and the constitutional committee into a new political dispensation—that forced the government into engaging directly with external stakeholders, many of whom suggested that the system itself needed much more than tweaking. It was both ironic and characteristic of Vorster's enigmatic tenure that he ended up laying much of the platform for P. W. Botha's signature reforms and for the NP's departure from his rigidly multinational vision.

The ideological legacies of this era were more significant still. The prime minister's abortive efforts to reframe the character of the polity were intended to provide a diversifying Afrikanerdom with a new mission. He doubled down on a vision of acceptance as an independent African state, shepherding the emergence of new *verligte* discourses through which Afrikaners rearticulated their communal identity. "Afrikaner nationalism and African nationalism are one family," wrote Schalk Pienaar in one of his widely read Nasionale Pers columns in late 1974, a claim that would scarcely have made sense to his readers just a few years earlier.[8] Expectations were raised. As late as September 1976, it bears recalling, Vorster told party delegates: "I do not want to put it any higher than this, but it can possibly flow from this that the matter of Southern Africa is settled."[9] Sky-high hopes followed by precipitous and undeniable failure only undermined the old frameworks of Verwoerdian white supremacy, leaving in their place nothing but a mirage of acceptance as an African nation.

This framework broadens our understanding of the changing fortunes of the apartheid state and the historical turning point that occurred in 1976. To read the wildly popular "rise and fall of apartheid" genre, the Soweto protests acted as singular jolt to the regime. The unrest galvanized black opposition, especially among the young. It undermined the regime's strength and stability. And it demanded the attention of the world's politicians, global civil society, and international media, all of whom became transfixed by developments in South Africa right up until the mid-1990s. In this telling, the crisis of apartheid was essentially functional: events made the grand plan harder (or impossible) to implement.

Yet at least as important as the functional crisis was the ideological crisis: the loss of faith among many of those within the Nationalist power structure in who they were, what they stood for, and why the social order that they lived in and preserved was worth persevering with. To understand why and how this process occurred, the regime's political and ideological agenda should not be understood narrowly, in a purely domestic perspective, but much more expansively, in the context of efforts to adapt existing forms of social order and identity to new, globalized notions of political organization and progress. A wider geographical lens reveals much. The Vorster government departed from its predecessor precisely in offering a vision for the polity's future that was integrated, both politically and conceptually. The regime's stewardship of the *volk*, its homeland policy, and its postcolonial statecraft would all be governed by the notion that national fulfillment was the ultimate desire of all "peoples" on the planet. This elevation of nationalism into the essential guiding principle of the regime in all spheres simultaneously was critical to winning over mainstream Afrikanerdom despite the transgression of established racial norms.

Statecraft was central to this project. Vorster utilized engagement with independent Africa to bolster the central supposition of the separate development scheme: that many blacks wanted the system of parallel nation-states as much as Afrikaners did. This moral justification for apartheid was a delusion, but no less tenaciously clung to by isolated Nationalists for that. However, Vorster's new focus on the terrain of foreign policy did not solve the central problems facing the polity, as advertised, but instead just entailed avoiding addressing them. Afrikaners were steadily less motivated by communal rather than material interests, while the blue-collar base felt steadily more disillusioned with the party's shift toward cosmopolitanism, the interests of capital, racial interdependence rather than unadulterated dominance, and a pan-white identity that corroded their privileged status as members of the *volk*. A younger black South Africa was increasingly dissatisfied with the homelands future sketched out for them, even as the economy's reliance on skilled black labor grew. And while the regime experienced some diplomatic successes on the bilateral level, the diversifying power structure of the global community of the 1970s coupled with the relentless march of nonracialism in global discourses posed a massive threat to the regime's viability. On all fronts, forces outside the regime's control were corroding the feasibility of the multinational project. Vorster not only ignored these trends, but sank more and more capital into a declining stock. Consequently, when his vision collapsed in 1976–77, it took more than just foreign policy with it. A profound ideological vacuum emerged, as Afrikaners lost faith in the capacity of nationalism to provide the guiding light for their future.[10] Though the underlying social and economic forces had been building over the preceding years, the final break was rather abrupt and decisive. To take one example, a 1977 study found that educated, better-off Afrikaners did not support homeland investment.[11] This was the exact same class that just a few years earlier had publicly begged the government to substantially increase investment in the homelands.[12] Afrikaner elites had decided that they were unwilling to pay for a vision that they no longer believed would ever materialize.

By widening the lens beyond domestic affairs to encompass the regime's broader quest for acceptance and survival, a subtly different picture emerges of the post-1976 period. The Soweto uprisings comprised the most important trigger event, ushering in what Hermann Giliomee has called the "rollercoaster years of hope and despair."[13] But it was not the only one. There was the

realization of geopolitical isolation engendered by Angola, the failure of the
Kissinger Initiatives, the humiliation of being lectured to at Vienna, the mandatory UN arms embargo, and the international backlash against the raid on
Cassinga. These public disasters cumulatively drove Afrikanerdom into demoralization, infighting, and existential fear, precisely because the viability of the
apartheid vision at home was intimately linked to its acceptance abroad. If the
regime's ability to continue imposing its rule through exercising its substantial
hard power began to evaporate during this window, so too did any semblance
of real consensus among the existing ruling elite about how to do so and what
end they were seeking beyond mere survival. Major questions also arose about
whether the existing program was right and moral. In short, the functional crisis
alone cannot explain why apartheid collapsed as it did; ideological erosion was
important too. After all, even after the Broederbond finally disavowed separate
development in 1986, the regime was able to hold onto power for several years
afterward, treading water with barely any plan for the future at all.[14] The ability
to keep going remained; it was the common purpose, will, and sense of direction
that disappeared first.

Yet this was not only a period of ideological erosion, but of political transformation too. The specific circumstances of Vorster's failure—including the
way in which the withdrawal from Angola was framed to the public and internalized by the regime, the decline of his control over national security policy,
and the disintegration of his authority and agenda—facilitated the emergence
of Botha's unique ideas as the glue needed to hold a demoralized and splintering Afrikanerdom together. These ideas did not elevate Afrikaners over
English-speakers in any significant way; they thus also hastened the political
rapprochement of the two white communities. As a state creed, total onslaught
later derived succor and even some limited credibility from the ideological atmosphere of the "Second Cold War," sustained by the Reagan Administration
and Thatcher government. But its origins lay in localized developments dating
back to the 1960s, specifically, strategic reimaginations of South Africa's security
conundrum in anticommunist and counterinsurgent frameworks, rather than in
purely racial terms. These reimaginations in turn reflected broader urges within
Afrikaner society to conceptualize racial differences in new ways, ones that did
not presuppose hostility and incompatibility between a white polity and African
states.

By the end of 1976, anticommunism was virtually the only ideological pillar
left entirely intact in a severely damaged Nationalist edifice. As Vorster's vision
for the future lost credibility among his constituents, anticommunism had to
bear a much larger share of the ideological weight for the regime.[15] Moreover,
anticommunism featured as not just the voice of the security establishment or
an approach to foreign policy, but as the starting point for the regime's entire

political agenda. P. W. Botha's biographers describe his approach to governance in telling terms:

> South Africa was now struggling for its life, and the total onslaught against it necessitated one thing above all others, namely change—rapid, visible change: the replacing of outdated political principles, the restructuring of race relations, the rejection of *baasskap*, the removal of humiliating discrimination and injustice, equal opportunity and rights, fewer restrictions—and a new [constitutional] disposition.[16]

As historian Peter Vale points out, beginning with the founding of the Institute for Strategic Studies in 1977, the study of "global communism" became a boom topic in academic circles in South Africa, attracting funding and support out of all proportion to its intellectual merit.[17] Just as a previous generation of academics had been a willing and important prop for the government's policies of racial separation,[18] their successors at the Institute for the Study of Marxism at Stellenbosch, or the Centre for Investigation into Revolutionary Activities and the Institute on the Total Onslaught, both at the Rand Afrikaans University, provided the intellectual heft to the new state-sanctioned worldview.

However, the more Botha's power-sharing boondoggle failed to win over voters' hearts and minds, and the more he abandoned traditional *volk* norms in order to appeal to new power bases, the more fear had to be used to muster political support and legitimize controversial reforms. Total onslaught defined what the polity was against precisely to compensate for the deep internal divisions over what, exactly, it was for. It fully externalized the mounting range of threats to the polity in ways that did not focus on race, mapped onto potent right-wing discourses of righteous isolationism, and animated currents of victimization coursing through the white polity. However, the casting of total onslaught in this pivotal role tethered the viability of the regime's new ideology to the existence of a viable communist enemy as a counterpoint. This had much to do with why the fall of apartheid was (roughly) contemporaneous with the fall of communism: once the existential foe was in terminal decline, the regime could no longer avoid confronting that it was too split on what the future of South African society should look like to endure.

The emergence of anticommunism in this guise had important consequences not only in the field of ideology, but for policy too. Total onslaught served as something of a Trojan horse for total strategy, as the two were conceptually and politically attached. Total strategy's improbable ascent from a doctrine shaped in obscure seminars on military strategy to a template of governance for the entire state had a major influence on the evolution of the regime in its era of decline. The new philosophy entailed the recasting of the regime's mission, the

restructuring of its administration, and the restaffing of much of its key personnel in the service of a singular goal: to neutralize the revolutionary challenge
to the regime. This entailed both mobilizing a broad array of state and private
resources to counter the immediate military threat, while simultaneously pioneering a substantial program of reforms in an effort to undercut the appeal to
blacks of revolutionary action.[19] There was no credible sense of the polity's mission as being *volk* advancement at all. National security became its own end. And
in its name, foreign and domestic policy were fused. In external affairs, the line
between foreign policy and military action was removed as both were subsumed
under the Beaufrean rubric of maintaining the strategic initiative. Preemptive
strikes, covert action, cross-border violence, and even targeted assassinations
became standard elements of the regime's statecraft. At home, domestic policy
was likewise treated as a strategic imperative. Total strategy became the central
political, ideological, and conceptual vehicle for P. W. Botha's signature efforts
to foster the emergence of a prosperous black middle class as a bulwark against
revolution. These included recognizing the existence and permanency of the
"urban black," acknowledging African labor rights, and investing in engines of
black social mobility through new education and employment policies.[20] Much
as the *verkramptes* predicted, these measures did little to coopt black South
Africans as a whole and fundamentally reshape their political aspirations, but
only fatally undermined the rationales for the entire system.

Decisions

How did this all come to pass? Even had Vorster managed to establish diplomatic relations with a handful of independent African states, the diffusion of
nonracialism as a normative foundation of postwar concepts of geopolitical
legitimacy meant that these victories would have ultimately been short-lived.
Ultimately, the NP of the Vorster era was delusional, constructing an evermore
elaborate ideological edifice out of constructs that had little or no enduring acceptance outside of the narrow conceptual realm in which they were forged. One
cannot but be struck by the massive intellectual energy and endless resources
invested (and wasted) in this endeavor. However, more explicit African recognition, or a favorable outcome in Angola, or successfully negotiated settlements
producing moderate black regimes in Rhodesia and SWA that refused support
to antiregime militants may have unleashed different ideological currents within
white South African circles. The small but vocal *verligte* community was clearly
energized by Vorster's outward policy; additional success on that front may have
prompted more enterprising conceptualizations of the *volk*'s future and its relationship to black Africans. Alternately, more foreign policy successes might have

merely seduced centrist Afrikaners into believing the *volk* could secure acceptance on the continent on its own terms, with no petty apartheid reforms needed at all. *Verkramptes* may have become even more alienated from a regime entering into extensive agreements with African governments, prompting a schism long before 1982. The events that helped Botha militarize the entire conversation about the polity's future and reboot his career, from the Angolan intervention to the raid on Cassinga, may never have happened, opening the political door to other emerging leaders and foreclosing the path to Vlakplaas. Or all of these simultaneously. Or something different entirely.

In hindsight, what was perhaps most remarkable about Pretoria's African outreach was not so much the regime's short-lived though still startling successes in opening lines of communication with independent Africa, but its inability to follow through and secure more tangible and public acknowledgments of the regime's viability and legitimacy. South Africa surely could have demanded an explicit quid pro quo of an exchange of ambassadors in exchange for, say, building Madagascar a new deep water harbor or committing its forces in Angola. But it did not. Vorster and his doves believed resolutely that if Pretoria showed its commitment to solving the continent's problems, moderate African leaders would inevitably come around of their own accord to recognizing the right of the Afrikaners to exist in Africa and maintain their own identity there. They wanted to be part of a real conversation about postcolonial African identity and refused to exert leverage or drive an explicit bargain. This "soft sell" was based on a consistent, though flawed, underlying logic: for Pretoria, African leaders could *recognize* the *volk's* right to exist in Africa, but they were not the *source* of that right. As early as 1967, United Party MP W. V. Raw berated the government for the lack of urgency in its African outreach: "Time is one of the factors of which we are short; time is one of the things that we cannot play with, because with each passing year we lose time which we can never regain." Muller's counter was emblematic of Vorster's entire attitude toward statecraft, governance, and leadership: "You cannot force the pace."[21] Botha's approach to foreign policy was very different. If Vorster wanted to be part of a conversation, Botha simply ejected from the conversation those whose opinions he did not like. Botha did meet with African leaders during his time as premier, which owed something to Vorster's example. But he never understood that strong-arming his interlocutors into talking to him meant that any exchanges were coercive and therefore failed to have any underlying impact on the discourses through which his polity was perceived. Bombing Lesotho into submission or providing extensive and barely concealed support for insurgents in Mozambique and Angola differed vastly from offering to build Malawi a new capital.

Never was Vorster's aversion to decisive action clearer than in his refusal to apply serious pressure on Smith in 1974–75. By the middle of December 1974, the broad framework for negotiations between Salisbury and the nationalists had been established, with Vorster and Kaunda prodding each faction toward the negotiating table. Yet no substantive progress at all was made toward bringing the parties together in person until August 1975. Even then, the parties never even started to talk about the outlines of an actual settlement. This was a colossal missed opportunity for Vorster: the types of settlement terms considered realistic by all parties in 1974–75 were much more favorable to both Salisbury and Pretoria than Annex C in 1976, and far more attractive than any subsequent proposals, like the Richard Plan or the Owen-Vance framework. If Vorster had worked successfully with Kaunda to secure a majority black polity in Rhodesia, he would have shattered international understandings of the geopolitical priorities of his regime. African moderates would have been heartened and radicals quelled, roughly the opposite of what happened in 1976. Vorster's already-burgeoning reputation as a peacemaker would have grown substantially, providing him with the personal stature to overcome the right-wing doubters at home. He may even have shared the Nobel Peace Prize with Kaunda; Rhodesia was, after all, one of the most intractable diplomatic issues of the day. Such events would have substantially influenced the ideological contests within white South Africa.

Vorster compounded this missed opportunity over Rhodesia with the intervention in Angola, which narrowed his subsequent room for diplomatic maneuver substantially. The entire endeavor was a mess. The regime had very few real strategic interests in Angola. Instead, its fears in winter 1975—particularly regarding the integrity of the SWA border and the border sites—were largely derived from two ideologically driven assumptions: that the rise of a local movement, the MPLA, represented the steady march of global communism; and, concomitantly, that a Marxist regime in Luanda would prove disastrous for South Africa. These assumptions dictated how events were processed and understood, corrupting subsequent decision making. Vorster was also seduced by the prospect of acting in concert with a number of African leaders. There was never anything resembling an overall strategic plan that drew upon a broad range of bureaucratic inputs to evaluate the feasibility of preventing the MPLA's success in the context of the military and diplomatic restrictions on Pretoria's statecraft. Instead, South Africa embarked upon an incremental intervention and ended up with a level of involvement that no- one had foreseen. Angola was, in many respects, Pretoria's Vietnam.

The consequences for Vorster's geopolitical vision and personal standing were disastrous. Angola drove the transition of South Africa's hawks from national security advisers to forthright advocates for an entirely different approach to the regime's long-term survival—one that was incompatible with and undermined his own program. The entire conversation on national security shifted toward hawkish recommendations of rearmament and confrontation, while on a more conceptual level, Vorster lost control of the conversation within Pretoria about the relationship between the regime and independent Africa in the context of the Cold War. Diplomatically, the exposure of South Africa's surreptitious intervention in Angola and its subsequent public withdrawal was the worst of all worlds: Pretoria was seen as having tried to interfere in a power struggle in black Africa and as having been too weak to have done so successfully. More broadly, so long as South Africa was being constructive, took the diplomatic initiative, and focused on bilateral relationships, it was an elusive target for anti-Pretoria opposition. It could even launch its own models of African identity governed by discourses of noninterference, mutual economic development, and anticommunism. But when it invaded Angola, that all changed: Vorster ended up offering his foes the opportunity to engage in an open diplomatic battle—and at the OAU, of all terrains. He duly lost, albeit narrowly, and paid a heavy price for it. American cables suggest that by late 1975, Houphouët-Boigny was on the verge of establishing full diplomatic relations with Pretoria.[22] It is hard to imagine that at least some of the other Conseil de l'Entente states under Abidjan's sway—Niger, Upper Volta, Dahomey, and Togo—would not have followed suit. Yet within weeks, such a prospect was once more fanciful.

The strategic shortcomings of Vorster's entire venture—based as it was on tenuous assumptions, flawed premises, long-odds bets, and outright delusions—should not obscure the tactical ineptitude. Vorster saw his state-building agenda like a game of chess, one of his favorite pastimes. He enjoyed creating strategies and displayed an entirely unexpected gift for them in the field of foreign affairs. But he needed someone else to play with. In 1974–75, it was Kaunda who filled this role; in 1976, it was Kissinger. During the Angolan intervention, the lack of clarity over Pretoria's precise purpose and strategy derived largely from Vorster's inability to find a reliable geopolitical partner. Kaunda, Mobutu, Savimbi, and Kissinger were all involved at times, but none of them stayed with him from start to finish. Unlike P. W. Botha, Vorster did not have the type of forceful leadership persona required to dictate events on his own; he was only driven to decisive action when events impelled him. When his political fortunes surged or he was under little pressure, Vorster's natural tendency was to enjoy the breathing space and think about the next move, rather than pressing ahead. He showed no more urgency in repealing elements of petty apartheid than he did in securing tangible recognition from African leaders, particularly during a second term in office in which he had few constraints on his power. Consequently, Vorster was never able to achieve the intermediate goals necessary to bolster his vision for the regime's future. He was ultimately unable to deliver settlements in SWA and Rhodesia to serve as concrete evidence of the distinction he was trying to draw between South Africa and its separate development system and its erstwhile partners in the white redoubt. Undoubtedly, he encountered substantial obstacles on both fronts. In Windhoek, the bitter division among the SWA whites proved a significant obstacle to South African efforts to establish a framework for an independent Namibia. Similarly, in Salisbury, Smith's intransigence as well as divisions between the various nationalists and Frontline presidents greatly hampered any agreement. But none of these obstacles were insuperable. Vorster had both the opportunity and the leverage to force a settlement in both places, but he proved reluctant to exert Pretoria's power in a swift, decisive fashion.

Vorster also failed on the home front, where he was unable either to develop an overwhelming consensus behind his vision or to neutralize, much less crush,

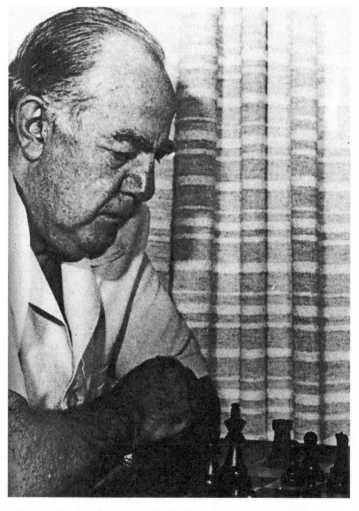

Figure 10.1 John Vorster saw his state-building agenda like a game of chess, one of his favorite pastimes. Source: Ernest Stanton Publishers.

opposition. The prime minister knew that he lacked widespread domestic support for his master plan, including as it did a shift away from fellow whites in Rhodesia and SWA. The hawks, led by Botha, exhibited barely concealed contempt for the détente agenda, which they saw as reckless appeasement of communist-backed African nationalism. They regularly undermined the prime minister's diplomacy, sometimes indirectly and at other times (particularly with the Rhodesians) overtly. Meanwhile, within the party, Schoeman, Treurnicht, and others all launched potent critiques of the prime minister's vision as being essentially incompatible with *volk* principles. In late 1976 Vorster's own brother, Koot, repudiated the entire notion that South Africa's different ethnic groups had similar nationalist rights, the very foundation of grand apartheid as the prime minister and *verligtes* understood it. Channeling *verkrampte* thinking, the reverend insisted that the sacred calling of Afrikaner fulfillment rendered the concerns of other South Africans irrelevant.[23] Preferring to see a broad monolith of Afrikaner racism, outside observers at the time were perhaps too dismissive of the depth of these divisions and the real constraints they placed on the Vorster government.

Vorster's solution to this problem was twofold. First, he stoked the publicity attracted by diplomatic coups to encourage white South Africans to believe that international rehabilitation was a possibility. Second, he worked in close quarters with a very small foreign policy team. This enabled him to circumvent opposition and avoid having to answer uncomfortable questions about his foreign policy agenda, even from his own Cabinet. This approach had its advantages. But simply allowing the hawks to continue their dissent and ignoring the disjuncture between his vision for the regime and the attitudes of many of his constituents did not make these problems disappear. Vorster could have reasserted his authority, reminding Biermann and Malan, if not Botha himself, that the military served the state as a defense force, not a think-tank for strategic policy of the broadest kind. Instead, he characteristically refused to take command and ensure that all elements of his government were working effectively toward the same goal. Vorster likewise failed spectacularly to neutralize the *verkrampte* critique on his right wing. It is true that many Nationalists were inherently sympathetic to the Afrikaner unilateralism that his critics invoked, but they also deferred readily to their elected leaders, particularly in times of crisis. This gave Vorster a great deal of leeway to use his leadership to set the agenda, and it was that leadership that Vorster was unable to consistently provide. Instead of proactively energizing key stakeholders across Afrikanerdom and mustering support for his vision of African outreach abroad and the dismantling of petty apartheid at home, he prioritized "party unity." The size of his massive electoral victories—118 out of 166 seats in 1970, 123 out of 171 in 1974, and 134 out of 165 in 1977—are testament to his ability to render the NP a broad church.

None of his predecessors or successors ever matched such a record. However, the landslides also reflect his inability and unwillingness to consistently provide the party with a narrower but clearer direction for the future—one that would inevitably have involved losing some supporters along the way.

To support the message of separation rather than domination, Vorster needed to at least tear down petty apartheid. He knew this, labeling such measures as "hurtful," "discriminatory," and "serving no purpose."[24] However, he was unwilling to do much beyond the desegregation of certain hotels, parks, and beaches. Separate facilities were the most prominent lightning rod for foreign antipathy, especially in the United States, where every photo recalled the pre-civil rights era and Jim Crow laws. Yet Vorster never had the courage to risk another intraparty confrontation and split Afrikanerdom definitively.

Reflections

The counterintuitive story told here offers new perspectives on Afrikanerdom and the apartheid regime. Vorster's new direction for the *volk* may have violated some existing racial norms, but it in fact grew out of a particular interpretation of the separate development model. That model, sketched out by Verwoerd, was intended as a mechanism to absolve the regime of any real responsibility for the advancement or welfare of South Africa's black population. Separate development remained a cruel farce: although Vorster greatly expanded upon Verwoerd's negligible investment in the homelands, his program never approached viability or plausibility. But the notion of parallel nationalisms that underpinned the logic of the separate development model prompted the emergence of a new discourse legitimizing the future of Afrikanerdom. Some elements of the new thinking, such as the paramountcy of group rights and national futures, had long histories in Nationalist political thought. But other elements—including the unlikely embrace of a particular version of African nationalism, the acknowledgment of the merits of interconnectedness among African peoples, and the recognition of the very existence of the modern African, the *évolué*—were sudden and substantial departures from the intellectual firmament of just a few years before. This new canon was inherently volatile. The corollaries of many of the new ideas, as the *verkramptes* pointed out, could readily be used to undermine the *volk*'s legitimacy and the separate development system. But, if manipulated just so, the new ideas formed a politically potent compound, one that Vorster temporarily used to bring Nationalists of all stripes (as well as a few non-Nationalist white politicians and even some black South Africans) together in 1974–75.

Although Vorster's African outreach was a top-down campaign, designed and executed by a tiny cabal of leaders and officials, it did not emerge out of a conceptual vacuum. How Afrikaner society understood what separate development meant was vital to the entire enterprise. The traction gained by African outreach at home in spite of the deeply ingrained fear and ignorance of Africa reflected a newly developing sense of *volk* identity, itself a product of major changes in the social and economic status of Afrikanerdom in the 1960s. Specifically, Vorster's new ideas resonated with three emerging constituencies in the Afrikaner community. The small but vocal *verligte* intelligentsia, heavily overrepresented in the media and decreasingly reliant upon traditional *volk* institutions for their platforms, was eager to develop a more moral basis for Afrikaner power. The new Afrikaner capitalist class was pioneering a new ethos of materialism and individual advancement that ultimately cut across existing canards on racial hierarchy and righteous isolation. And younger, urbanized, and educated Afrikaners understood their identity in ways that diverged from worldviews rooted in an earlier socioeconomic environment, one of small-scale farming that was uncompetitive without cheap black labor and of direct competition with urbanizing Africans for unskilled jobs in the towns. The new generation had never known the political, cultural, and economic precarity of the 1930s and 1940s that weighed so heavily on leaders of Vorster's and Botha's age. Instead, many knew only Nationalist hegemony, the security of a Republic, a growing and respected corpus of Afrikaans literature and poetry, foreign pop music and movies, white-collar employment, successful Afrikaans-language universities, consumer culture, booming incomes, multilingualism, even mini-skirts. These were the products not of the dark ages of Afrikanerdom, but its *risorgimento*. This security provided plenty of internal impetus for a foreign policy that reflected a *volk* that was confident and outward looking, determined to engage with and coexist alongside other peoples—even while suspicious of others' strange ideas on social organization and fiercely resistant to foreign interference. Just as ideology and society influenced foreign policy, so too can foreign policy serve as a lens through which to understand changes in ideology and society.

Scholars of apartheid have long acknowledged that for all its claims to be a nationalist movement, NP rule ultimately entrenched the interests of specific classes and racial groups. This study is a reminder that the discourses of the party itself, which focused relentlessly on nationalist teleologies, symbols, and appeals, shaped the regime's conduct in important ways too. Prior to 1976, at least, while NP leaders, ideological factions, and Afrikaner voters differed on the direction of the national strategy for survival, participants overwhelmingly engaged in debate from the same conceptual reference point: the fundamental primacy of the nation as the essential form of social organization and vessel for individual fulfilment. It was precisely Vorster's ability to tap into those discourses and use them to reframe the polity's mission and identity that enabled him to reach out to independent Africa: the inviolability of national communities and rights was central to the new understandings of African nationalism as a vehicle for Afrikaner advancement, rather than an existential threat. Vorster was even willing to abandon the racial bonds of the white redoubt in an effort to reconceptualize the category of "whiteness" in national rather than racially supremacist terms, trading in the anchor of "European" that had featured so prominently in the ideological legacy bequeathed to him by Verwoerd for the unlikely identity of "African."[25] Meanwhile, the emphasis on the polity's mission as a fundamentally national one was the political and conceptual key to transcending existing racial norms. Vorster's short-lived forays into the removal of petty apartheid served to underline the emerging *verligte* claim to a South Africa of horizontal national communities in conscious contradistinction to the old "colonialist" systems of vertical oppression based solely on racial distinctions. In the service of this ideal, Afrikanerdom was ultimately willing to stomach many things that would have been unthinkable under Hendrik Verwoerd. Their leaders met regularly with their counterparts from independent Africa and ate alongside black women. They themselves were introduced to multiracial hotels and theaters, as well as interracial sport and tours by foreign black entertainers. Many, particularly among the three constituencies referred to above, lauded these shifts. Some urged much more. Within the Nationalist community prior to 1976, racial thought was evidently malleable, whereas the goal of maintaining *volk* viability was much less so—even if the right-wing of the party saw little difference between the two. The former was remolded and redefined precisely to maintain the increasingly tenuous viability of the latter. This phenomenon was then essentially *reversed* under P. W. Botha. The pursuit of an Afrikaner national mission within a multinational framework receded from the regime's ideological corpus in favor of a new vision: a racially defined pan-white polity determined to undercut black unity not only along "national" cleavages, but increasingly economic ones too.

Verwoerdian apartheid could never have endured. The system produced a series of interlocking crises, in which ideological strictures impeded the government's ability to solve any one crisis without exacerbating others.[26] But the way in which the regime stumbled into its sunset years derived substantially from the abortive ideological renewal, audacious statecraft, and resulting political fallout detailed in this book. In the early 1970s, there were a range of future ideological platforms for the regime as different actors and power bases sought to reconcile the Verwoerdian vision of separate development to a modernizing South African society. Each of these conceptual networks sought to justify what Nationalist rule stood for and where the polity was going. Vorster's plan for the future aimed at nothing less than streamlining the regime's foreign and domestic policies under the overarching conceptual architecture of parallel nationalisms. Some elements of this plan were highly original, others deeply conservative and derivative. The death of that vision proved debilitating for the regime and its supporters, while creating a vacuum for the entrance of a different template for governance that proved hegemonic and a major obstacle to real change right up until F. W. de Klerk signed apartheid's death sentence in 1990.

NOTE ON SOURCES

Researching the history of the apartheid regime remains far from straightforward. Some of the reasons for this, such as logistical difficulties, cost, and language requirements, are obvious. Others, often deriving from the struggles of the new order in South Africa to process the history of the apartheid years, are more complex.[1] Moreover, officials in the apartheid regime were distinctly aware of how the outside world might later view its internal history. Cultures of secrecy and document destruction were the results.[2] Hopefully, this book will encourage others to overcome these obstacles and expand our understanding of how the apartheid regime operated. As many of the documents and files relied upon here have not before been used by other scholars, a brief outline of the nature (and limitations) of the source material utilized may help to contextualize this study for the reader, as well as illuminating future resources for the researcher.

This project's research program was originally based on three central premises. First, I surmised that much of the challenge (and value) would lie in bringing the different elements of the apartheid polity—domestic politics, intellectual history, foreign policy, national security theory, economic and social change—together into a unified whole. Scholarship existed on each of these, but precious few books explained how developments in one field influenced those in others. Second, as Afrikaans was the lingua franca of the National Party, I realized that if I was not prepared to learn the language then my understanding of the historical picture would have an unavoidable (and low) ceiling, quite apart from whatever shortcomings I brought to the process myself or other obstacles I encountered. As it turned out, the vast majority of the material I ended up encountering in the archives, as well as many of the memoirs and little-used secondary texts, were in Afrikaans. Finally, I rationalized that if I were to study how South Africa's leaders understood the threats to their regime and responded to them, I had to be able to set aside my own politics and appreciate the power structure's concerns in their own time and place. In this respect, being neither a South African nor a contemporary of the apartheid era may have been an advantage: apartheid is a scholarly field on which the weight of politics has been very substantial.

When I first began researching among the Department for Foreign Affairs (DFA) files in 2010, the archive had just been moved from the Union Buildings in Pretoria to a room off the underground car park of the brand new Department of International Relations and Cooperation, situated nearby on Soutpansberg Road in Rietondale. It was all very disorganized, with boxes strewn across corridors and in no logical order. After weeks of searching for a particular file series, I took it upon myself to go into the back rooms and manually write the relevant catalog numbers on each and every box. This took quite some time, but it enabled me (and, hopefully, future researchers) to have a much better idea of what the capacity of the archive actually was.

The material I subsequently found proved rich and revealing on some subject matters and frustratingly insufficient on others. All of the major decisions, on all issues, went through the office of the long-serving Secretary for Foreign Affairs, Brand Fourie. He kept the most important documentation in a personal safe[3]— a collection from which only a couple of boxes apparently survive. Efforts to try to locate the remainder of this material proved unsuccessful. Additionally, the department did not have a strong culture of document preservation. Many important conversations occurred either by telephone or in small high-level meetings with no departmental written record kept. For some years, at least, many of the documents on the most important issues—such as the future of South West Africa—were replicated in four copies, which went to Fourie, the foreign minister, the ambassador to the UN, and the decoding room.[4] As a matter of process, none went to the filing system. Finally, in the last years of the apartheid system, then head of the DFA, Rusty Evans, oversaw a purge of some key documentation.[5] Like most purges, this one was inconsistent and uneven, leaving somewhat ad hoc gaps in the documentary record. As a general rule, cables (and other documents attached to them) remain intact. But whatever existed in the way of policy-planning documents or records, which was limited in any case, as well as interchanges between DFA officials working within South Africa, has gone missing in the ensuing years. This was not the only confirmed document purge. Alongside Fourie, BOSS chief General Hendrik van den Bergh played a central role in Vorster's diplomacy during this period, especially on the African continent. One of his key officials, Piet de Wit, told me that he took custody of van den Bergh's filing cabinets upon the latter's retirement. He found them filled with evidence of the deep animosity between the General and his nemesis, P. W. Botha. Reasoning that such could never be of any help to anyone and would only be damaging to the Afrikaner cause, he shredded the entire contents.[6]

On their own, the DFA files provide a useful but limited yield. There was a marked looseness to how the regime formulated and executed foreign policy.

The DFA often did not play a central role. However, with reference to other documents, memoirs, or events, it becomes possible to deduce which cables had an important impact upon policy and which simply ended up in the files. A case in point is Pik Botha's "Long Telegram." On its own, it is not immediately apparent that this document played a key role in the government's response to the post-Soweto international condemnation of the regime. However, when read in the context of the minutes of the Cabinet meeting, my own interview with Pik Botha, and the SADF's Military Intelligence analysis of the cable (an unusual practice in 1976), the cable's true importance to the August 3 Cabinet meeting and its long-term significance in the fortunes of the polity becomes clear.

In anticipation of my longer research trip in South Africa in 2011, I applied for the declassification of some 150 files from the archives of the South African Defense Force (today the South African National Defense Force). The old SADF was one of the major targets of the Truth and Reconciliation Commission, both for its role in suppressing domestic and regional insurgency in the 1980s and for its close association with the government deemed responsible for the worst human rights abuses, that of P. W. Botha. Consequently, and in light of scholars' fairly limited use of its records for nonmilitary history, I expected that the SADF would keep a fairly close hold on most documentation, especially on anything regarded as sensitive.[7] Instead, the SADF fully declassified nearly every document that I requested. Many of these were classified Top Secret (*Uiters Geheim*). Unlike the DFA, the SADF did have a documentary culture and produced vast reams of paper, including reports from Military Intelligence, analyses of regional threats, strategic blueprints, reports from the various battlefields during the Angolan intervention, and so on.

If foreign affairs and national security were two dimensions of my topic, then political decision making was the third. It was here that archival sources proved most frustrating. The South African National Archives (SANA), which should hold the records of most apartheid-era government departments, proved vexing. Its central facility in Pretoria is poorly organized and staffed. Inventories are out of date, and archivists tend to see the researcher as an imposition rather than their raison d'être. The new(ish) digital search engine, to which the archivists constantly refer the inquisitive researcher, is all but useless. Doubtless the SANA holds many important files from this period, but it is currently impossible to know what the archive's holdings comprise. Meanwhile, efforts to obtain BOSS records through both the State Security Agency and SANA never got off the ground. Hopefully other scholars will have more success, enabling them to see much further into the past than I was able to.

Adding to the frustration with the SANA is that one of the most relevant accessible holdings, the Cabinet Minutes, is of limited use. Whereas in Westminster systems a Cabinet Secretary would take notes and later use these to compile extensive minutes of Cabinet meetings, in South Africa the custom was for junior ministers to only take handwritten notes in a bound volume. This was not a regulated or directed process. Certain meetings are recorded in useful and lengthy form, but in general the practice was simply to record under each minister's name whether his proposal was adopted, rejected, or postponed. The Cabinet Minutes themselves therefore comprise a useful microcosm of the chaotic and decentralized Vorster system of governance. On my most recent visit in October 2014, moreover, an archivist told me that the Cabinet Minutes had in fact been reclassified and would now require a high security clearance to be seen. Two esteemed researchers have recently informed me of a similar tightening of access to the DFA records, for reasons that remain unknown. This is a very worrying trend.

The limitations of these three repositories led to the realization that triangulation was going to be central to effectively utilizing the material that I had. Just because South African records of key diplomatic meetings were inaccessible or did not exist did not mean that their interlocutors did not take minutes for their own purposes. The exceptionally rich official records of the Ian Smith regime—smuggled out of Rhodesia in the last days of white rule, by the South African Air Force, no less—became of critical use in this regard. In contrast to the often lax record keeping in Pretoria, the Rhodesian civil service maintained meticulous records; they exhibited both the best and worst traits of the British colonial officials who trained them. The analysis of the détente negotiations of 1974–75 would have been impossible, or at least vastly weaker, without these Rhodesian records of Salisbury's countless meetings with South African representatives. Though these materials were initially deposited at Smith's alma mater at Rhodes University, Grahamstown, where I accessed them, they have since been repatriated to Zimbabwe. Future access is uncertain.

American research materials helped to flesh out another important part of the picture: South Africa's response to Washington's efforts to enlist it in managing transitions to majority rule in both Rhodesia and South-West Africa and thus stave off the prospect of a Cold War conflict fought along racial lines. I worked predominantly at the Ford Presidential Library and the Carter Presidential Library, as well as at the National Security Archive and National Archives II. Much as with the Rhodesian archives, I was usually able to locate the American records of meetings involving South African diplomats or politicians, such as the Kissinger-Vorster meetings in West Germany in 1976. I also utilized a number of digitized databases of American documents. Some of these were conventional, others were not. Just as I was completing my doctoral dissertation, WikiLeaks published a huge tranche of State Department cables from the 1973–76 period. Some of these helped to fill in important gaps in my existing analysis of the Washington-Pretoria relationship during the Angolan Civil War.

Over the subsequent years, my Freedom of Information Requests lodged at the Ford Library on this same topic were processed. These provided some useful contextual information, although most of the important and sensitive material remains redacted for national security reasons. I suspect that this material, when finally divulged, will confirm my thesis on Pretoria's military involvement in Angola: South Africa intervened—at first hesitantly, later more enthusiastically, always chaotically—based on the systems of threat perception and foreign policies that had evolved independently in Pretoria over the previous years; the Ford Administration, operating its own small-scale covert program, was content to allow the regime to do so and never had to provide the sort of explicit assurances that the South African government later claimed to have motivated its own intervention. I also suspect that further research will show that for John Vorster specifically, intimations of common cause from Lusaka and Kinshasa were of real importance.

Overall, my research in Washington, London, and Paris ended up playing a decidedly more peripheral role than I had originally envisaged. While telling me plenty about the context for various diplomatic encounters, they told me almost nothing about the underlying dynamics that were really at issue for this project. The ideas, opinions, ideologies, and worldviews of Western societies and their governments provided little insight into how Nationalists understood the world and their prospects for survival in it. The answers to these questions were to be found in South Africa, predominantly through exploring the political and intellectual universe of Afrikanerdom.

Over time, I began to realize that many of the ongoing difficulties I was having distinguishing between different factions and interests in Pretoria was due to my inability to develop the central figures of my book in three dimensions. To this end, I conducted interviews with more than twenty central figures from the South African government, diplomatic service, military, and BOSS. Some potential interviewees had recently passed away; Magnus Malan died less than a week before our scheduled session. I was nevertheless able to talk with a number of people who were involved at the highest level of government, including two former heads of the SADF, three former ambassadors to the United Nations, one former minister for foreign affairs, one former director-general of foreign affairs, numerous Nationalist MPs, and three former ambassadors to Washington. (Some individuals filled more than one of these roles at different times.) The resulting fifty-plus hours of recorded recollections was complemented by both written submissions and subsequent correspondence with the interviewees— to clarify this fact, or contextualize that point. There were also many hours of off-the-record discussions. The testimony of these interviewees provided an invaluable texture to the written record and opened up new avenues for my archival research. The vast majority of the interviewees were very forthcoming and cooperative. By contrast, nonregime actors featured in this story generally did not want to talk about their engagement with the apartheid regime. Henry Kissinger declined to be interviewed for this study, while Kenneth Kaunda and Mark Chona ignored repeated requests.

As this project evolved, I realized that the political dimension of my story was much more important than I had originally foreseen. I therefore sought to develop my understanding of the different figures within the regime and their conflicting motivations by conducting three separate trips to the Archive for Contemporary Affairs (ARCA) at the Instituut vir Eietydse Geskiedenis in Bloemfontein. ARCA contains the personal papers of many Afrikaner elites and Nationalist politicians dating back a century, including many of those who appear in this book. Documents acquired at ARCA, like the interviews, helped to illuminate new ideas or events whose significance I had not fully appreciated. Other files, such as the caucus minutes, revealed much about how the NP actually functioned, how leaders explained and justified policy to backbenchers, and how intraparty dynamics played out behind closed doors. During the course of my research, I played some small role in convincing Pik Botha to donate his massive collection of governmental records, housed in two sheds on his Pretoria property, to ARCA. These will take some time to catalog, but future researchers will hopefully be able to avail themselves of an extraordinary resource that will fill a major gap in our understanding of the regime and its foreign policy. I encourage all South Africans who worked in some capacity for the old regime, or their surviving family members, to donate all papers in their possession to ARCA so as to help create a one-stop-shop for future scholars of the regime.

From these files, it became clear that although the NP operated within Westminster structures (at least, prior to 1983), its culture was more like Vatican politics. For its members, the NP was more than a political party. It was dedicated to a higher mission, with a spiritual dimension: the fulfillment in perpetuity of the *volk*. Out of national solidarity and devotion to the mission, open disagreement with the *Hoofleier* was therefore very rare. Instead, the character of the party encouraged indirect attacks through carefully worded statements and scheming by party barons behind the scenes. However, the lack of transparency and accountability in the party's culture facilitated corruption, secrecy, and abuses of the *volk*'s trust. It was also apparent from the files that the flashpoints of Nationalist politics were not entirely dissimilar from those in the headlines today. Having recently moved to the United States, I did not have to look too far to see a model of economic change corroding old concepts of nationhood, with those left behind clinging to warped and outdated historical myths, and those whose fortunes were soaring pursuing their own interests and insistently imposing new forms of identity that were compatible with these. Equally, the class divides that largely dictated attitudes toward Vorster's state-building agenda were also roughly commensurate with urban-rural divides in Afrikaner society. Letters to the editor of *Die Afrikaner* came from places like Reivilo and Zastron, miniscule towns even today, where the faltering political economy of daily life would have mandated strong racial divisions to support white social status. As I finished writing this book from the Appalachian hill country of western Pennsylvania, amid the tumult of the 2016 US presidential campaign, it was hard not to see parallels.

Private memoranda, intraparty debates, and public speeches were not the only means of exchange and debate on political issues in this period. Another was print. (The regime owned the state radio service, rendering it essentially a one-way mouthpiece. Regular television service was introduced only in early 1976.) Historians have traditionally followed the English-language press in portraying the Afrikaans papers as little more than party-line sheets. Certainly, historic mainstream titles like *Die Burger* and *Die Transvaler* saw themselves as arms of the Afrikaner nationalist movement and were rarely openly critical of established party policy.[8] However, it was increasingly unclear by the mid-1970s what established party policy was. In order to make sense of the differences in coverage that ensued, political scientist Dan O'Meara pioneered a new framework, positioning newspapers as reflecting the interests of different owners, themselves part of broader concentrations of capital.[9] Another approach is to treat newspapers as reflecting (as well as shaping) the views of their readers, as much as the interests of their owners. If *Rapport*, say, pressed the government to embrace more reformist policies on petty apartheid measures, then this was indeed in part the result of decisions by its owners and editors. But these decisions did not exist in a vacuum: such papers only survived because their editorial lines and content resonated with a certain readership. Indeed, newspapers within the same ownership groups took different lines on the same issue. The venerable Free State daily *Die Volksblad* was much less supportive of Vorster's détente initiatives than its much newer Nasionale Pers stablemate *Beeld*, published out of Johannesburg, precisely because they targeted different markets. As such, historians can read Afrikaans newspapers as useful (if imperfect) proxies for the views of those who read them. For the same reason, historians can use white-owned papers like *The World* as reasonable (though far from flawless) barometers for black views on politics. If these papers were not broadly representative of their readership's views, people would not have bought them.

Nowhere is this approach more productive than in helping to recapture the views of the right-wing of Afrikaner politics. As the Nationalist community sought to isolate, discredit, and purge dissenters in the early 1970s, many HNP leaders and thinkers became more or less persona non grata in the forums of mainstream Afrikanerdom. For example, the giant radio tower in Brixton, Johannesburg, still standing today, was initially named after the then minister of post and telecommunications, Albert Hertzog. When he formed the HNP, he lost the naming rights. The footprints of the far-right are likewise found at best intermittently in the historical literature. However, journals like *Veg* and *Die Afrikaner* were published, written, and read for one reason: to express opposition to the policies of the Vorster government. They contain articles written by prominent HNP cheerleaders like B. M. Schoeman, long interviews with politicians such as Jaap Marais and Dr. Albert Hertzog, and letters to the editor from "ordinary" Afrikaners confused at their leaders' sudden rearticulation of the canards underpinning their identity and way of life. These journals therefore comprise a goldmine for understanding the content of a *verkrampte* discourse that resonated well beyond the narrow membership of the HNP.

Finally, I made extensive use of memoirs and similar sources. When read together, works such as Magnus Malan's autobiography, Donald Sole's unpublished memoirs, P. W. Botha's two authorized biographies (as well as his written submissions to the Truth and Reconciliation Commission), and Les de Villiers's excellent account of the Department of Information's secret projects provide fascinating insights into how the Vorster regime functioned. (I have placed considerably less faith in Eschel Rhoodie's various recollections than other chroniclers; it is just too hard to tell truth from self-serving fiction.) E. L. P. Stals's unpublished history of the Broederbond, grounded in unparalleled access to Bond archives, was highly revealing of debates among Afrikaner elites. Equally valuable was Brand Fourie's *Buitelandse Woelinge*, the extended manuscript from which his considerably shorter published account, *Brandpunte*, was drawn. *Buitelandse Woelinge* is exceptionally rare; I found only four manuscript copies in all of South Africa's libraries. Yet it proved a fascinating source, a first-hand account from the one man who featured in almost all of the key diplomatic meetings covered in this book. It is also evident that these memoirs were written on the basis of extensive written records. I have not lost hope of these, as well as many other primary source materials from the apartheid era, turning up somewhere.

ARCHIVAL ABBREVIATIONS

AB	Afrikaner Broederbond Archives
ARCA	Archive for Contemporary Affairs (Argief vir Eietydse Aangeleenthede)
BFF	Brand Fourie Files
CIARR	Central Intelligence Agency Reading Room
DFA	Department of Foreign Affairs
DFAA	South African Department of Foreign Affairs Archives
DNSA	Digital National Security Archive
FCO	Foreign and Commonwealth Office
GFL	Gerald R. Ford Presidential Library
HBA	Hastings Kamuzu Banda Collection, Herman B. Wells Library, Indiana University
ISP	Ian Smith Papers
JCL	Jimmy Carter Presidential Library
NARA	United States National Archives and Records Administration
NSA	National Security Archive
SAHA	South African History Archive
SANA	South African National Archives
SANDFA	South African National Defense Force Archives
WKL	WikiLeaks

NOTES

Terminology

1. Archive for Contemporary Affairs (ARCA), PV 203, 1/V9/1, P. W. Botha, 1 Onderwerpslêers, 1/V9 Vorster, adv. B. J., "Belangrike Doelstellings, Doelwitte en Beleide op die Nasionale Vlak soos Afgelei uit die Toesprake van Sy Edele Die Eerste Minister Adv B. J. Vorster," specific date unclear, 1977.
2. Hermann Giliomee, "The Beginnings of Afrikaner Ethnic Consciousness, 1850–1915," in *The Creation of Tribalism in Southern Africa*, ed. Leroy Vail (Berkeley: University of California Press, 1989).

Introduction

1. Account of Vorster-Kaunda meeting compiled from various newspaper reports.
2. Kenneth D. Kaunda, *Humanism and Apartheid* (Lusaka: The Veritas Corporation, 1971), n.p.
3. South African National Archives (SANA), MEM, 1/564, I13/2, Eerste Minister: Buitelandse Sake, Kenneth Kaunda, speech, "Southern Africa: A Time for Change," Lusaka, 26 October 1974.
4. James Barber and John Barratt, *South Africa's Foreign Policy: The Search for Status and Security, 1945–1988* (Johannesburg: Cambridge University Press, 1990), p. 105.
5. C. H. Feinstein, *An Economic History of South Africa: Conquest, Discrimination, and Development* (New York: Cambridge University Press, 2005), pp. 143–147.
6. For a stimulating discussion of the existential insecurity of "small peoples," see Uriel Abulof, "'Small Peoples': The Existential Uncertainty of Ethnonational Communities," *International Studies Quarterly* 53, no. 1 (2009).
7. Otto Krause, "Trends in Afrikaner Race Attitudes," in *South African Dialogue: Contrasts in South African Thinking on Basic Race Issues*, ed. Nicolaas Johannes Rhoodie (Johannesburg: McGraw-Hill Book Co., 1972), p. 534.
8. F. W. De Klerk, *The Last Trek: A New Beginning: The Autobiography* (London: Macmillan, 1998), p. 47.
9. South African National Defense Force Archives (SANDFA), Group 5—Minister van Verdediging, Box 8, MV/2/8/2, Eerste Minister, Volume 1, William E. Griffith, "Soviet-American Confrontation, 1970: In Sub-Saharan Africa, 1970: The Main Trends," attached to Kantoor van die Eerste Minister to Privaatsekretaris van die Minister van Verdediging, 22 January 1971.
10. Heribert Adam, *Modernizing Racial Domination: South Africa's Political Dynamics* (Berkeley; London: University of California Press, 1971), p. 111.
11. Norrie Macqueen, *The Decolonization of Portuguese Africa: Metropolitan Revolution and the Dissolution of Empire* (London; New York: Longman, 1997), p. 50.

12. See for instance Kenneth Maxwell, "Portugal and Africa: The Last Empire," in *Decolonization and African Independence: The Transfers of Power, 1960–1980*, ed. Prosser Gifford and William Roger Louis (New Haven, CT; London: Yale University Press, 1988). The title of the volume alone is instructive as to how decolonization was previously understood: as transfers of power, not multifaceted, messy contests that unfolded over periods of time. The eclipse of the older paradigm was foreshadowed in M. Crawford Young, "Nationalism, Ethnicity, and Class in Africa: A Retrospective," *Cahiers d'études africaines* (1986).

13. See Frederick Cooper, "Possibility and Constraint: African Independence in Historical Perspective," *Journal of African History* 49, no. 2 (2008). For area-specific studies building on this emerging consensus in different ways, see Brian Raftopoulos and Alois Mlambo, *Becoming Zimbabwe: A History from the Pre-Colonial Period to 2008* (Harare: Weaver Press, 2009); Jonathon Glassman, *War of Words, War of Stones: Racial Thought and Violence in Colonial Zanzibar* (Bloomington: Indiana University Press, 2011); Miles Larmer, *Rethinking African Politics: A History of Opposition in Zambia* (Farnham, UK: Ashgate, 2011); James R. Brennan, *Taifa: Making Nation and Race in Urban Tanzania* (Athens: Ohio University Press, 2012).

14. This approach is borrowed from Michael H. Hunt, *Ideology and U.S. Foreign Policy* (New Haven, CT: Yale University Press, 1987).

15. For studies of Vorster, see John D'Oliveira, *Vorster: The Man* (Johannesburg: Ernest Stanton, 1978); H. O. Terblanche, *John Vorster: OB-Generaal en Afrikanervegter* (Roodepoort: CUM-Boeke, 1983). For the much more extensive work on Botha, see Jan J. van Rooyen, *P.W. Botha: 40 Jaar* (Kaapstad: Hoofraad van die Kaaplandse Nasionale Party, 1976); Dirk de Villiers and Johanna de Villiers, *PW* (Kaapstad: Tafelberg, 1984); Deon Geldenhuys and Hennie Kotze, "P. W. Botha as Decision Maker: A Preliminary Study of Personality and Politics," *Politikon* 12 (June 1985); Brian Pottinger, *The Imperial Presidency: P.W. Botha the First 10 Years* (Johannesburg: Southern Book Publishers, 1988); Eschel M. Rhoodie, *PW Botha: The Last Betrayal* (Melville: S.A. Politics, 1989); Daan Prinsloo, *Stem uit die Wildernis: 'n Biographie van Oud-Pres. PW Botha* (Mossel Bay: Vaandel, 1997).

16. Ryan M. Irwin, *Gordian Knot: Apartheid and the Unmaking of the Liberal World Order* (New York: Oxford University Press, 2012). See also Roland Burke, *Decolonization and the Evolution of International Human Rights* (Philadelphia: University of Pennsylvania Press, 2010), pp. 59–91.

17. Vorster speech in Bloemfontein, 18 March 1967, in O. Geyser, ed. *Select Speeches* (Bloemfontein: INCH, 1977), p. 74.

18. Each of these programs was beset by obvious contradictions, as well as being substantially incompatible with the other. The relationship of the English-speaking newcomers to the *volk* and its mission remained deliberately unspecified by elites, capable of being articulated in divergent ways to different constituencies. Much the same ambiguity was also a feature of the Africanization of Afrikanerdom campaign and for the same reasons.

19. For core texts on the Vorster government's broader political, historical, and ideological contexts, see T. Dunbar Moodie, *The Rise of Afrikanerdom: Power, Apartheid, and the Afrikaner Civil Religion* (Berkeley: University of California Press, 1975); Heribert Adam and Hermann Giliomee, *The Rise and Crisis of Afrikaner Power* (Cape Town: David Philips, 1979); Hermann Giliomee, *The Afrikaners: Biography of a People* (Charlottesville: University of Virginia Press, 2003); Hermann Giliomee, *The Last Afrikaner Leaders: A Supreme Test of Power* (Cape Town: Tafelberg, 2012).

20. Henry Kissinger, *Years of Upheaval* (Boston: Little, Brown, 1982); Niall Ferguson et al., eds., *The Shock of the Global: The 1970s in Perspective* (Cambridge, MA; London: Belknap, 2010); W. W. Rostow, *The Diffusion of Power: An Essay in Recent History* (New York: Macmillan, 1972).

21. Paul Thomas Chamberlin, *The Global Offensive: The United States, the Palestine Liberation Organization, and the Making of the Post-Cold War Order* (Oxford; New York: Oxford University Press, 2012); Odd Arne Westad, *The Global Cold War: Third World Interventions and the Making of Our Times* (Cambridge: Cambridge University Press, 2007), pp. 73–109, 158–206.

22. South African National Archives (SANA), MEM, 1/572, 115/2, "Die Militêre Milieu in Suider-Afrika Waarin die RSA Hom Tans Bevind," attached to P. W. Botha to Vorster, 2 October 1974; SANDFA, Group 3- HSAW Chief of Defense Force, Box 181, Komp/503/1/8, SADF Five Year Plan, 27 May 1975.

23. While Pretoria certainly conflated a variety of ideological and political threats as "communist inspired," the alarmism and self-serving nature of this phenomenon should not obscure the important role played by communist ideas and parties in the anti-apartheid struggle. For recent work, see Irina Filatova and Apollon Davidson, *The Hidden Thread: Russia and South Africa in the Soviet Era* (Johannesburg: Jonathan Ball, 2013); Stephen Ellis, *External Mission: The ANC in Exile, 1960–1990* (London: Hurst, 2012).

24. Heribert Adam, "The South African Power-Elite: A Survey of Ideological Commitment," in *South Africa: Sociological Perspectives*, ed. Heribert Adam (Oxford: Oxford University Press, 1971), p. 91. The survey allowed respondents to select more than one option.

25. SANDFA, Group 4- P. W. Botha, Box 142, 76/1, Strategie: Algemeen, Volume 1, "Die Strategiese Waardering, SAW: Strategiese Benadering," 23 September 1975.

26. For leading works on total strategy, see Deon Geldenhuys, *Some Foreign Policy Implications of South Africa's Total National Strategy with Reference to the 12-Point Plan* (Braamfontein: South African Institute for International Affairs, 1981); Robert Davies and Dan O'Meara, "Total Strategy in Southern Africa: An Analysis of South African Regional Policy since 1978," *Journal of Southern African Studies* 11, no. 2 (April 1985); and especially Chris Alden, *Apartheid's Last Stand: The Rise and Fall of the South African Security State* (Basingstoke, UK: Macmillan, 1996).

27. Barber and Barratt, *South Africa's Foreign Policy: The Search for Status and Security, 1945–1988*, p. 7.

28. For the best overarching volumes, see Adam and Giliomee, *The Rise and Crisis of Afrikaner Power*; Hermann Giliomee, "Afrikaner Politics: How the System Works," in *The Rise and Crisis of Afrikaner Power*, ed. Heribert Adam and Hermann Giliomee (Cape Town: David Philips, 1979); Robert Schrire and Laurence Boulle, *Leadership in the Apartheid State: From Malan to De Klerk* (Cape Town: Oxford University Press, 1994); the incomparable Dan O'Meara, *Forty Lost Years: The Apartheid State and the Politics of the National Party, 1948–94* (Athens: Ohio University Press, 1996); Giliomee, *The Last Afrikaner Leaders*.

29. For the most important, see Sam C. Nolutshungu, *South Africa in Africa: A Study in Ideology and Foreign Policy* (Manchester: Manchester University Press, 1975); Gerrit Olivier, *Suid-Afrika se Buitelandse Beleid* (Pretoria: Academica, 1977); J. J. Swanepoel, "Die Diplomasie van Adv. B. J. Vorster" (PhD diss., University of the Orange Free State, 1982); Deon Geldenhuys, *The Diplomacy of Isolation: South African Foreign Policy Making* (Johannesburg: Macmillan South Africa, 1984); Barber and Barratt, *South Africa's Foreign Policy: The Search for Status and Security, 1945–1988*; Roger Pfister, *Apartheid South Africa and African States: From Pariah to Middle Power, 1961–1994* (London: I. B. Tauris, 2005).

30. Much of this corpus is aimed at the popular market. Of the scholarly literature, see Philip H. Frankel, *Pretoria's Praetorians: Civil-Military Relations in South Africa* (Cambridge: Cambridge University Press, 1984); Annette Seegers, *The Military in the Making of Modern South Africa* (London: Tauris Academic Studies, 1996); Gary Baines and Peter Vale, *Beyond the Border War: New Perspectives on Southern Africa's Late-Cold War Conflicts* (South Africa: Unisa Press, 2008); Leopold Scholtz, *The SADF in the Border War: 1966–1989* (Cape Town: Tafelberg, 2013).

31. Interview with Koos van der Merwe, Pretoria, 13 October 2014.

32. F. van Zyl Slabbert, *The Last White Parliament* (Johannesburg: J. Ball Publishers, 1985), p. 71.

33. See Hermann Giliomee, "The Afrikaner Economic Advance," in *Ethnic Power Mobilized: Can South Africa Change?* ed. Heribert Adam and Hermann Giliomee (New Haven, CT; London: Yale University Press, 1979); Stanley B. Greenberg, *Race and State in Capitalist Development* (New Haven, CT: Yale University Press, 1980); Stanley B. Greenberg, *Legitimating the Illegitimate: State, Markets, and Resistance in South Africa* (Berkeley: University of California Press, 1987); Robert M. Price, *The Apartheid State in Crisis: Political Transformation in South Africa, 1975–1990* (New York; Oxford: Oxford University Press, 1991); O'Meara, *Forty Lost Years*.

34. For the most prominent and comprehensive study of anti-apartheid activity, local and foreign, see South African Democracy Education Trust (SADET), *The Road to Democracy in South Africa*, vols. 1-6 (Pretoria: Unisa Press, 2004–2010). For criticism of the SADET volumes, see Martin Legassick, "Debating the Revival of the Workers' Movement in the 1970s:

The South African Democracy Education Trust and Post-Apartheid Patriotic History," *Kronos* 34, no. 1 (2008). For a sampling of the work on foreign anti-apartheid efforts, see Tor Sellström, *Sweden and National Liberation in Southern Africa* (Uppsala: Nordiska Afrikainstitutet, 1999); Roger Fieldhouse, *Anti-Apartheid: A History of the Movement in Britain* (London: Merlin Press, 2005); Håkan Thörn, *Anti-Apartheid and the Emergence of a Global Civil Society* (Basingstoke, UK: Palgrave Macmillan, 2006); Rob Skinner, *The Foundations of Anti-Apartheid: Liberal Humanitarians and Transnational Activists in Britain and the United States, c. 1919–64* (Basingstoke, UK; New York: Palgrave Macmillan, 2010); Christabel Gurney, "The 1970s: The Anti-Apartheid Movement's Difficult Decade," in *Southern African Liberation Struggles: New Local, Regional and Global Perspectives*, ed. Hilary Sapire and Christopher Saunders (Cape Town: UCT Press, 2013). For the local struggle, see as just a sampling Gail M. Gerhart, *Black Power in South Africa: The Evolution of an Ideology* (Berkeley: University of California Press, 1978); Robert Fatton, *Black Consciousness in South Africa: The Dialectics of Ideological Resistance to White Supremacy* (Albany: State University of New York Press, 1986); Thomas Karis and Gail M. Gerhart, eds., *Nadir and Resurgence, 1964–1979*, vol. 5, *From Protest to Challenge; a Documentary History of African Politics in South Africa, 1882–1964* (Bloomington: Indiana University Press, 1997); C. R. D. Halisi, *Black Political Thought in the Making of South African Democracy* (Bloomington: Indiana University Press, 1999); Craig Russell Charney, "Civil Society vs. the State: Identity, Institutions, and the Black Consciousness Movement in South Africa" (PhD diss., Yale University, 2000); Raymond Suttner, *The ANC Underground in South Africa, 1950–1976* (Boulder, CO: FirstForumPress, 2009); Daniel R. Magaziner, *The Law and the Prophets: Black Consciousness in South Africa, 1968–1977* (Athens: Ohio University Press, 2010); Thula Simpson, *Umkhonto We Sizwe: The ANC's Armed Struggle* (Cape Town: Penguin, 2016); Jacob Dlamini, *Askari: A Story of Collaboration and Betrayal in the Anti-Apartheid Struggle* (New York: Oxford University Press, 2015).

35. Giliomee, *The Last Afrikaner Leaders*, p. 12. For recent commentary on the difficulties of accessing the history of the apartheid regime, see Jamie Miller, "The Black Hole of Apartheid History" (Imperial and Global Forum, University of Exeter, https://imperialglobalexeter.com/2013/12/12/the-black-hole-of-apartheid-history/, 12 December 2013); Stephen Ellis, "ANC Suppresses Real History to Boost Its Claim to Legitimacy," *Mail & Guardian*, 3 January 2013.

36. Saul Dubow, *Racial Segregation and the Origins of Apartheid in South Africa, 1919–36* (Basingstoke, UK: Macmillan, 1989), p. ix.

37. Susan Pedersen, "What is Political History Now?," in *What is History Now?*, ed. David Cannadine (Basingstoke, Hampshire; New York: Palgrave Macmillan, 2002).

38. Important recent exceptions are Hermann Giliomee, *The Last Afrikaner Leaders: A Supreme Test of Power* (Cape Town: Tafelberg, 2012); Lindie Koorts, *D.F. Malan and the Rise of Afrikaner Nationalism* (Cape Town: Tafelberg, 2014).

39. Nolutshungu, *South Africa in Africa*, pp. 1–2.

40. P. Eric Louw, *The Rise, Fall, and Legacy of Apartheid* (Westport, CT: Praeger, 2004), p. xi.

41. For excellent recent work on "whiteness," see Bill Schwarz, *The White Man's World* (Oxford; New York: Oxford University Press, 2011); Marilyn Lake and Henry Reynolds, *Drawing the Global Colour Line: White Men's Countries and the International Challenge of Racial Equality* (Cambridge: Cambridge University Press, 2008).

42. See Joel S. Migdal, *Strong Societies and Weak States: State-Society Relations and State Capabilities in the Third World* (Princeton, NJ: Princeton University Press, 1988), pp. 259–278; Frederick Cooper, *Africa since 1940: The Past of the Present* (Cambridge: Cambridge University Press, 2002), pp. 91–132; Paul Nugent, *Africa since Independence: A Comparative History* (Basingstoke, UK; New York: Palgrave Macmillan, 2004), pp. 71–259.

43. M. Crawford Young, "Nationalism, Ethnicity, and Class in Africa: A Retrospective," *Cahiers d'études africaines* (1986): 425–428.

44. South African Department of Foreign Affairs Archives (DFAA), 1/157/3, AJ 1975, "Meeting between the Hon. Prime Minister and the Zambians," 15 October 1974.

45. Frederick Cooper, "Development and Disappointment: Social and Economic Change in an Unequal World, 1945–2000," in *Africa since 1940: The Past of the Present*, ed. Frederick Cooper (Cambridge, UK: Cambridge University Press, 2002), p. 39.

46. These literatures are vast. Good starting points are Westad, *The Global Cold War: Third World Interventions and the Making of Our Times*; Robert J. McMahon, *The Cold War in the Third World* (New York: Oxford University Press, 2013). While researchers have readily turned their gaze to the Middle East, Asia, and Latin America, Africa has lagged behind in their priorities. For overviews of the Cold War in Southern Africa and Africa respectively, see Westad, *The Global Cold War: Third World Interventions and the Making of Our Times*, pp. 207–249; Christopher Saunders and Sue Onslow, "The Cold War and Southern Africa, 1976–1990," in *The Cambridge History of the Cold War: Volume III: Endings*, ed. Melvyn P. Leffler and Odd Arne Westad (Cambridge; New York: Cambridge University Press, 2009); Jeffrey James Byrne, "Africa's Cold War," in *The Cold War in the Third World*, ed. Robert J. McMahon (New York: Oxford University Press, 2013).

47. Thomas J. Noer, *Cold War and Black Liberation: The United States and White Rule in Africa, 1948–1968* (Columbia: University of Missouri Press, 1985); Thomas Borstelmann, *Apartheid's Reluctant Uncle: The United States and Southern Africa in the Early Cold War* (New York; Oxford: Oxford University Press, 1993); Brenda Gayle Plummer, *Rising Wind: Black Americans and U.S. Foreign Affairs, 1935–1960* (Chapel Hill: University of North Carolina Press, 1996); Mary L. Dudziak, *Cold War Civil Rights: Race and the Image of American Democracy* (Princeton, NJ: Princeton University Press, 2000); Thomas Borstelmann, *The Cold War and the Color Line: American Race Relations in the Global Arena* (Cambridge, MA: Harvard University Press, 2001); Irwin, *Gordian Knot*.

48. Masuda Hajimu, *Cold War Crucible: The Korean Conflict and the Postwar World* (Cambridge, MA: Harvard University Press, 2015), p. 8.

49. For a superb analysis of the latter, see Ellen Schrecker, *Many Are the Crimes: McCarthyism in America* (Boston: Little, Brown, 1998).

50. Daniel J. Sargent, *A Superpower Transformed: The Remaking of American Foreign Relations in the 1970s* (New York: Oxford University Press, 2015).

51. John D. Kelly and Martha Kaplan, "Nation and Decolonization: Toward a New Anthropology of Nationalism," *Anthropological Theory* 1, no. 4 (2001).

52. See the analysis of distinctly nativist political violence in Taiwan and the Philippines in Masuda, *Cold War Crucible: The Korean Conflict and the Postwar World*, pp. 258–279.

53. And remains so. See for example Gérard Prunier, *Darfur: A 21st Century Genocide*, Crises in World Politics (Ithaca, NY: Cornell University Press, 2008); Mahmood Mamdani, *When Victims Become Killers: Colonialism, Nativism, and the Genocide in Rwanda* (Princeton, NJ: Princeton University Press, 2001). For an early prototype in this area, see Ben Kiernan, *The Pol Pot Regime: Race, Power, and Genocide in Cambodia under the Khmer Rouge, 1975–79* (New Haven, CT: Yale University Press, 2008), pp. 251–319. When first published, Kiernan's focus on race differed dramatically from existing understandings of the Khmer Rouge.

54. Glassman, *War of Words, War of Stones*; Brennan, *Taifa*.

55. Michael O'Brien, *Conjectures of Order: Intellectual Life and the American South, 1810–1860*, vol. 1 (Chapel Hill: University of North Carolina Press, 2004), pp. 2–7.

56. This study instead follows Saul Dubow's recent description of regime ideology as decidedly fluid, resting on a broad and shifting array of postwar logics. See Saul Dubow, *Apartheid, 1948–1994* (Oxford: Oxford University Press, 2014).

57. Notably, many of the best studies that engaged deeply with this unpleasant reality were by political scientists or economists: Robert H. Bates, *Markets and States in Tropical Africa: The Political Basis of Agricultural Policies* (Berkeley: University of California Press, 1981); Thomas M. Callaghy, *The State-Society Struggle: Zaire in Comparative Perspective* (New York: Columbia University Press, 1984); James S. Wunsch and Dele Olowu, *The Failure of the Centralized State: Institutions and Self-Governance in Africa* (Boulder, CO: Westview Press, 1990).

58. Timothy Burke, "Eyes Wide Shut: Africanists and the Moral Problematics of Postcolonial Societies," *African Studies Quarterly* 7, no. 2/3 (2003): 205. For an earlier, less strident iteration of many of Burke's points of departure see Young, "Nationalism, Ethnicity, and Class in Africa: A Retrospective."

59. Theda Skocpol, "Bringing the State Back In: Strategies of Analysis in Current Research," in *Bringing the State Back In*, ed. Peter B. Evans, Dietrich Rueschemeyer, and Theda Skocpol (Cambridge; New York: Cambridge University Press, 1985).

60. Jeffrey James Byrne, *Mecca of Revolution: Algeria, Decolonization, and the Third World Order* (New York: Oxford University Press, 2016), p. 9.

61. Bruce De Mesquita, "Foreign Policy Analysis and Rational Choice Models" in *International Studies Association Compendium Project* (2010), http://www.isadiscus sion.com/entry/c131-1/Foreign-Policy-Analysis-and-Rational-Choice-Models.html (accessed 11 January 2016).
62. I am indebted to Danelle van Zyl-Hermann for my use of "political imaginary" in this context.
63. Aletta J. Norval, *Deconstructing Apartheid Discourse* (London; New York: Verso, 1996), pp. 2–5.
64. Fred Halliday, *The Middle East in International Relations: Power, Politics and Ideology* (Cambridge, UK; New York: Cambridge University Press, 2005), p. 199.

Chapter 1

1. For the federal structure of NP and its influence upon party policies and practice, see Giliomee, "Afrikaner Politics: How the System Works," pp. 197–205. Each regional caucus had its own constitution and annual congress, usually held in August-September.
2. O'Meara, *Forty Lost Years*, pp. 104–109. The Natal NP, the fourth caucus, was both numerically small and politically weak.
3. Giliomee, *The Afrikaners*, pp. 522–523.
4. Figures from D'Oliveira, *Vorster: The Man*, p. 165. That Vorster would be the pioneer of such laws was deeply ironic. During the Second World War, he had been interned as an enemy of the state for his role in the OB, which opposed a British war effort that they saw as no concern of Afrikaners. He, like many of his later victims, was never tried in a court of law. Moreover, for decades the global press referred to Vorster as "pro-Nazi" or simply "a Nazi." Scholars have sometimes followed suit; see for instance O'Meara, *Forty Lost Years*, p. 152. The OB borrowed much fascist symbolism and loathed parliamentary democracy in favor of Afrikaner authoritarianism. But such pigeon-holing as a "Nazi" depended on much the same logic of association that Vorster later employed against the regime's "communist" foes.
5. D'Oliveira, *Vorster: The Man*, p. 134.
6. This account is largely based on O'Meara, *Forty Lost Years*, pp. 151–155. For a somewhat divergent account based on a narrower range of sources, see D'Oliveira, *Vorster: The Man*, pp. 181–197.
7. Albert Grundlingh, "'Are We Afrikaners Getting Too Rich?': Cornucopia and Change in Afrikanerdom in the 1960s," *Journal of Historical Sociology* 21, no. 2-3 (2008): 144.
8. Table 5 in Heribert Adam and Hermann Giliomee, *Ethnic Power Mobilized: Can South Africa Change?* (New Haven, CT; London: Yale University Press, 1979), p. 173.
9. Grundlingh, "'Are We Afrikaners Getting Too Rich?': Cornucopia and Change in Afrikanerdom in the 1960s": 150, 144.
10. Irwin, *Gordian Knot*, pp. 103–125.
11. Barber and Barratt, *South Africa's Foreign Policy: The Search for Status and Security, 1945–1988*, p. 9.
12. Robert S. Jaster, *South Africa's Narrowing Security Options* (London: International Institute for Strategic Studies, 1980), p. 16.
13. The framework of "the state" utilized here, with its emphasis on ideology and domestic politics, draws substantially on Tuong Vu, "Studying the State through State Formation," *World Politics* 62, no. 1 (2010). Specifically, it aims to historicize state formation in South Africa rather than generalizing, as well as treating states not as autonomous actors, but instead as institutional configurations in which different actors operate. To this the approach here adds an important third element: ideology, as the discourses through which those actors understand the world around them.
14. The first of these issues has been the subject of vast literatures and intense historiographical debates, for which there is scarcely space here. For useful analyses see Merle Lipton, *Liberals, Marxists and Nationalists: Competing Interpretations of South African History* (New York: Palgrave Macmillan, 2007); O'Meara, *Forty Lost Years*, pp. 419–489; Dan O'Meara, *Volkskapitalisme: Class, Capital, and Ideology in the Development of Afrikaner Nationalism, 1934–1948* (Cambridge, UK: Cambridge University Press, 1983), pp. 1–17.
15. Giliomee, *The Afrikaners*, pp. 355–402; Mariana Kriel, "Culture and Power: The Rise of Afrikaner Nationalism Revisited," *Nations & Nationalism* 16, no. 3 (2010). The rise of Afrikaner identity and political power must be seen in the circumstances of the day and in the context

of other identities and political platforms, rather than simply deduced from the prior existence of a proto-nationalist *ethnie*. See André Du Toit, "'Afrikaander Circa 1600': Reflections
and Suggestions Regarding the Origins and Fate of Afrikaner Nationalism," *South African
Historical Journal* 60, no. 4 (2008): 574–577; O'Meara, *Volkskapitalisme: Class, Capital, and
Ideology in the Development of Afrikaner Nationalism, 1934–1948*, pp. 6–7.

16. Allister Sparks, *The Mind of South Africa* (New York: Alfred A. Knopf, 1990), pp. 147–182;
    Giliomee, *The Afrikaners*, pp. 415–428, 464–471; Moodie, *The Rise of Afrikanerdom*.

17. See Norval, *Deconstructing Apartheid Discourse*, esp. pp. 142–151.

18. O'Meara, *Volkskapitalisme: Class, Capital, and Ideology in the Development of Afrikaner
    Nationalism, 1934–1948*, p. 3.

19. Philip Bonner, Peter Delius, and Deborah Posel, *Apartheid's Genesis, 1935–1962*
    (Braamfontein, South Africa: Ravan Press; Witwatersrand University Press, 1993).

20. See Miroslav Hroch, *Social Preconditions of National Revival in Europe: A Comparative Analysis
    of the Social Composition of Patriotic Groups among the Smaller European Nations* (Cambridge,
    UK; New York: Cambridge University Press, 1985).

21. E. J. Hobsbawm, *Nations and Nationalism since 1780: Programme, Myth, Reality*, 2nd ed.
    (Cambridge, UK; New York: Cambridge University Press, 1992), p. 12.

22. See for example Dubow, *Racial Segregation and the Origins of Apartheid in South Africa,
    1919–36*; Timothy J. Keegan, *Colonial South Africa and the Origins of the Racial Order*
    (Charlottesville: University Press of Virginia, 1996); Richard Elphick and Hermann Buhr
    Giliomee, *The Shaping of South African Society, 1652–1820* (Cape Town: Longman, 1979).

23. Frederick Cooper, *Decolonization and African Society: The Labor Question in French and British
    Africa* (Cambridge, UK: Cambridge University Press, 1996), pp. 110–175. There is a passing
    reference to South Africa on page 6.

24. Efforts to recruit black South Africans yielded limited results: Louis Grundlingh, "The
    Recruitment of South African Blacks for Participation in the Second World War," in *Africa
    and the Second World War*, ed. David Killingray and Richard Rathbone (New York: St. Martin's
    Press, 1986).

25. O'Meara, *Volkskapitalisme: Class, Capital, and Ideology in the Development of Afrikaner
    Nationalism, 1934–1948*, p. 226.

26. Dubow, *Apartheid, 1948–1994*, p. 5.

27. David Welsh, "Urbanisation and the Solidarity of Afrikaner Nationalism," *The Journal of
    Modern African Studies* 7, no. 2 (1969): 265–267.

28. Dubow, *Apartheid, 1948–1994*, p. 5.

29. Feinstein, *An Economic History of South Africa: Conquest, Discrimination, and Development*,
    pp. 126–127.

30. O'Meara, *Volkskapitalisme: Class, Capital, and Ideology in the Development of Afrikaner
    Nationalism, 1934–1948*, p. 228.

31. Dubow, *Apartheid, 1948–1994*, p. 6.

32. For more, see Philip Bonner, "African Urbanization on the Rand between the 1930s and
    1960s: Its Social Character and Political Consequences," *Journal of Southern African Studies*
    21(1995).

33. Excellent social history underlines that the rise of Afrikaner nationalism was accompanied
    and sometimes undercut by the growth of other ideas and identities on a more micro level.
    See Neil Roos, *Ordinary Springboks: White Servicemen and Social Justice in South Africa,
    1939–1951* (Aldershot, UK: Ashgate, 2005); Albert Grundlingh, "The King's Afrikaners?
    Enlistment and Ethnic Identity in the Union of South Africa's Defence Force During the
    Second World War, 1939–1945," *Journal of African History* 40, no. 3 (1999).

34. Giliomee, *The Afrikaners*, pp. 487–488.

35. O'Meara, *Volkskapitalisme: Class, Capital, and Ideology in the Development of Afrikaner
    Nationalism, 1934–1948*, p. 234.

36. B. M. Schoeman, *Die Broederbond in die Afrikaner-Politiek* (Pretoria: Aktuele Publikasies,
    1982), p. 27.

37. Giliomee, *The Afrikaners*, pp. 445–446.

38. The United Party's failure to resolve this political challenge was probably the central factor in
    its long, slow decline right through to its disintegration in 1977.

39. Dubow, *Apartheid, 1948–1994*, p. 15.

40. O'Meara, *Forty Lost Years*, pp. 446–447.

41. *Hansard*, House of Assembly Debates, 11 May 1949, col 5662.

42. Barber and Barratt, *South Africa's Foreign Policy: The Search for Status and Security, 1945–1988*, p. 67. See Chapter 3 for more.

43. Wessel Visser, "The Production of Literature on the 'Red Peril' and 'Total Onslaught' in Twentieth-Century South Africa," *Historia* 49, no. 2 (2004): 106–107. See also André van Deventer and Philip Nel, "The State and 'Die Volk' Versus Communism, 1922–1941," *Politikon* 17, no. 2 (1990).

44. Johannesburg District Committee of the Communist Party of South Africa, *Kommunisme en die Afrikaner* (Johannesburg 1940). Emphasis in the original. It was not until the Vorster era that educated Afrikaners began to seriously ruminate about their identity in these terms.

45. Alden, *Apartheid's Last Stand*, p. 32.

46. Welsh, "Urbanisation and the Solidarity of Afrikaner Nationalism": 268.

47. Gert Daniel Scholtz, *Dr. Hendrik Frensch Verwoerd, 1901–1966*, vol. 1 (Johannesburg: Perskor, 1974), p. 90.

48. Welsh, "Urbanisation and the Solidarity of Afrikaner Nationalism," p. 266.

49. de Villiers and de Villiers, *PW*, p. 365.

50. A. J. G. Oosthuizen, *Kommunisme en die Vakunies* (Heidelberg, South Africa: Voortrekkerpers, 1938).

51. For more, see Christopher Merrett, *A Culture of Censorship: Secrecy and Intellectual Repression in South Africa* (Cape Town: David Philip, 1994), pp. 21–27.

52. Visser, "The Production of Literature on the "Red Peril" and "Total Onslaught" in Twentieth-Century South Africa," pp. 115–119.

53. Masuda, *Cold War Crucible: The Korean Conflict and the Postwar World*, pp. 283–285. For an earlier venture in this direction, see Matthew Connelly, "Taking Off the Cold War Lens: Visions of North-South Conflict During the Algerian War for Independence," *The American Historical Review* 105, no. 3 (2000).

54. Giliomee, *The Afrikaners*, p. 447; Dubow, *Apartheid, 1948–1994*, p. 5.

55. O'Meara, *Forty Lost Years*, p. 36.

56. Kenneth A. Heard, *General Elections in South Africa, 1943–1970* (London; New York: Oxford University Press, 1974), p. 226.

57. Cited in Giliomee, *The Last Afrikaner Leaders*, p. 36. One of the more revealing derogatory terms used by Afrikaners to describe their anglophone allies in power was *soutpiel*, or "salt dick". This label derived from the notion that English-speakers only had one foot in South Africa and the other still in England, straddling the sea in between, juxtaposed with the Afrikaner's deep connection to Africa.

58. This doctrine was known as *sowereiniteit in eie kring*.

59. Deborah Posel, *The Making of Apartheid, 1948–1961: Conflict and Compromise* (Oxford: Clarendon Press, 1991).

60. O'Meara, *Forty Lost Years*, p. 60.

61. Heard, *General Elections in South Africa, 1943–1970*, p. 11.

62. Giliomee, *The Afrikaners*, pp. 349–353, 412–422, 447–486. See also Rebecca Davies, *Afrikaners in the New South Africa: Identity Politics in a Globalised Economy* (London; New York: Tauris Academic Studies, 2009), pp. 25–31.

63. Giliomee, *The Afrikaners*, p. 520.

64. Adriaan Nicolaas Pelzer, ed. *Verwoerd Speaks: Speeches, 1948–1966* (Johannesburg: APB Publishers,1966), pp. 206–211. As Roberta Balstad Miller has shown, that Verwoerd would become the pioneer of hardline Afrikaner nationalism was both ironic and revealing of his lust for power. His writings as an academic prior to 1937, when he moved to *Die Transvaler*, evinced positions that were fundamentally incompatible with many of the ideas and policies that he later spearheaded. See Roberta Balstad Miller, "Science and Society in the Early Career of H. F. Verwoerd," *Journal of Southern African Studies* 19, no. 4 (1993).

65. Much of this work was deeply reminiscent of the nineteenth-century European nationalism of authors like Johann Gottlieb Fichte. See Nico Diederichs, *Nasionalisme as Lewensbeskouing en sy Verhouding tot Internasionalisme* (Cape Town: Nasionale Pers, 1935); Geoffrey

Cronjé, 'n Tuiste vir die Nageslag: die Blywende Oplossing van Suid-Afrika se Rassevraagstukke (Johannesburg: Publicite Handelsreklamediens, 1945).

66. Barber and Barratt, South Africa's Foreign Policy: The Search for Status and Security, 1945–1988, pp. 89–91. For differing accounts of the role of religion in Afrikaner nationalism, see Andre du Toit, "No Chosen People: The Myth of the Calvinist Origins of Afrikaner Nationalism and Racial Ideology," American Historical Review 88, no. 4 (1983); Moodie, The Rise of Afrikanerdom, esp. pp. 22–38.

67. For a recent reconsideration of Verwoerd's efforts to entrench his brand of apartheid, see Giliomee, The Last Afrikaner Leaders, pp. 38–88. Opposition to Verwoerd's vision within the Party declined substantially over the same period: Giliomee, The Afrikaners, pp. 525–531, 534–536.

68. Heard, General Elections in South Africa, 1943–1970, pp. 143, 173.

69. Speech, Senate, 20 May 1959, in Pelzer, ed. Verwoerd Speaks: Speeches, 1948–1966, pp. 271–295.

70. Speech, London, 17 March 1961, in Pelzer, ed. Verwoerd Speaks: Speeches, 1948–1966, p. 509.

71. ARCA, PV 132, B. J. Vorster, 3/8/1, Toesprake, Verklarings en Boodskappe, Algemeen, Toesprake, Hendrik Verwoerd, "The Price of Appeasement in Africa," March 1960.

72. "Wyle Dr. H. F. Verwoerd," Volkshandel, September 1966.

73. "A heinous crime," editorial, Rand Daily Mail, 7 September 1966.

74. Giliomee, The Afrikaners, pp. 515–19; John Lazar, "Verwoerd Versus the 'Visionaries': The South African Bureau of Racial Affairs (Sabra) and Apartheid, 1948–1961," in Apartheid's Genesis, 1935–1962, ed. Philip Bonner, Peter Delius, and Deborah Posel (Braamfontein, South Africa: Ravan Press; Witwatersrand University Press, 1993).

75. J. L. Sadie, Projections of the South African Population, 1970–2020 (South Africa: Industrial Development Corporation of South Africa, 1970), pp. 36, 38.

76. Giliomee, The Last Afrikaner Leaders, pp. 100–101. Afrikaner capital was strongly supportive: "Eiesoortige ontwikkelingspatroon en ons toekoms," editorial, Volkshandel, November 1968.

77. Jan Lombard, "The Economic Philosophy of Homeland Development," in South African Dialogue: Contrasts in South African Thinking on Basic Race Issues, ed. Nicolaas Johannes Rhoodie (Johannesburg: McGraw-Hill Book Co., 1972), p. 171.

78. ARCA, PV 408, NP Caucus, Notule, 25 February 1975.

79. To the Point, 1 October 1976.

80. Vorster speech in Bloemfontein, 18 March 1967, in Geyser, ed. Select Speeches, p. 74. For more on invented traditions see E. J. Hobsbawm and T. O. Ranger, eds., The Invention of Tradition (Cambridge: Cambridge University Press,1983).

81. Interview with Albert Hertzog, Veg, 29 November 1969. See also Verwoerd's reply to Harold Macmillan's "wind of change" speech: Pelzer, ed. Verwoerd Speaks: Speeches, 1948–1966, pp. 336–339. Identifications as "white Africans" were also extant among Rhodesian political leaders, but these did not emanate from constructions of a white African nation, nor were they mobilized in support of a group claim to legitimacy as a postcolonial national community, as Vorster's autochthonous claims were. For Roy Welensky, see Timothy Scarnecchia, "The Congo Crisis, the United Nations, and Zimbabwean Nationalism, 1960–1963," African Journal on Conflict Resolution 11, no. 1 (2011): 67. For the Smith regime, see Luise White, Unpopular Sovereignty: Rhodesian Independence and African Decolonization (Chicago: University of Chicago Press, 2015).

82. Vorster speech in Bloemfontein, 18 March 1967, in Geyser, ed. Select Speeches, p. 74.

83. Geldenhuys, The Diplomacy of Isolation, p. 261.

84. Speech, London, 17 March 1961, in Pelzer, ed. Verwoerd Speaks: Speeches, 1948–1966, p. 509.

85. B. J. Vorster, South Africa's Outward Policy (Cape Town: Tafelberg, 1970), p. 10.

86. Hermann Giliomee, "The Making of the Apartheid Plan, 1929–1948," Journal of Southern African Studies 29, no. 2 (June 2003): 373–374.

87. Dubow, Racial Segregation and the Origins of Apartheid in South Africa, 1919–36, pp. 25–27.

88. Cited in Giliomee, "The Making of the Apartheid Plan, 1929–1948": 374.

89. Speech, Naboomspruit, 17 June 1971, in Geyser, ed. Select Speeches, pp. 144–147.

90. Speech, Naboomspruit, 17 June 1971, in Geyser, ed. Select Speeches, pp. 148. Emphasis added.

91. John Stuart Kane-Berman, *Soweto: Black Revolt, White Reaction* (Johannesburg: Ravan Press, 1978), p. 177.

92. Giliomee, "Afrikaner Politics: How the System Works": 240–253. For the churches' role in legitimizing apartheid, see Cecil Mzingisi Ngcokovane, "Religious and Moral Legitimations of Apartheid in Nederduitse Gereformeerde Kerk, Nationalist Party and Broederbond, 1948–Present" (PhD diss., Emory University, 1986), pp. 217–253; Tracy Kuperus, *State, Civil Society, and Apartheid in South Africa: An Examination of Dutch Reformed Church-State Relations* (New York: St. Martin's Press, 1999); J. H. P. Serfontein, *Apartheid Change and the NG Kerk* (Emmarentia, South Africa: Taurus, 1982). For work on the Broederbond see Schoeman, *Die Broederbond in die Afrikaner-Politiek*; J. H. P. Serfontein, *Brotherhood of Power: An Exposé of the Secret Afrikaner Broederbond* (Bloomington: Indiana University Press, 1978); Ivor Wilkins and Hans Strydom, *The Super-Afrikaners* (Johannesburg: Jonathan Ball, 1978); Nico Smith, *Die Afrikaner Broederbond: Belewinge van die Binnekant* (Pretoria: LAPA Uitgewers, 2009).

93. Serfontein, *Brotherhood of Power: An Exposé of the Secret Afrikaner Broederbond*, p. 27.

94. André P. Brink, *A Fork in the Road: A Memoir* (London: Harvill Secker, 2009), p. 347.

95. The deep impact of this crisis within the NP and Afrikanerdom generally is a major theme in O'Meara, *Forty Lost Years*; Adam and Giliomee, *The Rise and Crisis of Afrikaner Power*; Hermann Giliomee, *The Parting of the Ways: South African Politics 1976–82* (Cape Town: David Philips, 1982); Price, *The Apartheid State in Crisis: Political Transformation in South Africa, 1975–1990*.

96. D'Oliveira, *Vorster: The Man*, p. 229.

97. de Villiers and de Villiers, *PW*, p. 99. Others have seen this approach as something of a "chairman of the board" style of governance: Giliomee, "Afrikaner Politics: How the System Works": 202–203; O'Meara, *Forty Lost Years*, pp. 205–7.

98. Hilton Hamann, *Days of the Generals: The Untold Story of South Africa's Apartheid-Era Military Generals* (Cape Town: Zebra Press, 2001), p. 7.

99. Henry Kenney, *Power, Pride and Prejudice*, pp. 224.

100. The most colorful account of the notorious bitterness among these bureaucracies remains O'Meara, *Forty Lost Years*, pp. 210–19.

101. Interview with Jeremy Shearar, Pretoria, 23 August 2011.

102. Price, *The Apartheid State in Crisis: Political Transformation in South Africa, 1975–1990*, p. 29.

103. Merle Lipton, *Capitalism and Apartheid: South Africa, 1910–1986* (Aldershot, UK: Wildwood House, 1986), p. 251.

104. Price, *The Apartheid State in Crisis: Political Transformation in South Africa, 1975–1990*, p. 20.

105. Barber and Barratt, *South Africa's Foreign Policy: The Search for Status and Security, 1945–1988*, p. 346.

106. Greenberg, *Legitimating the Illegitimate: State, Markets, and Resistance in South Africa*, p. 22.

107. For more, see the excellent Ian Macqueen, "Black Consciousness in Dialogue in South Africa: Steve Biko, Richard Turner and the 'Durban Moment,' 1970–1974," *Journal of Asian and African Studies* 49, no. 5 (2014).

108. de Villiers and de Villiers, *PW*, pp. 156–164; Nic Olivier, "The Head of Government and the Party," in *Leadership in the Apartheid State: From Malan to De Klerk*, ed. Robert Schrire and Laurence Boulle (Cape Town: Oxford University Press, 1994), p. 92; O'Meara, *Forty Lost Years*, p. 159.

109. For more, see Giliomee, *The Afrikaners*, pp. 542–560; O'Meara, *Forty Lost Years*, pp. 115–148; J. H. P. Serfontein, *Die Verkrampte Aanslag* (Cape Town: Human & Rousseau, 1970), pp. 84–117; André du Pisani, *John Vorster en die Verlig-Verkrampstryd* (Bloemfontein: Instituut vir Eietydse Geskiedenis, 1988), pp. 56–87.

110. Most Afrikaners belonged to a few different though closely related Calvinist churches, which enabled perceptions of a common faith and divine cause to remain tenable.

111. Hermann Giliomee, "Ethnic Business and Economic Empowerment: The Afrikaner Case, 1915–1970," *South African Journal of Economics* 76, no. 4 (2008): 768.

112. Table 7 in Adam and Giliomee, *Ethnic Power Mobilized: Can South Africa Change?* p. 174.

113. Table 5 in Adam and Giliomee, *Ethnic Power Mobilized: Can South Africa Change?* p. 173.

114. J. L. Sadie, "Die Ekonomiese Faktor in die Afrikaner-Gemeenskap," in *Identiteit en Verandering*, ed. Hendrik W. van der Merwe (Kaapstad: Tafelberg, 1975), p. 94.
115. Table 2 in Adam and Giliomee, *Ethnic Power Mobilized: Can South Africa Change?* p. 169.
116. Tjaart Steenekamp, "Discrimination and the Economic Position of the Afrikaner," *South African Journal of Economic History* 5, no. 1 (1990): 63.
117. Welsh, "Urbanisation and the Solidarity of Afrikaner Nationalism": 267.
118. J. L. Sadie, "The Fall and Rise of the Afrikaner in the South African Economy," *Annale* 1(2002), p. 33.
119. Giliomee, *The Afrikaners*, p. 490.
120. Keith Breckenridge, "Hopeless Entanglement: The Short History of the Academic Humanities in South Africa," *American Historical Review* 120, no. 4 (2015): 1258.
121. ARCA, PV 132, B. J. Vorster, 3/8/1, 3 Toesprake, Verklarings en Boodskappe 3/8 Kanselier, Notes for Commencement Address at Stellenbosch University, 1971.
122. Grundlingh, "'Are We Afrikaners Getting Too Rich?': Cornucopia and Change in Afrikanerdom in the 1960s," p. 154.
123. Giliomee, *The Afrikaners*, p. 554.
124. Brink, *A Fork in the Road: A Memoir*, p. 218.
125. Giliomee, "Ethnic Business and Economic Empowerment: The Afrikaner Case, 1915–1970."
126. Cited in O'Meara, *Forty Lost Years*, p. 123.
127. Grundlingh, "'Are We Afrikaners Getting Too Rich?': Cornucopia and Change in Afrikanerdom in the 1960s," pp. 148–149.
128. "Aanbidders van Mammon," *Die Transvaler*, 31 August 1968.
129. Gert Daniel Scholtz, *Dr. Hendrik Frensch Verwoerd, 1901–1966*, vol. 2 (Johannesburg: Perskor, 1974), p. 162.
130. It is worth stressing that Vorster initially sought to obfuscate such views. He resolutely denied that apartheid was divisible and that there was any such thing as "petty apartheid"— all while he was working behind the scenes in the Broederbond to effect just such a divide. See Japie Basson, *State of the Nation: As Viewed from a Front Bench in Parliament, 1969–1981* (Camps Bay, South Africa: Politika, 2008), pp. 31–34, 194–196.
131. David Welsh, *The Rise and Fall of Apartheid* (Charlottesville: University of Virginia Press, 2009), p. 83. Vorster's use here of "apartheid *and* separate development" is in itself telling.
132. Botha had long disagreed with party policy on Coloreds, for instance. See de Villiers and de Villiers, *PW*, pp. 66–73.
133. D'Oliveira, *Vorster: The Man*, pp. 57, 109–111.
134. ARCA, PV 819, Alf Ries, Box 1, "Statement on the Conference of Homeland Leaders with the Prime Minister," 22 January 1975.
135. Interview with Stoffel van der Merwe, Pretoria, 13 October 2014.
136. For three different accounts, each useful in its own way, see du Pisani, *John Vorster en die Verlig-Verkrampstryd*; B. M. Schoeman, *Vorster se 1000 Dae* (Cape Town: Human & Rousseau, 1974); Serfontein, *Die Verkrampte Aanslag*.
137. "J. Mijer, Krugersdorp," *Die Afrikaner*, 11 May 1973.
138. A. P. Treurnicht, *Credo van 'n Afrikaner* (Kaapstad: Tafelberg, 1975), p. 22.
139. Wilkins and Strydom, *The Super-Afrikaners*, p. 185.
140. "Feeskongres," editorial, *Hoofstad*, 9 September 1969.
141. "Dobbelhuise en Toneelstuk oor 'n Kommunis," editorial, *Die Afrikaner*, 22 January 1971.
142. "Die jaar 1971 kan dalk politieke drama bring," *Die Afrikaner*, 15 January 1971.
143. O'Meara, *Forty Lost Years*, p. 266.
144. "Arm man wurg onder rykmansparty," *Die Afrikaner*, 15 January 1971.
145. Welsh, *The Rise and Fall of Apartheid*, p. 84.
146. *Veg*, 29 November 1969.
147. Giliomee, *The Afrikaners*, p. 549.
148. Louis Louw, *Dawie, 1946–1964* (Cape Town: Tafelberg-Uitgewers, 1965), pp. 285–290.
149. Krause, "Trends in Afrikaner Race Attitudes," p. 536–537.
150. Krause, "Trends in Afrikaner Race Attitudes," p. 536–537.
151. Giliomee, *The Afrikaners*, p. 550.

152. Willem de Klerk, "The Concepts 'Verkramp' and 'Verlig,'" in *South African Dialogue: Contrasts in South African Thinking on Basic Race Issues*, ed. Nicolaas Johannes Rhoodie (Johannesburg: McGraw-Hill Book Co., 1972), pp. 523–524. De Klerk was also the brother of F. W. de Klerk, though they were very far apart politically.

153. Alex Mouton, *Voorloper: die Lewe van Schalk Pienaar* (Cape Town: Tafelberg, 2002), p. 132.

154. Krause, "Trends in Afrikaner Race Attitudes," p. 537.

155. Hermann Giliomee, "'Survival in Justice': An Afrikaner Debate over Apartheid," *Comparative Studies in Society and History* 36, no. 3 (1994): 537.

156. Lombard, "The Economic Philosophy of Homeland Development," p. 169.

157. Cited in Giliomee, "'Survival in Justice': An Afrikaner Debate over Apartheid," p. 538.

158. de Klerk, "The Concepts 'Verkramp' and 'Verlig,'" p. 530.

159. E. L. P. Stals, "Geskiedenis van die Afrikaner-Broderbond, 1918–1994," p. 366.

160. Stals, "Geskiedenis van die Afrikaner-Broderbond, 1918–1994," p. 369.

161. "Blanke Kapitaal en Inisiatief vir Bantoe-tuislande," editorial, *Volkshandel*, February 1967.

162. "Bloudruk en Meesterplan vir Ontwikkeling," editorial, *Volkshandel*, November 1970.

163. "The key to continued White existence," editorial, *Volkshandel*, August 1971.

164. "Arm man wurg onder rykmansparty," *Die Afrikaner*, 15 January 1971.

165. "R40 000 000 vir Bantoe-onderwys in een jaar uit die blankes sak," *Die Afrikaner*, 22 January 1971.

166. "R40 000 000 vir Bantoe-onderwys in een jaar uit die blankes sak," *Die Afrikaner*, 22 January 1971.

167. "'Witter' stede word toe 'n swarter stroom": editorial, *Die Afrikaner*, 19 February 1971.

168. Welsh, "Urbanisation and the Solidarity of Afrikaner Nationalism": 273–274.

169. Welsh, "Urbanisation and the Solidarity of Afrikaner Nationalism": 273–274.

170. Wilkins and Strydom, *The Super-Afrikaners*, p. 177.

171. Wilkins and Strydom, *The Super-Afrikaners*, pp. 187–190.

172. "Feeskongres," editorial, *Hoofstad*, 9 September 1969.

173. See, for instance, B. M. Schoeman, *Die Geldmag: SA se Onsigbare Regering* (Pretoria: Aktuele Publikasies, 1980).

174. Basson, *State of the Nation: As Viewed from a Front Bench in Parliament, 1969–1981*, p. 55.

175. Krause, "Trends in Afrikaner Race Attitudes," p. 536–537.

176. de Klerk, "The Concepts 'Verkramp' and 'Verlig,'" p. 522. Emphasis added.

177. Adam, *Modernizing Racial Domination: South Africa's Political Dynamics*, p. 178; Adam and Giliomee, *The Rise and Crisis of Afrikaner Power*, p. 215.

178. Wilkins and Strydom, *The Super-Afrikaners*, pp. 202–204.

179. O'Meara, *Forty Lost Years*, pp. 138–142.

180. Nasionalis, Reivilo, letter to the editor, *Die Afrikaner*, 15 January 1971.

181. Alf Ries and Ebbe Dommisse, *Broedertwis: die Verhaal van die 1982-Skeuring in die Nasionale Party* (Kaapstad: Tafelberg, 1982), p. 67.

182. Welsh, *The Rise and Fall of Apartheid*, p. 87.

Chapter 2

1. Piet Meiring, *Die Lewe van Hilgard Muller* (Silverton: Promedia Publikasies, 1985), p. 77.

2. From 1974 onward, the Department of Information launched parallel covert overtures to Africa as part of its policy remit. For the most reliable account, see Les de Villiers, *Secret Information* (Cape Town: Tafelberg, 1980).

3. This premise was the golden thread running through all incarnations of Vorster's foreign policy until the game-changing Soweto riots of 1976.

4. The counterintuitive scene that followed, as the architects of apartheid developed relationships with the leaders of independent African states, has attracted no shortage of attention from scholars. For the relevant historiography, see Jamie Miller, "Africanising Apartheid: Identity, Ideology, and State-Building in Post-Independence Africa," *Journal of African History* 56, no. 3 (2015).

5. Meiring, *Die Lewe van Hilgard Muller*, pp. 56–57.

6. Kenneth W. Grundy, *Confrontation and Accommodation in Southern Africa: The Limits of Independence* (Berkeley; London: University of California Press, 1973), p. 241.

7. Adrian Guelke, "Africa as a Market for South African Goods," *The Journal of Modern African Studies* 12, no. 1 (1974): 80.

8. Pfister, *Apartheid South Africa and African States*, pp. 45–46.

9. John Lonsdale and Bruce Berman, "Coping with the Contradictions: The Development of the Colonial State in Kenya, 1895–1914," *Journal of African History* 20, no. 4 (1979): 491.

10. Glassman, *War of Words, War of Stones*; Brennan, *Taifa*.

11. Ian Smith Papers (ISP), Deposit 4, Box 4, Rhodesia Settlement: Meetings with African National Council, Volume 2, Notes of Meeting between Smith and Muzorewa, 12 June 1974.

12. See Chapter 4.

13. World Bank, *World Development Report 1980* (New York: Oxford University Press, 1980), p. 99.

14. Bates, *Markets and States in Tropical Africa: The Political Basis of Agricultural Policies*. See also Catherine Boone, "State Building in the African Countryside: Structure and Politics at the Grassroots," *The Journal of Development Studies* 34, no. 4 (1998).

15. For a succinct but stimulating overview, see Cooper, "Development and Disappointment: Social and Economic Change in an Unequal World, 1945–2000."

16. Speech, Naboomspruit, 17 June 1971, in Geyser, ed. *Select Speeches*, pp. 148–149.

17. Pfister, *Apartheid South Africa and African States*, pp. 50–104.

18. *Hansard*, House of Assembly Debates, 6 August 1974, col 123.

19. DFAA, 1/157/3, AJ 1975, "Meeting between the Hon. Prime Minister and the Zambians," 15 October 1974.

20. For more on development from this perspective, see Michael E. Latham, *The Right Kind of Revolution: Modernization, Development, and U.S. Foreign Policy from the Cold War to the Present* (Ithaca, NY: Cornell University Press, 2011).

21. "'n Statebond vir Suider-Afrika," editorial, *Volkshandel*, January 1975.

22. "'n Statebond vir Suider-Afrika," editorial, *Volkshandel*, January 1975.

23. "Blanke Kapitaal en Inisiatief vir Bantoe-tuislande," editorial, *Volkshandel*, February 1967.

24. See James C. Scott, *Seeing Like a State: How Certain Schemes to Improve the Human Condition Have Failed* (New Haven, CT: Yale University Press, 1998); Nick Cullather, *The Hungry World: America's Cold War Battle against Poverty in Asia* (Cambridge, MA: Harvard University Press, 2010); Allen Isaacman and Barbara Isaacman, *Mozambique: From Colonialism to Revolution, 1900–1982* (Boulder, CO: Westview, 1983).

25. The classic account is Westad, *The Global Cold War: Third World Interventions and the Making of Our Times*. For an overdue focus on the Eastern bloc, see Jeremy Friedman, *Shadow Cold War: The Sino-Soviet Split and the Third World* (Chapel Hill: University of North Carolina Press, 2015).

26. The most enduring rulers were often precisely those who maintained the largest degree of ideological maneuverability. See Callaghy, *The State-Society Struggle: Zaire in Comparative Perspective*.

27. Byrne, "Africa's Cold War," pp. 107–109.

28. Nugent, *Africa since Independence: A Comparative History*, pp. 141–143; Crawford Young, *Ideology and Development in Africa* (New Haven, CT: Yale University Press, 1982), p. 326.

29. Westad, *The Global Cold War: Third World Interventions and the Making of Our Times*, pp. 108–109, 180–206.

30. The term *françafrique* soon came to acquire negative connotations of personal patronage, protection, and corruption, but a more neutral substitute has yet to be identified. See François-Xavier Verschave, *La Françafrique: Le Plus Long Scandale de La République* (Paris: Stock, 1998).

31. Jean-Pierre Bat, *Le Syndrome Foccart: La Politique Française en Afrique, de 1959 à nos Jours* (Paris: Gallimard, 2012), pp. 340–341.

32. John Chipman, *French Power in Africa* (Oxford, UK; Cambridge, MA: Basil Blackwell, 1989), p. 169.

33. Bat, *Le Syndrome Foccart*, pp. 340–341.

34. For new perspectives on Guinea's unique postcolonial path, see Elizabeth Schmidt, "Anticolonial Nationalism in French West Africa: What Made Guinea Unique?" *African Studies Review* 52, no. 2 (2009); Elizabeth Schmidt, *Cold War and Decolonization in Guinea, 1946–1958* (Athens: Ohio University Press, 2007).

35. Vorster speech at Goodwood, 31 May 1971, Geyser, ed. *Select Speeches*, p. 139.

36. Vorster speech in the House of Assembly, 4 February 1974, Geyser, ed. *Select Speeches*, pp. 212–213.

37. Pretoria explicitly classified African states according to this radical-moderate dichotomy: DFAA, 1/99/19, 13, Africa: SA Policy in Africa and Relations with African States, report, author unclear, "Houding van Afrika-State teenoor Suid-Afrika," April 1972. For all its oversimplifications, this classification was a reasonable means of distinguishing between the different ideological blocs of postindependence Africa. See Nugent, *Africa since Independence: A Comparative History*, pp. 142–143.

38. Meredith Terretta, "Cameroonian Nationalists Go Global: From Forest Maquis to a Pan-African Accra," *Journal of African History* 51, no. 2 (2010); Frederick Cooper, *Citizenship between Empire and Nation: Remaking France and French Africa, 1945–1960* (Princeton, NJ: Princeton University Press, 2015); Joseph S. Nye, *Pan-Africanism and East African Integration* (Cambridge, MA: Harvard University Press, 1965). See also Kelly and Kaplan, "Nation and Decolonization: Toward a New Anthropology of Nationalism."

39. Jeffrey Herbst, *States and Power in Africa: Comparative Lessons in Authority and Control* (Princeton, NJ: Princeton University Press, 2000), 100–101.

40. Herbst, *States and Power in Africa: Comparative Lessons in Authority and Control*, p. 111.

41. Nicolas van de Walle, *African Economies and the Politics of Permanent Crisis, 1979–1999* (Cambridge, UK; New York: Cambridge University Press, 2001), pp. 113–151; Robert H. Jackson and Carl G. Rosberg, "Personal Rule in Black Africa: Prince, Autocrat, Prophet, Tyrant," (Berkeley: University of California Press, 1982); Jean-François Médard, "The Underdeveloped State in Africa: Political Clientelism or Neo-Patrimonialism?" in *Private Patronage and Public Power: Political Clientelism in the Modern State*, ed. Christopher S. Clapham (London: Pinter, 1982).

42. Robert H. Jackson and Carl G. Rosberg, "Why Africa's Weak States Persist: The Empirical and the Juridical in Statehood," *World Politics* 35, no. 1 (October 1982).

43. Cooper, *Africa since 1940: The Past of the Present*, pp. 156–157.

44. For more on the tension between pan-African and state-bounded conceptions of postcolonial society, see Cooper, "Possibility and Constraint: African Independence in Historical Perspective," pp. 170, 176, 179.

45. Vorster, *South Africa's Outward Policy*, p. 10.

46. C. David Dalcanton, "Vorster and the Politics of Confidence," *African Affairs* 75, no. 299 (April 1976): 169.

47. Fifth Summit Conference of East and Central African States, "Manifesto on Southern Africa," (Lusaka: April 1969). Though more than pleased in private, Pretoria actually formally rejected the Manifesto, refusing to condone any hint of African interference in its internal affairs.

48. "Beware the temptor," editorial, *Sechaba*, 5, 1, January 1971.

49. *Sechaba*, 5, 7, July 1971.

50. These were Dahomey, Niger, Swaziland, Togo, and Upper Volta: Pfister, *Apartheid South Africa and African States*, p. 58.

51. DFAA, 1/99/19, 13, Africa: SA Policy in Africa and Relations with African States, report, author unclear, "Houding van Afrika-State teenoor Suid-Afrika," April 1972.

52. Ian Smith, *The Great Betrayal: The Memoirs of Ian Douglas Smith* (London: Blake, 1997), p. 197.

53. Hastings Kamuzu Banda Collection (HBA), Box 1, Correspondence, 3, Banda to Muller, 29 February 1968.

54. "Solving problems in Southern Africa not by shouting," *Malawi News*, 22 May 1970.

55. "Banda vandag in Kaapstad," *Hoofstad*, 17 August 1971; "Le président Banda en Afrique du Sud," *Fraternité-Matin*, 17 August 1971.

56. "Le président Banda en Afrique du Sud," *Fraternité-Matin*, 17 August 1971.

57. "Africans in S. Africa support of dialogue," *Malawi News*, 24 August 1971.

58. "Le président Banda en Afrique du Sud," *Fraternité-Matin*, 17 August 1971.

59. "Levée de boucliers contre la visite de Vorster à Blantyre," *Le Soleil*, 22 May 1970.

60. "'El Moudjahid' et le voyage de M. Banda en Afrique du Sud," *L'Essor*, 20 August 1971.

61. "M. Banda n'a été accueilli que par son propre ambassadeur à Pretoria," *L'Essor*, 18 August 1971. The title of the article itself was pure fiction.

62. For more on Banda's rule, see Philip Short, *Banda* (London, Boston: Routledge & Kegan Paul, 1974), pp. 251–282.

63. HBA, Box 2, Writings, 2, Banda speech, "A Threat to World Peace," Zomba, 29 April 1964. See also Short, *Banda*, pp. 173–178.

64. Carolyn McMaster, *Malawi: Foreign Policy and Development* (London: Julian Friedmann Publishers Ltd., 1974), p. 59.

65. HBA, Box 1, Correspondence, 2, Banda to Kaunda, 28 November 1967.

66. James Barber, *South Africa's Foreign Policy, 1945–1970* (London: Oxford University Press, 1973), pp. 268–269. For a rich overview of Abidjan's engagement with Pretoria, though with conclusions that ultimately diverge from those here, see A. B. Bamba, "An Unconventional Challenge to Apartheid: The Ivorian Dialogue Diplomacy with South Africa, 1960–1978," *International Journal of African Historical Studies* 47, no. 1 (2014).

67. *New York Times*, 29 April 1971.

68. "Solving problems in Southern Africa not by shouting," *Malawi News*, 22 May 1970.

69. "Le Président K. Banda en Afrique du Sud," *Fraternité-Matin*, 13 August 1971; "M. K. Banda aujourd'hui a Johannesbourg," *Fraternité-Matin*, 16 August 1971.

70. "Contact and Dialogue," *Malawi News*, 22 February 1975.

71. "Ngwazi's main priority is to improve living standards of his people," *Malawi News*, 13 December 1975.

72. "Banda," editorial, *Hoofstad*, 17 August 1971. Treurnicht had just stepped down as editor to enter politics.

73. "Swart en wit ontmoet mekaar," *Beeld*, 15 May 1975.

74. Vorster, *South Africa's Outward Policy*, p. 10.

75. ARCA, PV 528, MB 10/1/2, Hilgard Muller, Korrespondensie, Fourie to A. M. Mogwe, Permanent Secretary to the President, 24 February 1971, p. 11.

76. Ton Vosloo, ed. *Schalk Pienaar: 10 Jaar Politieke Kommentaar* (Cape Town: Tafelberg,1975), p. 73.

77. "R. A. S., Pretoria," letter to the editor, *Die Afrikaner*, 15 January 1971.

78. Rian Malan, *My Traitor's Heart: A South African Exile Returns to Face His Country, His Tribe, and His Conscience* (New York: Atlantic Monthly Press, 1990), p. 41.

79. *Hansard*, House of Assembly Debates, 15 September 1970, col 4209.

80. Speech, Pretoria, 28 June 1971, in Geyser, ed. *Select Speeches*, p. 158.

81. "Arm man wurg onder rykmansparty," *Die Afrikaner*, 15 January 1971.

82. "Bittere Vrugte," editorial, *Die Afrikaner*, 14 September 1973.

83. A. Rossouw, Kimberley, letter to the editor, *Die Afrikaner*, 22 January 1971.

84. ARCA, PV 132, B. J. Vorster, 3/6/119, Toesprake, Verklarings en Boodskappe, Eerste Minister, Kongresse, "Beantwoording van Beskrywingspunte deur Sy Edele Die Eerste Minister op die Kongres van die Nasionale Party – Transvaal – Pretoria," 12 September 1968.

85. Interview with Albert Hertzog, *Veg*, 29 November 1969.

86. "Bittere Vrugte," editorial, *Die Afrikaner*, 14 September 1973.

87. "Arm man wurg onder rykmansparty," *Die Afrikaner*, 15 January 1971.

88. Ontnugter, Zastron, letter to the editor, *Die Afrikaner*, 29 January 1971.

89. Lombard, "The Economic Philosophy of Homeland Development," pp. 536–537.

90. de Klerk, "The Concepts 'Verkramp' and 'Verlig,'" p. 530. Emphasis in original.

91. "Steun Suid-Afrika se Afrika-beleid," *Volkshandel*, July 1967.

92. "Groot uitdagings wag," *Volkshandel*, May 1974.

93. R. McLachlan, ed. *Vrugte van die Nasionale Bewind* (Kaapstad: Inligtingdiens van die Nasionale Party,1974), p. 26.

94. ARCA, PV 132, B. J. Vorster, 3/6/119, Toesprake, Verklarings en Boodskappe, Eerste Minister, Kongresse, "Beantwoording van Beskrywingspunte deur Sy Edele Die Eerste Minister op die Kongres van die Nasionale Party – Transvaal – Pretoria," 12 September 1968.

95. *Hansard*, House of Assembly Debates, 12 March 1971, col 2666.
96. *Hansard*, House of Assembly Debates, 11 September 1974, col 2647.
97. de Klerk, "The Concepts 'Verkramp' and 'Verlig,'" p. 525.
98. *Hansard*, House of Assembly Debates, 6 August 1974, col 122–3.
99. "Klein Apartheid," editorial, *Die Transvaler*, 20 August 1973.
100. Editorial, *Die Transvaler*, 17 October 1973.
101. "Integrasie op die sportveld," *Die Afrikaner*, 26 October 1973.
102. "Address by Dr. The Hon. C.P. Mulder, at the Royal Institute of International Affairs, London, 5th July, 1971" (Johannesburg: South African Institute for International Affairs, 1971).
103. Kaunda to Vorster, 15 August 1968, in Kenneth D. Kaunda and B.J. Vorster, *Dear Mr Vorster...: Details of Exchanges between President Kaunda of Zambia and Prime Minister Vorster of South Africa* (Lusaka: Zambia Information Services, 1971).
104. Fifth Summit Conference of East and Central African States, "Manifesto on Southern Africa."
105. *Hansard*, House of Assembly Debates, 28 October 1974, cols. 6576–6577.
106. It is unclear who was giving this foreign aid or how much ultimately ended up in the homelands.
107. *New York Times*, 29 April 1971.
108. *To the Point*, 21 April 1973, p. 20.
109. Pfister, *Apartheid South Africa and African States*, p. 70.
110. HBA, Box 1, Correspondence, 3, Nkrumah to Banda, 24 April 1965.
111. National Archives of Malawi, 45/1/13, V, John R. Ngwiri, Secretary for External Affairs, to Minister for External Affairs, "Report of a Mission to the United Nations," April 1972.
112. Speech to Parliament, 11 January 1966, cited in Short, *Banda*, pp. 289–290.
113. HBA, Box 3, unpublished autobiographical manuscript, 1959–1960, p. 554.
114. HBA, Box 2, Writings, 3, Banda speech, Liwonde, 4 July 1970.
115. Chamberlin, *The Global Offensive*.
116. DFAA, 1/99/19, 14, Africa: SA Policy in Africa & Relations with African States, "Situasie in Afrika (Franssprekende en Noord-Afrika), Afdeling 30," March 1973.
117. DFAA, 1/99/19, 14, Africa: SA Policy in Africa & Relations with African States, DFA report, "Die Afrika State se Houding oor die Kwessie van 'Dialoog' met die Republiek: Die Huidige Posisie," 29 August 1972; DFAA, 1/99/19, 14, Africa: SA Policy in Africa & Relations with African States, DFA report, " 'Dialoog' met Afrika," 29 August 1972.
118. "Is Dialogue Dying?" *Financial Mail*, 19 May 1972.
119. Johannesburg *Star*, editorial, 6 October 1972.
120. DFAA, 1/99/19, 14, Africa: SA Policy in Africa & Relations with African States, Report, "Agtergrond Dokument oor die Situasie in Afrika vir Sover dit Bedreigings vir die RSA Inhou," January 1973.
121. Maxime Rodinson, "Israél, fait colonial?" *Les Temps modernes* 22 (1967). See also George Jabbour, *Settler Colonialism in Southern Africa and the Middle East* (Khartoum: University of Khartoum, 1970).
122. DFAA, 1/99/19, 15, Africa: SA Policy in Africa and Relations with African States, Zdenek Cervenka, "The Afro-Arab Alliance," *Africa and the World*, Issue 31, March 1974.
123. "5 in Black Africa Keep Israel Ties: Ruptures Seen As Response to Pressure by Arabs," *New York Times*, 6 November 1973.
124. Ties between Tel Aviv and Pretoria duly strengthened: Sasha Polakow-Suransky, *The Unspoken Alliance: Israel's Secret Relationship with Apartheid South Africa* (New York: Pantheon, 2010), pp. 69–74.
125. Theresa Papenfus, *Pik Botha and His Times* (Pretoria: Litera, 2010), pp. 132–133. The walk-out included outward policy stalwarts like Côte d'Ivoire.
126. DFAA, 1/14/10, 1, Portugal's African Territories, SA Mission to the UN, New York, to the Secretary for Foreign Affairs, "Lisbon, Lourenco Marques, and Luanda, Special Committee of Twenty-Four: Consideration of the Question of Territories under Portuguese Administration," 15 March 1974.
127. *Hansard*, House of Assembly Debates, 9 September 1974, col 2486.
128. ARCA, PV 528, Hilgard Muller, MB 8/4, 18, Poslêer, "Geheim: Amptelike Kontak met Afrika-State Gedurende Die Periode 1 Julie 1973 tot 31 Julie 1974," undated, post-July 1974.

129. Compare DFAA, 1/99/19, 16, Africa: SA Policy in Africa and Relations with African States, "RSA Invoer van en Uitvoer na Afrikalande 1972 en 1973" with Guelke, "Africa as a Market for South African Goods," p. 85.

130. DFAA, 1/99/19, 14, Africa: SA Policy in Africa & Relations with African States, Speech by Muller at Opening of Stellenbosch University, 19 February 1973.

131. Pfister, *Apartheid South Africa and African States*, pp. 68–79; de Villiers, *Secret Information*; Mervyn Rees, *Muldergate: The Story of the Info Scandal* (Johannesburg: Macmillan South Africa, 1980).

Chapter 3

1. Pierre Hugo, "Towards Darkness and Death: Racial Demonology in South Africa," *The Journal of Modern African Studies* 26, no. 4 (1988): 571.

2. Hugo, "Towards Darkness and Death: Racial Demonology in South Africa": 572–573.

3. Heard, *General Elections in South Africa, 1943–1970*, p. 164.

4. Likewise, *volkseie* would later shape official perceptions of the various pretenders to power in Angola as essentially ethnically based national movements. See Chapter 5.

5. Norval, *Deconstructing Apartheid Discourse*, p. 158.

6. Eugene Paul Dvorin, *Racial Separation in South Africa: An Analysis of Apartheid Theory* (Chicago: University of Chicago Press, 1952), p. 97.

7. For more, see Norval, *Deconstructing Apartheid Discourse*, pp. 151–161.

8. Deon Geldenhuys, *South Africa's Search for Security since the Second World War* (Braamfontein: South African Institute of International Affairs, 1978), p. 1.

9. Irwin, *Gordian Knot*. See also Verwoerd speech in the House of Assembly, 10 April 1961 in Pelzer, ed. *Verwoerd Speaks: Speeches, 1948–1966*, pp. 549–566.

10. DFAA, 1/99/19, 14, Africa: SA Policy in Africa & Relations with African States, Speech by Muller at Opening of Stellenbosch University, 19 February 1973.

11. DFAA, 1/33/3, 18, United States of America Relations With South Africa, Vorster to Nixon, March 1971.

12. United States National Archives Access to Archival Databases (NARA AAD), Central Foreign Policy Files, Record Group 59, Records of State Department, Hurd, US Embassy, Pretoria, to State Department, "US Policy Towards the Indian Ocean: South African Government's Unique View," 3 May 1974.

13. For the best account of the campaign of the Department of Information by an outsider see Rees, *Muldergate: The Story of the Info Scandal*; for the best account by an insider, see de Villiers, *Secret Information*. See also Hendretia Marwick, "Dr C. P. Mulder as Minister van Inligting, 1968–1978" (MA thesis, University of the Orange Free State, 1982), pp. 85–100.

14. The fascinating records of the Department of Information can be found in the MNL series at the South African National Archives, finding aid S180.

15. See Irwin, *Gordian Knot*; Noer, *Cold War and Black Liberation*; Philip E. Muehlenbeck, *Betting on the Africans: John F. Kennedy's Courting of African Nationalist Leaders* (Oxford; New York: Oxford University Press, 2012).

16. DDRS, Summary of Senior Interdepartmental Group meeting on US Policy Towards South Africa's Racial Problems, State Department, 9 December 1968.

17. DDRS, State Department Policy Planning Council report, "National Policy Paper—Southern Africa," 1 November 1968.

18. For analysis of the formation of NSSM 39, see Witney W. Schneidman, *Engaging Africa: Washington and the Fall of Portugal's Colonial Empire* (Lanham, MD; Oxford: University Press of America, 2004), pp. 112–121.

19. Mohamed El-Khawas and B. Cohen, *The Kissinger Study of Southern Africa* (Westport, CT: Lawrence Hill, 1976). For an overview of Nixon's policies on sub-Saharan Africa, see Borstelmann, *The Cold War and the Color Line: American Race Relations in the Global Arena*, pp. 222–237; Alex Thomson, *U.S. Foreign Policy Towards Apartheid South Africa, 1948–1994: Conflict of Interests* (Basingstoke, UK: Palgrave Macmillan, 2008), pp. 63–83.

20. DFAA, 1/33/3, 18, United States of America Relations With South Africa, H. L. T. Taswell, SA Ambassador, Washington, D. C., to Secretary for Foreign Affairs, Pretoria, June 1971; Digital National Security Archive (DNSA), Secretary of State, Washington, D. C., to

American Consulate, Cape Town, "Minint [Minister of Interior] and Mininfo [Minister of Information] Mulder's Pentagon Meeting," 25 January 1974.

21. de Villiers, *Secret Information*.

22. DFAA, 1/33/8/3, 22, USA: Policy on Africa, Buro vir Staatsveiligheid (BOSS) report, "'n Sowjet-Waardering van Dr. H. Kissinger se Siening van Afrika Suid van die Sahara," 30 January 1974.

23. DNSA, *South Africa: The Making of US Policy 1962–1989*, Peter Hooper, US Consulate, Cape Town, to State Department, 20 February 1970.

24. DFAA, 1/33/3, 28, USA Relations With South Africa, Report, "VSA Verhoudings," author unknown, date unknown, presumably early 1974.

25. DFAA, 1/33/3, 28, USA Relations With South Africa, "Report: Relations With the USA," author unknown, presumably early 1974.

26. DFAA, 1/33/3, Volume 18, United States of America Relations With South Africa, Nixon to Vorster, 3 March 1971.

27. CIARR, National Intelligence Estimate, "South Africa in a New Decade," April 1972.

28. See for instance DFAA, 1/33/3, 28, USA Relations With South Africa, D. V. Louw, South African Ambassador to the United States, Washington, D. C., to Fourie, Pretoria, "Siening van Staatsdepartment Amptenare oor Suid-Afrika," 31 December 1973.

29. Anna-Mart van Wyk, "South Africa's Nuclear Programme and the Cold War," *History Compass* 8, no. 7 (2010); Anna-Mart van Wyk, "Ally or Critic? The United States Response to South African Nuclear Development, 1949–1980," *Cold War History* 7, no. 2 (2007).

30. Monica Wilson and Leonard Thompson, *The Oxford History of South Africa* (Oxford: Clarendon Press, 1971), pp. 424–476.

31. For more on the genesis of the cooperation between South Africa and Portugal, see Jamie Miller, "Things Fall Apart: South Africa and the Collapse of the Portuguese Empire, 1973–74," *Cold War History* 11, no. 2 (2012). South Africa did provide Portugal with some unspecified aid prior to 1964: Paulo Correia and Grietjie Verhoef, "Portugal and South Africa: Close Allies or Unwilling Partners in Southern Africa During the Cold War?," *South African Journal of Military Studies* 37, no. 1 (2009): 58–59.

32. DFAA, 1/14/3, 1, Portugal Relations With SA, Full Report, "Onderhoud Met Dr. Salazar," H. L. T Taswell, full report, 14 and 19 August 1964. Pretoria had already allowed numerous South African mercenaries to head to the Congo to assist Tshombe. See United States National Archives II (NARA), Central Foreign Policy Files, Record Group 59, Records of the State Department, Records of the Bureau of African Affairs, 1958–1966, Box 51, Def-19 Military Assistance (SA-Congo) 1964, Peter Hooper, Deputy Director, Office of Southern African Affairs, Bureau of African Affairs, State Department, to Governor Mennen Williams, Assistant Secretary of State for African Affairs, "Tshombe Request for South African Assistance," 11 August 1964; Piero Gleijeses, *Conflicting Missions: Havana, Washington, and Africa, 1959–1976* (Chapel Hill; London: University of North Carolina Press, 2002), p. 126.

33. DFAA, 1/14/3, 1, Portugal Relations With SA, H. L. T. Taswell, "Onderhoud Met Dr. Salazar," full report, 14 and 19 August 1964. For Salazar's similar statements to the Rhodesians, see Smith, *The Great Betrayal*, p. 72; Ken Flower, *Serving Secretly: An Intelligence Chief on Record: Rhodesia into Zimbabwe, 1964 to 1981* (London: Murray, 1987), pp. 32–33.

34. DFAA, 1/14/3, 1, Portugal Relations With SA, H. L. T. Taswell, "Onderhoud Met Dr. Salazar," full report, 14 and 19 August 1964.

35. DFAA, 1/14/3, 1, Portugal Relations With SA, H. L. T. Taswell, "Onderhoud Met Dr Salazar," top secret report of meetings with Salazar, late August 1964.

36. Correia and Verhoef, "Portugal and South Africa: Close Allies or Unwilling Partners in Southern Africa During the Cold War?": 59–60.

37. SANDFA, Group 2—MVV/P. W. Botha, Box 155, BGG/203/3/3/1, Defense Headquarters report, Appendix A: Cost Analysis of Operation Bombay in Respect of Support to the Portuguese: Period Jun 68–Dec 69, "A Review of the Campaign in East and South East Angola 1968 to End of January 1970," March 1970.

38. DFAA, 1/14/3, 1, Portugal Relations With SA, unknown DFA official to J. E. De Meneses Rosa, Ambassador of Portugal, "R25 Million Military Loan to Portugal," 16 July 1969.

39. DFAA, 1/14/3, 1, Portugal Relations With SA, Loan Agreement Between the South African Reserve Bank and the Govt of the Republic of Portugal, 12 February 1970.
40. Allen F. Isaacman and Barbara S. Isaacman, "Extending South Africa's Tentacles of Empire: The Deterritorialisation of Cahora Bassa Dam," *Journal of Southern African Studies* 41, no. 3 (2015): 547.
41. Interview with Kaas van der Waals, Centurion, 15 August 2011.
42. For good accounts of Rhodesia's control of the security situation before December 1972, see Flower, *Serving Secretly*; J. K. Cilliers, *Counter-Insurgency in Rhodesia* (London: Croom Helm, 1985).
43. *Hansard*, House of Assembly Debates, 25 January 1966, cols 49–56.
44. Brand Fourie, *Brandpunte: Agter die Skerms met Suid-Afrika se Bekendste Diplomaat* (Cape Town: Tafelberg, 1991), p. 108.
45. M. Tamarkin, *The Making of Zimbabwe: Decolonization in Regional and International Politics* (London: Cass, 1990), p. 4.
46. "Onafhanklike Rhodesië," editorial, *Die Volksblad*, 12 November 1965.
47. "Is min Vorster ten gunste van 'n swart meerderheidsregering?" *Veg*, December 1968.
48. Sue Onslow, "A Question of Timing: South Africa and Rhodesia's Unilateral Declaration of Independence, 1964–1965," *Cold War History* 5, no. 2 (2005): 132–33; Flower, *Serving Secretly*, p. 28.
49. White, *Unpopular Sovereignty: Rhodesian Independence and African Decolonization*, pp. 5, 33.
50. For Rhodesian perceptions of apartheid, see Smith, *The Great Betrayal*, p. 107. For South African perceptions of the Rhodesian model, see Onslow, "A Question of Timing: South Africa and Rhodesia's Unilateral Declaration of Independence, 1964–1965": 132–133. The South Africans and the Portuguese also looked down upon each other's systems of racial governance. For Portuguese perceptions of the South Africans, see NARA AAD, Central Foreign Policy Files, Record Group 59, Records of State Department, US Embassy, Lisbon, to State Department, "Conversations With Portuguese," 20 March 1973. For South Africa's views on the Portuguese assimilation model, see Isaacman and Isaacman, "Extending South Africa's Tentacles of Empire: The Deterritorialisation of Cahora Bassa Dam": 548–549, 552.
51. Stals, "Geskiedenis van die Afrikaner-Broderbond, 1918–1994," unpublished manuscript, p. 435.
52. See also Caroline Elkins, "Race, Citizenship, and Governance: Settler Tyranny and the End of Empire," in *Settler Colonialism in the Twentieth Century: Projects, Practices, Legacies*, ed. Caroline Elkins and Susan Pedersen (New York: Routledge, 2005).
53. White, *Unpopular Sovereignty: Rhodesian Independence and African Decolonization*, p. 4.
54. White, *Unpopular Sovereignty: Rhodesian Independence and African Decolonization*, p. 310.
55. Onslow, "A Question of Timing: South Africa and Rhodesia's Unilateral Declaration of Independence, 1964–1965": 133.
56. Zambian Government Official Statement, 15 August 1968, in Kaunda and Vorster, *Dear Mr Vorster . . .: Details of Exchanges between President Kaunda of Zambia and Prime Minister Vorster of South Africa*.
57. Onslow, "A Question of Timing: South Africa and Rhodesia's Unilateral Declaration of Independence, 1964–1965"; Flower, *Serving Secretly*, pp. 31–32; A. S. Mlambo, "'We Have Blood Relations over the Border': South Africa and Rhodesian Sanctions, 1965–1975," *African Historical Review* 40, no. 1 (2008).
58. Filipe Ribeiro de Meneses and Robert McNamara, "The Origins of Exercise Alcora, 1960–1971," *International History Review* 35, no. 5 (2013).
59. ISP, Deposit 5, Box 16, Defense Matters with RSA, Jack Howman, Rhodesian Minister for Defense, to Muller, 1 May 1973.
60. ISP, Deposit 5, Box 16, Defense Matters with RSA, Vorster to Howman, 21 May 1973.
61. ISP, Deposit 5, Box 16, Defense Matters with RSA, Vorster to Howman, 21 May 1973.
62. SANDFA, Group 3 (Volume 1)—AMI/HSI, Box 391, MI/STRAT/1/7, Afdeling Militêre Inligting, "Die Militêre Bedreiging Teen die RSA," October 1973.
63. Vorster speech in the House of Assembly, 15 September 1970, Geyser, ed. *Select Speeches*, p. 111.

64. SANDFA, Group 2—MVV/P. W. Botha, Box 23, MV 56/5, Portugal: Samewerking, Volume 3, "Global Strategy in the ALCORA Territories," c. May 1972; Alden, *Apartheid's Last Stand*, pp. 36–38.
65. The best discussion of the shortcomings of total onslaught as an ideology remains DFAA, 1/99/19, 16, Africa: SA Policy in Africa and Relations with African States, John Seiler, "The South African Perspective of the World: Can It Serve as the Basis of a Productive Foreign Policy?" unpublished paper, 1974.
66. DFAA, 1/99/12, 22, Africa: Communism in Africa, Buro vir Staatsveiligheid to Fourie, "People's Republic of China: Infiltration into Africa," 1 November 1973.
67. DFAA, 1/99/12, 22, Africa: Communism in Africa, Buro vir Staatsveiligheid, "Soviet Penetration South of the Sahara," 13 November 1973 (forwarded to DFA 18 March 1974).
68. DFAA, 1/99/12, 22, Africa: Communism in Africa, Buro vir Staatsveiligheid, "Sjina: Nuwe Tendense in Afrika-Beleid," 27 July 1973.
69. DFAA, 1/99/12, 22, Africa: Communism in Africa, Buro vir Staatsveiligheid, "Sjina: 'n Evaluasie van die 'Bevrydingstryd' teen die RSA en SWA," 24 August 1973.
70. SANDFA, Group 2—MVV/P. W. Botha, Box 23, MV 56/5, Portugal: Samewerking, Volume 3, "Global Strategy in the ALCORA Territories," c. May 1972.
71. SANDFA, Group 3 (Volume 1)—AMI/HSI, Box 391, MI/STRAT/1/7, Afdeling Militêre Inligting, "Die Militêre Bedreiging teen die RSA," October 1973.
72. Prinsloo, *Stem uit die Wildernis*, p. 63.
73. de Villiers and de Villiers, *PW*, p. 96.
74. Prinsloo, *Stem uit die Wildernis*, pp. 21–31.
75. de Villiers and de Villiers, *PW*, pp. 123–124.
76. SANA, 1/1/7, Kabinet Notuleregister, 3 October 1978; SANA, 1/1/7, Kabinet Notuleregister, 24 October 1978; SANA, 1/1/7, Kabinet Notuleregister, 14 November 1978.
77. *Hansard*, House of Assembly Debates, 23 July 1970, cols 292–3.
78. ARCA, PV 203, P. W. Botha, 4/2/60, Toesprake, Boksburg, 20 October 1973.
79. ARCA, PV 203, P. W. Botha, 4/2/60, Toesprake, "Toespraak Gelwer Deur Sy Edele P. W. Botha, Minister van Verdediging, Tydens die Opening van Die Kaapse Landbouskou op 2 Maart 1974 te Goodwood," 2 March 1974.
80. See for instance H. H. Smit, MP for Stellenbosch, *Hansard*, House of Assembly Debates, 27 February 1973, col 1514, or 7 June 1973, col 8465.
81. CIARR, National Intelligence Estimate, "South Africa in a New Decade," April 1972. See also DNSA, Secretary of State, Washington, D. C., to American Consulate, Cape Town, "Minint [Minister of Interior] and Mininfo [Minister of Information] Mulder's Pentagon Meeting," 25 January 1974.
82. DFAA, BFF, unlabeled box, Folder 25, General C. A. Fraser, "Revolutionary Warfare: Basic Principles of Counter-Insurgency," undated, late 1960s. Fraser was General Officer Commanding Joint Combat Forces, a position analogous to Head of the Army. Emphasis added.
83. Interview with Deon Fourie, Pretoria, 8 July 2011.
84. André Beaufre, *An Introduction to Strategy* (New York: Praeger, 1965). For more on Beaufre, see Alden, *Apartheid's Last Stand*, pp. 41–45; O'Meara, *Forty Lost Years*, pp. 259–263.
85. Prinsloo, *Stem uit die Wildernis*, p. 63.
86. Interview with Deon Fourie, Pretoria, 8 July 2011. See also Alden, *Apartheid's Last Stand*, p. 44.
87. DFAA, BFF, unlabeled box, Folder 25, General C. A. Fraser, "Revolutionary Warfare: Basic Principles of Counter-Insurgency," undated, late 1960s.
88. DFAA, BFF, unlabeled box, Folder 25, General C. A. Fraser, "Revolutionary Warfare: Basic Principles of Counter-Insurgency," undated, late 1960s.
89. The Directorate for Strategic Studies was founded at Fraser's urging: SANDFA, Group 4-P. W. Botha, Box 142, 76/1, Strategie: Algemeen, Volume 1, Lt. Gen. C. A. Fraser, "Formation of a South African Institute for Defense and Strategic Studies," attached to Commandant General, SADF, to Military Secretary, 1 December 1972.
90. SANDFA, Group 1- HSAW Chief of Defense Force, Box 112, HSAW/303/3/2, Beplanning: Strategiese: Beleid, Volume 1, speech, "Total Strategic Policy," 19 June 1973. The audience and location of this speech is unclear.

91. Flower, *Serving Secretly*, p. 138.

92. Magnus Malan, *My Life with the SA Defence Force* (Pretoria: Protea Book House, 2006), p. 187.

93. Interview with Deon Fourie, Pretoria, 8 July 2011.

94. DFAA, BFF, unlabeled box, Folder 25, General C. A. Fraser, "Revolutionary Warfare: Basic Principles of Counter-Insurgency," undated, late 1960s.

95. Breyten Breytenbach, "The Alienation of White South Africa," in *Apartheid*, ed. Alex La Guma (New York: International Publishers, 1977), p. 142.

96. Correia and Verhoef, "Portugal and South Africa: Close Allies or Unwilling Partners in Southern Africa During the Cold War?": 64–65.

97. Correia and Verhoef, "Portugal and South Africa: Close Allies or Unwilling Partners in Southern Africa During the Cold War?": pp. 62–63.

98. SANDFA, Group 2—MVV/P. W. Botha, Box 155, BGG/203/3/3/1, Defense Headquarters report, "A Review of the Campaign in East and South East Angola 1968 to End of January 1970," March 1970.

99. SANDFA, Group 2—MVV/P. W. Botha, Box 155, BGG/203/3/3/1, Defense Headquarters report, "A Review of the Campaign in East and South East Angola 1968 to End of January 1970," March 1970.

100. SANDFA, Group 3 (vol 1)—HSI/AMI, Box 394, Volume 18, "Portugal en die Oorsese Provinsies," 31 July 1970.

101. Deduced from tables in Price, *The Apartheid State in Crisis: Political Transformation in South Africa, 1975–1990*, p. 44.

102. DFAA, 1/14/3, 1, Portugal Relations With SA, Departement van Verdediging, Report, "Versoek om Bystand: Portugal," 13 March 1969.

103. DFAA, 1/14/3, 1, Portugal Relations With SA, Departement van Verdediging, Report, "Versoek om Bystand: Portugal," 13 March 1969.

104. SANDFA, Group 1- VBR/VBK (DSC), Box 3, VBK Notules 1-21, Chief of Staff Logistics to Chief of Staff Operations, "Op Tower: Return of Equipment and Stores by Portugal," 18 August 1976, attached to "Minutes of the 20th Meeting of the DPC 23 August 76," 23 August 1976.

105. SANDFA, Group 2—MVV/P. W. Botha, Box 23, MV 56/5, Portugal: Samewerking, Volume 3, General C. A. Fraser, Commander Joint Combat Forces, to Biermann, "Meeting of Ministers of Defense of RSA and Portugal: 21–22 June 1972," 1 June 1972.

106. SANDFA, Group 2—MVV/P. W. Botha, Box 23, MV 56/5, Portugal: Samewerking, Volume 3, General C. A. Fraser, Commander Joint Combat Forces, to Biermann, "Meeting of Ministers of Defense of RSA and Portugal: 21–22 June 1972," 1 June 1972.

107. SANDFA, Group 2—MVV/P. W. Botha, Box 23, MV 56/5, Portugal: Samewerking, Volume 3, General C. A. Fraser, Commander Joint Combat Forces, to Biermann, "Meeting of Ministers of Defense of RSA and Portugal: 21–22 June 1972," 1 June 1972.

108. SANDFA, Group 2—MVV/ P. W. Botha, Box 23, MV/56/5, Portugal: Samewerking, Volume 4, Annex 1, "Permanent ALCORA Planning Organization (PAPO): Background and Organization," attached to "Oefening ALCORA: Notule van die Vergadering van die Ministers van Verdediging van Portugal en die RSA Gehou in Lissabon 29 November 1973," 29 November 1973.

109. SANDFA, Group 2—MVV/ P. W. Botha, Box 23, MV/56/5, Portugal: Samewerking, Volume 4, "Notule van die Vergadering van die Ministers van Verdediging van Portugal en die RSA Gehou in Lissabon 29 November 1973," 29 November 1973.

110. SANDFA, Group 2—MVV/ P. W. Botha, Box 23, MV/56/5, Portugal: Samewerking, Volume 4, Komptroleur SAW to P. W. Botha, "Hulp aan Buurstate," 14 September 1973.

111. SANDFA, Group 2—MVV/P. W. Botha, Box 23, MV 56/5, Portugal: Samewerking, Volume 3, Portuguese Minister of Defense to P. W. Botha, 21 August 1973.

112. SANDFA, Group 2—MVV/P. W. Botha, Box 23, MV 56/5, Portugal: Samewerking, Volume 3, Biermann to P. W. Botha, "Portugese Navraag vir Materiele Uitrusting," 11 May 1973. Emphasis added.

113. SANDFA, Group 2—MVV/ P. W. Botha, Box 23, MV/56/5, Portugal: Samewerking, Volume 4, Ministro da Defesa Nacional to Ministerie van Verdediging, 4 March 1974.

114. SANDFA, Group 2—MVV/P. W. Botha, Box 23, MV 56/5, Portugal: Samewerking, Volume 3, Biermann to P. W. Botha, "Portugese Navraag vir Materiele Uitrusting," 11 May 1973.

115. SANDFA, Group 2—MVV/ P. W. Botha, Box 23, MV/56/5, Portugal: Samewerking, Volume 4, H. J. Samuels, President, Krygskor, to General Ivo Ferreira, Secretary General for Defense, 7 March 1974.

116. Cooperation increased only in fits and starts. Each country had its own interests and ideas, while bilateral relations within the triangular structure were often difficult. See Filipe Ribeiro de Meneses and Robert McNamara, "Exercise Alcora: Expansion and Demise, 1971–1974," *International History Review* 36, no. 1 (2013); Correia and Verhoef, "Portugal and South Africa: Close Allies or Unwilling Partners in Southern Africa During the Cold War?"

117. Jaster, *South Africa's Narrowing Security Options*, p. 16.

118. SANDFA, Group 3 (Volume 1)—AMI/HSI, Box 391, MI/STRAT/1/7, Afdeling Militêre Inligting, "Die Militêre Bedreiging teen die RSA," October 1973; SANDFA, Group 1—Chief of Staff Operations, Box 3, Waardering: Die Militêre Bedreiging teen die RSA, "Waardering: Die Militêre Bedreiging teen die RSA," November 1973.

119. "Boodskap vir SA," *Die Afrikaner*, 25 May 1973.

120. "Is min Vorster ten gunste van 'n swart meerderheidsregering?" *Veg*, December 1968.

121. SANDFA, Group 3 - HSAW Chief of Defense Force, Box 180, Kabinetsmemorandum No. 3/74, "Maatreëls om die Mannekragsituasie in die Staande Mag te Verbeter," 14 May 1974.

122. SANDFA, Group 3- HSAW Chief of Defense Force, Box 181, Komp/503/1/8, SADF Five Year Plan, 27 May 1975.

123. Vorster speech at Naboomspruit, 17 June 1971, in Geyser, ed. *Select Speeches*, p. 147–148.

124. Flower, *Serving Secretly*, p. 140.

125. Flower, *Serving Secretly*, p. 140.

126. ISP, Deposit 5, Box 16, Defense Matters with RSA, Ministry of Defense, "Brief for the Prime Minister," 23 May 1973.

127. ISP, Deposit 5, Box 16, Defense Matters with RSA, Ministry of Defense, "Brief for the Prime Minister," 23 May 1973.

128. SANDFA, Group 3 (Volume 1)—AMI/HSI, Box 391, MI/STRAT/1/7, Afdeling Militêre Inligting, "Die Militêre Bedreiging Teen die RSA," October 1973; SANDFA, Group 1— Chief of Staff Operations, Box 3, Waardering: Die Militêre Bedreiging teen die RSA, "Waardering: Die Militêre Bedreiging teen die RSA," November 1973.

129. ISP, Deposit 5, Box 16, Defense Matters with RSA, Vorster to Howman, 21 May 1973.

130. *Hansard*, House of Assembly Debates, 11 September 1974, col 2652.

Chapter 4

1. An authorized biography of P. W. Botha suggests that in 1973 he presciently saw that the Portuguese were fighting a 'lost cause': de Villiers and de Villiers, *PW*, pp. 236–238. The archival evidence does not appear to support this contention.

2. DFAA, 1/14/10, 1, Portugal's African Territories, R. J. Montgomery, Ambassador, Lisbon, to Sekretaris van Buitelandse Sake, Pretoria, "Die Toestand in Portugal: Dr Caetano se Familie-Praatjie," 3 April 1974.

3. DFAA, 1/22/1 OS, 16, Angola: Political Situation and Developments, E. M. Malone, SA Consul-General, Luanda, to Secretary for Foreign Affairs, Pretoria, "Portugal and the Overseas Territories," 12 March 1974; DFAA, 1/14/10, 1, Portugal's African Territories, SA Mission to the UN, New York, to Secretary for Foreign Affairs Lisbon, Lourenco Marques, and Luanda, "Special Committee of Twenty-Four: Consideration of the Question of Territories Under Portuguese Administration," 15 March 1974.

4. DFAA, 1/22/1 OS, 16, Angola: Political Situation and Developments, Malone to Secretary for Foreign Affairs, Pretoria, "Angola: The Progress of the War," 27 November 1973.

5. DFAA, 1/22/1 OS, 16, Angola: Political Situation and Developments, Malone to Secretary for Foreign Affairs, Pretoria, "Angola: The Progress of the War," 4 February 1974. BOSS reports corroborated Malone's optimism: DFAA, 1/22/1 OS, 16, Angola: Political Situation and Developments, Buro vir Staatsveiligheid, Afdeling G: Weeklikse Oorsig Nr. 1/74, 17 January 1974, sent to Sekretaris van Buitelandse Sake, Pretoria, 30 January 1974.

6. Interview with Kaas van der Waals, Centurion, 15 August 2011.
7. DFAA, 1/22/1 OS, 16, Angola: Political Situation and Developments, "Military and Socio-Political Situation in Moçambique and Angola," author unknown, September 1973.
8. DFAA, 1/22/1 OS, 16, Angola: Political Situation and Developments, R. J. Montgomery, SA Ambassador, Lisbon, to Sekretaris van Buitelandse Sake, "Besoek aan Angola en Mosambiek: Augustus 1973," 12 September 1973.
9. SANDFA, Group 2 – MVV/P. W. Botha, Box 23, MV 56/5, Portugal: Samewerking, Volume 3, Director-General Military Intelligence to H SAW, "Huidige Terroriste-Situasie in Mosambiek, Angola en Rhodesië," 3 April 1973.
10. "Africa: The Persistent Empire," *Time*, 31 December 1973, p. 21. See also NARA AAD, Central Foreign Policy Files, Record Group 59, Records of State Department, Hendrik van Oss, US Consul-General, Lourenco Marques, to State Department, "Portugal- Africa-Brazil and US Policy," 4 January 1974: "Even after ten years of armed struggle, Frelimo still does not control significant portions of country or command substantial support among [the] populace. Portuguese seem strong enough to hang on indefinitely, barring unforeseen developments."
11. Interview with Jeremy Shearar, Pretoria, 18 August 2011.
12. SANA, 1/1/5, 2, Kabinet Notuleregister, 4 June 1974. For Pretoria's defense spending throughout the 1970s see Jaster, *South Africa's Narrowing Security Options*, p. 16.
13. DFAA, 1/14/3, 5, Portugal Relations with South Africa, SA Mission to the UN, New York, to Secretary for Foreign Affairs, Pretoria, 13 June 1974.
14. Magaziner, *The Law and the Prophets: Black Consciousness in South Africa, 1968–1977*, p. 151.
15. DFAA, 1/14/10, 1, Portugal's African Territories, Jeremy Shearar, Chargé d'Affaires, South African Embassy, London, to the Secretary for Foreign Affairs, Pretoria, "Portugal and Africa," 1 August 1974.
16. DFAA, 1/14/10, 1, Portugal's African Territories, "Record of Discussion Between the Secretary for Foreign Affairs and the American Ambassador," 30 May 1974; DFAA, 1/14/10, 1, Portugal's African Territories, R. J. Montgomery, SA Ambassador to Portugal, Lisbon, to die Sekretaris van Buitelandse Sake, Pretoria, "Die Toestand in Portugal," 18 June 1974.
17. DFAA, 1/14/10, 1, Portugal's African Territories, Ambassador to France, Paris, to Secretary for Foreign Affairs, Pretoria, 12 July 1974.
18. Private communication, 2 March 2013.
19. Interview with Neil van Heerden, Hermanus, 6 September 2011.
20. SANA, 1/1/5, 2, Kabinet Notuleregister, 14 May 1974.
21. SANA, MEM, 1/564, I13/2, Eerste Minister: Buitelandse Sake, "Moçambique," draft speech for Vorster, late 1974.
22. DFAA, 1/14/10, 1, Portugal's African Territories, "Record of Discussion Between the Secretary for Foreign Affairs and the American Ambassador," 30 May 1974. The policy was widely publicized: "Swartes Kan in Angola Regeer, As . . . Hul Bestending Is – Premier," *Die Transvaler*, 30 May 1974; "Vorster and Smith Agree: Black Rule in LM 'No Worry,' " *Star*, 29 May 1974; NARA AAD, Central Foreign Policy Files, Record Group 59, Records of State Department, State Department to US Embassy, Pretoria, "Assessment of SAG Views on Changing Situation North of Border," 17 June 1974.
23. SANA, MEM, 1/564, I13/2, Eerste Minister: Buitelandse Sake, "Moçambique," draft speech for Vorster, late 1974.
24. "Chaos or Stability?" editorial, *Cape Times*, 9 September 1974.
25. DFAA, 1/113/3, 9, Mocambique: Relations with SA, Muller to Louis Nel, 21 August 1975.
26. DFAA, 1/33/8/3, 23, USA: Policy on Africa, Kantoornota, Cape Town, 1 August 1974; NARA AAD, Central Foreign Policy Files, Record Group 59, Records of State Department, Kissinger to many posts, "Foreign Minister Expresses SAG Concern about Communist Influence over Future Government in Mozambique," 8 August 1974.
27. DFAA, 1/33/8/3, 23, USA: Policy on Africa, Hurd to Muller, 13 August 1974.
28. NARA AAD, Central Foreign Policy Files, Record Group 59, Records of State Department, Walker, US Consulate, Lourenco Marques, to State Department, "SAG Concern about Communist Influence over Future Government of Mozambique," 7 August 1974.
29. Magaziner, *The Law and the Prophets: Black Consciousness in South Africa, 1968–1977*, p. 152.

30. DFAA, 1/14/10, 1, Portugal's African Territories, "Record of Discussion Between the Secretary for Foreign Affairs and the American Ambassador," 30 May 1974. Portugal likewise saw the situation in Angola as much less problematic than in Mozambique: DFAA, 1/14/3, 5, Portugal Relations with South Africa, South African Ambassador, Lisbon, R. J. Montgomery, to Secretary for Foreign Affairs, "Interview with Portuguese Foreign Minister," 29 May 1974.

31. DFAA, 1/22/1 OS, 16, Angola: Political Situation and Developments, Malone, Luanda, to Secretary for Foreign Affairs, Pretoria, "The Situation in Angola," 2 May 1974.

32. DFAA, 1/22/1 OS, 17, Angola: Political Situation and Developments, Malone, Luanda, to Secretary for Foreign Affairs, Pretoria, "Events in Luanda," 7 August 1974.

33. DFAA, 1/14/10, 1, Portugal's African Territories, R. J. Montgomery, SA Ambassador to Portugal, Lisbon, to Sekretaris van Buitelandse Sake, Pretoria, "Die Toestand in Portugal," 18 June 1974.

34. SANDFA, Group 3 (Volume 1) – HSI/AMI, Box 158, Portugal (Information Documents), Volume 2, W. A. Kempen, Militêre Attaché, Lisbon, to Hoof van Staf Inligting, "Portugese Kabinet," 26 July 1974.

35. SANDFA, Group 1- AMI/HSI, Box 50, AMI/SK/1/8/3, Eie MA: Angola: Algemene Inligting ex Angola, Volume 1, Oelschig, Vice-Consul, Luanda, to Chief of Staff Intelligence, "The Situation in Angola," 25 July 1974.

36. DFAA, 1/113/3, 6B, Mocambique: Relations with SA, Kotzé to Sekretaris van Buitelandse Sake, "Mosambiek Verhoudings met Suid-Afrika," 6 September 1974.

37. See Vorster's reiteration of the noninterference policy in Parliament: Hansard, House of Assembly Debates, 30 August 1974, cols 1857–60.

38. DFAA, 1/14/10, 1, Portugal's African Territories, "Record of Discussion between the Secretary for Foreign Affairs and the American Ambassador," 30 May 1974; DFAA, 1/22/1 OS, 17, Angola: Political Situation and Developments, Malone, Luanda, to the Secretary for Foreign Affairs, Pretoria, "The Situation in Angola," 28 August 1974; NARA AAD, Central Foreign Policy Files, Record Group 59, Records of State Department, US Embassy, Paris, to State Department, "French Views on Portuguese Territories and South Africa," 10 May 1974; DNSA, Kissinger Transcripts, Minutes of Secretary Kissinger's Staff Meeting, 10 July 1974; NARA AAD, Central Foreign Policy Files, Record Group 59, Records of State Department, State Department to US Embassy, Lusaka, "SAG Views of Developments in Mozambique," 26 June 1974.

39. DFAA, 1/14/10, 1, Portugal's African Territories, Brand Fourie to van den Bergh, 10 September 1974.

40. Smith, The Great Betrayal, pp. 160–161.

41. "South Africa Will Defend Itself," Newsweek, 16 September 1974.

42. DFAA, 1/113/3, 6B, Mocambique: Relations with SA, R. J. Montgomery, South African Ambassador, Lisbon, to Secretary of the Department of Foreign Affairs, 10 September 1974.

43. ARCA, PV 408, NP Caucus, Notule, 25 February 1975.

44. SANDFA, Group 3 - HSAW Chief of Defense Force, Box 180, Kabinetsmemorandum No. 3/74, "Maatreëls om die Mannekragsituasie in die Staande Mag te Verbeter," 14 May 1974.

45. SANDFA, Group 3 (Volume 1) – AMI/HSI, Box 417, HS 11/1/2/2 DG OPS, Operasie Waardering van die RSA se Moontlike Aktiewe Militêre Betrokkenheid in Mosambiek, Volume 5, Kolonel J. F. J. van Rensburg to Biermann, "Operasie waardering van die RSA se Moontlike Aktiewe Militêre Betrokkenheid in Mosambiek," 21 May 1974. Rumors continued to circulate that Botha actually ordered troops into Mozambique, but Vorster sent van den Bergh to the eastern Transvaal to halt the invasion: Harvey Tyson, Editors under Fire (Sandton, South Africa: Random House, 1993), p. 186.

46. SANDFA, Group 3 (Volume 1) – AMI/HSI, Box 403, MI/STRAT/1/4, Direktoraat Militêre Inligting, "Die Terrorisbedreiging teen die RSA en SWA: Huidige Stand en Verwagte Uitbreiding," August 1974.

47. SANDFA, Group 3 (Volume 1) – AMI/HSI, Box 403, MI/STRAT/1/4, Direktoraat Militêre Inligting, "Die Terrorisbedreiging teen die RSA en SWA: Huidige Stand en Verwagte Uitbreiding," August 1974.

48. SADF Chief of Staff General Ray Armstrong, Head of Military Intelligence General Heinrich du Toit, and Head of the Army General Magnus Malan were the others present: ARCA, PV 132, B. J. Vorster, 5/1/19–22, Aantekeninge en Dagboeke, Vorster's Dagboek.

49. SANA, MEM, 1/572, I15/2, "Die Militêre Milieu in Suider-Afrika Waarin die RSA Hom Tans Bevind," attached to P. W. Botha to Vorster, 2 October 1974.

50. SANA, MEM, 1/572, I15/2, "Die Militêre Milieu in Suider-Afrika Waarin die RSA Hom Tans Bevind," attached to P. W. Botha to Vorster, 2 October 1974.

51. SANA, MEM, 1/572, I15/2, "Die Militêre Milieu in Suider-Afrika Waarin die RSA Hom Tans Bevind," attached to P. W. Botha to Vorster, 2 October 1974.

52. SANDFA, Group 3 - HSAW Chief of Defense Force, Box 168, SWA I, "Onderhoud met Eerste Minister," 3 October 1974.

53. The 1971 Home-Smith proposals had allowed for the achievement of majority rule, but following their rejection by the UK this principle had never been enacted into law.

54. See John Comaroff, "Government, Materiality, Legality, Modernity: On the Colonial State in Africa," in *African Modernities: Entangled Meanings in Current Debate*, ed. Jan-Georg Deutsch, Peter Probst, and Heike Schmidt (Portsmouth, NH; Oxford: Heinemann, 2002); Daniel Branch, *Defeating Mau Mau, Creating Kenya: Counterinsurgency, Civil War, and Decolonization*, African Studies (Cambridge; New York: Cambridge University Press, 2009), p. 7. This was a much more explicit feature of settler rule than, say, in much of French West Africa, where educational opportunities and full citizenship were eventually possible for a thin elite. See Cooper, *Citizenship between Empire and Nation*.

55. Tamarkin, *The Making of Zimbabwe: Decolonization in Regional and International Politics*, p. 16.

56. ISP, Deposit 4, Box 4, Rhodesia Settlement: Meetings with African National Council, Volume 2, Notes of meeting between Smith and Muzorewa, 12 June 1974.

57. Fourie, *Brandpunte*, p. 109.

58. At van Wyk, *Dirk Mudge: Reënmaker van die Namib* (Pretoria: J.L. van Schaik, 1999), p. 31.

59. Interview with Riaan Eksteen, Swakopmund, 2 August 2011. See also van Wyk, *Dirk Mudge: Reënmaker van die Namib*, pp. 34–47.

60. Interview with Riaan Eksteen, Swakopmund, 2 August 2011. See also interview with Dirk Mudge, Otjiwarongo, 2 August 2011.

61. SANDFA, Group 4 - P. W. Botha, Box 153, 48/3, Inligtingsoorsig: DMI, Volume 9, "Voorligting te VHK," 29 August 1975.

62. DFAA, 1/99/19, 16, Africa: SA Policy in Africa and Relations with African States, SA Ambassador to the UN, Pik Botha, to Sekretaris van Buitelandse Sake, 4 November 1974.

63. Interview with Pik Botha, Pretoria, 11 August 2011.

64. ISP, Deposit 3, Box 1, Rhodesia Government: Cabinet Minutes (Secretary's Standard File), Volume 5, Annexure to 11th Meeting, 21 March 1975.

65. ISP, Deposit 4, Box 6, Détente: Official Communications with South Africa, Volume 1, Hawkins to Smith, 15 October 1974.

66. *Hansard,* House of Assembly Debates, 7 February 1975, cols 397–8.

67. ARCA, PV 408, NP Caucus, Notule, 8 April 1975.

68. *Hansard,* House of Assembly Debates, 10 September 1974, col 2608. De Villiers later became a minister in the Botha and de Klerk governments, as well as in the postapartheid Government of National Unity.

69. Journalists often conflated the two terms and programs, while scholars have signally failed to provide any real definition since to the distinction between the two. See especially Pfister, *Apartheid South Africa and African States*, p. 93–104. See also "South Africa," *Financial Times* (London), 25 February 1975; D. Hirschmann, "Southern Africa: Detente?" *Journal of Modern African Studies* 14 (1976): 107–126; Barber and Barratt, *South Africa's Foreign Policy: The Search for Status and Security, 1945–1988*, pp. 181–186; Tamarkin, *The Making of Zimbabwe: Decolonization in Regional and International Politics*, p. 21.

70. The story later broke with much fanfare: "Vorster se Reis na Donker Afrika," *Die Oosterlig*, 16 May 1975.

71. "Vorster's Secret Visit to Liberia," *Argus*, 17 February 1975. Over the same 1974–75 time period, Information organized for Mulder to visit the United States twice, as well as Israel, Taiwan, Hong Kong, and Japan: de Villiers, *Secret Information*, pp. 102–103.

72. For this definition of détente, see John Lewis Gaddis, *Strategies of Containment: A Critical Appraisal of American National Security Policy During the Cold War* (New York: Oxford University Press, 2005), p. 277.

73. Fourie, *Brandpunte*, p. 108.
74. DFAA, 1/14/3, 1, Portugal Relations With SA, "Discussion between the Minister of Foreign Affairs, Dr The Hon. H. Muller and the Minister of Foreign Affairs of Portugal, His Excellency Dr Rui D'Espiney Patricio," Pretoria, 23–24 June 1971.
75. Kaunda and Vorster, *Dear Mr Vorster . . .: Details of Exchanges between President Kaunda of Zambia and Prime Minister Vorster of South Africa*.
76. Tamarkin, *The Making of Zimbabwe: Decolonization in Regional and International Politics*, pp. 24–5.
77. Larmer, *Rethinking African Politics*, p. 188.
78. Douglas Anglin and Timothy M. Shaw, *Zambia's Foreign Policy: Studies in Diplomacy and Dependence* (Boulder, CO: Westview Press, 1979), pp. 13–17; Larmer, *Rethinking African Politics*, pp. 187–188.
79. James Ferguson, *Expectations of Modernity: Myths and Meanings of Urban Life on the Zambian Copperbelt* (Berkeley, CA: University of California Press, 1999), p. 6.
80. United Kingdom National Archives (UKNA), Foreign and Commonwealth Office (FCO) 45/1323, Political Relations between South Africa and Zambia, Julian Amery, Minister of State, FCO, to Foreign Secretary, 29 May 1973.
81. Hugh Macmillan, *The Lusaka Years: The ANC in Exile in Zambia, 1963–1994* (Auckland Park, South Africa: Jacana Media, 2013), p. 114.
82. ARCA, PV 132, B. J. Vorster, 5/1/19-22, Aantekeninge en Dagboeke, Vorster's Dagboek.
83. DFAA, 1/157/3, AJ 1975, "Meeting between the Hon. Prime Minister and the Zambians," 15 October 1974.
84. Macmillan, *The Lusaka Years: The ANC in Exile in Zambia, 1963–1994*.
85. UKNA, FCO 45/1760, Visit by Secretary of State to Southern Africa: Policy, "Record of Conversation between Callaghan and Kaunda," 2 January 1975.
86. *Hansard*, House of Assembly Debates, 9 September 1974, col 2471.
87. DFAA, 1/99/19, 16, Africa: SA Policy in Africa and Relations with African States, SA Ambassador to the UN, Pik Botha, to Sekretaris van Buitelandse Sake, Pretoria, 4 November 1974.
88. ISP, Deposit 4, Box 6, Détente: Official Communications with South Africa, Volume 1, Hawkins to Smith, 15 October 1974. Lacking international recognition, Salisbury was represented by accredited diplomatic representatives rather than ambassadors.
89. ARCA, PV 132, B. J. Vorster, 5/1/19-22, Aantekeninge en Dagboeke, Vorster's Dagboek.
90. Tamarkin, *The Making of Zimbabwe: Decolonization in Regional and International Politics*, pp. 33–34.
91. Fourie, *Brandpunte*, p. 112.
92. The term "Frontline Presidents" was more widely used during the P. W. Botha years, but for ease of reference it is employed here.
93. DFAA, 1/99/19, 16, Africa: SA Policy in Africa and Relations with African States, Vorster speech, Senate, 23 October 1974.
94. DFAA, 1/99/19, 16, Africa: SA Policy in Africa and Relations with African States, Vorster speech, Senate, 23 October 1974.
95. DFAA, 1/99/19, 16, Africa: SA Policy in Africa and Relations with African States, Vorster speech, Senate, 23 October 1974.
96. Papenfus, *Pik Botha and His Times*, p. 142.
97. SANA, MEM, 1/564, I13/2, Eerste Minister: Buitelandse Sake, Kenneth Kaunda, speech, "Southern Africa: A Time for Change," Lusaka, 26 October 1974.
98. Fourie, *Brandpunte*, pp. 191–193.
99. DFAA, 1/113/3, 7, Mocambique: Relations with SA, I. A. Kotzé, Lourenco Marques, to Secretary for Foreign Affairs, Pretoria, "Pronouncements by Mr. Chissano," 25 November 1974.
100. DFAA, 1/113/3, 7, Mocambique: Relations with SA, Killen to Fourie, 13 February 1975; "SAR aid is keeping LM railways line open," *Pretoria News*, 14 April 1975.
101. DFAA, 1/113/3, 7, Mocambique: Relations with SA, B. F. Theron, Sekretaris van Nywerheidswese, to Fourie, "Verskaffing van Kunsmis aan Mosambiek," 19 February 1975; Fourie 191–3.

102. Martin Meredith, *The Past is Another Country: Rhodesia, 1890–1979* (London: A. Deutsch, 1979), p. 150.
103. Flower, *Serving Secretly*, p. 108.
104. Interview with Pik Botha, Pretoria, 5 April 2013; Smith, *The Great Betrayal*, p. 165.
105. du Pisani, *John Vorster en die Verlig-Verkrampstryd*, p. 183.
106. *Hansard*, House of Assembly Debates, 25 April 1975, col 4820-22.
107. "Een mens een stem in Suidwes-Afrika," editorial, *Die Afrikaner*, 5 February 1971.
108. "Konferensie oor toekoms van Suidwes," *Die Afrikaner*, 26 October 1973.
109. Ben Schoeman, *My Lewe in die Politiek* (Johannesburg: Perskor, 1978), p. 408.
110. "South Africa's Trade Routes to Détente," *Financial Times*, 15 October 1975. See also "South Africa," *Financial Times*, 25 February 1975.
111. "Rhodesië: Ons moes vroeër gepraat het," *Die Transvaler*, 21 January 1975.
112. Schoeman, *My Lewe in die Politiek*, p. 410.
113. One exception to this was the Bloemfontein daily *Die Volksblad*, whose editorials were consistently more skeptical that détente with Africa could ever be achieved. In his memoirs, Harvey Tyson, editor of the *Johannesburg Star*, famously wrote that "The English-language press in no way and at no stage colluded with the apartheid regime." However, the anglophone press was certainly not as forthright in denouncing Vorster's détente initiatives, with their goal of entrenching the regime's control, as it could have been. See Harvey Tyson, *Editors under Fire* (Sandton, SA: Random House, 1993), p. 401.
114. On 17 February 1975, he briefed the Afrikaans editors in the morning and the English-speaking editors in the afternoon: ARCA, PV 132, B. J. Vorster, 5/1/19-22, Aantekeninge en Dagboeke, Vorster's Dagboek.
115. "Schoeman Speech Ignored," *Sunday Times*, 8 December 1974.
116. "'n blanko tjek vir Rhodesië?" *Hoofstad*, 24 February 1975.
117. Schoeman, *My Lewe in die Politiek*, p. 411.
118. "Rhodesië: Ons moes vroeër gepraat het," *Die Transvaler*, 21 January 1975.
119. Serfontein, *Brotherhood of Power: An Exposé of the Secret Afrikaner Broederbond*, p. 123.
120. Afrikaner Broederbond (AB), 1975/1-5URanotDB, Box 1/1/23, 1 Besluite: Agendas & Notules, "Verslag van Samesprekings wat by die UR plaasgevind het," 28 February 1975.
121. AB, 3/75/Staat, Box 3/1/8, Staat: Détente in Suider-Afrika, "Détente in Suider-Afrika," May 1975.
122. ARCA, PV 408, NP Caucus, Notule, 25 February 1975.
123. For Fourie, see interview with Neil van Heerden, Hermanus, 6 September 2011, and interview with Riaan Eksteen, Swakopmund, 30 March 2013. For van den Bergh, see interview with Riaan Eksteen, Swakopmund, 2 August 2011, and interview with Kaas van der Waals, Centurion, 15 August 2011.
124. Interview with C. A. "Bastie" Bastiaanse, Centurion, 28 July 2011.
125. Interview with Neil van Heerden, Hermanus, 6 September 2011.
126. Interview with J. S. F. "Frikkie" Botha, Cape Town, 7 September 2011.
127. Interview with Neil van Heerden, Hermanus, 6 September 2011.
128. Flower, *Serving Secretly*, p. 157.
129. Fourie, *Brandpunte*, pp. 112–116.
130. SANA, MEM, 1/564, I13/2, Eerste Minister: Buitelandse Sake, Kaunda to Vorster, 15 November 1974.
131. ARCA, PV 132, B. J. Vorster, 5/1/19-22, Aantekeninge en Dagboeke, Vorster's Dagboek. On both 15 and 25 November, Fourie met no fewer than three times in one day with the prime minister. Muller met with Vorster only four times over all of November 1974, indicating his more peripheral role in the détente demarches.
132. SANA, MEM, 1/564, I13/2, Eerste Minister: Buitelandse Sake, Kaunda to Vorster, 15 November 1974.
133. ISP, Deposit 5, Box 10, Reports of Meeting with Zambian Reps and ANC from October 1974 to June 1975: "Détente," Record of Meeting Between Mark Chona and George Chipambata, Jack Gaylard and E. A. T. Smith, and Brand Fourie, Pretoria, 4 November 1974. Kaunda and Nyerere told the British the same thing: UKNA, PREM 16/634, Rhodesia Part II, James Callaghan, Nairobi, to UK Embassy, Cape Town, 8 January 1975.

134. ISP, Deposit 5, Box 10, Reports of Meeting with Zambian Reps and ANC from October 1974 to June 1975: "Détente," Meeting between Nyerere, Kaunda, Seretse Khama, Gaylard, E. A. T. Smith and others, Lusaka, 6 December 1974.
135. ISP, Deposit 4, Box 6, Détente: Official Communications with South Africa, Volume 1, Gaylard to Hawkins, 20 February 1975.
136. ISP, Deposit 4, Box 6, Détente: Official Communications with South Africa, Volume 1, Gaylard to Rhodesian Diplomatic Mission, 6 November 1974.
137. Fourie, *Brandpunte*, pp. 114–118. See also "Kaunda wys hy wil weer praat: Hoe swart eise was 'misverstaan,'" *Die Burger*, 11 December 1974.
138. "Détente in Africa: How the Lusaka talks came about," *Malawi News*, 21 December 1974.
139. Tamarkin, *The Making of Zimbabwe: Decolonization in Regional and International Politics*, p. 39.
140. The headlines alone convey the mood of the times. For the domestic press, see "Secret SA trip . . . Vorster summit next," *Sunday Times*, 24 November 1974; "Vorster 'Questioned': Secret Zambia Mission to SA," *Cape Times*, 25 November 1974; "Vorster se 'Geheime tog': Diep in Afrika vir vrede, sê gerug," *Die Burger*, 30 November 1974; "Well-planned move led to détente," *Sunday Times*, 1 December 1974; "Nog groot deurbrake vir SA kom gou: Vorster in Swart Afrika: 'n Naweek-reis na Ivoorkus," *Rapport*, 1 December 1974; "Vorster was twee keer in Afrika," *Die Volksblad*, 2 December 1974; "Did PM visit Ivory Coast?," *Cape Times*, 3 December 1974; "Rhodesië bespreek? Swart leiers byeen in Lusaka," *Die Burger*, 5 December 1974; "Dit is vir SA einde van 'n lang swart tonnel," *Hoofstad*, 12 December 1974; "Einde aan terreur: Swart leiers praat," *Die Burger*, 13 December 1974. For the international press see "Vorster in talks with Zambia," London *Observer*, 24 November 1974; "Kaunda 'has sent envoy for Détente talks with Vorster,'" London *Financial Times*, 25 November 1974; "Vorster's Secret Trip Might Bring African Summit," London *Daily Telegraph*, 2 December 1974; "Mr. Vorster's Secret Diplomacy," editorial, London *Times*, 2 December 1974; "Secret Diplomacy," editorial, *Scotsman*, 3 December 1974; "Lusaka Waits for 'Historic' Summit Talks," London *Financial Times*, 5 December 1974; "Is the Grand Plan For a 'Southern African United Nations' Nearing Fruition?" London *Times*, 6 December 1974; "Vorster Aim is Normal Links With Black Africa," *Times*, 21 February 1975.
141. "Liberië-besoek 'ongelooflik,'" *Hoofstad*, 17 February 1975.
142. Speech, Nigel, 5 November 1974, in Geyser, ed. *Select Speeches*, p. 226–240.
143. Cited in Tamarkin, *The Making of Zimbabwe: Decolonization in Regional and International Politics*, p. 47.
144. Cited in Tamarkin, *The Making of Zimbabwe: Decolonization in Regional and International Politics*, p. 47.
145. *Hansard*, House of Assembly Debates, 4 February 1975, col. 157–8.
146. *Hansard*, House of Assembly Debates, 28 October 1974, col. 6640. A close ally of Treurnicht, Langley was a founding member of the Conservative Party in 1982.
147. ARCA, PV 408, NP Caucus, Notule, 13 May 1975.
148. Interview with Stoffel van der Merwe, Pretoria, 13 October 2014.
149. ARCA, PV 819, Alf Ries, Box 1, "Statement on the Conference of Homeland Leaders with the Prime Minister," 22 January 1975.
150. Vosloo, ed. *Schalk Pienaar: 10 Jaar Politieke Kommentaar*, p. 107.
151. "Détente is ons erns," editorial, Die Transvaler, 1 February 1975.
152. *Hansard*, House of Assembly Debates, 22 August 1974.
153. *Hansard*, House of Assembly Debates, 10 September 1974, col 2613.
154. *Cape Times*, editorial, 7 January 1975.
155. "Statesman Vorster gambles all for peace in Southern Africa," *Sunday Times*, 23 February 1975.
156. UKNA, PREM 16/634, Rhodesia Part II, UK Embassy, Blantyre, to FCO, Record of Callaghan-Vorster meeting in Port Elizabeth, 5 January 1975.
157. For emergence of obstacles, see ISP, Deposit 5, Box 10, Reports of Meeting with Zambian Reps and ANC from October 1974 to June 1975: "Détente," Record of Meeting Between Gaylard, E. A. T. Smith, Muzorewa, Mugabe, Sithole, Nkomo, and others, Salisbury, 20 January 1975.

158. ISP, Deposit 4, Box 2, Records of Meetings 1973–1978, Record of Discussion between Smith, Gaylard, Fourie, van den Bergh, and others, 27 January 1975.

159. ISP, Deposit 4, Box 6, Détente: Official Communications with South Africa, Volume 1, Gaylard to Rhodesian Diplomatic Mission, 23 January 1975.

160. ISP, Deposit 4, Box 6, Détente: Official Communications with South Africa, Volume 1, Gaylard to Rhodesian Diplomatic Mission, 23 January 1975.

161. ISP, Deposit 5, Box 10, Reports of Meeting with Zambian Reps and ANC from October 1974 to June 1975: "Détente," Meeting between Gaylard, E. A. T. Smith, Chona, Chipambata, Fourie and van den Bergh, Lusaka, 4 February 1975.

162. This was the first official visit by a South African minister to Zambia: Meredith, *The Past is Another Country: Rhodesia, 1890–1979*, p. 153.

163. Tamarkin, *The Making of Zimbabwe: Decolonization in Regional and International Politics*, pp. 61–63; Meredith, *The Past is Another Country: Rhodesia, 1890–1979*, 172–173.

164. ISP, Deposit 4, Box 6, Détente: Official Communications with South Africa, Volume 1, Hawkins, Pretoria, to O'Donnell, Salisbury, "Settlement," 11 February 1975.

165. Smith, *The Great Betrayal*, pp. 167–173.

166. ISP, Deposit 4, Box 2, Records of Meetings 1973–1978, Record of Discussion between Smith, Gaylard, Fourie, van den Bergh, and others, 27 January 1975.

167. Fourie, *Brandpunte*, p. 120.

168. See for instance ISP, Deposit 4, Box 6, Détente: Official Communications with South Africa, Volume 2, Rhodesian Diplomatic Mission to O'Donnell, 16 June 1975.

169. Flower, *Serving Secretly*, pp. 107–109; Fourie, *Brandpunte*, p. 108.

170. ISP, Deposit 4, Box 6, Détente: Official Communications with South Africa, Volume 1, Hawkins to Stan O'Donnell, Secretary for Foreign Affairs, "Settlement," 11 February 1975.

171. ISP, Deposit 4, Box 6, Détente: Official Communications with South Africa, Volume 1, Gaylard to Hawkins, 20 February 1975.

172. Flower, *Serving Secretly*, p. 158–159.

173. Botha said very little: Smith, *The Great Betrayal*, pp. 169–170.

174. ISP, Deposit 3, Box 1, Rhodesia Government: Cabinet Minutes (Secretary's Standard File), Volume 5, Annexure to 6th Meeting, 18 February 1975. See also Smith, *The Great Betrayal*, pp. 168–171.

175. ISP, Deposit 3, Box 1, Rhodesia Government: Cabinet Minutes (Secretary's Standard File), Volume 5, Annexure to 6th Meeting, 18 February 1975; Fourie, *Brandpunte*, p. 117.

176. ISP, Deposit 3, Box 1, Rhodesia Government: Cabinet Minutes (Secretary's Standard File), Volume 5, Annexure to 6th Meeting, 18 February 1975.

177. ISP, Deposit 4, Box 6, Détente: Official Communications with South Africa, Volume 1, Rhodesian Diplomatic Mission to Gaylard, 5 March 1975. See also Muller's statement in Parliament in *Hansard*, House of Assembly Debates, 7 March 1975, cols 2189–2190.

178. Tamarkin, *The Making of Zimbabwe: Decolonization in Regional and International Politics*, p. 63.

179. ARCA, PV 132, B. J. Vorster, 5/1/19-22, Aantekeninge en Dagboeke, Vorster's Dagboek.

180. ISP, Deposit 3, Box 1, Rhodesia Government: Cabinet Minutes (Secretary's Standard File), Volume 5, Annexure to 11th Meeting, 21 March 1975.

181. ISP, Deposit 3, Box 1, Rhodesia Government: Cabinet Minutes (Secretary's Standard File), Volume 5, Annexure to 11th Meeting, 21 March 1975.

182. ISP, Deposit 3, Box 1, Rhodesia Government: Cabinet Minutes (Secretary's Standard File), Volume 5, Annexure to 11th Meeting, 21 March 1975.

183. ISP, Deposit 4, Box 2, Records of Meetings 1973–1978, Minutes of Meeting between Smith, Fourie, Muller, and others, Salisbury 3 April 1975.

184. ISP, Deposit 3, Box 1, Rhodesia Government: Cabinet Minutes (Secretary's Standard File), Volume 5, Annexure to 11th Meeting, 21 March 1975.

185. See ISP, Deposit 3, Box 1, Rhodesia Government: Cabinet Minutes (Secretary's Standard File), Volume 5, Annexure to 11th Meeting, 21 March 1975; ISP, Deposit 3, Box 1, Rhodesia Government: Cabinet Minutes (Secretary's Standard File), Volume 5, Annexure to 27th Meeting, 22 July 1975; ISP, Deposit 4, Box 6, Détente: Official Communications with South Africa, Volume 2, Smith to Vorster, 22 July 1975.

186. See, for instance, Carl Peter Watts, *Rhodesia's Unilateral Declaration of Independence: An International History* (New York: Palgrave Macmillan, 2012), p. 20.

187. Meredith, *The Past is Another Country: Rhodesia, 1890–1979*, p. 183.

188. DFAA, 1/156/3, 13, Rhodesia: Relations with South Africa, P. Snyman, SA Diplomatic Mission, Salisbury, to Secretary for Foreign Affairs, Pretoria, "Reaction in Rhodesia to the Release of the Rev. Sithole to attend the OAU meeting in Dar-es-Salaam," 7 April 1975.

189. ISP, Deposit 3, Box 1, Rhodesia Government: Cabinet Minutes (Secretary's Standard File), Volume 5, Annexure to 11th Meeting, 21 March 1975.

190. ISP, Deposit 3, Box 1, Rhodesia Government: Cabinet Minutes (Secretary's Standard File), Volume 5, Annexure to 11th Meeting, 21 March 1975.

191. SANDFA, Group 4- P. W. Botha, Box 142, 76/1, Strategie: Algemeen, Volume 1, P. W. Botha, Speech, "RSA se Strategiese Posisie," 1–3 September 1975.:

192. South African History Archive (SAHA), AL 3060, The State v. P. W. Botha and Appeal, Volumes 28 to 31, "Antwoorde op Vrae Deur die Waarheids- en Versoeningskommissie aan Oud-Staatspresident P. W. Botha," date unknown, pp. 89–90.

193. SANDFA, Group 3 – HSI/AMI (Volume 1), Box 407, Direktoraat Militêre Inligting, "Die Militêre Bedreiging Teen die RSA," 15 November 1974.

194. ARCA, PV 203, P. W. Botha, 4/2/66, Toesprake, Notes for Speech to the House of Assembly, 6 February 1975.

195. SANDFA, Group 4 – Chief of Staff Operations, Box 3, DGSS/2/2/27, Studies: Waardering: Détente, Volume 1, Major General J. H. Robbertze to Geoffrey Stewart-Smith, Foreign Affairs Publishing Co., London, 18 June 1975.

196. *Hansard*, House of Assembly Debates, 6 February 1975, col 291.

197. See Botha's handwritten notes in ARCA, PV 203, P. W. Botha, 4/2/66, Toesprake, Cape Town, 14 May 1975.

198. ARCA, PV 203, P. W. Botha, 4/2/66, Toesprake, Cape Town, 14 May 1975.

199. SANDFA, Group 3 (Volume 1) - AMI/HSI, Box 380, The Current Military Threat to the RSA and Rhodesia February 1975, Volume 14, "The Current Military Threat to the RSA and Rhodesia February 1975," 12 February 1975.

200. SANDFA, Group 3 – HSI/AMI (Volume 1), Box 407, Direktoraat Militêre Inligting, "Die Militêre Bedreiging Teen die RSA," 15 November 1974.

201. SANDFA, Group 2 – MVV/ P. W. Botha, Box 153, MV 48/3, Inligtingsoorsig: DMI, Volume 9, DMI report, "RSA: SA ANC Bedrywighede," 17 June 1975.

202. SANDFA, Group 4 – MVV/ P. W. Botha, Box 153, MV 48/3, Inligtingsoorsig: DMI, Volume 9, AMI report, "Oorsig: Toestand in Suider Afrika en die Veiligheidsituasie van die RSA," June 1975.

203. SANDFA, Group 3 (Volume 1) - AMI/HSI, Box 380, The Current Military Threat to the RSA and Rhodesia February 1975, Volume 14, "The Current Military Threat to the RSA and Rhodesia February 1975," 12 February 1975.

204. SANA, MEM, 1/563, I13/2, Eerste Minister: Buitelandse Sake, Dar es Salaam Declaration on Southern Africa, 10 April 1975.

205. SANA, 1/1/6, 1, Kabinet Notuleregister, 16 April 1975.

206. Fourie, *Brandpunte*, p. 125.

207. ISP, Deposit 4, Box 6, Détente: Official Communications with South Africa, Volume 1, Rhodesian Diplomatic Mission to O'Donnell, Salisbury, 2 April 1975.

208. ISP, Deposit 4, Box 6, Détente: Official Communications with South Africa, Volume 2, Rhodesian Diplomatic Mission to O'Donnell, Salisbury, 15 May 1975.

209. ISP, Deposit 4, Box 6, Détente: Official Communications with South Africa, Volume 2, Rhodesian Diplomatic Mission to O'Donnell, 15 May 1975.

210. ISP, Deposit 4, Box 6, Détente: Official Communications with South Africa, Volume 2, Rhodesian Diplomatic Mission to O'Donnell, Salisbury, 16 June 1975; ISP, Deposit 4, Box 6, Détente: Official Communications with South Africa, Volume 2, Smith to Vorster, contained in Gaylard to Rhodesian Diplomatic Mission, Pretoria, 30 May 1975.

211. ISP, Deposit 4, Box 6, Détente: Official Communications with South Africa, Volume 2, Smith to Vorster, contained in Gaylard to Rhodesian Diplomatic Mission, 30 May 1975.

212. ISP, Deposit 4, Box 6, Détente: Official Communications with South Africa, Volume 1, Gaylard to Hawkins, 20 February 1975; Smith, *The Great Betrayal*, p. 174.
213. ISP, Deposit 3, Box 1, Rhodesia Government: Cabinet Minutes (Secretary's Standard File), Volume 5, Annexure to 23rd Meeting, 1 July 1975.
214. ISP, Deposit 3, Box 1, Rhodesia Government: Cabinet Minutes (Secretary's Standard File), Volume 5, Annexure to 23rd Meeting, 1 July 1975.
215. ISP, Deposit 4, Box 6, Détente: Official Communications with South Africa, Volume 2, Smith to Vorster, 22 July 1975.
216. ISP, Deposit 4, Box 6, Détente: Official Communications with South Africa, Volume 2, Smith to Vorster, 22 July 1975.
217. Smith would state more bluntly to his Cabinet that "the South African Government's policy in drawing back its forces in the interests of Détente was wrong": ISP, Deposit 3, Box 1, Rhodesia Government: Cabinet Minutes (Secretary's Standard File), Volume 5, Annexure to 27th Meeting, 22 July 1975.
218. Fourie, *Brandpunte*, p. 124.
219. As late as October, Smith again insisted that Vorster had made this assurance: ISP, Deposit 3, Box 1, Rhodesia Government: Cabinet Minutes (Secretary's Standard File), Volume 5, Annexure to 45th Meeting, 28 October 1975.
220. ISP, Deposit 4, Box 6, Détente: Official Communications with South Africa, Volume 2, South African Accredited Diplomatic Representative, Salisbury, to Smith, 5 August 1975.
221. ISP, Deposit 4, Box 6, Détente: Official Communications with South Africa, Volume 2, South African Accredited Diplomatic Representative, Salisbury, to Smith, 5 August 1975.
222. The reaction in Rhodesia was sharp: "Don't do it, Mr. Vorster," Salisbury *Sunday Mail*, 3 August 1975; DFAA, 1/156/3, 13, Rhodesia: Relations with South Africa, P. Snyman, SA Diplomatic Mission, Salisbury, to Sekretaris van Buitelandse Sake, Pretoria, 20 August 1975.
223. ISP, Deposit 4, Box 6, Détente: Official Communications with South Africa, Volume 2, South African Accredited Diplomatic Representative, Salisbury, to Smith, 5 August 1975.
224. Fourie, *Brandpunte*, p. 126.
225. ISP, Deposit 3, Box 1, Rhodesia Government: Cabinet Minutes (Secretary's Standard File), Volume 5, Annexure to 31st Meeting, 11 August 1975.
226. ISP, Deposit 4, Box 4, Victoria Falls Conference August 1975, Pretoria Agreement, 9 August 1975.
227. ISP, Deposit 3, Box 1, Rhodesia Government: Cabinet Minutes (Secretary's Standard File), Volume 5, Annexure to 31st Meeting, 11 August 1975.
228. ISP, Deposit 3, Box 1, Rhodesia Government: Cabinet Minutes (Secretary's Standard File), Volume 5, Annexure to 31st Meeting, 11 August 1975.
229. ISP, Deposit 4, Box 6, Détente: Official Communications with South Africa, Volume 3, Gaylard to Hawkins, 19 August 1975.
230. "Die brugberaad," editorial, *Hoofstad*, 25 August 1975.
231. Macmillan, *The Lusaka Years: The ANC in Exile in Zambia, 1963–1994*, pp. 117–119.
232. *Sechaba*, 9, 8/9, Aug-Sep 1975.
233. ISP, Deposit 4, Box 4, Victoria Falls Conference Background Papers, Record of Victoria Falls Conference, 25 August 1975.
234. ISP, Deposit 4, Box 4, Victoria Falls Conference Background Papers, Record of Victoria Falls Conference, 25 August 1975. See also ISP, Deposit 4, Box 4, Victoria Falls Conference August 1975, "Excerpts from Victoria Falls Bridge Conference," recorded by tape recorder, 25 August 1975; and National Security Archive (NSA), Incoming FOIAs, Box 6, Wilkowski to Secretary of State, "Victoria Bridge Talks: A Zambian Description," 30 August 1975.
235. Fourie, *Brandpunte*, p. 129.
236. ISP, Deposit 4, Box 6, Détente: Official Communications with South Africa, Volume 3, Gaylard to Rhodesian Diplomatic Mission, 29 August 1975.
237. ISP, Deposit 4, Box 6, Détente: Official Communications with South Africa, Volume 3, Rhodesian Diplomatic Mission to Gaylard, 13 October 1975; Fourie, *Brandpunte*, pp. 133–140.

238. Gerald R. Ford Presidential Library (GFL), National Security Adviser Memoranda of Conversations, Ford Administration, Box 11, Conversation between Ford, Kissinger, Kaunda, and others, 19 April 1975.

Chapter 5

1. Macqueen, *The Decolonization of Portuguese Africa: Metropolitan Revolution and the Dissolution of Empire*, pp. 179–185.
2. DFAA, 1/22/1 OS, 19, Angola: Political Situation and Developments, E. M. Malone, SA Consul-General, Luanda, to the Secretary for Foreign Affairs, Pretoria, "Developments in Angola," 20 May 1975. Asterisks in the original.
3. This had been predicted early on by Malone: DFAA, 1/22/1 OS, 17, Angola: Political Situation and Developments, Malone, Luanda, to the Secretary for Foreign Affairs, Pretoria, "Events in Luanda," 7 August 1974. For a more extensive outline of the three groups and their respective strengths, see Gleijeses, *Conflicting Missions*, pp. 235–245. For a BOSS evaluation of the three movements, see DFAA, 1/22/1 OS, 18, Angola: Political Situation and Developments, Buro vir Staatsveiligheid, Weeklikse Oorsig Nr. 2 vir die Week Eindigende 9 Januarie 1974.
4. Odd Arne Westad, "Moscow and the Angolan Crisis, 1974–1976: A New Pattern of Intervention," *Cold War International History Project Bulletin* 8–9 (Winter 1996–1997): 23–24; Jeremy Friedman, "Reviving Revolution: The Sino-Soviet Split, the 'Third World,' and the Fate of the Left" (Princeton University, 2011), pp. 392, 439–446. See also CWIHP, *The Cold War in Africa*, Russian State Archive of Contemporary History (RGANI), fond 5, opis 68, delo 1962, ll. 157–159, Soviet Ambassador to the People's Republic of Angola E.I. Afanasenko, "Memorandum of Conversation with President of the Movement for the Popular Liberation of Angola, Agostinho Neto," 4 July 1975.
5. SANDFA, Group 3 (vol 2)—HSI/AMI, Box 637, MI/PLANS/8/1/2, "Waardering oor die Moontlike Gebruik/Aanwending van Chipenda/FNLA tot Voordeel van RSA," 25 June 1975.
6. SANDFA, Group 1- AMI/HSI, Box 50, AMI/SK/1/8/3, Eie MA: Angola: Algemene Inligting ex Angola, Volume 1, Oelschig, Luanda, to Chief of Staff Intelligence, "Liberation Movement Activity in Angola," 11 July 1974.
7. I am indebted to Nat Powell for sending me this document.
8. Interview with Constand Viljoen, Pretoria, 13 July 2011.
9. Interview with Koos van der Merwe, Pretoria, 13 October 2014.
10. For the increasing white flight see: DFAA, 1/113/3, 6B, Mocambique: Relations with SA, "Note for File," 13 September 1974; SANDFA, Group 1- AMI/HSI, Box 50, AMI/SK/1/8/3, Eie MA: Angola: Algemene Inligting ex Angola, Volume 1, Oelschig, Luanda, to Hoof van Staf Inligting, "Die Situasie in Luanda en Angola," 4 September 1974; DFAA, 1/22/3, 5, Angola: Relations with South Africa, Dirk Visser, Consulate-General, Luanda, to the Secretary for Foreign Affairs, 10 May 1975.
11. DFAA, 1/22/1 OS, 18, Angola: Political Situation and Developments, Malone, Luanda, to the Secretary for Foreign Affairs, Pretoria, "Text of the Agreement Signed Between Portugal and the Angolan Liberation Movements: January 1975," 21 January 1975.
12. SANDFA, Group 3 (vol 2) - AMI/HSI, Box 601, MI/INT/1/5, Aktiwiteite in Angola, Volume 1, Marius Oelschig, Vice-Consul, Luanda, to Chief of Staff Intelligence, "The Week in Angola," 26 June 1975.
13. DFAA, 1/22/3, 4, Angola: Relations with South Africa, Malone, Luanda, to Secretary for Foreign Affairs, Pretoria, "Angolan National Union," 12 July 1974.
14. DFAA, 1/22/1 OS, 18, Angola: Political Situation and Developments, Malone, Luanda, to the Secretary for Foreign Affairs, Pretoria, Developments in Angola, 9 April 1975.
15. DFAA, 1/22/1 OS, 18, Angola: Political Situation and Developments, Malone, Luanda, to the Secretary for Foreign Affairs, Pretoria, "Developments in Angola," 19 March 1975.
16. DFAA, 1/22/1 OS, 16, Angola: Political Situation and Developments, Malone, Luanda, to the Secretary for Foreign Affairs, Pretoria, The Situation in Angola, 2 May 1974.
17. Marius Oelschig, private communication, 2 March 2013.
18. Marius Oelschig, private communication, 2 March 2013.

19. "VSA, China en Rusland Betrokke: Wapenwedloop in Afrika," Pretoria *Hoofstad*, 8 July 1975. See also "Onrus in Afrika," Pretoria *Oggendblad*, 8 July 1975; "Flashpoint Somalia," Johannesburg *Star*, 17 July 1975; "Horing van Afrika is Reeds Rooi Satelliet," Pretoria *Hoofstad*, 22 July 1975.

20. W. A. Dorning, "A History of Co-Operation: The South African Defence Force's Involvement with the Angolan Resistance Movement Unita—Volume One, 1976–1980" (Universiteit van die Oranje-Vrystaat, 1986), pp. 19–20.

21. Sophia du Preez, *Avontuur in Angola: Die Verhaal van Suid-Afrika se Soldate in Angola 1975–1976* (Pretoria: J. L. van Schaik, 1989), pp. 13–15; F. J. du Toit Spies, *Operasie Savannah: Angola 1975–1976* (Pretoria: S. A. Weermag, 1989), pp. 60–65.

22. Spies, *Operasie Savannah*, pp. 60–65. When Chipenda met SA officials in SWA later in the year, he did much the same: Spies, *Operasie Savannah*, p. 63. All three leaders were willing to promise just about anything to get external support.

23. Spies, *Operasie Savannah*, p. 62.

24. Spies, *Operasie Savannah*, p. 62.

25. DFAA, 1/22/1 OS, 18, Angola: Political Situation and Developments, BOSS, Weeklikse Oorsig Nr. 2 vir die Week Eindigende 9 Januarie 1974.

26. DFAA, 1/22/1 OS, 18, Angola: Political Situation and Developments, Malone, Luanda, to the Secretary for Foreign Affairs, Pretoria, Developments in Angola, 19 March 1975.

27. DFAA, 1/22/1 OS, 19, Angola: Political Situation and Developments, Buro vir Staatsveiligheid message, Dirk Visser to Wilson, 14 July 1975; SANDFA, Group 3- HSAW Chief of Defense Force, Box 420, MI/STRAT/1/7, Die Militêre Bedreiging teen die RSA, Volume 51, Direktoraat Militêre Inligting study, "Die Militêre Bedreiging teen die RSA," 24 October 1975.

28. Spies, *Operasie Savannah*, p. 63.

29. DFAA, 1/22/3, 5, Angola Relations with South Africa, aide-mémoire, author unknown, April 1975; DFAA, 1/22/3, 5, Angola Relations with South Africa, Departement van Buitelandse Sake, Pretoria, to Departement van Buitelandse Sake, Kaapstad, 8 April 1975.

30. ARCA, PV 408, NP Caucus, Notule, 8 April 1975.

31. du Preez, *Avontuur in Angola*, p. 17.

32. SANDFA, Group 3 (vol 2)—HSI/AMI, Box 637, MI/PLANS/8/1/2, "Waardering oor die Moontlike Gebruik/Aanwending van Chipenda/FNLA tot Voordeel van RSA," 25 June 1975.

33. Paraphrased from SANDFA, Group 3 (vol 2)—HSI/AMI, Box 637, MI/PLANS/8/1/2, "Waardering oor die Moontlike Gebruik/Aanwending van Chipenda/FNLA tot Voordeel van RSA," 25 June 1975.

34. Dorning, "A History of Co-Operation: The South African Defence Force's Involvement with the Angolan Resistance Movement Unita—Volume One, 1976–1980," p. 22.

35. *Hansard*, House of Assembly Debates, 26 January 1976, col 50. The first claim was particularly specious: such was the three-way balance of power, an alliance between any two of the movements would have commanded a majority of popular support.

36. Brand Fourie, "Buitelandse Woelinge om Suid-Afrika, 1939–1985," p. 194.

37. Gleijeses, *Conflicting Missions*, pp. 247–256.

38. For Cuba's support of the MPLA, see Castro's monologue in CWIHP, *Cuba in the Cold War*, Central State Archive, Sofia, Fond 1-B, Record 60, File 194, Minutes of the meeting between Todor Zhivkov and Fidel Castro, Sofia, 11 March 1976; Gleijeses, *Conflicting Missions*, pp. 246–265. Almost five hundred Cuban advisers—several times what the MPLA had requested—arrived to staff four different training centers, but these were only up and running by 18–20 October.

39. SANDFA, Group 1- HSAW Chief of Defense Force, Box 172, HSAW/82/1/1, Terroriste Bedrywighede en Onluste: Angola, Volume 1, "Op Savannah: Opsomming van Gebeure tot 10 Jan 76," 13 January 1976. The Americans were equally unsure of the nature of Cuban involvement in Angola. As late as the end of October, the CIA National Intelligence Bulletin outlined that there "may" have been a delivery of Cuban arms and personnel in Congo recently, though they "may" have actually just been there to assist the Congolese; and Havana "appears to have secretly sent" the arms and personnel via a ship that "may" have docked in

Angola though those getting off the ship "may" have been Angolans: NSA, South Africa and the United States, Box 1, CIA National Intelligence Bulletin, 25 October 1975. At Kissinger's staff meeting ten days later, he twice asked his staff whether Cuban troops were indeed in Angola: DNSA, *Kissinger Transcripts*, Minutes of Secretary Kissinger's Staff Meeting, 5 November 1975.

40. du Preez, *Avontuur in Angola*, p. 16. Du Preez was part of the committee chaired by Professor F. J. du Toit Spies that researched the official SADF account of Operation Savannah referred to in this chapter. Like Spies's, du Preez's book, which focuses on the military rather than political dimensions of the conflict, does not contain reference notes that might allow other historians to verify her sources and conclusions. However, archival research for this book suggests that both can be considered broadly reliable.

41. SANDFA, Group 3 (vol 2)—HSI/AMI, Box 637, MI/PLANS/8/1/2, "Waardering oor die Moontlike Gebruik/Aanwending van Chipenda/FNLA tot Voordeel van RSA," 25 June 1975.

42. SANDFA, Group 4—P. W. Botha, Box 153, 48/3, Inligtingsoorsig: DMI, Volume 9, Chief of Staff Intelligence, to Military Secretary, "Intrep 168/75," 11 September 1975; SANDFA, Group 1- HSAW Chief of Defense Force, Box 174, HSAW/82/1/1, Volume 1, Terroriste Bedrywighede en Onluste: Angola, Hoof van Staf Inligting to Military Secretary and other senior military officers, Intrep 248/75, "Friction between FNLA/UNITA," 10 November 1975.

43. SANDFA, Group 3 (vol 2)—HSI/AMI, Box 637, MI/PLANS/8/1/2, "Waardering oor die Moontlike Gebruik/Aanwending van Chipenda/FNLA tot Voordeel van RSA," 25 June 1975.

44. SANDFA, Group 1- HSAW Chief of Defense Force, Box 174, HSAW/82/1/1, Volume 1, Terroriste Bedrywighede en Onluste: Angola, Hoof van Staf Inligting to Military Secretary and other senior military officers, "SWAPO/SADF Activities South Angola," 13 November 1975.

45. SANDFA, Group 3 (vol 2)—HSI/AMI, Box 637, MI/PLANS/8/1/2, "Waardering oor die Moontlike Gebruik/Aanwending van Chipenda/FNLA tot Voordeel van RSA," 25 June 1975.

46. SANDFA, Group 3 (vol 2)—HSI/AMI, Box 637, MI/PLANS/8/1/2, "Waardering oor die Moontlike Gebruik/Aanwending van Chipenda/FNLA tot Voordeel van RSA," 25 June 1975; ARCA, PV 203, P. W. Botha, 4/2/60, Toesprake, "RSA en Betrokkenheid by Angola," late 1975 or early 1976; SANDFA, Group 3- HSAW Chief of Defense Force, Box 420, MI/STRAT/1/7, Die Militêre Bedreiging teen die RSA, Volume 51, Direktoraat Militêre Inligting study, "Die Militêre Bedreiging teen die RSA," 24 October 1975.

47. DFAA, 1/22/3, 5, Angola Relations with South Africa, aide-mémoire, author unknown, April 1975; DFAA, 1/22/3, 5, Angola Relations with South Africa, Departement van Buitelandse Sake, Pretoria, to Departement van Buitelandse Sake, Kaapstad, 8 April 1975.

48. See Chapter 4.

49. SANA, MEM, 1/572, I15/2, "Die Militêre Milieu in Suider-Afrika Waarin die RSA Hom Tans Bevind," attached to P. W. Botha to Vorster, 2 October 1974.

50. Interview with Constand Viljoen, Pretoria, 13 July 2011. In this interview, Viljoen repeatedly recalled Cuban support as an important factor in the SADF's calculus when, as explained above, it only materialized later.

51. Spies, *Operasie Savannah*, p. 65.

52. DFAA, 1/22/1 OS, 19, Angola: Political Situation and Developments, Buro vir Staatsveiligheid cable, Visser to Wilson, 14 July 1975 (second message).

53. *Die Burger*, editorial, 21 July 1975.

54. ARCA, PV 132, B. J. Vorster, 5/1/19–22, Aantekeninge en Dagboeke, Vorster's Dagboek.

55. du Preez, *Avontuur in Angola*, p. 18; Spies, *Operasie Savannah*, p. 65. Other documents confirm that van den Bergh spent almost all of June and July in Europe: ISP, Deposit 4, Box 6, Détente: Official Communications with South Africa, Volume 2, Rhodesian Diplomatic Mission, Pretoria, to Gaylard, 28 July 1975.

56. Dorning, "A History of Co-Operation: The South African Defence Force's Involvement with the Angolan Resistance Movement Unita—Volume One, 1976–1980," p. 22.

57. Interview with Constand Viljoen, Pretoria, 13 July 2011.

58. Spies, *Operasie Savannah*, p. 55.
59. GFL, US National Security Institutional Files, 1974–1977, Box 10, Senior Review Group Meeting 19 June 1975—Angola (NSSM 224) (2), Memorandum to the National Security Adviser, "NSSM 224: United States Policy toward Angola," 16 June 1975.
60. GFL, National Security Adviser Memoranda of Conversations, Ford Administration, Box 13, Conversation between Ford and Kissinger, 18 July 1975.
61. John Stockwell, *In Search of Enemies: A CIA Story* (London: Futura Publications, 1979), p. 86.
62. Spies, *Operasie Savannah*, p. 65.
63. Private communication, Johan Mostert, 25 January 2012.
64. Interview with Piet de Wit, Pretoria, 2 April 2013.
65. Interview with Piet de Wit, Pretoria, 2 April 2013.
66. SANA, MEM, 1/572, I15/2, DG Ops, Viljoen, to H SAW, Malan, "Op Savannah—Hulp aan FNLA," 3 September 1975.
67. SANDFA, Group 5—Minister van Verdediging, Box 22, MV/21/11, Kabinet en Parlement: Verdedigingsgroep, Volume 1, Biermann, "Briefing for Defense Group of the United Party," 25 March 1976.
68. SANDFA, Group 4- P. W. Botha, Box 142, 76/1, Strategie: Algemeen, Volume 1, "Die Strategiese Waardering, SAW: Strategiese Benadering," 23 September 1975.
69. See Seegers, *The Military in the Making of Modern South Africa*, pp. 131–132; Hamann, *Days of the Generals*, pp. 7–9.
70. Flower, *Serving Secretly*, p. 154.
71. Interview with Piet de Wit, Pretoria, 1 April 2013.
72. Spies, *Operasie Savannah*, p. 61.
73. ARCA, PV 132, B. J. Vorster, 5/1/19-22, Aantekeninge en Dagboeke, Vorster's Dagboek.
74. For the broad structure of the seizure of the border sites, other than where specified, see du Preez, *Avontuur in Angola*, pp. 22–25; Spies, *Operasie Savannah*, pp. 46–48.
75. For Cabinet being informed in broad terms of the seizure of the border sites see SANA, 1/1/6, 1, Kabinet Notuleregister, 19 August 1975, and more fully only on 9 September: SANA, 1/1/6, 1, Kabinet Notuleregister, 9 September 1975. For the DFA, see DFAA, 1/22/3 OS, 6, Angola: Relations with South Africa. For the press and the public see "Keeping public informed," editorial, *Pretoria News*, 8 September 1975 and "Min. P. W. oor SA troepe in Angola," *Die Transvaler*, 9 September 1975.
76. Historian Norrie Macqueen has convincingly pointed out that while the government in Lisbon was widely expected to further the MPLA's aims, in reality Portugal's impact upon anything happening in Angola in winter 1975 was very limited, such was its desire to divest itself of responsibilities there. Lisbon was not even invited to the last-ditch Nakuru meeting convened in July with a view to bringing the three factions together. See Macqueen, *The Decolonization of Portuguese Africa: Metropolitan Revolution and the Dissolution of Empire*, p. 182. This does not change the fact that the South Africans consistently perceived Portugal as favoring the MPLA due to the close relations between the MFA-led government and the Portuguese Communist Party: SANDFA, Group 4–P. W. Botha, Box 153, 48/3, Inligtingsoorsig: DMI, Volume 9, "Voorligting te VHK," 25 July 1975.
77. SANDFA, Group 4–P. W. Botha, Box 153, 48/3, Inligtingsoorsig: DMI, Volume 9, "Voorligting te VHK," 25 July 1975.
78. Fourie, *Brandpunte*, p. 200.
79. DFAA, 1/22/3 OS, 6, Angola: Relations with South Africa, Minutes, "Vergadering Oor Kunene-Skema, Union Buildings, Pretoria, 11 August 1975.
80. de Villiers and de Villiers, *PW*, p. 243.
81. DFAA, 1/22/3 OS, 6, Angola: Relations with South Africa, Minutes, "Vergadering Oor Kunene-Skema, Union Buildings, Pretoria, 11 August 1975.
82. DFAA, 1/22/3 OS, 6, Angola: Relations with South Africa, Minutes, "Vergadering Oor Kunene-Skema, Union Buildings, Pretoria, 11 August 1975.
83. See especially DFAA, 1/22/3 OS, 6, Angola: Relations with South Africa, handwritten notes, Hilgard Muller and P. W. Botha, mid-August 1975; DFAA, 1/22/3 OS, 6, Angola: Relations with South Africa, B. G. Fourie, Sekretaris van Buitelandse Sake, to Admiral H. H. Biermann, Hoof van die Suid-Afrikaanse Weermag, Pretoria, 21 August 1975; DFAA, 1/22/3

OS, 6, Angola: Relations with South Africa, Kommandement South-West Africa to H Leer, "Minutes of Meeting with SA and Portuguese Personnel," 27 August 1975.

84. SANA, 1/1/6, 1, Kabinet Notuleregister, 19 August 1975. Riaan Eksteen recalls that DFA and the Bronze committee were both strongly against the banning of SWAPO as a move that would have gained little while attracting substantial criticism from abroad: Riaan Eksteen, private communication, 20 May 2013.

85. DFAA, 1/22/3 OS, 6, Angola: Relations with South Africa, HSAW to Militêre Sekretaris and Departement van Buitelandse Sake, 22 August 1975.

86. Hamann, *Days of the Generals*, pp. 22–23. See also interview with Constand Viljoen, Pretoria, 13 July 2011: the seizure of the sites was "just the explanation, it was not really the case."

87. Spies, *Operasie Savannah*, pp. 66–68.

88. SANDFA, Group 1- HSAW Chief of Defense Force, Box 172, HSAW/82/1/1, Terroriste Bedrywighede en Onluste: Angola, Volume 1, "Op Savannah: Opsomming van Gebeure tot 10 Jan 76," 13 January 1976; de Villiers and de Villiers, *PW*, p. 248.

89. du Preez, *Avontuur in Angola*, p. 27; Spies, *Operasie Savannah*, pp. 66–67.

90. Spies, *Operasie Savannah*, p. 67.

91. SANA, MEM, 1/572, I15/2, DG Ops, Viljoen, to H SAW, Malan, "Op Savannah—Hulp aan FNLA," 3 September 1975. This document, written by Viljoen, was based on Breytenbach's original recommendations, and forwarded by P. W. Botha to Vorster.

92. Spies, *Operasie Savannah*, p. 67.

93. SANA, MEM, 1/572, I15/2, DG Ops, Viljoen, to H SAW, Malan, "Op Savannah—Hulp aan FNLA," 3 September 1975.

94. SANDFA, Group 4- P. W. Botha, Box 142, 76/1, Strategie: Algemeen, Volume 1, P. W. Botha, speech, "RSA se Strategiese Posisie," 1–3 September 1975. If Cuban intervention in Angola had been a factor in Pretoria's thinking in early September, Botha surely would have mentioned it in this speech.

95. SANA, MEM, 1/572, I15/2, DG Ops, Viljoen, to H SAW, Malan, "Op Savannah—Hulp aan FNLA," 3 September 1975.

96. ARCA, PV 132, B. J. Vorster, 5/1/19-22, Aantekeninge en Dagboeke, Vorster's Dagboek; du Preez, *Avontuur in Angola*, p. 28.

97. Figures from SANDFA, Group 1- HSAW Chief of Defense Force, Box 172, HSAW/82/1/1, Terroriste Bedrywighede en Onluste: Angola, Volume 1, "Op Savannah: Opsomming van Gebeure tot 10 Jan 76," 13 January 1976. For UNITA's consistent inability to keep appointments or stay in touch with the South Africans, see Dorning, "A History of Co-Operation: The South African Defence Force's Involvement with the Angolan Resistance Movement Unita—Volume One, 1976–1980," pp. 19–24.

98. DFAA, 1/22/1 OS, 19, Angola: Political Situation and Developments, Malone, Luanda, to the Secretary for Foreign Affairs, Pretoria, "The Situation in Angola," 3 June 1975; NSA, Incoming FOIAs, Box 2A, Joint Chiefs of Staff to Secretary of State, "PRC Military Presence in Zaïre," 4 June 1974; CIARR, National Intelligence Bulletin, "China-Angola," 25 August 1975; NSA, Incoming FOIAs, Box 2A, Joint Chiefs of Staff to Secretary of State, "PRC Military Equipment to FNLA," 16 September 1974.

99. SANA, MEM, 1/572, I15/2, DG Ops, Viljoen, to H SAW, Malan, "Op Savannah—Hulp aan FNLA," 3 September 1975.

100. de Villiers and de Villiers, *PW*, pp. 246–261. See also O'Meara, *Forty Lost Years*, pp. 222–223; James Michael Roherty, *State Security in South Africa: Civil-Military Relations under P.W. Botha* (Armonk, NY; London: M. E. Sharpe, 1992), p. 73.

101. This important point is also clear from Spies, *Operasie Savannah*, p. 147.

102. Prinsloo, *Stem uit die Wildernis*. This title is also a pun on the Wilderness region, located in Botha's constituency of George in the Cape Province.

103. ARCA, PV 528, Hilgard Muller, 3/2/51, Toesprake, Address to the Foreign Affairs Club, Waldorf Hotel, London, 22 September 1975.

104. SANDFA, Group 1- HSAW Chief of Defense Force, Box 172, HSAW/82/1/1, Terroriste Bedrywighede en Onluste: Angola, Volume 1, "Op Savannah: Opsomming van Gebeure tot 10 Jan 76," 13 January 1976.

105. O'Meara, *Forty Lost Years*, pp. 206–207.

106. ARCA, PV 132, B. J. Vorster, 5/1/19-22, Aantekeninge en Dagboeke, Vorster's Dagboek.

107. Seegers, *The Military in the Making of Modern South Africa*, p. 186.
108. Spies, *Operasie Savannah*, p. 147.
109. SANA, 1/1/5-6, 1, Kabinet Notuleregister.
110. Malan, *My Life with the SA Defence Force*, p. 113.
111. Nerys John offers the best summary of the legal basis for Pretoria's wide remit in this area. "[T]he Official Secrets Act (No. 16 of 1956) in conjunction with the Defense Amendment Act (No. 85 of 1967) prohibited the publication of virtually all matters concerned with South Africa's defense, without the express permission of the Minister of Defense. 'Official secrets' were widely defined to include 'anything relating to munitions of war or any military, police, or security matter.' The Defense Act prohibited newspapers from publishing any statement 'relating to any member of the SADF or any activity of the SADF or any force of a foreign country which is calculated to prejudice or embarrass the government in its foreign relations or to alarm or depress members of the public.' The broad scope, and intentional vagueness, of this legislation led newspapers to refer all matters connected with defense, no matter how tenuously, to the defense authorities prior to publication. In this way the press employed what became, in effect, self-censorship." See Nerys John, "South African Intervention in the Angolan Civil War, 1975–1976: Motivations and Implications" (University of Cape Town, 2002), pp. 79, 82.
112. SANA, MEM, 1/572, I15/2, DG Ops, Viljoen, to H SAW, Malan, "Op Savannah—Hulp aan FNLA," 3 September 1975.
113. Interview with Kaas van der Waals, Centurion, 15 August 2011.
114. SANDFA, Group 1- HSAW Chief of Defense Force, Box 172, HSAW/82/1/1, Terroriste Bedrywighede en Onluste: Angola, Volume 1, "Op Savannah: Opsomming van Gebeure tot 10 Jan 76," 13 January 1976.
115. Hamann, *Days of the Generals*, p. 32.
116. Interview with Constand Viljoen, Pretoria, 13 July 2011.
117. Dorning, "A History of Co-Operation: The South African Defence Force's Involvement with the Angolan Resistance Movement Unita—Volume One, 1976–1980," pp. 27–28.
118. Interview with Kaas van der Waals, Centurion, 15 August 2011.
119. Jan Breytenbach, *They Live by the Sword* (Alberton, South Africa: Lemur, 1990), p. 13.
120. Gleijeses, *Conflicting Missions*, pp. 265–272.
121. SANDFA, Group 3- HSAW Chief of Defense Force, Box 420, MI/STRAT/1/7, Die Militêre Bedreiging teen die RSA, Volume 51, Direktoraat Militêre Inligting study, "Die Militêre Bedreiging teen die RSA," 24 October 1975.
122. Spies, *Operasie Savannah*, p. 82.
123. ARCA, PV 132, B. J. Vorster, 5/1/19-22, Aantekeninge en Dagboeke, Vorster's Dagboek.
124. SANA, 1/1/6, 1, Kabinet Notuleregister, 7 October 1975.
125. GFL, National Security Adviser Memoranda of Conversations, Ford Administration, Box 11, Conversation between Ford, Kissinger, Kaunda, and others, 19 April 1975. That Kinshasa might have been willing to abandon its client, the FNLA, is notable here, as is Dar es Salaam's supposed openness to ditching the MPLA. Both points suggest, once more, the ideological fluidity of African politics at this time.
126. Interview with Constand Viljoen, Pretoria, 13 July 2011
127. Spies, *Operasie Savannah*, pp. 82, 147.
128. SANA, MEM, 1/572, I15/2, Wet op Veiligheidsinligting en die Staatsveiligheidsraad, Number 64 of 1972, June 1972.
129. SANA, MEM, 1/572, I15/2, P. W. Botha to Vorster, "Voorlegging aan die Staatsveiligheidsraad Aangaande die Bestaande Gesamentlike Interdepartementele Teen-Insurgensie Komitee," 14 June 1974; SANDFA, Group 3—HSAW Chief of Defense Force, Box 168, SWA I, "Onderhoud met Eerste Minister," 3 October 1974.
130. Interview with Niël Barnard, Cape Town, 11 October 2011.
131. Spies, *Operasie Savannah*, p. 83. The Bloemfontein squadron did not actually enter Angola for several days due to the presence of an OAU fact-finding team in southern Angola.
132. Spies, *Operasie Savannah*, p. 87. Zulu left Rundu at 2 p.m., but it travelled parallel to the border until it arrived at the crossing at Katwitwi (also spelled Katuitui) at 10 p.m. and entered Angola shortly afterward, by which stage SSC authorization would have been given.

133. ARCA, PV 132, B. J. Vorster, 5/1/19-22, Aantekeninge en Dagboeke, Vorster's Dagboek.

134. The course of the open warfare stage of the Angolan Civil War is well known. See Spies, *Operasie Savannah*, pp. 86–129; du Preez, *Avontuur in Angola*; Gleijeses, *Conflicting Missions*, pp. 300–321.

135. Spies, *Operasie Savannah*, p. 149.

136. Interview with Constand Viljoen, Pretoria, 13 July 2011.

137. Spies, *Operasie Savannah*, p. 147.

138. SANDFA, Group 1—HSAW Chief of Defense Force, Box 174, HSAW/82/1/1, Volume 1, Terroriste Bedrywighede en Onluste: Angola, Afdeling Militêre Inligting Weekly Report No 12/75, "Situation in Angola," 31 October 1975, attached to Chief of Staff Intelligence to Chief of the SA Defense Force, 6 November 1975.

139. GFL, National Security Adviser, Presidential Country Files for Africa, 1974–1977, Box 7, Zaïre (3), US Embassy, Kinshasa, to Secretary of State, "Mulcahy Meeting with Holden Roberto," 28 November 1975; SANDFA, Group 1- HSAW Chief of Defense Force, Box 174, HSAW/82/1/1, Volume 1, Terroriste Bedrywighede en Onluste: Angola, Hoof van Staf Inligting to Military Secretary and other senior military officers, Intrep 282/75, "The Situation in Angola," 28 November 1975.

140. SANDFA, Group 1- HSAW Chief of Defense Force, Box 174, HSAW/82/1/1, Volume 1, Terroriste Bedrywighede en Onluste: Angola, Hoof van Staf Inligting to Military Secretary and other senior military officers, Intrep 282/75, "The Situation in Angola," 28 November 1975.

141. ARCA, PV 132, B. J. Vorster, 5/1/19-22, Aantekeninge en Dagboeke, Vorster's Dagboek; Spies, *Operasie Savannah*, pp. 148–149.

142. SANA, 1/1/6, 1, Kabinet Notuleregister, 18 November 1975.

143. Spies, *Operasie Savannah*, pp. 148–149.

144. ARCA, PV 132, B. J. Vorster, 5/1/19-22, Aantekeninge en Dagboeke, Vorster's Dagboek; Spies, *Operasie Savannah*, p. 149.

145. Spies, *Operasie Savannah*, pp. 150, 258.

146. SANDFA, War Diaries (OD), G/Ops/3/3, Box 88, Major W. G. Lombard to Commandant M. Fourie, "Persoonlike Waarnemings: Ops Savannah," 5 March 1976; SANDFA, OD, Box 91, "Werksdokument: Nabetragting: Operasie Savannah," March 1976.

147. ARCA, PV 132, B. J. Vorster, 5/1/19-22, Aantekeninge en Dagboeke, Vorster's Dagboek. The "consensus" did not mean that enthusiasm was equal across the board. There is no reason to think that Fourie or Muller, for example, were as enthused about a military escalation as Viljoen or Botha.

148. Memorandum of Conversation, 40 Committee Meeting, 14 November 1975, in *Foreign Relations of the United States: Southern Africa, 1969–1976*, vol. XXVIII (Washington, DC: State Department, Office of the Historian, 2011), pp. 336–337.

149. The redacted sections of the minutes of the 40 Committee meetings strongly suggest that van den Bergh was Potts's point of contact, as Stockwell suggests: Stockwell, *In Search of Enemies: A CIA Story*, p. 187.

150. Minutes of NSC Meeting, "Angola," 27 June 1975, *Foreign Relations of the United States: Southern Africa, 1969–1976*, p. 269. This bears out Gleijeses's intuition in *Conflicting Missions*: "It is difficult to believe that the CIA did not approach the South Africans. (Relations between BOSS and the CIA were notoriously close.)" See Gleijeses, *Conflicting Missions*, p. 291.

151. Memorandum of Conversation, 40 Committee Meeting, 14 November 1975, in *Foreign Relations of the United States: Southern Africa, 1969–1976*, p. 342.

152. Gleijeses, *Conflicting Missions*, pp. 329–330.

153. "The US government urged South Africa, which might otherwise have hesitated, to act," Piero Gleijeses claims: Piero Gleijeses, "Moscow's Proxy?" *Journal of Cold War Studies* 8, no. 4 (2006): 5–6. See also Gleijeses, *Conflicting Missions*, pp. 273–299.

154. DNSA, *Kissinger Transcripts*, Minutes of Secretary Kissinger's Staff Meeting, 30 January 1976. Nevertheless, American officials' efforts to distance themselves from accusations of cooperation with the toxic apartheid regime were far from truthful. For instance, Ford instructed his African embassies at the height of the diplomatic furor over South Africa's intervention: "The US in no way sought or encouraged the South Africans to become involved in Angola

nor was our advice sought." See GFL, National Security Adviser, Presidential Country Files for Africa, 1974–1977, Box 2, Angola: Presidential Message, Secretary of State to African Embassies, "Presidential Message on Angola," 3 January 1976. Kissinger likewise recalled in his memoirs: "South Africa had opted for intervention without prior consultation with the United States." See Henry Kissinger, *Years of Renewal* (New York: Simon & Schuster, 1999), p. 820. Neither statement was true.

155. GFL, National Security Adviser, Presidential Country Files for Africa, 1974–1977, Box 5, South Africa (2), Horan to Scowcroft, "South Africa Ambassador Johan Botha's Farewell Call on You," 6 June 1975

156. ARCA, PV 132, B. J. Vorster, 5/1/19-22, Aantekeninge en Dagboeke, Vorster's Dagboek.

157. WKL, Public Library of US Diplomacy, Kissinger Cables, Bowdler to State Department, "Angola Situation: Conversation with the Prime Minister," 14 November 1975.

158. WKL, Public Library of US Diplomacy, Kissinger Cables, Bowdler to State Department, "Angola Situation: Conversation with the Prime Minister," 14 November 1975.

159. WKL, Public Library of US Diplomacy, Kissinger Cables, Bowdler to State Department, "Angola: South African Approach to French," 21 November 1975.

160. WKL, Public Library of US Diplomacy, Kissinger Cables, Bowdler to State Department, "Angola Situation: Conversation with the Prime Minister," 14 November 1975.

161. "Mystery of South African Accent in Armored Units," London *Times,* 15 November 1975.

162. *West Africa*, 1 December 1975.

163. London *Times*, 8 and 10 December 1975.

164. DFAA, 1/112/3, 7, Zaïre: Relations with SA, "Note from Zaïre Embassy, Bangui, to Diplomatic and Consular Missions and Representative of International Organizations, Bangui," December 1975.

165. *Pretoria News*, editorial, 17 November 1975.

166. *Star*, editorial, 17 November 1975.

167. For P. W. Botha, see "White troops among forces advancing on Angolan capital," *Times*, 17 November 1975. For Muller, see "Three South African soldiers killed in Angolan border clash," *Times*, 19 November 1975, and "Our forces are not involved in this war," *Rand Daily Mail*, 20 November 1975.

168. DFAA, 1/22/3, 7, Angola: Relations with SA, Secretary for Foreign Affairs, Pretoria, to Ambassador, Ottawa, 19 November 1975, DFAA, 1/22/3, 7, Angola: Relations with SA, Secretary for Foreign Affairs, Pretoria, to Ambassador, Rome, 20 November 1975, DFAA, 1/22/3, 7, Angola: Relations with SA, Secretary for Foreign Affairs, Pretoria, to Ambassador, Washington, 25 November 1975.

169. SANA, 1/1/6, 1, Kabinet Notuleregister, 18 November 1975. While the full details of the intervention only came later, nevertheless the Cabinet was informed of South Africa's role in Angola much earlier than January, as suggested in Geldenhuys, *The Diplomacy of Isolation*, p. 81; John, "South African Intervention in the Angolan Civil War, 1975–1976: Motivations and Implications," p. 87.

170. ARCA, PV 132, B. J. Vorster, 5/1/19-22, Aantekeninge en Dagboeke, Vorster's Dagboek. The outlets invited represented all but the most *verkrampte* viewpoints, and came from both the Perskor and Nasionale Pers conglomerates: *Die Vaderland, Oggendblad, Hoofstad, Die Transvaler, Beeld, Rapport*, and the South African Broadcasting Corporation. Over the ensuing weeks, Botha, SADF officers, and the Prime Minister conducted regular briefings along the same lines. See SANDFA, Group 3 (Volume 1)—AMI/HSI, Box 442, MI/OPS/3/9, Operasies (Spesifiek) Op Savannah, Volume 1, "Vergadering van Minister van Verdediging met Koerant-Redakteurs op Dinsdag, 9 Des 75," 9 December 1975; Spies, *Operasie Savannah*, p. 152; Hamann, *Days of the Generals*, p. 34.

171. Papenfus, *Pik Botha and His Times*, p. 495.

172. SANDFA, Group 35, Box 3, Volume 8, MAN/S/37/2/1, Afdeling Militêre Inligting, Intelligence—Monthly Reports—AFA, H. R. Meintjies, Weermagsattache, to Hoof van Staf Inligting, "Verslag vir November 1975," 4 December 1975.

173. SANA, 1/1/6, 1, Kabinet Notuleregister, 18 November 1975.

174. DFAA, 1/22/3, 7, Angola: Relations with SA, "Risks for détente in Angolan war," *Financial Times*, 18 December 1975.

175. "SA must keep out," editorial, *World*, 22 December 1975. See also John, "South African Intervention in the Angolan Civil War, 1975–1976: Motivations and Implications," pp. 96–97.

176. Spies, *Operasie Savannah*, p. 260.

177. "Angola comes home to roost," *Guardian*, 27 January 1976.

178. Interview with Kaas van der Waals, Centurion, 15 August 2011.

179. Spies, *Operasie Savannah*, p. 153.

180. WKL, Public Library of US Diplomacy, Kissinger Cables, Bowdler to State Department, "Angola: SAG suggests USG provide FNLA/UNITA with badly needed military equipment," 20 November 1975; WKL, Public Library of US Diplomacy, Kissinger Cables, Kissinger to several posts, "Angolan Situation—French Ambassador Approached by Vorster," 20 November 1975.

181. Bat, *Le Syndrome Foccart*, pp. 391–392. For France's program, see Alexandre de Marenches and Christine Ockrent, *Dans Le Secret Des Princes* (Paris: Stock, 1986), pp. 181–194. French archives currently offer little illumination either of the Service de Documentation Extérieure et de Contre-Espionnage (SDECE) program or Paris' diplomatic contacts with Pretoria concerning the Angolan Civil War.

182. Memorandum of Conversation, 40 Committee Meeting, 14 November 1975, in *Foreign Relations of the United States: Southern Africa, 1969–1976*, pp. 339, 341.

183. Memorandum of Conversation, 40 Committee Meeting, 21 November 1975, in *Foreign Relations of the United States: Southern Africa, 1969–1976*, p. 348.

184. GFL, National Security Adviser Memoranda of Conversations, Ford Administration, Box 16, Conversation between Ford and Kissinger, 19 November 1975.

185. Kissinger, *Years of Renewal*, p. 821.

186. DNSA, *Conflicting Missions: Secret Cuban Documents on History of Africa Involvement*, Electronic Briefing Book No. 67, National Archives Record Group 59, Records of the Department of State, Policy Planning Staff, Director's Files (Winston Lord), 1969–1977, Box 373, White House Memorandum of Conversation with Chinese Officials in Beijing, "The Soviet Union; Europe; the Middle East; South Asia; Angola," 3 December 1975; GFL, National Security Adviser, Trip Briefing Books and Cables for Henry Kissinger, 1974–1976, Kissinger Trip File, Box 25, December 10–17, 1975—Europe (Brussels, London, Paris, Nuremberg) TOSEC (3), Ingersoll to Secretary of State Delegation, "Briefing Memorandum," 12 December 1975.

187. WKL, Public Library of US Diplomacy, Kissinger Cables, State Department to US Delegation, Secretary of State, "Action Memorandum—Talking Points for Ambassador Schaufele's Meeting with the French," 1 January 1976.

188. GFL, Remote Archive Capture Series, NSA Backchannel Messages, Box 20, Kissinger to Giscard d'Estaing, 18 December 1975.

189. DNSA, State Department report, "Discussion of Soviet Involvement in Angola," presumably late January or February 1976.

190. DNSA, Secretary of State to US Embassy, Pretoria, "Angola: SAG Requests USG Provides FNLA/UNITA with Military Equipment," 27 November 1975.

191. Hamann, *Days of the Generals*, pp. 40–41.

192. GFL, National Security Adviser, Presidential Country Files for Africa, 1974–1977, Box 6, South Africa: State Department Telegrams: To SECSTATE NODIS (1), Bowdler to Secretary of State, "Angola: Conversation with Prime Minister Vorster," 29 November 1975.

193. SANA, 1/1/6, 1, Kabinet Notuleregister, 3 December 1975.

194. Botha's plan for "Angola-ization" and increased Western economic assistance in the south drew directly on the fourth phase of the original Viljoen-Breytenbach recommendations and the orders given to van Deventer's 101 Taskforce on 14 November. It is unclear whether Botha at this juncture envisaged the carving out of a new and pliant buffer state in southern Angola.

195. Spies, *Operasie Savannah*, p. 259.

196. Gleijeses, *Conflicting Missions*, pp. 316–317.

197. SANDFA, Group 1- HSAW Chief of Defense Force, Box 174, HSAW/82/1/1, Volume 1, Terroriste Bedrywighede en Onluste: Angola, H SAW to P. W. Botha, "HS/11/3/14 Op Savannah(.) Eksklusief vir Minister," 17–19 December 1975. See also SANDFA,

Group 1- HSAW Chief of Defense Force, Box 174, HSAW/82/1/1, Volume 1, Terroriste Bedrywighede en Onluste: Angola, Afdeling Militêre Inligting to Hoof van die SA Weermag, "Situasie in Angola: Weeklikse Oorsig No 18/75," 18 December 1975.

198. SANDFA, Group 3 (Volume 1)—AMI/HSI, Box 442, MI/OPS/3/9, Operasies (Spesifiek) Op Savannah, Volume 1, report, "'n Besoek op 12/13 Desember," late 1975.

199. DFAA, 1/22/3, 7, Angola: Relations with SA, SA Embassy, Washington, to Secretary for Foreign Affairs, 12 December 1975.

200. DNSA, Minutes of Conversation between Kissinger and Mandungu Bula Nyati, Zairean Minister for Foreign Affairs, US Embassy, Paris, 17 December 1975.

201. Interview with Pik Botha, Pretoria, 11 August 2011.

202. Papenfus, *Pik Botha and His Times*, p. 496.

203. DFAA, 1/22/3, 7, Angola: Relations With SA, SA Embassy, Washington, to Die Sekretaris van Buitelandse Sake, 17 December 1975.

204. The better known Clark Amendment of June 1976 extended the applicability of the Tunney Amendment indefinitely.

205. Malan, *My Life with the SA Defence Force*, pp. 130–131.

206. Fourie, "Buitelandse Woelinge om Suid-Afrika, 1939–1985," pp. 195–198.

207. GFL, National Security Adviser, Trip Briefing Books and Cables for Henry Kissinger, 1974–1976, Kissinger Trip File, Box 26, December 26, 1975—Jamaica: TOHAK (3), Scowcroft to Kissinger, likely 26–28 December 1975; Spies, *Operasie Savannah*, pp. 260–263.

208. Fourie, "Buitelandse Woelinge om Suid-Afrika, 1939–1985," pp. 199, 201. See also SANA, 1/1/6, 1, Kabinet Notuleregister, 14 January 1976. For American role, see GFL, National Security Adviser, Trip Briefing Books and Cables for Henry Kissinger, 1974–1976, Kissinger Trip File, Box 25, December 26, 1975—Jamaica: TOHAK (1), Schaufele, Situation Room, to Kissinger, 28 December 1975.

209. "Vingt pays membres de l'OUA acceptent le sommet extraordinaire," *L'Essor*, 19 November 1975.

210. CIARR, Weekly Review, 21 November 1975.

211. DDRS, State Department, Memorandum, "OAU-Angola," 12 January 1976.

212. Westad, *The Global Cold War: Third World Interventions and the Making of Our Times*, p. 237.

Chapter 6

1. Spies, *Operasie Savannah*, p. 313.

2. Alden, *Apartheid's Last Stand*, p. 46.

3. Vladimir Zubok, *A Failed Empire: The Soviet Union in the Cold War from Stalin to Gorbachev* (Chapel Hill: University of North Carolina Press, 2007), pp. 251, 253.

4. See Castro's monologue in CWIHP, *Cuba in the Cold War*, Central State Archive, Sofia, Fond 1-B, Record 60, File 194, Minutes of the meeting between Todor Zhivkov and Fidel Castro, Sofia, 11 March 1976; Gleijeses, *Conflicting Missions*, pp. 246–265.

5. DNSA, *Conflicting Missions: Secret Cuban Documents on History of Africa Involvement*, Electronic Briefing Book No. 67, Centro de Informacion de la Defensa de las Fuerzas Armadas Revolucionarias, Major Raúl Díaz Argüelles to Major Raúl Castro Ruiz, "Report on visit to Angola," 11 August 1975.

6. For scholars, the more pertinent question is not just why the apartheid regime found it impossible to perceive events through a different prism, but why the other actors, ideological counterpoints in the Cold War dichotomy, reacted in much the same way. See Masuda, *Cold War Crucible: The Korean Conflict and the Postwar World*. Such realizations might provide entry points for others to extend Masuda's findings beyond Western countries to those from the other side of the Cold War, thereby greatly expanding the reach and significance of his framework.

7. GFL, National Security Adviser, Presidential Country Files for Africa, 1974–1977, Box 6, South Africa (4), Bowdler to Secretary of State, "Conversation with PM Vorster," 19 February 1976.

8. ISP, Deposit 4, Box 6, Détente: Official Communications with South Africa, Volume 3, Rhodesian Diplomatic Mission to Gaylard, 3 February 1976.

9. *Newsweek*, 17 May 1976.

10. *Hansard*, House of Assembly Debates, 17 April 1978, col 4852. It should be noted that by the time Botha made these comments, the regime's relationship with Washington was in a terrible state. This helps explain why he was taking the extreme step of hanging the US out to dry at this time, in contrast to his more carefully worded statements in 1976.

11. Jannie Geldenhuys, *A General's Story: From an Era of War and Peace* (Johannesburg: Jonathan Ball, 1995), p. 54.

12. Given the minimalist South African Cabinet minutes, the dearth of available American cables to and from South Africa during this period, the informal and undocumented nature of much of Pretoria's decision making, our limited understanding of the van den Bergh–Vorster channel, and the substantial redactions in many of the currently available American documents, our understanding of US–South Africa cooperation in Angola remains unavoidably incomplete. For instance, in the thirty-five-page official CIA history of the conflict, a sizeable section remains fully withheld, covering precisely the area in the narrative where one would expect to find mention of coordination with the South Africans. See CIARR, CIA Office of Regional and Political Analysis, Section B in "Soviet and Cuban Intervention in the Angolan Civil War," March 1977.

13. SANDFA, Group 3 (vol 2)—HSI/AMI, Box 637, MI/PLANS/8/1/2, "Waardering oor die Moontlike Gebruik/Aanwending van Chipenda/FNLA tot Voordeel van RSA," 25 June 1975.

14. WKL, Public Library of US Diplomacy, Kissinger Cables, Bowdler to Secretary of State and others, "USG Connection with South African Involvement in Angola," 11 May 1976.

15. Gerhart, *Black Power in South Africa: The Evolution of an Ideology*; Fatton, *Black Consciousness in South Africa: The Dialectics of Ideological Resistance to White Supremacy*; Halisi, *Black Political Thought in the Making of South African Democracy*; Magaziner, *The Law and the Prophets: Black Consciousness in South Africa, 1968–1977*.

16. Thula Simpson, "Military Combat Work: The Reconstitution of the ANC's Armed Underground, 1971–1976," *African Studies* 70, no. 1 (2011).

17. Charney, "Civil Society vs. the State: Identity, Institutions, and the Black Consciousness Movement in South Africa," pp. 438–463.

18. Magaziner, *The Law and the Prophets: Black Consciousness in South Africa, 1968–1977*, pp. 144–145.

19. "'SA will never be the same again,'" *Weekend World*, 22 August 1971.

20. "What Blacks Think of Vorster," letters to the editor, M. J. Pitso, Bloemfontein, and Isaac Moeletsi, Pretoria, *World*, 14 January 1976. Polling took place from November 1975 onwards.

21. "Don't miss this chance, Mr. Vorster," editorial, *World*, 15 January 1976.

22. The literature on the rise of black militancy has traditionally given Angola short shrift in favor of focusing on the transformative effect of Soweto. See the BCM literature cited at note 15. For an exception, see O'Meara, *Forty Lost Years*, p. 180.

23. "Black S. Africans cool on Angola," *Guardian*, 24 January 1976.

24. "It's time to consult urban Blacks," editorial, *World*, 7 April 1976.

25. "Get rid of this curse," editorial, *World*, 10 March 1976.

26. "Give urban Blacks something to defend," editorial, *World*, 12 March 1976. See also Grundlingh, "The Recruitment of South African Blacks for Participation in the Second World War."

27. "Buthelezi speaks out on Mangope's move for independence," *World*, 11 November 1975.

28. "Zulu chief attacked for majority rule demand," London *Times*, 19 March 1976.

29. GFL, National Security Adviser, Presidential Country Files for Africa, 1974–1977, Box 6, South Africa (4), Bowdler to Secretary of State, "Conversation with PM Vorster," 19 February 1976.

30. *Hansard*, House of Assembly Debates, 30 January 1976, col 375.

31. SANDFA, Group 4—P. W. Botha, Box 143, 76/1, Strategie: Algemeen, Volume 2, Direkteur Strategiese Studies, "Huidige Stand van Militêre Bedreiging teen die RSA," March 1976.

32. DFAA, 1/99/12, 23, Africa: Communism in Africa, Secretary for Foreign Affairs, Cape Town, to All Heads of Mission, "Soviet and Cuban Involvement and Objectives in Southern Africa," 4 May 1976.

33. SANDFA, OD, Box 91, "Werksdokument: Nabetragting: Operasie Savannah," March 1976.

34. Malan, *My Life with the SA Defence Force*, pp. 138–9. See also SANDFA, Group 4—P. W. Botha, Box 143, 76/1, Strategie: Algemeen, Volume 2, Direkteur Strategiese Studies, "Huidige Stand van Militêre Bedreiging teen die RSA," March 1976; Interview with Constand Viljoen, Pretoria, 13 July 2011.

35. SANDFA, OD, Box 133, "Voorligting Gegee Deur Generaal van Deventer," 18 March 1977.

36. SANA, 1/1/6, 1, Kabinet Notuleregister, 2 December 1975.

37. SANDFA, Group 3 (Volume 1)—AMI/HSI, Box 442, MI/OPS/3/9, Operasies (Spesifiek) Op Savannah, Volume 1, report, "'n Besoek op 12/13 Desember," late 1975.

38. de Villiers and de Villiers, *PW*, p. 241.

39. *Hansard*, House of Assembly Debates, 29 January 1976, col 296.

40. de Villiers and de Villiers, *PW*, p. 241.

41. ARCA, PV 408, NP Caucus, Notule, 22 January 1976.

42. ARCA, PV 408, NP Caucus, Notule, 22 January 1976.

43. *Hansard*, House of Assembly Debates, 26 January 1976, col 72; Botha made much the same claim, 6 May 1976, col 6210. For the government's defense of Operation Savannah generally, see 26–30 January 1976, cols 24–396.

44. *Hansard*, House of Assembly Debates, 26 January 1976, col 54.

45. *Hansard*, House of Assembly Debates, 6 May 1976, col 6211.

46. *Hansard*, House of Assembly Debates, 6 May 1976, cols 6211–2.

47. *Hansard*, House of Assembly Debates, 6 May 1976, cols 6209–6211, 6227. The Progressive Reform Party, home at the time of Helen Suzman and Colin Eglin, comprised the third most represented party in Parliament. Unlike the NP and the UP, it approached what today would be recognized as a form of liberal democratic inclusiveness.

48. *Hansard*, House of Assembly Debates, 30 January 1976, col 369. The reference here is to the Afrikaans edition of *Hansard*, so as to capture the exact words of Vorster's insult: "Laat ek, soos ons dit in die volksmond het, vir hom dit sê: 'Waarom gaan sit jy nie waar jou mond is nie?'" This is represented in the English edition as: 'Why don't you take your seat where your mouth is?' I have opted for a more colloquial translation that I hope better captures the deliberate crudeness of the original.

49. John, "South African Intervention in the Angolan Civil War, 1975–1976: Motivations and Implications," p. 97. There was also a difference in response based on culture and language. Afrikaners were more likely to approve of the government's actions than English-speakers (70 to 55 percent) and less likely to disapprove (14 to 22 percent).

50. AB, 3/84/1 Afrikaner, Box 3/1/2, Algemeen: Ons betrokkenheid in Angola, "Ons Betrokkenheid in Angola," March 1976. Emphasis in the original.

51. AB, 3/84/1 Afrikaner, Box 3/1/2, Algemeen: Ons betrokkenheid in Angola, "Ons Betrokkenheid in Angola," March 1976. Emphasis in the original.

52. SANA, 1/1/6, 1, Kabinet Notuleregister, 14 January 1976; Jaster, *South Africa's Narrowing Security Options*, p. 25.

53. AB, 3/84/1 Afrikaner, Box 3/1/2, Algemeen: Ons betrokkenheid in Angola, "Ons Betrokkenheid in Angola," March 1976.

54. SANDFA, Group 3- HSAW Chief of Defense Force, Box 181, Komp/503/1/8, SADF Five Year Plan, 27 May 1975.

55. Calculating how much money Defense received in various budgets is difficult. First, a distinction must be drawn between what Defense asked for and what it actually received. Second, care must be taken to use like-for-like figures, as some are calculated in current rand and and others in real terms. Third, inflation was a serious problem at this time, reaching 15.5 percent in 1975–76: ARCA, PV 203, P. W. Botha, C3/6/2/2, Politieke Aangeleenthede: Kongresse: NP van Kaapland, Head of the SADF to Private Secretary, "Beskrywingspunte: Nasionale Party Kongres van Kaapland," 15 August 1977. Finally, Defense received funds from the Main Budget, the Supplementary Budget, and, from 1976 onward, on an ad hoc basis for specific necessities. Every effort has been made here to take these issues into consideration.

56. SANA, MEM, 1/572, I15/2, P. W. Botha to Vorster, 30 October 1975.

57. SANA, 1/1/6, Kabinet Notuleregister, 3 December 1975.

58. SANA, MEM, 1/572, I15/2, P. W. Botha to Vorster, 30 October 1975.

59. SANA, 1/1/6, Kabinet Notuleregister, 25 February 1976.

60. SANA, 1/1/6, Kabinet Notuleregister, 3 March 1976.

61. SANDFA, Group 1- HSAW Chief of Defense Force, Box 172, HSAW/82/1/1, Terroriste Bedrywighede en Onluste: Angola, Volume 1, "Meningspeiling vir Rapport," April 1976.

62. SANA, 1/1/6, Kabinet Notuleregister, 15 June 1976.

63. SANDFA, Group 1—HSAW Chief of Defense Force, Box 150, HSAW/14/1/1, Volume 1, Lëerwapens: Beleid, HS to HSAW Kaapstad, May 1976.

64. SANDFA, Group 1—HSAW Chief of Defense Force, Box 150, HSAW/14/1/1, Volume 1, Lëerwapens: Beleid, HS to HSAW Kaapstad, May 1976.

65. ARCA, PV 203, PS 6/12/3, P. W. Botha, Politiek en Algemeen, Minutes of Meeting of the Krygstuigraad, Annexure A, 14 April 1976; Malan, *My Life with the SA Defence Force*, pp. 231–237.

66. SANDFA, Group 1- HSAW Chief of Defense Force, Box 172, HSAW/82/1/1, Terroriste Bedrywighede en Onluste: Angola, Volume 1, Biermann to P. W. Botha, "Toekomstige RSA Handelswyse in die Suid Angola/Noord SWA Grensgebied," 10 February 1976.

67. SANDFA, Group 1- HSAW Chief of Defense Force, Box 172, HSAW/82/1/1, Terroriste Bedrywighede en Onluste: Angola, Volume 1, Biermann to P. W. Botha, "Toekomstige RSA Handelswyse in die Suid Angola/Noord SWA Grensgebied," 10 February 1976.

68. SANDFA, Group 1- HSAW Chief of Defense Force, Box 172, HSAW/82/1/1, Terroriste Bedrywighede en Onluste: Angola, Volume 1, Biermann to P. W. Botha, "Toekomstige RSA Handelswyse in die Suid Angola/Noord SWA Grensgebied," 10 February 1976.

69. Interview with Chris Thirion, Pretoria, 6 July 2011.

70. For South Africa, see DFAA, 1/22/3 OS, 8, Angola: Relations with SA, SA Ambassador, Rome, to Sekretaris van Buitelandse Sake, Pretoria, 2 February 1976; NSA, Incoming FOIAs, Box 2A, Defense Intelligence Agency to US European Command, "Angola-South Africa: Aid For UNITA," 3 November 1976; GFL, National Security Adviser, Presidential Country Files for Africa, 1974–1977, Box 6, South Africa (3), Robert S. Smith to William Hyland, "South African Military Links with UNITA (Angolan Opposition Movement)—Implications of Namibia's Independence on Struggle within Angola," 27 October 1976. As for the Americans, they were very reluctant to keep using unreliable Zaïre as a primary conduit to anticommunist groups in Angola: GFL, National Security Adviser, Presidential Country Files for Africa, 1974–1977, Box 1, Angola (3), Clinton E. Granger and Les Janka to Brent Scowcroft, "Overt Funding for Angola," 16 January 1976. Nevertheless, they ultimately turned to Mobutu once more, this time to funnel support to UNITA: GFL, National Security Adviser, Presidential Country Files for Africa, 1974–1977, Box 7, Zaïre (3), Secretary of State to US Embassy, Kinshasa, "Message for President Mobutu from the Secretary," 18 February 1976.

71. NSA, Incoming FOIAs, Box 2A, Defense Intelligence Agency to US European Command, "Angola-South Africa: Aid For UNITA," 3 November 1976.

72. This was the forerunner of the infamous "destabilization" strategy that would become a hallmark of the security policies of the P. W. Botha era (1978–89).

73. DFAA, 1/156/3, 14, Rhodesia: Relations with SA, Daantjie Olivier, SA Consul, Salisbury, to Fourie, 7 April 1976.

74. "SA détente jolted: 'We can no longer talk to racists,'" *Times of Zambia*, 1 August 1976.

75. GFL, National Security Adviser, Presidential Country Files for Africa, 1974–1977, Box 6, South Africa: State Department Telegrams: To SECSTATE EXDIS, US Embassy, Pretoria, to Secretary of State, "Responsiveness of South African Military to Civilian Control," 25 August 1976.

76. NSA, Incoming FOIAs, Box 2A, Defense Intelligence Agency to US European Command, "Angola-South Africa: Aid For UNITA," 3 November 1976.

77. *Hansard*, House of Assembly Debates, 30 January 1976, col 356.

78. DFAA, 1/99/19, 18, Africa: SA Policy in Africa and Relations with African States, Tom Wheeler, SA Embassy, London, to Secretary for Foreign Affairs, Pretoria, "IISS Discussion: 'Is Détente Dead?'" 31 March 1976.

79. DFAA, 1/14/3, 5, Portugal Relations with South Africa, Secretary for Foreign Affairs to All Heads of Mission, "Extracts from Thirtieth Session of the United Nations General Assembly 6–9 October," 28 October 1975.

80. DFAA, 1/14/3, 5, Portugal Relations with South Africa, Secretary for Foreign Affairs to All Heads of Mission, "Extracts from Thirtieth Session of the United Nations General Assembly 6–9 October," 28 October 1975.

81. ISP, Deposit 4, Box 2, Records of Meetings 1973–1978, First Record of Meeting between Smith, Vorster, and others, Pretoria, 13 June 1976.

82. ISP, Deposit 4, Box 4, Negotiations with ANC (Nkomo) Minutes, Record of Meeting between Representatives of the Rhodesian Government and the African National Council, 19 March 1976.

83. ISP, Deposit 4, Box 4, Negotiations with ANC (Nkomo) Minutes, Record of Meeting between Representatives of the Rhodesian Government and the African National Council, 7 January 1976; ISP, Deposit 4, Box 4, Negotiations with ANC (Nkomo) Minutes, Annexure "C," Record of Meeting between Representatives of the Rhodesian Government and the African National Council, 16 January 1976.

84. ISP, Deposit 4, Box 4, Negotiations with ANC (Nkomo) Minutes, Record of Meeting between Representatives of the Rhodesian Government and the African National Council, 22 January 1976.

85. ISP, Deposit 4, Box 4, Negotiations with ANC (Nkomo) Minutes, Record of Meeting between Representatives of the Rhodesian Government and the African National Council, 22 January 1976.

86. ISP, Deposit 4, Box 4, Negotiations with ANC (Nkomo) Minutes, Record of Meeting between Representatives of the Rhodesian Government and the African National Council, 26 February 1976; SANA, 1/1/6, 1, Kabinet Notuleregister, 17 March 1976.

87. ISP, Deposit 5, Box 22, Prime Minister's Personal File: General Correspondence, Press Interview with Smith, 20 March 1976.

88. Tamarkin, *The Making of Zimbabwe: Decolonization in Regional and International Politics*, p. 111.

89. ARCA, PV 408, NP Caucus, Notule, 22 January 1976.

90. ARCA, PV 408, NP Caucus, Notule, 24 March 1976.

91. SANA, 1/1/6, 1, Kabinet Notuleregister, 14 January 1976.

92. SANDFA, Group 4 - P. W. Botha, Box 171, MV/56/6/1, Volume 3, Afdeling van Militêre Inligting, Weekly Report 2/76, 16 January 1976, attached to Hoof van die SA Weermag to Die Militêre Sekretaris, "Situasie in Angola," 29 January 1976.

93. AB, 3/84/1 Afrikaner, Box 3/1/2, Algemeen: Ons betrokkenheid in Angola, "Ons Betrokkenheid in Angola," March 1976. Emphasis in original.

94. DFAA, 1/156/3, 14, Rhodesia: Relations with SA, SA Embassy, London, to Secretary for Foreign Affairs, 10 February 1976.

95. AB, 1976/2-5URanotDB, Box 1/1/23, 1 Besluite: Agendas & Notules, "Gesprek oor Angola," 13 February 1976.

96. CWIHP, *Cuba in the Cold War*, Central State Archive, Sofia, Fond 1-B, Record 60, File 194, Minutes of the meeting between Todor Zhivkov and Fidel Castro, Sofia, 11 March 1976.

97. DFAA, 1/113/3, 10, Mocambique: Relations with SA, Nico Nel to Sekretaris van Buitelandse Sake, "Skakeling met die Mosambiekse Regering," 4 March 1976.

98. ISP, Deposit 3, Box 1, Rhodesia Government: Cabinet Minutes (Secretary's Standard File), Volume 5, Annexure to 11th Meeting, 16 March 1976

99. DFAA, 1/156/3, 14, Rhodesia: Relations with SA, BOSS report, B. P. De V. Campbell, undated, likely early March.

100. ARCA, PV 132, B. J. Vorster, 2/6/1/51, Korrespondensie, "Russ Tanks for Mozambique," *Los Angeles Times*, 8 March 1976.

101. GFL, National Security Adviser, Presidential Country Files for Africa, 1974–1977, Box 6, South Africa (4), Bowdler to Secretary of State, "Conversation with PM Vorster," 19 February 1976.

102. SANDFA, Group 3 (Volume 1)- AMI/HSI, Box 403, INT/37/6, report, "The Effect of the Developments in Angola on the Security Situations of Rhodesia and the RSA," 27 February 1976.

103. DFAA, 1/113/3, 10, Mocambique: Relations with SA, Killen to Fourie, "Direct Contact with Mosambique Government," 5 February 1976.

104. SANA, MEM, 1/563, I13/2, Eerste Minister: Buitelandse Sake, Minister van Buitelandse Sake to Vorster, 28 April 1976; Fourie, "Buitelandse Woelinge om Suid-Afrika, 1939–1985," pp. 208–211. See also Christopher Saunders, "The South Africa-Angola Talks, 1976–1984: A Little-Known Cold War Thread," *Kronos* 37 (November 2011).

105. The costs involved, all borne by Pretoria, were substantial: 438,000 rand to convert the venue into a suitable facility, and a further 315,000 rand for travel costs for delegates as well as a budget for the white constitutional gathering. See van Wyk, *Dirk Mudge: Reënmaker van die Namib*, p. 50.

106. AB, 1976/2-5URanotDB, Box 1/1/23, 1 Besluite: Agendas & Notules, "Gesprek oor Angola," 13 February 1976.

107. GFL, National Security Adviser Memoranda of Conversations, Ford Administration, Box 18, Conversation between Kissinger, Scowcroft, and Pik Botha, 15 April 1976. Vorster reiterated this timetable to Smith in June: ISP, Deposit 4, Box 2, Records of Meetings 1973–1978, Second Record of Meeting between Smith, Vorster, and others, Pretoria, 13 June 1976.

108. "1976: SA se beslissingsjaar," editorial, *Volkshandel*, March 1976.

109. Turnhalle was far more successful in repealing petty apartheid in SWA than Pretoria was in South Africa. See Christopher Ford, "South African Foreign Policy since 1965: The Cases of Rhodesia and Namibia" (PhD diss., Oxford University, 1991), p. 135.

110. Interview with Dirk Mudge, Otjiwarongo, 1 August 2011.

111. ARCA, PV 203, P. W. Botha, 1/V9/1, 1 Onderwerpslêers, 1/V9 Vorster, adv. B. J., Press Conference of the Honorable B. J. Vorster, Zürich, 6 September 1976.

112. AB, 1976/2-5URanotDB, Box 1/1/23, 1 Besluite: Agendas & Notules, "Gesprek oor Angola," 13 February 1976.

113. DFAA, 1/22/3, 8A, Angola Relations With South Africa, "Soviet Advance in Africa," Interview with John Vorster, *Sunday Telegraph*, 14 March 1976.

114. SANDFA, Group 1- HSAW Chief of Defense Force, Box 175, HSAW/82/1/3, Terroriste Bedrywighede en Onluste: Rhodesië, Volume 1, "Rhodesië: Militêre Bedreiging en Veiligheidsmagte," attached to Chief of Staff, Intelligence, to Malan, 23 April 1976.

115. SANDFA, Group 1- HSAW Chief of Defense Force, Box 175, HSAW/82/1/3, Terroriste Bedrywighede en Onluste: Rhodesië, Volume 1, "Rhodesië: Militêre Bedreiging en Veiligheidsmagte," attached to Chief of Staff, Intelligence, to Malan, 23 April 1976.

116. ISP, Deposit 4, Box 6, Détente: Official Communications with South Africa, Volume 3, Rhodesian Diplomatic Mission to Gaylard, 26 January 1976; Smith, *The Great Betrayal*, p. 191.

117. This was a recurrent theme in the *Times of Zambia*, late January and early February 1976.

118. SANA, 1/1/6, Kabinet Notuleregister, 3 March 1976.

119. In his memoirs, Kissinger tellingly labeled Kaunda "the closet moderate": Kissinger, *Years of Renewal*, p. 937.

120. SANA, 1/1/6, Kabinet Notuleregister, 3 March 1976; ISP, Deposit 4, Box 6, Détente: Official Communications with South Africa, Volume 3, Rhodesian Diplomatic Representative, Hawkins, to Gaylard, 3 March 1976.

121. GFL, National Security Adviser Memoranda of Conversations, Ford Administration, Box 17, Conversation between Ford, Kissinger, and Rumsfeld, 26 February 1976; GFL, US National Security Institutional Files, 1974–1977, Box 44, NSSM 241—United States Policy in Southern Africa (1), Interagency Review, "Southern Africa: Contingencies and Options," 11 March 1976.

122. GFL, Minutes of National Security Council Meeting, 7 April 1976, at http://www.fordlibrarymuseum.gov/library/document/0312/nscmin.asp.

123. NSA, Incoming FOIAs, Box 7C, Winston Lord to Kissinger, "The Soviets and Southern Africa," 12 March 1976.

124. GFL, US National Security Institutional Files, 1974–1977, Box 44, NSSM 241—United States Policy in Southern Africa (1), Interagency Review, "Southern Africa: Contingencies and Options," 11 March 1976.

125. UKNA, FCO 82/662, Messages Passed between Henry Kissinger and Secretary of State for Foreign and Commonwealth Affairs, FCO to UK Embassy, Washington DC, 15 March 1976. For a detailed analysis of the British angle of the Kissinger Initiatives, see Sue Onslow,

"'We Must Gain Time': South Africa, Rhodesia, and the Kissinger Initiative of 1976," *South African Historical Journal* 56 (2006).

126. GFL, Minutes of National Security Council Meeting, 7 April 1976, at http://www.fordlibrarymuseum.gov/library/document/0312/nscmin.asp.

127. ISP, Deposit 4, Box 6, Détente: Official Communications with South Africa, Volume 4, Rhodesian Diplomatic Mission to Gaylard, 21 May 1976.

128. ARCA, PV 408, NP Caucus, Notule, 22 January 1976.

129. GFL, National Security Adviser, Trip Briefing Books and Cables for Henry Kissinger, 1974–1976, Kissinger Trip File, Box 38, June 6–13, 1976—Latin America—TOSEC (5), Briefing Book for HAK—Vorster Meeting (1), Roger Harrison to Scowcroft, "Briefing Book for the Kissinger-Vorster Meeting," 21 June 1976.

130. GFL, National Security Adviser Memoranda of Conversations, Ford Administration, Box 17, Conversation between Scowcroft, Arthur House, NSC Fellow, John McGoff of Panex Corporation, and Les de Villiers, South African Deputy Secretary of Information, 21 January 1976.

131. DNSA, *Kissinger Transcripts*, Minutes of Meeting between Pik Botha, Kissinger, Scowcroft, and Rodman, Washington, D. C., 13 July 1976.

132. DNSA, *Kissinger Transcripts*, Memorandum of Conversation between Smith, Kissinger, and Vorster, 19 September 1976.

133. GFL, National Security Adviser Memoranda of Conversations, Ford Administration, Box 18, Conversation between Kissinger, Scowcroft, and Pik Botha, 15 April 1976.

134. GFL, National Security Adviser Memoranda of Conversations, Ford Administration, Box 18, Conversation between Kissinger, Scowcroft, and Pik Botha, 15 April 1976. The Carter Administration would draw no such distinction, instead insisting upon tangible progress toward majority rule in all three places simultaneously. This cost it South Africa's cooperation in the region.

135. DNSA, Transcript of Kissinger's Speech in Lusaka, 27 April 1976.

136. "Kissinger's African Speech," editorial, *Washington Post*, 29 April 1976.

137. GFL, National Security Adviser, Presidential Country Files for Africa, 1974–1977, Box 6, South Africa: State Department Telegrams: SECSTATE NODIS, Bowdler to Secretary of State, "Vorster-Kissinger Meeting: Strategy Considerations," 12 June 1976.

138. SANA, 1/1/6, 1, Kabinet Notuleregister, 3 August 1976.

139. GFL, National Security Adviser, Presidential Country Files for Africa, 1974–1977, Box 6, South Africa: State Department Telegrams: SECSTATE NODIS, Bowdler to Secretary of State, "Vorster-Kissinger Meeting: Strategy Considerations," 12 June 1976.

140. ISP, Deposit 4, Box 2, Records of Meetings 1973–1978, Second Record of Meeting between Smith, Vorster, and others, Pretoria, 13 June 1976.

141. GFL, National Security Adviser Memoranda of Conversations, Ford Administration, Box 18, Conversation between Kissinger, Scowcroft, and Pik Botha, 15 April 1976.

142. ARCA, PV 408, NP Caucus, Notule, 22 January 1976.

143. SANDFA, Group 4—Chief of Staff Operations, Box 12, DGSS/4/3/2, Doktrine Totale Strategiese Beleid, SA Verdedigingsverdrag, report, "The Joint Defense of Southern Africa," February 1976.

144. SANDFA, Group 4—Chief of Staff Operations, Box 12, DGSS/4/3/2, Doktrine Totale Strategiese Beleid, SA Verdedigingsverdrag, report, "The Joint Defense of Southern Africa," February 1976. Ironically, the hawks would end up championing a variant of this policy in the form of the Constellation of Southern African States just a few years later: Alden, *Apartheid's Last Stand*, pp. 103–104.

145. Smith, *The Great Betrayal*, pp. 193–194.

146. DFAA, 1/22/3, 8A, Angola Relations with South Africa, "Soviet Advance in Africa," Interview with John Vorster, *Sunday Telegraph*, 14 March 1976.

147. Ford, "South African Foreign Policy since 1965: The Cases of Rhodesia and Namibia," p. 37.

148. SANA, 1/1/6, Kabinet Notuleregister, 3 March 1976. See also SANA, 1/1/6, Kabinet Notuleregister, 3 August 1976 and 28 September 1976; ARCA, PV 408, NP Caucus, Notule, 24 March 1976.

149. This was roughly what ended up transpiring over the next few years.

150. GFL, National Security Adviser, Presidential Country Files for Africa, 1974–1977, Box 6, South Africa (4), Bowdler to Secretary of State, "Conversation with PM Vorster," 19 February 1976. For more, see Ford, "South African Foreign Policy since 1965: The Cases of Rhodesia and Namibia," pp. 85–8.
151. SANA, 1/1/6, Kabinet Notuleregister, 3 March 1976. Emphasis in the original.
152. ISP, Deposit 4, Box 6, Détente: Official Communications with South Africa, Volume 3, Rhodesian Diplomatic Representative, Hawkins to Gaylard, 3 March 1976.
153. ARCA, PV 408, NP Caucus, Notule, 24 March 1976.
154. Smith, The Great Betrayal, pp. 186–188.
155. ISP, Deposit 3, Box 1, Rhodesia Government: Cabinet Minutes (Secretary's Standard File), Volume 5, Annexure to 45th Meeting, 28 October 1975.
156. Smith, The Great Betrayal, pp. 183, 228.
157. Smith, The Great Betrayal, pp. 196–197.
158. Flower, Serving Secretly, p. 157.
159. Smith, The Great Betrayal, p. 228.

Chapter 7

1. DNSA, Transcript of Kissinger's Speech in Lusaka, 27 April 1976.
2. DFAA, 1/156/3, 14, Rhodesia: Relations with SA, "South Africa to End All Military Aid to Rhodesia," London Times, 10 May 1976.
3. ISP, Deposit 4, Box 6, Détente: Official Communications with South Africa, Volume 3, Hawkins to Gaylard, 30 April 1976.
4. ISP, Deposit 4, Box 2, Records of Meetings 1973–1978, First Record of Meeting between Smith, Vorster, and others, Pretoria, 13 June 1976.
5. ISP, Deposit 4, Box 2, Records of Meetings 1973–1978, First Record of Meeting between Smith, Vorster, and others, Pretoria, 13 June 1976.
6. ISP, Deposit 4, Box 6, Détente: Official Communications with South Africa, Volume 3, Gaylard to Rhodesian Diplomatic Mission, 9 February 1976.
7. ISP, Deposit 4, Box 2, Records of Meetings 1973–1978, First Record of Meeting between Smith, Vorster, and others, Pretoria, 13 June 1976; Fourie, "Buitelandse Woelinge om Suid-Afrika, 1939–1985," p. 215.
8. Fourie, "Buitelandse Woelinge om Suid-Afrika, 1939–1985," p. 216.
9. Kissinger's memoirs do provide some detail of the private meetings: Kissinger, Years of Renewal, pp. 968–972. It must be stressed, however, that Kissinger's memoirs repeatedly deviate from or do not accurately reflect the existing archival record, especially in instances where American power was closely aligned with that of the apartheid regime. Therefore, where no archival record exists or is available, as for the private meetings with Vorster, the memoirs should at least be read with caution.
10. Donald Sole, "This Above All": Reminiscences of a South African Diplomat, p. 333.
11. GFL, National Security Adviser Memoranda of Conversations, Ford Administration, Box 20, Minutes of Meeting between Kissinger, Vorster, and others, Bodenmais, Bavaria, West Germany, 23 June 1976.
12. GFL, National Security Adviser Memoranda of Conversations, Ford Administration, Box 20, Minutes of Meeting between Kissinger, Vorster, and others, Bodenmais, Bavaria, West Germany, 23 June 1976.
13. Fourie, "Buitelandse Woelinge om Suid-Afrika, 1939–1985," p. 217.
14. GFL, National Security Adviser, Presidential Country Files for Africa, 1974–1977, Box 6, South Africa: State Department Telegrams: SECSTATE NODIS, Bowdler to Secretary of State, "Vorster-Kissinger Meeting: Strategy Considerations," 12 June 1976.
15. GFL, National Security Adviser Memoranda of Conversations, Ford Administration, Box 20, Minutes of Meeting between Kissinger, Vorster, and others, Bodenmais, Bavaria, West Germany, 23 June 1976.
16. GFL, National Security Adviser Memoranda of Conversations, Ford Administration, Box 20, Minutes of Meeting between Kissinger, Vorster, and others, Bodenmais, Bavaria, West Germany, 23 June 1976.

17. GFL, National Security Adviser, Trip Briefing Books and Cables for Henry Kissinger, 1974–1976, Kissinger Trip File, Box 38, June 20–28, 1976—Paris, Munich, et al., HAK Messages for the President, Scowcroft to Ford, 24 June 1976.
18. DNSA, *Kissinger Transcripts*, Minutes of Conversation between Kissinger, Botha, Scowcroft, Schaufele, and Rodman, 26 July 1976.
19. DNSA, *Kissinger Transcripts*, Minutes of Meeting between Pik Botha, Kissinger, Scowcroft, and Rodman, Washington, D. C., 13 July 1976.
20. ISP, Deposit 4, Box 6, Détente: Official Communications with South Africa, Volume 4, Rhodesian Diplomatic Mission to Gaylard, 29 June 1976.
21. ISP, Deposit 4, Box 6, Détente: Official Communications with South Africa, Volume 4, Rhodesian Diplomatic Mission to Gaylard, 29 June 1976.
22. ISP, Deposit 4, Box 6, Détente: Official Communications with South Africa, Volume 4, Rhodesian Diplomatic Mission to Gaylard, 29 June 1976.
23. ISP, Deposit 4, Box 6, Détente: Official Communications with South Africa, Volume 4, Rhodesian Diplomatic Mission to Gaylard, 8 July 1976.
24. R. W. Johnson, *How Long Will South Africa Survive?* (New York: Oxford University Press, 1977), pp. 216–220.
25. GFL, National Security Adviser, Presidential Country Files for Africa, 1974–1977, Box 6, South Africa: State Department Telegrams: SECSTATE NODIS, Bowdler to Secretary of State, "Vorster-Kissinger Meeting: Strategy Considerations," 12 June 1976.
26. Dirk Mudge, "From South-West Africa to Namibia: My Experiences Along a Crooked Road to an Unknown Destination," (Unknown), p. 3.
27. *Hansard*, House of Assembly Debates, 30 January 1976, col. 361.
28. ARCA, PV 203, P. W. Botha, 1/V9/1, 1 Onderwerpsléers, 1/V9 Vorster, adv. B. J., Onderhoud met sy Edele Die Eerste Minister deur Morkel van Tonder, SAUK, 13 September 1976.
29. GFL, National Security Adviser, Presidential Country Files for Africa, 1974–1977, Box 6, South Africa: State Department Telegrams: SECSTATE NODIS, Bowdler to Secretary of State, "Vorster-Kissinger Meeting: Strategy Considerations," 12 June 1976.
30. SANDFA, Group 3—HSAW Chief of Defense Force, Box 168, SWA I, "Samesprekings Eerste Minister," 24 November 1976.
31. DNSA, *Kissinger Transcripts*, Minutes of Meeting between Kissinger, Vorster, and others, Grafenau, Bavaria, West Germany, 24 June 1976.
32. DNSA, *Kissinger Transcripts*, Minutes of Meeting between Kissinger, Vorster, and others, Grafenau, Bavaria, West Germany, 24 June 1976. Kissinger later told Pik Botha that during their private meeting on June 24, Vorster agreed "with extremely bad grace" to allow SWAPO participation: DNSA, *Kissinger Transcripts*, Minutes of Meeting between Pik Botha, Kissinger, Scowcroft, and Rodman, Washington, D. C., 13 July 1976.
33. SANDFA, Group 1—HSAW Chief of Defense Force, Box 164, HSAW/11/5/1, Volume 1, Bedreiging Teen die RSA: Beleid, R. F. Botha, SA Permanent Representative to the UN, New York, to Sekretaris van Buitelandse Sake, 31 July 1976; ISP, Deposit 4, Box 2, Records of Meetings 1973–1978, First Record of Meeting between Smith, Vorster, and others, Pretoria, 13 June 1976.
34. Of the substantial literature on Soweto, see especially Alan Brooks and Jeremy Brickhill, *Whirlwind before the Storm* (London: International and Defence Aid Fund for Southern Africa, 1980); Kane-Berman, *Soweto: Black Revolt, White Reaction.*
35. Christi van der Westhuizen, *White Power & the Rise and Fall of the National Party* (Cape Town: Zebra Press, 2007), pp. 102–3.
36. ARCA, PV 408, NP Caucus, Notule, 15 June 1976.
37. "They must act to save South Africa," editorial, *World*, 21 June 1976.
38. SANA, 1/1/6, Kabinet Notuleregister, 3 August 1976.
39. SANDFA, Group 1—HSAW Chief of Defense Force, Box 164, HSAW/11/5/1, Volume 1, Bedreiging Teen die RSA: Beleid, R. F. Botha, SA Permanent Representative to the UN, New York, to Sekretaris van Buitelandse Sake, 31 July 1976.
40. Interview with Pik Botha, Pretoria, 11 August 2011.
41. SANDFA, Group 1—HSAW Chief of Defense Force, Box 164, HSAW/11/5/1, Volume 1, Bedreiging Teen die RSA: Beleid, R. F. Botha, SA Permanent Representative to the UN, New York, to Sekretaris van Buitelandse Sake, 31 July 1976.

42. SANDFA, Group 1—HSAW Chief of Defense Force, Box 164, HSAW/11/5/1, Volume 1, Bedreiging Teen die RSA: Beleid, R. F. Botha, SA Permanent Representative to the UN, New York, to Sekretaris van Buitelandse Sake, 31 July 1976.

43. SANDFA, Group 1—HSAW Chief of Defense Force, Box 164, HSAW/11/5/1, Volume 1, Bedreiging Teen die RSA: Beleid, R. F. Botha, SA Permanent Representative to the UN, New York, to Sekretaris van Buitelandse Sake, 31 July 1976.

44. SANDFA, Group 1—HSAW Chief of Defense Force, Box 164, HSAW/11/5/1, Volume 1, Bedreiging Teen die RSA: Beleid, R. F. Botha, SA Permanent Representative to the UN, New York, to Sekretaris van Buitelandse Sake, 31 July 1976.

45. SANA, 1/1/6, Kabinet Notuleregister, 3 August 1976.

46. SANDFA, Group 1—HSAW Chief of Defense Force, Box 164, HSAW/11/5/1, Volume 1, Bedreiging Teen die RSA: Beleid, R. F. Botha, SA Permanent Representative to the UN, New York, to Sekretaris van Buitelandse Sake, 31 July 1976.

47. SANDFA, Group 1—HSAW Chief of Defense Force, Box 164, HSAW/11/5/1, Volume 1, Bedreiging Teen die RSA: Beleid, R. F. Botha, SA Permanent Representative to the UN, New York, to Sekretaris van Buitelandse Sake, 31 July 1976.

48. SANDFA, Group 1—HSAW Chief of Defense Force, Box 164, HSAW/11/5/1, Volume 1, Bedreiging Teen die RSA: Beleid, Military Intelligence Section to Chief of Staff Intelligence, "Komentaar op Ambassadeur Botha se Telegram van 31 Jul 76 tov die Militêre Situasie," 17 August 1976

49. SANDFA, Group 1—HSAW Chief of Defense Force, Box 164, HSAW/11/5/1, Volume 1, Bedreiging Teen die RSA: Beleid, Military Intelligence Section to Chief of Staff Intelligence, "Komentaar op Ambassadeur Botha se Telegram van 31 Jul 76 tov die Militêre Situasie," 17 August 1976.

50. SANA, 1/1/6, Kabinet Notuleregister, 3 August 1976.

51. SANA, 1/1/6, Kabinet Notuleregister, 3 August 1976.

52. See Chapter 5.

53. Stals, "Geskiedenis van die Afrikaner-Broderbond, 1918–1994," p. 435.

54. In accordance with his desire to avoid a total Rhodesian Front (RF) collapse, Vorster instructed the South African Air Force (SAAF) to begin training Rhodesian helicopter and light aircraft crews to take their place and later donated to Salisbury the South African aircraft that the SAAF flight crews were currently operating. See SANDFA, Group 3- HSAW Chief of Defense Force, Box 182, HSAW/101/15/1, "Minutes of First Meeting of the SADF Command Council: 9 August 1976," 12 August 1976; Smith, *The Great Betrayal*, p. 196.

55. ISP, Deposit 4, Box 6, Détente: Official Communications with South Africa, Volume 4, Rhodesian Diplomatic Mission to Gaylard, 8 July 1976. The Rhodesians made similar pleas to the Americans. "Hawkins argued that if moribund Rhodesian patient is to be disposed of, he has right to know what is to be done with his remains": DNSA, US Embassy, Pretoria, to Secretary of State, Washington, D. C., "Vorster-Kissinger Talks," 10 July 1976.

56. SANDFA, Group 3—HSAW, Box 137, HSAW/311/1/23, Verdediging Samewerking: Rhodesië: Korrespondensie, Volume 1, "Minutes of Third Meeting of the SADF Command Council: 9 August 1976," 16 August 1976.

57. ISP, Deposit 4, Box 6, Détente: Official Communications with South Africa, Volume 4, Rhodesian Diplomatic Mission to Gaylard, 12 August 1976.

58. For Vorster, see SANDFA, Group 3—HSAW, Box 137, HSAW/311/1/23, Verdediging Sam ewerking: Rhodesië: Korrespondensie, Volume 1, "Minutes of Third Meeting of the SADF Command Council: 9 August 1976," 16 August 1976; for Fourie, see DNSA, US Embassy, Pretoria, to Secretary of State, Washington, D. C., "Vorster-Kissinger Talks," 10 July 1976; for van den Bergh, see ISP, Deposit 4, Box 6, Détente: Official Communications with South Africa, Volume 4, Rhodesian Diplomatic Mission to Brice, 1 July 1976.

59. ISP, Deposit 4, Box 6, Détente: Official Communications with South Africa, Volume 4, Gaylard to Rhodesian Diplomatic Mission, 13 August 1976.

60. ISP, Deposit 4, Box 6, Détente: Official Communications with South Africa, Volume 4, Gaylard to Rhodesian Diplomatic Mission, 13 August 1976.

61. ISP, Deposit 4, Box 6, Détente: Official Communications with South Africa, Volume 4, Gaylard to Rhodesian Diplomatic Mission, 13 August 1976.

62. DNSA, Minutes of Conversation between Kissinger, Botha, and others, Washington, D. C., 12 August 1976.
63. ARCA, PV 528, Hilgard Muller, 3/2/56, Toesprake, speech, "Suid-Afrika se Verhoudings met die Wêreld as Bydrae tot Interne Stabiliteit," Congress of the Natal National Party, 13 August 1976.
64. DFAA, 1/156/3, 14, Rhodesia: Relations with SA, P. Snyman, SA Diplomatic Mission, Salisbury, to Secretary for Foreign Affairs, "Minister Hilgard Muller's Durban Speech," 19 August 1976.
65. DNSA, *Kissinger Transcripts*, Minutes of Meeting between Kissinger and Botha, 17 August 1976.
66. DNSA, *Kissinger Transcripts*, Minutes of Meeting between Kissinger, Crosland, and others, London, 4 September 1976.
67. DNSA, *Kissinger Transcripts*, Minutes of Meeting between Kissinger, Crosland, and others, London, 4 September 1976.
68. DNSA, *Kissinger Transcripts*, Minutes of Meeting between Vorster, Kissinger, and others, Zurich, 4 September 1976.
69. Fourie, "Buitelandse Woelinge om Suid-Afrika, 1939–1985," pp. 219–220.
70. DNSA, *Kissinger Transcripts*, Minutes of Meeting between Vorster, Kissinger, and others, Zurich, 4 September 1976.
71. DNSA, *Kissinger Transcripts*, Minutes of Meeting between Vorster, Kissinger, and others, Zurich, 4 September 1976.
72. SANA, 1/1/6, Kabinet Notuleregister, 7 September 1976.
73. GFL, National Security Adviser, Trip Briefing Books and Cables for Henry Kissinger, 1974–1976, Kissinger Trip File, Box 39, September 3–7, 1976—London, Zurich, HAK Messages for the President, Scowcroft to Ford, 5 September 1976.
74. GFL, National Security Adviser, Trip Briefing Books and Cables for Henry Kissinger, 1974– 1976, Kissinger Trip File, Box 39, September 3–7, 1976—SECTO (1), Secretary of State Delegation, Zurich, to US Mission to the UN, "Namibia: Public Statement by Sean Macbride," 5 September 1976.
75. DNSA, *Kissinger Transcripts*, Minutes of Meeting between Vorster, Kissinger, and others, Zurich, 4 September 1976.
76. SANA, 1/1/6, Kabinet Notuleregister, 7 September 1976.
77. DNSA, Secretary of State to US Embassy, Pretoria, "Vorster Speeches," 7 September 1976; DNSA, Bowdler, US Embassy, Pretoria, to Secretary of State, "Prime Minister Vorster's Speeches on September 8 and 13," 7 September 1976..
78. DNSA, Secretary of State Delegation, Lusaka, to US Embassy, Pretoria, "Message to Prime Minister Vorster," 20 September 1976.
79. ARCA, PV 203, P. W. Botha, 1/V9/1, 1 Onderwerpslêers, 1/V9 Vorster, adv. B. J., "Toespraak Deur Sy Edele Die Eerste Minister Tydens Die Nasionale Party Kongres in die Callie Humansaal, Bloemfontein," 8 September 1976.
80. GFL, National Security Adviser, Trip Briefing Books and Cables for Henry Kissinger, 1974– 1976, Kissinger Trip File, Box 41, September 13–24, 1976—South Africa, London, HAK Messages to the President, Scowcroft to Ford, 15 September 1976 and 17 September 1976.
81. Paraphrased from ISP, Deposit 4, Box 6, Rhodesia: Official Communications with South Africa, Volume 5, Rhodesian Diplomatic Mission to Gaylard, "International Economic Support for Rhodesian Settlement," 15 September 1976.
82. Flower, *Serving Secretly*, p. 164.
83. ISP, Deposit 4, Box 6, Rhodesia: Official Communications with South Africa, Volume 5, Rhodesian Diplomatic Mission to Gaylard, 17 September 1976.
84. *Die Burger*, 18 September 1976.
85. Elsabé Brink, *Soweto, 16 June 1976: Personal Accounts of the Uprising* (Cape Town: Kwela Books, 2006), p. 10.
86. "Our Blacks will watch Dr K closely," editorial, *World*, 17 September 1976.
87. Wilkins and Strydom, *The Super-Afrikaners*, pp. 235–236.
88. DNSA, *Kissinger Transcripts*, Memorandum of Conversation between Kissinger and Vorster, 17 September 1976.

89. GFL, National Security Adviser, Trip Briefing Books and Cables for Henry Kissinger, 1974–1976, Kissinger Trip File, Box 41, September 13–24, 1976—South Africa, London, HAK—Messages to the President, Scowcroft to Ford, 19 September 1976; Fourie, "Buitelandse Woelinge om Suid-Afrika, 1939–1985," pp. 220–223.

90. Smith, *The Great Betrayal*, pp. 201–202. Smith's recollection is inconsistent with other accounts that suggest that Kissinger berated Smith into compliance: Andrew DeRoche, *Black, White, and Chrome: The United States and Zimbabwe, 1953 to 1998* (Trenton, NJ: Africa World Press, 2001), p. 220.

91. DNSA, *Kissinger Transcripts*, Memorandum of Conversation between Smith, Kissinger, and Vorster, 19 September 1976. See also Fourie, "Buitelandse Woelinge om Suid-Afrika, 1939–1985," pp. 224–225.

92. ISP, Deposit 4, Box 6, Rhodesia: Official Communications with South Africa, Volume 5, Rhodesian Diplomatic Mission to Gaylard, 22 September 1976.

93. Sue Onslow, "Dr Kissinger, I Presume?" (unpublished paper).

94. Smith, *The Great Betrayal*, p. 202.

95. DNSA, *Kissinger Transcripts*, Memorandum of Conversation between Smith, Kissinger, and Vorster, 19 September 1976.

96. Smith, *The Great Betrayal*, p. 202.

97. Flower, *Serving Secretly*, p. 134; Ford, "South African Foreign Policy since 1965: The Cases of Rhodesia and Namibia," p. 43.

98. Smith, *The Great Betrayal*, p. 207.

99. GFL, Ronald H. Nessen Files, Box 64, Transcript of Interview with John Vorster on *Face the Nation*, 7 November 1976.

100. Onslow, "Dr Kissinger, I Presume?"

101. ISP, Deposit 4, Box 6, Rhodesia: Official Communications with South Africa, Volume 5, Rhodesian Diplomatic Mission to Gaylard, 20 September 1976.

102. GFL, National Security Adviser, Trip Briefing Books and Cables for Henry Kissinger, 1974–1976, Kissinger Trip File, Box 43, September 13–24, 1976—South Africa, London, SECTO (6), Secretary of State Delegation to US Embassy, Pretoria, "Smith Speech," 21 September 1976. See also ISP, Deposit 4, Box 6, Rhodesia: Official Communications with South Africa, Volume 5, Rhodesian Diplomatic Mission to Gaylard, 22 September 1976.

103. DNSA, *Kissinger Transcripts*, Memorandum of Conversation between Kissinger and Vorster, 19 September 1976.

104. ISP, Deposit 3, Box 1, Rhodesia Government: Cabinet Minutes (Secretary's Standard File), Volume 5, Annexure to 35th Meeting, 21 September 1976

105. Flower, *Serving Secretly*, p. 153.

106. Smith, *The Great Betrayal*, p. 228.

107. ISP, Deposit 3, Box 1, Rhodesia Government: Cabinet Minutes (Secretary's Standard File), Volume 5, Annexure to 36th Meeting, 22 September 1976.

108. Paraphrased from GFL, National Security Adviser, Trip Briefing Books and Cables for Henry Kissinger, 1974–1976, Kissinger Trip File, Box 41, September 13–24, 1976—South Africa, London, HAK—Messages to the President, "Basis for a Proposal for Namibia," 21 September 1976.

109. GFL, National Security Adviser, Trip Briefing Books and Cables for Henry Kissinger, 1974–1976, Kissinger Trip File, Box 44, September 29–30, 1976—USUN: TOSEC, State Department to Secretary of State Delegation, "Namibia: South Africa Positions," 29 September 1976.

110. DNSA, *Kissinger Transcripts*, Memorandum of Conversation between Kissinger and Vorster, 19 September 1976.

111. DNSA, Secretary of State, Washington, DC, to US Embassy, Pretoria, "Message for Fourie," 18 October 1976.

112. SANA, 1/1/6, Kabinet Notuleregister, 31 August 1976.

113. van Wyk, *Dirk Mudge: Reënmaker van die Namib*, pp. 61, 66, 85.

114. ARCA, PV 698, A. H. du Plessis, Korrespondensie NP 1 NP 2, NP 8: NP van SWA: notules, omsendbriewe ens., Interview with Dirk Mudge and Mr. X, Windhoek, 15 September 1976.

115. van Wyk, *Dirk Mudge: Reënmaker van die Namib*, pp. 65, 85, 87.

116. SANDFA, Group 5- Minister van Verdediging, Box 78, MV/28/14, Politiek Ander Departemente: Buitelandse Sake, Volume 2, Billy Marais, Sekretaris Staatkundige Beraad, Windhoek, to Sekretaris van Buitelandse Sake, "Persverklaring," 9 December 1976.

117. SANA, 1/1/6, Kabinet Notuleregister, 19 October 1976.

118. ARCA, PV 698, A. H. du Plessis, Korrespondensie NP 1 NP 2, NP 8: NP van SWA: notules, omsendbriewe ens., Interview with Dirk Mudge and Mr. X, Windhoek, 15 September 1976.

119. ARCA, PV 698, A. H. du Plessis, Korrespondensie NP 1 NP 2, NP 8: NP van SWA: notules, omsendbriewe ens., handwritten note, Mudge to du Plessis, 7 October 1976.

120. van Wyk, *Dirk Mudge: Reënmaker van die Namib*, p. 89.

121. DNSA, US Embassy, Pretoria, to Secretary of State, Washington, DC, "Namibia: Turnhalle at Fragile Stage," 15 November 1976.

122. SANDFA, Group 3—HSAW Chief of Defense Force, Box 168, SWA I, "Samesprekings Eerste Minister," 24 November 1976.

123. SANA, MEM, 1/572, I15/2, P. W. Botha to Vorster, 26 November 1976.

124. SANDFA, Group 3—HSAW Chief of Defense Force, Box 168, SWA I, "Samesprekings Eerste Minister," 24 November 1976.

125. ARCA, PV 698, A. H. du Plessis, Korrespondensie NP 1 NP 2, NP 8: NP van SWA: notules, omsendbriewe ens., handwritten note, A. H. du Plessis to Vorster, 17 November 1976.

126. SANDFA, Group 3—HSAW Chief of Defense Force, Box 168, SWA I, "Samesprekings Eerste Minister," 24 November 1976.

127. SANDFA, Group 3—HSAW Chief of Defense Force, Box 168, SWA I, "Samesprekings Eerste Minister," 24 November 1976.

128. Jimmy Carter Library (JCL), Donated Historical Material: Zbigniew Brzezinski Collection, Subject File, Box 24, Meetings—PRC 3: 2/8/77, Special Coordination Committee Meeting on South Africa and Rhodesia, 8 February 1977.

129. DNSA, US Embassy, Pretoria, to Secretary of State, Washington, DC, "Namibia: Turnhalle at Fragile Stage," 15 November 1976.

130. Interview with Dirk Mudge, Otjiwarongo, 1 August 2011.

131. DNSA, Bowdler to Secretary of State, "Turnhalle Adjourns Without Finding Solutions: SWAPO Threatens Greater Pressure," 7 January 1977.

132. JCL, Collection 7, NSA Brzezinski Material, Subject File, Box 34, Memcons: President, 3/77, Memorandum of Conversation between Carter, Mondale, Vance, Brzezinski, Schaufele, Pik Botha, Jeremy Shearar, 23 March 1977.

133. Meredith, *The Past is Another Country: Rhodesia, 1890–1979*, p. 260.

134. Fourie, "Buitelandse Woelinge om Suid-Afrika, 1939–1985," p. 231.

135. ISP, Deposit 4, Box 5, Kissinger Proposals: Geneva Conference—Background Papers, Statement by Smith, 6 October 1976.

136. In the days preceding Smith's announcement, both Kaunda and Nyerere had assented to the Five Points providing the basis of any future settlement. However, Kaunda had said he needed to talk to the other presidents, while Nyerere signposted that the nationalists would probably wish to bring up both the security ministries and the Council of State (the two issues that ultimately became problematic). For Kaunda, see GFL, National Security Adviser, Trip Briefing Books and Cables for Henry Kissinger, 1974–1976, Kissinger Trip File, Box 41, September 13–24, 1976—South Africa, London, HAK—Messages to the President, Scowcroft to Ford, 21 September 1976; and for Nyerere, see GFL, National Security Adviser, Trip Briefing Books and Cables for Henry Kissinger, 1974–1976, Kissinger Trip File, Box 41, September 13–24, 1976—South Africa, London, HAK—Messages to the President, Scowcroft to Ford, 21 September 1976.

137. Onslow, "Dr Kissinger, I Presume?; Susan Crosland, *Tony Crosland* (London: Cape, 1982), pp. 362–365.

138. Kissinger, *Years of Renewal*, pp. 1003–1012.

139. David Scott, *Ambassador in Black and White: Thirty Years of Changing Africa* (London: Weidenfeld and Nicolson, 1981), p. 189.

140. The evidence consistently shows that Kissinger tried hard to bring London with him, including conducting very regular briefings and keeping them in the loop. However, when the British responded by showing little sense of urgency, Kissinger pushed ahead regardless.

141. UKNA, FCO 73/224, S/S Messages to & From the USA, Part I, FCO to UK Embassy, Dar es Salaam, 21 September 1976.
142. UKNA, FCO 73/224, S/S Messages to & From the USA, Part I, Kissinger to Callaghan, 21 October 1976.
143. DeRoche, *Black, White, and Chrome: The United States and Zimbabwe, 1953 to 1998*, pp. 224–5.
144. SANA, 1/1/6, Kabinet Notuleregister, 28 September 1976.
145. Smith, *The Great Betrayal*, p. 212.
146. GFL, National Security Adviser, Presidential Country Files for Africa, 1974–1977, Box 6, South Africa: State Department Telegrams: SECSTATE NODIS, Secretary of State to US Embassy, Pretoria, "Secretary's Response to Personal Message From Ian Smith," 1 October 1976.
147. GFL, National Security Adviser, Presidential Country Files for Africa, 1974–1977, Box 6, South Africa: State Department Telegrams: To SECSTATE NODIS (2), Schaufele, US Embassy, Pretoria, to Secretary of State, "Meeting with Brand Fourie," 5 October 1976.
148. ISP, Deposit 4, Box 5, Geneva Conference: Record of Meetings (British)—Informal, Record of Bilateral Meeting, Palais des Nations, Geneva, 1 December 1976.
149. Fourie, "Buitelandse Woelinge om Suid-Afrika, 1939–1985," pp. 232–233.
150. ISP, Deposit 4, Box 6, Rhodesia Settlement: Communications with South Africa, Volume 7, Rhodesian Diplomatic Mission to Gaylard, 19 January 1977.
151. "SA explodes," *Times of Zambia*, 18 June 1976.
152. "Support reforms in Southern Africa, says Tolbert," *Malawi News*, 25 September 1976.
153. "South African Cabinet Reshuffle Likely," London *Times*, 25 June 1976.
154. ARCA, PV 408, NP Caucus, Notule, 8 June 1976 and 15 June 1976.
155. Interview with Koos van der Merwe, Pretoria, 13 October 2014.
156. Botha did something similar in 1982 and, while costing him a schism, the move made it much easier to push through the party room reforms far more controversial than anything Vorster was considering.
157. "Dit is tyd vir herwaardering," editorial, *Volkshandel*, July 1976.
158. *Die Burger*, "Nuwe magte vir swartes," 21 October 1976.
159. Stals, "Geskiedenis van die Afrikaner-Broderbond, 1918–1994," p. 375.
160. Stals, "Geskiedenis van die Afrikaner-Broderbond, 1918–1994," pp. 379–382.
161. Johnson, *How Long Will South Africa Survive?* p. 276.
162. Johnson, *How Long Will South Africa Survive?* p. 276.
163. Stals, "Geskiedenis van die Afrikaner-Broderbond, 1918–1994," p. 382.
164. O'Meara, *Forty Lost Years*, p. 197.
165. ARCA, PV 408, NP Caucus, Notule, 16 February 1977. Emphasis added.
166. Johnson, *How Long Will South Africa Survive?* p. 275.
167. "Redakteur is dislojaal, sê Raubenheimer," *Die Burger*, 27 November 1976.
168. JCL, Collection 24, NSA Brzezinski Material, Country File, Box 69, South Africa 1–4/77, Bowdler to Secretary of State, "Comment on Talks with Scott and Hawkins," 22 January 1977.
169. GFL, National Security Adviser, Presidential Country Files for Africa, 1974–1977, Box 6, South Africa: State Department Telegrams: To SECSTATE NODIS (4), Edmondson, US Embassy, Pretoria, to Schaufele, "Richard Sees Vorster on Rhodesia," 3 January 1977; Fourie, "Buitelandse Woelinge om Suid-Afrika, 1939–1985," p. 236.
170. Fourie, "Buitelandse Woelinge om Suid-Afrika, 1939–1985," p. 233.
171. Johnson, *How Long Will South Africa Survive?* p. 277.
172. Fourie, "Buitelandse Woelinge om Suid-Afrika, 1939–1985," p. 233.
173. JCL, Collection 24, NSA Brzezinski Material, Country File, Box 69, South Africa 1-4/77, Secretary of State to US Consulate, Cape Town, "South African Ambassador's January 25 Call on the Secretary," 26 January 1977.
174. ISP, Deposit 4, Box 6, Rhodesia Settlement: Communications with South Africa, Volume 7, Rhodesian Diplomatic Mission to Gaylard, 11 January 1977.

175. ISP, Deposit 4, Box 6, Rhodesia Settlement: Communications with South Africa, Volume 7, Rhodesian Diplomatic Mission to Gaylard, 11 January 1977. See also Fourie, "Buitelandse Woelinge om Suid-Afrika, 1939–1985," p. 235.

176. ISP, Deposit 4, Box 6, Rhodesia Settlement: Communications with South Africa, Volume 7, Rhodesian Diplomatic Mission to Gaylard, 11 January 1977.

177. Fourie, "Buitelandse Woelinge om Suid-Afrika, 1939–1985," p. 236.

178. ISP, Deposit 4, Box 6, Rhodesia Settlement: Communications with South Africa, Volume 7, Rhodesian Diplomatic Mission to Gaylard, 19 January 1977.

179. JCL, Collection 24, NSA Brzezinski Material, Country File, Box 69, South Africa 1-4/77, Bowdler to Secretary of State, "Rhodesia: Smith May See Richard Twice," 20 January 1977; JCL, Collection 24, NSA Brzezinski Material, Country File, Box 69, South Africa 1-4/77, Secretary of State to US Consulate, Cape Town, "South African Ambassador's January 25 Call on the Secretary," 26 January 1977.

180. ISP, Deposit 4, Box 6, Rhodesia Settlement: Communications with South Africa, Volume 7, Rhodesian Diplomatic Mission to Gaylard, 19 January 1977.

181. ISP, Deposit 4, Box 5, Geneva Conference: Record of Meetings (British)—Informal, Record of Meeting held in Cabinet Room, Milton Building, 24 January 1977.

Chapter 8

1. See Chapter 1.

2. Adapted from T. J. Steenekamp, "'n Ekonomiese Ontleding van Sosio-Politieke Groepvorming met Spesiale Verwysing na die Afrikaner" (PhD diss., University of South Africa, 1989), p. 193.

3. Stals, "Geskiedenis van die Afrikaner-Broderbond, 1918–1994," p. 374.

4. Given the social context of segregation, "public" goods were created for the benefit of either Afrikaner advancement or the broader white power structure, and were of course not "public" among the population as a whole.

5. The only substantial outlier was public sector employment within the state itself, whether in politics or the civil service. Both continued to attract educated Afrikaners.

6. O'Meara, Forty Lost Years, pp. 145–146.

7. In some ways, this scenario was a redux of the similar political impasse that had doomed the UP's ruling consensus in 1948. See Chapter 1.

8. Vorster speech in the House of Assembly, 15 September 1970, Geyser, ed. Select Speeches, p. 118.

9. "Realistiese vertroue in toekoms," editorial, Volkshandel, November 1976; "Mededeelsame welvaart," editorial, Volkshandel, March 1978.

10. "Bantoes in Tuislande kry R104 000 000 van Blankes," Die Afrikaner, 29 January 1971.

11. SANDFA, Group 4—P. W. Botha, Box 142, 76/1, Strategie: Algemeen, Volume 2, "Notes on Total Strategy," July 1977.

12. "Sal Afrikaans nader aan Engels kom?" editorial, Volkshandel, October 1975.

13. South African Institute of Race Relations, A Survey of Race Relations in South Africa (Johannesburg 1982), pp. 274–275.

14. This is a major theme of O'Meara, Forty Lost Years.

15. Vorster speech in the House of Assembly, 15 September 1970, Geyser, ed. Select Speeches, p. 114.

16. Sometimes, depending on the location and audience, they threw in a few paragraphs in English somewhere in the middle. But almost none of the elected Nationalist leaders or the nonelected elites in other arms of the volksbeweging had English as their mother tongue. Indeed, a few MPs of the older generation appear to have spoken the language only with a notable lack of fluency.

17. Adam and Giliomee, Ethnic Power Mobilized: Can South Africa Change? p. 129.

18. Giliomee, The Afrikaners, pp. 545–547, 550.

19. Craig Charney, "Class Conflict and the National Party Split," Journal of Southern African Studies 10, no. 2 (1984).

20. WKL, Public Library of US Diplomacy, Kissinger Cables, State Department to US Embassy, Pretoria, "Congressman Young's Reply to Joseph Rhodes," 6 December 1976.
21. SML, MS 1664, Vance Papers, Box 8, 6, Joseph Rhodes to Andrew Young, "The Mulder Overture," 25 December 1976.
22. DDRS, Brzezinski to Carter, Follow-up to the NSC meeting on South Africa, White House Memorandum, 1 April 1977.
23. Heribert Adam, "Survival Politics: In Search of a New Ideology," in *Ethnic Power Mobilized: Can South Africa Change?*, ed. H. Adam and H. Giliomee (Cape Town: David Philips, 1979), p. 132.
24. Wilkins and Strydom, *The Super-Afrikaners*, p. 214.
25. O'Meara, *Forty Lost Years*, pp. 196–203.
26. Malan, *My Life with the SA Defence Force*, p. 144. Malan's accession to the top job had been public since early May. When Biermann went on leave on July 30, Malan became acting chief before formally assuming the top job on September 1. See *Hansard*, House of Assembly Debates, 6 May 1976, cols 6157–8.
27. SANDFA, Group 4- P. W. Botha, Box 142, 76/1, Strategie: Algemeen, Volume 1, Biermann to P. W. Botha, "Koördinasie van Beplanning en Optrede," 20 July 1976.
28. SANDFA, Group 4—P. W. Botha, Box 142, 76/1, Strategie: Algemeen, Volume 2, Malan to P. W. Botha, "Memo Oor Totale Strategie," 26 November 1976.
29. SANDFA, Group 1- VBR/VBK (DSC), Box 3, VBK Notules 1-21, Minutes of the 10th Meeting of the DPC: 14 June 1976, 16 June 1976.
30. ARCA, PV 203, P. W. Botha, PS 6/12/3, Politiek en Algemeen, "Notule van Samesprekings tussen die Minister van Verdediging en die Minister van Finansies Gehou ten Kantore van Eersgenoemde," 27 July 1976; ARCA, PV 203, P. W. Botha, PS 6/12/3, Politiek en Algemeen, P. W. Botha to Vorster, "Finansiële Behoeftes van Verdediging: Huidige en Volgende Boekjare," 15 September 1976; PV 203, PS 6/12/3, P. W. Botha, Politiek en Algemeen, P. W. Botha to Horwood, "Finansiële Behoeftes van Verdediging: Huidige en Volgende Boekjare," 15 September 1976.
31. SANDFA, Group 4- P. W. Botha, Box 142, 76/1, Strategie: Algemeen, Volume 1, Biermann to P. W. Botha, "Koördinasie van Beplanning en Optrede," 20 July 1976.
32. SANDFA, Group 4- P. W. Botha, Box 142, 76/1, Strategie: Algemeen, Volume 1, Biermann to P. W. Botha, "Koördinasie van Beplanning en Optrede," 20 July 1976.
33. Interview with Deon Fourie, Pretoria, 8 July 2011.
34. SANDFA, Group 1- VBR/VBK (DSC), Box 3, VBK Notules 1-21, Minutes of the 10th Meeting of the DPC: 14 June 1976, 16 June 1976.
35. SANDFA, Group 4- P. W. Botha, Box 142, 76/1, Strategie: Algemeen, Volume 1, Biermann to P. W. Botha, "Koördinasie van Beplanning en Optrede," 20 July 1976.
36. ARCA, PV 203, P. W. Botha, PS 6/12/3, Politiek en Algemeen, P. W. Botha to Vorster, "Finansiële Behoeftes van Verdediging: Huidige en Volgende Boekjare," 15 September 1976.
37. Interview with Chris Thirion, Pretoria, 20 July 2011.
38. Interview with Stoffel van der Merwe, Pretoria, 13 October 2014.
39. Unlike most other government departments, Defense had no secretary, which facilitated a close Malan-Botha axis.
40. Interview with Deon Fourie, Pretoria, 6 July 2011.
41. SANA, MEM, 1/572, 115/2, P. W. Botha to Vorster, "Voorlegging aan die Staatsveiligheidsraad Aangaande die Bestaande Gesamentlike Interdepartementele Teen-Insurgensie Komitee," 14 June 1974.
42. SANA, MEM, 1/572, 115/2, P. W. Botha to Vorster, "Voorlegging aan die Staatsveiligheidsraad Aangaande die Bestaande Gesamentlike Interdepartementele Teen-Insurgensie Komitee," 14 June 1974.
43. SANA, 1/1/5, 2, Kabinet Notuleregister, 19 June 1974.
44. SANDFA, Group 4- P. W. Botha, Box 142, 76/1, Strategie: Algemeen, Volume 1, Biermann to P. W. Botha, "Koördinasie van Beplanning en Optrede," 20 July 1976.
45. Hamann, *Days of the Generals*, pp. 53–54.
46. Interview with Niël Barnard, Cape Town, 11 October 2011.
47. The date of Botha's actual presentation to Cabinet is unclear.

48. SANDFA, Group 4- Chief of Staff Operations, Box 12, DGSS/4/3/1, Doktrine Totale Strategiese Beleid: Algemeen, Departement van Verdediging Kabinetsraadmemorandum, "Koördinasie van Beplanning en Optrede Tussen Staatsdepartemente," 12 August 1976.

49. ARCA, PV 203, P. W. Botha, 1/W1/8, 1 Onderwerpslêers: 1/W1 Weermag, Magnus Malan, speech, "Skouer aan die Wiel," Rustenberg, 12 August 1976.

50. SANDFA, Group 4- Chief of Staff Operations, Box 12, DGSS/4/3/1, Doktrine Totale Strategiese Beleid: Algemeen, Departement van Verdediging Kabinetsraadmemorandum, "Koördinasie van Beplanning en Optrede Tussen Staatsdepartemente," 12 August 1976.

51. SANDFA, Group 4- Chief of Staff Operations, Box 12, DGSS/4/3/1, Doktrine Totale Strategiese Beleid: Algemeen, Departement van Verdediging Kabinetsraadmemorandum, "Koördinasie van Beplanning en Optrede Tussen Staatsdepartemente," 12 August 1976.

52. SANDFA, Group 4- Chief of Staff Operations, Box 12, DGSS/4/3/1, Doktrine Totale Strategiese Beleid: Algemeen, "Notas vir Voorligting aan Staatsveiligheidsraad oor die Noodsaaklikheid van Totale Strategie," Magnus Malan, 6 August 1976.

53. For more on the Venter Commission, see Alden, *Apartheid's Last Stand*, pp. 70–71.

54. SANDFA, Group 4- P. W. Botha, Box 142, 76/1, Strategie: Algemeen, Volume 1, Malan to P. W. Botha, "Voorligting oor Totale Strategie op 21 Sept 76 by die SA Verdedigingskollege," 11 August 1976.

55. SANDFA, Group 4- Chief of Staff Operations, Box 12, DGSS/4/3/1, Doktrine Totale Strategiese Beleid: Algemeen, "Notas vir Voorligting aan Staatsveiligheidsraad oor die Noodsaaklikheid van Totale Strategie," Magnus Malan, 6 August 1976.

56. Malan to Sekretaris van die Eerste Minister, Kabinetsmemorandum, "Staatsoorlogboek," August 1976.

57. SANDFA, Group 4- Chief of Staff Operations, Box 12, DGSS/4/3/1, Doktrine Totale Strategiese Beleid: Algemeen, Departement van Verdediging Kabinetsraadmemorandum, "Koördinasie van Beplanning en Optrede Tussen Staatsdepartemente," 12 August 1976.

58. SANDFA, Group 4- Chief of Staff Operations, Box 12, DGSS/4/3/1, Doktrine Totale Strategiese Beleid: Algemeen, Malan to P. W. Botha, "Simposium oor die Nasionale Strategie," Magnus Malan, late September 1976.

59. SANDFA, Group 4- Chief of Staff Operations, Box 12, DGSS/4/3/1, Doktrine Totale Strategiese Beleid: Algemeen, Departement van Verdediging Kabinetsmemorandum, "Simposium oor die Nasionale Beveiligingsopset," 11 August 1976. The symposium was held on 21 September 1976.

60. SANDFA, Group 4—P. W. Botha, Box 142, 76/1, Strategie: Algemeen, Volume 2, P. W. Botha to Vorster and others, 1 September 1976.

61. SANDFA, Group 4- Chief of Staff Operations, Box 12, DGSS/4/3/1, Doktrine Totale Strategiese Beleid: Algemeen, Malan to P. W. Botha, "Simposium oor die Nasionale Strategie," Magnus Malan, late September 1976; SANDFA, Group 4- Chief of Staff Operations, Box 12, DGSS/4/3/1, Doktrine Totale Strategiese Beleid: Algemeen, Departement van Verdediging Staatsveiligheidsraadmemorandum, "Daarstelling van 'n Komitee om Aspekte Rakende Nasionale Veiligheid te Ondersoek," October 1976.

62. Interview with Deon Fourie, Pretoria, 6 July 2011.

63. Interview with Deon Fourie, Pretoria, 6 July 2011.

64. SANDFA, Group 4- Chief of Staff Operations, Box 12, DGSS/4/3/1, Doktrine Totale Strategiese Beleid: Algemeen, Departement van Verdediging Staatsveiligheidsraadmemorandum, "Daarstelling van 'n Komitee om Aspekte Rakende Nasionale Veiligheid te Ondersoek," October 1976.

65. SANDFA, Group 4- Chief of Staff Operations, Box 12, DGSS/4/3/1, Doktrine Totale Strategiese Beleid: Algemeen, Departement van Verdediging Staatsveiligheidsraadmemorandum, "Daarstelling van 'n Komitee om Aspekte Rakende Nasionale Veiligheid te Ondersoek," October 1976. In fact, this view on the unsuitability of the Westminster system was that of none other than Botha and he later jettisoned major features of that system.

66. Interview with Deon Fourie, Pretoria, 6 July 2011.

67. Interview with Chris Thirion, Pretoria, 20 July 2011.

68. SANDFA, Group 4- Chief of Staff Operations, Box 12, DGSS/4/3/1, Doktrine Totale Strategiese Beleid: Algemeen, Departement van Verdediging Staatsveiligheidsraadmemorandum,

"Nasionale Strategie," 13 October 1976. It is not clear who did or did not actually attend the symposium, but it can be reasonably assumed that several of the civilians invited did not while all of the military did.

69. The program was: Malan (lecturing on the development of strategy in the context of the evolution of war); J. J. Venter (the existing national structures for national security and their shortcomings); M. H. A. Louw (the goals of a modern state in an international context); Captain G. Nieuwoudt, Military Intelligence (enemy strategy and the prevention of RSA's national goals); Brigadier G. M. C. Wassenaar, Military Intelligence (enemy propaganda); Dr W. J. de Villiers (the principles of planning); Dr S. S. Brandt, Adjunct Head of the PM's Economic Advice Board (the economy as an instrument of national strategy); Wassenaar again (propaganda as an instrument of RSA national strategy); and Colonel J. F. Huyser, Operations (the role of logistics). See SANDFA, Group 4- Chief of Staff Operations, Box 12, DGSS/4/3/1, Doktrine Totale Strategiese Beleid: Algemeen, Departement van Verdediging Staatsveiligheidsraadmemorandum, "Nasionale Strategie," 13 October 1976.

70. SANDFA, Group 4- Chief of Staff Operations, Box 12, DGSS/4/3/1, Doktrine Totale Strategiese Beleid: Algemeen, "'n Voorbeeld van Moontlike Beleidsriglyne vir die RSA se Totale Strategie," attached to Departement van Verdediging Kabinetsraadmemorandum, "Koördinasie van Beplanning en Optrede Tussen Staatsdepartemente," 12 August 1976.

71. SANDFA, Group 4- Chief of Staff Operations, Box 12, DGSS/4/3/1, Doktrine Totale Strategiese Beleid: Algemeen, Departement van Verdediging Kabinetsmemorandum, "Totale Strategie: Jongste Gebeure in Angola," precise date unclear, late spring 1976.

72. Malan, *My Life with the SA Defence Force*, pp. 150–153.

73. Hamann, *Days of the Generals*, p. 61.

74. Beaufre, *An Introduction to Strategy*, p. 30.

75. Alden, *Apartheid's Last Stand*, p. 44.

76. Interview with Chris Thirion, Pretoria, 20 July 2011.

77. O'Meara, *Forty Lost Years*, p. 256.

78. SANDFA, Group 4- Chief of Staff Operations, Box 12, DGSS/4/3/1, Doktrine Totale Strategiese Beleid: Algemeen, "Nasionale Strategie vir Rhodesië," September 1976.

79. SANDFA, Group 4- Chief of Staff Operations, Box 12, DGSS/4/3/1, Doktrine Totale Strategiese Beleid: Algemeen, "Notas vir Voorligting aan Staatsveiligheidsraad oor die Noodsaaklikheid van Totale Strategie," Magnus Malan, 6 August 1976. In this aspect, they resembled Beaufre's own texts.

80. SANDFA, Group 4- Chief of Staff Operations, Box 12, DGSS/4/3/1, Doktrine Totale Strategiese Beleid: Algemeen, "'n Voorbeeld van Moontlike Beleidsriglyne vir die RSA se Totale Strategie," attached to Departement van Verdediging Kabinetsraadmemorandum, "Koördinasie van Beplanning en Optrede Tussen Staatsdepartemente," 12 August 1976. The latter had already begun in 1974: Malan, *My Life with the SA Defence Force*, p. 107.

81. Interview with Deon Fourie, Pretoria, 8 July 2011.

82. Interview with Chris Thirion, Pretoria, 20 July 2011.

83. SANDFA, Group 4- Chief of Staff Operations, Box 12, DGSS/4/3/1, Doktrine Totale Strategiese Beleid: Algemeen, Departement van Verdediging Staatsveiligheidsraadmemorandum, "Daarstelling van 'n Komitee om Aspekte Rakende Nasionale Veiligheid te Ondersoek," October 1976.

84. SANDFA, Group 3- HSAW Chief of Defense Force, Box 420, MI/STRAT/1/7, Die Militêre Bedreiging teen die RSA, Volume 54, Direktoraat Militêre Inligting study, "Die Militêre Bedreiging teen die RSA," 29 October 1976.

85. SANDFA, Group 3- HSAW Chief of Defense Force, Box 420, MI/STRAT/1/7, Die Militêre Bedreiging teen die RSA, Volume 54, Direktoraat Militêre Inligting study, "Die Militêre Bedreiging teen die RSA," 29 October 1976.

86. SANDFA, Group 4- Chief of Staff Operations, Box 12, DGSS/4/3/1, Doktrine Totale Strategiese Beleid: Algemeen, Departement van Verdediging Staatsveiligheidsraadmemorandum, "Nasionale Strategie," 13 October 1976.

87. SANDFA, Group 4- Chief of Staff Operations, Box 12, DGSS/4/3/1, Doktrine Totale Strategiese Beleid: Algemeen, Departement van Verdediging Staatsveiligheidsraadmemorandum,

"Daarstelling van 'n Komitee om Aspekte Rakende Nasionale Veiligheid te Ondersoek," October 1976.

88. SANDFA, Group 4-Chief of Staff Operations, Box 12, DGSS/4/3/1, Doktrine Totale Strategiese Beleid: Algemeen, Departement van Verdediging Staatsveiligheidsraadmemorandum, "Daarstelling van 'n Komitee om Aspekte Rakende Nasionale Veiligheid te Ondersoek," October 1976.

89. See also SANDFA, Group 4- Chief of Staff Operations, Box 12, DGSS/4/3/1, Doktrine Totale Strategiese Beleid: Algemeen, Departement van Verdediging Staatsveiligheidsraad-memorandum, "Daarstelling van 'n Komitee om Aspekte Rakende Nasionale Veiligheid te Ondersoek," October 1976.

90. Republic of South Africa, "White Paper on Defense and Armaments Production," (Pretoria: Government Printing Office), p. 5.

91. There is little in the personal files of Botha and his political allies, the SADF archives, or interviews with those individuals most involved in these events to suggest that total strategy originated anywhere else.

92. Pierre Hugo, "The Politics of Untruth: Afrikaner Academics for Apartheid," *Politikon* 25, no. 1 (1998).

Chapter 9

1. Tamarkin, *The Making of Zimbabwe: Decolonization in Regional and International Politics*, p. 180.

2. DNSA, Bowdler to Secretary of State, "Turnhalle Adjourns Without Finding Solutions: SWAPO Threatens Greater Pressure," 7 January 1977.

3. Interview with C. A. Bastiaanse, Centurion, 28 July 2011; Fourie, "Buitelandse Woelinge om Suid-Afrika, 1939–1985," p. 292.

4. JCL, CREST, NLC-18-4-6-1-1, Presidential Review Memorandum/ NSC-4, "Rhodesia, Namibia and South Africa," 21 January 1977.

5. Cyrus R. Vance, *Hard Choices: Critical Years in America's Foreign Policy* (New York: Simon & Schuster, 1983), pp. 257, 262–263.

6. DNSA, *Kissinger Transcripts*, Minutes of Meeting between Kissinger, Vorster, and others, Grafenau, Bavaria, West Germany, 24 June 1976.

7. ARCA, PV 408, NP Caucus, Notule, 8 April 1975.

8. SANDFA, Group 1—HSAW Chief of Defense Force, Box 98, HSAW/311/1/29, Volume 1, Verdedigingsamewerking: VSA Korrespondensie, CSI to Military Secretary, Department of Military Intelligence (AMI) Report, circa 16 August 1976.

9. GFL, National Security Adviser: Presidential Country Files for Africa, 1974–1977, Box 7, Cutler to Secretary of State, Washington, DC, "Angola: GOZ Contemplates UN Action," 16 January 1976.

10. DFAA, 1/33/3, 28, USA Relations With South Africa, J. S. F. Botha, Embassy of South Africa, Washington, DC, to Secretary for Foreign Affairs, US/SA Relations, 6 February 1974.

11. JCL, Donated Historical Material: Zbigniew Brzezinski Collection, Subject File, Box 24, Meetings—PRC 3: 2/8/77, Special Coordination Committee Meeting on South Africa and Rhodesia, 8 February 1977.

12. JCL, Collection 24, NSA Brzezinski Material, Country File, Box 69, South Africa 1-4/77, Vance to Carter, "Farewell Call by South African Ambassador R. F. Botha," c. 23 March 1977.

13. JCL, CREST, NLC-16-108-6-21-6, Secretary of State to US Embassy, Pretoria, 14 October 1977.

14. DDRS, Zbigniew Brzezinski to President Carter, Summary of Policy Review Committee meeting on Southern Africa, 9 February 1977; JCL, CREST, NLC-132-3-9-1-1, NSC Memorandum to Brzezinski, "Response to Presidential Directive—NSC-5: Southern Africa" 29 March 1977.

15. Carter's handwritten comment on JCL, CREST, NLC-17-1-5-8-9, Brzezinski to Carter, "NSC Meeting on South Africa," 4 March 1977. Emphasis in the original.

16. JCL, Collection 24, NSA Brzezinski Material, Country File, Box 69, South Africa 6/77, Richardson to Aaron, "Talkers for Your Dinner With Botha," 22 June 1977. See also Vance, *Hard Choices: Critical Years in America's Foreign Policy*, p. 262; David Owen, *Time to Declare* (London: Joseph, 1991), p. 310.

17. Even in the last days of the Ford Administration, Kissinger and Ford would agree to a one-time exception to the embargo for C-130 navigational equipment in order to encourage future cooperation by Pretoria on Rhodesia and SWA. There would be no such carrots from the Carter White House. See GFL, National Security Adviser, Presidential Country Files for Africa, 1974–1977, Box 6, South Africa (4), Scowcroft to Kissinger, 14 January 1977.

18. DDRS, Minutes, NSC Meeting on South Africa, 3 March 1977.

19. JCL, CREST, NLC-132-3-9-1-1, NSC Memorandum to Brzezinski, "Response to Presidential Directive—NSC-5: Southern Africa," 29 March 1977.

20. JCL, CREST, NLC-132-3-9-1-1, NSC Memorandum to Brzezinski, "Response to Presidential Directive—NSC-5: Southern Africa," 29 March 1977.

21. JCL, Collection 7, NSA Brzezinski Material, Subject File, Box 34, Memcons: President, 3/77, Memorandum of Conversation between Carter, Mondale, Vance, Brzezinski, Schaufele, Pik Botha, Jeremy Shearar, 23 March 1977.

22. Interview with Jeremy Shearar, Pretoria, 18 August 2011.

23. JCL, White House Central Files, Subject File, Countries, Box CO-50, CO 141 Executive 1/20/77-5/31/77, Vorster to Carter, 23 March 1977.

24. Interview with Riaan Eksteen, Swakopmund, 2 August 2011.

25. Donald Sole, *"This Above All": Reminiscences of a South African Diplomat* (Archive for Contemporary Affairs), pp. 366–367.

26. JCL, Collection 24, NSA Brzezinski Material, Country File, Box 69, South Africa 6/77, Minutes of First Meeting between Vorster and Mondale, Vienna, 19 May 1977.

27. JCL, CREST, NLC-7-6-10-1-6, Mondale to Vance, Young, Brzezinski, "Southern Africa—US Strategy and Meeting with Prime Minister Vorster," 4 April 1977.

28. JCL, Donated Historical Material: Zbigniew Brzezinski Collection, Geographic File, Box 14, Southern Africa—3/77-4/77, Secretary of State to White House, "Rhodesia: Owen's Brief," 1 April 1977. See also Vance, *Hard Choices: Critical Years in America's Foreign Policy*, pp. 263–265.

29. JCL, Collection 24, NSA Brzezinski Material, Country File, Box 69, South Africa 1-4/77, Bowdler to Secretary of State, "Comment on Talks with Scott and Hawkins," 22 January 1977.

30. JCL, Collection 24, NSA Brzezinski Material, Country File, Box 69, South Africa 6/77, Minutes of First Meeting between Vorster and Mondale, Vienna, 19 May 1977.

31. JCL, Collection 24, NSA Brzezinski Material, Country File, Box 69, South Africa 6/77, Minutes of First Meeting between Vorster and Mondale, Vienna, 19 May 1977.

32. JCL, Collection 24, NSA Brzezinski Material, Country File, Box 69, South Africa 6/77, Minutes of Second Meeting between Vorster and Mondale, Vienna, 19 May 1977.

33. DDRS, Papers for the Policy Review Committee Meeting 22/7/77 on Southern Africa, 19 July 1977.

34. DDRS, Minutes, NSC Meeting on South Africa, 3 March 1977.

35. JCL, CREST, NLC-7-6-10-1-6, Mondale to Vance, Young, Brzezinski, "Southern Africa—US Strategy and Meeting with Prime Minister Vorster," 4 April 1977.

36. JCL, Collection 24, NSA Brzezinski Material, Country File, Box 69, South Africa 6/77, Minutes of Second Meeting between Vorster and Mondale, Vienna, 19 May 1977.

37. JCL, Collection 24, NSA Brzezinski Material, Country File, Box 69, South Africa 6/77, Minutes of Third Meeting between Vorster and Mondale, Vienna, 19 May 1977.

38. GFL, National Security Adviser, Presidential Country Files for Africa, 1974–1977, Box 6, South Africa: State Department Telegrams: SECSTATE NODIS, Bowdler to Secretary of State, "Vorster-Kissinger Meeting: Strategy Considerations," 12 June 1976.

39. JCL, Collection 24, NSA Brzezinski Material, Country File, Box 69, South Africa 6/77, Minutes of Third Meeting between Vorster and Mondale, Vienna, 19 May 1977.

40. ARCA, PV 203, 1/V2/2, P. W. Botha, 1 Onderwerpslêers 1/V2 Verenigde State van Amerika, Press Conference with Vice President Mondale, Vienna, 20 May 1977.

41. See Colin Eglin (Progressive Reform Party), *Hansard*, House of Assembly Debates, 27 May 1977, col. 8370 and J. W. E. Wiley (South African Party), 27 May 1977, cols. 8733–4.

42. Sole, *"This Above All": Reminiscences of a South African Diplomat*, p. 367.

43. "Nooit ooit! sê min. Pik Botha," *Beeld*, 23 June 1977.

44. ISP, Deposit 4, Box 2, Records of Meetings 1973–1978, Record of Meeting between Smith, Vorster, and others, 12 September 1977.

45. ISP, Deposit 4, Box 2, Records of Meetings 1973–1978, First Record of Meeting between Smith, Pik Botha, Fourie, and others, Salisbury, 15 June 1977.

46. JCL, Collection 24, NSA North-South File, Funk: Subject File, Box 119, Rhodesia 4-10/77, Thornton to Brzezinski, "Elections in Africa," 1 April 1977.

47. DFAA, BFF, Kernkrag, South African Embassy, Washington, DC, to Fourie, "South Africa and the Bomb," 31 August 1977.

48. JCL, Collection 24, NSA Brzezinski Material, Country File, Box 69, South Africa 6/77, Minutes of Third Meeting between Vorster and Mondale, Vienna, 19 May 1977.

49. See also, for instance, DNSA, US Embassy, Pretoria, to Secretary of State, Washington, D. C., "Fonmin Botha Terms US Arms Embargo Decision 'Unacceptable,'" 28 October 1977.

50. Robert H. Bates, *Markets and States in Tropical Africa: The Political Basis of Agricultural Policies* (Berkeley: University of California Press, 2014), p. 131.

51. *Hansard*, House of Assembly Debates, 24 January 1977, col. 49.

52. See Giliomee, *The Afrikaners*, especially pp. 487–494; Moodie, *The Rise of Afrikanerdom*, especially pp. 1–21.

53. Jaap Marais and B. M. Schoeman, *Stryd is Lewe* (Pretoria: Aktuele Publikasies, 1980), p. 105.

54. A. Hertzog, *Oproep tot die Stryd* (Waterkloof, Pretoria: M. M. Hertzog, 1985), p. 2.

55. Hertzog, *Oproep tot die Stryd*, p. 35.

56. Hertzog, *Oproep tot die Stryd*, pp. 40–41.

57. Marais and Schoeman, *Stryd is Lewe*, p. 105.

58. "Regse winde waai nou sterk," *Die Vaderland*, 24 June 1977.

59. "Prog" was the widespread label used to denote the Progressive agenda, in its various political incarnations. It carried universally understood connotations that the target was "soft" on racial identity issues, did not represent the interests of the existing white power structure, and ultimately supported a one-man-one-vote polity.

60. Interview with Dirk Mudge, Otjiwarongo, 1 August 2011.

61. Ries and Dommisse, *Broedertwis*, p. 1.

62. Interview with Deon Fourie, Pretoria, 8 July 2011.

63. Interview with Koos van der Merwe, Pretoria, 13 October 2014.

64. Interview with Stoffel van der Merwe, Pretoria, 13 October 2014.

65. Interview with Stoffel van der Merwe, Pretoria, 13 October 2014.

66. ARCA, PV 408, NP Caucus, Notule, 22 June 1977.

67. "Beperkings op die Swart sakeman," *Volkshandel*, June 1977.

68. "SA moet tot vergelyk kom met nie-blanke middelstand," *Volkshandel*, September 1977.

69. ARCA, PV 408, NP Caucus, Notule, 20 April 1977.

70. Vance, *Hard Choices: Critical Years in America's Foreign Policy*, p. 265.

71. *Hansard*, House of Assembly Debates, 13 June 1977, col. 10005. See also 10085-92.

72. SANA, MEM, 1/565, I13/2, Eerste Minister: Buitelandse Sake, Tolbert to Vorster, 14 September 1977. Emphasis in the original.

73. Sole, *"This Above All": Reminiscences of a South African Diplomat*, p. 371.

74. SANA, MEM, 1/564, I13/2, Eerste Minister: Buitelandse Sake, Secretary for Foreign Affairs to All Heads of Mission, 18 October 1977.

75. This was the first ever time that Chapter VII sanctions were imposed upon a member state (Rhodesia being neither a member nor a state). See UN Security Council Resolution 418, 4 November 1977.

76. SANA, MEM, 1/565, I13/2, Eerste Minister: Buitelandse Sake; SANDFA, Group 5- Minister van Verdediging, Box 78, MV/28/14, Politiek Ander Departemente: Buitelandse Sake, Volume 2, Sole to Fourie, "Reaksie op 19 Oktober-Gebeure," 11 November 1977.

77. Papenfus, *Pik Botha and His Times*, p. 223.

78. "Pretoria se sterk rol," editorial, *Hoofstad*, 18 October 1977.

79. Interview with Koos van der Merwe, Pretoria, 13 October 2014.
80. Leonard Thompson, *A History of South Africa* (New Haven, CT: Yale University Press, 2001), p. 221.
81. Geldenhuys, *The Diplomacy of Isolation*, p. 64.
82. ARCA, PV 408, NP Caucus, Notule, 25 May 1977.
83. Interview with Koos van der Merwe, Pretoria, 13 October 2014.
84. Interview with Stoffel van der Merwe, Pretoria, 13 October 2014.
85. Interview with Koos van der Merwe, Pretoria, 13 October 2014.
86. Prinsloo, *Stem uit die Wildernis*, p. 71.
87. O'Meara, *Forty Lost Years*, p. 195.
88. ISP, Deposit 4, Box 6, Communications with ADR (SA), Volume 9, Rhodesian Diplomatic Mission to Gaylard, 18 July 1977.
89. Dan Slater, *Ordering Power: Contentious Politics and Authoritarian Leviathans in Southeast Asia* (Cambridge, UK; New York: Cambridge University Press, 2010).
90. Table 7 in Adam and Giliomee, *Ethnic Power Mobilized: Can South Africa Change?* p. 174.
91. SAHA, AL 3060, The State v. P. W. Botha and Appeal, Volumes 28 to 31, Antwoorde op Vrae Deur die Waarheids- en Versoeningskommissie aan Out-Staatspresident P. W. Botha, date unknown, pp. 95–96; Alden, *Apartheid's Last Stand*, pp. 46–49.
92. Republic of South Africa, "White Paper on Defense and Armaments Production," p. 4.
93. Republic of South Africa, "White Paper on Defense and Armaments Production," p. 7.
94. Republic of South Africa, "White Paper on Defense and Armaments Production," p. 4.
95. SANDFA, Group 4—P. W. Botha, Box 143, 76/1, Strategie: Algemeen, Volume 3, Malan to P. W. Botha, "Strategiese Riglyne," August 1977. Aanhangsel A.
96. SANDFA, Group 4—P. W. Botha, Box 142, 76/1, Strategie: Algemeen, Volume 2, "Notes on Total Strategy," July 1977.
97. SANDFA, Group 4—P. W. Botha, Box 143, 76/1, Strategie: Algemeen, Volume 3, Malan to P. W. Botha, "Strategiese Riglyne," August 1977. Aanhangsel B.
98. SANDFA, Group 3—HSAW Chief of Defense Force, Box 168, SWA I, HS Ops to Malan, "Riglyne vir Verdere Onderhandelings met "S" tov SAW Teenwoordigheid in SWA," 28 December 1978.
99. SANDFA, Group 4—P. W. Botha, Box 143, 76/1, Strategie: Algemeen, Volume 3, Malan to P. W. Botha, "Strategiese Riglyne," August 1977. Aanhangsel B.
100. SANDFA, Group 4—P. W. Botha, Box 143, 76/1, Strategie: Algemeen, Volume 3, Malan to P. W. Botha, "Strategiese Riglyne," August 1977. Aanhangsel B.
101. SANDFA, Group 4—P. W. Botha, Box 143, 76/1, Strategie: Algemeen, Volume 3, "Riglyne vir 'n Strategie tov Rhodesië," 13 July 1977. For Rhodesia policy see also SANDFA, Group 4—P. W. Botha, Box 143, 76/1, Strategie: Algemeen, Volume 3, Malan to P. W. Botha, "Strategiese Riglyne," August 1977. Aanhangsel D.
102. SANDFA, Group 4—P. W. Botha, Box 143, 76/1, Strategie: Algemeen, Volume 3, "Riglyne vir 'n Strategie tov Rhodesië," 13 July 1977. Emphasis added.
103. SANDFA, Group 4—P. W. Botha, Box 143, 76/1, Strategie: Algemeen, Volume 3, "Riglyne vir 'n Strategie tov Rhodesië," 13 July 1977.
104. "Politiek oorheers die ekonomie," editorial, *Volkshandel*, June 1977.
105. SANDFA, Group 4—P. W. Botha, Box 143, 76/1, Strategie: Algemeen, Volume 3, Malan to P. W. Botha, "Strategiese Riglyne," August 1977.
106. Interview with Niël Barnard, Cape Town, 11 October 2011.
107. Interview with Chris Thirion, Pretoria, 20 July 2011.
108. Prinsloo, *Stem uit die Wildernis*, p. 69.
109. ISP, Deposit 4, Box 2, Records of Meetings 1973–1978, Record of Meeting between Smith, Vorster, and others, 12 September 1977.
110. ISP, Deposit 4, Box 2, Records of Meetings 1973–1978, Record of Meeting between Smith, Hawkins, Pik Botha, and Fourie, Cape Town, 31 March 1977.
111. ARCA, PV 408, NP Caucus, Notule, 24 March 1976.
112. SANDFA, Group 3—HSAW, Box 137, HSAW/311/1/23, Verdediging Samewerking: Rhodesië: Korrespondensie, Volume 1, "Bookvalue of Material Assistance by RSA to Rhodesia: Period 1 January 1977 to 31 December 1977," 6 January 1978.

113. ISP, Deposit 4, Box 6, Communications with ADR (SA), Volume 10, Gaylard to Rhodesian Diplomatic Mission, 16 December 1977.
114. ISP, Deposit 4, Box 6, Communications with ADR (SA), Volume 10, Rhodesian Diplomatic Mission to Gaylard, 5 December 1977. See also ISP, Deposit 4, Box 6, Communications with ADR (SA), Volume 10, Gaylard to Rhodesian Diplomatic Mission, 6 December 1977.
115. Interview with Piet van Vuuren, Pretoria, 27 July 2011; Smith, *The Great Betrayal*, p. 253.
116. Interview with Dirk Mudge, Otjiwarongo, 1 August 2011.
117. SANDFA, Group 3—HSAW, Box 169, SWA II, "Samewatting van Samesprekings met Minister Pik Botha, BG SWA, Mnr Mudge en Generaals Viljoen en Boshoff," 20 December 1977.
118. Papenfus, *Pik Botha and His Times*, p. 235.
119. Interview with C. A. "Bastie" Bastiaanse, Centurion, 28 July 2011.
120. ARCA, PV 408, NP Caucus, Notule, 20 April 1977.
121. Interview with C. A. "Bastie" Bastiaanse, Centurion, 28 July 2011.
122. Interview with Neil van Heerden, Hermanus, 6 September 2011.
123. "Is the Afrikaner's choice between change and national suicide," *Times*, 23 May 1977.
124. "Is the Afrikaner's choice between change and national suicide," *Times*, 23 May 1977.
125. "Ontugwet is vir voortbestaan nie nodig—Pik," *Beeld*, 7 July 1977.
126. Interview with Neil van Heerden, Hermanus, 6 September 2011.
127. Papenfus, *Pik Botha and His Times*, p. 431.
128. de Villiers and de Villiers, *PW*, p. 124.
129. O'Meara, *Forty Lost Years*, p. 235.
130. SANDFA, Group 3—HSAW Chief of Defense Force, Box 168, SWA I, "Notas Oor Vergadering te Oubos," 29 December 1977.
131. SANDFA, Group 3—HSAW Chief of Defense Force, Box 168, SWA I, "Notas Oor Vergadering te Oubos," 29 December 1977.
132. SANDFA, Group 6—DMI, Box 125, MI/303/3/2, "Strategiese riglyne vir Optrede teen Terroriste wat die RSA Bedreig maar Hulle Oorkant die Grense van die RSA/SWA Bevind," 12 December 1977.
133. Interview with Jannie Geldenhuys, Pretoria, 18 July 2011.
134. SANDFA, Group 3—HSAW Chief of Defense Force, Box 168, SWA I, "Notas Oor Vergadering te Oubos," 29 December 1977.
135. SANDFA, Group 3—HSAW Chief of Defense Force, Box 168, SWA I, "Notas Oor Vergadering te Oubos," 29 December 1977.
136. SANDFA, Group 3—HSAW Chief of Defense Force, Box 168, SWA I, "Notas Oor Vergadering te Oubos," 29 December 1977. Despite his best efforts to achieve a balance, the reality was that the SADF had won a major victory. The decision is foregrounded in Malan's autobiography: Malan, *My Life with the SA Defence Force*, pp. 192–193.
137. DNSA, UN Document S/12636, "Namibia, 1977–1980: Document 18: Proposal Transmitted by the Contact Group to the UN General Assembly," 10 April 1978.
138. Fourie, *Brandpunte*, p. 170.
139. Interview with Riaan Eksteen, Swakopmund, 2 August 2011.
140. Fourie, *Brandpunte*, p. 169.
141. SANA, 1/1/7, Kabinet Notuleregister, 18 April 1978.
142. Sole, *"This Above All": Reminiscences of a South African Diplomat*, pp. 432.
143. Interview with Riaan Eksteen, Swakopmund, 2 August 2011.
144. Interview with Pik Botha, Pretoria, 11 August 2011.
145. Fourie, *Brandpunte*, p. 169; Papenfus, *Pik Botha and His Times*, p. 234.
146. *Hansard*, House of Assembly Debates, 24 August 1988, col 15969. Both Bothas were later proved to be "right." Into the 1980s, South Africa prevaricated extensively on the meaning and implementation of Resolution 435, but the framework Pretoria committed to in 1978 did ultimately provide much of the basis for Namibian independence in 1990.
147. See Piero Gleijeses, *Visions of Freedom: Havana, Washington, Pretoria and the Struggle for Southern Africa, 1976–1991* (Chapel Hill: The University of North Carolina Press, 2013).
148. Interview with Dirk Mudge, Otjiwarongo, 1 August 2011.
149. Interview with Neil van Heerden, Hermanus, 6 September 2011.

150. SANDFA, Group 3—HSAW, Box 169, SWA II, Malan to Fourie, "Weermagsvereistes ten Opsigte van Onderhandelings oor Suidwes-Afrika," 14 March 1978.

151. SANDFA, Group 3—HSAW, Box 169, SWA II, "Proposal for a Settlement of the Namibian Situation," 31 January 1978.

152. SANDFA, Group 6—MID/MI, Box 125, MI/303/3/2, Strategiese Beplanning: SWA, Volume 2, Malan to P. W. Botha, "Brief van Mnr R. F. Botha aan Dr K. Waldheim tov die Waldheimverslag," September 1978.

153. SANDFA, Group 3—HSAW Chief of Defense Force, Box 143, HSOPS/DES/303/5/11/1, Die Militêre Standpunt tov SWA 8 Des 1978, TNSD 15/78, "National Strategic Guidelines for the Implementation of a Forward Defense Strategy in SWA, Angola and Zambia," 9 August 1978.

154. SANDFA, Group 6—MID/MI, Box 125, MI/303/3/2, Strategiese Beplanning: SWA, Volume 2, Malan to P. W. Botha, "Brief van Mnr R. F. Botha aan Dr K. Waldheim tov die Waldheimverslag," September 1978.

155. SANDFA, Group 3—HSAW, Box 169, SWA II, "SAW optrede teen SWAPO Basisse in Angola en Zambië," 16 February 1978.

156. SANDFA, Group 3—HSAW, Box 169, SWA II, Malan to P. W. Botha, "Militêr Politieke Situasie in Suidwes-Afrika: Oorsig van die Situasie," 27 February 1978.

157. SANDFA, Group 3—HSAW, Box 169, SWA II, Malan to P. W. Botha, "Militêr Politieke Situasie in Suidwes-Afrika: Oorsig van die Situasie," 27 February 1978.

158. SANDFA, Group 3—HSAW, Box 169, SWA II, AMI to Malan, "Studiestukke tov SWA en Botswana," 6 February 1978.

159. DNSA, Bowdler to State Department, "Namibia: Clarification of Proposal," 27 February 1978.

160. Responsibility for the killing remains unclear today: Jan-Bart Gewald, "Who Killed Clemens Kapuuo?" *Journal of Southern African Studies* 30, no. 3 (September 2004): 573.

161. SANA, 1/1/8, Kabinet Notuleregister, 29 March 1978.

162. SANA, 1/1/7, Kabinet Notuleregister, 11 April 1978. See also Malan, *My Life with the SA Defence Force*, pp. 191–194.

163. SANA, 1/1/8, Kabinet Notuleregister, 2 May 1978.

164. Interview with Pik Botha, Pretoria, 11 August 2011.

165. Sole, *"This Above All": Reminiscences of a South African Diplomat*, p. 432.

166. Peter Stiff, *The Silent War: South African Recce Operations, 1969–1994* (Alberton: Galago, 1999), p. 205. For a stimulating overview of the controversy surrounding the attack, see Gary Baines, *South Africa's "Border War": Contested Narratives and Conflicting Memories* (London: Bloomsbury, 2014), pp. 89–104.

167. "SA slaan hard," editorial, *Hoofstad*, 8 May 1978.

168. Interview with Constand Viljoen, Pretoria, 13 July 2011.

169. Papenfus, *Pik Botha and His Times*, p. 528.

170. DNSA, State Department to many posts, "Namibia: Comments by Defense and Foreign Ministers," 18 May 1978.

171. SANA, 1/1/7, Kabinet Notuleregister, 9 May 1978. See also De Klerk, *The Last Trek*, p. 59.

172. SANA, 1/1/7, Kabinet Notuleregister, 13 June 1978.

173. André du Pisani, *SWA/Namibia, the Politics of Continuity and Change* (Johannesburg: J. Ball Publishers, 1985), pp. 405–406.

174. Interview with Riaan Eksteen, Swakopmund, 2 August 2011.

175. Interview with Constand Viljoen, Pretoria, 13 July 2011.

176. Interview with Jeremy Shearar, Pretoria, 23 August 2011.

177. Interview with Chris Thirion, Pretoria, 20 July 2011

178. Interview with Constand Viljoen, Pretoria, 13 July 2011.

179. O'Meara, *Forty Lost Years*, pp. 230–249; de Villiers and de Villiers, *PW*, pp. 95–138.

180. Papenfus, *Pik Botha and His Times*, pp. 245–252.

181. de Villiers and de Villiers, *PW*, p. 105.

182. The former editor of the *Rand Daily Mail*, Allister Sparks, contends that, if not for the scandal, Mulder, with his old ally van den Bergh, would have led the polity in a very different

direction (though what direction that was remains unsaid). See Sparks, *The Mind of South Africa*, p. 307.

183. Anna Starcke, *Survival: Taped Interviews with South Africa's Power Elite* (Cape Town: Tafelberg, 1978).

184. For an extensive discussion, see Ries and Dommisse, *Broedertwis*.

185. *Hansard*, House of Assembly Debates, 9 February 1977, col. 1112.

186. Interview with Koos van der Merwe, Pretoria, 13 October 2014.

187. Interview with Stoffel van der Merwe, Pretoria, 13 October 2014.

188. For divergent perspectives, see Welsh, *The Rise and Fall of Apartheid*, pp. 233–237; Malan, *My Life with the SA Defence Force*, pp. 320–327; Papenfus, *Pik Botha and His Times*, pp. 423–428.

189. SANDFA, Group 3—HSAW, Box 169, SWA II, "Opsomming van Bespreking op 17 Februarie 1978 Tussen die Ministers van Verdediging, Ekonomiese Sake, Buitelandse Sake en hul Departementshoofde," 17 February 1978.

Conclusion

1. D'Oliveira, *Vorster: The Man*, p. 256.

2. Papenfus, *Pik Botha and His Times*.

3. One 1975 entry in Vorster's diary, for instance, notes a "conversation about yearly report on Information's secret projects" featuring himself, Minister for Finance Owen Horwood, Mulder, van den Bergh, and Eschel Rhoodie. See ARCA, PV 132, 5/1/19, Aantekeninge en Dagboeke, Vorster's Dagboek, 1 October 1975.

4. Rudolf Erasmus, *Supplementary Report of the Commission of Inquiry into Alleged Irregularities in the Former Department of Information* (Pretoria: Government Printer, 1979).

5. O'Meara, *Forty Lost Years*, pp. 243–244, 305–308.

6. Lawrence Schlemmer, "Change in South Africa: Opportunities and Restraints," in *The Apartheid Regime: Political Power and Racial Domination*, ed. Robert M. Price and Carl Gustav Rosberg (Berkeley: Institute of International Studies, University of California, 1980), p. 251.

7. SANA, 1/1/6, Kabinet Notuleregister, 3 August 1976.

8. Vosloo, ed. *Schalk Pienaar: 10 Jaar Politieke Kommentaar*, p. 100.

9. ARCA, PV 203, P. W. Botha, 1/V9/1, 1 Onderwerpsleers, 1/V9 Vorster, adv. B. J., "Toespraak Deur Sy Edele Die Eerste Minister Tydens Die Nasionale Party Kongres in die Callie Humansaal, Bloemfontein," 8 September 1976.

10. English-speaking whites had long since lost any such faith, if they had it in the first place.

11. Schlemmer, "Change in South Africa: Opportunities and Restraints," pp. 260–261.

12. "Dis kwart voor middernag: waarheen nou met Bantoebeleid," editorial, *Volkshandel*, July 1973.

13. Giliomee, *The Parting of the Ways: South African Politics 1976–82*, p. ix.

14. Welsh, *The Rise and Fall of Apartheid*, pp. 201–202. See also Christopher Saunders, "The Ending of the Cold War and Southern Africa," in *The End of the Cold War and the Third World: New Perspectives on Regional Conflict*, ed. Artemy M. Kalinovsky and Sergey Radchenko (London; New York: Routledge, 2011), p. 268.

15. A decent case could even be made that the NP moved away from Afrikaner exclusivity under Vorster and from a solely white power structure under P. W. Botha, but never abandoned anticommunism in any way, shape, or form. If so, what did the regime ultimately stand for?

16. de Villiers and de Villiers, *PW*, p. 151.

17. Peter Vale, "The Cold War and South Africa: Repetitions and Revisions on a Prolegomenon," in *Beyond the Border War: New Perspectives on Southern Africa's Late-Cold War Conflicts*, ed. Gary Baines and Peter Vale (South Africa: Unisa Press, 2008), pp. 31–32.

18. Hugo, "The Politics of Untruth: Afrikaner Academics for Apartheid."

19. Alden, *Apartheid's Last Stand*, p. 51.

20. O'Meara, *Forty Lost Years*, pp. 271–287.

21. *Hansard*, House of Assembly Debates, 31 January 1967, col 441–2.

22. WKL, Public Library of US Diplomacy, Kissinger Cables, US Embassy, Pretoria, to State Department, "South African Policy Review," 7 November 1975.

23. *Rand Daily Mail*, 28 and 29 December 1976. See especially the Bob Connelly cartoon on 29 December.

24. O'Meara, *Forty Lost Years*, p. 197.

25. I am grateful to Daniel Magaziner for discussions on this point.

26. Price, *The Apartheid State in Crisis: Political Transformation in South Africa, 1975–1990.*

Note on Sources

1. Miller, "The Black Hole of Apartheid History."

2. Verne Harris, "'They Should Have Destroyed More': The Destruction of Public Records by the South African State in the Final Years of Apartheid, 1990–1994," in *Archives and the Public Good: Accountability and Records in Modern Society*, ed. Richard J. Cox and David A. Wallace (Westport, CT: Quorum Books, 2002).

3. Interview with Riaan Eksteen, Swakopmund, 2 August 2011; Interview with C. A. "Bastie" Bastiaanse, Centurion, 28 July 2011.

4. Interview with Riaan Eksteen, Swakopmund, 2 August 2011.

5. Interview with Tom Wheeler, Johannesburg, 21 July 2011.

6. Interview with Piet de Wit, Pretoria, 2 April 2013.

7. See Dlamini, *Askari: A Story of Collaboration and Betrayal in the Anti-Apartheid Struggle*, p. 119.

8. Welsh, *The Rise and Fall of Apartheid*, pp. 173–175.

9. O'Meara, *Forty Lost Years.*

BIBLIOGRAPHY

Primary Sources

ARCHIVAL SOURCES

South Africa

Afrikaner Broederbond Archives, Pretoria
    3/75/Staat
    3/84/1 Afrikaner
    1975/1-5UranotDB
    1976/2-5UranotDB

Archive for Contemporary Affairs, Institute for Contemporary History, University of the Free State, Bloemfontein
    PV 132, B. J. Vorster
    PV 203, P. W. Botha
    PV 408, NP Caucus
    PV 528, Hilgard Muller
    PV 698, A. H. du Plessis
    PV 819, Alf Ries

Ian Smith Papers, Cory Library, Rhodes University, Grahamstown
    Communications with ADR (SA)
    Defense Matters with RSA
    Détente: Official Communications with South Africa
    Geneva Conference: Record of Meetings (British)—Informal
    Kissinger Proposals: Geneva Conference—Background Papers
    Negotiations with ANC (Nkomo) Minutes
    Prime Minister's Personal File: General Correspondence
    Records of Meetings 1973–1978
    Reports of Meeting with Zambian Reps and ANC from October 1974 to June 1975: "Détente"
    Rhodesia Government: Cabinet Minutes (Secretary's Standard File)
    Rhodesia Settlement: Meetings with African National Council
    Victoria Falls Conference August 1975
    Victoria Falls Conference Background Papers

South African Department of Foreign Affairs Archives, Pretoria
    1/14/3, Portugal Relations with South Africa

1/14/10, Portugal's African Territories
1/22/1 OS, Angola: Political Situation and Developments
1/22/3, Angola: Relations with South Africa
1/33/3, United States of America Relations with South Africa
1/33/8/3, USA: Policy on Africa
1/99/12, Africa: Communism in Africa
1/99/19, Africa: SA Policy in Africa & Relations with African States
1/112/3, Zaïre: Relations with SA
1/113/3, Moçambique: Relations with SA
1/156/3, Rhodesia: Relations with South Africa
1/157/3, Zambia: Relations with South Africa
Brand Fourie Files

South African History Archive, William Cullen Library, Witwatersrand University, Johannesburg
AL 3060, The State v. P. W. Botha and Appeal

South African National Archives
1/1/5, Kabinet Notuleregister
1/1/6, Kabinet Notuleregister
MEM, I15/2
MEM, I13/2

South African National Defense Force Archives, Pretoria
Group 1—VBR/VBK (DSC)
Group 1—Chief of Staff Operations
Group 1—AMI/HIS
Group 1—HSAW Chief of Defense Force
Group 2—MVV/P. W. Botha
Group 3—HSAW Chief of Defense Force
Group 3 (Volume 1)—AMI/HSI
Group 3 (Volume 2)—HSI/AMI
Group 4—P. W. Botha
Group 4—MVV/ P. W. Botha
Group 4—Chief of Staff Operations
Group 5—Minister van Verdediging
War Diaries (OD)
Group 35

United Kingdom

National Archives, Kew
FCO 45/1323, Political Relations between South Africa and Zambia
FCO 45/1760, Visit by Secretary of State to Southern Africa: Policy
FCO 82/662, Messages Passed between Henry Kissinger and Secretary of State for Foreign and Commonwealth Affairs
FCO 73/224, S/S Messages to & from the USA
PREM 16/634, Rhodesia Part II

United States

Gerald R. Ford Presidential Library, Ann Arbor, Michigan
Freedom of Information Act documents
National Security Adviser Memoranda of Conversations, Ford Administration
National Security Adviser, Presidential Country Files for Africa, 1974–1977
National Security Adviser, Trip Briefing Books and Cables for Henry Kissinger, 1974–1976
National Security Council Meeting Minutes

Remote Archive Capture Series, NSA Backchannel Messages
Ronald H. Nessen Files
US National Security Institutional Files, 1974–1977

Herman B. Wells Library, Indiana University, Bloomington, Indiana
Hastings Kamuzu Banda Collection

Jimmy Carter Presidential Library, Atlanta, Georgia
Donated Historical Material: Zbigniew Brzezinski Collection
NSA Brzezinski Material
NSA North-South File

National Archives II, College Park, Maryland
Record Group 59, Records of the Department of State

National Security Archive, George Washington University, Washington, DC
Incoming FOIAs
South Africa and the United States

Sterling Memorial Library, Yale University, New Haven, Connecticut
Cyrus R. and Grace Sloane Vance Papers

Malawi

National Archives of Malawi
Ministry of External Affairs

Online Databases

Association for Diplomatic Studies and Training Foreign Affairs Oral History Project
Central Intelligence Agency Reading Room
Digital National Security Archive
    Conflicting Missions: Secret Cuban Documents on History of Africa Involvement
    Kissinger Transcripts
    South Africa: The Making of US Policy 1962–1989
    National Security Archive Electronic Briefing Book No. 454
United States National Archives Access to Archival Databases
WikiLeaks
    Public Library of US Diplomacy: Kissinger Cables

Memoirs

Basson, Japie. *State of the Nation: As Viewed from a Front Bench in Parliament, 1969–1981.* Camps Bay, SA: Politika, 2008.

Beukes, Herbert. *From Garies to Washington.* Milnerton, SA: CED Book Printers, 2011.

Breytenbach, Jan. *They Live by the Sword.* Alberton, SA: Lemur, 1990.

Brink, André P. *A Fork in the Road: A Memoir.* London: Harvill Secker, 2009.

De Klerk, F. W. *The Last Trek: A New Beginning: The Autobiography.* London: Macmillan, 1998.

De Villiers, Les. *Secret Information.* Cape Town: Tafelberg, 1980.

Easum, Donald. *Hard Times for the Africa Bureau, 1974–1976.* Chapel Hill, NC: American Diplomacy Publishers, 2010, at http://www.unc.edu/depts/diplomat/item/2010/0406/fsl/fsl_hardtimes.html.

Fourie, Brand. *Brandpunte: Agter Die Skerms met Suid-Afrika se Bekendste Diplomaat.* Kaapstad: Tafelberg, 1991.

———. *Buitelandse Woelinge om Suid-Afrika, 1939–1985.* unknown: unknown, unknown.

Flower, Ken. *Serving Secretly: An Intelligence Chief on Record; Rhodesia into Zimbabwe, 1964 to 1981.* London: Murray, 1987.

Geldenhuys, Jannie. *At the Front: A General's Account of South Africa's Border War.* Jeppestown: Jonathan Ball, 2009.

————. *Dié Wat Gewen Het: Feite en Fabels Van Die Bosoorlog.* Pretoria: Litera, 2007.

Graaff, De Villiers. *Div Looks Back: The Memoirs of Sir De Villiers Graaff.* Cape Town: Human & Rousseau, 1993

Hertzog, A. *Oproep Tot Die Stryd.* Waterkloof, Pretoria: M.M. Hertzog, 1985.

Kissinger, Henry. *Years of Renewal.* New York: Simon & Schuster, 1999.

————. *Years of Upheaval.* Boston: Little, Brown, 1982.

Malan, Magnus. *My Life with the SA Defense Force.* Pretoria: Protea Book House, 2006.

Marais, Jaap, and B. M. Schoeman. *Stryd Is Lewe.* Pretoria: Aktuele Publikasies, 1980.

Marenches, Alexandre de, and Christine Ockrent. *Dans Le Secret Des Princes.* Paris: Stock, 1986.

Mudge, Dirk. "From South-West Africa to Namibia: My Experiences Along a Crooked Road to an Unknown Destination." Unpublished manuscript, date unknown.

Muzorewa, Abel Tendekayi. *Rise up & Walk: The Autobiography of Bishop Abel Tendekai Muzorewa.* Nashville: Abingdon, 1978.

Nkomo, Joshua. *Nkomo: The Story of My Life.* London: Methuen, 1984.

Nujoma, Sam. *Where Others Wavered: The Autobiography of Sam Nujoma,* Panaf Great Lives. London: Panaf, 2001.

Owen, David. *Time to Declare.* London: Joseph, 1991.

Rhoodie, Eschel M. *P. W. Botha: The Last Betrayal.* Melville: S.A. Politics, 1989.

Schoeman, Ben. *My Lewe in Die Politiek.* Johannesburg: Perskor, 1978.

Scott, David. *Ambassador in Black and White: Thirty Years of Changing Africa.* London: Weidenfeld and Nicolson, 1981.

Slabbert, F. van Zyl. *The Last White Parliament.* Johannesburg: J. Ball Publishers: H. Strydom Publishers, 1985.

Smith, Ian. *The Great Betrayal: The Memoirs of Ian Douglas Smith.* London: Blake, 1997.

Smith, Nico. *Die Afrikaner Broederbond: Belewinge van Die Binnekant.* Pretoria: LAPA Uitgewers, 2009.

Sole, Donald. *"This above All": Reminiscences of a South African Diplomat.* Unpublished manuscript, date unknown.

Tyson, Harvey. *Editors under Fire.* Sandton, SA: Random House, 1993.

Vance, Cyrus R. *Hard Choices: Critical Years in America's Foreign Policy.* New York: Simon & Schuster, 1983.

Wolvaardt, Pieter, Tom Wheeler, and Werner Scholtz. *From Verwoerd to Mandela: South African Diplomats Remember.* 3 vols. Pretoria: Crink, 2010.

Woods, Donald. *Asking for Trouble: Autobiography of a Banned Journalist.* 1st American ed. New York: Atheneum, 1981.

Interviews (all locations in South Africa unless otherwise specified)

Niël Barnard, Cape Town, 11 October 2011

C. A. "Bastie" Bastiaanse, Centurion, 28 July 2011

J. H. A. "Herb" Beukes, Somerset West, 7 September 2011

J. S. F. "Frikkie" Botha, Cape Town, 7 September 2011

Roelof "Pik" Botha, Pretoria, 11 August 2011 and 5 April 2013

Riaan Eksteen, Swakopmund, Namibia, 2 and 3 August 2011, 30 March 2013

Deon Fourie, Pretoria, 8 July 2011

Deon Geldenhuys, Johannesburg, 28 July 2011

Jannie Geldenhuys, Pretoria, 18 July 2011

Neil van Heerden, Hermanus, 6 September 2011

Hennie de Klerk, Pretoria, 20 September 2011

Dirk Mudge, Otjiwarongo, Namibia, 1 August 2011

Barend du Plessis, Pretoria, 5 April 2013

Jeremy Shearar, Pretoria, 18 and 23 August 2011

Maritz Spaarwater, Onrusrivier, 6 September 2011
Chris Thirion, Pretoria, 19 July 2011
Constand Viljoen, Pretoria, 13 July 2011
Piet van Vuuren, Pretoria, 27 July 2011
Koos van der Merwe, Pretoria, 14 October 2014
Stoffel van der Merwe, Pretoria, 14 October 2014
W. S. "Kaas" van der Waals, Centurion, 15 August 2011
Tom Wheeler, Johannesburg, 21 July 2011
Piet de Wit, Pretoria, 2 April 2011

Personal Communications (in addition to the above)

Fred Bridgland
Sean Cleary
Walter Cutler
Robert Hultslander
F. W. de Klerk (c/o Dave Steward)
Johan Mostert
Marius Oelschig
Daan Prinsloo
David Tothill

Newspapers and Periodicals

Argus
Beeld
Cape Times
Daily News
Die Afrikaner
Die Beeld
Die Burger
Die Oosterlig
Die Transvaler
Die Vaderland
Die Volksblad
Daily Telegraph (London)
Financial Times (London)
Fraternité-Matin (Abidjan)
Guardian (London)
Hoofstad
L'Essor (Bamako)
Le Soleil (Dakar)
Malawi News (Blantyre)
Newsweek
New York Times
Observer (London)
Oggendblad
Pretoria News
Rand Daily Mail
Rapport
Rhodesia Herald (Salisbury)
Scotsman (Edinburgh)
Sechaba
Sunday Times (London)
Time
Times (London)

Times of Zambia (Lusaka)
To the Point
Veg
Volkshandel
Washington Post
Weekend World (Johannesburg)
West Africa (London)
World (Johannesburg)

Official Publications

Fifth Summit Conference of East and Central African States. "Manifesto on Southern Africa." Lusaka, April 1969.

Foreign Relations of the United States: Southern Africa, 1969–1976, vol. XXVIII. Washington, DC: State Department, Office of the Historian, 2011.

Kaunda, Kenneth D., and B. J. Vorster. *Dear Mr Vorster . . .: Details of Exchanges between President Kaunda of Zambia and Prime Minister Vorster of South Africa.* Lusaka: Zambia Information Services, 1971.

Republic of South Africa, *Hansard,* House of Assembly Debates.

Republic of South Africa, *Hansard,* Debates of the Senate.

Republic of South Africa. *White Paper on Defense and Armaments Production.* Pretoria: Government Printing Office, 1977.

United Nations Security Council, Official Records, Thirty-First Year.

United States Senate, Committee on Foreign Relations, Subcommittee on African Affairs, *Angola,* 94th Congress, 2nd Session (Washington, DC: GPO, 1976)

United States House of Representatives, Committee on International Relations, *United States Policy on Angola,* 94th Congress, 2nd Session (Washington, DC: GPO, 1976)

World Bank, *World Development Report 1980.* New York: Oxford University Press, 1980.

Other Published Primary Sources

"Address by Dr. The Hon. C.P. Mulder, at the Royal Institute of International Affairs, London, 5th July, 1971." Johannesburg: South African Institute for International Affairs, 1971.

Geyser, O., ed. *Select Speeches.* Bloemfontein: INCH, 1977.

Johannesburg District Committee of the Communist Party of South Africa. *Kommunisme en Die Afrikaner.* Johannesburg 1940.

Kaunda, Kenneth D. *Humanism and Apartheid.* Lusaka: The Veritas Corporation, 1971.

Louw, Louis. *Dawie, 1946–1964.* Cape Town: Tafelberg-Uitgewers, 1965.

McLachlan, R., ed. *Vrugte van Die Nasionale Bewind.* Kaapstad: Inligtingdiens van die Nasionale Party, 1974.

Oosthuizen, A. J. G.. *Kommunisme en die Vakunies.* Heidelberg, South Africa: Voortrekkerpers, 1938.

Pelzer, Adriaan Nicolaas, ed. *Verwoerd Speaks: Speeches, 1948–1966.* Johannesburg: APB Publishers, 1966.

Scholtz, J. J. J., ed. *Vegter en hervormer: grepe uit die toesprake van P.W. Botha.* Cape Town: Tafelberg, 1988

Vorster, B. J. *South Africa's Outward Policy.* Cape Town: Tafelberg, 1970.

Vosloo, Ton, ed. *Schalk Pienaar: 10 Jaar Politieke Kommentaar.* Cape Town: Tafelberg, 1975.

Secondary Sources

Abulof, Uriel. "'Small Peoples': The Existential Uncertainty of Ethnonational Communities." *International Studies Quarterly* 53, no. 1 (2009): 227–248.

Adam, Heribert. *Modernizing Racial Domination: South Africa's Political Dynamics.* Berkeley; London: University of California Press, 1971.

———. "The South African Power-Elite: A Survey of Ideological Commitment." In *South Africa: Sociological Perspectives*, edited by Heribert Adam, 73–102. London: Oxford University Press, 1971.

———. "Survival Politics: In Search of a New Ideology." In *Ethnic Power Mobilized: Can South Africa Change?*, edited by H. Adam and H. Giliomee, pp. 128–144. Cape Town: David Philips, 1979.

Adam, Heribert, and Hermann Giliomee. *Ethnic Power Mobilized: Can South Africa Change?* New Haven, CT; London: Yale University Press, 1979.

———. *The Rise and Crisis of Afrikaner Power*. Cape Town: David Philips, 1979.

Alden, Chris. *Apartheid's Last Stand: The Rise and Fall of the South African Security State*. Basingstoke: Macmillan, 1996.

Anglin, Douglas, and Timothy M. Shaw. *Zambia's Foreign Policy: Studies in Diplomacy and Dependence*. Boulder, CO: Westview Press, 1979.

Baines, Gary. *South Africa's "Border War": Contested Narratives and Conflicting Memories*. London: Bloomsbury, 2014.

Baines, Gary, and Peter Vale. *Beyond the Border War: New Perspectives on Southern Africa's Late-Cold War Conflicts*. South Africa: Unisa Press, 2008.

Bamba, A. B. "An Unconventional Challenge to Apartheid: The Ivorian Dialogue Diplomacy with South Africa, 1960–1978." *International Journal of African Historical Studies* 47, no. 1 (2014): 77–99.

Barber, James. *South Africa's Foreign Policy, 1945–1970*. London: Oxford University Press, 1973.

Barber, James, and John Barratt. *South Africa's Foreign Policy: The Search for Status and Security, 1945–1988*. Johannesburg: Cambridge University Press, 1990.

Barratt, John. "South Africa's Outward Policy: From Isolation to Dialogue." In *South African Dialogue: Contrasts in South African Thinking on Basic Race Issues*, edited by Nicolaas Johannes Rhoodie, 543–561. Johannesburg: McGraw-Hill Book Co., 1972.

Bat, Jean-Pierre. *Le Syndrome Foccart: La Politique Française en Afrique, de 1959 à nos Jours*. Paris: Gallimard, 2012.

Bates, Robert H. *Markets and States in Tropical Africa: The Political Basis of Agricultural Policies*. Berkeley: University of California Press, 1981.

———. *Markets and States in Tropical Africa: The Political Basis of Agricultural Policies*. Berkeley: University of California Press, 2014.

Beaufre, André. *An Introduction to Strategy*. New York: Praeger, 1965.

Bethencourt, Francisco. *Racisms: From the Crusades to the Twentieth Century*. Princeton, NJ: Princeton University Press, 2013.

Bonner, Philip. "African Urbanization on the Rand between the 1930s and 1960s: Its Social Character and Political Consequences." *Journal of Southern African Studies* 21 (1995): 115–129.

Bonner, Philip, Peter Delius, and Deborah Posel. *Apartheid's Genesis, 1935–1962*. Braamfontein, South Africa: Ravan Press; Witwatersrand University Press, 1993.

Boone, Catherine. "State Building in the African Countryside: Structure and Politics at the Grassroots." *Journal of Development Studies* 34, no. 4 (1998): 1–31.

Borstelmann, Thomas. *Apartheid's Reluctant Uncle: The United States and Southern Africa in the Early Cold War*. New York; Oxford: Oxford University Press, 1993.

———. *The Cold War and the Color Line: American Race Relations in the Global Arena*. Cambridge, MA: Harvard University Press, 2001.

Branch, Daniel. *Defeating Mau Mau, Creating Kenya: Counterinsurgency, Civil War, and Decolonization*, African Studies. Cambridge; New York: Cambridge University Press, 2009.

Breytenbach, Breyten. "The Alienation of White South Africa." In *Apartheid*, edited by Alex La Guma, pp. 137–148. New York: International Publishers, 1977.

Brink, Elsabé. *Soweto, 16 June 1976: Personal Accounts of the Uprising*. Cape Town: Kwela Books, 2006.

Brooks, Alan, and Jeremy Brickhill. *Whirlwind before the Storm*. London: International and Defense Aid Fund for Southern Africa, 1980.

Burke, Roland. *Decolonization and the Evolution of International Human Rights*. Philadelphia: University of Pennsylvania Press, 2010.

Burke, Timothy. "Eyes Wide Shut: Africanists and the Moral Problematics of Postcolonial Societies." *African Studies Quarterly* 7, no. 2/3 (2003): 205–209.

Byrne, Jeffrey James. "Africa's Cold War." In *The Cold War in the Third World*, edited by Robert J. McMahon, 101–123. New York: Oxford University Press, 2013.

———. *Mecca of Revolution: Algeria, Decolonization, and the Third World Order*. New York: Oxford University Press, 2016.

Callaghy, Thomas M. *The State-Society Struggle: Zaire in Comparative Perspective*. New York: Columbia University Press, 1984.

Chafer, Tony. *The End of Empire in French West Africa: France's Successful Decolonization?* Oxford; New York: Berg, 2002.

Chamberlin, Paul Thomas. *The Global Offensive: The United States, the Palestine Liberation Organization, and the Making of the Post-Cold War Order*. Oxford; New York: Oxford University Press, 2012.

Charney, Craig. "Class Conflict and the National Party Split." *Journal of Southern African Studies* 10, no. 2 (1984): 269–282.

Charney, Craig Russell. "Civil Society vs. the State: Identity, Institutions, and the Black Consciousness Movement in South Africa." PhD diss., Yale University, 2000.

Chipman, John. *French Power in Africa*. Oxford, UK; Cambridge, MA: Basil Blackwell, 1989.

Cilliers, J. K. *Counter-Insurgency in Rhodesia*. London: Croom Helm, 1985.

Comaroff, John. "Government, Materiality, Legality, Modernity: On the Colonial State in Africa." In *African Modernities: Entangled Meanings in Current Debate*, edited by Jan-Georg Deutsch, Peter Probst and Heike Schmidt, pp. 107–134. Portsmouth, NH; Oxford: Heinemann, 2002.

Cooper, Frederick. *Africa since 1940: The Past of the Present*. Cambridge, UK: Cambridge University Press, 2002.

———. *Citizenship between Empire and Nation: Remaking France and French Africa, 1945–1960*. Princeton, NJ: Princeton University Press, 2015.

———. *Decolonization and African Society: The Labor Question in French and British Africa*. Cambridge, UK: Cambridge University Press, 1996.

———. "Development and Disappointment: Social and Economic Change in an Unequal World, 1945–2000." In *Africa since 1940: The Past of the Present*, edited by Frederick Cooper, 91–132. Cambridge, UK: Cambridge University Press, 2002.

———. "Possibility and Constraint: African Independence in Historical Perspective." *Journal of African History* 49, no. 2 (2008): 167–196.

Correia, Paulo, and Grietjie Verhoef. "Portugal and South Africa: Close Allies or Unwilling Partners in Southern Africa During the Cold War?" *South African Journal of Military Studies* 37, no. 1 (2009): 50–72.

Cronjé, Geoffrey. *'n Tuiste vir Die Nageslag: Die Blywende Oplossing van Suid-Afrika se Rassevraagstukke*. Johannesburg: Publicite Handelsreklamediens, 1945.

Crosland, Susan. *Tony Crosland*. London: Cape, 1982.

Cullather, Nick. *The Hungry World: America's Cold War Battle against Poverty in Asia*. Cambridge, MA: Harvard University Press, 2010.

D'Oliveira, John. *Vorster: The Man*. Johannesburg: Ernest Stanton, 1978.

Dalcanton, C. David. "Vorster and the Politics of Confidence." *African Affairs* 75, no. 299 (April 1976): 163–181.

Davies, Rebecca. *Afrikaners in the New South Africa: Identity Politics in a Globalised Economy*. London; New York: Tauris Academic Studies, 2009.

Davies, Robert, and Dan O'Meara. "Total Strategy in Southern Africa: An Analysis of South African Regional Policy since 1978." *Journal of Southern African Studies* 11, no. 2 (April 1985): 183–211.

de Klerk, Willem. "The Concepts 'Verkramp' and 'Verlig.'" In *South African Dialogue: Contrasts in South African Thinking on Basic Race Issues*, edited by Nicolaas Johannes Rhoodie, 519–531. Johannesburg: McGraw-Hill Book Co., 1972.

de Mesquita, Bruce Bueno. "Foreign Policy Analysis and Rational Choice Models" In *International Studies Association Compendium Project*, 2010. http://www.isadiscussion.com/entry/c131-1/Foreign-Policy-Analysis-and-Rational-Choice-Models.html (accessed 11 January 2016).

de Villiers, Dirk, and Johanna de Villiers. *PW*. Kaapstad: Tafelberg, 1984.

DeRoche, Andrew. *Black, White, and Chrome: The United States and Zimbabwe, 1953 to 1998*. Trenton, NJ: Africa World Press, 2001.

Diederichs, Nico. *Nasionalisme as Lewensbeskouing en Sy Verhouding Tot Internasionalisme*. Cape Town: Nasionale Pers, 1935.

Dlamini, Jacob. *Askari: A Story of Collaboration and Betrayal in the Anti-Apartheid Struggle*. New York: Oxford University Press, 2015.

Dorning, W. A. "A History of Co-Operation: The South African Defense Force's Involvement with the Angolan Resistance Movement Unita—Volume One, 1976–1980." PhD diss., Universiteit van die Oranje-Vrystaat, 1986.

du Pisani, André. *John Vorster en Die Verlig-Verkrampstryd*. Bloemfontein: Instituut vir Eietydse Geskiedenis, 1988.

———. *SWA/Namibia, the Politics of Continuity and Change*. Johannesburg: J. Ball Publishers, 1985.

du Preez, Sophia. *Avontuur in Angola: Die Verhaal van Suid-Afrika se Soldate in Angola 1975–1976*. Pretoria: J. L. van Schaik, 1989.

du Toit, Andre. "No Chosen People: The Myth of the Calvinist Origins of Afrikaner Nationalism and Racial Ideology." *American Historical Review* 88, no. 4 (1983): 920–952.

Dubow, Saul. *Apartheid, 1948–1994*. Oxford: Oxford University Press, 2014.

———. *Racial Segregation and the Origins of Apartheid in South Africa, 1919–36*. Basingstoke, UK: Macmillan, 1989.

Dudziak, Mary L. *Cold War Civil Rights: Race and the Image of American Democracy*. Princeton, NJ: Princeton University Press, 2000.

Dvorin, Eugene Paul. *Racial Separation in South Africa: An Analysis of Apartheid Theory*. Chicago: University of Chicago Press, 1952.

El-Khawas, Mohamed, and B. Cohen. *The Kissinger Study of Southern Africa*. Westport, CT: Lawrence Hill, 1976.

Ellis, Stephen. "ANC Suppresses Real History to Boost Its Claim to Legitimacy." *Mail & Guardian*, 3 January 2013.

———. *External Mission: The ANC in Exile, 1960–1990*. London: Hurst, 2012.

Elphick, Richard, and Hermann Buhr Giliomee. *The Shaping of South African Society, 1652–1820*. Cape Town: Longman, 1979.

Erasmus, Rudolf. *Supplementary Report of the Commission of Inquiry into Alleged Irregularities in the Former Department of Information*. Pretoria: Government Printer, 1979.

Fatton, Robert. *Black Consciousness in South Africa: The Dialectics of Ideological Resistance to White Supremacy*. Albany: State University of New York Press, 1986.

Feinstein, C. H. *An Economic History of South Africa: Conquest, Discrimination, and Development*. New York: Cambridge University Press, 2005.

Ferguson, James. *Expectations of Modernity: Myths and Meanings of Urban Life on the Zambian Copperbelt*. Berkeley: University of California Press, 1999.

Ferguson, Niall, Charles S. Maier, Erez Manela, and Daniel Sargent, eds. *The Shock of the Global: The 1970s in Perspective*. Cambridge, MA; London: Belknap, 2010.

Fieldhouse, Roger. *Anti-Apartheid: A History of the Movement in Britain*. London: Merlin Press, 2005.

Filatova, Irina, and Apollon Davidson. *The Hidden Thread: Russia and South Africa in the Soviet Era*. Johannesburg: Jonathan Ball, 2013.

Ford, Christopher. "South African Foreign Policy since 1965: The Cases of Rhodesia and Namibia." PhD diss., Oxford University, 1991.

Frankel, Philip H. *Pretoria's Praetorians: Civil-Military Relations in South Africa*. Cambridge: Cambridge University Press, 1984.

Friedman, Jeremy. "Reviving Revolution: The Sino-Soviet Split, the 'Third World,' and the Fate of the Left." PhD diss., Princeton University, 2011.

———. *Shadow Cold War: The Sino-Soviet Split and the Third World*. Chapel Hill, NC: University of North Carolina Press, 2015.

Gaddis, John Lewis. *Strategies of Containment: A Critical Appraisal of American National Security Policy During the Cold War*. New York: Oxford University Press, 2005.

Geldenhuys, Deon. *The Diplomacy of Isolation: South African Foreign Policy Making*. Johannesburg: Macmillan South Africa, 1984.

———. *Some Foreign Policy Implications of South Africa's Total National Strategy with Reference to the 12-Point Plan*. Braamfontein: South African Institute for International Affairs, 1981.

———. *South Africa's Search for Security since the Second World War*. Braamfontein: South African Institute of International Affairs, 1978.

Geldenhuys, Deon, and Hennie Kotze. "P. W. Botha as Decision Maker: A Preliminary Study of Personality and Politics." *Politikon* 12 (June 1985): 30–42.

Gerhart, Gail M. *Black Power in South Africa: The Evolution of an Ideology*. Berkeley: University of California Press, 1978.

Gewald, Jan-Bart. "Who Killed Clemens Kapuuo?" *Journal of Southern African Studies* 30, no. 3 (September 2004): 559–576.

Giliomee, Hermann. "The Afrikaner Economic Advance." In *Ethnic Power Mobilized: Can South Africa Change?* edited by Heribert Adam and Hermann Giliomee, pp. 145–176. New Haven, CT; London: Yale University Press, 1979.

———. "Afrikaner Politics: How the System Works." In *The Rise and Crisis of Afrikaner Power*, edited by Heribert Adam and Hermann Giliomee, 196–257. Cape Town: David Philips, 1979.

———. *The Afrikaners: Biography of a People*. Charlottesville: University of Virginia Press, 2003.

———. "The Beginnings of Afrikaner Ethnic Consciousness, 1850–1915." In *The Creation of Tribalism in Southern Africa*, edited by Leroy Vail, 21–54. Berkeley: University of California Press, 1989.

———. "Ethnic Business and Economic Empowerment: The Afrikaner Case, 1915–1970." *South African Journal of Economics* 76, no. 4 (2008): 765–788.

———. *The Last Afrikaner Leaders: A Supreme Test of Power*. Cape Town: Tafelberg, 2012.

———. "The Making of the Apartheid Plan, 1929–1948." *Journal of Southern African Studies* 29, no. 2 (June 2003): 373–392.

———. *The Parting of the Ways: South African Politics 1976–82*. Cape Town: D. Philip, 1982.

———. "'Survival in Justice': An Afrikaner Debate over Apartheid." *Comparative Studies in Society and History* 36, no. 3 (1994): 527–548.

Glassman, Jonathon. *War of Words, War of Stones: Racial Thought and Violence in Colonial Zanzibar*. Bloomington: Indiana University Press, 2011.

Gleijeses, Piero. *Conflicting Missions: Havana, Washington, and Africa, 1959–1976*. Chapel Hill; London: University of North Carolina Press, 2002.

———. *Visions of Freedom: Havana, Washington, Pretoria and the Struggle for Southern Africa, 1976–1991*. Chapel Hill: University of North Carolina Press, 2013.

Greenberg, Stanley B. *Legitimating the Illegitimate: State, Markets, and Resistance in South Africa*. Berkeley: University of California Press, 1987.

———. *Race and State in Capitalist Development*. New Haven, CT: Yale University Press, 1980.

Grundlingh, Albert. "'Are We Afrikaners Getting Too Rich?': Cornucopia and Change in Afrikanerdom in the 1960s." *Journal of Historical Sociology* 21, nos. 2–3 (2008): 143–165.

———. "The King's Afrikaners? Enlistment and Ethnic Identity in the Union of South Africa's Defense Force During the Second World War, 1939–1945." *Journal of African History* 40, no. 3 (1999): 351–365.

Grundlingh, Louis. "The Recruitment of South African Blacks for Participation in the Second World War." In *Africa and the Second World War*, edited by David Killingray and Richard Rathbone, 181–203. New York: St. Martin's Press, 1986.

Grundy, Kenneth W. *Confrontation and Accommodation in Southern Africa: The Limits of Independence*. Berkeley; London: University of California Press, 1973.

Guelke, Adrian. "Africa as a Market for South African Goods." *Journal of Modern African Studies* 12, no. 1 (1974): 69–88.

Gurney, Christabel. "The 1970s: The Anti-Apartheid Movement's Difficult Decade." In *Southern African Liberation Struggles: New Local, Regional and Global Perspectives*, edited by Hilary Sapire and Christopher Saunders, 229–250. Cape Town: UCT Press, 2013.

Hajimu, Masuda. *Cold War Crucible: The Korean Conflict and the Postwar World*. Cambridge, MA: Harvard University Press, 2015.

Halisi, C. R. D. *Black Political Thought in the Making of South African Democracy*. Bloomington: Indiana University Press, 1999.

Halliday, Fred. *The Middle East in International Relations: Power, Politics and Ideology*. Cambridge, UK; New York: Cambridge University Press, 2005.

Hamann, Hilton. *Days of the Generals: The Untold Story of South Africa's Apartheid-Era Military Generals*. Cape Town: Zebra Press, 2001.

Harris, Verne. "'They Should Have Destroyed More': The Destruction of Public Records by the South African State in the Final Years of Apartheid, 1990–1994." In *Archives and the Public Good: Accountability and Records in Modern Society*, edited by Richard J. Cox and David A. Wallace, 205–228. Westport, CT: Quorum Books, 2002.

Heard, Kenneth A. *General Elections in South Africa, 1943–1970*. London; New York: Oxford University Press, 1974.

Herbst, Jeffrey. *States and Power in Africa: Comparative Lessons in Authority and Control*. Princeton, NJ: Princeton University Press, 2000.

Hirschmann, D. "Southern Africa: Detente?" *Journal of Modern African Studies* 14 (1976): 107–126.

Hobsbawm, E. J. *Nations and Nationalism since 1780: Program, Myth, Reality*. 2nd ed. Cambridge, UK; New York: Cambridge University Press, 1992.

Hobsbawm, E. J., and T. O. Ranger, eds. *The Invention of Tradition*. Cambridge: Cambridge University Press, 1983.

Hroch, Miroslav. *Social Preconditions of National Revival in Europe: A Comparative Analysis of the Social Composition of Patriotic Groups among the Smaller European Nations*. Cambridge, UK; New York: Cambridge University Press, 1985.

Hugo, Pierre. "The Politics of Untruth: Afrikaner Academics for Apartheid." *Politikon* 25, no. 1 (1998): 31–55.

———. "Towards Darkness and Death: Racial Demonology in South Africa." *Journal of Modern African Studies* 26, no. 4 (1988): 567–590.

Hunt, Michael H. *Ideology and U.S. Foreign Policy*. New Haven, CT: Yale University Press, 1987.

Irwin, Ryan M. *Gordian Knot: Apartheid and the Unmaking of the Liberal World Order*. New York: Oxford University Press, 2012.

Isaacman, Allen F., and Barbara S. Isaacman. "Extending South Africa's Tentacles of Empire: The Deterritorialisation of Cahora Bassa Dam." *Journal of Southern African Studies* 41, no. 3 (2015): 541–560.

———. *Mozambique: From Colonialism to Revolution, 1900–1982*. Boulder, CO: Westview, 1983.

Jabbour, George. *Settler Colonialism in Southern Africa and the Middle East*. Khartoum: University of Khartoum, 1970.

Jackson, Robert H., and Carl G. Rosberg. "Why Africa's Weak States Persist: The Empirical and the Juridical in Statehood." *World Politics* 35, no. 1 (October 1982): 1–24.

———. *Personal Rule in Black Africa: Prince, Autocrat, Prophet, Tyrant*. Berkeley: University of California Press, 1982.

Jaster, Robert S. *South Africa's Narrowing Security Options*. London: International Institute for Strategic Studies, 1980.

John, Nerys. "South African Intervention in the Angolan Civil War, 1975–1976: Motivations and Implications." MA thesis, University of Cape Town, 2002.

Johnson, R. W. *How Long Will South Africa Survive?* New York: Oxford University Press, 1977.

Kane-Berman, John Stuart. *Soweto: Black Revolt, White Reaction.* Johannesburg: Ravan Press, 1978.

Karis, Thomas, and Gail M. Gerhart, eds. *From Protest to Challenge; A Documentary History of African Politics in South Africa, 1882–1964.* Vol. 5, *Nadir and Resurgence, 1964–1979.* Bloomington: Indiana University Press, 1997.

Keegan, Timothy J. *Colonial South Africa and the Origins of the Racial Order.* Charlottesville: University Press of Virginia, 1996.

Kelly, John D., and Martha Kaplan. "Nation and Decolonization: Toward a New Anthropology of Nationalism." *Anthropological Theory* 1, no. 4 (2001): 419–437.

Kenney, Henry. *Power, Pride and Prejudice.* Johannesburg: J. Ball Publishers, 1991.

Kiernan, Ben. *The Pol Pot Regime: Race, Power, and Genocide in Cambodia under the Khmer Rouge, 1975–79.* New Haven, CT: Yale University Press, 2008.

Killingray, David, and Martin Plaut. *Fighting for Britain: African Soldiers in the Second World War.* Oxford: James Currey, 2010.

Koorts, Lindie. *D.F. Malan and the Rise of Afrikaner Nationalism.* Cape Town: Tafelberg, 2014.

Krause, Otto. "Trends in Afrikaner Race Attitudes." In *South African Dialogue: Contrasts in South African Thinking on Basic Race Issues,* edited by Nicolaas Johannes Rhoodie, 532–539. Johannesburg: McGraw-Hill Book Co., 1972.

Kriel, Mariana. "Culture and Power: The Rise of Afrikaner Nationalism Revisited." *Nations & Nationalism* 16, no. 3 (2010): 402–422.

Kuperus, Tracy. *State, Civil Society, and Apartheid in South Africa: An Examination of Dutch Reformed Church-State Relations.* New York: St. Martin's Press, 1999.

Lake, Marilyn, and Henry Reynolds. *Drawing the Global Colour Line: White Men's Countries and the International Challenge of Racial Equality.* Cambridge: Cambridge University Press, 2008.

Larmer, Miles. *Rethinking African Politics: A History of Opposition in Zambia.* Farnham, Surrey, UK: Ashgate, 2011.

Latham, Michael E. *The Right Kind of Revolution: Modernization, Development, and U.S. Foreign Policy from the Cold War to the Present.* Ithaca, NY: Cornell University Press, 2011.

Lazar, John. "Verwoerd versus the "Visionaries": The South African Bureau of Racial Affairs (Sabra) and Apartheid, 1948–1961." In *Apartheid's Genesis, 1935–1962,* edited by Philip Bonner, Peter Delius and Deborah Posel, 362–392. Braamfontein, South Africa: Ravan Press; Witwatersrand University Press, 1993.

Legassick, Martin. "Debating the Revival of the Workers' Movement in the 1970s: The South African Democracy Education Trust and Post-Apartheid Patriotic History." *Kronos* 34, no. 1 (2008): 240–266.

Lipton, Merle. *Capitalism and Apartheid: South Africa, 1910–1986.* Aldershot: Wildwood House, 1986.

———. *Liberals, Marxists and Nationalists: Competing Interpretations of South African History.* New York: Palgrave Macmillan, 2007.

Lombard, Jan. "The Economic Philosophy of Homeland Development." In *South African Dialogue: Contrasts in South African Thinking on Basic Race Issues,* edited by Nicolaas Johannes Rhoodie, 168–181. Johannesburg: McGraw-Hill Book Co., 1972.

Lonsdale, John, and Bruce Berman. "Coping with the Contradictions: The Development of the Colonial State in Kenya, 1895–1914." *Journal of African History* 20, no. 4 (1979): 487–505.

Louw, P. Eric. *The Rise, Fall, and Legacy of Apartheid.* Westport, CT: Praeger, 2004.

MacMillan, Hugh. *The Lusaka Years: The ANC in Exile in Zambia, 1963–1994.* Auckland Park, SA: Jacana Media, 2013.

Macqueen, Ian. "Black Consciousness in Dialogue in South Africa: Steve Biko, Richard Turner and the 'Durban Moment,' 1970–1974." *Journal of Asian and African Studies* 49, no. 5 (2014): 511–525.

Macqueen, Norrie. *The Decolonization of Portuguese Africa: Metropolitan Revolution and the Dissolution of Empire.* London; New York: Longman, 1997.

Magaziner, Daniel R. *The Law and the Prophets: Black Consciousness in South Africa, 1968–1977.* Athens: Ohio University Press, 2010.

Malan, Rian. *My Traitor's Heart: A South African Exile Returns to Face His Country, His Tribe, and His Conscience.* New York: Atlantic Monthly Press, 1990.

Mamdani, Mahmood. *When Victims Become Killers: Colonialism, Nativism, and the Genocide in Rwanda*. Princeton, NJ: Princeton University Press, 2001.

Marwick, Hendretia. "Dr C. P. Mulder as Minister van Inligting, 1968–1978." MA thesis, University of the Orange Free State, 1982.

Maxwell, Kenneth. "Portugal and Africa: The Last Empire." In *Decolonization and African Independence: The Transfers of Power, 1960–1980*, edited by Prosser Gifford and William Roger Louis, pp. 337–385. New Haven, CT; London: Yale University Press, 1988.

McMahon, Robert J. *The Cold War in the Third World*. New York: Oxford University Press, 2013.

McMaster, Carolyn. *Malawi: Foreign Policy and Development*. London: Julian Friedmann Publishers Ltd., 1974.

Médard, Jean-François. "The Underdeveloped State in Africa: Political Clientelism or Neo-Patrimonialism?" In *Private Patronage and Public Power: Political Clientelism in the Modern State*, edited by Christopher S. Clapham, 162–192. London: Pinter, 1982.

Meiring, Piet. *Die Lewe van Hilgard Muller*. Silverton: Promedia Publikasies, 1985.

Meredith, Martin. *The Past Is Another Country: Rhodesia, 1890–1979*. London: A. Deutsch, 1979.

Migdal, Joel S. *Strong Societies and Weak States: State-Society Relations and State Capabilities in the Third World*. Princeton, NJ: Princeton University Press, 1988.

Miller, Jamie. "Africanising Apartheid: Identity, Ideology, and State-Building in Post-Independence Africa." *Journal of African History* 56, no. 3 (2015): 449–470.

———. "The Black Hole of Apartheid History." Imperial and Global Forum, University of Exeter, https://imperialglobalexeter.com/2013/12/12/the-black-hole-of-apartheid-history/, 12 December 2013.

———. "Things Fall Apart: South Africa and the Collapse of the Portuguese Empire, 1973–74." *Cold War History* 11, no. 2 (2012): 183–204.

Miller, Roberta Balstad. "Science and Society in the Early Career of H.F. Verwoerd." *Journal of Southern African Studies* 19, no. 4 (1993): 634–661.

Mlambo, A. S. "'We Have Blood Relations over the Border': South Africa and Rhodesian Sanctions, 1965–1975." *African Historical Review* 40, no. 1 (2008): 1–29.

Moodie, T. Dunbar. *The Rise of Afrikanerdom: Power, Apartheid, and the Afrikaner Civil Religion*. Berkeley: University of California Press, 1975.

Mouton, Alex. *Voorloper: Die Lewe van Schalk Pienaar*. Cape Town: Tafelberg, 2002.

Muehlenbeck, Philip E. *Betting on the Africans: John F. Kennedy's Courting of African Nationalist Leaders*. Oxford; New York: Oxford University Press, 2012.

Ngcokovane, Cecil Mzingisi. "Religious and Moral Legitimations of Apartheid in Nederduitse Gereformeerde Kerk, Nationalist Party and Broederbond, 1948-Present." PhD diss., Emory University, 1986.

Noer, Thomas J. *Cold War and Black Liberation: The United States and White Rule in Africa, 1948–1968*. Columbia: University of Missouri Press, 1985.

Nolutshungu, Sam C. *South Africa in Africa: A Study in Ideology and Foreign Policy*. Manchester, UK: Manchester University Press, 1975.

Norval, Aletta J. *Deconstructing Apartheid Discourse*. London; New York: Verso, 1996.

Nugent, Paul. *Africa since Independence: A Comparative History*. Basingstoke, UK; New York: Palgrave Macmillan, 2004.

Nye, Joseph S. *Pan-Africanism and East African Integration*. Cambridge, MA: Harvard University Press, 1965.

O'Brien, Michael. *Conjectures of Order: Intellectual Life and the American South, 1810–1860*. Vol. 1. Chapel Hill: University of North Carolina Press, 2004.

O'Meara, Dan. *Forty Lost Years: The Apartheid State and the Politics of the National Party, 1948–94*. Athens: Ohio University Press, 1996.

———. *Volkskapitalisme: Class, Capital, and Ideology in the Development of Afrikaner Nationalism, 1934–1948*. Cambridge, UK: Cambridge University Press, 1983.

Olivier, Gerrit. *Suid-Afrika se Buitelandse Beleid*. Pretoria: Academica, 1977.

Olivier, Nic. "The Head of Government and the Party." In *Leadership in the Apartheid State: From Malan to De Klerk*, edited by Robert Schrire and Laurence Boulle, 80–101. Cape Town: Oxford University Press, 1994.

Onslow, Sue. "Dr Kissinger, I Presume?" unpublished paper.

———. "A Question of Timing: South Africa and Rhodesia's Unilateral Declaration of Independence, 1964–1965." *Cold War History* 5, no. 2 (2005): 129–159.

———. "'We Must Gain Time': South Africa, Rhodesia, and the Kissinger Initiative of 1976." *South African Historical Journal* 56 (2006): 123–153.

Papenfus, Theresa. *Pik Botha and His Times*. Pretoria: Litera, 2010.

Pedersen, Susan. "What is Political History Now?" In *What is History Now?*, edited by David Cannadine, 36–56. Basingstoke, Hampshire; New York: Palgrave Macmillan, 2002.

Pfister, Roger. *Apartheid South Africa and African States: From Pariah to Middle Power, 1961–1994*. London: I. B. Tauris, 2005.

Plummer, Brenda Gayle. *Rising Wind: Black Americans and U.S. Foreign Affairs, 1935–1960*. Chapel Hill: University of North Carolina Press, 1996.

Polakow-Suransky, Sasha. *The Unspoken Alliance: Israel's Secret Relationship with Apartheid South Africa*. New York: Pantheon, 2010.

Posel, Deborah. *The Making of Apartheid, 1948–1961: Conflict and Compromise*. Oxford: Clarendon Press, 1991.

Pottinger, Brian. *The Imperial Presidency: P.W. Botha the First 10 Years*. Johannesburg: Southern Book Publishers, 1988.

Price, Robert M. *The Apartheid State in Crisis: Political Transformation in South Africa, 1975–1990*. New York; Oxford: Oxford University Press, 1991.

Prinsloo, Daan. *Stem uit Die Wildernis: 'n Biographie van Oud-Pres. PW Botha*. Mossel Bay: Vaandel, 1997.

Prunier, Gérard. *Darfur: A 21st Century Genocide*. 3rd ed., Crises in World Politics. Ithaca, NY: Cornell University Press, 2008.

Raftopoulos, Brian, and Alois Mlambo. *Becoming Zimbabwe: A History from the Pre-Colonial Period to 2008*. Harare: Weaver Press, 2009.

Rees, Mervyn. *Muldergate: The Story of the Info Scandal*. Johannesburg: Macmillan South Africa, 1980.

Ribeiro de Meneses, Filipe, and Robert McNamara. "Exercise Alcora: Expansion and Demise, 1971–1974." *International History Review* 36, no. 1 (2013): 89–111.

———. "The Origins of Exercise Alcora, 1960–1971." *International History Review* 35, no. 5 (2013): 1113–1134.

Ries, Alf, and Ebbe Dommisse. *Broedertwis: Die Verhaal van Die 1982-Skeuring in Die Nasionale Party*. Kaapstad: Tafelberg, 1982.

Rodinson, Maxime. "Israël, fait colonial?" *Les Temps modernes* 22 (1967): 17–88.

Roherty, James Michael. *State Security in South Africa: Civil-Military Relations under P.W. Botha*. Armonk, NY; London: M. E. Sharpe, 1992.

Roos, Neil. *Ordinary Springboks: White Servicemen and Social Justice in South Africa, 1939–1951*. Aldershot, UK: Ashgate, 2005.

Rostow, W. W. *The Diffusion of Power: An Essay in Recent History*. New York: Macmillan, 1972.

Sadie, J. L. "Die Ekonomiese Faktor in Die Afrikaner-Gemeenskap." In *Identiteit en Verandering*, edited by Hendrik W. van der Merwe, 84–101. Kaapstad: Tafelberg, 1975.

———. "The Fall and Rise of the Afrikaner in the South African Economy." *Annale* 1 (2002).

———. *Projections of the South African Population, 1970–2020*. South Africa: Industrial Development Corporation of South Africa, 1970.

Sargent, Daniel J. *A Superpower Transformed: The Remaking of American Foreign Relations in the 1970s*. New York: Oxford University Press, 2015.

Saunders, Christopher. "The South Africa-Angola Talks, 1976–1984: A Little-Known Cold War Thread." *Kronos* 37 (November 2011): 104–119.

———. "The Transitions for Apartheid to Democracy in Namibia and South Africa in the Context of Decolonization." *Journal of Colonialism and Colonial History*, 1, 1 (2000).

Saunders, Christopher, and Sue Onslow. "The Cold War and Southern Africa, 1976–1990." In *The Cambridge History of the Cold War: Volume III: Endings*, edited by Melvyn P. Leffler and Odd Arne Westad, 222–243. Cambridge; New York: Cambridge University Press, 2009.

Scarnecchia, Timothy. "The Congo Crisis, the United Nations, and Zimbabwean Nationalism, 1960–1963." *African Journal on Conflict Resolution* 11, no. 1 (2011): 63–86.

Schlemmer, Lawrence. "Change in South Africa: Opportunities and Restraints." In *The Apartheid Regime: Political Power and Racial Domination*, edited by Robert M. Price and Carl Gustav Rosberg. Berkeley: Institute of International Studies, University of California, 1980.

Schmidt, Elizabeth. "Anticolonial Nationalism in French West Africa: What Made Guinea Unique?" *African Studies Review* 52, no. 2 (2009): 1–34.

———. *Cold War and Decolonization in Guinea, 1946–1958*. Athens: Ohio University Press, 2007.

Schneidman, Witney W. *Engaging Africa: Washington and the Fall of Portugal's Colonial Empire*. Lanham, MD; Oxford: University Press of America, 2004.

Schoeman, B. M. *Die Broederbond in Die Afrikaner-Politiek*. Pretoria: Aktuele Publikasies, 1982.

———. *Die Geldmag: SA se Onsigbare Regering*. Pretoria: Aktuele Publikasies, 1980.

———. *Vorster se 1000 Dae*. Cape Town: Human & Rousseau, 1974.

Scholtz, Gert Daniel. *Dr. Hendrik Frensch Verwoerd, 1901–1966*. 2 vols. Johannesburg: Perskor, 1974.

Scholtz, Leopold. *The SADF in the Border War: 1966–1989*. Cape Town: Tafelberg, 2013.

Schrecker, Ellen. *Many Are the Crimes: McCarthyism in America*. Boston: Little, Brown, 1998.

Schrire, Robert, and Laurence Boulle. *Leadership in the Apartheid State: From Malan to De Klerk*. Cape Town: Oxford University Press, 1994.

Schwarz, Bill. *The White Man's World*. Oxford; New York: Oxford University Press, 2011.

Scott, James C. *Seeing Like a State: How Certain Schemes to Improve the Human Condition Have Failed*. New Haven, CT: Yale University Press, 1998.

Seegers, Annette. *The Military in the Making of Modern South Africa*. London: Tauris Academic Studies, 1996.

Sellström, Tor. *Sweden and National Liberation in Southern Africa*. Uppsala: Nordiska Afrikainstitutet, 1999.

Serfontein, J. H. P. *Apartheid Change and the NG Kerk*. Emmarentia, SA: Taurus, 1982.

———. *Brotherhood of Power: An Exposé of the Secret Afrikaner Broederbond*. Bloomington: Indiana University Press, 1978.

———. *Die Verkrampte Aanslag*. Cape Town: Human & Rousseau, 1970.

Short, Philip. *Banda*. London; Boston: Routledge & Kegan Paul, 1974.

Simpson, Thula. "Military Combat Work: The Reconstitution of the ANC's Armed Underground, 1971–1976." *African Studies* 70, no. 1 (2011): 103–122.

———. *Umkhonto We Sizwe: The ANC's Armed Struggle*. Cape Town: Penguin, 2016.

Skinner, Rob. *The Foundations of Anti-Apartheid: Liberal Humanitarians and Transnational Activists in Britain and the United States, c. 1919–64*. Basingstoke, UK; New York: Palgrave Macmillan, 2010.

Skocpol, Theda. "Bringing the State Back In: Strategies of Analysis in Current Research." In *Bringing the State Back In*, edited by Peter B. Evans, Dietrich Rueschemeyer and Theda Skocpol, 3–37. Cambridge; New York: Cambridge University Press, 1985.

Slabbert, F. van Zyl. *The Last White Parliament*. Johannesburg: J. Ball Publishers, 1985.

Slater, Dan. *Ordering Power: Contentious Politics and Authoritarian Leviathans in Southeast Asia*. Cambridge, UK; New York: Cambridge University Press, 2010.

Smith, Nico. *Die Afrikaner Broederbond: Belewinge van Die Binnekant*. Pretoria: LAPA Uitgewers, 2009.

South African Democracy Education Trust. *The Road to Democracy in South Africa*. Vols. 1–6. Pretoria: Unisa Press, 2004–2010.

South African Institute of Race Relations. *A Survey of Race Relations in South Africa*. Johannesburg 1982.

Sparks, Allister. *The Mind of South Africa*. New York: Alfred A. Knopf, 1990.

Spies, F. J. du Toit. *Operasie Savannah: Angola 1975–1976*. Pretoria: S. A. Weermag, 1989.

Stals, E. L. P. "Geskiedenis van Die Afrikaner-Broderbond, 1918–1994." Unpublished manuscript, 1998.

Starcke, Anna. *Survival: Taped Interviews with South Africa's Power Elite.* 1st ed. Cape Town: Tafelberg, 1978.

Steenekamp, T. J. "'n Ekonomiese Ontleding van Sosio-Politieke Groepvorming met Spesiale Verwysing na Die Afrikaner." PhD diss., University of South Africa, 1989.

Steenekamp, Tjaart. "Discrimination and the Economic Position of the Afrikaner." *South African Journal of Economic History* 5, no. 1 (1990): 49–66.

Stiff, Peter. *The Silent War: South African Recce Operations, 1969–1994.* Alberton: Galago, 1999.

Stockwell, John. *In Search of Enemies: A CIA Story.* London: Futura Publications, 1979.

Suttner, Raymond. *The ANC Underground in South Africa, 1950–1976.* Boulder, CO: FirstForumPress, 2009.

Swanepoel, J. J. "Die Diplomasie van Adv. B. J. Vorster." PhD diss., University of the Orange Free State, 1982.

Tamarkin, M. *The Making of Zimbabwe: Decolonization in Regional and International Politics.* London: Cass, 1990.

Terblanche, H. O. *John Vorster: OB-Generaal en Afrikanervegter.* Roodepoort: CUM-Boeke, 1983.

Terretta, Meredith. "Cameroonian Nationalists Go Global: From Forest Maquis to a Pan-African Accra." *Journal of African History* 51, no. 2 (2010): 189–212.

Thompson, Leonard. *A History of South Africa.* New Haven, CT: Yale University Press, 2001.

Thomson, Alex. *U.S. Foreign Policy Towards Apartheid South Africa, 1948–1994: Conflict of Interests.* Basingstoke, UK: Palgrave Macmillan, 2008.

Thörn, Håkan. *Anti-Apartheid and the Emergence of a Global Civil Society* Basingstoke, UK: Palgrave Macmillan, 2006.

Toit, André Du. "'Afrikaander Circa 1600': Reflections and Suggestions Regarding the Origins and Fate of Afrikaner Nationalism." *South African Historical Journal* 60, no. 4 (2008): 562–578.

Treurnicht, A. P. *Credo van 'n Afrikaner.* Kaapstad: Tafelberg, 1975.

Vale, Peter. "The Cold War and South Africa: Repetitions and Revisions on a Prolegomenon." In *Beyond the Border War: New Perspectives on Southern Africa's Late-Cold War Conflicts,* edited by Gary Baines and Peter Vale, 22–41. South Africa: Unisa Press, 2008.

van de Walle, Nicolas. *African Economies and the Politics of Permanent Crisis, 1979–1999.* Cambridge, UK; New York: Cambridge University Press, 2001.

van der Westhuizen, Christi. *White Power & the Rise and Fall of the National Party.* Cape Town: Zebra Press, 2007.

van Deventer, André, and Philip Nel. "The State and 'die Volk' Versus Communism, 1922–1941." *Politikon* 17, no. 2 (1990): 64–81.

van Rooyen, Jan J. *P.W. Botha: 40 Jaar.* Kaapstad: Hoofraad van die Kaaplandse Nasionale Party, 1976.

van Wyk, Anna-Mart. "Ally or Critic? The United States Response to South African Nuclear Development, 1949–1980." *Cold War History* 7, no. 2 (2007): 195–225.

———. "South Africa's Nuclear Program and the Cold War." *History Compass* 8, no. 7 (2010): 562–572.

van Wyk, At. *Dirk Mudge: Reënmaker van die Namib.* Pretoria: J.L. van Schaik, 1999.

Verschave, François-Xavier. *La Françafrique: Le Plus Long Scandale de la République.* Paris: Stock, 1998.

Visser, Wessel. "The Production of Literature on the 'Red Peril' and 'Total Onslaught' in Twentieth-Century South Africa." *Historia* 49, no. 2 (2004): 105–128.

Vu, Tuong. "Studying the State through State Formation." *World Politics* 62, no. 1 (2010): 148–175.

Watts, Carl Peter. *Rhodesia's Unilateral Declaration of Independence: An International History.* New York: Palgrave Macmillan, 2012.

Welsh, David. *The Rise and Fall of Apartheid.* Charlottesville: University of Virginia Press, 2009.

———. "Urbanisation and the Solidarity of Afrikaner Nationalism." *Journal of Modern African Studies* 7, no. 2 (1969): 265–276.

Westad, Odd Arne. *The Global Cold War: Third World Interventions and the Making of Our Times.* Cambridge, UK: Cambridge University Press, 2007.

————. "Moscow and the Angolan Crisis, 1974–1976: A New Pattern of Intervention." *Cold War International History Project Bulletin* 8–9 (Winter 1996–1997): 21–37.

White, Luise. *Unpopular Sovereignty: Rhodesian Independence and African Decolonization*. Chicago: University of Chicago Press, 2015.

Wilkins, Ivor, and Hans Strydom. *The Super-Afrikaners*. Johannesburg: Jonathan Ball, 1978.

Wilson, Monica, and Leonard Thompson. *The Oxford History of South Africa*. Oxford: Clarendon Press, 1971.

Wunsch, James S., and Dele Olowu. *The Failure of the Centralized State: Institutions and Self-Governance in Africa*. Boulder, CO: Westview Press, 1990.

Young, M. Crawford. "Nationalism, Ethnicity, and Class in Africa: A Retrospective." *Cahiers d'études africaines* (1986): 421–495.

————. "Nationalism, Ethnicity, and Class in Africa: A Retrospective." *Cahiers d'études africaines* (1986): 421–495.

Zubok, Vladimir. *A Failed Empire: The Soviet Union in the Cold War from Stalin to Gorbachev*. Chapel Hill: University of North Carolina Press, 2007.

INDEX

Adam, Heribert, 4
African National Congress (South Africa), 70, 125,
    131, 155, 158
African National Congress (Rhodesia), 143, 160
African nationalism, 10–12, 17, 30, 40, 43, 63, 75,
    89, 91, 95, 102–103, 114, 324
Afrikaner Freedom Front, 322
Afrikaner nationalism, 6, 8, 20, 31–38, 39, 42–43,
    45, 48, 52–59, 61, 63, 66, 78, 80, 82, 90,
    257, 263–270, 293–294, 296, 318–319,
    320, 323–325, 334–336
    and Christian Nationalism, 5, 31–32, 34, 39, 47
Afrikaner Party, 34
Afrikaners, (see also *volk*) xvii–xviii, 4, 7, 8, 16,
    34–35, 37, 46, 57
    and anti-colonialism, 8, 21, 42, 81, 56, 266
    and communism, 35–38
    and decolonization, response to, 39–40, 88–91
    and shifting group identity, 6, 21, 31–33, 42, 44, 45,
        48–51, 54–55, 59–60, 80, 129–130, 265, 335
    and socio-economic diversification of, 8, 31–33,
        47–48, 49–50, 263–264, 317, 320, 325, 335
    and youth, 76, 267, 335
Alliance Against the Rebellions in Africa
    (ALCORA), 112, 113
Angola, 4, 11, 65–66, 95–96, 111–113, 118,
    119–124, 125–127, 130, 150, 155, 161,
    165–198, 199–205, 206–208, 208–213,
    213–218, 219–221, 225–226, 229, 232,
    237, 241, 249–250, 253, 267, 270–271,
    273, 274, 277, 280, 290, 294, 301–302,
    304, 308–309, 312, 315, 318–319, 326,
    328–331, 341–343
    Operation Savannah, 180, 182–187, 194–195,
        199–201, 206–208, 312 (*see also* South
        African Defense Force)
Anti-communism, 7, 10, 16, 18–19, 81, 281, 318,
    326–327 (*see also* Cold War)
    and Afrikaner unity, 10, 11, 19, 20, 318, 326–327
    as means of social control, 18–19, 37, 326–327

Apartheid, 6, 20, 31, 37
    downfall of, 324, 326–327
    historiography of, 14–16, 22–23, 25
    Immorality and Prohibition of Mixed Marriages
        Act, 38, 268, 307
    implementation of, 38, 46, 47
    Masters and Servants Act, 145
    origins of, 34–35, 37
    petty apartheid, 80–81, 83, 134–135, 146, 287,
        323, 329, 334, 336
    and post-colonialism, 2, 7, 8–9, 10, 15–17,
        23–24, 63, 123
    separate development, 2, 8, 15, 39, 40, 54–56,
        63, 286–287, 293, 295, 320–321, 323,
        325, 334–335
    Tomlinson Commission, 57
    Verwoerdian apartheid, 9, 13, 39–40, 42, 47,
        51–52, 54–55, 61, 75, 82, 108, 222, 255,
        269, 334, 336, 269, 317, 323–324, 336
Ashe, Arthur, 76
Atomic Energy Agency, 291

Banda, Hastings, 76–78, 204
    South Africa, relationship with, 71–74, 83–84
        (*see also* outward policy)
    visit to Pretoria, 71–72
Barnard, Niël, 272, 304, 322
Bastiaanse, C.A., 140–141, 306
Beaufre, Andre, 108–109, 272, 277–279,
    309, 328
Biermann, Hugo, 109–110, 113, 115–116, 124–125,
    128, 177, 187, 211, 270–272, 333
Black Consciousness Movement, 120, 122, 203
    Steve Biko's death in custody 296–297
Botha, P.W., 36, 47, 86, 97, 105, 222, 292
    Angola, approach to, 175, 177–179, 180–182,
        184–185, 191, 194–195, 205–206, 208
    détente, approach to, 153–155
    and Magnus Malan, 271–273, 300–301
    political career of, 13, 103, 181

Botha, P.W. (*Cont.*)
  and Soweto uprising, 234, 273–274
  South-West Africa, approach to, 308, 310–313
  total onslaught ideology, promotion of, 11–13,
    19, 106–107, 113, 117, 125–126, 318–319,
    320–321, 326–328
  total strategy, promotion of, 236, 272–278,
    301–302, 314–315
Botha, Pik, 128–129, 133–135, 196, 228, 233–236,
  252, 258, 286–287, 289–291, 296–297,
  299, 304–308, 310–311, 313, 319, 322
  Kissinger Initiatives, participation in, 219–220
  Long Telegram 233–234
Bowdler, William, 188–189, 192–194, 201–202,
  205, 212, 220, 224, 229, 241, 250–251,
  288, 290, 297
Bridgland, Fred, 189, 191–194, 206
British government 135
  Kissinger Initiatives, involvement in, 246,
    251, 253
Broederbond, 38, 45, 54, 57, 237, 243, 255–256,
  259, 263–264, 326
  Executive Council, 139–140, 207–208, 215
Brzezinski, Zbigniew, 284–286
Bureau for State Security (BOSS), 46, 87, 102,
  132, 174–175, 180, 281–282
Buthelezi, Mangosuthu, 204–205

Callaghan, James, 147, 219, 252
capitalism
  and Afrikaner society, 49–51, 335 (*see also*
    socio-economic diversification)
Carter, Jimmy
  Southern Africa, policy towards, 268–269,
    284–293, 296
  South-West Africa, policy towards, 231–232,
    234, 250–251
Castro, Fidel, 283
Censorship, 95, 189–191, 264
Chad, 65
China, 68, 73, 81, 102–103, 115, 122, 125, 153,
  163, 173, 179, 187, 186
Chipenda, Daniel, 168–169, 171, 178–179, 182, 186
Chissano, Joaquim, 132, 135, 155
Chitepo, Herbert, 155
Chona, Mark 143, 156–157
  and John Vorster, 65–66, 132–133
Cillié, Piet, 38, 56, 119
Coetsee, Kobie, 207
Colby, William, 188, 193
Cold War, 6, 37
  in Angola, 171–173, 179–180, 194, 200
  and National Party ideology, 18–20 (*see also*
    anti-communism)
  in post-colonial Africa 66–68
communism, 15, 35–36, 52–53, 68, 102–103,
  106–107, 110, 199, 330

Congo, 35, 88, 165, 173, 177, 184, 194, 195, 197,
  215, 284 (*see also* Mobutu)
  Simba Rebellion, 95
Conservative Party, 318–319
Cooper, Frederick 17–18
Cuba, 85, 170, 172–173, 180, 183–184, 186, 189,
  194–195, 199–201, 205, 207, 210–212,
  216, 218–219, 221, 225, 249–250, 283, 302

d'Estaing, Valéry Giscard, 192, 194
de Klerk, F.W., 4, 335
de Klerk, Willem, 57, 60, 78, 80–81, 257, 295
de Villiers, Dawie, 81, 130
development (*see also* homelands, separate
    development)
  aid, 63, 65–66, 80, 81 (*see also* outward policy)
  in post-colonial Africa, 15–16, 64
de Wit, Piet, 174, 180, 340
Defense Planning Committee, 270–271
defense,
  spending on, 30, 114, 208–210, 212, 208–210
Democratic Turnhalle Alliance, 305–306, 310, 313
  (*see also* Dirk Mudge)
Department of Foreign Affairs, 62, 92, 282, 315
Department of Information, 46, 62, 87, 92–93
  Information Scandal, 316, 322
Die Afrikaner, 54–55, 58–61, 77–79, 115,
  136–137, 265
Die Beeld, 49, 75
Die Burger, 56, 88, 173, 242–243, 255
Die Transvaler, 32–33, 39, 49, 52, 80, 90, 137–138,
  145–146, 148, 257
Die Vaderland, 49, 145, 294
Die Volksblad, 97
Dönges, Eben, 29, 103
du Plessis, A.H., 248–250, 305
du Plessis, J.C., 44
du Preez, Sophia, 170, 176, 182
du Toit, Heinrich, 46
Dutch Reformed Church, 36

economic change,
  and apartheid 46–47
  income levels, 8, 30, 47, 263–264 (*see also*
    Afrikaners and socio-economic
    diversification)
  post-colonial Africa, 17, 64–65
  1960s South Africa, 2, 30
  and World War II, 32
Eglin, Colin, 118, 133, 146
Elections
  1948 General Elections, 37
  1958 General Elections, 37
  1961 General Elections, 40
  1966 General Elections, 41, 264
  1970 General Elections, 61
  1977 General Elections, 265, 297

Equatorial Guinea, 123
Erasmus, Rudolph, 322

Flower, Ken, 110, 116, 141, 148–149, 175,
        242, 246
Ford, Gerald, 184, 228,
    South Africa, approach to, 173–174, 193–194,
        197, 207, 218–219, 221, 223, 229, 239–241,
        250, 268, 284–286
Foster, Bob 76
Fourie, Brand, 10, 62, 74–75, 127–128, 131, 135,
        140–141, 143–144, 148, 151–152, 155–157,
        160, 170, 173, 175, 177, 180–181, 184, 197,
        223–224, 226, 228-229, 235, 238, 242, 258,
        272, 275–277, 279, 295, 308–310, 322,
        340, 346
Fourie, Deon, 108–110, 272, 275–276, 279, 294–295
Fourie, Pierre, 76
France, 67, 108, 135–136, 156, 173, 188, 192–193,
        195, 198, 289, 291, 313
Fraser, Alan, 107–109, 111–113, 116
Frontline Presidents
    détente negotiations, participation in, 134,
        141–142, 148, 151

Gabon, 65
Gaylard, Jack, 143, 148–149, 157, 226
Geldenhuys, Jannie, 201, 309
Giliomee, Hermann, 33, 325

Hawkins, Harold, 133, 149, 229, 237–238
Herenigde Nasionale Party, 34
Herstigte Nasionale Party, 54, 59, 60, 61, 258,
        294–295, 297
Hertzog, Albert, 34, 42, 54, 56, 78, 293, 346
Hertzog, Barry, 60, 294
homelands, 3, 11, 15, 17, 40–41, 75, 145, 203, 232,
        255, 265
    development of, 57–58, 70
Hoofstad, 54–55, 59, 61, 75, 138, 158, 167,
        296–297, 314
Horan, Hal, 188
Houphouët-Boigny, Félix, 67, 73–75, 83, 87, 130,
        143–144, 331
Howman, Jack, 116, 154,
Hupkes, Jan, 295
Hurd, John, 92, 122

Israel, 85–86, 292

Kapuoo, Clemens, 313
Kaunda, Kenneth, 12, 16, 25, 65, 69, 71, 73, 85,
        131–132, 137, 161, 198, 218, 227, 253,
        319, 330–331
    apartheid, approach toward, 1, 82
    détente, engagement in, 132, 135, 141–143,
        148–149, 151, 155–157, 184, 218

and John Vorster, 1–2, 69, 99, 100, 131
    Kissinger Initiatives, approach to, 242, 251
Kissinger, Henry 173, 188, 193–195, 201, 203,
        207–208, 217, 219, 223, 238, 287, 290–291,
        298, 314
    Lusaka Address, 225
    Kissinger Initiatives, 12, 23, 94, 220–221,
        225–259, 283–284, 287, 326, 331
    collapse of, 250–253, 257–259
        Annex C/Five Points, 242, 245–246, 330
        question of South-West Africa, 240–241,
        246–251
    and Ian Smith, 244–246
    South Africa, approach to, 193–194,
        219, 220, 226–228, 238,
        242–243, 287
Krause, Otto, 3–4, 56–57, 60, 78, 137, 139
Kruger, Jimmy, 148–149, 151, 236, 296

labor, 32, 47
Langley, Tom, 145–146
Lord, Winston, 219
Lusaka Manifesto, 69–70, 82–83, 132, 135, 140

MacMillan, Harold, 4, 39, 147
Madagascar, 63, 160
Malan, D.F., 34–36, 44, 60, 76, 294
Malan, Magnus, 110–111, 182, 196–197, 205,
        236, 249, 309, 311–312, 322
    and P.W. Botha, 271–276, 280, 301–302
Malan, Rian 76
Malone, Mike, 119, 122–123, 165–166,
        168–169
Marais, Jaap, 55, 59, 293–294
Matanzima, Chief Kaiser, 3
Mau Mau, 88–89
McBride, Sean, 240
Mobutu Sese Seko, 165, 177, 197, 331
Mondale, Walter, 285, 290
Montgomery, J. R., 119–120
Mostert, Johan, 174, 180
Mozambique Liberation Front (FRELIMO),
        119–125, 127, 132, 135, 155, 158, 167,
        216, 238, 280
Mozambique, 4, 11, 23, 48, 65–66, 71, 96,
        112–113, 118–127, 130, 132, 134–136,
        150, 154–155, 157–158, 160, 165, 167,
        171, 176, 184, 205, 212–213, 215–216,
        218, 225, 238, 253, 277, 280, 282, 294,
        301, 303–304, 329
Mudge, Dirk, 217, 230, 247–250, 284, 294,
        305–306, 310–311
Mugabe, Robert, 127, 133, 288
Mulder, Connie, 81–82, 92–94, 222, 234, 236,
        257, 268–270, 308, 322–323
    candidacy following Vorster resignation,
        316–317

Muller, Hilgard, 2, 10, 62, 74–76, 86–87, 92, 94, 122, 131, 138, 148–152, 156, 175, 177–178, 180, 184, 187–188, 191, 197, 216–217, 221, 223, 228, 235, 238, 244, 283, 306, 322, 329
Muller, Louwrens, 236, 323
Muzorewa, Abel, 64, 127, 147, 159–160, 283, 305

nation-state, 20
    Afrikaner understanding of, 21, 24, 55, 69
        (see also volk)
    in post-colonial Africa, 56, 68–69
National Front for the Liberation of Angola (FNLA) 165–174, 178–180, 182–189, 192–197, 199–203, 215, 303
    South African support for, 172, 178–179, 182–183, 185–187
National Party, 2, 6–7, 9–10, 13, 19, 29–30, 34, 37–41, 44–47, 52, 54–57, 60–61, 78, 80–81, 93, 103, 107, 128–129, 136–137, 140, 153, 179, 206, 221–222, 231, 236, 238, 241, 243, 254–255, 264–266, 268–270, 282–284, 291, 294–295, 297, 307, 318, 328, 333, 335
    changing identity of, 265–269, 321, 328
        (see also Afrikaners, shifting group identity)
    'doves', 10–11, 23, 116–118, 153–155, 161, 175, 177, 181, 187, 205, 212, 235, 329
    relationship with the 'hawks' faction, 275–278, 281, 308–309
    'hawks', 11, 23, 24, 110, 115–118, 125, 136, 153–155, 170–171, 177, 179, 181, 187, 205, 208, 212, 235, 235–236, 270–271, 273, 302, 308, 310–311, 330–331, 333
    advancement of total strategy, 276–282
    right-wing ascendancy, 293–295, 299–300
    Soweto Uprising, response to, 255–256, 259, 273
National Union for the Total Independence of Angola (UNITA), 165–174, 176, 199–203, 250, 312
    South African support for, 172, 178–180, 182–189, 192–197, 211–212, 215, 247, 303
Nel, Louis, 83, 256, 268–269
New Republic Party, 297
Nigeria, 82, 192, 197
Nixon, Richard, 268, 285
    apartheid, approach towards, 7–8, 93–95
    Byrd Amendment, 94
    National Security Study Memorandum 39 (NSSM 39), 93
Nkomo, Joshua, 127, 133–134, 141, 143, 156, 189, 213–214, 218, 227–229, 288
Nkrumah, Kwame, 64, 83–84
nuclear capacity 108
    Nuclear Non-Proliferation Treaty, 95
    South African nuclear weapons program, 95
Nujoma, Sam, 231, 240, 313
Nuwe Orde, 34

Nyerere, Julius, 69, 71, 85, 132, 143, 148, 218, 242, 251

O'Meara, Dan, 181
Oelschig, Marius, 121, 123, 165–167
oorstroming, 33, 318
Organization for African Unity (OAU), 10, 17, 39, 75, 84–85, 87, 103, 126, 131–132, 140, 144, 146, 148–155, 157, 160–161, 193, 197–198, 215, 222, 230
    and African liberation movements, 69–73, 85, 111, 115, 280, 283, 331
    Dar es Salaam Declaration 155
    Mogadishu Declaration, 86, 140
    OAU Charter 68
Organization of Petroleum Exporting Countries (OPEC), 86
Ossewabrandwag, 34, 52, 62, 103

pan-white nationalism, 9, 60, 92, 97, 100, 117, 125, 138, 160, 266, 293, 317, 321, 325, 336
Paulus, Arrie, 307
People's Movement for the Liberation of Angola (MPLA), 165–173, 176–180, 183–187, 189–194, 197–200, 202, 204, 206–207, 211–212, 215–216, 249, 302–303, 330
    Cuban support for, 184, 186, 200–201, 215
Phatudi, Cedric, 146
Pienaar, L.A., 65, 80
Pienaar, Schalk, 56–57, 76, 146, 206, 324
Podgorny, Nikolai, 283
Portugal 15, 23, 65, 82, 86, 94, 107, 122–125, 127, 165, 167, 177, 184, 200
    Carnation Revolution, 4–6, 9, 11, 64, 87, 118–121, 129, 132, 160
    counter-insurgency efforts, 96–97, 111–114
    relationship with South Africa, 86, 95–97, 99–100, 103, 111–114, 116, 118–124, 130–131, 173, 176, 182, 211
Potgieter Commission, 174
Potts, Jim, 187
Progressive Reform Party, 133, 207

Rand Daily Mail, 30, 39, 189–191, 207, 285
Rapport 76, 255, 257
Raubenheimer, Braam, 257
Rhodes, Joseph, 268–269
Rhodesia, 1, 4, 11, 23, 64, 86, 91, 94, 96, 131, 135, 142–144, 161, 184, 189, 215, 216, 219–223, 239–240, 243, 247, 257, 271, 284–288, 293–294, 299–301, 322, 330–331, (see also Ian Smith)
    Annex C/Five Points, 242, 245–246, 330
    détente, approach to, 131–134, 147–148, 213–214, 225
    domestic insurgency, 127, 205, 216, 218, 238, 283

electoral system, 127, 143, 213–214, 225
Kissinger Initiatives, approach to, 237–238, 242, 244–246, 251–253
Owen-Vance Proposals, 288, 330
relations with South Africa, 15, 20, 23, 71, 82, 97–101, 103, 107, 112–113, 115–116, 118, 126–129, 136–141, 143–144, 149–152, 154–157, 160, 165, 171, 174–175, 201, 211–213, 216–218, 223–231, 233–237, 241, 252, 258–259, 277, 279, 291, 293–294, 300, 303–305, 319, 321, 333
Richard Plan, 253, 258–259, 288, 305, 330
Universal Declaration of Independence (UDI), 96–97
Zimbabwe Development Fund (Zimbabwe Adjustment Fund), 239, 242, 288–289
Richard, Ivor, 253, 257 (*see also* Rhodesia) and Vorster, 257–259
Robbertze, Jan, 109–110, 153
Roberto, Holden, 165, 171–172
Rhoodie, Eschel 92, 275, 346
Rupert, Anton, 66

Salazar, Antonio, 96
Savimbi, Jonas, 166, 170–172, 179, 181, 183–185, 187, 189, 191, 195–196, 211, 331
Schaufele, Bill, 194, 253
Schlebusch, Alwyn, 270, 316
Schoeman, Ben, 29, 93, 137–139, 333, 346
Scowcroft, Brent, 193, 197, 219
Senghor, Léopold, 67, 75, 83, 87, 130, 143–144
Sestigers 49
settler society 123–124, 250
in Rhodesia, 98–99
in South Africa, 21,
Sharpeville massacre, 2, 29, 39, 62, 232, 263
Shearar, Jeremy, 46, 120, 287, 316
Sithole, Ndabaningi, 127, 133–134, 141, 143, 151–152, 155, 160, 227
Slabbert, van Zyl, 13
Smith, Ian, 64, 71, 74, 96–98, 100, 116, 123, 127, 129, 220–221, 241, 257–259, 283, 288–289, 291–292, 305, 329, 332, 342
and détente, 133, 136, 141–143, 146, 148–152, 154–157, 160–161, 177, 189, 213–214,
and Kissinger Initiatives, 222–228, 239–246, 251–253
Smuts, Jan, 35
Sole, Donald, 226, 287, 290–291, 297, 310, 313, 346
South African Broadcasting Corporation, 48, 61, 231, 313
South African Communist Party, 35
South African Defense Force, 46, 96–97, 100, 105, 112–113, 120–121, 123, 125–126, 140, 150, 152–156, 193, 201–203, 205–206, 210–212, 216, 218, 221, 224, 247, 249, 265, 271, 301, 309, 311–316, 341

Angola, approach to and engagement in, 165–177, 179–187, 191, 194–197, 203, 208–209, 270–281
Breytenbach-Vijoen Recommendations, 178–180, 182
South-West Africa, approach to, 303–304, 309, 311, 312
total onslaught theory, 101–103, 108–110, 112–118, 211, 216, 221–222, 272, 275–276, 279, 300 (*see also* total onslaught, P. W. Botha)
South African Police, 97, 99, 136, 148–149, 151, 155–157, 218
South West Africa People's Organization (SWAPO), 101, 125, 128, 167–169, 171, 176, 178–180, 199, 205, 211–212, 216, 230–232, 238–240, 247–251, 259, 283, 291, 302–303, 306, 308–313, 315
South-West Africa, 4, 11, 65, 82, 96, 112, 128, 131, 134, 136–137, 150, 161, 169, 171–172, 176–180, 182, 189, 196, 199, 202, 203, 208–209, 211, 216–217, 223, 226, 229–231, 233, 234–237, 240–241, 246–251, 259, 267, 283, 286–289, 294, 299, 302–306, 308–315, 321, 330–333,
Operation Reindeer, 313–315, 317, 319
United Nations Transition Assistance Group, 310
Western Contact Group 289, 308–311, 314–315
See also Turnhalle Conference
Soviet Union, 11, 36, 65, 68, 73, 81, 86, 99, 101–102, 111, 115, 122, 125, 153, 155, 165, 167, 170, 172–173, 177–179, 186–189, 193–195, 200–201, 205, 207, 211, 215–216, 218–221, 225, 236, 250, 283, 301, 303, 318
Soweto uprising, 232–234, 236, 239, 241, 243, 250, 253–257, 259, 266, 271, 273, 317, 324–325
Spies, F.J. du Toit, 167, 173–175, 182, 192
Spínola, Antonio, 114, 119–121, 125, 132
sports, 53, 76, 256, 291
State Security Council, 185, 194, 272–276, 280, 316
state-building, 24, 63, 325
and apartheid state, 72, 75 (*see also* apartheid and post-colonialism)
in post-colonial Africa, 21

Tanzania, 69, 106, 115, 127, 132, 134, 184, 192, 225, 284
Thirion, Chris, 211, 272, 276, 278–279, 304, 316
Tolbert, William, 74, 254, 297
Tomlinson Commission (1955) 41, 57
total onslaught, 11, 23, 101–102, 107, 110, 117, 169, 170–172, 186, 200, 205, 236, 249, 271, 274–280, 283, 300–304, 317, 319, 326–327

total strategy, 11, 12, 23, 101–102, 108–110,
111–113, 117–118, 124, 181, 271, 276–283,
301–304, 314–317, 319, 327–328
Transkei, 3, 204, 232, 241, 299
Treurnicht, Andries, 54, 59–61, 136, 222, 254,
257, 294–295, 318, 323, 333
Tshombe, Moïse, 95–96, 173
Turnhalle Conference, 217, 229–231, 240–241,
247–250, 283, 289–291, 302, 305

United Nations, 130, 230–231
General Assembly, 39, 70, 86, 311, 314
economic sanctions, 314
Security Council, 100, 128, 134, 157, 198, 232,
234, 247, 289, 313, 314, 316
Resolution 385, 216
Resolution 435, 311
UN Declaration of Human Rights, 307
United Party, 33–34, 37, 80, 146, 207, 329, 397
United States government (see also Nixon, Ford,
Kissinger, Carter)
National Security Council (NSC), 291
University of Zambia, 135
urbanization, 31–33, 36–37, 48, 263
Uys, Stanley, 147

van den Bergh, Hendrik, 10, 62, 102, 128, 140,
144, 148, 173–175, 177, 179–180, 182,
184, 187, 194–195, 223, 238, 242, 275,
304, 317, 340, 322
van den Vyver, Johan, 206
van der Merwe, Koos, 13, 166, 254, 272, 295, 297,
299, 318
van der Merwe, Stoffel, 53–54, 145, 272, 295,
299, 318
van der Waals, Kaas, 97, 119, 182–184, 192
van Deventer, Andre, 187, 195–196, 206
van Heerden, Neil, 121, 141, 306–308, 311
van Zyl, Eben, 248, 305
Veg, 56, 97–98, 104, 115, 346
verkramptes, 13, 76, 115, 145–146, 161, 233, 236, 240,
254–255, 265–266, 268–269, 298, 323, 346
détente, response to, 161
ideology, 53–56, 58, 60–61, 293–295
opposition to Vorster, 59, 254–257, 328–329,
333–334
outward policy, response to, 77–78
verlig-verkrampstryd, 51–61, 80
verligtes, 13, 236–237, 254–257, 264, 268–269,
278, 282, 294, 307, 320, 335–336
détente, response to, 137, 146, 217
ideology, 53, 55–58, 60–61, 66, 80, 83, 98, 268,
294–295, 316–317, 323–324, 328–329, 333
outward policy, response to, 76, 78
Verwoerd, Hendrik, 8, 36, 40–44, 51–58, 77,
88–89, 91–92, 103, 146, 255, 264, 266,
318, 323, 334, 336 (see also apartheid)

Blood River Speech, 39, 80,
foreign policy, 62
style of governance, 38, 45
succession to, 29–30, 44
Vietnam War 9, 67, 93, 196
Viljoen, Constand, 166, 172–173, 178–180,
182–187, 195–197, 278, 308,
314–316, 322
Viljoen, Gerrit, 237, 255
Viljoen, Pieter, 322
volk
conceptualizations of, 6, 15–16, 19, 20, 21, 31,
45, 46, 54–56, 59, 61, 265–266, 320, 323,
324, 328, 335–336 (see also Afrikaner
nationalism)
volkseie, 31, 89, 95, 170, 267
Volkshandel, 40, 58, 66, 79, 217, 255, 304
Vorster, John, 2, 30, 48, 304
Angola, approach to, 169, 173, 177–179, 184,
186–189, 195–197, 201, 205–206, 215
and P. W. Botha, 7, 11, 301–302, 304, 331
détente, 141–142, 146, 152, 156–157, 160,
215–216
Lusaka Agreement, 143, 145–146
Pretoria Agreement, 157–158
stumbling blocks, 143, 147–150
Victoria Falls Meeting 157–160
domestic opposition to, 53–55, 254, 298, 333
(see also verkramptes and 'hawks')
and domestic press, 138–141, 161, 191
foreign policy team, 10, 62, 141, 175, 223
on homelands, 11, 41
and Ian Smith, 149–151, 156–157, 226, 228,
239, 245–246, 258
Kissinger Initiatives, participation in, 223–224,
226–227, 239–241, 243, 250–251
as minister of justice, 39–40, 52, 105–106
and Walter Mondale, 287–291, 299
Mozambique, approach to, 123–124
outward policy, 12, 70–73, 78–80, 134
attraction to independent Africa, 63–70,
197–198
domestic response to, 74–78
downfall, 85–87
undermining factors, 82–84
on petty apartheid, 145, 256
political downfall, 255–259, 298, 316, 321–322,
330–331
Rhodesia, approach to, 99–101, 116, 127–128,
132–133, 136, 136, 148–150, 157, 239,
291, 329–330
South-West Africa, approach to, 231, 240–241,
247, 291, 289–290, 308–309
Soweto uprising, response to, 233, 255–257, 271
style of governance, 13, 45–46, 52, 87, 103,
140–141, 181, 256, 306–309, 312–314,
331–334

Vorster doctrine, 7–11, 15, 18, 21, 42, 54, 59, 62, 65–66, 250, 265–269, 281, 320–321, 323–325, 334, 336–337
   and Cold War, 101, 107, 110, 117
   multi-nationalism and race, 41, 43, 75–76, 77, 90, 268, 299
   non-interference, 69, 121–122, 186, 222
   separate development, 41–42, 44, 58, 256, 290
Vorster, Koot, 138, 333

Washington Post, 193, 220
World War II, 33–36, 47, 62, 103, 204,

   and social change, 19, 32 (*see also* economic change)
World, 192, 203–204, 243, 297

Yom Kippur War, 85–86

Zambia, 64, 106, 115, 127, 157–158, 184, 187, 194, 197, 212, 215, 218, 225, 238, 302, 304, 319,
   détente, participation in, 131–134, 148, 157 (*see also* Kaunda)
   domestic politics, 131, 135
Zionism, 85–86